INDUSTRIAL RELATIONS

INDUSTRIAL RELATION

THEORY AND PRACTICE

Third Edition

EDITED BY
TREVOR COLLING AND MICHAEL TERRY

WILEY

John Wiley & Sons, Inc.

CONTENTS

FIGURES AND TABLES

Figures

Tables

FIGURES AND TABLES

Figures

Tables

COMMON ABBREVIATIONS

ACAS	Advisory Conciliation and Arbitration Service
BERR	Department for Business, Enterprise and Regulatory Reform (formerly DTI now the Department for Business, Innovation and Skills (BIS))
CAC	Central Arbitration Committee
CBI	Confederation of British Industry
CRE	Commission for Racial Equality
DfES	Department for Education and Skills
DoH	Department of Health
Donovan Commission	Royal Commission on Trade Unions and Employers' Associations, chaired by Lord Donovan, 1965–68
DRC	Disability Rights Commission
DTI	Department of Trade and Industry
EAT	Employment Appeal Tribunal
EC	European Commission
ECJ	European Court of Justice
EHRC	Equalities and Human Rights Commission
EOC	Equal Opportunities Commission
ET	Employment Tribunal
EU	European Union
EWC	European Works Council
HRM	Human Resource Management
HSE	Health and Safety Executive
ILO	International Labour Organization
LFS	Labour Force Survey
MNC	Multinational Company
NES	New Earnings Survey
NHS	National Health Service
NMW	National Minimum Wage

NVQ	National Vocational Qualification
SME	Small and Medium-Sized Enterprises
TUC	Trades Union Congress
ULF/ULR	Union Learning Fund/Union Learning Representative
VET	Vocational Education and Training
WERS	Workplace Employee Relations Survey

CONTRIBUTORS

James Arrowsmith is Professor in the Department of Management and International Business, Massey University, New Zealand and an Associate Fellow of the Industrial Relations Research Unit, University of Warwick.

Stephen Bach is Professor of Employment Relations at the Department of Management, King's College, London.

William Brown is the Master of Darwin College and Professor of Industrial Relations at Cambridge University.

Andy Charlwood is Senior Lecturer in HRM at the York Management School, University of York.

Trevor Colling is Senior Lecturer in the Industrial Relations and Organizational Behaviour Group, Warwick Business School, University of Warwick and Director of Masters Programmes in Industrial Relations.

Colin Crouch is Professor of Governance and Public Management at Warwick Business School, University of Warwick. He is External Scientific Member of the Max Planck Institute for Social Research.

Deborah Dean is Senior Lecturer in the Industrial Relations and Organizational Behaviour Group, Warwick Business School, University of Warwick.

Linda Dickens is Professor of Industrial Relations at Warwick Business School, University of Warwick.

Paul Edwards is Professor of Industrial Relations at Warwick Business School, University of Warwick. He is former Director of the Industrial Relations Research Unit.

Damian Grimshaw is Professor of Employment Studies and Director of EWERC (European Work and Employment Research Centre) at the Manchester Business School, University of Manchester.

Mark Hall is Professorial Fellow at the Industrial Relations Research Unit, Warwick Business School, University of Warwick.

Jason Heyes is Reader in Human Resource Management and Head of the International Management and Organization Group at Birmingham Business School, University of Birmingham.

Richard Hyman is Professor of Industrial Relations at the London School of Economics and Editor of the *European Journal of Industrial Relations*.

Ewart Keep is Deputy Director of the ESRC Centre on Skills, Knowledge and Organizational Performance (SKOPE), School of Social Sciences, Cardiff University.

Sonia Liff is an independent researcher in the fields of social inclusion, community action and environmental sustainability. She is an Associate Fellow of the Industrial Relations Research Unit at Warwick Business School, University of Warwick.

Caroline Lloyd is Senior Research Fellow at the Economic and Social Research Council Centre on Skills, Knowledge and Organizational Performance (SKOPE) and a Senior Lecturer at the School of Social Sciences at Cardiff University.

Paul Marginson is Professor of Industrial Relations at Warwick Business School, University of Warwick, and Director of the Industrial Relations Research Unit.

Guglielmo Meardi is Associate Professor/Reader in Industrial Relations at Warwick Business School, University of Warwick.

Peter Nolan is the Montague Burton Professor of Industrial Relations, University of Leeds, the former Director of the ESRC Future of Work Programme.

Jonathan Payne is Senior Research Fellow with the ESRC Centre on Skills, Knowledge and Organizational Performance (SKOPE), School of Social Sciences, Cardiff University.

John Purcell is Research Professor at the Industrial Relations Research Unit, Warwick Business School and the Strategic Academic Adviser for ACAS.

Monder Ram is Professor of Small Business and Director of the Centre for Ethnic Minority Entrepreneurship Research at De Montfort University.

Jill Rubery is Professor of Comparative Employment Systems at the Manchester Business School, University of Manchester and Co-director of the European Work and Employment Research Centre.

Sukanya Sengupta is Associate Professor in the Industrial Relations and Organizational Behaviour Group, Warwick Business School, University of Warwick.

Melanie Simms is Associate Professor in the Industrial Relations and Organizational Behaviour Group, Warwick Business School, University of Warwick.

Keith Sisson is Emeritus Professor of Industrial Relations at the University of Warwick. He is a former director of the Industrial Relations Research Unit and Head of Strategy Development at ACAS.

Michael Terry is Emeritus Professor of Industrial Relations in the Industrial Relations Research Unit at Warwick Business School, University of Warwick.

PREFACE

The first of Warwick's Industrial Relations Research Unit's series of advanced texts in industrial relations and related topics was the 1983 collection *Industrial Relations in Britain*, edited by George Bain. Its successor, *Industrial Relations: Theory and Practice*, followed in 1995 with a second edition in 2003, both under Paul Edwards' editorship. From the start these books aimed to provide, through 'comprehensiveness and an authoritative blend of description and analysis', in the words of the preface to the first volume, a series of advanced essays designed for final-year undergraduate and postgraduate students, researchers and teachers of industrial relations. Each chapter contains detailed contemporary analysis of its chosen topic, informed by rich research data.

The present volume owes much to its predecessors both in approach and content. Several of the chapters are substantial rewrites of chapters in the last edition but we have also made several structural changes, as with earlier editions, to reflect the ever-changing terrain and priorities of the subject. First, while this is explicitly a book about industrial relations in Great Britain, the need to set the national experience in comparative conceptual and empirical frameworks has become ever more pressing, both as a consequence of the growing significance of the country's membership of the EU and of the influence of the 'Varieties of Capitalism' debate that is deployed in several chapters; hence, the two context-setting chapters by Crouch and Hyman that start the book and the frequent references to international comparative experience in many of the contributions.

Second, two new chapters in particular, those by Arrowsmith and by Ram and Edwards, provide a more differentiated account of the private sector of employment than previously, segmenting it by sector and by size, to reflect the growing diversity of employment structures and the continuing decline of the large manufacturing workplace, once taken as the paradigm for private sector industrial relations. Similarly, the chapter on unions by Simms and Charlwood explicitly takes account of the challenges they face in seeking to attract and unite an increasingly differentiated and individualized workforce. All these chapters insist on the capacity of an explicitly industrial relations analysis to deal with this growing complexity and differentiation.

Third, the role of law features ever more prominently in this edition, with two chapters explicitly devoted to capturing the ever-growing importance of legal enactment and process in UK industrial relations, and with virtually all chapters devoting space to consideration of the importance of legal intervention in particular areas of activity. Finally, we have expanded a number of chapters dealing with industrial relations outcomes. There is a growing conviction that the subject of industrial relations needs to shift focus away from analysis of institutions and processes, important though those remain, and engage to a greater extent than in recent decades with the consequences of the operation of industrial relations processes for employers, employees and their families as well as the broader economy and society. In recent years several leading industrial relations scholars have noted our collective failure to convince academics, commentators and policy makers concerned with issues of social and economic policy to engage seriously with industrial relations analyses. The final chapters in this book represent a first attempt to rectify this fault; no doubt further volumes will take this further.

As with all previous books in this series, this is very much a Warwick-based collection, in that most authors have either current or past connections here. Since the publication of the second edition several colleagues who have contributed to this and to earlier volumes have left Warwick. Ewart Keep, Caroline Lloyd and Jonathan Payne moved as the Warwick 'wing' of the ESRC Centre for Skills, Knowledge and Organizational Performance (SKOPE) was relocated to Cardiff, and Sonia Liff left the university after many years. Their contributions to Warwick's reputation for teaching, mentoring and research are widely recognized and we are grateful for their continued engagement with this volume. We are also deeply grateful to Jo Sheehan of the Industrial Relations and Organisational Behaviour Group, Warwick Business School, for her hard work and invaluable contribution in liaising with authors and keeping successive drafts in proper order.

Twelve years passed between the publication of *Industrial Relations in Great Britain* and the first edition of *Industrial Relations: Theory and Practice* and a further eight years before the second edition. This third edition will appear seven years after the second. The gradually increasing frequency of publication reflects the speed at which the world of work is changing and the consequent need to revise and update texts such as this more often, so that students and researchers have access to up-to-date information and ideas. No doubt, despite our best efforts, events will have overtaken some of the data and analysis presented here by the time of publication. That is unavoidable. But our central purpose in this volume, reflected in our introductory chapter, is to demonstrate the continuing capacity of the intellectual study of industrial relations to provide a framework both for understanding change and for providing a basis for progressive policy.

Trevor Colling
Michael Terry

INTRODUCTION

1

WORK, THE EMPLOYMENT RELATIONSHIP AND THE FIELD OF INDUSTRIAL RELATIONS

TREVOR COLLING AND MICHAEL TERRY

Introduction

Rarely have the insights of industrial relations been more timely or necessary for students of business or society at large. Such a bold claim may surprise those who have only encountered the term in the journalistic context of strikes and trade union activity. Since both of these have been dramatically in decline (and only patchily resurgent in the recent crisis) the relevance of the subject to current concerns may be called into question. Our objectives in this chapter are to explore changes in the world of work and to demonstrate the rich perspectives offered by a revitalized industrial relations approach.

Why have such reassertions become necessary? There is an important defensive task, a need to address the historical weaknesses of the subject and to ensure its fitness for purpose in exploring the rapidly changing world of work in which we are engaged. For the British Universities' Industrial Relations Association (see Darlington (ed.) 2009) this requires a response to the argument, forwarded in the context of the proposed closure of one of the UK's most important centres for the academic study of the subject, that 'academic industrial relations is now outdated; either the problems of the "human factor" in work have all been solved, or they are better addressed by new approaches such as "human resource management" (HRM) or "organisational behaviour" (OB)'. For many, this response involves remedying the subject's predominant focus upon *collective* institutions and processes (trade unions, collective bargaining and strikes) which has rendered it increasingly irrelevant as all three have diminished and left it susceptible to the challenge from HRM: 'management activity outside of collective bargaining (including non-union companies) became no concern of IR . . . leaving large conceptually "empty" areas to be colonized by HRM' (Ackers and Wilkinson 2003: 8).

But there is an important positive case to be made too, that the subject is uniquely placed to explore and understand current developments. As Kaufman (2008) argues, in moving to address that wider range of actors and institutions now involved in the world of work, the subject is merely returning to its founding paradigm, which he terms 'original industrial relations', having being diverted for much of the post-Second World War period into a narrower focus on collective institutions and processes ('modern industrial relations'). Paradoxically, the strength and vitality of the original field is now backlit by the potentially narrow and impoverished nature of alternative perspectives such as HRM, which can reduce workers to one of several *resources* to be blended in production and take the concerns of *management* as the first and sometimes exclusive point of departure in such processes. The risk here is that the pressure to provide responses to practical problems of business performance draws the subject away from its foundations in social science. As Jacoby (2003) has observed in the North American context, the development of *human resource management* in practice has been halting, its role contingent upon external crises and susceptible to challenge from other management functions with more tangible claims to production expertise: 'HR's problems are partly of its own making. It does not have strong and consistent theories that would justify its expertise inside the corporation' (ibid.: 170).

To the extent that this risk is less apparent so far in Britain, and this is debatable, it is because HRM departments and journals have been taken forward by researchers able to retain, deploy and develop frameworks from industrial relations. Critically important here is the focus on the employment relationship as a set of interactions, rather than exclusively a management process, and a multidisciplinary approach to teaching and research which locates these processes in social context. It has become commonplace to note that industrial relations is not a discipline in its own right, but a *field of study* drawing upon perspectives from core disciplines including sociology, political science, economics, history and law. This provides relatively fragmented boundaries from which to defend and advance understanding of the subject but also generates strong centripetal forces, drawing contending and complementary perspectives from social science to bear on problems manifest in the workplace: 'the value of the multidisciplinary approach is not that it denies or minimizes the contributions and insights of the various disciplines but that it builds on and integrates prior and current work from these fields' (Kochan 1998: 35). The central contention of this chapter, and the approach of the book, is that only such multidisciplinary and critical approaches are capable of capturing the range of change evident in today's workplaces and highlighting the reciprocal connections between them and other aspects of social and economic development.

This introductory chapter starts by restating the central importance of work to employees, employers and the wider society and the profound importance of understanding the forces that shape its nature. We go on to argue that an industrial relations perspective can provide a powerful tool for the understanding of work through an analysis rooted in identifying the complex and dynamic phenomenon that is the *employment relationship*. The chapter then establishes the potential for industrial relations analysis that goes beyond its historical terrain of collective relationships and action and provides a basis for understanding and analysing many of the issues that arise from the profound changes affecting work and its regulation in the UK in the early years of the 21st century. It concludes by outlining the structure of the present volume.

The Centrality of Work to Society and Business

In this section, we make a case for exploring the world of work from a social scientific perspective: one that acknowledges connections with dimensions of social and economic activity beyond the specific management problems in question. This is far from an original project. Scholars involved in the initial development of industrial relations as a field of study started from just such a vantage point. Beatrice Webb, who co-authored with her husband Sidney the seminal *Industrial Democracy*, came from a background in broader social policy as did John R. Commons in the United States (see Hyman 1989; Kaufman 2004). To begin, we can identify four factors that underpin the centrality of work to contemporary society.

First, work is the dominant activity in the lives of most people between the end of full-time education and their retirement. Britain's adult population, meaning those over 16 years of age and under 65, comprises some 30 million people. Four fifths of them are economically active, meaning that they are engaged in some way in securing income for their work, and the vast majority of this group is in paid employment (Hughes 2009). As Grimshaw and Rubery make clear (this volume), work provides the predominant waking activity for most of those engaged in it – three quarters of all employees work more than 31 hours per week, and one in five works more than 45 hours. These figures become even more significant when viewed from the perspective of the household, rather than the individual employee. Many families depend on two incomes, with both parents increasingly involved in paid work. As a consequence of greater flexibility of production and variation in employment contracts, these households now supply more hours to the labour market than ever before and in more complex working patterns (Warren 2003). Considerable expertise is devoted to 'juggling' home and work lives. Research quoted by Edwards and Wajcman (2005: 49) refers to the growth of 'shift-parenting', 'where parents do back-to-back shifts, passing the children between them'. Developments such as these have fuelled the growing public policy concern with 'work–life' balance (see Dean and Liff, this volume).

Second, the social, family and personal lives of most adults depend critically on the income derived from their employment. Three quarters of the income going to households with two adults with dependent children derives from wages and salaries and this figure rises to four fifths for adult households without children, reflecting the absence there of benefits supporting childcare (Hughes 2009: 69). Employees are concerned not only with the size of their income but with its security and predictability, increasingly so as they acquire long-term financial responsibilities (see below). But, depending upon how it is organized, the quality and duration of work may also influence their sense of physical and emotional well-being. Work can provide social contact and fulfilment, beneficial activity and stimulation, but can also be 'miserable, toxic, soul-destroying, inadequately rewarded and at times dangerous' (Bolton and Houlihan 2009: 3). In 2007/8, over two million people were suffering an illness they believed was caused or made worse by work, a growing proportion accounted for by depression and mental ill-health (HSE 2008). Overall, 34 million working days were lost, 28 million due to work-related illness and 6 million to injuries (ibid.). Work-related stress may be related to many factors, one of which is the growing perception among employees of a loss of autonomy in and control over work as it becomes increasingly subject to managerial direction (Bunting 2004).

Third, for reasons foreshadowed above, our sense of personal and community identity is closely conditioned by our work. 'And what do you do for a living?' enquiries are amongst the first to be fielded in social exchange and the answers provide the foundation for relationships that ensue, offering clues about status, lifestyles and class position. This capacity for work to provide broader collective identities and a sense of shared interests has long been noted: 'while one's social experience determines one's consciousness, a major component of that social experience is the specific things that one does in one's occupational and professional practice' (Bensman and Lilienfeld 1975: 186). Such *occupational attitudes* (ibid.) have underpinned individual and collective identities in the workplace and suffused the communities to which they have given rise. In these contexts and more generally, the unexpected loss of paid work, for whatever reason, is often a cause of personal crisis that goes beyond mere financial security.

Finally, for all of these reasons, work is also critically important for employers and for the state. Business viability and growth depends upon the availability of suitably skilled workers willing to be engaged in paid work and their application to their tasks while at the workplace. For governments, the plentiful supply of jobs lowers demands on the public purse: if citizens are able to support themselves through paid work, they are less likely to call upon costly support from the state, in terms of welfare benefits, for example. Increasingly, this capacity for self-support is seen as central to social capital and cohesion too. Particularly in the USA and Britain, widespread and long-term reliance upon welfare is seen as perpetuating a 'dependency culture', a debilitating social state sapping human character and potential: '[dependency] is an incomplete state in life; normal in the child, abnormal in the adult' (Moynihan in Sennet 2003: 103). Work, on the other hand, is said to offer security and purpose: 'as well as underpinning our economic growth, employment is the best route to independence, enables people to keep their children out of poverty, lays the foundation for successful retirement and enables people to develop their potential' (DTI in Sisson 2008: 4). Public policy since 1997 has focused upon maximizing employment and removing barriers to those minorities of people not yet fully engaged in the labour market. Labour governments have invested tremendous sums in a variety of *New Deal* and *Connexions* programmes to encourage into paid work young people, workers over 50, single parents and the disabled (Blundell *et al.* 2003; Toynbee and Walker 2001).

In a context where labour markets have been buoyant and expanding, and therefore unproblematic, the central significance of work to social stability and personal security has been masked. The focus of popular and social scientific debate has shifted from the world of production towards consumption. Yet, as Crouch makes clear (this volume), these worlds are closely connected and inter-dependent, held together by patterns of economic growth founded centrally on the expansion of the financial services sector. Household debt-to-income ratios remain very high in Britain, due in large part to the growth in the incidence and extent of mortgage lending. But this has been underpinned by growth in employ-ment and household income, increasing volumes of which have been channelled into servicing debt; both income and debt have increased more than three-fold since the 1980s. Most has been secured on property but unsecured personal debt has also increased and much of this borrowing is driven by lifestyle consumption. Household expenditure on subsistence living costs (such as food) has been relatively stable or in decline since the 1970s while spending on communications (including personal computing and telephony) increased almost ten-fold; clothing and footwear five-fold; and recreation and culture eight-fold (Hughes 2009: 83). In short, households have invested more in property and consumer durables and have been prepared to go into debt to do so, provided their incomes were rising and secure.

Ultimately, this context amplifies further the significance of work; it under-writes significant improvement in the quality of life but the risk associated with loss of jobs or income is increased and privatized. Just as the benefits of property wealth and consumer goods tend to accrue privately, so does the risk associated with their loss with wide ranging consequences. It is a critical aspect of the social change said to be undermining collective identities and interest recognition required for collective bargaining and trade union activity (summarized by Simms and Charlwood, this volume). The collapse of the viability of such a debt-based system of consumption captured in the phrase 'credit crunch' has, as Heyes and Nolan argue in this volume, propelled issues of employment (and unemployment) back onto the political and personal agenda.

An Industrial Relations Perspective

Industrial relations as an academic discipline provides a particular and unique insight into the forces and processes that shape these vital issues. Its particular contribution, which marks it out from different disciplinary approaches such as sociology, psychology and economics, is its insistence on the central analytical importance of the employment relationship (or *employment relations* as in several contributions to this volume) and the forces and processes that shape it.

It is important to note three aspects of the employment relationship empha-sized by those utilizing an industrial relations perspective. The first of these is *indeterminacy*, which derives from the fact that, unlike virtually every other form of contract evident in production, the labour contract involves the exchange of money not for actual goods or services, but for the *capacity* to provide something desired by the purchaser. In other words, employers wishing to secure the full value of their purchased labour power must ensure that workers are willing or somehow required to perform it. 'In the labour contract, the worker sells an ability to work, which is translated into actual labour only during the course of the working day. Expectations about standards of performance have to be built up during the process of production' (Edwards 2003: 14).

The second is that the employment relationship is *unequal*. As we have seen, in order to provide for themselves and their families, most workers have no choice but to engage in paid work and, in practice, many workers will have relatively limited choices between potential employers. In contrast, employers enjoy considerable resources and can often replace unwilling workers with other people or with technology. Of course, these relative power resources vary over time (employees may be easier to replace when unemployment increases, and harder when labour markets tighten) and between contexts (highly skilled staff are replaced less easily and their departure may incur a financial loss to the employer, when they have invested in training). Nevertheless, the employment relationship is generally one in which the employee is subjugated to the employer and consents to their control during the working day.

The third defining feature of the employment relationship arises from the first two; it is *dynamic* in the sense that it is driven forward by the coexistence of both conflict and cooperation in varying degrees. As Edwards notes, ultimately all 'managerial strategies are about the deployment of workers' labour power in ways which permit the generation of a surplus' (Edwards 2003: 16–17). Yet employers cannot rely solely upon the subjugation inherent in the employment relationship. Employers willing to press their power advantage too hard run the risk that workers will act likewise should the opportunity arise. Even relatively unskilled workers can find moments to do this, for example by refusing to work overtime to meet a pressing order target. Increasingly, in those areas of work requiring some element of *emotional labour*, in call centres, for example, employers will understand the benefits of customers encountering contented workers. Thus, while the opportunity to act coercively is nearly always available to employers, such strategies are not cost free and there are incentives to cooperate with workers. These factors impinge equally upon the behaviour of employees. They have an abiding interest in cooperating to ensure the viability and success of the firm, and thereby their employment, but they will guard against arbitrary or excessive demands placed upon them. In Edwards' term (1986), therefore, the employment relationship is characterized by 'structured antagonism'. There is an underlying conflict of interest between employers and workers but it is not always apparent. Contingent pressures may act on the parties to induce high levels of cooperation but tensions may remain beneath the surface and emerge during moments of crisis or change. An ability to understand and anticipate changes in the character and perception of employment relations is thus an important requirement of those involved in them.

Such a perspective provides an analytical tool for understanding the nature of work processes, the forces that shape them and the rewards and benefits deriving from them. In particular it suggests that one response to the uncertainty inherent in the employment relationship is to generate rules governing behaviour in the workplace, and this is the activity that provides the focal point for the study of industrial relations. Formally, in capitalist societies, ownership confers on employers the right unilaterally to specify the rules of employment; the terms of the employment relationship. However, an industrial relations analysis, centred on these features of the employment relationship, draws our attention also to the potential for negotiation in the specification of rules (see Brown, this volume).

Rules may be of different kinds and generated at different levels. Distinctions can be drawn between *managerial* and *market* relations, for example. Rules of the first kind govern the prerogatives of the actors and the ways in which these can be used legitimately. They may confirm the power of managers to make decisions on how production should be organized, while offering some assurances to employees that this control will be implemented with respect and consideration for the interests of employees. Those rules concerned with market relations will stipulate relative rewards available to workers engaged in different tasks. Again, these may confirm the power of managers to make key decisions, such as the allocation of jobs or particular earning opportunities, but they may also make clear the criteria affecting such decisions and even offer scope for negotiation.

This argument indicates a need to specify both the actors involved in these rule-making processes and the level at which they operate. The first and most obvious is at the level of the workplace, where employers and workers develop and codify shared understandings. Such is the context affecting large numbers of those employed in small and medium-sized enterprises (see Ram and Edwards, this volume), where processes can be based often on tacit agreements between workgroups and their managers. In large, complex organizations these kinds of understandings are more usually formalized into written procedures and agreements. Employees have often sought representative agents to act on their behalf in such processes, in part for the negotiating expertise they bring to bear but also to mitigate the power imbalance between individual workers and their employer. This is the kind of rule-making experienced under *collective bargaining* between employers and trade unions which has provided the formal focus of much industrial relations research.

But bargaining of this kind has never taken place purely in isolation; it is affected by processes below and above formal negotiations. Even in large organizations, codified understandings have often been derived from and supplemented by informal compromises with workgroups, managers turning a 'blind-eye' to minor infringements, for example. Conversely, the rights and duties of parties to the employment relationship may be defined above the level of the workplace and enshrined in law. Rule-making of this kind, referred to often as *legal enactment*, may perform an auxiliary role, establishing the context with which such rule-making takes place, and furnishing only minimum rights and protections, or may go beyond this to intervene directly in the employment relationship and establish standards governing key aspects of managerial or market relations (see Colling; Dickens and Hall, this volume). Thus, the state may establish rules governing the procedures through which workers can be disciplined and dismissed or even influence the length and composition of working time and the calculation of pay.

This then is the terrain of industrial relations and it should be clear by now that it is not as narrow as critics sometime suggest. It is true that the subject in Britain and North America *became* geared closely to specific systems of formal regulation based on collective bargaining. This was to the neglect in practice of large sections of the economy where such regulation was underdeveloped (e.g. the service sector) and large parts of the workforce (e.g. women who tended to work in the service sector). Such weaknesses can be explained partly by the context of *voluntarism* in which the subject developed. The innate and often visceral hostility of Britain's system of common law to collective rights fostered a deep mistrust of employment regulation by state and judicial mechanisms amongst all parties (for a full account, see Deakin and Morris 2005: 5–42). For most of the 20th century, therefore, the policy emphasis in the UK was on facilitating voluntary self-regulation of employment by employers and worker representatives through collective bargaining and this provided the research focus for students of industrial relations. As Kaufman puts it (2008: 317), 'the field's shift towards unions was not only a pragmatic accommodation but an intellectual and ideological commitment on the part of many scholars, not only to collective bargaining but to larger programmes of social democracy and collective organization of the economy'.

But it is important to distinguish between this focus in practice and the underlying, if neglected, conceptual foundations of the subject. In describing industrial relations *systems*, Dunlop (1958) attempted to locate exchanges within the institutions of job regulation in their wider societal context, identifying the key components of the employment relationship and the layers around it influencing their interaction. Significantly, macro-level analysis of this kind has been resurgent within industrial relations more recently, as a response to the challenge of globalization and international integration. Debate about whether these pressures will force convergence in employment systems, for example, requires that their basic elements can be identified and connections explored with processes of social and economic change (e.g. see Ludlum *et al.* 2003; Streeck and Thelen 2005). It has become common, therefore, to distinguish between the full range of *actors* involved in the process, including employers, the state, workers and their representatives. At the same time, the *processes* are not axiomatically focused on collective bargaining. Different regulatory mechanisms were recognized by the earliest pioneers in the subject, the Webbs famously distinguishing between legal enactment and collective bargaining at the end of the 19th century (Hyman 2003). Balances between actors and processes are known to depend on *context*. Critically, the balance between law and collective bargaining has varied by national context, subject to differences in legal and political systems (see Colling, this volume). But also within these arenas, the public sector is different to the private sector; parts of the private sector are subject to quite different pressures; and small firms are engaged in different ways with both of these broader parts of the economy (see Arrowsmith; Bach; Ram and Edwards, this volume). Finally, and most critically, a range of social and policy *outcomes* cannot be understood without a thoroughgoing understanding of the employment relationship, a theme to which we must return.

Studying Employment in Transition

This strand in our argument has a deliberate double meaning. One reading points to the magnitude of change in employment, another to the crisis affecting ideas about how best to understand and study such changes. While perhaps distinctively blunt, the conclusion of one leading management commentator has resonated widely in recent years: 'there seems little energy left in a distinctive industrial relations field of study and few managers look to the literature for inspiration about how to manage better' (Emmott 2005: 15). Policy makers have also in recent years adopted the view that approaches rooted in industrial relations perspectives – for example, in dealing with issues such as productivity and conflict – are less relevant than in earlier decades; a misapprehension dealt with by Keep *et al.* and by Heyes and Nolan in this volume. The 'productivity debate' has shifted to an interest in the relationship between so-called 'strategic human resource management' and corporate performance (analysed in this volume by Edwards and Sengupta) and to a preoccupation with supply-side factors such as skills and competencies (addressed here by Keep *et al.*). Analyses of conflict have shifted to some extent from the collective to the individual, reflected, for example, in the inexorably growing list of grievances and complaints taken to Employment Tribunals (see the chapter by Colling).

Likewise, the political economy of universities increasingly has prioritized the practical concerns of (putative) managers. Courses on industrial relations have been displaced by others using the terminology of *human resource management*. The reasons are easy to understand. At the most superficial level, managers comprise a greater proportion of the workforce than they once did, and so provide a viable market for higher education. More significantly, shifts in the way that the employment relationship is now managed mean that unequivocally, 'the principal actor in employee relations is in fact management' (Blyton and Turnbull 2004: 99). One consequence of this shift in power and authority within the employment relationship has been the ill-founded claim that changes in the world of paid work are so substantial that the concerns of traditional industrial relations research are no longer useful or even generally applicable.

Changing Work, Employment and Regulation

There is no doubt that work has been changing in important respects and very rapidly on some dimensions. The attention of industrial relations scholars has been forced away from traditional concerns, focused on the underlying homogeneity of employment in large, stable, UK-owned workplaces, towards the greater number of actors and processes now at play (see Freeman *et al.* 2005; Heery and Frege 2006).

Let us first take labour market participation. The overall rise in economic activity towards the levels indicated above has been gradual, but shifts within this total have been very significant. In the 1950s, around one third of women were economically active while the majority of men entered employment immediately on leaving school and stayed there until they reached retirement age, usually working full-time (Crompton 1997: 25). This pattern was seen to justify 'breadwinner' status; wages offered to men were higher on the ground that they secured the 'family wage', whereas women's work was understood to provide only supplementary income (Barrett and McIntosh 1982). This model of standard employment provided the mainstay of industrial relations but has now changed almost out of all recognition (Dean and Liff, this volume). The bastions of male employment have gone into decline, particularly in manufacturing industry (see below) and young men and those approaching retirement age have begun to fall out of formal employment. At the same time, women have been drawn back into the labour market in substantial numbers and across all age ranges. There are now as many jobs performed mainly by women as there are performed by men (Hughes 2009: 53) and most women will be involved in paid work of some sort for most of their adult lives.

At the same time, as Crouch makes clear (this volume), the British labour market has become more diverse in terms of race. Immigrants from the former Commonwealth countries have formed a significant component for some time, comprising about 4% of the total population in the 1950s (Rutter and Latorre 2009: 202). In recent years inward migration has increased significantly and migrants now come from a much broader range of countries, including new EU member states from Eastern Europe often referred to as the A8 countries. Precise measures are difficult, because many of these workers stay for only short periods, but it is estimated that the foreign-born population now comprises 11% of the total (ibid.). That nearly all of those coming from the A8 countries arrived in the UK after 1999 is to be expected, but significant proportions of those from the Middle East and Africa (48%), from India (53%), and from Australia (50%) and North America (50%) also arrived only recently (Khan and Kerr 2009: 5).

Distinct from the composition of the labour market, the occupational roles into which workers are recruited have also changed substantially, as a consequence of economic restructuring deep enough to connote for some the arrival of the *post-industrial* society (Bell 1973). Over 25 years between 1981 and 2006, employment in primary (e.g. mining and agriculture) and secondary industries (e.g. manufacturing and construction) more or less halved to 4.7 million jobs (Self and Zealey 2007: 46). The implosion of British manufacturing employment has been especially dramatic, falling by 58% between 1978 and 2008 to just 2.9 million employees (Hughes 2009: 53). Overwhelmingly, the long-term shift has been inexorably towards service sector employment. Reflecting the trends in consumer credit and consumption outlined above, financial services alone now employ 5.4 million people – more than the combined total of primary and secondary industries and almost twice the size of the manufacturing workforce.

The occupational roles required by these industries are substantially different as a consequence. In the 1950s, two thirds of workers were employed in manual occupations, principally in manufacturing; a proportion cut in half since then. In the final quarter of 2008, manual work (machine operatives, elementary occupations and skilled trades together) accounted for only 29% of the labour market

(Hughes 2009: 46). Conversely, only small minorities in the 1950s were employed in management positions (6%) or professional and technical occupations (7%) (Gallie 2001: 2). The number of managers has tripled now to 15% of the workforce and over a quarter (27%) now work either in the professions (e.g. lawyers) or associate professions (e.g. teachers).

A third axis of significant change is the trading environment in which companies operate and employ their staff. Britain has always had a relatively open and internationalized economy, as a consequence of its naval prowess, economic aspirations and consequently its empire: 'the demand for sugar drew merchants to the Caribbean. The demand for spices, tea and textiles drew them to Asia' (Ferguson 2003: xxv). As Marginson and Meardi make clear (this volume), the outward orientation of Britain's latter-day merchants is still more marked: overseas investment by British companies increased six-fold between 1990 and 2006. Just as important is the relatively unchecked influx into Britain of investment from overseas competitors, which also increased six-fold over the same time period (ibid.). Such investment trends are closely implicated in the industrial restructuring explored above. Though many prominent British manufacturing companies have succumbed to international competition, it is not always the case that manufacturing work is no longer being done; as British firms have acquired production capacity abroad, it is just not being done in Britain any longer. Two fifths of manufactured imports into OECD countries come from developing economies, such as India and China, suggesting a new international division of labour (McGrew 2008: 284). Similarly, the shift to financial services employment in particular has been fuelled by the arrival of multinational banks and financial institutions, attracted by deregulation in the City of London and the open market for mortgage and consumer credit. And thus to a further dimension of change, international competition has increased in capital markets as well as product markets. Open share markets means that there are relatively few barriers to mergers and acquisitions in Britain, and investors can move their funds between public companies in pursuit of the best financial returns (see Sisson and Purcell, this volume). This short-term approach to investment has intensified as a consequence of innovation in investment vehicles. Private equity firms, for example, borrow money to buy companies outright with a view to removing liabilities in the businesses and selling them again for a profit within a short time frame (Peston 2008: 29). As a consequence, as Thompson notes (2003: 366), 'capital markets are no longer merely intermediaries in relations between economic actors, but a regulator of firm and household behaviour'. Shifts in product and capital market competition intensify further the pressure on managers to maintain short-run financial performance and to remove any obstacles that might constrain their ability to do so.

Fourth, organizations have changed substantially in response to these pressures. For much of the 20th century, it was common to distinguish between market and bureaucratic models and to trace a line of development towards the latter. Most workers in Britain were employed in large, integrated firms with an unmistakable single identity, and the same was true in the public sector. Competitive pressures have changed this scenario in favour of flexible or 'network' organizations. Two lines of organizational change have become particularly apparent. First, accountability for business and financial performance has been divisionalized within companies. While investment and strategic decisions may be taken at higher levels, brand identities and operational decisions including those affecting employment are taken at the level of individual businesses, and often at relatively decentralized levels within them. Second, interactions within companies are characterized more and more by markets rather than hierarchies. Divisions and business units, for example, are invited to vet the performance and costs of the services they source from within the firm, and to switch to external providers if this delivers improvements. In the public sector particularly, but also across large private corporations, businesses increasingly *outsource* important business services, such as buildings maintenance, customer enquiries, even elements of the HRM function. Other newer business may never seek to provide them internally in the first place but to *insource* the service from a specialist third party. Again, the consequences for employment and the way it is regulated are stark:

> [Organizations] are no longer so clearly or permanently defined, their hierarchical organization has been challenged, their size has been reduced and the exposure to risks has increased. This is why the protections that belong to these institutions afforded in the long term have been greatly eroded: both at home and at work a general principle of uncertainty has spread over everyone's lives, while the number of people seesawing in and out of insecurity has grown steadily. (Supiot 2002: 219)

Finally, and perhaps most significantly for our purposes, these combined pressures have been strongly associated with the declining purchase of collective bargaining as an effective means of regulation (see, Brown; Simms and Charlwood; Sisson and Purcell, this volume). While collective bargaining established the terms and conditions of employment for two thirds of the workforce in 1980, now just over one third are in this position (Brown and Nash 2008: 95). Research suggests this decline has now stabilized. In part, unions have become adept at using a more favourable legislative climate (including statutory rights to trade union recognition) but it also seems likely that the need for coordinated pay setting is acknowledged and accepted broadly in those sectors where it remains, including the public sector (see Bach, this volume). Nevertheless, only one in five private sector workers is covered by a collective agreement. Manufacturing industry, once the focal point for formal industrial relations, now has a lower unionization rate than the rest of the economy (Metcalf 2005: 3). Areas of employment growth, small firms and those in the service sector remain especially impervious to joint regulation (outside of those providing public services, where outsourced staff retain rights to trade union representation).

In summary, virtually all the actors and institutions of employment have been through dramatic and turbulent change over the last 30 years, involving complex processes delivering important challenges to those studying employment and its regulation. More even distribution of work across labour markets potentially masks significant polarization and differentiation within them (Humphries and Rubery 1992). Any attempt to engage with these important developments takes researchers immediately away from the established terrain of formal industrial relations. Though as Dean and Liff make clear (this volume), collective bargaining has been associated with lower levels of gendered inequality, for example, many women and most migrant workers are employed in areas beyond the reach of formal agreements. As has always been the case, the law and statutory intervention play critical roles in defining and diffusing employment standards in these areas. Both have grown substantially as a result of recent developments and extended beyond equality policy to establish key employment standards once set by collective bargaining (see Colling; Dickens and Hall; Grimshaw and Rubery; Hyman, this volume). Re-engagement with the state and the mechanisms of legal regulation have become inescapable in this context.

Industrial and occupational trends carry important implications for social identity, and thereby relationships in the workplace, but these need careful interpretation (see Simms and Charlwood, this volume). Employment structures in the 1950s supported relatively clear *occupational attitudes* (see above) for significant parts of the workforce, able to distinguish clearly their working and family lives from the privileged minorities engaged to manage them. Particularly in comparatively homogeneous occupational communities built around mining, shipbuilding and steel, this underpinned demand for union representation and collective bargaining. But it is important to avoid 'dualistic historical thinking whereby a communitarian and solidaristic proletariat of some bygone heyday of class antagonism is set against the atomised and consumer-oriented working class of today' (Marshall *et al.* in Butler and Watt 2007: 179). Occupational change is a constant feature of capitalist development and has long provided puzzles for commentators interested in the responses of workers and their institutions. Questions about growing affluence and its impact on class identity were rife even during the high points of collective bargaining, providing the focal point of studies in coal fields and car plants, for example (see Dennis *et al.* 1969; Goldthorpe and Lockwood 1969). Moreover, new occupational identities emerge continually: collective bargaining and industrial action these days are focused principally in the public sector, amongst professionals and associate professionals as much as manual workers, and it is often overlooked that more than one in five workers in financial services, the totem of the new service economy, is a trade union member (Barratt 2009: 10, 12). The fact that union membership even in these new mainstays continues to decline, coupled with the trends in private consumption noted above, confirms that the class identity is shifting constantly with important consequences for workplace dynamics (Botero 2009). And, of course, this opens questions about representation, involvement and the processes of conflict and accommodation in the new workplaces and communities that have developed in the wake of re-structuring (Terry, this volume).

A final set of challenges arises from the definition of the employment relationship in these environments. Usually, this has relied upon the binary identification of workers and their employer, allowing the allocation of rights and responsibilities between them. Newly flexible working arrangements and complex organizations make this process problematic. Growing proportions of the labour market are engaged by intermediaries, such as employment agencies. Employees subject to outsourcing find themselves transferred from one organization to another, with possible consequences for their contracts of employment, the organization of their work, and the way that they are managed. Those employed by providers of *insourced* services may be deployed in a range of companies simultaneously, call centres taking enquiries on behalf of a range of clients, for example. Responsibility for control and direction of staff is diffused up and down and across organizations. Critically, these developments potentially obscure the identity of the employer and the nature of the employment relationship, a process epitomized in the increasingly necessary request from employment advisers, 'will the real employer please stand up?' (Wynn and Leighton 2006).

The Resilience of Industrial Relations Approaches

Our argument so far has acknowledged the need for industrial relations analysis to move beyond the concerns that dominated the subject for half a century and to rediscover a more expansive and inclusive approach to employment relations. Substantial strengths inherent in the approach derive principally from a focus on the employment relationship in its social context and a multidisciplinary perspective which brings a range of social scientific concepts to bear on workplace matters. In this penultimate section, we substantiate these claimed strengths with reference to two stubbornly enduring policy challenges: employment quality and social inequality. Attempts to address them recently have cohered around improving the supply of skills to the labour market; encouraging further inward investment; and by ensuring fairness in employment through the growth of minimum statutory rights. These have met with modest results overall. An industrial relations perspective, by contrast, lays emphasis on the centrality of regulation in the workplace (for a fuller exploration than is possible here, see Sisson 2008).

As we have seen, current policy trajectories have proved effective in promoting employment growth and integration. Employment growth has been guaranteed by the removal of obstacles to inward investment, so that employment in services in particular has been boosted by international companies locating in Britain. Industrial restructuring of this kind has been associated with occupational restructuring: the decline in manual and elementary roles and increased demand for managerial and professional expertise is said to constitute an 'upskilling' of the workforce. Integration has involved drawing into the labour market large numbers of women and migrant workers, often on flexible employment contracts. Though these positions in themselves are often precarious and insecure, policy makers take great pride in the supposed absence of obstacles to more secure work. That is, there is an expectation of flexible labour markets in Britain, enabling workers to move between different kinds of contractual arrangements.

Yet this positive picture requires some qualification: it certainly cannot be concluded that the underlying character of work and employment relations has been transformed by any general upskilling or by consequent improvement in rewards from employment. The skill requirements of many jobs remain relatively menial (see Keep *et al.*, this volume) and there is limited evidence of management strategies based on job enrichment. One common characterization of the 'hourglass labour market' suggests that there has been an expansion both of good and of poor jobs, with relatively well-paid mid-ranking jobs being squeezed (Goos and Manning 2003). Alternative readings suggest that even this may prove too optimistic. Let us take the issue of employment security and job tenure, for example. Longer job tenures may indicate 'good' work, to the extent that it suggests satisfaction with the role and a willingness to stay. Conversely, it may still be associated with employment insecurity where alternative employment is hard to find and cherished features of the present job are perceived to be under threat (Burchell 2002). As Coats puts it (2009: 25), 'it is quite possible for a skilled and apparently well-paid employee to believe that their job is insecure, that they lack autonomy and control, that the workplace is unfair, and that they cannot rely on either their colleagues or their employer'.

Certainly, the general picture emerging from survey data is one of marked intensification of work effort (with increases of up to one third) between 1992 and 1997 compensated for to some extent by a levelling of this trend since then: 'work has become much more pressurised and more demanding, with workers subject to increasing levels of stress and anxiety at work' (Brown *et al.* 2007: 6). For example, 40% of workers feel that they never have enough time to get work done and more than one quarter say that they worry a lot about work outside of work hours (ibid.: 19). Significantly, both of these measures increased between 1998 and 2004 and were more likely to be a feature of new workplaces than older ones. The prospects for high-skill and high-commitment workplaces are not strong overall and are contingent on specific circumstances (see Edwards and Sengupta, this volume).

A similarly chequered analysis emerges when considering inequality. New Labour came to power in 1997 determined to reverse increases in absolute poverty witnessed during the 1980s and 1990s. Policy focused on widening access to work (see above) and increasing the returns from paid work through the introduction of the national minimum wage and reform of the tax system (see Grimshaw and Rubery, this volume). Opportunities to work have undoubtedly increased and preceding incremental trends towards greater social equality have been re-established and accelerated since 1997. The incomes of the poorest sections of the labour market were lifted and measures of absolute poverty fell: 'income growth at the bottom in the New Labour period represents the first sustained rise in living standards since the 1960s and early 1970s' (Hills *et al.* 2009: 342).

Yet social mobility has not recovered in the same way, even in a context until recently of economic expansion. Indeed, it may have worsened on some counts, as government commissioned reports concede frankly:

> It has long been recognised that the UK is a highly unequal society in which class background still too often determines life chances. Hence the welcome focus in recent years on tackling poverty and disadvantage. But we need to recognise too that a closed shop mentality in our country means too many people, from middle income as well as low income families, encounter doors that are shut to their talents. (Cabinet Office 2009: 6–7)

Persistent poverty, meaning income below a set standard for three of the four preceding years, has fallen but is still entrenched in Britain (Hills *et al.* 2009: 344). The number of workless households (where no one over the age of 16 is in employment) has remained at about the 16% level throughout this period and a further 27% of households contain one or more members who are out of work (Jenkins 2008: 3). More important, the growth of 'poor work' at the bottom of the earnings scales means that there is real doubt about whether work any longer provides a route out of poverty for significant proportions of the workforce. Ten low-paying industries identified by the Low Pay Commission account for one third of all jobs in the UK and 70% of those working at or below the national minimum wage (Low Pay Commission 2009: 58). Three fifths of workers at this earnings level across the economy have been in that employment for more than one year (ibid.: 19) and reviews of 'in-work poverty' conclude that, 'Poor children are increasingly likely to come from a working family. Today, 50 per cent of all poor children live in families where at least one parent works. This compares with 40 per cent ten years ago' (Tripney *et al.* 2009: 7).

Despite investment in economic regeneration, these patterns of worklessness and poor work are intractably focused on particular regions (Dorling *et al.* 2007; Low Pay Commission 2009). Managers and professionals may be willing to move for work opportunities but only minorities of people overall will do so. Manual workers are three times less likely to move for work and those with school level or no qualifications are half as likely to do so as those with degrees (Dixon 2003: 195). Job horizons for these groups are confined not just by what is available locally, but by the knowledge contained in networks of friends and family which tends also to be highly localized: 'because those that helped in finding jobs were also typically confined to the same sectors of the labour market as them, our interviewees remained constrained to work at the bottom of the labour market that offered little chance of personal progression' (MacDonald *et al.* 2005: 884).

While these poorest groups have benefited in *absolute* terms of their minimum pay, their *relative* position has barely improved and has deteriorated markedly on some measures. This is usually considered the more robust indicator of equality since 'a relative standard is a moving target, one reduces poverty only if one generates a larger increase in incomes of the poor than is achieved by the middle class' (Dickens and Ellwood 2003: 225). This has proved difficult in Britain, where improving relative income has relied almost exclusively on setting minimum pay and redistributive tax and benefit measures. There has been a marked reluctance to intervene in decision-making over pay at any level above this minimum floor, either in terms of promoting joint regulation between trade unions and employers or establishing meaningful procedures to limit executive pay. Relative measures in this context have benefited to the extent that income growth amongst middle-earners has slowed, particularly as the growing numbers of degree-qualified workers has reduced the returns from education (Machin 2003). But this effect has been swept away by striking and sustained income increases at the upper end of the scale. Between 1997 and 2005, income for the top 10% of earners increased faster than for the rest of the population, and 'the average earnings of a top 100 CEO was more than £2.2 million per annum, or nearly 100 times the average for all full-time employees' (Sefton *et al.* 2009: 26). Consequently, the UK is one of only eight countries above the European Union average on measures of the proportion of individuals with incomes below 60% of the median (Self and Zealey 2007: 68) and one of only two countries from the EU15 where relative inequality has worsened since 1998 (Hills *et al.* 2009: 343).

Our understanding of the roots of these issues can again be enhanced through industrial relations analysis and by a revitalized focus upon the employment relationship at the heart of these developments. They draw our attention to the need to understand the indeterminate nature of the design and organization of work, the division of labour between workers and the intensity of production. There is a tendency to subscribe to a form of determinism in which the nature of work (the 'bundle' of tasks brought together to constitute particular jobs) and the rewards offered in exchange flow directly from the prevailing technology or market pressures. Industrial relations analysis acknowledges the importance of such factors but also insists that the way in which, for example, employers choose between production technologies (and the influence of employees over such choices) also has to be understood as part of the working-through of the tensions involved in the employment relationship.

Decisions about the complexity of technology and the level of investment required in order to remain competitive will be subject to environmental circumstances, such as the relative availability and cost of labour and the ease with which it can be engaged and dismissed. Britain's flexible labour markets and weakened employee voice provide relatively few obstacles to 'low-road' competitive strategies, founded on cheap labour performing unskilled tasks. Recent change has had the effect of diminishing the countervailing power of workers and expanding the role of managers and the pressure upon them to sustain financial performance above other measures. As Sisson has argued repeatedly, Britain's managerial culture, with its continuous emphasis on year-on-year profitability, predisposes employers towards short-term 'fixes' in times of economic turbulence – use of overtime, work intensification, layoff and dismissal – rather than longer-term strategies of work redesign in capital investment more characteristic of some other northern European economies: 'there is a massive tension between the degree of stability necessary for HRM and HPWS to operate effectively and the insecurity inherent in current forms of corporate governance' (Thompson 2003: 365). Arguably, the enthusiasm for so-called 'lean production' in the 1990s, with its catchy slogan 'work smarter – not harder', failed to translate into anything more than work intensification precisely because of weaknesses in the regulation of employment (Rees *et al.* 1997). The growth of 'poor work' and the persistence of poverty must be understood partly in that context (see Edwards and Sengupta; Keep *et al.*, this volume).

Income inequality was for much of the 1960s and 1970s, an area of industrial relations attention, in particular insofar as the maintenance of 'differentials' (income relationships between different categories of employees in the same enterprise) and 'relativities' (pay relationships within sectors) formed part of pay claims in collective bargaining and, on occasion, the reason for pay conflict. The overall dynamic of collective bargaining is to restrain pay dispersion:

> This is because unions protect the pay of those on low earnings and because unionized workplaces make more use of objective criteria – seniority for example – in setting pay rather than subjective factors – like merit – preferred in non-union establishments. Unions also compress the pay structure between different groups in the labour market: women and men, blacks and whites, and those with health problems and the healthy. (Metcalf 2005: 15)

Such processes are still at work across important parts of the economy, particularly in the public sector (see Bach; Dean and Liff, this volume). Elsewhere, pay determination is at the discretion of management, subject principally to market pressures, the requirements of equality legislation, and at the very lowest level, the national minimum wage. An industrial relations analysis of the actions and interests of the actors in these processes therefore can provide some insight into both the reasons for wage dispersion and the mechanisms to address at least some of its negative social consequences.

Two implications flow from examples such as these, both of great importance to students of industrial relations. The first is that policy makers concerned with the issues dealt with above should recognise that insofar as the problems derive in part from the regulation (or lack of regulation) of the employment relationship, they need to understand the workings of industrial relations processes and institutions if they wish to propose serious remedies. The second is that those wishing to understand and explain interactions in the workplace, whether as students, policy makers or managers, cannot work within a framework that stops 'at the factory gate' (or more likely the office door). The study of industrial relations reveals that problems experienced in specific workplaces often have deep roots in other aspects of social and economic life and can rarely be resolved without such an understanding. As several of the authors in this volume demonstrate, however, such perspectives on these issues have not adequately caught the imagination and attention of those preoccupied with policy in vital social areas and that remains a key challenge for the subject.

The Structure of the Book

This book, like its predecessors in this series, is about industrial relations in Britain but it aims to locate developments here in their international context. The chapters, all written by leading authorities in the field, most of them members of or closely associated with the Industrial Relations Research Unit at the University of Warwick, follow the established tradition of developing an understanding of key issues in industrial relations through conceptual development grounded in the best empirical research.

The chapters fall under five major headings. The first acknowledges explicitly the importance of the international context for interactions in British workplaces, a theme which then runs through several contributions (most obviously, Marginson and Meardi). The subsequent four sections are derived from the 'systems approach' discussed above and adopted in many industrial relations texts: context, actors, processes and outcomes. The advantages of structure and order this provides potentially masks important connections and overlap between the sections. Chapters by Crouch and Hyman, for example, both locate UK industrial relations within explicit comparative contexts – of labour market dynamics and of European politics and regulatory frameworks respectively – and in doing so make clear both the universal application of industrial relations approaches and the need to understand sources of national variation. But they also necessarily provide information on key actors and processes, anticipating subsequent discussion. The sensitivity to context revealed in these chapters also informs many of the subsequent chapters dealing with actors. Thus, for example, the chapter on management by Sisson and Purcell locates its analysis of managerial action firmly within the context of changing structural and financial environments while those by Arrowsmith, Bach, Marginson and Meardi and Ram and Edwards all stress the need to understand industrial relations action, particularly that of management, the 'dominant actor' within specific contexts of ownership, sector, geography and size.

In different ways all these illustrate a central theme of this chapter, the need to abandon assumptions, often implicit, of some earlier approaches, that the terrain for industrial relations analysis could be reduced to that of a large UK-based manufacturing plant or a national public sector service. Similarly, the chapter by Simms and Charlwood argues for an analytical approach to trade union decline, identifying sources of power and linking *actors* to *contexts*.

The chapters on process illustrate two further issues that reflect the need for industrial relations to abandon earlier limiting assumptions. First is the explicit recognition that an emphasis on collective bargaining between employers and trade unions as the dominant process – possibly even the sole process – of regulation of the employment relationship has to give way to a more diversified approach that embraces other modes of regulation. The second, particular to the UK within a European context, is the ever-greater emphasis placed on understanding the more complex and interventionist role of legal intervention into employment regulation. Thus while some of the tensions and dynamics within contemporary UK industrial relations can only be understood by reference to its 'voluntarist' past, the idea, once widespread, that law plays only a minor, auxiliary role in employment regulation has to be fully abandoned. Dickens and Hall and Colling provide overviews of the UK legal framework, linking references in virtually every other chapter in the book to the role of law in helping understanding of current developments.

The final section on 'outcomes' is conceived much more broadly than in Dunlop's treatment, which focused on the hierarchies of rules affecting employment. Rather, the chapters evaluate current policy results in four critical areas: skills; economic performance; pay and working time; and equality and diversity. Readers may be frustrated by the selectivity required in a volume of this size: there is no chapter on health and safety or on conflict, though this latter theme is discussed in other substantive chapters (e.g. Simms and Charlwood; Colling; Dean and Liff). Another criticism of the classification deployed by the editors here must be accepted – many of the issues discussed under this heading might be considered issues of *context* as much as *outcomes*. Social inequality, for example, structures approaches to the labour market as much as it is perpetuated by it. Such is the rich terrain of industrial relations analysis, however, and we must hope at least that it helps to stimulate further debate.

This is not a book to be read from cover to cover, except perhaps by book reviewers; but the reading of one chapter alone is unlikely to be sufficient for students of the subject to grasp all the key issues relating to that topic. Pay and pay structures provide one example of this. Readers interested in the subject may well start with the chapter by Grimshaw and Rubery and, having read it, will know that they also need to read those by Keep *et al.* on skills, by Dean and Liff on gendered pay and by Brown on the decline of collective bargaining for a more comprehensive grasp of the issues involved. We have tried to illustrate the importance of these interconnections by cross-referencing throughout but engaged readers will, we hope, be able to use the richness of the chapters to establish their own patterns of search and discovery.

References

Ackers, P. and Wilkinson, A. 2003: The British industrial relations tradition – formation, breakdown and salvage. In Ackers, P. and Wilkinson, A. (eds) *Understanding Work and Employment: Industrial Relations in Transition*. Oxford, Oxford University Press, pp. 1–30.

Barratt, C. 2009: *Trade Union Membership 2008*. Department for Business, Enterprise and Regulatory Reform, London.

Barrett, M. and McIntosh, M. 1982: *The Anti-social Family*. London, Verso.

Bell, D. 1973: *The Coming of Post-Industrial Society*. London, Heinemann.

Bensman, J. and Lilienfeld, R. 1975: Craft and consciousness. In Salaman, G. and Speakman, M. (eds) *People and Work*. Milton Keynes, Open University Press, pp. 186–196.

Blundell, R., Reed, H., Van Reenen, H. and Shepherd, A. 2003: The impact of the new deal for young people on the labour market: a four year assessment. In Dickens, R., Gregg, P. and Wadsworth, J. (eds) *The Labour Market Under New Labour: The State of Working Britain*. Basingstoke, Palgrave Macmillan, pp. 17–32.

Blyton, P. and Turnbull, P. 2004: *The Dynamics of Employee Relations*. Basingstoke, Palgrave Macmillan.

Bolton, S. and Houlihan, M. 2009: Work, workplaces, and workers: the contemporary experience. In Bolton, S. and Houlihan, M. (eds) *Work Matters: Critical Reflections on Contemporary Work*. Baskingstoke, Palgrave Macmillan, pp. 1–20.

Botero, W. 2009: Class in the 21st century. In Sveinsson, K. (ed.) *Who Cares about the Working Class?* London, Runnymede Trust, pp. 7–15.

Brown, A., Charlwood, A., Forde, C. and Spencer, D. 2007: Changing Job Quality in Great Britain 1998–2004. *Employment Relations Research Series*. London, Department of Trade and Industry.

Brown, W. and Nash, D. 2008: What has been happening to collective bargaining under New Labour? Interpreting WERS 2004. *Industrial Relations Journal*, 39 (2), 91–103.

Bunting, M. 2004: *Willing Slaves: How the Overwork Culture is Ruling Our Lives*. London, Harper Collins.

Burchell, B. 2002: The prevalence and redistribution of job insecurity and work intensification. In Burchell, B., Lapido, D. and Wilkinson, D. (eds) *Job Insecurity and Work Intensification*. London, Routledge, pp. 61–78.

Butler, T. and Watt, P. 2007: *Understanding Social Inequality*. London, Sage.

Cabinet Office 2009: *Unleashing Aspiration: The Final Report of the Panel on Fair Access to the Professions*. London, Her Majesty's Government.

Coats, D. 2009: The sunlit uplands or Bleak House? Just how good are today's workplaces? In Bolton, S. and Houlihan, M. (eds) *Work Matters: Critical Reflections on Contemporary Work*. Baskingstoke, Palgrave Macmillan, pp. 21–37.

Crompton, R. 1997: *Women and Work in Modern Britain*. Oxford, Oxford University Press.

Darlington, R. (ed.) 2009: *What's the Point of Industrial Relations? In Defence of Critical Social Science*. Manchester: British Universities' Industrial Relations Association.

Deakin, S. and Morris, G. 2005: *Labour Law*. Fourth Edition. Oxford, Hart.

Dennis, N., Henriques, F. and Slaughter, C. 1969: *Coal is our Life*. Tavistock Press, London.

Dickens, R. and Ellwood, D. 2003: Child poverty in Britain and the United States. *The Economic Journal*, 113, June, 219–239.

Dixon, S. 2003: Migration within Britain for job reasons. *Labour Market Trends*, April, 191–201.

Dorling, D., Rigby, J., Wheeler, B., Ballas, D., Thomas, B., Fahmy, E., Gordon, D. and Lupton, R. 2007: *Poverty, Wealth and Place in Britain 1968–2005*. York, Joseph Rowntree Foundation.

Dunlop, J.T. 1958: *Industrial Relations Systems*. Carbondale, Southern Illinois University Press.

Edwards, P.K. 1986: *Conflict at Work*. Oxford, Blackwell.

Edwards, P.K. 2003: The employment relationship and the field of industrial relations. In Edwards, P.K. (ed.) *Industrial Relations: Theory and Practice*. Second Edition. Oxford, Blackwell, pp. 1–36.

Edwards, P. and Wajcman, J. 2005: *The Politics of Working Life*. Oxford, Oxford University Press.

Emmott, M. 2005: What is employee relations? *Change Agenda*. London, Chartered Institute of Personnel and Development.

Ferguson, N. 2003: *Empire: How Britain Made the Modern World*. London, Penguin.

Freeman, R., Hersch, J. and Mishel, L. (eds) 2005: *Emerging Labor Market Institutions for the Twenty First Century*. Chicago, Chicago University Press.

Gallie, D. 2001: Skill change and the labour market: gender, class and unemployment. Paper given at the National Institute for Economic and Social Research conference *Disadvantage in the Labour Market: Diversity and Commonality in Causes, Consequences and Redress*, 15 June.

Goldthorpe, J. and Lockwood, D. 1969: *The Affluent Worker*. Cambridge, Cambridge University Press.

Goos, M. and Manning, A. 2003: McJobs and MacJobs: the growing polarisation of jobs in the UK. In Dickens, R., Gregg, P. and Wadsworth, J. (eds) *The Labour Market Under New Labour: The State of Working Britain*. Basingstoke, Palgrave MacMillan, pp. 70–85.

Health and Safety Executive (HSE) 2008: *Health and Safety Statistics 2007–08*. London, HSE.

Heery, E. and Frege, C. 2006: New actors in industrial relations. *British Journal of Industrial Relations*, 44 (4), 601–604.

Hills, J., Sefton, T. and Stewart, K. 2009: Climbing every mountain or retreating from the foothills? In Hills, J., Sefton, T. and Stewart, K. (eds) *Towards a More Equal Society? Poverty, Inequality and Policy Since 1997*. Bristol, Polity Press, pp. 341–360.

Hughes, M. 2009: *Social Trends*, 39, 2009 Edition. London, Office for National Statistics.

Humphries, J. and Rubery, J. 1992: The legacy for women's employment: integration, differentiation and polarisation. In Michie, J. (ed.) *The Economic Legacy 1979–1992*. London, Academic Press, pp. 236–254.

Hyman, R. 1989: *The Political Economy of Industrial Relations: Theory and Practice in a Cold Climate*. Basingstoke, Macmillan.

Hyman, R. 2003: The historical evolution of British industrial relations. In Edwards, P.K. (ed.) *Industrial Relations: Theory and Practice*. Second Edition. Oxford, Blackwell, pp. 37–57.

Jacoby, S. 2003: A century of human resource management. In Kaufman, B., Beaumont, R. and Helfgoot, R. (eds) *Industrial Relations to Human Resources and Beyond*. New York, M.E. Sharpe, pp. 147–171.

Jenkins, J. 2008: *Work and Worklessness amongst Households*. London, Office for National Statistics.

Kaufman, B. 2004: *The Global Evolution of Industrial Relations: Events, Ideas and the IIRA*. International Labour Office, Geneva.

Kaufman, B. 2008: Paradigms in industrial relations: original, modern and versions in-between. *British Journal of Industrial Relations*, 46, 314–339.

Khan, K. and Ker, D. 2009: *Employment of Foreign Workers: Period of Arrival*. London, Office for National Statistics.

Kochan, T. 1998: What is distinctive about industrial relations research? In Whitfield, K. and Strauss, G. (eds) *Researching the World of Work*. Ithaca, Cornell University Press.

Low Pay Commission 2009: *National Minimum Wage: Low Pay Commission Report 2009*. London, The Stationery Office.

Ludlum, S., Wood, S., Heery, E. and Taylor, A. 2003: Politics and employment relations. *British Journal of Industrial Relations*, 41 (4), 609–616.

MacDonald, R., Shildrick, T., Webster, C. and Simpson, D. 2005: Growing up in poor neighbourhoods: the significance of class and place in the extended transitions of 'socially excluded' young adults. *Sociology*, 39 (5), 873–891.

Machin, S. 2003: Wage inequality since 1975. In Dickens, R. Gregg, P. and Wadsworth, J. (eds) *The Labour Market Under New Labour: The State of Working Britain*. Basingstoke, Palgrave Macmillan, pp. 191–200.

McGrew, A. 2008: The logics of economic globalisation. In Ravenhill, J. (ed.) *Global Political Economy*. Oxford, Oxford University Press, pp. 277–313.

Metcalf, D. 2005: *British Unions: Resurgence or Perdition?* Provocation Series, 1.1. London, The Work Foundation.

Peston, R. 2008: *Who Runs Britain? And Who's to Blame for the Economic Mess We're In*. London, Hodder and Stoughton.

Rees, C., Scarbrough, H. and Terry, M. 1997: The people management implications of leaner ways of working. *Issues in People Management*, No. 15, London: Institute of Personnel and Development.

Rutter, J. and Latorre, M. 2009: Migration, migrants and inequality. In Hills, J., Sefton, T. and Stewart, K. (eds) *Towards a More Equal Society? Poverty, Inequality and Policy Since 1997*. Bristol, Polity Press, pp. 201–220.

Sefton, T., Hills, J. and Sutherland, H. 2009: Poverty, inequality and redistribution. In Hills, J., Sefton, T. and Stewart, K. (eds) *Towards a More Equal Society? Poverty, Inequality and Policy Since 1997*. Bristol, Polity Press, pp. 21–46.

Self, A. and Zealey, L. 2007: *Social Trends*. Basingstoke, Palgrave Macmillan.

Sennet, R. 2003: *Respect: The Formation of Character in an Age of Inequality*. London, Penguin.

Sisson, K. 2008: *Why employment relations matters*. Seminar paper given to the Industrial Relations Research Unit, University of Warwick, November.

Streeck, W. and Thelen, K. (eds) 2005: *Beyond Continuity: Institutional Change in Advanced Political Economies*. Oxford, Oxford University Press.

Supiot, A. 2002: Synthesis. In Auer, P. and Gazier, B. (eds) *The Future of Work, Employment and Social Protection: The Dynamics of Change and the Protection of Workers*. Geneva, International Labour Organisation, pp. 217–228.

Thompson, P. 2003: Disconnected capitalism: or why employers can't keep their side of the bargain. *Work, Employment and Society*, 17 (2), 359–378.

Toynbee, P. and Walker, D. 2001: *Did Things Get Better? An Audit of Labour's Successes and Failures*. London, Penguin.

Tripney, J., Newman, M., Bangpan, M., Hempel-Jorgensen, A., Mackintosh, M., Tucker, H. and Sinclair, J. 2009: *In-Work Poverty – A Systematic Review*. London, Department for Work and Pensions.

Warren, T. 2003: Class and gender based working time? Time poverty and the division of domestic labour. *Sociology*, 37 (4), 733–752.

Wynn, M. and Leighton, P. 2006: Will the real employer please stand up? Agencies, client companies and the employment status of the temporary agency worker. *Industrial Law Journal*, 35, 301–320.

SECTION ONE

BRITISH INDUSTRIAL RELATIONS IN COMPARATIVE CONTEXT

2

BRITISH INDUSTRIAL RELATIONS: BETWEEN SECURITY AND FLEXIBILITY

COLIN CROUCH

Introduction

The term 'industrial relations' emerged as denoting a specialized field of study in the mid-20th century, initially as an Anglo-American concept. During the 1960s it spread to other European countries, often as a literal and sometimes obviously foreign translation: *industrielle Beziehungen* in German; *relazioni industriali* in Italian. The French retained some autonomy with *relations professionnelles* (*professionnel* meaning 'occupational' in French rather than 'professional'). The development of the specialized field was part of a general trend of the 20th century in both science and policy to specialize and compartmentalize. Such specialization represented a certain progress in focus and the precision of knowledge. However, compartmentalization is always artificial, as life does not appear in segregated compartments. This is especially true at times when certain taken-for-granted fixed horizons enter a state of flux. This is the case today for many issues, including industrial relations. There is therefore a need for innovation, which is itself partly a return to an older tradition, in how we view the field of industrial relations and its appropriate wider context. This chapter proposes an attempt at such an innovation.

It was not the case that, before they acquired the Anglo-American term, people in other countries and languages had no conception of the field of organized relations between employers and trade unions as a field of study or public policy. It was, however, seen within a broader canvas of issues. From the late 19th century onwards German scholars and policy makers used the idea of *Sozialpolitik* – social policy – to embrace the full range of issues that we would today separate as industrial relations, the welfare state and citizenship rights. The policies and approaches concerned tried to provide an answer to the *soziale Frage* (*question sociale* in French), the 'social question'. That question was the integration of the increasingly disaffected manual working class that was being created by industrialization. Once universal citizenship had been more or less achieved, different fields of social policy had become fields for professional and technical administration, and collective and individual work relations had become primarily matters for negotiated or legal resolution, this ensemble fell apart and became detached from its original major social and political significance. The working class and its integration were increasingly taken for granted. Hence 'industrial relations'.

The first major change from this perspective went in the opposite direction from that being proposed here. Starting in the USA and spreading to the UK and beyond during the 1980s, the term 'human resource management' began to replace both 'industrial relations' and 'personnel management' in the names of both corporate departments and university courses. This signified a further compartmentalization, to the extent that workers were both decollectivized and depersonalized. The detailed reasons for this and its implications are beyond our scope here, except to note the change that it marked in the conception of issues, and the now complete disappearance of any perceived links between the world of work and wider socio-political life.

But the change that was taking place in the relationship between work and wider life was in fact making necessary a re-engagement of the two. The manual working class was declining considerably in size, making it no longer possible to take for granted a certain set of mid-20th century relations between citizenship, welfare state and working life. Technological change, the globalization of economic relations and the entry of women into the labour force in very large numbers were together producing changes in the balance between work and the rest of life. Questions which 30 years ago seemed to require an answer solely at the level of industrial relations today need them at a far broader level, certainly closer to the level of the original social question than to that of human resource management. A major example of such a question is the one which is our focus in this chapter: how are people to manage new demands placed upon them for flexibility, adaptability and frequent change, in their working lives, when for many reasons they also seek stability and freedom from anxiety? Below we shall first elaborate a potential model for bringing together a diverse range of fields which contain different components of answers to this question. Several different ensembles may result from an analysis based on such a model, which will have implications for different kinds of capitalism. While some general implications of this kind flow from the discussion, our primary task here is to examine the British case as one important example.

That UK public policy has during the past 30 years favoured 'flexibility' over 'security' in employment relations more strongly than most of its western European neighbours has become so taken for granted that its meaning needs to be questioned. Grounds for questioning are provided by the fact that British consumers, like Americans, demonstrated stronger consumer confidence from the mid-1990s until the late 2000s than many of their European counterparts. If British and American workers had such insecure labour market positions, how was this possible? The simple answer to this question from neo-classical economic theory would be that, once labour markets are made fully flexible, they are unlikely to suffer shocks, and therefore there is no contradiction between employment insecurity and consumer confidence. Closer inspection reveals this to be an oversimplification. In the following I shall try to formulate a more realistic expression of the confrontation, in order to relocate the British case on a more complex comparative map.

One important implication of the neo-classical view is that industrial relations institutions can do little about employment security in any case, as the market will eventually trump any attempt by other institutions to distort it. This argument has to be taken seriously, if only to show the need for industrial relations to be set in a wider context. Not only stable markets, but corporate policy, the support available through the welfare state, and several other factors may affect the dependence that given groups of workers may place on industrial relations institutions as such in search of a preferred balance between security and flexibility.

Coordination, Governance and Industrial Relations

Elsewhere (Crouch 2008, 2009) I have argued that the confrontation between flexibility and security should not be presented solely as one between the needs of the market economy and the search by workers for certainty in their lives. A modern market economy based on mass consumption itself requires the majority of workers to have enough sense of certainty in their economic lives to be confident consumers. Resolutions of the confrontation do not therefore stem solely from various compromises between the market on the one hand and social policy and/or industrial relations on the other. Table 2.1 presents a range of potential

Table 2.1 Policies and practices for combining flexibility and security

Governance modes	Policies and practices	Limitations
Various	1 Elite consumers, insecure workers	Limited growth prospects; long-term social control problems
	2 Export consumption, insecure workers	Dependent on non-synchronized trade cycles; limits to long-term viability
	3 Demographic structure segments population	Dependent on durability of demographic patterns
Market	4 Individuals insure against instability	Inadequate incentives for individuals to realize collective goods aspects; myopic individuals
	5 Private unsecured debt supports consumption of insecure workers	Limited capacity of economy to support unsecured debt

(Continued)

Table 2.1 (Continued)

Market + corporate hierarchy	6 Management apportions security levels, including use of external supply chains	Dependent on viability of firm; insider/outside divisions
Market + networks	7 Clusters, industrial districts provide opportunities for insecure workers	Limited to niche economies; insider/outsider divisions
Associations	8 Collective bargaining seeks to balance flexibility/security	Dependent on neo-corporatist structures of bargaining
Government + market	9 Government maintains stable demand levels	Ratchet effect in face of inflationary tendencies
Government	10 Government favours key industries/firms	Distorts competition; produces insider/outsider effects
	11 State provides labour market insurance and/or income support, reducing workers' dependence on labour market for standard of living	Limited capacity when operating alone; or reduce labour market incentives
	12 State supplies certain services outside market, reducing workers' dependence on labour market for standard of living	
	13 State supports workers' attempts to improve their employability/adaptability	Limited reach
Law	14 Law provides framework of employment rights and limits to them	Difficulty of engaging law in collective action tasks

resolutions, together with the forms of governance that produce them, with an indication of their limitations.

The first seven types must count as practices rather than as public policies, in that either they are not associated with any particular modes of governance, or the modes associated with them do not provide scope for strategic decisions about macro-economic governance – though as we shall see explicit policy-making does become mixed with some of them. Type 8 (collective bargaining) can under certain circumstances acquire such a strategic role, and it therefore comes here as a bridge type linking practices to the explicit public policies embodied in types 9–14.

Type 1: Elite consumers, insecure workers   Type 1 constitutes the mode of resolving the confrontation which has dominated for most of human history, including the early stages of industrial development. Elites, themselves protected from the labour market, confidently consume; workers work flexibly and can hardly afford to consume beyond subsistence levels. The approach was cast aside by capitalist economies when they entered the Fordist period of mass production at various points during the 20th century. However, its solution to the confrontation – the flexible labour force has sufficiently weak purchasing power for its lack of consumer confidence not to present a macro-economic problem – can apply to poor minorities within modern workforces. This type may therefore continue to appear as an aspect of type 2.

Type 2: Demographic structure segments population   In this second type, demographic characteristics mark off sections of the population whose labour is flexible and purchasing power relatively low. In advanced economies the main relevant divisions are gender, immigrant/ethnic minorities and certain age groups (see Dean and Liff, this volume). Women, more specifically mothers, are often regarded as not being in the same labour-force position as men; their redundancy, reduced hours or periods of unemployment are not seen as problematic, and their incomes tend to be low. Immigrant, and even some settled ethnic minority, workers may function in the same way. Their positions are in general far less secure and less well remunerated than the majority population, but while they remain *de facto* segregated from that majority, their lack of security does not threaten that of the majority. This will be particularly the case with illegal immigrants, who provide the most flexible of all kinds of labour, imposing no costs on public assistance and insurance systems if they lose their jobs. Sometimes young and/or old workers are also likely to be found in both insecure and low-paid employment – the former because they are seen as waiting for a chance to establish themselves on the occupational ladder; the latter because they are stepping off it.

Type 3: Export consumption, insecure workers   Here the economy is export oriented, and therefore dependent on consumer confidence in other societies, the insecurity of the domestic workforce not being relevant. This has been important to many instances of rapid economic growth amongst newly industrializing countries with flexible labour. It is currently important in both the Far East and central and eastern Europe. It was also a fundamental feature of the initial post-war recovery of West Germany.

Type 4: Individuals insure against instability   The 'individual insurance' pattern, type 4, is the purest neo-liberal approach. In a free market, individuals insure themselves against risk. In a perfect labour market therefore people would set aside from their current incomes in order to protect themselves from the adverse consequences of flexibility. Such behaviour is vulnerable to three market failures.

First, such insurance would be very expensive for the people most likely to need it, those on modest incomes, so they tend not to undertake it. Second, individuals are myopic in relation to likely major economic developments and would find it hard to make rational calculations concerning their insurance needs. Third, given that there is a collective interest in resolving the flexibility/security confrontation, and that individuals must be expected to take precautions below the level needed for this collective purpose, this is an area where governments have intervened. They have done so by providing social insurance (see type 11 below), which may in turn have crowded out any tendencies there might have been amongst the workforce to undertake private insurance.

Such insurance might take the form of using current income to invest in future retraining and mid-life education in order to prepare for economic change. This is subject to exactly the same market failures as in the general case, and has also been an area for government intervention. We shall encounter this as type 13.

Type 5: Private unsecured debt supports consumption of insecure workers   While insurance against labour market risk has not been a significant approach, another market-compatible practice has been to separate individuals' consumption behaviour from their labour market income. This involves facilitating consumer debt backed by collateral that is independent of labour market position (type 5). This has developed in a major way in a number of countries, principally the USA, the UK and Ireland. It has required three conditions. The first was a general rise in home ownership funded by mortgages, giving individuals on moderate and even low incomes forms of collateral partly independent of labour market position. The second was the growth of secondary financial markets that enabled the risks associated with housing and other forms of debt (such as credit cards, which were growing during the same period) to be shared amongst an increasing number of players in the financial markets. The third is a gradual deregulation of financial markets on a global scale, which enabled more and more players and holders of different kinds of funds to enter these markets. Eventually risks were being shared so widely that collateral requirements on mortgages, credit cards and other forms of debt became nugatory. The sums that people could borrow both rose strongly and – the point that is relevant to our present discussion – became detached from their labour market positions.

The system can be seen as a market-generated functional equivalent of government demand management – a form of 'house price Keynesianism' (Hay *et al.* 2008), or 'privatized Keynesianism' (Bellofiore and Halevi 2009; Crouch 2008). Whereas under straight Keynesianism government sustains mass demand through its own borrowing, here the borrowing is undertaken by individuals themselves, incurring mass individual debt. The collective goods element in this practice – the maintenance of consumer confidence – has meant that public policy eventually became involved in sustaining it. The model depends on continued housing market buoyancy, and governments may intervene to ensure this situation. This regime is vulnerable to eventual questioning of the value of the risks being traded, as was demonstrated in 2007–08 in a financial crisis of global scale.

Type 6: Management apportions security levels, including use of external supply chains Resolutions to the confrontation may be found at the level of the individual corporation, where firms develop internal markets, sub-contracting and supply chains offering explicit or implicit guarantees of employment and/or stable incomes to sections of the workforce (type 6). Such corporate policies will depend on distinctions being made (again, either explicitly or implicitly) between insiders and outsiders. The protection offered to insiders is partly dependent on outsiders bearing the full brunt of any difficulty encountered in maintaining the stability guarantee given major market fluctuations. Unless this is the case, these policies have not resolved the confrontation between flexibility and security, but have sacrificed flexibility. Demographic distinctions of type 2 might be used for this purpose. For example, workers of different ages, ethnicities and genders might be typically found working for sub-contractors rather than in leading firms' core business. Use can be made of illegal workers (usually illegal immigrants) in order to concentrate insecurity in particular groups and provide reassurance to others. Most important of all, global supply chains produce a mirror image of type 3 practices, with insecure workers being located outside the economy in which the corporation is based.

Type 7: Industrial districts provide opportunities for insecure workers An alternative form of perceived stability of employment chances in the face of market fluctuations can occur where large numbers of firms, particularly but not solely small and medium-sized enterprises (SMEs), in related areas of activity, cluster within geographical areas (type 7). Major instances are found in the Italian industrial districts (Pyke *et al.* 1990), in Denmark (Kristensen 1992) and in California (Kenney 2000). Such clusters provide security at a level above that of the individual enterprise. Workers perceive that they have a diversity of employment opportunities available to them within a geographical range and within social networks. The fragility of individual firms does not therefore necessarily threaten employment and income levels of either the economic activities or the areas concerned.

While such situations provide robust solutions to the security/flexibility problem, they have two weaknesses as general models. First, SME clusters are normally found in niche economies and are not likely to exist at a national level. They are most likely to thrive in activities involving new scientific knowledge or fashion-conscious design, where there are particular gains to be had from innovation based on tacit knowledge. Second, districts and other clustered activities move from being particularly resilient to being particularly brittle when there is a collapse of the whole sector in which the area is specializing, as this frequently leaves few employment opportunities, leading to a crisis of confidence and a decline in purchasing power.

Type 8: Collective bargaining seeks to balance flexibility/security Collective bargaining between trade unions and either individual firms or groups of employers (type 8) is normally associated with reinforcing labour-market stability of a kind that can support consumer confidence, but at the expense of flexibility. However, because collective bargaining involves negotiation and is capable of operating at a strategic level, it is possible for the participants in bargaining to trade flexibility and security.

This can happen under a variety of contexts, but not all. For example, when bargaining takes place at the level of the individual firm, workers' representatives may have to trade the short-term protection of their members' security against possible needs for flexibility if the firm is to survive and thrive. This is generally known as concession bargaining. Alternatively, unions may protect the positions of current insiders at the expense of outsiders, through such formulae as 'first in, last out' (which tends to discriminate against young workers – another example of type 2), or discriminating between a permanent core workforce and one on temporary contracts. Economists' theories of trade unions regard these practices as axiomatic (e.g. Blanchard and Summers 1986; Rueda 2005, 2007). This is because they assume a model of company-level bargaining (as in the US and Japanese cases). But a union with members across an entire industry or other generally defined labour market is likely to see such arrangements as leading eventually to employers preferring the creation of temporary and insecure contracts over stable ones (Watanabe 2009). For example, in Spain, the European country where most use is made of temporary contracts, unions oppose the strategy (Talani and Cerviño 2003: 214–215).

Above individual firm level, collective bargaining may be involved in explicit flexibility/security trade-offs, but only where bargaining takes a centralized form, with unions and employers associations being so structured that they cannot easily avoid taking responsibility for macro-economic consequences of their actions (Traxler 2003; Traxler *et al.* 2001).

Type 9: Government maintains stable demand levels   We now turn to explicit public-policy measures, the first being Keynesian demand management (type 9). Here government uses its own spending to boost the economy to avert recession and to cool the economy during inflation. By damping the impact of the trade cycle it seeks to reduce the degree of insecurity in the labour market. This was the main macro-economic strategy pursued in the USA, the UK and the Nordic countries for the first three decades after World War II. It fell into relative disuse after it was considered to have worsened the inflationary crises of the 1970s.

Type 10: Government favours key industries/firms   Governments may also stabilize economic activity by intervening to protect industries seen as of particular importance (type 10). Workers in these industries have a strong expectation of security, while the burden of flexible adjustment is borne by those in other sectors. This was a strategy particularly favoured in France and Italy after World War II, as an alternative to Keynesianism. It is becoming increasingly difficult to maintain, particularly in the European Union, as it breaks many rules of competition law. It is also another approach that generates divisions between insiders (in the protected industries) and outsiders (in the non-strategic industries, usually light manufacturing and sectors dominated by small firms).

Type 11: State provides labour market insurance and/or income support; Type 12: State supplies certain services outside market   Classic social policy measures appear as types 11 and 12. Under the former come direct measures to sustain purchasing power under conditions of instability or disappearance of employment income: unemployment, sickness and retirement insurance; public assistance; statutory minimum wages. These are the main public policy equivalents of the 'missing' market practices of type 4. They constitute the main historical forms of governments' own attempts to resolve the flexibility/security confrontation.

Whereas type 11 policies supplement labour-market income (or compensate financially for lack of it), those of type 12 decommodify such basic services as health and education, separating consumption from income where they are concerned and thereby alleviating anxiety. However, the main practical significance of the distinction for contemporary labour markets has been a secondary, originally accidental consequence. Public services offered in kind include a range of care services: child care, sickness care, elderly care. Where these services are provided by the market, they tend to be too expensive for people on modest incomes, so there is underprovision. They are often provided, as in much of southern Europe, within the family, primarily by women. In that case the provision exists, but not as part of the labour market. Where government provides or subsidizes services, they are still primarily provided by women, but within the labour force, generating jobs, incomes and therefore purchasing power. Further, other women relieved of family caring roles by the availability of the public services enter other parts of the labour force. This leads to a kind of femino-multiplier of job creation. Within Europe, those economies that provide high levels of publicly funded direct services have higher levels of female *and aggregate* employment (Esping-Andersen 1999).

Type 13: State supports workers' attempts to improve their employability/adaptability   Type 11 policies are in many countries increasingly being linked to active labour market policy (ALMP) measures (type 13). Activation measures are often linked to official encouragement of type 4 practices, particularly via training and education. There is an important triangle linking types 4, 11 and 13. To the extent that type 13 policies are linked to type 11, ALMP takes the form of 'workfare' threatening loss of benefit if advantage is not taken of activation opportunities. If they are more linked to improved access to type 4, we may speak of Danish and Dutch 'flexicurity' measures, though the distinction is far from clear (Muffels 2008; Rogowski 2008).

Type 14: Law provides framework of employment rights and limits to them   Finally, account must be taken of the role of labour law (type 14). During at least democratic periods, the main purpose of labour law in most countries has been to protect the rights of employees against employers who are regarded as being *prima facie* more powerful than they are (Davies and Freedland 2007). Labour law has therefore been a force on the security side of the flexibility/security equation. As such, it has come under sustained criticism from economists and others during recent years when increasing employment has been seen to depend on increasing flexibility. The aim of much of this criticism has been to encourage labour law to accept a role in achieving a balance between security and flexibility. This is sometimes expressed in terms of degrees of deregulation, but deregulation nearly always requires some re-regulation, as maintenance of the market order itself requires a framework of rules (Majone 1990).

Types of Policy and Practice and Varieties of Capitalism

It will readily be seen that some of the differences amongst types of policy and practice outlined above resonate with analyses of different forms of capitalism. Those types most closely related to market governance (4 and 5, possibly 6) would seem to fit with what Hall and Soskice (2001) have called liberal market economies. Types 8–14 cannot, however, be aligned simply to their rival concept of coordinated market economies, as this oversimplified concept cannot cope with differences between the role of organized interests or different kinds of government action. More purchase can be had by applying Esping-Andersen's (1990) distinction between corporatist (more or less type 8) and social democratic (various combinations of 9–14). However, this too fails to deal with the fact that many countries that have featured strong social-democratic policies (mainly the Nordic countries) also have corporatist (type 8) forms of industrial relations. Also, Esping-Andersen's modelling of welfare states is concerned overwhelmingly with income-maintenance policies and cannot cope with differences between policies of types 11–14, though these are becoming highly important. His account is also not well suited to distinguishing between the strong interventionist policies of type 10 (mainly associated with France and Italy, which are not normally defined as social democratic), and those of 11–13.

Varieties of capitalism theories are in general not sufficiently nuanced to deal with important differences emerging amongst advanced industrial societies today. This is not surprising. Esping-Andersen's model is based on certain stylized differences emerging amongst different national systems depending on different configurations of power relations amongst traditional elites, capitalists and workers' organizations during the early stages of industrialization. It would be surprising if these differences proved adequate to deal with different approaches being taken within societies experiencing economic globalization and a transition to a post-industrial economy. This chapter is not the place to take up the challenge of providing a new general theory of different policy trajectories during these major historical processes, as we are concerned primarily with just one country, the UK. We can, however, note certain complexities in the British case as we discuss it below. According to both Hall and Soskice and Esping-Andersen, the UK is a liberal, that is, market-based, society. The discussion below will corroborate much of that analysis. Certainly the UK today stands closer to that model than it did in the 1970s, when collective bargaining played a far bigger role in regulating the labour market. There are, however, certain points of departure from that model, in particular in relation to active government policy in shaping the workforce.

Flexibility and Security in British Employment

We can now locate the British case within this wider framework, exploring one by one the roles of the different policy and practice approaches from Table 2.1. The results are shown in summary form in Table 2.2.

Table 2.2   UK policies and practices for combining flexibility and security

Policies and practices	British experience since 1980s
1 Elite consumers, insecure workers	Some return, through rising inequalities – mainly linked to position of recent immigrants (type 2)
2 Demographic structure segments population	**Major part-time role for female workers; also for immigrants**
3 Export consumption, insecure workers	No importance
4 Individuals insure against instability	A policy aspiration, combined with type 13
5 Private unsecured debt supports consumption of insecure workers	**Very major importance from mid-1980s; supported by government policy**
6 Management apportions security levels, including use of external supply chains	Important in individual firms; nothing nationally specific
7 Clusters, industrial districts provide opportunities for insecure workers	Very rare
8 Collective bargaining seeks to balance flexibility/security	Some examples of concession bargaining
9 Government maintains stable demand levels	Continuing minor importance
10 Government favours key industries/firms	Rarely used, except for finance sector
11 State provides labour market insurance and/or income support, reducing workers' dependence on labour market for standard of living	Less important than in Nordic countries, Germany or France; more important than in central and southern Europe. Minimum wage legislation since 1997
12 State supplies certain services outside market, reducing workers' dependence on labour market for standard of living	Less important than in Nordic countries; more important than in rest of Europe
13 State supports workers' attempts to improve their employability/ adaptability	Strong policy emphasis, but low levels of actual support; combined with type 4 policies as 'workfare'
14 Law provides framework of employment rights and limits to them	Strong role of law in encouraging labour force participation, combined with type 2 practices; declining role of law supporting employment rights as such

Type 1   These practices are typical of societies where a rich minority contributes enough to consumption to compensate for the fact that some other members of the society, in insecure economic positions, are in poverty. This does not apply to British society in the late 20th and early 21st centuries. However, an element of it has been marginally present. Along with the USA,

the UK did become a highly unequal society during these decades, with a high and conspicuously consuming wealthy elite and some 'working poor' in flexible labour market positions and on very low incomes. However, the 1997 Labour government enacted minimum wage legislation early on (see Grimshaw and Rubery, this volume), which placed a floor under low incomes, with the exception of course of those of illegal immigrants. Also, if this type of practice was in evidence in the UK, it did not affect the position of the mass of worker-consumers.

Type 2   In common with many countries that have achieved high levels of labour-force participation, the UK has important segmented labour forces based on gender and ethnic or migration status. Type 2 practices have therefore been more important. The country has a high level of female participation, the majority of it part-time (Table 2.3). Part-time work in the UK is not necessarily precarious, and its hours are often regular (Blossfeld and Hakim 1997; Ginn *et al.* 1996; Hakim 1995), but it provides a flexible form of employment for employers. Whether or not part-time work is a source of security or insecurity for the people, primarily women, who undertake it, is not easy to determine. Where it is undertaken because of difficulties in finding child care, and particularly in the case of the UK's relatively large population of single mothers, it is a source of low incomes. In some other cases, income from part-time work may provide a useful but not vital supplement to a partner's full-time work, improving a household's security while offering a flexible form of employment to the economy. However, as noted above, the principal contribution of part-time work to the flexibility/security balance at macro-level operates similarly to type 1.

The UK also has relatively large ethnic minority and recent immigrant populations, who are often found in insecure labour market positions and on low incomes. They therefore also contribute to flexibility in the same way. It is possible to give comparative statistics of immigrant (strictly speaking, foreign-born) populations (Table 2.4), but not of ethnic minorities, as countries use such different definitions for these. The UK does not have a particularly high foreign population, compared with most of the rest of western Europe, but it does also have a large settled population of ethnic minority origin.

Type 3   Long a weak performer in manufacturing and net exports, the UK has not been a locus of type 3 practices throughout its industrial history. This position has become more exaggerated in recent years, leading the country to rely on domestic consumption of domestically produced services for growth. Table 2.5 presents very recent data for the balance of payments of various countries, but the UK's deficit position here is a long-term one. This presents *prima facie* a major paradox, since British workers enjoyed less formal job protection than their counterparts in many other European countries, and yet maintained higher levels of consumer confidence, enough to maintain higher levels of economic growth than several of these others (also shown in Table 2.5). Given that much British consumer spending is devoted to exports, this means that people were also spending considerably on each others' traded services. They displayed greater consumer confidence than

Table 2.3   Female participation in employment (2007), European countries and the USA

% women in employment		% employed women who are part-time	
Norway	74.0	Netherlands	75.0
Denmark	73.2	Switzerland	59.0
Sweden	71.8	Germany	45.8
Switzerland	71.6	Norway	44.1
Netherlands	69.6	**UK**	**42.2**
Finland	68.5	Austria	41.2
Estonia	65.9	Belgium	40.6
USA	65.9	Sweden	40.0
UK	**65.5**	Denmark	36.2
Austria	64.4	France	30.2
Latvia	64.4	Italy	26.9
Germany	64.0	Spain	22.8
Slovenia	62.6	Turkey	19.7
Lithuania	62.4	Finland	19.3
Portugal	61.9	Portugal	16.9
Ireland	60.6	Poland	12.5
France	60.0	Estonia	12.1
Japan	59.4	Croatia	11.3
Bulgaria	57.6	Slovenia	11.3
Czech R	57.3	Romania	10.4
Belgium	55.3	Lithuania	10.2
Spain	54.7	Greece	10.1
Slovakia	53.0	Czech R	8.5
Romania	52.8	Latvia	8.0
Hungary	50.9	Hungary	5.8
Poland	50.6	Slovakia	4.5
Croatia	50.0	Bulgaria	2.1
Greece	47.9		
Italy	46.6		
Turkey	23.8		

Source: Eurostat
Data refer to women between the ages of 15 and 64. Figures for part-time employment follow national definitions of part-time.

their counterparts in France, Germany, Italy and Spain, despite the higher levels of formal job protection and (in the case of France and Germany) more generous public income maintenance programmes enjoyed by these others.

Type 4   These practices should be particularly characteristic of neo-liberal economies, as the UK is often characterized. However, the market failures associated with

Table 2.4   Percentage foreign population (2007), European countries

Switzerland	20.20
Latvia	19.27
Estonia	17.73
Spain	9.87
Austria	9.83
Ireland	9.80
Germany	8.83
Belgium	8.64
Greece	7.85
UK	**5.90**
France	5.83
Sweden	5.29
Denmark	5.05
Norway	4.95
Italy	4.90
Netherlands	4.13
Portugal	4.06
Czech R	2.85
Slovenia	2.63
Finland	2.28
Hungary	1.67
Lithuania	1.19
Slovakia	0.59
Bulgaria	0.34
Poland	0.14
Romania	0.12

Source: Eurostat

this approach are as evident here as elsewhere. Also as elsewhere, British governments have historically intervened to bridge the gap, first by providing national insurance systems for protection against certain risks; second by providing free or heavily subsidized education to high levels. During recent years UK governments have moved to reduce any possible crowding-out effects of this by reducing state provision, as will be discussed with reference to types 11 and 13 below. It is notable that type 4 does not therefore appear as pure market practice, but as the market strongly encouraged by explicit public policy.

Action has concentrated at two points. First, government has encouraged employees to take out third-tier pensions, that is, pensions funded entirely by their own rather than by employers' or state contributions. Alongside this, employers have been reducing the coverage of second-tier, or occupational pensions, again throwing the emphasis on to employees' own provision. The UK has moved further in this direction than in countries where unions have a role in the

Table 2.5   Balance of trade as % of GDP (2007) and average annual growth rates (%) (1999–2008), advanced economies

Balance of trade		*Annual growth*	
Norway	18.05	Ireland	5.7
Netherlands	6.11	Greece	4.0
Germany	5.59	Spain	3.5
Finland	3.63	Finland	3.2
Denmark	3.33	Sweden	2.8
Austria	1.82	**UK**	**2.6**
France	−1.75	USA	2.5
Italy	−1.82	Netherlands	2.4
UK	**−2.12**	Norway	2.4
USA	−4.95	Austria	2.4
Ireland	−4.98	Belgium	2.2
Belgium	−6.89	France	2.0
Spain	−8.36	Denmark	1.6
Greece	−9.12	Portugal	1.5
Portugal	−10.15	Japan	1.3
		Germany	1.2
		Italy	1.2

Source: Eurostat

management of pension schemes (Ebbinghaus 2006). Pension reform in the UK has been a discussion between ministers and the major insurance firms, focused on the investment potential of insurance funds. There has certainly been a decline in the coverage of second-tier pensions in the UK. On the other hand, while first-tier pensions are less generous than in most other western European countries, they have increased in recent years (see discussion of type 11). However, there has been little increase in the take-up of third-tier pensions (Clark and Emmerson 2003; Taylor-Gooby 2002). Overall therefore there has been a weakening of private pension provision, whether funded by employers and employees together or by employees alone. The recent decline in share markets and other investment opportunities has further reduced incentives to insure one's own future income streams. Overall it would therefore seem that changes in practices and policies in relation to type 4 action have weakened rather than strengthened the market's own capacity to resolve the confrontation between flexibility and security.

More prominent in public debate has been the question of individuals investing in their own future enhanced employability. As indicated above, there are several obstacles to this happening within the market alone, and it is therefore not surprising that governments in the UK have also intervened here to stimulate and support the market. They have done this partly by introducing student fees for university education alongside a strong expansion of that education. In further education outside universities the record has been considerably less successful.

Historically the UK has had low levels of apprenticeship and other vocationally oriented forms of training and education. This area continues to be weak in performance, despite or because of repeated reorganizations of the sector by government (Grugulis 2003; Steedman 2001; see also Keep *et al.*, this volume).

Type 5   If insurance forms of market solutions to the flexibility/security confrontation have had a mixed record in the UK, debt-based market solutions have been particularly strong. With Ireland, Hungary and Latvia (Hay *et al.* 2008; Bohle 2009), and outside Europe the USA, the UK developed particularly strongly the model of 'privatized Keynesianism' based on mortgage and credit card debt, but particularly the former, from the mid-1980s onwards. As explained above, this model depended on the coincidental expansion of home ownership and other forms of credit to households on moderate incomes and of secondary risk trading in an increasingly deregulated global financial market. The UK was exceptionally well placed to participate in this process, with the financial sector being larger in relation to the rest of the economy than in any other European country (Table 2.6). By 2007 household mortgage indebtedness had reached exceptionally high levels, larger even than in the USA, this debt providing strong support to the maintenance

Table 2.6   Annual balance sheet totals of credit institutions as % of GDP (2006 or 2005), European countries

UK	**2095**
Switzerland	1578
Denmark	1323
Netherlands	1317
Belgium	1290
Germany	1170
France	1107
Austria	1092
Portugal	954
Spain	912
Italy	679
Norway	530
Greece	514
Finland	500
Estonia	384
Slovenia	314
Hungary	284
Czech R	280
Slovakia	223
Lithuania	210
Poland	182

Source: Eurostat

of purchasing power (Table 2.7). The low role of exports in UK economic performance meant that British people were maintaining each other in employment by extending their credit lines. As a consequence their *de facto* employment security became stronger than that in economies where legal protection was stronger but economic growth lower. As housing and other debt relieved the labour market of the strain of sustaining consumption, the British economy enjoyed its first period of relative success over the other large western European economies for decades.

By the turn of the century this process had developed sufficiently strongly for it to be described it as a 'model'. Overall it must be classified as a market practice rather than as public policy, as it developed gradually, and without anyone ever planning that it would play the role that it did. It was in fact fundamentally related to the concept of 'liberal market economies' – discussed above – that has been proposed as a model of an entire economic system distinguishing the Anglophone countries from almost everywhere else (Hall and Soskice 2001). The authors of this concept included as parts of an integrated whole both deregulated, short-term-oriented financial markets and flexible labour markets, though they did not perceive the link forged between these two components by extended household debt.

Certain acts of government policy promoted the model, at first accidentally. First, the sale of local authority homes to their tenants at low prices from the 1980s onwards opened the possibility of residential property ownership and access to property-based mortgages to people on modest incomes. Second, the 'Big Bang' deregulation of the City of London in 1985 enabled financial firms based in the UK to take early advantage of the new possibilities of the global financial system. However, after a time easing access to housing debt became more explicitly a means whereby governments could sustain demand without using Keynesian policies. Maintaining the buoyancy of the housing market became an objective of government – signs of a slow-down in house-price inflation being viewed negatively. Consistent with this view, the British government began to prefer the retail price index over the consumer price index as its measure of inflation. The latter includes house prices, where inflation was officially viewed with favour.

By 2007 the housing-based credit system had become so important to UK economic health that the imminent collapse of a building society specializing in

Table 2.7   Mortgages as a % of disposable income (2006), selected countries

UK	**129.2**
USA	104.8
Germany	70.9
Japan	65.1
Italy	39.4

Source: OECD Economic Outlook, December 2008

The countries listed were the only ones for which OECD could collect statistics. The Italian figure is for all medium- and long-term loans.

extended credit to relatively poor families (Northern Rock) led rapidly to a government rescue operation. This was soon realized to be the start of the general global financial crisis and collapse of the unsecured credit markets and associated secondary risk trading, a crisis powered primarily by the collapse of the US sub-prime housing market – the equivalent phenomenon, serving the same consumer market function, in the USA. The future of this component of the UK system is therefore, at the time of writing, uncertain.

Type 6   These practices, involving the differential allocation of security and flexibility of employment through sub-contracting and supply chains, exist in the UK just as they do in most other advanced countries. As corporations develop global supply chains, the impact on workers in wealthy countries is ambiguous. There is probably a net flow of jobs towards developing economies, which will be associated with declining employment, redundancies and plant closures – increases in uncertainty. However, the posts that are retained in the richer economies tend to be the high-productivity, higher-paid, more secure ones, low wages and low employment security being borne by workers in second and third world economies – which are in turn primarily dependent on types 1 and 3 models for their own reconciliation of the security/flexibility confrontation.

The UK is host to a large number of TNCs, but it underwent its crisis of a decline in manufacturing and the associated uncertainty during the 1980s and early 1990s. While the impact of supply-chain shifts continues to affect certain parts of the services sectors (e.g. call centres), the country has probably reached a position where it gains more from the reorganization of global supply chains than it loses.

Type 7   There are very few examples of networked industrial districts or clustered economies in the UK (type 7), apart from a small number of niches (Crouch and Farrell 2001).

Type 8   As discussed in other chapters in this volume, collective bargaining has undergone considerable decline in the UK since its peak during the 1970s, partly as an indirect consequence of the decline in manufacturing in which private-sector bargaining was concentrated (see Arrowsmith; Brown, this volume). Changes in the role of bargaining in resolving the flexibility/security confrontation are more difficult to trace. On the one hand, if collective industrial relations decline overall, the contribution that they might make to macro-economic goals will also decline. On the other hand, bargaining during the 1960s and 1970s heyday only occasionally contributed to any such reconciliation. This was partly because the order of the day during that period was combating inflation and not flexibility/security reconciliation, and partly because neo-corporatist collaboration was weak in the UK in any case (Crouch 1993). More recently, concession bargaining, whereby unions agree to changes in working practices in exchange for employment stability, has become important. This has been facilitated by the trend to single-employer rather than associational bargaining – a general tendency, but particularly in evidence in the UK, which within Europe ranks alongside only France and central European economies for the scarcity of bargaining above the level of the individual firm (European

Commission 2009: 76). The country also has a low level of collective bargaining coverage similar to that in central Europe (ibid.: 78).

Type 9   Keynesian demand management declined in the UK from the mid-1970s onwards as part of the international reaction against its apparent inability to cope with major inflationary crises. It did, however, make something of a return from the late 1990s, particularly in contrast with the situation in European countries that joined the single European currency. The latter became (more or less) tied to a monetary regime of the European Central Bank that targeted price levels alone (Dyson 2008; Talani and Casey 2008), while the Bank of England (like the US Federal Reserve) was also able to have regard to unemployment levels. Keynesian demand management therefore survived in the UK in a minor form, though not as strongly as in the Scandinavian economies.

Type 10   Policies favouring particular sectors or national champion firms have not featured in British policy during the past 30 years. There is one major exception to this in the special status of the 'City of London', or the financial sector, where successive governments have seen a source of major comparative advantage for the UK economy. This in turn partly accounts for the large size of this sector and the particular prominence enjoyed by type 5 practices. The favoured sector has therefore been relevant to explaining the British resolution of the flexibility/security confrontation, but in an indirect way, not as a means for differentiating between favoured (secure) and unfavoured (flexible) industries as in France and Italy.

Types 11–13   These types are best discussed together, as they constitute the ensemble of public social policy, though differences in the balance amongst them are fundamental to international comparisons. The UK is amongst those European countries whose welfare states provide services (type 12) as well as money transfers (type 11). The indirect contribution that this difference can make to levels of female labour force participation was discussed above. The UK has been an example of a strong direct service-delivery welfare state, with a relatively high proportion of its total workforce being women in various care and other public service delivery occupations (Table 2.8). It is not as high as in the Nordic countries, but is amongst the highest overall.

Type 11 policies as such have been less generous in the UK than almost anywhere else in north-western European countries, but they have been higher than in southern Europe (Table 2.9).

As noted above, social security payments are everywhere increasingly being linked to active labour market policy (ALMP) measures (type 13). There has been considerable discussion of activation policies in the UK, though a comparison of expenditure on ALMP as a percentage of GDP showed the UK spending less than a quarter of that achieved in Belgium, Denmark, France, Germany, the Netherlands, and Sweden – though the figures date from 2000 (OECD 2002, cited in De Lathouwer 2008: 239). Overall, since the 1980s British employment services have gradually moved away from helping those having trouble finding work

Table 2.8   Women employed in health and other care occupations as % of all persons employed (2007), European and selected other countries

Norway	16.05
Denmark	14.81
Sweden	13.23
Finland	13.18
Netherlands	13.02
France	9.66
Switzerland	9.63
USA	9.61
UK	**9.51**
Canada	9.04
Germany	8.70
Ireland	8.30
Japan	6.86
Austria	6.60
Russia	5.97
Lithuania	5.61
Czech R	5.51
Portugal	5.40
Slovakia	5.40
Hungary	5.18
Estonia	4.88
Serbia	4.83
Spain	4.62
Poland	4.61
Italy	4.58
Slovenia	4.53
Croatia	4.34
Bulgaria	3.84
Latvia	3.82
Greece	3.41
Romania	3.11
Turkey	1.36

Source: ILO Yearbook 2008

towards 'workfare', cajoling those who did not necessarily see themselves as in the labour market (Davies and Freedland 2007: 174).

Type 14   Finally, the UK is remarkable for the emphasis placed in its public policies on re-equilibrating labour's legal rights to security. The country participated in, and in many respects led, the general process of deregulation, or the gradual removal of protection from employees. The UK has consistently been ranked as

Table 2.9   Social protection payments per capita in € (2006), European Union

Luxembourg	13458.3
Norway	9900.6
Switzerland	9126.8
Netherlands	9099.4
Sweden	8897.5
Denmark	8601.4
Austria	8523.9
Belgium	8520.3
France	8199.8
Germany	7705.8
UK	**7410.3**
Finland	7215.3
Iceland	6535.4
Italy	6476.3
Ireland	6320.7
Greece	5525.2
Spain	5162.7
Slovenia	4792.9
Portugal	4450.6
Cyprus	3993.7
Czech R	3439.3
Hungary	3400.6
Malta	3297.8
Slovakia	2387.2
Poland	2373.1
Estonia	1976.0
Lithuania	1770.0
Latvia	1547.3
Bulgaria	1294.1
Romania	1277.0

Source: Eurostat

an unrestricted labour market by the OECD and the EU, though the gap between it and other European nations has narrowed as others have imitated many of its approaches. This is consistent with a model of labour law as acting solely on the 'security' side; flexibility is served by reducing its role (see chapters by Colling; Dickens and Hall, this volume).

However, alongside this process has gone an extraordinary amount of new labour-market regulation. Some of this has been in compliance with European Union directives, which until recently continued to follow the concept of a 'European Social Model', offering workers a more favourable security/flexibility trade-off to that typical of Anglophone countries. But, as Davies and Freedland

(2007) show, many provisions do not follow this course. In the first years of New Labour government (1997–99) some elements of the collectivist agenda, and an individual agenda based on rights as countervailing power against the employer, remained in play. Then began a shift which Davies and Freedland analyse as one from treating workers' rights as a form of countervailing power against employers to that of devices designed to maximize labour-force participation. Rights increasingly took the form of increasing labour market 'inclusion' rather than the granting of substantive rights (ibid.: 81). The late 19th century idea of government as 'model employer' shifted from referring to government wages practice to meaning encouraging the disabled, single parents and other groups to enter employment (ibid.: 202–203). Within a context of weakening employee rights in general, those of some groups were enhanced – again, groups like parents of young children who might be inclined otherwise to leave the labour force (ibid.: 64). The authors ask why:

> did the voluntary principle continue to play a greater part in the arrangements for lone parents [in labour-force participation] as compared with disabled, especially as moving lone parents into work was seen as the main mechanism for relieving child poverty? (ibid.: 179)

The reason seems to be that the former had been more adept at getting into jobs without much policy support, so needed less pressure. This ceases to be problematic if one sees that the priority of government policy has been, not to provide a regime of overall balanced rights based on entitlements *per se*, but to maximize labour-force participation. In activating women and ethnic minorities in particular, these new trends in law provide certain kinds of security to sections of the labour force which are, in terms of type 2 practices, particularly flexible.

Conclusions: How Distinctive is the British Model?

The core of the British approach to combining flexibility with security runs across two axes. The first links certain demographic characteristics of the labour force with welfare state care services and changes in the character of labour law (types 2, 12 and 14). This combination has enabled the economy to bring into active employment highly flexible kinds of worker – women and ethnic minorities – who have had difficulties in entering employment in some other European economies. The second uses household debt (type 5) to decouple in part consumption and the labour market. This has enabled the country to reduce dependence on collective bargaining, demand management, or generous income maintenance programmes. However, this model is currently in a state of crisis. A third strand looms large in the rhetoric of public policy, but has been weaker in practical effect. This is the strand linking ALMP to benefit restrictions and encouragement of individuals to invest in their own futures (types 10, 12, 14). The resources devoted to the positive measures have been relatively weak.

None of the individual practices and policies that are distinctive of the British pattern are unique to it, but the overall combination may be unique – an observation that can probably be made about every country. Elements of the first strand – in particular the relationship between female employment and strong welfare services (the femino-multiplier) – are shared with the Nordic countries and, to a lesser extent, the Netherlands. In fact, the British case is a weaker instance of this pattern than the Nordics. Also, in those countries and the Netherlands much more reliance is placed on the collective bargaining system sharing a role in achieving the flexibility/security balance. The UK resembles Denmark, but not the other countries usually placed with it, in having labour law that supports flexibility rather than security. But in the Danish case this runs alongside strong collective bargaining and a considerably more generous income maintenance system; it also has a networked economy of industrial districts. While these comparator countries have, particularly in the Nordic cases, even stronger records of bringing women into paid employment than the British, the UK has until now enjoyed greater success in activating ethnic minorities as a flexible labour force without creating ethnic tensions. The reasons for this are beyond our scope here.

As already noted, the distinctive British 'privatized Keynesian' or mortgage-debt based consumption model is shared with some other European countries: Ireland, Hungary and Latvia. All three share the effects of the current crisis of this pattern. However, in Ireland, the country which probably comes closest to the UK within Europe, there is also a strong role for neo-corporatist collective bargaining. That country is also more dominated by TNC supply-chain management than is the UK, though in recent years it moved from being a cheap-labour supplier to being at the other end of the chain – a shift made easier by the housing credit model, which in Ireland (unlike the UK) was also associated with a boom in activity and employment in house-building. Hungary and Latvia are not strongly comparable, as they are both export-dependent economies with employment at the insecure end of supply chains. They were able to accommodate eventual pressures for increased domestic consumption only through the debt model, while balance of payments problems showed that the export model was not working.

The UK has remained very different from its more obvious comparators: the other large countries of western Europe. Germany in particular is a mirror image, having particularly low profiles at the points of strong emphasis in the UK. The femino-multiplier has until recently been relatively weak in Germany. This can be partly attributed to the reluctance of Catholic social policy to encourage women into the paid workforce (an attribute shared with Italy, Spain and post-communist Poland); and partly to the important role played by (largely male) income-maintaining social insurance in the welfare state, which crowds out potential public care service provision and/or funding. Germans also have relatively low levels of home ownership and strong debt-avoidance preferences. These have combined to give privatized Keynesianism a virtually non-existent place in the German economy. (German banks became heavily involved in secondary markets in 'poisoned paper', but they were investing in US, UK and Irish unsecured debt, not that of German citizens.) Instead Germany has relied on measures to balance flexibility and security that are weakly developed in the British case: strong export dependence (which becomes problematic when national trade cycles becoming increasing synchronized), a strong training system (which functions as ALMP *avant la lettre*), and continuing reliance on income maintenance and corporatist collective bargaining.

In this context, it is not surprising that attempts by Germany to imitate certain aspects of British policy were not particularly successful. In particular, none of the policy-commending processes, such as the Open Method of Coordination of the European Union, or the *OECD Jobs Study*, which have been influential in popularizing and encouraging various British practices, ever included massive housing debt in the list of commendable British activities, if only because the link between it and the country's ability to sustain consumer confidence amidst flexible labour markets was never perceived.

In terms of varieties of capitalism, the UK emerges from the above analysis as clearly displaying certain attributes of liberal market capitalism. However, to be content with just applying that label would be to miss the important nuances discussed above, which are fundamental to describing precisely how the liberal market components of the British ensemble interact with others. Also highly problematic is the extent to which the role of mortgage debt constitutes an example of how the liberal market works or an unsustainable distortion of it.

References

Bellofiore, R. and Halevi, J. 2009: Deconstructing Labor. A Marxian-Kaleckian perspective on what is 'new' in contemporary capitalism and economic. In Gnos, C. and Rochon, L.-P. (eds), *Employment, Growth and Development. A Post-Keynesian Approach*. Cheltenham: Elgar.

Blanchard, O. and Summers, L.H. 1986: Hysteresis and the European unemployment problem. *NBER Macroeconomics Annual*.

Blossfeld, H.-P. and Hakim, C. 1997: *Between Equalization and Marginalization: Women Working Part-Time in Europe and the United States of America*. Oxford: Oxford University Press.

Bohle, D. 2009: East European capitalism: what went wrong? *Intervention*, 1.

Clark, T. and Emmerson, C. 2003: Privatizing provision and attacking poverty? The direction of UK pensions policy under new Labour. *Journal of Pension Economics and Finance*, 2 (1), 67–89.

Crouch, C. 1993: *Industrial Relations and European State Traditions*. Oxford: Oxford University Press.

Crouch, C. 2008: What will follow the demise of privatised Keynesianism? *The Political Quarterly*, 79 (4), 476–487.

Crouch, C. 2009: Towards a theoretical framework for modelling the flexibility-security trade-off. GUSTO Working Paper 2:1. Coventry: Warwick Business School, mimeo.

Crouch, C. and Farrell, H. 2001: Great Britain: falling through the holes in the network concept. In Crouch, C. *et al.* (eds) *Local Production Systems in Europe*. Oxford: Oxford University Press, pp. 154–211.

Davies, P. and Freedland, M. 2007: *Towards a Flexible Labour Market: Labour Legislation and Regulation since the 1990s*. Oxford: Oxford University Press.

De Lathouwer, L. 2008: Making work pay, making transitions flexible: the case of Belgium in a comparative perspective. In Rogowski, R. (ed.) *The European Social Model and Transitional Labour Markets*. Farnham: Ashgate, pp. 227–265.

Dyson, K. (ed.) 2008: *The Euro at 10: Europeanization, Power, and Convergence* Oxford: Oxford University Press.

Ebbinghaus, B. 2006: The politics of pension reform: managing interest group conflicts. In Clark, G.L., Munnell, A.H. and Orszag, J.M. (eds) *The Oxford Handbook of Pensions and Retirement Income*, pp. 759–777.

Esping-Andersen, G. 1990: *The Three Worlds of Welfare*. Cambridge: Polity Press.

Esping-Andersen, G. 1999: *Social Foundations of Post-Industrial Economies*. Oxford: Oxford University Press.

European Commission 2009: *Industrial Relations in Europe 2008*. Luxembourg: The Commission.

Ginn, J., Arber, S., Brannen, J., Dale, A. and others 1996: Feminist fallacies: a reply to Hakim on women's employment. *British Journal of Sociology*, 47 (1), 167–174.

Grugulis, I. 2003: The contribution of National Vocational Qualifications to the growth of skills in the UK. *British Journal of Industrial Relations*, 41, 457–475.

Hakim, C. 1995: Five feminist myths about women's employment. *British Journal of Sociology*, 46 (3), 429–455.

Hall, P.H. and Soskice, D. (eds) 2001: *Varieties of Capitalism*. Oxford: Oxford University Press.

Hay, C., Riiheläinen, J.M., Smith, N.J. and Watson, M. 2008: Ireland: the outside inside. In Dyson, K. (ed.) *The Euro at 10: Europeanization, Power, and Convergence* Oxford: Oxford University Press.

Kenney, M. (ed.) 2000: *Understanding Silicon Valley: The Anatomy of an Entrepreneurial Region*. Stanford: Stanford University Press.

Kristensen, P.H. 1992: Industrial districts in West Jutland. In Pyke, F. and Sengenberger, W. (eds) *Industrial Districts and Economic Regeneration*. Geneva: Institute of International Labour Studies.

Majone, G. 1990: *Deregulation or Reregulation? Regulatory Reform in Europe and the United States*. Basingstoke: Palgrave Macmillan.

Muffels, R.J.A. (ed.) 2008: *Flexibility and Employment Security in Europe: Labour Markets in Transition*. Cheltenham: Edward Elgar.

OECD 2002: *Economic Outlook 2002*. Paris: OECD.

Pyke, F., Beccatini, G. and Sengnberger, W. 1990: *Industrial Districts in Italy*. Geneva: Institute of International Labour Studies.

Rogowski, R. (ed.) 2008: *The European Social Model and Transitional Labour Markets*. Farnham: Ashgate.

Rueda, D. 2005: Insider-outsider politics in industrialized democracies: the challenge to social democratic parties. *American Political Science Review*, 99 (1), 61–74.

Rueda, D. 2007: *Social Democracy Inside Out: Partisanship and Labour Market Policy in Advanced Industrialized Democracies*. Oxford: Oxford University Press.

Steedman, H. 2001: *Benchmarking Apprenticeship: The UK and Continental Europe Compared*. London: LSE, CEP.

Talani, L.S. and Casey, B. 2008: *Between Growth and Stability: The Demise and Reform of the European Union's Stability and Growth Pact*. Cheltenham: Elgar.

Talani, L.S. and Cerviño, E. 2003: Mediterranean labour and the impact of economic and monetary union: mass unemployment or labour market flexibility? In Overbeek, H. (ed.) *The Political Economy of European Employment*. London: Routledge.

Taylor-Gooby, P. 2002: Policy change at a time of retrenchment: recent pensions reform in France, Germany, Italy and the UK. *Social Policy and Administration*, 33 (1), 1–19.

Traxler, F. 2003: Bargaining, (de)centralization, macroeconomic performance and control over the employment relationship. *British Journal of Industrial Relations*, 41, 1–27.

Traxler, F., Blaschke, S. and Kittel, B. 2001: *National Labour Relations in Internationalized Markets*. Oxford: Oxford University Press.

Watanabe, H. 2009: Politics of labour market deregulation in Italy and Japan: labour market flexibility and worker protection in an era of globalisation. Unpublished DPhil thesis, University of Oxford.

3

BRITISH INDUSTRIAL RELATIONS: THE EUROPEAN DIMENSION

RICHARD HYMAN

The United Kingdom has been a member of the European Union (EU) since 1973, and in a number of important respects its institutions and processes of industrial relations are shaped by European law. The aim of this chapter is to explore some of the ways in which EU has contributed to the transformation of employment regulation in Britain.

The relationship between Britain and the rest of Europe has always been problematic. The old newspaper headline, 'Fog in Channel: continent cut off' is probably apocryphal but is symptomatic of a view that island Britain is not really part of the European continent. It was commonly said that the UK 'joined Europe' in 1973; but what exactly did this imply? 'Europe' itself is an ambiguous and disputed concept. Attali (1994: 9) cautions that 'Europe, evidently, does not exist. It is neither a continent, nor a culture, nor a people, nor a history. It is neither defined by a single frontier nor by a common destiny or dream.' For Delanty (1995: 49), 'it was always politics masquerading as geography that determined the definition of Europe'. Certainly, the relationship between Britain and the EU has always been politically loaded and politically contentious.

This chapter begins with a brief stylized account of the contrast in approaches to employment regulation in continental western Europe as against the UK. It then outlines the development of the EU, its institutional architecture and its role in shaping a supranational level of industrial relations. After a summary of the changing orientations towards European regulation amongst the main UK 'actors', the body of the chapter examines the regulation of specific aspects of employment relations: working time, job security and 'atypical' employment, information and consultation and equal opportunities. The conclusion considers how far British industrial relations have been 'Europeanized' and, conversely, how far the UK approach to labour market regulation has influenced EU developments.

Varieties of Capitalism, Varieties of Industrial Relations

A central theme in the recent literature on comparative political economy is the existence of different varieties of capitalism, with distinctive institutional configurations which shape the operation of markets (including labour markets). The simplest presentation of this approach is by Hall and Soskice (2001), who outline a contrast between liberal market economies (LMEs) and coordinated market economies (CMEs). In the former, the functioning of markets is subject to few institutional constraints, and in consequence the unequal control of economic resources shapes market outcomes; in addition, collective action problems are hard to overcome. In the latter, a range of institutions – in some countries the government, in others private associations or networks – sets tight limits to the autonomy of individual economic actors. Many subsequent critics have pointed to inadequacies in this dichotomy. First, markets require some form of institutional coordination even in LMEs; second, it makes a considerable difference whether coordination is effected primarily by the state, or by other social institutions.

Nevertheless, the stylized contrast between 'Anglo-Saxon' and 'Rhineland' capitalisms (Albert 1993) does have heuristic value. Britain, like other English-speaking countries, has a common law system and a bias within economic jurisprudence towards the primacy of individual contracts (see Colling, this volume). Private companies are the exclusive property of their owners, and the duty of managers is with few qualifications to maximize the financial returns to shareholders. This distinguishes the UK from the civil law regimes in most of western Europe, where the interests of other stakeholders are a legitimate concern of managements and where freedom of contract has less iconic status. An additional factor of importance is that while the British electoral system with its 'first-past-the-post' method normally results in single-party majorities in parliament, in many European countries proportional representation typically leads to coalition government, creating an inbuilt bias against radical change in the institutional order of the kind seen in Britain in recent decades.

This contrast underlies significant differences in approaches to industrial relations. 'There is no such thing as society', notoriously proclaimed a former British prime minister: an assertion which in much of Europe would be taken as evidence of insanity. The idea that employment relations are embedded in broader social foundations connects closely to the notion of a 'European social model' of industrial relations (Ebbinghaus 1999), which links in turn to the longer-standing German concept of a 'social market economy'. It is interesting that, in most of western Europe, the English term industrial relations is commonly understood through the notion of 'social affairs' or some analogue. Similarly, government responsibility for industrial relations is typically vested in a ministry of labour and social affairs. Employment is perceived as a social relation, not simply a contractual issue. Partly as a corollary, it is taken for granted that industrial relations is an arena for collective actors: trade unions and employers' organizations are described in much of Europe as 'social partners', a term which at one and the same time expresses an aspiration that conflicts of interest should be resolved cooperatively but also an assumption that collective representation is a necessary and important basis for agreement between employers and workers.

In much of western Europe, both socialist and catholic traditions have viewed the individual employee as at a serious disadvantage in attempting to achieve an equitable contract with the employer, and have thus encouraged a wide range of market-correcting interventions. To take two examples, the principles of a national minimum wage and of a universal limit to working time are uncontentious in the majority of countries, whereas they have only recently been applied in the UK, against significant resistance. Two other features deserve mention. The first is the high degree of employer solidarity in most of western Europe, so that multi-employer collective bargaining remains an important practice even if, increasingly, company-level bargaining occurs in parallel: a marked contrast to the virtual collapse of multi-employer bargaining in Britain (see Brown, this volume) and the absence of effective employers' associations in most of eastern Europe. A consequence is that the coverage of collective bargaining tends to be high, even in countries where union membership is far lower. The second is the existence of standardized systems of workplace representation (established by law or peak-level collective agreement, or both), which entail that employees are collectively represented whether or not strong union organization exists in their workplace.

Yet if the organized capitalisms of western Europe share important common features in their industrial relations systems, there are also major differences. Crouch (1993) has argued that every national system of industrial relations is distinctive, in that the historical evolution of employment regulation has been shaped by specific national 'state traditions'; and Turner has written (2002: 165) that 'there is no one European and social model but many different national models common only at the level of objectives and broad approaches'. To simplify this diversity, one might suggest that mainland (western) Europe seems to encompass three subsidiary 'models' (though with many 'mixed cases'): a 'Mediterranean' (or 'southern') model, with elaborate legal regulation of substantive employment conditions; a 'Germanic' model, in which the actors and procedures of industrial relations are juridically defined, with varying degrees of substantive regulation of employment conditions but a bias towards 'free collective bargaining'; and a 'Nordic' model, more 'voluntaristic' than in Germanic systems but based on strong collective organization on either side, reinforced by institutional integration in para-state labour market regulation bodies. Such cross-national differences have made it very difficult to 'harmonize' institutions and processes within the EU. However, Britain is clearly an 'outlier': it possesses neither a tradition of extensive state regulation, nor strong central organizations of unions and employers; in consequence it is scarcely possible to speak of a national system, since there is large scope for each company to establish its own employment regime.

The EU and its Role in Employment Regulation

The Treaties of Rome, signed by Belgium, France, Italy, Luxembourg, the Netherlands and West Germany in 1957, established the European Economic Community

(EEC); Denmark, Ireland and the UK joined in 1973, Greece in 1981 and Portugal and Spain in 1986. After the Maastricht Treaty of 1991 introduced the current title of EU (for simplicity, in this chapter I use this title even when referring to earlier periods), Austria, Finland and Sweden joined in 1995. A further ten countries (mainly from eastern Europe) joined in May 2004 (Cyprus, the Czech Republic, Estonia, Hungary, Latvia, Lithuania, Malta, Poland, Slovakia and Slovenia), and Bulgaria and Romania in January 2007. In addition, since 1994 EU law has applied to the three other members (Iceland, Liechtenstein and Norway) of the European Economic Area (EEA). Further enlargement is envisaged.

The EU is something of an enigma for political (and other social) scientists. It is not just a regional trading bloc; unlike, for example, the North American Free Trade Area, it possesses a significant administrative infrastructure with authority of a political nature. But nor is it, as sometimes asserted, a 'super-state': the competence of the EU institutions is limited to the agenda specified in the governing Treaties, and the principle of 'subsidiarity' insists that the European level should regulate only when this cannot be accomplished effectively at national level.

Almost from the formation of the EEC, analysts debated the nature of the EU polity. Much of the early academic discussion assumed that the political authority and competence of the European level would inevitably expand, because powers to regulate in one policy field would 'spill over' into other fields. This would obviously favour harmonization of employment systems. But scholars soon insisted that there would never be a truly federal Europe, because national governments were effective protectors of their own autonomy. Europe was not a super-state in the making, but an arena governed by the diplomatic manoeuvres of the member states – hence the emphasis on subsidiarity. The obvious corollary was that national employment systems would remain distinctive. More recently, attempts have been made to bridge these conflicting positions: the fashionable notion of 'multi-level governance' (Marks *et al.* 1996; see also Heyes and Nolan, this volume) implies that both national and European (and also sub-national) levels have an important influence, and that it is the *interaction* between levels which is crucial. Moreover, the primary locus of power may shift over time, and may also vary according to policy issue.

A second key question is the character of European integration. For many commentators it once seemed self-evident that if the importance of the European level increased, this would entail a growing body of European rules, including those regulating employment and the labour market. But subsequently a more sceptical position was developed, based on the concept of 'negative integration' (Scharpf 1999). The argument here was that integration has occurred primarily through weakening or eliminating national rules, without necessarily establishing supranational rules in their place. For example, central to the single European market are the 'four freedoms' of movement (for goods, services, capital and labour). Freedom of movement meant eliminating national barriers; but for neo-liberals and advocates of flexibility, it was neither necessary nor desirable to create positive regulation at European level. I will say more about this issue below.

This question overlaps with the relationship between *economic* and *social* integration. What was established in 1957 was a 'common market', and market integration was in the eyes of many observers (both supporters and opponents) the be-all and end-all. Is the 'social dimension' simply a fig-leaf to make a neo-liberal economic project more acceptable, or is it a thing of substance? How far has the relationship between economic and social changed over time? If the whole idea of a social dimension is little more than rhetoric, the possibility of significant European employment regulation is minimal; if it has real meaning, then the Europeanization of industrial relations seems more feasible. In terms of the EU 'constitution', the Single European Act (SEA) prescribes a large agenda of economic integration, with disagreements in many instances resoluble by qualified majority voting (QMV); the Treaty imposes fewer obligations concerning social regulation, and most decisions require unanimity (though as outlined below, Maastricht and Amsterdam increased the scope for QMV on employment issues).

Many observers see a contradiction between 'broadening' and 'deepening' of the EU. The original Six were relatively homogeneous, economically and politically. Each enlargement has increased the internal diversity and made effective govern-ance more difficult, threatening policy-making deadlock in the absence of further weakening (or removal) of national veto powers. In 2003 the *Convention on the Future of Europe* drafted a series of reforms, the basis for the 'Constitutional Treaty' which in 2005 was rejected in referendums in France and the Netherlands. In 2007 there was agreement in Lisbon on a 'Reform Treaty' incorporating many of the same features. Its future was also thrown in doubt in June 2008 by the referendum rejection in Ireland (the only country to hold such a vote), but this was reversed in October 2009 and the Treaty is now in force.

The EU Institutions

The constitutional arrangements of the EU are extremely complex, but there are four key institutions:

The *Commission* consists of a nominee from each member state, including a presi-dent, with a five-year term of office. Commissioners' portfolios are linked to the Directorates-General (quasi-ministries). The Commission is usually seen as the 'motor' of European integration, since its own status is enhanced as EU competence expands. It has the power to initiate policy but not decide, and has been described as a 'policy entrepreneur' (Majone 1996). Its budget is limited but can be used to 'win friends' within the member states, creating a 'policy community' which may influence national governments.

The *Council of Ministers* comprises the heads of state and/or government, who meet in the 'European Council'. It is in effect the legislative and decision-making forum, receiving and deciding upon proposals from the Commission. For a long period there was a unanimity rule, which allowed a veto to any individual member state. This has been increasingly replaced by qualified majority voting (QMV) on specific issues: in this case the larger countries have more votes and a roughly two thirds majority is required for a decision.

The *European Parliament* (EP) has far fewer powers than most national parlia-ments. Initially, it had a very limited consultative role in the legislative process, but it now possesses some veto powers, and has acquired an important role in the appointment of the Commission.

The *European Court of Justice* (ECJ) adjudicates on complaints by the Commission of breaches of EU obligations by member states and on appeals on points of EU law from within member states. Its rulings in turn set guidelines for subsequent decisions by national courts; indeed, if UK law, for example, is incompatible with EU law as interpreted by the ECJ, 'the national court must disapply the UK law' (Samuels 1998: 84). Lately, it has become a source of 'judge-made law'.

The main regulatory instrument is the directive, which is binding as to the result to be achieved but leaves the method of implementation to member states. Legislation involves complicated interaction between Commission, Council and EP, with much delicate manoeuvring and diplomacy, often within specialist committees. There is also a requirement for detailed consultation with interest groups affected by any legislation.

The 'Treaty Base' and the development of EU social regulation

The principle of 'subsidiarity' imposes constraints on the capacity of the EU to adopt supranational regulatory instruments. Moreover, the EU possesses legal competence to regulate only insofar as such capacity is formally assigned in the Treaties which constitute the EU 'constitution'. Initially, it was generally assumed that economic integration would bring social progress without the need for specific regulation at European level. However, there were some fears that countries with inferior employment conditions would gain an unfair advantage in the common market (what would later be described as 'social dumping'). For this reason, the original Treaty of Rome included Article 117 (now 151) on the need to facilitate the improvement and harmonization of working conditions; article 118 (now 153), requiring the Commission to promote 'close co-operation between member states in the social field, particularly in matters relating to: employment; labour law and working conditions; basic and advanced vocational training; social security; prevention of occupational accidents and diseases; occupational hygiene; the right of association, and collective bargaining between employers and workers'; and Article 119 (now 157) prescribing equal pay for women. In addition, Articles 48–51 (now 45–8) mandated the free movement for workers. Any legislation required unanimity in the Council. (Note that the Treaty of Amsterdam changed the numbers of most Articles and the Lisbon Treaty has done so once more.) In the 1970s (when centre–left governments were in power in many member states) there were more ambitious efforts to adopt directives which would ensure upwards harmonization of employment regulations. But this was halted with a shift to the right in European politics (notably Thatcher's election in Britain in 1979) and a more general enthusiasm for labour market deregulation.

A new phase began when Jacques Delors became Commission President in 1985. He helped drive the single market project, but also insisted that greater economic integration must possess a 'social dimension'. The SEA, which came into force in 1987, enlarged Community competence in the industrial relations arena.

Notably, it introduced a somewhat ambiguous Article (118a, now 153) which amplified 117 by encouraging 'improvements, especially in the working environment, as regards the health and safety of workers'; while Article 118b (now 154–5) mandated the Commission to 'develop the dialogue between management and labour at European level which could, if the two sides consider it desirable, lead to relations based on agreement'. The SEA also introduced the procedure of qualified majority voting (QMV) and specified this (Article 100a) 'for measures which have as their object the establishing and functioning of the internal market'; this clause was, however, not to apply to measures 'relating to the rights and interests of employed persons'. However, QMV *did* apply to Article 118a.

Delors also pressed the initiative for a European 'social charter', eventually adopted by 11 member states in December 1989 (with the UK dissenting). This had no binding status, but gave a green light for further Commission initiatives. This was followed by the 'social chapter' agreed at Maastricht in December 1991, which enlarged EU competence in the employment field, and extended the range of such issues on which directives could be adopted by QMV. (Though this provision did 'not apply to pay, the right of association, the right to strike or the right to impose lock-outs'.) It also created the 'social partners' route' to EU legislation, discussed below. Initially, most of the new measures were contained in the 'social policy protocol' of the Maastricht Treaty, in which the UK was allowed an 'opt-out'. This was ended after the election of the Blair government in 1997, and these provisions were incorporated into the Amsterdam Treaty. As discussed below, this Treaty radically extended equality provisions, prescribing 'appropriate action to combat discrimination based on sex, racial or ethnic origin, religion or belief, disability, age or sexual orientation'; and also introduced the 'Employment Chapter'.

After Maastricht – which was also notable for the agreement on Economic and Monetary Union (EMU), from which the UK also obtained an opt-out – there was a considerable acceleration in employment legislation by the EU, but from the late 1990s the pace slowed again. Many argue that the accession of the new member states from central and eastern Europe has now created a large bloc without the traditions of 'social Europe' and with a competitive interest in preventing new employment regulation (though they have been required to adopt the rules already in place). However, a difficult question is whether EU rules are actually observed if they conflict with the interests/preferences of individual governments. The Commission monitors whether directives are transposed into national law, but not whether these laws are then enforced. As noted above, national courts may (and indeed should) take EU law as their point of reference; and in Britain this has had some important consequences for industrial relations, as discussed below. How far this is true in other member states is difficult to judge.

The 'Charter of Fundamental Rights' adopted in 2000 includes wide-ranging provisions on information and consultation, right of collective bargaining and action, protection against unfair dismissal and 'fair and just working conditions'. However, attempts to give this force of law in the Nice Treaty the same year failed, as did the subsequent 'Constitutional Treaty' which would have incorporated the Charter but succumbed to the referendum defeats in France and the Netherlands in 2005. The Lisbon Reform Treaty states that 'the rights, freedoms and principles set out in the Charter of Fundamental Rights . . . shall have the same legal value as the Treaties', but controversially contains an ambiguous opt-out for the UK and Poland.

The 'social partners' and the 'social dialogue'

The notion that trade unions and employers' organizations are 'social partners' is familiar in most of the 'old' member states. This does *not* necessarily mean that unions and employers cooperate in a spirit of mutual friendship; rather, that the organizations of capital and labour are 'partners' of the state in formulating and administering social policy. This conception was reflected in the creation of what is now the European Economic and Social Committee (EESC) as one of the institutions of the original EEC. It represents a wide variety of economic interest groups, and is a consultative body with no power and little influence.

Although there is a proliferation of organizations representing worker and (particularly) employer interests, there are just three major players:

The *ETUC* (European Trade Union Confederation) was founded in 1973, initially including only confederations affiliated to the International Confederation of Free Trade Unions (ICFTU). All the major 'Christian' unions were admitted in 1974; subsequently all main (ex-) communist confederations have been allowed in. Its affiliates are national confederations and the 12 European Industry Federations (EIFs); hence national trade unions have a dual channel of representation. In the 1990s, ETUC admitted members and associates from eastern Europe. It has 82 member confederations from 36 countries and covers the large majority of unionized workers in the EU. It is strongly in favour of enhanced social regulation at EU level; but arguably there is a lack of internal consensus on what, and how, to regulate.

BusinessEurope (until 2007 known as *UNICE*) was founded in 1958. It comprises 39 national business/employer confederations, and is as much (or more) concerned with issues of trade and business as with employment. It has loose links to sectoral business organizations (FEBIs), but the coverage of these is uneven: in many key sectors (such as metal-working), there is no real equivalent to trade union organization at European level. BusinessEurope is resistant to social regulation, and national employers' organizations are often reluctant to give it a mandate to negotiate. There is an asymmetry between the representation of unions and employers, since larger companies typically have their own lobbying facilities in Brussels.

CEEP (*Centre européen des entreprises à participation publique*) covers nationalized and semi-nationalized enterprises. It has shown more support than UNICE for the social dimension.

The notion of 'social dialogue' was invented, and strongly promoted, by the Delors Commission as a precursor – or perhaps an alternative – to EC legislation. The assumption was that if the 'social partners' agreed on the need for regulation at European level, this would make it easier to win agreement in the Council (or might enable them to regulate matters themselves). As noted above, the SEA mandated the Commission to 'endeavour to develop the dialogue between management and labour at European level' which could, if the two sides consider it desirable, lead to relations based on agreement. Social dialogue also takes place at *sectoral* level: joint committees or informal working parties have been created in a range of sectors. But in many sectors, 'social partner' organizations are weak or absent – particularly amongst employers.

A key development was the *social partners' agreement* of October 1991, on the eve of the Maastricht summit. UNICE abandoned its traditional opposition to the whole principle of European-level agreements, prompted by the prospect of treaty revisions enabling extensive use of QMV for employment legislation. Maastricht boosted the role of the social partners: as well as being guaranteed consultative input during the framing of Commission legislative proposals, they acquired a new right to opt to deal with an issue by means of European-level agreements. Such agreements could be implemented either 'in accordance with procedures and practices specific to management and labour in the member states' or, at the joint request of the signatory parties and on a proposal from the Commission, by a 'Council decision'.

This new 'social partners' route' to legislation has had limited results. UNICE failed to agree with ETUC on the European Works Council proposal; the first agreement reached was on the less contentious issue of parental leave (December 1995), subsequently implemented as a directive. Since then there have been several agreements on aspects of 'atypical' employment. In December 2001 ETUC, UNICE and CEEP declared their continuing commitment to the social dialogue process, and in November 2002 they adopted a joint work programme for the following three years (2003–05). This marked a new departure in that, whereas previous discussions had taken place on an issue-by-issue basis, it was now agreed to maintain a continuing dialogue on a broad agenda encompassing employment, enlargement and mobility. This was followed by framework agreements on telework and work-related stress; neither was subsequently adopted as a directive. There have also been two 'frameworks of actions', on the lifelong development of competencies and qualifications (2002) and gender equality (2005). A second three-year programme was agreed in 2006. Since then there was agreement in 2007 on a set of guidelines on 'flexicurity' and a framework covering harassment and violence at work, and in 2009 on a revised framework for parental leave.

Some commentators have seen this process as signalling the emergence of a 'corporatist policy community' (Falkner 1998). Others are more sceptical, suggesting that social dialogue can actually delay EU legislation ('double subsidiarity'), and that those agreements reached so far have occurred 'in the shadow of the law': if legislation seemed imminent, UNICE saw agreement on terms it could directly influence as a preferable alternative to an externally imposed directive. Since enlargement, this 'shadow' has been lifted. The fact that the last two peak-level agreements did not result in directives is consistent with this view. Some, such as Marginson and Sisson (2004), argue that broad framework agreements, even though lacking strong prescriptive content, can have a significant impact. This links to a broader debate about the role of 'soft law' – decisions, recommendations or guidelines which are backed by no direct sanctions but which, in some interpretations, can nevertheless shape behaviour. One variant of soft law is the 'open method of coordination' (OMC), which is applied in particular in the field of employment policy. Can 'soft law' have hard effects, and how do we judge?

Britain in Europe

The UK did not participate in the construction of the EEC in 1957, partly because of opposition to the founders' 'federalist' ambitions; instead it took the lead in creating the European Free Trade Area (EFTA) in 1960, providing the first two secretaries-general. However, the government rapidly changed its mind and applied for membership in 1961, and again in 1967, on both occasions being blocked by the French veto. A third application (after de Gaulle's departure) was successful, accession taking place in January 1973.

Britain is widely regarded as the 'awkward' member of the EU, resistant to the desire of most other members for enhanced regulatory competence. This was one of de Gaulle's stated reasons for opposing the UK attempts to become a member in the 1960s, a view which seemed strongly validated by the Thatcher government two decades later. Britain has been described as a 'Eurosceptic state' (George 2000), with widespread doubts about the value of EU membership and resistance to any further transfer of powers to supranational level. In both main political parties there has been a wide spectrum of views on EU membership (the Liberals have predominantly, though not universally, been strongly pro-EU; conversely, a single-issue fringe party, the UK Independence Party, which campaigns for withdrawal from the EU, won almost 17% of the national vote in the 2004 EP elections and 16% in 2009).

Amongst the Conservatives, Edward Heath was the most pro-European of any party leader, before or after. He led the abortive negotiations in 1960s and signed the eventual accession agreement. But Thatcher and her successors were far more suspicious, or simply hostile, to European integration. In particular, the Thatcher and Major governments usually headed the resistance to proposals for strengthened employment regulation at EU level, as well as refusing to participate in EMU. Thatcher's 'free market' ideology was at odds with the prevailing 'social market' orientation of most continental member states, even those with conservative governments; and this encouraged a broader hostility to what were seen as the 'federal' ambitions of the Commission and other EU governments, and a strong assertion of the primacy of national sovereignty. In opposition, the 'Eurosceptic' tendency within the Conservative Party has been reinforced, and it strenuously opposed ratification of the Lisbon Treaty.

Labour has always possessed a strong anti-EU tendency, partly because many on the left have viewed 'Europe' as incorrigibly business-oriented and have seen national autarchy as a basis for more progressive social and economic policy. Though the Wilson government of 1964–70 initiated the successful accession negotiations, the party in opposition rejected the terms agreed. When Labour was re-elected in 1974 the government attempted to renegotiate these, and held a referendum the following year on continued membership; the result was a two-to-one vote to remain in the EU. By the 1990s Labour was denouncing Conservative 'negative posturing' and insisting that the UK should be more positively involved in EU policy-making in order to 'set the agenda' (Hindmoor 2004: 150–151). But while the Blair government, elected in 1997, reversed the 'opt-out' from the Maastricht social chapter, the UK continued to resist new employment legislation; and though not opposing EMU in principle, the government set stringent conditions for joining the euro. Blair undertook to hold a referendum on the Constitutional Treaty, before the French and Dutch 'no' votes made this superfluous; but the Brown government refused to do so in the case of the Lisbon Treaty.

British employers' organizations have always adopted a predominantly positive view of the EU. The Confederation of British Industry (CBI) established a Brussels office in 1971 as a base for lobbying the EU institutions, and became a member of UNICE the following year. As an influential member of UNICE/BusinessEurope the CBI has been notable for the intensity of its hostility to EU social regulation, for example being generally regarded as the main obstacle to negotiations with the ETUC over the European Works Council (EWC) proposals. From the outset the CBI has supported the principle of monetary union, while also urging caution over the process (Grant and Marsh 1977: 180–184); but more recently, a strong minority grouping of employers has opposed UK entry to the euro (Forster 2002: 113–117).

Amongst trade unions, as within the Labour Party, views of the EU have been sharply divided. Though a minority, primarily on the right of the movement, has been strongly in favour of European integration, while a mainly left-wing grouping has been strongly opposed, much of the leadership of the Trades Union Congress (TUC) has been more pragmatic. Official TUC policy throughout the 1960s was to approve EEC membership, but only if the conditions of accession were acceptable. By the time that accession was negotiated, several major unions had shifted to the left, and in 1971 the TUC decided to oppose membership on the terms negotiated (Rosamond 1993). In the following two years the annual Congress voted to oppose membership in principle, and in 1975 it campaigned for a 'no' vote in the referendum. However, the TUC also played an active role in the creation of the ETUC in 1973.

From 1980, Congress repeatedly voted once more for withdrawal – though the TUC secretariat maintained a far more positive view. In any event, union views were redefined by the experience of the Thatcher government. As employment legislation in Britain, and the monetarist bias of social and economic policy, became increasingly hostile to union aspirations, so EU membership could be perceived in an altered light. In 1988 the TUC agreed to invite Delors to address the annual conference, and his speech – delivered in English – was both a challenge to Thatcher's obstructionism (she made her notorious Bruges speech in the same month) and an appeal to British unions to support both the single market and the social dimension (MacShane 1991). As so often, official TUC policy shifted radically and rapidly, with minimal debate. As Mullen (2005, 2007) has demonstrated, debates on European issues at the TUC from 1988 onwards have stressed overwhelmingly the importance of the 'European social model' in providing a bulwark against the advance of Anglo-Saxon neo-liberalism and as a source of new employment rights for British workers. The TUC has pressed strongly to counteract the opposition of both Conservative and Labour governments to effective European legislation on such questions. More generally it opposed the UK opt-out from the Maastricht social chapter and supported the inclusion of an employment chapter in the Amsterdam Treaty.

Other issues have been more divisive. In 1989, the General Council offered 'conditional support for EMU' (Mullen 2005: 182), and this was approved by Congress. In subsequent years the TUC gave greater backing to EMU entry. Nevertheless, there was opposition: in particular the then largest affiliate, UNISON, regarded entry into EMU as a threat to public expenditure and hence its members' jobs. In 1999 a campaign group was established, 'Trade Unionists against the Single Currency'. In 2005 Congress rejected the Constitutional Treaty (already seemingly dead as a result of the French and Dutch votes) because it was seen as entrenching economic liberalization; and in September 2007 it voted in favour of a referendum on the Reform Treaty, largely as a protest against the UK opt-out from the charter of fundamental rights – although a motion to campaign for a 'no' vote in any referendum was defeated.

Key Areas of EU Influence on British Industrial Relations

Given the obstacle-ridden framework of EU decision-making, particularly in the social field, regulation of employment issues is often viewed as the adoption of a 'lowest common denominator' of existing practice in the member states. However, because of the contrast between 'Anglo-Saxon' and 'Rhineland' capitalisms, regulation of the labour market which is commonplace in most of western Europe is harder to accommodate within the 'lightly regulated' British system. Below I examine the impact in several distinct policy areas.

Working time

Historically, British law has regulated working time only for specific categories of employee (women and young workers) and in occupations with significant safety implications; whereas in most continental countries, maximum working hours for all employees have been prescribed by law (see Grimshaw and Rubery, this volume). EU regulation in this area has therefore been contentious. As noted above, the SEA provided for legislation (which could be adopted by QMV) in pursuit of 'improvements, especially in the working environment, as regards the health and safety of workers'. Yet while 'working environment' seems to cover most aspects of employment conditions, 'health and safety' seems much narrower in scope. The Commission argued that it was entitled to use a broad interpretation – which would enable the UK veto to be by-passed in the Council.

The 1989 social charter (which had no binding effect, but legitimized many subsequent Commission proposals for directives) included a clause insisting that 'approximation of living and working conditions' must be part of the internal market process, 'as regards in particular the duration and organisation of working time'. There was specific mention of the need for a weekly rest period and annual paid leave, 'the duration of which must be progressively harmonised in accordance with national practices'. A draft directive was published in 1990, and was adopted in 1993 against the opposition of the UK – despite the dilution of a number of its provisions in response to British objections. Key provisions included a maximum working week of 48 hours including overtime (though this could be averaged over a 'reference period' of 4 months); a maximum of 8 hours' night work on average; a minimum daily rest period of 11 consecutive hours; a rest break where the working day is longer than 6 hours; a minimum rest period of 1 day per week (in principle Sunday) plus 11 hours; and minimum annual paid leave of 4 weeks. The working time directive (WTD) allowed for variation in these provisions via collective agreements, and for working hours above the 48-hour maximum with an employee's agreement. The directive did not apply to a number of transport sectors or to junior hospital doctors; but these groups were covered by extension directives in 2000 and 2004.

The UK challenged the validity of the QMV treaty basis, arguing that working time was an issue of social policy rather than health and safety. This challenge was almost wholly rejected by the ECJ in November 1996 (ironically, this was widely seen as strengthening the hand of the Commission by confirming the broad scope of Article 118a). The Conservative government then pressed for the directive to be 'disapplied' from the UK, before drafting regulations which fell short of the directive's requirements. The Labour government elected in 1997 accepted the directive, and issued regulations in October 1998 which 'took full advantage of the derogations and exemptions in the WTD'. In particular, the UK was the only member state to include a blanket provision for an individual opt-out. Its restrictive interpretation of the right to holiday entitlement was successfully challenged in the ECJ (Geyer *et al.* 2005: 131).

At the start of 2004 the Commission launched a consultation process on the revision of the directive. Key questions were whether the individual opt-out should be retained; whether time spent 'on call' should count as working time – as the ECJ had ruled in 2003; and what should be the 'reference period' over which working time is averaged. The Commission subsequently issued proposals which would retain the opt-out, narrow the definition of on-call time which would count as working time, and extend the reference period from 4 to 12 months. The ETUC considered this 'very unsatisfactory', and in 2005 the EP proposed major changes to the Commission's draft. Currently, the issue is still deadlocked: in June 2008 the Council of Ministers agreed on proposals broadly in line with the earlier Commission draft, but these were again rejected by the EP; and attempts to negotiate a compromise broke down, largely because of UK insistence on retaining the opt-out.

What is the practical significance of the WTD? In most member states, the 48-hour ceiling is above, or equal to, the maximum normally permitted under national working-time law, while collectively agreed limits are usually significantly lower. In the UK by contrast, the directive required the introduction of a completely new statutory framework because of the absence of any universal legislation on working time issues. And because of the British 'overtime culture', the average working week (for full-time employees) is considerably above the European norm. Yet because of the widespread use of individual opt-outs (and the weakness of enforcement mechanisms) the impact of the directive seems to have been minimal. Official statistics show that in the first six years after the regulations took effect, the proportion of the workforce normally working over 45 hours a week did decline (from 37% in 1998 to 31% in 2004) but the figure has since stabilized. Whether this reduction was actually caused by the regulations is uncertain: a survey by the CIPD (2001) after the regulations had been in place for two years found that the majority of workers who had been working over 48 hours a week were still doing so, while only 2% were working reduced hours because of the directive. Analysing unpublished official data, the TUC (2008) reported that those recorded as working over 48 hours a week fell from 3.8 million in 1998 to 3.1 million in 2007, but rose to 3.3 million in 2008 (see discussion in Grimshaw and Rubery, this volume).

Employment protection and 'atypical' work

In Britain, the contract of employment was traditionally open to termination by either side, subject only to the period of notice which it specified. Legislation in 1965 established a statutory system of compensation in cases of redundancy, and the principle of unfair dismissal was introduced by the 1971 Industrial Relations Act (both subject to a minimum length of service). Much subsequent legislation on employment protection has, however, stemmed from EU directives (see Dickens and Hall, this volume).

One initiative with an important impact in the UK was the 1977 Acquired Rights Directive (ARD, revised in 1998 and 2001). This was implemented in the UK as the Transfer of Undertakings (Protection of Employment) Regulations 1981 (amended several times between 1995 and 2006), usually known simply as TUPE. The aim was to ensure that when an undertaking was transferred, in whole or in part, to another firm, employees' continuity of employment and their associated terms and conditions should be protected.

In implementing the directive in 1981, the Thatcher government defined its scope to apply solely to 'commercial' undertakings. This meant, in particular, that it did not cover activities 'outsourced' under the compulsory competitive tendering (CCT) imposed in the NHS from 1983 and local government from 1988. A decade later, this narrow interpretation was shown to be inconsistent with the meaning of the ARD, through a series of ECJ rulings and a Commission report critical of TUPE. In consequence, the government was obliged to widen the scope of TUPE as part of the 1993 Trade Union Reform and Employment Rights Act (Cutler and Waine 1998: 93). The impact 'on the "property" rights of UK firms initially produced shocks of a seismic scale' (Anderman 2004: 107). Since much of the logic of CCT was to enable outside contractors to cut labour costs, this radically diluted a key element of Conservative strategy towards public services. However, in practice this did not prevent the new employer from 'negotiating' inferior conditions with the workforce, and new employees lacked any protection, often leading to the development of a 'two-tier' workforce with different contractual provisions (see Bach, this volume).

For many observers, the ARD was internally inconsistent and contained many ambiguities, for example over the continuity of pension entitlements. Rulings by the ECJ compounded the uncertainties (Davies 1993; McMullen 1996; Shrubshall 1998). A decade ago, Adnett (1998: 79) wrote that 'nearly twenty years after its introduction the ARD is still a significant source of confusion and uncertainty in European labour markets. Nowhere is the confusion greater than in the UK.' Though recent revisions of the directive and the Regulations have clarified some of the uncertainties, complexities remain; nevertheless, the ARD has certainly imposed significant limits on the ability of employers – whether in the private or the public sector – to use subcontracting as a simple cost-cutting measure. In this respect, a 'liberal market economy' has become more coordinated.

The treatment of 'atypical' employment – usually understood as involving contracts which are not full-time and permanent – has long been a contentious issue in the EU. One rationale for regulation has been the argument of a 'level playing field'; if 'atypical' workers have inferior terms and conditions of employment to 'standard' workers, and if such contracts are more common in some member states than others (both of which are indeed the case), competition will be distorted. Another concerns equal opportunities, particularly in the case of part-time work, which disproportionately involves women; for this reason I discuss this aspect in a separate section (see also Dean and Liff, this volume). The Commission first proposed the regulation of the conditions of part-time and temporary workers – primarily in respect of statutory and contractual employment rights – in 1982, but without success. The initiative was revived as a package of three directives on 'atypical employment' in 1990, of which only the health and safety element was adopted. Subsequently, the Commission consulted the social partners on a proposed initiative on 'flexible working time and security for workers'. Negotiations between the social partners began in October 1996 separately (at UNICE insistence) over part-time and temporary work. In June 1997 they reached an agreement on part-time work (see below), and in March 1999 on fixed-term contracts; the Council adopted both agreements as directives.

Talks on a directive regulating temporary agency work broke down in May 2001; the Commission issued its own draft in March 2002, but this was blocked, mainly because of opposition by the UK. However, in May 2008 an agreement was reached between the TUC and CBI, in part brokered by the government. This reflected an assessment that, within the horse-trading processes of the EU, the UK government would only sustain the 48-hour opt-out if it was willing to agree a directive on agency work. The key points in the agreement were that after 3 months in a given job, an agency worker would be entitled to equal treatment – at least as regards 'basic employment and working conditions' – with directly employed workers. The following month there was 'political agreement' in the European Council on equal rights on core employment conditions without any waiting period, and these terms were approved by the EP in October 2008, paving the way for formal adoption of the directive. There is, however, provision for variation of the terms of the directive by collective agreement, which means that in the case of the UK the 12-week waiting period agreed in May 2008 will apply.

The fixed-term directive has a relatively limited impact in the UK, where the proportion of such contracts is only about half the EU average. This reflects the fact – linked to the contrast between varieties of capitalism – that 'permanent' contracts of employment are in practice far easier to terminate in the UK than in many other member states. Conversely, the impact of an agency worker directive would be far greater – the main reason for UK government opposition – because the incidence of such work is far higher than in most of the EU. On some estimates, agency work covers 5% of the UK force, by far the highest proportion amongst the member states.

Information and consultation

As noted above, most countries of continental western Europe have long-established national systems of company-level employee representation – with works councils or similar channels of 'industrial democracy' (see Terry, this volume). Yet attempts to generalize such arrangements by EU legislation have proved particularly contentious; despite continuous debate since the 1960s, no breakthrough was achieved until the EWC directive of September 1994. A major reason for the long deadlock was the lack of any analogous arrangements in the UK. But though all the original six members of the EEC possessed standardized works councils or committees, their composition and powers differed significantly; and this diversity was increased with each round of enlargement. In particular, company-level representation in the Nordic countries rested on peak-level collective agreements rather than legislation and usually involved a 'single channel' structure based on trade unions.

During the 1970s and 1980s the Commission launched three main initiatives, with drafts of the European company statute (1970 and 1975); the Fifth company law directive, providing for board-level employee representation (1972 and 1983); and the 'Vredeling' directive concerning information and consultation in multinationals (1980 and 1983). All were blocked as a result of employer opposition (including strong lobbying by US firms), resistance by some governments (primarily the UK) and problems in 'harmonizing' diverse national practice. Early drafts tended to attempt to generalize the 'German model'; later drafts were more flexible, but still 'alien' for many member states.

The Single European Market, which was expected to lead to an acceleration of cross-border mergers and acquisitions, encouraged new Commission proposals on transnational information and consultation procedures: a revised collective redundancies directive (adopted in 1992); successive drafts of the EWC directive; and new proposals for a European company statute (1989 and 1991).

The rationale for Vredeling, and subsequently the *EWC directive*, was that nationally based rights of employee participation were being outflanked by the transnationalization of corporate structures; and there was a political need for 'social acceptability' of such restructuring. Also important was trade union pressure, and the precedent set by the voluntary establishment of 'prototype' EWCs in some (mainly French- and German-owned) companies. The Commission proposal of December 1990 had an Article 100 treaty basis and therefore required unanimity; it went through the initial stages of the legislative procedure, but UK opposition (and also reservations on the part of Portugal) was sufficient to prevent adoption. Prospects were transformed by the ratification of the Maastricht treaty. Since measures adopted under the social chapter were not directly applicable in the UK, Britain had no formal role in the legislative process; and directives concerning information and consultation of workers were subject to QMV amongst the 11 other member states. Talks between ETUC, UNICE and CEEP about a Community-level agreement on transnational information and consultation procedures broke down in March 1994 (partly because the British CBI stiffened UNICE resistance). An amended directive was adopted by Council in September 1994, applying to all members of the by now enlarged EU, except for the UK, plus the three other members of the EEA.

The aim of the EWC directive was to coordinate national provisions in order to create a European legal framework for transnational information and consultation within 'community-scale' enterprises (with at least 1000 employees in the EEA countries, including 150 in at least two of these) (see Marginson and Meardi, this volume). On a request by employee representatives, companies were to set up EWCs or transnational information and consultation procedures. There was considerable flexibility for the negotiation of company-specific arrangements, but the directive defined a standard EWC package as a 'default option' in the absence of agreement. This provided for an EWC of up to 30 members drawn from existing employee representatives, to discuss transnational issues in an annual information and consultation meeting with central management. The operating costs were to be met by the enterprise. In line with 'subsidiarity', member states were given considerable scope for ensuring that the legal framework for EWCs reflected national traditions and practices.

The effect of the UK 'opt-out' was only partial: the UK government did not have to implement the directive, but UK-based multinationals with requisite employment figures in the other countries concerned were still obliged to establish EWCs in respect of their non-UK operations within the EEA. In such cases there was inevitable and usually successful pressure to include UK representatives voluntarily in the EWC. Following the election of the Labour government with a commitment to end the Maastricht opt-out, an extension directive was agreed in December 1997. Enlargement in 2004 and 2007 has extended its scope.

What do EWCs mean in practice? Streeck (1997) argued that they were 'neither European nor works councils' but mere token mechanisms, lacking the powers of national representative institutions and typically ancillary to national procedures in the companies' home country. Subsequent research has revealed a slightly more nuanced picture. First, the complexity of the procedure for establishing an EWC (and the scope for hostile managements to obstruct the process) means that only just over a third of the companies that meet the size thresholds in the directive actually possess an EWC – though coverage of larger multinationals is far greater. Interestingly, the proportion of UK-owned firms with an EWC is above the average. There is evidence that most EWCs are either marginalized by management, or else incorporated into a process of instilling 'company culture'. Problems of language and of different national industrial relations backgrounds inhibit cross-national unity amongst employee representatives, and in times of restructuring and redundancy, representatives are often preoccupied with protecting their 'national interests'. Nevertheless, there is evidence that in a minority of cases, EWCs have developed into genuine transnational actors with a quasi-bargaining role (Fitzgerald and Stirling 2004; Lecher *et al.* 1999; Whittall *et al.* 2007). In any event, the EWC gave roughly a thousand UK employees (mainly trade unionists) – and also managers – the experience of 'continental' representative mechanisms which were previously unfamiliar (Marginson *et al.* 2004).

The ETUC has pushed for a decade for stronger powers, more resources and a lowering of the employment threshold for the establishment of EWCs, but without success. In February 2008 the Commission announced a new consultation process on possible revision of the directive, and issued detailed proposals. On this occasion, the 'social partners' at European level were able to agree a common position on at least some elements of revision. Though the UK government was reported to be lobbying hard to block or minimize any changes, a 'recast' directive was approved in December 2008.

Potentially more radical in its impact on the UK is the 2002 directive establishing 'a general framework setting out minimum requirements for the right to information and consultation of employees in undertakings or establishments within the Community'. This was proposed by the Commission in November 1995 as a revival of the initiatives on this theme in the 1970s, and (after negotiations between the 'social partners' failed to take off), a draft directive was issued in November 1998.

There were considerable differences of opinion within Council, with strong UK opposition in particular, reflecting a powerful campaign by the CBI; but 'political agreement' on a revised (and diluted) text was reached in June 2001. The EP pressed for amendments, a 'conciliated' text was agreed in December 2001, and the directive was adopted in March 2002.

The directive applies to undertakings with at least 50 employees, with a phased introduction of application to firms with under 150 employees in countries without established information and consultation arrangements (the UK and Ireland). It creates an obligation to inform and consult employee representatives on recent and foreseeable developments in the firm's financial situation, employment and work organization; with opportunities for the representatives to respond and seek agreement before implementation of changes.

In practice, the UK was the main country where significant institutional innovation was required – though after EU enlargement in 2004 most of the new member states also had to introduce new mechanisms. The government brokered an (unprecedented) agreement between the TUC and the CBI on the detailed arrangements for transposition and legislation was implemented by regulations issued in 2004, which took effect in April 2005. This provides that a request by 10% of employees can 'trigger' negotiations to establish an information and consultation procedure. A fall-back mechanism is prescribed for cases where no agreement can be reached, and 'pre-existing agreements' are protected. In line with the requirements of the directive, the employment threshold for application of the regulations was reduced to 100 in 2007 and 50 in 2008.

In formal terms, the information and consultation legislation entails a major institutional innovation in the UK (see Terry, this volume). The practical significance is far harder to assess. Certainly, the procedures specified in the directive fall far short of the rights of employee representatives in most of western Europe, and the UK regulations make extensive use of the flexibility which the directive permits – indeed, some consider that it fails to comply fully with the requirements. In the debates before the adoption of the directive, some observers suggested that the election of employee representatives might provide a bridgehead for unionization, while others on the contrary saw this as a means for anti-union employers to bypass union representation. At this stage there is little indication that either scenario will be common. One of the few studies of the implementation of the new provisions (Hall *et al.* 2007) indicates that the regulations have provided an additional communication channel for management but have failed to provide new opportunities for employee consultation (Taylor *et al.* 2009).

Equal opportunities

Equality between women and men is the area of social policy where EU law has had the most sustained and profound influence (see Dean and Liff; Dickens and Hall, this volume). As noted above, the Treaty of Rome embodied the principle of equal pay for equal work – the springboard for all subsequent developments in this area. However, for almost two decades the formal commitment to this principle had little practical effect. This changed in the 1970s and 1980s, with the adoption of directives in 1975 prescribing equal pay for work of equal value, and in 1976 banning sex discrimination in all aspects of employment. The ECJ also played a path-breaking role with a series of landmark rulings interpreting and developing EC equality law. In some cases it ruled that treaty provisions and certain aspects of directives had a 'direct effect': in other words, they should inform national judicial decisions even if national law had not been brought into conformity.

This had a significant impact on the development of equality law in the UK. The 1970 Equal Pay Act was adopted before membership of the EEC but after accession negotiations had commenced, and the need to comply with forthcoming Treaty obligations was one argument for the new law. The 1975 Sex Discrimination Act anticipated the directive adopted the following year, but the UK failed to implement the equal value requirements of the 1975 Equal Pay Directive. The government's argument that 'equal value' could be demonstrated only if an employer had undertaken a systematic evaluation of grading procedures – which no employer was obliged to do – was contested by the Commission and firmly rejected by the ECJ in 1982 (Kilpatrick 1997; Stone Sweet and Caporaso 1998: 124–125). Accordingly, the Thatcher government found itself obliged to amend the 1970 Act to take account of the ruling, resulting in a series of successful equal value claims (Schofield 1988).

In the 1980s the Commission introduced a series of five-year Action Programmes on Equal Opportunities, containing detailed proposals for legislative and other measures to promote the integration of women in the labour market. In 1990 the NOW programme (New Opportunities for Women) was launched. An annual Commission report on equal opportunities has been published since 1996.

Directives concerning 'equality between men and women with regard to labour market opportunities and treatment at work' were earmarked for QMV under the Maastricht social chapter, making legislation easier to achieve. A directive was adopted in 1992 covering maternity leave, prohibition of dismissal on grounds of pregnancy, maternity pay and health and safety provision for new and expectant mothers, and one on parental leave in 1996 following the first Community-level agreement between the social partners. A directive on the reversal of the burden of proof in sex discrimination cases (putting the onus on the employer to rebut a claim), first proposed in 1988, was adopted in 1997 under the Maastricht 'social chapter' procedures; and extended to the UK in July 1998. The social partners' agreement on equal treatment for part-time work – which particularly involves women – was implemented as a directive in December 1997. This was particularly important for the UK, where 44% of women workers are part-time – a proportion exceeded only in the Netherlands. Another proposal, to outlaw sexual harassment, was initiated in 1996 but made slow progress, eventually leading to an amendment to the Equal Treatment Directive in 2002.

The Amsterdam Treaty radically extended the EU's formal commitment to 'eliminate inequalities, and to promote equality, between men and women'. But the focus was greatly enlarged, authorizing 'appropriate action to combat discrimination based on sex, racial or ethnic origin, religion or belief, disability, age or sexual orientation'. A framework directive on equal treatment was adopted in November 2000, covering age, disability, race/ethnicity and sexual orientation; and in 2006 a Consolidated Equal Treatment Directive was adopted, strengthening some of the provisions against gender discrimination, in particular in terms of legal remedies in national courts. The UK was one of the few member states with a tradition of legislation against racial or ethnic discrimination, dating back to the 1976 Race Relations Act; while the Disability Discrimination Act was passed in 1996; but three new sets of Regulations were required to meet the other anti-discrimination requirements. The 2006 Age Regulations (issued almost three years after the implementation deadline), which permit employers to maintain a mandatory retirement age of 65, were challenged in the ECJ; it ruled that this provision could be upheld if the national courts considered it necessary and appropriate for achieving 'legitimate social policy objectives'.

The Charter of Fundamental Rights contains a chapter on equality which is more comprehensive still: 'any discrimination based on any ground such as sex, race, colour, ethnic or social origin, genetic features, language, religion or belief, political or any other opinion, membership of a national minority, property, birth, disability, age or sexual orientation shall be prohibited'. As noted above, this will take effect now that the Lisbon Treaty has been adopted, but with a UK opt-out which may be subject to legal challenge.

Equal opportunities is certainly the area of employment relations where the EU has had the most substantial impact, not just in the UK but in member states more generally. The 'European social model', particularly in countries with a conservative religious tradition, has been oriented to the 'male breadwinner' rather than to workers in general. Achieving 'hard law' on equality issues has been slow and partial, but nevertheless there is an extensive body of regulation. As in so many other policy areas, one can ask the question: is the glass half-full or half-empty? In the case of gender equality the history of regulation is long enough to make a reasonable assessment of its impact. As noted above, UK governments of both parties have been forced reluctantly to change national law to meet EU requirements. Critics argue that the main focus of regulation has been on formal equality within the labour market, rather than on the social institutions outside the labour market which prevent most women from participating on equal terms. As Mósesdóttir (2006) puts it, most EU initiatives have been concerned to give women 'the same rights as men insofar as they behave like men on the labour market'.

But real advances have been made, and at first sight the extent of current EU regulation is surprising. Given the strength in many EU countries of ideologies defining domestic responsibilities as essentially female, the wide range of legislation on gender issues is noteworthy. And the degree of prejudice on questions of sexual orientation means that many countries would not voluntarily have adopted national legislation. So one could ask why socially conservative governments have signed up to such regulation at EU level. In many respects, equal opportunities is an issue on which a coordinated and determined campaign can exert a substantial impact on EU policy, in the absence of a similarly organized counter-movement. Some speak of an 'advocacy coalition' (Sabatier 1987) involving women Commissioners, the EP Committee for Women's Rights, the European Women's Lobby (EWL, which receives Commission funding), and actors at national level. Since 1995, a 'Group of Commissioners' on equal opportunities has held regular meetings with the EP Women's Rights Committee and the EWL. As van der Vleuten (2005) suggests, one can detect a 'pincer movement' at national level with governments under pressure from the EU institutions above and equal opportunities organizations below.

The Europeanization of British Industrial Relations or the Liberalization of the European Social Model?

The British system of industrial relations has been radically transformed since the early 1970s. Many of the changes reflect social, economic and political developments in the UK in the intervening period. But EU membership has also had a significant impact, as the previous sections have shown. Given the resistance of both Conservative and Labour governments to statutory regulation of the labour market, it is very improbable that legislation on working time and information and consultation would have been enacted voluntarily, and the same is true of much of the legislation on employment security and equal opportunities. Indeed, the virulence of UK governments' resistance to most EU social legislation, and their minimalist approach to implementing those directives which are nevertheless adopted, indicates that British labour law today would be very different but for EU membership. Kicking and screaming, British governments have been obliged to move closer to the 'European social model' of individual employment rights – though the EU has little capacity to shape collective industrial relations, and the actual enforcement of individual rights is largely dependent on national regulatory institutions.

The EU has clearly added a new level above, and influencing, national industrial relations systems: there are new rules, new pressures, new actors and a new agenda. For most countries – at least before enlargement – 'Europeanization' has probably had limited impact, except over issues which were previously not seriously addressed at national level. This is most obviously the case as regards equal opportunities: here, the EU has been the matrix of a 'policy community' (Falkner 1998; Heclo and Wildavsky 1974) which has driven initiatives which would have been far less likely to achieve results at the level of individual member states. The impact of EU regulation has, however, been more general in countries like Britain and to a lesser extent Ireland, where the 'voluntarist' tradition has meant that areas of employment relations controlled by law in most of continental Europe were left to regulation (or not) through collective bargaining.

Yet it is also possible to speak of a reverse process, the 'Anglicization' of continental employment relations. As indicated earlier, European integration has always involved a contradictory mix of market liberalization and social regulation. The Thatcher government was willing to endorse the SEA because, for all the rhetoric concerning the 'social dimension', its core objective was to enshrine the 'four freedoms' characteristic of a liberal market economy. Two decades later, the ECJ is increasingly interpreting these principles as overriding national employment protection rules (Höpner and Schäfer 2007). The landmark decisions of the ECJ in the Viking and Laval cases in 2007 adopted the principle that, irrespective of national law, industrial action which interfered with freedom of movement was legitimate only if it satisfied a 'proportionality' test (Davies 2008a; Joerges and Rödl 2009). These were followed in 2008 by the Rüffert and Luxembourg cases, which set very strict limits on the extent to which public authorities could prescribe minimum employment standards if these interfered with the freedom to provide services, hence severely restricting the protections contained in the 1996 Posted Workers Directive (Davies 2008b; Deakin 2008). A direct consequence in the UK was the inability of the airline pilots' union BALPA to call a strike against plans by British Airways to offshore part of its operations.

The complex interaction between 'Europeanization' and 'Anglicization' can also be seen in the development of the European Employment Strategy (EES). This dates from the 1993 Delors White Paper 'Growth, Competitiveness and Employment', which was an uneasy compromise between demands for a positive programme of public expenditure and active labour market and incomes policies, and calls – particularly from the UK government – for deregulation and 'flexibility'. The Amsterdam Treaty, and the subsequent 'jobs summit', gave the EES a formal basis: the Commission was to draft annual guidelines for employment policy, and member states were to produce national action plans which would be reviewed by the Commission and Council, which could issue recommendations to individual governments. The Luxembourg jobs summit in November 1997 adopted 19 employment guidelines with four main 'pillars': employability, entrepreneurship, adaptability and equal opportunities. (These were radically revised in 2003, and the whole structure of the EES was transformed in 2005.) The predominant focus on supply-side measures closely matched the priorities of the new Blair government.

The EES was amplified at the Lisbon summit of March 2000, which famously declared that Europe should become by 2010 'the most competitive and dynamic knowledge-based economy in the world, capable of sustained economic growth with more and better jobs and greater social cohesion, and respect for the environment'. Here, in an approach which I have elsewhere termed the 'composite resolution' (Hyman 2005), essentially competing aims were subsumed in a manner which delegated the choice of priorities to administrative discretion. Lisbon also introduced the concept of the OMC, whereby information exchange, peer review and the highlighting of 'best practice' were expected to guide national policy without the need for coercive sanctions: an approach consistent with the UK government's preference for exhortation rather than regulation. And as Offe has suggested (2003: 463), the 'hidden curriculum' of the OMC may be to encourage governments with strongly regulated labour markets to '"unlearn" and partially demolish entrenched institutional patterns'.

A further boost to UK government conceptions of labour market flexibility derived from the European Employment Taskforce under former Dutch premier Wim Kok, which was appointed by the Council in March 2003 and reported that EU policies should focus on increasing adaptability of workers and enterprises, attracting more people to the labour market, investing more, and more effectively, in human capital and ensuring effective implementation of reforms through better governance. The current Commission under Barroso has intensified the pressure for flexibility – presented in the now fashionable language of 'flexicurity'. Its Green Paper on Modernising Labour Law, issued in November 2006, placed central emphasis on this concept – but was far more concrete in its prescriptions for flexibility than in those for security (Keune and Jepsen 2007). Indeed, Ashiagbor (2007: 110, 113) has remarked that the final version of the Green Paper reflected 'fierce criticisms from Member States, in particular the UK, as well as concerted lobbying from business organisations, above all UNICE'. She added that 'there are marked similarities between British discourse on labour market policy, and EU-level discourse on the need to remove labour market "rigidities"' (113).

'No-one is forcing the European Union to become more competitive than the United States in nine years time', declared Frits Bolkestein (2000), who as Commissioner responsible for the internal market pushed for the radical liberalization of services. 'But if that is what we really want, we must leave the comfortable surroundings of the Rhineland and move closer to the tougher conditions and cold climate of the Anglo-Saxon form of capitalism.' Though Bolkestein failed to realize his objectives during his period as Commissioner, the balance of forces within the EU is increasingly favourable to the agenda which he – in common with UK governments – espoused.

The ambiguous and multifaceted character of the 'European social model' (Jepsen and Serrano Pascual 2006) makes it vulnerable to erosion. UK governments have shown some skill in exploiting this vulnerability, and particularly since enlargement have increasingly found allies in other member states. Thus we can discern a form of double movement. British industrial relations have in significant measure been Europeanized, despite the strenuous resistance of both Conservative and Labour governments. But the European social model has become in key respects increasingly Anglo-Saxon. Complete convergence is unlikely, but it no longer makes much sense to speak of a clash of systems.

References

Adnett, N. 1998: The Acquired Rights Directive and compulsory competitive tendering in the UK: an economic perspective. *European Journal of Law and Economics*, 6 (1), 69–81.

Adnett, N. and Hardy, S. 2001: Reviewing the Working Time Directive: rationale, implementation and case law. *Industrial Relations Journal*, 32 (2), 114–125.

Albert, M. 1993: *Capitalism against Capitalism*. London: Whurr.

Anderman, S. 2004: Termination of employment: whose property rights? In Barnard, C., Deakin, S.F. and Morris, G.S. (eds) *The Future of Labour Law: Liber Amicorum Bob Hepple QC*. Oxford: Hart, pp. 101–128

Ashiagbor, D. 2007: Statement of written evidence. In House of Lords, *Modernising European Union Labour Law: Has the UK Anything to Gain?* London: Stationery Office, pp. 110–113.

Attali, J. 1994: *Europe(s)*. Paris: Fayard.

Bolkestein, F. 2000: The future of the social market economy. http://europa.eu/rapid/pressReleasesAction.do?reference=SPEECH/00/487&format=HTML&aged=1&language=EN&guiLanguage=en

CIPD 2001: *Working Time Regulations: Have they Made a Difference?* London: CIPD.

Crouch, C. 1993: *Industrial Relations and European State Traditions*. Oxford: Clarendon Press.

Cutler, T. and Waine, B. 1998: *Managing the Welfare State*. Oxford: Berg.

Davies, A.C.L. 2008a: One step forward, two steps back? The Viking and Laval cases in the ECJ. *Industrial Law Journal*, 37 (2), 126–148.

Davies, P. 1993: Transfers Again: contracting out and the employee's option. *Industrial Law Journal*, 22 (2), 151–163.

Davies, P. 2008b: Case C-346/06, *Rüffert v Land Niedersachsen* [2008] IRLR 467 (ECJ). *Industrial Law Journal*, 37 (3), 293–295.

Deakin, S. 2008: Regulatory competition in Europe after *Laval*. Cambridge: CBR Working Paper 364.

Delanty, G. 1995: *Inventing Europe: Idea, Identity, Reality*. London: Macmillan.

Ebbinghaus B. 1999: Does a European social model exist and can it survive? In Huemer, G., Mesch, M. and Traxler, F. (eds) *The Role of Employer Associations and Labour Unions in the EMU*. Aldershot: Ashgate, pp. 1–26.

Falkner, G. 1998: *EU Social Policy in the 1990s Towards a Corporatist Policy Community*. London: Routledge.

Fitzgerald, I. and Stirling, J. (eds) 2004: *European Works Councils: Pessimism of the Intellect, Optimism of the Will?* London: Routledge.

Forster, A. 2002: *Euroscepticism in Contemporary British Politics*. London: Routledge.

George, S. 2000: Britain: anatomy of a Eurosceptic state. *European Integration* 22 (1), 15–33.

Geyer, R., Mackintosh, A. and Lehmann, K. 2005: *Integrating UK and European Social Policy*. Oxford: Radcliffe.

Grant, W. and Marsh, D. 1977: *The Confederation of British Industry*. London: Hodder and Stoughton.

Hall, M.J., Hutchinson, S., Parker, J., Purcell, J. and Terry, M.A. 2007: *Implementing Information and Consultation: Early Experience under the ICE Regulations*. London: BERR.

Hall, P.A. and Soskice, D. (eds) 2001: *Varieties of Capitalism: The Institutional Foundations of Comparative Advantage*. Oxford: Oxford UP.

Heclo, H. and Wildawsky, A.B. 1974: *The Private Government of Public Money*. London: Macmillan.

Hindmoor. A. 2004: *New Labour at the Centre. Constructing Political Space*. Oxford: OUP.

Höpner, M. and Schäfer, A. 2007: A new phase of European integration: organized capitalisms in post-Ricardian Europe. Cologne: MPIfG Discussion Paper 07/4.

Hyman, R. 2005: Trade unions and the politics of European integration. *Economic and Industrial Democracy*, 26 (1), 9–40.

Jepsen, M. and Serrano Pascual, A. (eds) 2006: *Unwrapping the European Social Model*. Bristol: Policy Press.

Joerges, C. and Rödl, F. 2009: Informal politics, formalised law and the 'social deficit' of European integration: reflections after the judgments of the ECJ in *Viking* and *Laval*. *European Law Journal*, 15 (1), 1–19.

Keune, M. and Jepsen, M. 2007: Not balanced and hardly new: the European Commission's quest for flexicurity. In Jørgensen, H. and Madsen, P.K. (eds) *Flexicurity and Beyond*. Copenhagen: DJØF Publishing.

Kilpatrick, C. 1997: Effective utilisation of equality rights. In Gardiner, F. (ed.) *Sex Equality Policy in Western Europe*. London: Routledge, pp. 25–45.

Lecher, W., Nagel, B. and Platzer, H.-W.1999: *Establishment of European Works Councils: From Information Committee to Social Actor*. Aldershot: Ashgate.

MacShane, D. 1991: British unions and Europe. In Pimlott, B. and Cook, C. (eds) *Trade Unions and British Politics*. London: Longman, pp. 286–306.

Majone, G. 1996: *Regulating Europe*. London: Routledge.

Marginson, P., Hall, M., Hoffmann, A. and Müller, T. 2004: The impact of European works councils on management decision-making in UK and US-based multinationals. *British Journal of Industrial Relations*, 42 (2), 209–233.

Marginson, P. and Sisson, K. 2004: *European Integration and Industrial Relations: Multi-Level Governance in the Making*. Basingstoke: Palgrave.

Marks, G., Hooghe, L. and Blank, K. 1996: European integration from the 1980s: state-centric vs multi-level governance. *Journal of Common Market Studies*, 34 (3), 341–378.

McMullen, J. 1996: Atypical transfers, atypical workers and atypical employment structures: a case for greater transparency in transfer of employment issues. *Industrial Law Journal*, 25 (4), 286–307.

Mósesdóttir, L. 2006: The European social model and gender equality. In Jepsen, M. and Serrano Pascual, A. (eds) *Unwrapping the European Social Model*. Bristol: Policy Press, pp. 145–166.

Mullen, A. 2005: The British Left's 'Great Debate' on Europe. PhD thesis, University of Leeds.

Mullen, A. 2007: The British Left: for and against Europe? *Capital and Class*, 93, 217–231.

Offe, C. 2003: The European Model of "Social" Capitalism: Can it Survive European Integration? *Journal of Political Philosophy* 11(4), 437–69.

Rosamond, B. 1993: National labour organizations and European integration: British trade unions and '1992'. *Political Studies*, 41, 420–434.

Sabatier, P.A. 1987: Knowledge, policy-oriented learning, and policy change: an advocacy coalition framework. *Science Communication*, 8, 649–692.

Samuels, A. 1998: Incorporating, translating or implementing European Union law into UK law. *Statute Law Review*, 19 (2), 80–92.

Scharpf, F. 1999: *Governing in Europe: Effective and Democratic?* Oxford: Oxford University Press.

Schofield, P. 1988: Recent cases: equal pay. *Industrial Law Journal*, 17 (1), 241–244.

Shrubshall, V. 1998: Competitive tendering, out-sourcing and the Acquired Rights Directive. *Modern Law Review*, 61, 85–92.

Stone Sweet, A. and Caporaso, J. 1998: From free trade to supranational polity: the European Court and integration. In Sandholtz, W. and Stone Sweet, A. (eds) *European Integration and Supranational Governance*. Oxford: Oxford University Press, pp. 92–133.

Streeck, W. 1997: Neither European nor works councils: a reply to Paul Knutsen. *Economic and Industrial Democracy*, 18 (2), 325–337.

Taylor, P., Baldry, C., Danford, A. and Stewart, P. 2009: 'An umbrella full of holes?': corporate restructuring, redundancy and the effectiveness of ICE Regulations. *Relations Industrielles/Industrial Relations*, 64 (1), 27–49.

TUC 2008: The return of the long hours culture. http://www.tuc.org.uk/extras/longhoursreturn.pdf

Turner, A. 2002: *Just Capital: The Liberal Economy*. Basingstoke: Macmillan.

van der Vleuten, A. 2005: Pincers and prestige. Explaining implementation of EU gender equality legislation. *Comparative European Politics*, 3 (4), 464–488.

Whittall, M., Knudsen, H. and Huijgen, F. (eds) 2007: *Towards a European Labour Identity: The Case of the European Work Council*. London: Routledge.

SECTION TWO

ACTORS

4

MANAGEMENT: CAUGHT BETWEEN COMPETING VIEWS OF THE ORGANIZATION

KEITH SISSON AND JOHN PURCELL

Introduction

Until the 1980s, most employment relations commentators paid no more than perfunctory attention to management's role. By comparison to trade unions and the state, management seemed to be a relatively unproblematic, if not unimportant, actor. It was management, defined as a group of people with responsibility to the board of directors or its equivalent for running the organization, which exercised the discretionary rights that are the employment relationship's distinguishing feature. Yet it seemed to have settled for a particular way of doing things and to be more concerned with maintaining the status quo than changing it. To paraphrase Dunlop (1958), management was one of a number of actors working within an *industrial relations system* of institutions, processes and rules shaped by technology, markets and the balance of power in the wider society: it was assumed to share the same interests or 'ideology' of the state and trade unions in having a relatively stable framework within which it could get on with the tasks of planning, controlling and coordinating the business's activities. From the 1980s, interest in management moved centre-stage reflecting a consensus that it had become the major force for change in the arrangements governing the employment relationship. In one direction, the emphasis is on the universal: management is seen as a strategic actor responding to increasingly global product market competitive pressures (see, for example, Kochan *et al.* 1986). In a second, the focus is more on the particular: management is viewed as an agent of the prevailing form of capital. It is driven by a logic of efficiency shaped by the interplay between two sets of deeply embedded institutions: on the one hand, the institutions, processes and rules of employment relations and, on the other, the structures of corporate governance and finance. Here the particular 'variety of capitalism' to be found in the UK and the USA, 'shareholder' capitalism, is contrasted with the more 'stakeholder' approach found in Japan (Jacoby 2005) and in continental Europe (Sisson and Marginson 1994, 2003; Hall and Soskice 2001; Gospel and Pendleton 2003).

The argument of this chapter is that these approaches are not incompatible – it is a question of balance, which also depends on the different levels of management. There are universal pressures, above all on workplace managers, reflecting product market competition – to paraphrase Herriot (1998) and his colleagues, they have to reconcile two seemingly conflicting requirements intrinsic to the employment relationship: to cut costs to the bone and yet at the same time promote the commitment necessary for innovation. Traditionally, company managers confronted the same requirements. Over the past two decades, however, above all in the UK and USA, the basis of competition for them has increasingly shifted to financial results in the form of current and projected cash returns on investment, almost regardless of product or service. The effect of what has come to be known as 'financialization' has been more or less 'permanent restructuring', making it increasingly difficult for workplace managers to develop any consistency in approach. Moreover, the tension between the two positions finds expression in very different views of the work organization, with important implications for future developments: the resource-based view, which stresses the importance of developing the capability of the organization and its employees; and the doctrine of the firm as a nexus of contracts, which views the organization as a 'contracting site', with the parties owing no responsibilities to one another beyond those expected of participants acting in good faith.

The argument is reflected in the chapter's structure. The first section reviews the nature and extent of the changes in the management of the employment relationship at workplace level, drawing on the evidence of the most recent Workplace Employment Relations Survey (WERS 2004) (Kersley *et al.* 2006). The second moves on to discuss the 'permanent restructuring' of the multi-establishment organizations that dominate employment in the UK, focusing on 'financialization' and the main instruments of coordination and control, i.e. divisionalization, budgetary devolution and 'marketization'. The third highlights the two very different views of the organization lying at the heart of the tensions between the workplace and company levels, with the fourth reviewing future prospects in the light of the banking and credit crisis of 2007–08. The main focus is on the private sector, although many of the trends observed are also evident in the public sector.

HRM: A Case of More of the Same?

Recognition that the employment relationship is not automatic in effect and involves 'managerial' as well as 'market' relations is a key distinguishing feature of employment relations analysis. Workers do not 'sell' a finite amount of work, as they do in the case of the labour service contract. Rather they 'sell' the *ability to work* or labour power. Motivating employees to do what managers want is far from being a straightforward matter. As Brown and Walsh (1994: 440) suggest, 'the act of hiring . . . is not sufficient to ensure that the job gets done in an acceptable way . . . the employee has to be motivated – by encouragement, threats, loyalty, discipline, money, competition, pride, promotion, or whatever else is deemed effective to work with the required pace and care'.

Managing the employment relationship, defined here as human resource management or HRM, is also massively contradictory. It is not just that employees represent both a cost and an investment, which means constantly making compromises between the two. In Edwards' words (2003: 16), 'managements have to pursue the objectives of control and releasing creativity . . . [and] the problem is that these involve very different and conflicting strategies'. Very tight monitoring is not only costly, but also can reduce the prospects of employees using their initiative. But lax control can mean that different groups and/or individuals may pursue aims and objectives that are incompatible with one another.

Initially, fear of 'organized' or collective conflict ensured that HRM figured prominently on companies' agendas. In some cases, for example in the USA, the determination to keep trade unions out of the workplace was a major factor in the development of welfare practices (Jacoby 2004). In others, for example where craft unions were firmly entrenched in the workplace as metalworking in the UK, management agreed to make many of the rules and procedures of bureaucratic control the subject of collective bargaining with trade unions as a means of legitimating their authority (Edwards *et al.* 1992). In most countries, governments also championed collective bargaining as a means of institutionalizing conflict, particularly at times of crisis such as at the end of the two World Wars (Sisson 1987). One result is that HRM effectively became equated with collective relations with trade unions. Meanwhile, its individual dimension came to be seen largely as an administrative function involving first-line managers supported by relatively low status personnel managers, many of whom were involved in welfare activities (Sisson 1989; Jacoby 2003).

In the case of the UK, two features in the complex of institutions, processes and rules making up the national employment relations system need to be highlighted in the light of later developments. The first was *the tradition of 'voluntarism'* discussed in Dickens and Hall (this volume). The legal framework of employment of rights and obligations (individual and collective) that emerged was minimal and offered little counterweight to the privileges of shareholders. The second was a highly decentralized and diverse structure of collective bargaining embedded in procedural rather than substantive rules. This meant that, save for a few exceptions, the UK did not develop the detailed and legally enforceable multi-employer agreements that supplement and extend the legislative framework in most other European Union (EU) member countries.

From the 1980s onwards, with the decline of trade unions and collective bargaining, the focus of attention shifted on to the individual dimension, the aim being to secure a highly committed and adaptable workforce. A widespread consensus seemingly emerged amongst analysts, governments and international agencies about the need to move away from the traditional control structures of hierarchy, bureaucracy and specialization. The starting point was the recognition that people were not simply one of the factors of production along with money and machinery, but the major source of competitive advantage – *People: The Key to Success* was the title of a 1987 National Economic Development Office/Manpower Services publication. The prescription implied not just a change in beliefs and assumptions. In the case of work organization, increasing employees' participation in the design of work processes was recommended, along with the sharing of task-specific knowledge, with the emphasis on semi-autonomous team working with managers assuming the role of enablers and developers. In the case of HR policies and practices, the emphasis was to be on 'high performance working' – coupling team working with individualized training and development, along with performance management linked to reward systems to enhance commitment and involvement (see Edwards and Sengupta, this volume). The specialist function was also to drop its 'Cinderella' image and shift from the largely administrative role associated with personnel management and take on responsibility for ensuring a more strategic approach that aligned policies and practices with business strategy – be it 'best practice' or 'best fit' (for further details, see Sisson 1994; Boxall and Purcell 2008; see also European Commission 1997; ILO 2002; OECD 1997).

Much of the thinking had its roots in the neo-human relations school associated with the likes of Maslow (1943), Herzberg (1966) and McGregor (1960), which recognized that labour was not a commodity and motivation was management's main problem. Also increasingly important was the resource-based approach discussed later. It was the changing context of business, however, that provided the impetus. Especially important here was the growing dominance of Japanese companies in highly visible sectors such as cars and electronics arising from their use of new 'lean production' methods such as 'just-in-time', *kaizen* ('continuous improvement'), and the direct participation of the workforce. Bearing in mind the emergence of low cost manufacturers, above all in China, the status quo was deemed to be unsustainable: the future lay with quality products and a quality workforce. Moving into the new millennium, intensifying competition and/or pressure on scarce resources, coupled with the growing importance attached to the notions of the 'knowledge organization' and 'knowledge economy', supposedly reinforced these imperatives.

Work organization

In practice, most features of traditional HRM have proved to be extremely durable. In overviewing developments in work organization, one commentator puts it like this:

> When compared with the momentous changes we've witnessed over the past half century in technology, life styles, and geo-politics, the practice of management seems to have evolved at a snail's pace. While a suddenly resurrected 1960s era CEO would undoubtedly be amazed by the flexibility of today's real-time supply chains and the ability to provide 24/7 customer service, he or she would find a great many of today's management rituals little changed from those that governed corporate life a generation or two ago. Hierarchies may have gotten flatter but they haven't disappeared. Front-line employees may be smarter and better trained, but

they're still expected to line up obediently behind executive decisions. Lower-level managers are still appointed by more senior managers. Strategy still gets set at the top. (Hamel 2007: 4)

Recent years have certainly seen reductions in the tiers of managers in some organizations – British Steel, which is now a subsidiary of Tata Steel, is a good example (Overell 1998). These have rarely been accompanied, however, by the widely promoted semi-autonomous team working. According to the 2004 WERS (Kersley *et al.* 2006: 89), around three quarters of workplaces (72%) reported that some employees were involved in formally designated teams. Yet only a small number of these, just 6%, said that employees were allowed to appoint their own team leaders. Other data, from the 2001 Skills Survey, also suggest that, although there had been some increase in team working in the 1990s, there had been a substantial decline in task discretion (Gallie *et al.* 2004: 256). Less than half of employees said that they had a lot of influence on how work was done or the order in which tasks were undertaken; only a third said so in relation to the tasks performed (Kersley *et al.* 2006: 95–97).

HR policies and practices

Individualism rather than collectivism?   There has certainly been a shift in emphasis to individual employment relations. One indicator is the number of workplaces covered by collective bargaining (see Brown, this volume). In 1980, some nine out of ten workplaces in the private sector were covered. In 2004, this had dropped to less than two in ten (16%) (Kersley *et al.* 2006: 179–184). In other words, management determines pay unilaterally in just under three quarters of private sector workplaces. Paralleling this development has been an increasing emphasis on performance management. This is manifest in the use of performance appraisal for all types of employees, individual performance related pay and direct communications between front line managers and their teams as well as the introduction of a wider range of communication methods focused on the individual. In part the logic is to manage, or manipulate, the psychological contract and seek to improve the sense of commitment felt by the individual to his or her employer, what is often nowadays called 'engagement'. Even where unions are recognized, as in the public sector, this rhetoric of individualism has been much in evidence, too, seen in the growth of individual performance related pay and associated techniques linked to performance management such as appraisal.

Yet, for all the talk of the individualization of the employment relationship, transaction costs considerations mean that, in the majority of cases, it is inefficient for employers to differentiate between individual employees. For example, pay systems may have been taken out of collective bargaining and wider pay bands adopted ('broad banding'). In theory, this makes it much easier to differentiate between each individual and pay him or her according to their performance. In practice, it is rare to find any difference between the pay of most employees and what there is, is most likely to be linked to length of service. 'Merit pay' awards for most have an uncanny similarity to movements in inflation and should more accurately be called 'cost of living awards'. Where there is variety, it is found only at the extremes: amongst poor performers (who rarely constitute more than 5% of the workforce) and high performers (usually constituting less than 10%). As for the individualized contracts advocated by some free market commentators, these are very rarely found beyond the higher echelons of senior executives. Essentially, most contracts of employment tend to take a 'standard form' (Collins 2007: 2), the written statement usually requiring the consultation of other documents that are expressly incorporated, such as staff handbooks and occupational pension schemes composed on advice from lawyers.

'High performance working'? In recent years, there has been considerable emphasis on how HRM contributes to organizational performance (see Edwards and Sengupta, this volume) – indeed establishing the link has been described as the 'holy grail' of HRM researchers. Although individual studies show positive relationships, for example, between team working, employee commitment and performance (European Foundation, 1997; Defarue *et al.* 2008), the numerous reviews of the evidence (see, for example, Wright and Boswell 2002, Wall and Wood 2005 and Boselie *et al.* 2005) have been disappointing for those seeking a definitive, causal link (Purcell and Kinnie 2007). Arguably, however, what is interesting is not so much the confusion of the evidence, but the fact that, despite the rhetoric and strong public policy support for the adoption of an integrated bundle of high performance or high involvement practices, the take-up has been low. In 1998, WERS reported that 'high commitment management practices are associated with better economic performance, better workplace well being and a better climate of employment relations, *but just 14 percent of all work-places have a majority of them in place*' (Cully *et al.* 1999: 291 emphasis added). Despite the widespread rhetoric promoting the adoption of 'high performance working', it seems that the increasing levels of work intensity reported in the 1990s (Green 2001; Kersley *et al.* 2006) reflected employees having to work harder rather than smarter.

WERS 2004 suggests very little evidence to indicate that the take-up quickened in recent years. Take the three practices that, on this occasion, it uses as indicators of 'high performance working', i.e. team working, multi-skilling and problem-solving groups. The proportion of continuing workplaces combining these three practices rose from 22 to 29% between 1998 and 2004, but the increase was much smaller (from 15 to 19%) if team working was restricted to groups exercising a degree of autonomy (Kersley *et al.* 2006: 97).

A strategic approach? The need for management to develop a more integrated approach to employment relations has been a constant theme since the publication of the Donovan Royal Commission report (1968) four decades ago. Yet review after review has concluded that, although some individual cases stand out, it is very difficult to identify any general patterns or styles in British management's approach (Sisson and Marginson 2003; Colling 2003; Purcell and Kessler 2003). WERS 2004 showed that only four out of ten (38%) of workplaces were accredited by Investors in People (IiP), which requires them to have a planned approach to setting and communicating business objectives and developing people to meet those objectives (Kersley *et al.* 2006: 67). Less than two thirds of workplaces (61%) reported having a strategic plan covering just one of three employment relations issues, i.e. employee development, employee job satisfaction, and employee diversity (Kersley *et al.* 2006: 62).

The results of devising a simple 'strategic' HR index giving workplaces a point each for having a strategic plan covering employment relations matters, for involving managers responsible for employment relations matters in its preparation, and for IiP accreditation are also instructive. One quarter (28%) of workplaces scored zero, 16% scored one, one third (34%) scored two and only one fifth (22%) scored three (most of which were the larger unionized workplaces in the public sector).

Perhaps most interesting are the data on the workplaces that do appear to be pursuing a strategic approach. There are four findings that are important. First, there is no clear link between the measures of HRM strategies and product market strategies – quality, it seems, is not as critical in this context as many people believe. Second, there is a positive relationship between these measures and the amount of change that management has introduced at the workplace – the more changes being experienced, the greater the likelihood of a strategic approach to HRM. Furthermore, this positive relationship between HR integration and the probability of making changes held across eight types of change. Third, there is also a positive relationship between these measures and labour costs. Workplaces whose labour costs exceeded half their sales revenue or operating costs were significantly more likely than those with lower labour costs to have a strategic plan covering HRM, to involve specialist managers in its preparation and to be IiP qualified. Fourth, higher scores on the HR integration index were also associated with a higher incidence of contracted-out services. Attention to change, labour costs and contracting-out are wholly consistent with the pressures for restructuring that many UK organizations have been experiencing for the reasons considered below.

The HRM function: more than personnel management by another name?   The WERS findings in respect of the specialist function are largely consistent with the picture emerging so far. Overall, it seems that the function continues to struggle to achieve the position and status associated with strategic HRM. Only just over one in four workplaces had a specialist manager who spent more than half of their time on HR matters (Kersley *et al.* 2006: 41). In the economy as a whole, managers responsible for employment relations were involved in the preparation of a strategic plan in around half (53%) of all workplaces (Kersley *et al.* 2006: 64). In multi-establishment companies, only three out of five of private sector respondents reported having someone responsible for employment relations on the board of directors or top governing body: this is important because workplaces with board-level employment relations representation were much more likely to include employment relations in a strategic business plan (Kersley *et al.* 2006: 62, 64).

Yet many more workplaces had specialists in 2004 (28%) than in 1998 (17%) (Kersley *et al.* 2006: 39). Moreover, not only had the proportion with 'human resource managers' increased – there are more 'human resource managers' than there are 'personnel managers' – they were also likely to be better qualified (especially the female specialists who considerably outnumber their male counterparts); spend more time on employment relations issues; have more staff assisting them; and are more likely to be responsible for pay and pension entitlements than personnel managers. The HR label also made a difference in terms of the autonomy that local managers have when making decisions about employment relations matters. Specialist managers were also likely to seek advice from external sources. Overall, if there is no great evidence of concern with 'grand' strategy, the specialist function does appear to be developing the all-round competence that commentators have advocated (see, for example, Ulrich 1998). Equally, it does not appear that there has been any increase in the unloading of key responsibilities to either line managers or external agencies.

Summary

Changes in the policies and practices directly involved in managing the employment relationship turn out to be nowhere near as dramatic as many pundits have proclaimed. There is little evidence of autonomous team working and 'high performance working'; the number of workplaces with a comprehensive strategy also appears to be very small. At the same time, however, it appears that there has been a considerable increase in performance management; there is also a close relationship between those that adopt a more strategic approach and two key variables: the extent of changes taking place and the significance of labour costs. There have also been developments in the specialist function: there appears to be a new breed of HR managers, who are better qualified and have greater responsibilities.

Permanent Restructuring?

Our attention now shifts to the higher levels of the organizations of which workplaces are subsidiaries – important though the workplace is, it is not enough to look there to understand the conduct of the employment relationship. In the UK, some 68% of UK workplaces were part of larger organizations in 2004 (Kersley *et al.* 2006: 20), the size of the workplaces involved suggesting that the proportion of employees was higher still. More than half of workplaces in the private sector, i.e. 57%, were also part of international companies, around 38% being UK owned and 19% foreign owned. Adding to the significance of the larger organization is that many small businesses are their suppliers and/or customers; employment relations in the small business in no small measure directly depend on what happens in the larger organization.

If there is one phrase that sums up developments in large UK organizations in recent years, it would be 'permanent restructuring' (Folkman *et al.* 2006). In the private sector, a major source has been merger and acquisition (M&A) and disposal, with redundancy becoming the accepted way in which firms handle the consequences regardless of the overall economic situation (McGovern *et al.* 2007: 134). Indeed, 'headcount' reductions are typically put forward as a major consideration in justifying the initiative. A second source, affecting the public as well as the private sector (see Bach, this volume), has been major changes in the arrangements for coordination and control with significant implications for the way organizations are run. The overall effect, with wide-ranging implications for HRM, has been to exaggerate the importance of measurable results and targets.

An era of 'financialization'

Previous versions of this chapter (Sisson and Marginson 1994, 2003) emphasized that there were a number features of the UK's 'shareholder capitalism' that were important in understanding management's employment relations behaviour. These included, first, a privileged position for shareholders and an overwhelming emphasis on shareholder value as the key business driver, as opposed to the interests of other stakeholders. Second, a focus on short-term profitability, rather than long-term market share or added value, as the key index of business performance has been encouraged by high concentrations of institutional share ownership by investment trusts and pension funds. Third, takeovers are relatively easy, which not only reinforces the pressure on short-term profitability to maintain share price, but also encourages expansion by M&A rather than by internal growth, while reconfiguring the corporation through outsourcing, off-shoring and restructuring to remove parts of the business from the portfolio. Finally, there tends to be a premium on 'financial engineering' as the core organizational competence, the domination of financial management over other functions and numbers driven as opposed to issue-driven planning.

The pressures on company managers from these features intensified in recent years. Some idea of the sheer scale of the M&As taking place in the UK can be gauged by studying Table 4.1, which shows acquisitions by foreign-owned and domestically owned companies over the period 1997–2006. Fundamentally important, however, is that whereas in earlier decades, market position was the main driver, in the 1990s, financial considerations came to the fore.

A walk down any high street brings life to the statistics. Even before the banking and credit crisis of 2007–08, many building societies had become banks and part of larger groups. Abbey National belongs to Spain's Banc Santander, Cheltenham and Gloucester to LloydsTSB, and the Woolwich to Barclays, while Halifax is part of a wider group involving the Bank of Scotland. The banks themselves have not been immune: NatWest is part of Royal Bank of Scotland Group and the Midland has been absorbed by HSBC.

Table 4.1 Mergers and acquisitions in the UK, 1997–2006

	By UK companies		By foreign companies	
	Number	*Value £ billion*	*Number*	*Value £ billion*
1997	506	26.829	193	15.717
1998	635	29.525	252	32.413
1999	493	26.163	252	60.860
2000	587	106.916	227	64.618
2001	493	28.994	162	24.382
2002	430	25.236	117	16.798
2003	558	18.679	129	9.309
2004	741	31.408	178	29.928
2005	769	25.134	242	50.280
2006	739	27.694	242	75.511

Source: ONS, 2007

In manufacturing, the change is, if anything, even more dramatic. Many companies that were once household names have simply disappeared. Courtaulds, the chemicals/textile manufacturer, was split into two independent companies in 1990 and subsequently absorbed by Akzo-Nobel and Sara Lee, respectively. Lucas Industries, the engineering company, merged with the USA's much smaller Verity in 1996, the merged company being taken over three years later by the TWR, which proceeded to divest most of the businesses. British Steel merged with the Dutch company Hoogovens in 1999 to form the Corus Group, which was bought by Tata Steel of India in 2007. GEC, the UK's largest engineering company in its day, is no more after a disastrous restructuring at the time of the dotcom boom/ bust in 2001. Even the mighty bell-weather of British business that was ICI has gone: a division into heavy and specialty chemicals in the 1990s was followed by absorption into Akzo-Nobel and AstraZenica, respectively.

Since the mid-1980s traditional M&A forms have been joined by other kinds of investment/divestment (Froud 2000a, 2000b). These include inter-business sell-offs, where ownership of a particular unit changes hands; spin-offs, where the divested part of the company is floated and shares distributed to shareholders of the parent; and purchases by internal management buyouts (MBOs) or external management buyins (MBI). Leveraged buyouts (LBOs), which are heavily financed by debt, have also figured.

There was also a fundamental shift in the logic of much investment/divestment activity, leading to a redefinition of the nature of competition itself, which has come to be known as 'financialization'. In the 1970s and 1980s, to paraphrase Froud (2000a), competition was based on product and process, most notably in sectors such as cars and consumer electronics; pressure was exerted through the product market, with consumers making firms winners or losers by virtue of their combined purchasing power; the management challenge was represented in physical terms – 'lean production' was about better factories with lower build hours, less inventory and higher quality; and there was a leading role for Japanese companies such as Toyota whose practices were widely imitated and transplanted. By the late 1990s, the emphasis of competition shifted to financial results in the form of current and projected cash returns on investment using cross-sector league tables such as MVA (market value added) and EVA™ (economic value added), with the returns on investment in one firm explicitly compared against all others regardless of product or sector; pressure was exerted through the capital market by shareholders via buy, sell and hold decisions; the management challenge came to be represented in narrow financial terms; and there was a renewed leadership role for US companies. Overall, a key consequence was to intensify the pressure on managers to increase returns to shareholders: the proportion of profits paid out to shareholders in the form of dividends and share 'buy-backs' rose from just over 40% in the 1960s and 1970s to around 70% in the 1980s and 1990s (Lazonick and O'Sullivan 2000).

Promoting many of these developments have been new forms of private investment funds, which have assumed an increasingly 'active' role in seeking to influence company share performance. Hedge funds, for example, are aggressively managed with the aim of delivering the highest returns for their members, typically wealthy individuals or professional investors such as insurance companies and pension funds. Essentially, they make sophisticated bets on the future direction of an asset or even a whole financial market. They invest in stock, bonds, currencies, futures, options, indexes, using techniques such as short selling (selling borrowed securities when prices are considered overvalued and then repurchasing them after an anticipated drop in value) and leveraging (borrowing money to invest). Similarly, private equity groups typically take a controlling interest in a business with a view to delisting it from public stock exchanges, holding it private during which time they may restructure its reserve capital management and internal organization, and relisting it through an initial public offer (Froud and Williams 2007). High profile businesses taken over in recent years include the AA motoring organization, Boots the chemist and the department store chain Debenhams. Finally, sovereign investment funds are state-backed funds that governments use to reinvest for the longer term some of the returns from depleting assets such as oil and gas. Notable examples include the Norwegian Government's Pension Fund, the Abu Dhabi Investment Authority and the China Investment Corporation. Their investment strategies tend to more long term, but their size means they can be critical in particular takeover situations.

The immediate catalyst creating 'financialization' was deregulation of the financial sector in the 1980s (so-called 'Big Bang') and the accompanying globalization of capital markets. Not only was the City of London given much freer rein, access to credit and credit markets was substantially eased across the world. The effect was to increase opportunities to borrow (leverage) on the basis of expected rises in asset values. As well as giving a very considerable boost to the activities of private equity groups and hedge funds, it also fuelled the growth of a veritable 'industry' of business intermediaries who derive their income from share price-related activities ranging from the buying and selling of shares to M&A. As Folkman (2006) and his colleagues argue, while senior managers in major companies benefited considerably from the incentive schemes and share options they were encouraged to put into place, their numbers at around 500 were hardly sufficient to carry the full weight of responsibility for what was happening. Rather, it was senior investment bankers, city analysts and traders, accounting and law partners, consultants and senior advertising and PR executives who provided much of the impetus. In the case of M&A, for example, they could typically expect to make in fees 2 to 3% of the value of the transaction (Doran 2008). In 2003, their numbers were estimated to be around 20 000 on the basis of tax returns of those earning more than £250 000 a year (Erturk *et al.* 2006).

From management by task to management by performance

Paralleling 'financialization' have been changes in the internal coordination and control structures of large organizations that add up to little short of a revolution in the ways they are being managed. Above all, they involve a fundamental shift from the management by task characteristic of traditional organizational structures to management by performance. Critically, too, these changes affect the public as well as the private sector (see Bach, this volume).

Three related changes in particular deserve attention. First, *divisionalization* involves dividing the large-scale hierarchical organization into a number of semi-autonomous business units or executive agencies (the civil service) or trusts (the National Health Service) that operate as individual profit and/or cost centres. These may be product and/or territory based. In a phrase the organization becomes 'decentralised operationally, but centralised strategically' (Whittington and Mayer 2000). Critically important is that headquarters retains control over target setting and resource allocation, with all profits returned to the centre for reallocation according to strategic priorities, in effect operating as a 'central banker' shifting resources to and from the divisions depending on achievement of specified targets and/or return on investment.

Second, *budgetary devolution* involves the allocation of responsibility for managing activities within financial resources or targets. Like divisionalization, with which it nearly always goes hand in hand, budgetary devolution can operate at a number of levels: it can relate to a business unit within a company, or an executive agency within the civil service or a trust within the NHS. It can also relate to the internal units within such divisions, and even to bundles of activities. Budget formulation and control constitute one of the most important regular activities that corporate offices undertake. They establish key performance indicators (KPIs) for strategic business units (SBUs) and for managers themselves. These KPIs emphasize financial performance with corporate managers often 'managing by numbers'. Intangible, more human assets and behaviour tend therefore to be ignored since they cannot be 'counted' (Boxall and Purcell 2008: 263). Thus budget meetings at both corporate and SBU levels are of prime importance yet HR people attend these relatively rarely (Marginson *et al.* 1993).

Finally, *marketization* is short-hand for the greater application of market principles to decision making. Externally, it is reflected in developments such as 'competitive tendering', 'market testing' and the subcontracting or outsourcing of activities previously undertaken in-house, very often involving 'off-shoring' to another country where labour costs are much lower. Internally, it involves the introduction of 'markets', with different units being regarded as 'purchasers' and 'providers' trading products and services with one another. This has led to the fragmentation of work and contracts, blurring organizational boundaries and the disordering of hierarchies, raising questions about the continuing validity of models of employment focused on a single employer (Marchington *et al.* 2005).

In particular, multiple patterns of interlocking ownership and the provision of goods and services through intermediary companies, often employing people who previously worked for the single large integrated firm, make the control of employment relations more complex and often at arm's length. This has been vividly seen in recent months in 2008 in two labour disputes that mirrored the earlier major strike in Gate Gourmet, which supplied aircraft meals to British Airways. In the Shell Petroleum drivers' dispute, the workers were employed by a subcontractor. This was also the case in the Grangemouth BP oil refinery, which had been sold to a private equity company. In each case it was the fragmentation of the employment relationship now involving three parties that exacerbated the dispute and made settlement much harder to achieve – the immediate employer no longer controlled the purse strings.

Although the thinking behind these changes is not new – General Motors pioneered divisionalization as a means of instilling greater accountability more than 80 years ago (Chandler 1962) – there are two main reasons behind their adoption in recent years. One is the pressure of competition, which puts a premium on managing performance. In the private sector, this comes from the process of 'financialization' discussed above. In the public sector, it comes from competition for scarce resources. In both circumstances, traditional management by task structures is said to be not only costly and inefficient but also a major barrier to the management of performance.

The second reason is the revolution in information processing facilities made possible by the coming of the microchip and associated developments in computer software. These have provided managers with instruments of arm's-length control and coordination that are far more effective and efficient than task-based structures. More or less instant up-to-date data on activity and costs can be used not only to monitor performance against targets, but also to make 'coercive comparisons' between individual units leading to the continuous stretching of targets.

Also important was the further diminution in the countervailing power of the employment relations framework (see Brown, this volume). Unions such as the GMB campaigned vigorously for greater transparency and control of the activities of private equity groups, but the main preoccupation has been with halting membership decline. Moreover, as the overall balance of membership shifted from the private to the public sector, many unions become preoccupied with the changes that the government was trying to implement. Large-scale immigration also made its contribution, helping to minimize the wage pressures in a relatively buoyant economy that might otherwise have helped to bring about change.

Implications   It is difficult to underestimate the impact of these changes on HRM. Many employees find themselves working for very different organizations from the ones they joined, with significant implications for their pay, career prospects and pensions (Clark 2008). Some are now in jobs where the employer who pays may be different from the one who directs (Marchington *et al.* 2005). Employees are also being encouraged to take responsibility for their careers and pension funding – tangible benefits of the employment relationship that many employers have been providing, but no longer feel they can afford. As authoritative bodies such as the Audit Commission (2003, 2006) and the House of Commons Public Administration Select Committee (2003) have recognized in the case of public services, centralized and detailed targets, very often reflecting short-term political pressures, have considerably distorted management priorities as well as riding roughshod over local consultative processes. In Caulkin's (2008) words, 'today's employment anxieties are not about being out of work: they're about the job itself being more demanding, and the rewards more unequal'.

Immediately relevant are the implications of the sheer pace and extent of the change that these developments have encouraged. Crucially, as Marginson *et al.* (1994: 26) suggest, it has made it very difficult for operating managers to develop any consistency in approach to HRM, let alone create the long-term relationships that 'high performance working' entails. Inevitably, the time and energies of human resource specialists tend to be consumed in managing the operational implications of restructuring, helping to explain the significance of the extent of change cited in the previous section. Indeed, many large organizations are littered with half-finished initiatives that had to be interrupted because of M&A or divestment activity (Storey *et al.* 1997). In these circumstances, it is not surprising that operational managers seem to be 'muddling through' – they cannot do much else.

Arguably, too, the business environment in which UK managers have to work does not encourage business policies that emphasize quality products and services, helping to explain the lack of a clear link between the measures of HRM strategies and product market strategies mentioned earlier (see Edwards and Sengupta, this volume). Certainly, the UK has a concentration of businesses in sectors with low R&D. Moreover, within these sectors, many UK managers continue to compete on the basis of low-skill, low-wage labour (Delbridge *et al.* 2006).

Even in service industries involving a high level of customer contact, the commitment to quality is far from absolute. In many cases, as Batt's (2007) summary of the extensive literature reminds us, the HR function is caught between the competing claims of marketing strategies, which prioritize the quality of customer contact, and operational strategies, which are primarily concerned with efficiency and costs. In many cases it was operational strategies that won out. In practice, this took the form of the widespread adoption of segmentation strategies with a targeted customer approach. Put simply, more costly approaches based on relationship management are reserved for customers with high value accounts, particularly business clients. By contrast, more cost-driven approaches that emphasize technology and require greater input from customers are applied to low-value mass market activities. It was the latter that very often involved outsourcing and off-shoring in the form of burgeoning call centres.

The developments described here have also had implications for our understanding of the nature of management. It has long been recognized that management is not a homogeneous group, comprising a range of positions from that of supervisor through to chief executive. Yet the assumption was that a common thread was present, making it possible to think in terms of a professional body of expertise involving planning, controlling, coordinating, developing, motivating, leading, etc. For most managers directly involved in managing operations, this continues to be the case. Arguably, however, 'financialization' and 'divisionalization' mean that, unlike their forebears, very senior managers are increasingly detached from these processes, along with the communities in which they take place – in Khurana's (2007: 364) words, they are like 'hired hands', with their job boiling down to financial engineering and/or target setting, coupled with extreme risk taking (Froud *et al.* 2000a: 109).

The Resource-based View versus the Firm as a Nexus of Contracts

Arguably, the different pressures being experienced by workplace and company managers reflect two very contrasting views of the organization: the resource-based view and the doctrine of the firm as a nexus of contracts. These are rarely articulated in any detail, let alone juxtaposed as they are here, and yet are fundamental to our understanding of what has been happening, along with the prospects for the future. Table 4.2 sets out the two positions schematically, along with some of their key implications. To begin with the resource-based view (RBV), in the words of Martin-Alcazar (2008:112) and his colleagues, 'scholars relied heavily on this framework to justify the strategic importance of human resources and to identify which particular characteristics supported this role'. RBV is an 'inside-out theory' focusing on the sources of internal strengths and weakness of the corporation – in a phrase the organization is a 'capability structure' (Morgan *et al.* 2005: 5). This is in contrast to more traditional approaches, which are 'outside-in' assessments of market threats and opportunities and externally focused strategic responses or 'positioning'. In the case of the RBV, the single firm is the focus of attention, albeit in its industry context, with interest devoted to the achievement of sustained competitive advantage over the medium and long term. It thus seeks to eschew short-termism and look for the sources of competitive advantage that come from within the firm. In most

Table 4.2 Competing views of the work organization

	Resource-based view	*Nexus of contracts doctrine*
Role of the organization	providing goods and services	vehicle for contracting
Role of managers	direct and support	coordinate contacts
Responsibilities	multiple stakeholders	shareholders only
Main focus	product market	capital market
Main form of competition	internal growth/process and product development	external/merger and takeover
Performance measures	market share	share price
Scope for coordinated action	significant	limited
Horizons	medium/long term	short term
Relationship between management and employees	market and managerial	purely market
View of labour	resource to be developed	commodity whose cost is to be minimized
Methods of securing commitment	financial plus training and development/voice/ consultation	financial/use of market type devices such as stock options

cases this will be from the combination of people and processes within the firm with attractive implications for strategic human resource management. Here the emphasis is on core competencies in the sense that they deliver superior competitive results and are both rare and inimitable so that others cannot gain similar levels of talent and cannot copy the work processes. These resources are also appropriable in the sense of the firm and its shareholders gaining value from them. This in turn places an emphasis on organizational culture and learning over time in unique ways, what is called path dependency, all of which make it hard for others to copy (for a full elaboration of the RBV see Boxall and Purcell 2008: 85–110).[1]

Company managers may make statements suggesting they are motivated by the RBV, but their behaviour is much more consistent with the strongly contrasting doctrine of the firm as a nexus of contracts, which has been described as the 'dominant legal and economic perspective' in the UK and the USA (Parkinson 2003: 485). This doctrine, which has largely developed as the result of economists grappling with the need to accommodate the organization into neo-classical thinking, starts from the proposition that the firm is a legal fiction to which the term ownership cannot be meaningfully applied – it is a 'contracting site at which the parties to a business enterprise agree the terms on which they are prepared to supply the firm's inputs and which they are to be rewarded for doing so' (Parkinson 2003: 485). The employment contract is no different from other contracts – it is purely a market relationship and the parties owe no responsibilities to one another beyond those expected of participants acting in good faith. There is no 'unique relationship between an organisational leader and other constituents' and, supposedly, issues of 'power, coercion and exploitation' do not figure (Khurana 2007: 325). In the words of Alchian and Demsetz (1972), who were responsible for much of the initial thinking, the organization is merely 'the centralised contractual agent in a team productive process – not some superior authoritarian directive or disciplinary process'. Exclusive residual rights are vested in shareholders on efficiency grounds, managers are the shareholders 'agents', with responsibilities to them only, and the share price is the measure of performance. Overall, market competition is the basis of governance, with the emphasis on 'pay for performance schemes such as stock option grants, an active market for corporate control, and the fiscal discipline of leverage' (Khurana 2007: 325).

It might have been expected that the return in 1997 of the first of four Labour governments would have swung policy support behind the RBV. Certainly, ministers have espoused the 'high performance working' and the 'knowledge organization' associated with it. Yet they have showed little appreciation of the barriers to bringing them about, let alone an appetite to do anything to overcome them. Arguably, this is because the dominant neo-liberal approach to running the economy they have espoused is much more compatible with the NOC doctrine than the RBV, seeing a relatively limited role for government. The emphasis is on markets and ensuring that they work effectively, with attention primarily focused on the quantity rather than the quality of employment, which is regarded as a matter for the parties. Significantly, the government department with prime responsibility for the area, the Employment Relations Directorate, sits within the 'Fair Markets' group of the Department of Business, Enterprise and Regulatory Reform, one of its major tasks being to encourage 'confident participants' in the labour market and introduce any regulation in a business-friendly or 'light touch' way. The handling of change in the public services similarly suggests little understanding of, let alone support for, the RBV: the main vehicle for change, the setting and resetting of highly detailed quantitative targets from the centre, has led not just to cynicism and low staff morale, but also a widespread view that much of the recent increase in expenditure in public services has been wasted.

Future Prospects

Arguably, the credit and banking crisis that swept through the world in 2007–08, engulfing major financial businesses and drawing attention to the 'casino capitalism' in which many had been engaged, will have major implications for the management of employment relations. To begin with, it is likely to mean the end of the era of 'financialization', along with a shrinking in the size and influence of the financial sector more generally. Coupled with a shortage of credit to fuel M&A activity, there are likely to be major controls over short selling, the ability to leverage debt-related activities and a bonus culture that encourages excessive risk. Hedge fund groups, along with investment banks, have an uncertain future; private equity groups are expected to have to return to nurturing and investing in the companies they buy. Overall, it might be expected that there will be a refocusing on product and process as the main forms of competition and, in terms of horizons, greater emphasis on the long as opposed to the short term. It may be even be that there will be changes in the corporate governance framework emphasizing the fundamental role of business in providing goods and services to customers rather than just returns to shareholders.

The second outcome is a recognition that the 'efficient markets' approach that underpins the NOC doctrine has serious limitations. 'Markets' need institutions, i.e. 'rules of the game', to give them shape and structure and, above all, help ensure that individuals and businesses behave responsibly. 'Light touch' regulation, which is widely seen to have been a major factor in contributing to the crisis, is no longer the mantra it was.

In these circumstances, it is tempting to speculate that the RBV might begin to have a serious impact on employment relations practice and policy, with recognition that work organizations are a major source as well as consumer of social capital. Certainly, there is no shortage of proposals to this end – these embrace an increase in individual employment rights, greater support for employee 'voice', compulsory social reporting of HR policies and practice, the return of a leadership role for the public sector reflecting its procurement powers and uprating of the role and status of specialist HR managers (see, for example, Sisson 2006; Kochan 2007). Yet it is difficult to see how the necessary institutional framework is to be translated into practice, bearing in mind the considerable opposition likely from employers. The HRM function does not have the authority and its energies are likely to be absorbed in dealing with the redundancy and insecurity following the financial crisis. Trade unions are too weak to promote anything like the level of challenge necessary for change and, in any event, are likely to be primarily concerned to promote collective bargaining. Looking at government, there is no evidence that the lessons from the financial crisis are being read across to employment – with the recession biting, there is likely to be even more emphasis on the quantity rather than the quality, of employment; the government is reported to be already rowing back on its commitments to more flexible working as this chapter was being prepared. Conceivably, there could be EU initiatives that promote the RVB or 'capability approach'[2] as it is more commonly known in mainland Europe. But this raises the UK's vexed relationship with Europe, which could change substantially if there is a return of a Conservative government. It is highly likely, then, that the tensions in management's employment relations behaviour will be ongoing.

Notes

1   Complicating matters is that the RBV is a very seductive theory with a range of interpretations, some of which can be made compatible with 'nexus of contract' thinking. Although many HR scholars use it to emphasize the inclusive nature of the firm and critical role of its human resources, a closer reading of some treatments also suggests

that it is far from the case that all the firm's human resources are deemed to have core competencies. Leonard (1998) made a distinction between core capabilities, which are superior and cannot be easily imitated; supplemental, which add value to core capabilities but can easily be copied; and enabling, which are necessary conditions for being in the industry. It is only the core competencies which have to be obtained and nurtured. Others may be obtained elsewhere. The Shell tanker drivers found this out and indeed all petroleum producers have outsourced their drivers since their competencies are 'enabling' while those in IT, facilities, HR and other non-core functions can be outsourced since they are 'supplementary'. Using the logic of RBV many organizations have shrunk in size as they have outsourced and off-shored. High performance working, high commitment strategies and high involvement policies are, in effect, limited under the logic of RBV to those with core competencies who need to be valued and nurtured. This is far from the inclusive view of RBV often espoused in the HR literature, yet the focus on the single firm with single contracts with all its employees remains a powerful image of how the world ought to be.

It is also possible to conceive of the RBV in much broader terms than most of the management-oriented literature does. Work organizations, it can be argued, are a major source as well as consumers of human and social capital, with implications for anti-social behaviour, crime and participation in civil society as well as life chances and the quality of family life. The costs to society of work organizations foregoing any responsibility for the development of such capital are immense (for further details, see Coats 2004; Sisson forthcoming).

2 In contrast to the 'activation' route, which sees the objective as maximizing the macro rate of employment regardless of its quality, the 'capability' approach seeks to improve living and working conditions, along with social protection, both as an end and a means to an end: what matters is what a person can do and be, given the appropriate resources. Similarly, the source of a firm's competitiveness resides not in cost minimization, but in its capacity to innovate, learn from and cooperate with others. Consequently, rather than deregulating labour markets, structural policies should be designed to improve capabilities – of firms, sectors and territories as well as individual citizens. Overall, the approach is seen as central to economic growth and the role of Europe in globalization, offering the basis for endogenous development that prioritizes specialization in products and services reflecting the region's specific advantages (for further details, see Salais and Villeneuve 2005; Deakin 2005).

References

Alchian, A. and Demsetz, H. 1972: Production, information costs, and economic organization. *The American Economic Review*, Vol. 62, 777–795.

Audit Commission 2003: *Targets in the public sector. Public sector briefing*. Available at www.audit-commission.gov.uk.

Audit Commission/National Audit Office 2006: *Delivering efficiently: strengthening the links in public service delivery chains*. Available at www.nao.org.uk.

Batt, R. 2007: Service strategies: marketing, operations, and human resources policies. In Boxall, P., Purcell, J. and Wright, P. (eds) *The Oxford Handbook of Human Resource Management*. Oxford: Oxford University Press, pp. 428–459.

Boselie, P., Deitz, G. and Boon, C. 2005: Commonalities and contradictions. In Research in Human Resource Management and Performance, *Human Resource Management Journal*, 13 (3), 67–94.

Boxall, P. and Purcell, J. 2008: *Strategies and Human Resource Management*. 2nd edition. Basingstoke: Palgrave Macmillan.

Brown, W. and Walsh, J. 1994: Managing pay in Britain. In Sisson, K. (ed.) *Personnel Management*. 2nd edition. Oxford: Blackwell.

Caulkin, S. 2008: Why big brother makes an uneasy workmate. *The Observer*, 13 January.

Chandler, A. 1962: *Strategy and Structure: Chapters in the History of the Industrial Enterprise*. Cambridge, MA: MIT Press.

Clark, I. 2008: Private equity and the 'take private' private equity business model: the implications for industrial relations? Plenary paper for the 2008 annual BUIRA Conference, Bristol.

Coats, D. 2004: *Speaking Up! Voice, Industrial Democracy and Organisational Performance*. London: The Work Foundation.

Colling, T. 2003: Managing without unions: the sources and limits of individualism. In Edwards, P.K. (ed.) *Industrial Relations Theory and Practice*. 2nd edition. Oxford: Blackwell.

Collins, H. 2007: Legal responses to the standard form contract of employment. *Industrial Law Journal*, 36 (1), 2–18.

Cully, M., Woodland, S., O'Reilly, A and Dix, G. 1999: *Britain at Work: As Depicted by the Workplace Employee Relations Survey*. London: Routledge.

Deakin, S. 2005: The 'capability' concept and the evolution of European social policy, ESRC Centre for Business Research, Working Paper No. 303, University of Cambridge.

Defarue, A., Van Hootegem, G., Proctor, S. and Burridge, M. 2008: Teamworking and organizational performance: a review of survey-based research. *International Journal of Management Reviews*. 10 (2), 127–148.

Delbridge, R., Edwards, P., Forth, J., Miskell, P. and Payne, J. 2006: *The Organisation of Productivity: Re-thinking Skills and Work Organisation*. London: Advanced Institute of Management Research.

Doran, J. 2008: Advisers set for 1bn Yahoo bonanza. *The Observer*, 3 February.

Dunlop, J.T. 1958: *Industrial Relations Systems*. New York: Holt.

Edwards, P.K. 2003: The employment relationship and the field of industrial relations. In Edwards, P.K. (ed.) *Industrial Relations: Theory and Practice*. 2nd edition. Oxford: Blackwell.

Edwards, P.K., Hall, M., Hyman, R., Marginson, P., Sisson, K., Waddington, J. and Winchester, D. 1992: Great Britain: still muddling through. In Ferner, A. and Hyman, R. (eds) *Industrial Relations in the New Europe*. Oxford: Blackwell.

Erturk, I., Froud, J., Johal, S., Leaver, A. and Williams, K. 2006: Agency, the romance of management pay and an alternative explanation, CRESC Working Paper Series Working Paper No. 23. CRESC, University of Manchester.

European Commission 1997: *Partnership for a New Organisation of Work*. Brussels: European Commission.

European Foundation 1997: *New forms of work organisation. Can Europe realise its potential? Results of a survey of direct employee participation in Europe*. Luxembourg: Office for the Official Publications of the European Communities.

Folkman, P., Froud, J., Johal, S. and Williams, K. 2006: Working for themselves? Capital market intermediaries and present day capitalism. *CRESC Working Paper* No. 25. CRESC, University of Manchester.

Froud, J., Haslam, C., Johal, S. and Williams, K. 2000a: Shareholder value and financialisation: consultancy promise, management moves. *Economy and Society*, 29 (1), 80–111.

Froud, J., Haslam, C., Johal, S. and Williams, K. 2000b: Restructuring for shareholder value and its implications for labour. *Cambridge Journal of Economics*, 24, 771–797.

Froud, J. and Williams, K. 2007: Private equity and the culture of value extraction. *CRESC Working Paper No. 31*. CRESC, University of Manchester.

Gallie, D., Felstead, A. and Green, F. 2004: Changing Patterns of Task Discretion in Britain. *Work, Employment and Society*, 18 (2), 243–266.

Gospel, H. and Pendleton, A. 2003: Finance, corporate governance and the management of labour: a conceptual and comparative analysis. *British Journal of Industrial Relations*, 42 (3), 211–228.

Green, R. 2001: It's been a hard day's night: the concentration and intensification of work in late twentieth century Britain. *British Journal of Industrial Relations*, 39 (1), 53–80.

Hall, P. and Soskice, D. 2001: An introduction to varieties of capitalism. In Hall, P. and Soskice, D. (eds) *Varieties of Capitalism: The Institutional Foundations of Comparative Advantage*. Oxford: Oxford University Press.

Hamel, G. 2007: *The Future of Management*. Boston, Mass: Harvard University Business Press.

Herriot, P., Hirsch, W. and Reily, P. 1998: *Trust and Transitions: Managing the Employment Relationship*. Chichester: John Wiley & Sons.

Herzberg, F. 1966: *Work and the Nature of Man*. Cleveland, Ohio: World Publishing.

House of Commons Public Administration Select Committee. 2003: *On target? Government by measurement*. Available at www.publications.parliament.uk.

ILO (Ashton, D. and Sung, J.) 2002: *Supporting Workplace Learning for High Performance Working*. Geneva: International Labour Organization.

Jacoby, S. 2003: Industrial relations to human resources and beyond. In Kaufmann, B.E., Beaumont, R.A. and Helfgott, R.B. (eds) *The Evolving Process of Employee Relations Management*. Armonk, New York: M.E. Sharpe.

Jacoby, S. 2004: *Employing Bureaucracy: Managers, Unions, and the Transformation of Work in the 20th Century*. Mahwah, NJ: Lawrence Erlbaum.

Jacoby, S. 2005: *The Embedded Corporation: Corporate Governance and Employment Relations in Japan and the United States*. Princeton, NJ: Princeton University Press.

Kersley, B., Alpin, C., Forth, J., Bryson, A., Bewley, H., Dix, G. and Oxenbridge, S. 2006: *Inside the Workplace: Findings from the 2004 Workplace Employment Relations Survey*. London: Routledge.

Khurana, R. 2007: *From Higher Aims to Hired Hands. The Social Transformation of American Business Schools and the Unfulfilled Promise of Management as a Profession*. Princeton: Princeton University Press.

Kochan, T.A. 2007: Social legitimacy of the HRM profession. In Boxall, P., Purcell, J. and Wright, P. (eds) *The Oxford Handbook of Human Resource Management*. Oxford: Oxford University Press.

Kochan, T.A., Katz, H.C. and McKersie, R.B. 1986: *The Transformation of American Industrial Relations*. New York: Basic Books.

Lazonick, W. and O'Sullivan, M. 2000: Maximising shareholder value: a new ideology for corporate governance. *Economy and Society*, 29 (1), 13–35.

Leonard, D. 1998: *Wellsprings of Knowledge: Building and Sustaining the Sources of Innovation*. Boston, MA. Harvard Business School Press.

Marchington, M., Grimshaw, D., Rubery, J. and Wilmott, H. 2005: *Fragmenting Work: Blurring Organisational Boundaries and Disordering Hierarchies*. Oxford: Oxford University Press.

Marginson, P., Armstrong, P., Edwards, P. and Purcell, J. with Hubbard, N. 1993: The control of industrial relations in large companies: an initial analysis of the second company level industrial relations survey. *Warwick Papers in Industrial Relations* No. 45. Coventry: University of Warwick.

Marginson, P., Olsen, L. and Tailby, S. 1994: The eclecticism of managerial policy towards labour regulation: three case studies. *Warwick Papers in Industrial Relations* No. 47. Coventry: Industrial Relations Research Unit: University of Warwick.

Martin-Alcazar, F., Romero-Fernandez, P. and Sanchez-Gardey, G. 2008: Human resource management as a field of research. *British Journal of Management*, 19 (2), 103–119.

Maslow, A.H. 1943: A theory of motivation. *Psychological Development*, 50, 370–396.

McGovern, P., Hill, S., Mills, C. and White, M. 2007: *Market, Class, and Employment*. Oxford: Oxford University Press.

McGregor, D.C. 1960: *The Human Side of the Enterprise*. New York: McGraw-Hill.

Morgan, G., Whitley, R. and Moen, E. 2005: *Changing Capitalisms? Internationalisation, Institutional Change and Systems of Economic Organisation*. Oxford: Oxford University Press.

Office for National Statistics (ONS) 2007: Mergers and Acquisitions involving UK Companies: 4th Quarter 2006. First Release. London, ONS.

Organisation for Economic Cooperation and Development and Government of Canada. 1997: Changing workplace strategies: achieving better outcomes for enterprises, workers, and society. Report of the International Conference organised by the Government of Canada and the Organisation for Economic Cooperation and Development, Ottawa, Canada, 2–3 December, 1996. Quebec: Government of Canada.

Overell, S. 1998: Delayering to drive steel profits drive. *People Management*, 25 June, 12.

Parkinson, J. 2003: Models of the company and the employment relationship. *British Journal of Industrial Relations*, 41 (3), 481–510.

Purcell, J. and Kessler, I. 2003: Individualism and collectivism in industrial relations. In Edwards, P.K. (ed.) *Industrial Relations Theory and Practice*. 2nd edition. Oxford: Blackwell.

Purcell, J. and Kinnie, N. 2007: HRM and business performance. In Boxall, P., Purcell, J. and Wright, P. (eds) *The Oxford Handbook of Human Resource Management*. Oxford: Oxford University Press, pp. 533–551.

Salais, R. and Villeneuve, R. 2005: Introduction: Europe and the politics of capabilities. In Salais, R. and Villeneuve, R. (eds) *Europe and the Politics of Capabilities*. Cambridge: Cambridge University Press.

Sisson, K. 1987: The *Management of Collective Bargaining: An International Comparison*. Oxford: Blackwell.

Sisson, K. 1989: Personnel management in perspective. In Sisson, K. (ed.) *Personnel Management in Britain*. Oxford: Blackwell, pp. 3–21.

Sisson, K. 1994: Personnel management in Britain: paradigms, practice and practice. In Sisson, K. (ed.) *Personnel Management: A Comprehensive Guide to Theory and Practice in Britain*. Oxford: Blackwell, pp. 3–50.

Sisson, K. 2006: Responding to Mike Emmott: What 'industrial relations' suggests should be at the heart of 'employee relations'. Available at buira.org.uk/index.php?option=com_docman&task=doc_view&gid=26

Sisson, K. forthcoming: Why employment relations matter. *Warwick Papers in Industrial Relations*, Coventry: Industrial Relations Research Unit, University of Warwick.

Sisson, K. and Marginson, P. 1994: Management: systems, structures and strategy. In Edwards, P.K. (ed.) *Industrial Relations: Theory and Practice*. Oxford: Blackwell.

Sisson, K. and Marginson, P. 2003: Management: systems, structures and strategy. In Edwards, P.K. (ed.) *Industrial Relations: Theory and Practice*. 2nd edition. Oxford: Blackwell.

Storey, J., Edwards, P.K. and Sisson, K. 1997: *Managers in the Making: Management and Management Development in Britain and Japan*. London: Sage.

Ulrich, D. 1998: A new mandate for human resources. *Harvard Business School Review*, 63 (2), 124–134.

Wall, T. and Wood, S. 2005: The romance of HRM and business performance, and the case for big science. *Human Relations*, 58 (4), 429–462.

Whittington, R. and Mayer, M. 2000: *The European Corporation: Strategy, Structure and Social Science*. Oxford: Oxford University Press.

Wright, P. and Boswell, W. 2002: Desegregating HRM: a review and synthesis of micro and macro human resource management research. *Journal of Management*, 28 (3), 247–276.

5

STATE, CAPITAL AND LABOUR RELATIONS IN CRISIS

JASON HEYES AND PETER NOLAN

Introduction

The state's role in industrial relations has been drawn in narrow terms, typically limited to specific, policy-focused issues. Established textbooks thus include chapters on the extent, character and effects of legislation on individual and collective employment rights; the role of governments in slicing national income between wages and profits; and the state as the major employer and exemplar of good practice. These are vital issues that extend the understanding of the state's role in contemporary capitalist societies, but do not include an explicit discussion of the nature, origins and economic significance of the state itself. The case for such a treatment has never been more compelling.

There is a broader political economy of the state in the social sciences that transcends previous discipline-based narratives. Theory is in flux. Recognition that research on work, employment and industrial relations should directly address the role of the state as actor, architect and respondent to material and social developments is now reflected in new debates on the 'varieties' of capitalism, social capital, modes of governance and the impacts of globalization and new information and communication technologies on the circuits of capital.

The minimalist state theories that dictated policy and practice for three decades – no more evidently than in the US and the UK – are now facing a period of unprecedented scrutiny. Some contemporary accounts suggest their time has passed. Although this assessment is almost certainly premature, the contemporary crisis of unleashed capitalism has dealt a severe blow to the conventional wisdom in recent policy debates. Current economic and political upheavals call for a new research agenda, and an urgent reassessment of the state's past and present role in the restructuring of the employment relationship, if a better understanding of future problems, possibilities and contradictions is to be achieved.

This chapter, contrary to recent narratives stressing the limited role of the state in Britain and elsewhere, argues that states in the advanced economies are poised to consolidate and extend their position as guarantor of the employment relationship.

The concept of the minimalist state was at best a partial truth masking the extensive involvement of state agencies in the organization of class relations. The first section accordingly examines competing theories of the state, the second looks at the recent history of state intervention in the UK, and the third examines the shifting tensions between nation state and the forces of globalization. The fourth section considers the potential contribution of the concept of varieties of capitalism in aiding understanding of the current government's economic and social policy record. The analysis shifts in section five to look in more detail at the UK's system of labour administration and the respective roles that the state, employer organizations and trade unions play in processes of policy formation and policy implementation. This section provides an overview of public administration reforms introduced by Conservative and New Labour governments over the past three decades and considers the extent to which they have diminished the state's role in the development and implementation of public policies relating to industrial relations.

The State in Theory and Practice

The 'state' is amongst the most elusive concepts in the social sciences. Why does the state command a dominant role in civil society, and which institutions, class formations and elites construct, fashion and refashion the formulation and execution of state policies? What do states do, for whom and why? With whose support and against which forces of opposition does the state exercise authority in society? These questions have taken on new layers of complexity in an age of globalization and the weakening of boundaries between nation states. How have the movements of capital and labour and the wider diffusion of advanced technology influenced and constrained traditional public policy objectives and modes of delivery at regional, national and local levels? How have social scientists addressed these challenging questions?

An important departure point is economics. Economists strip the origins and the role of the state in contemporary capitalist societies to their irreducible minimum. The standard neo-classical theory accordingly gives priority (and approval) to the free working of unregulated market relations, and highlights two *prima facie* cases in which state intervention may be appropriate: that is where markets are rendered 'imperfect' by natural monopoly and the presence of externalities.

Natural monopoly – however innocuous its reference may suggest – has important implications for the organization of work and employment in contemporary economies, yet its treatment in intermediate textbooks is minimized. Natural monopoly refers to the prevalence of increasing returns (diminishing costs) to output increases in industries and large companies where technological conditions advantage one or a few, rather than multiple, producers. If market forces dictated the provision of such services (gas, electricity, rail, water and telecommunications, for example), private suppliers would most likely exploit their position at the expense of consumers. Technologically induced market failures thus provide the context for state intervention to prevent monopoly suppliers from departing from socially efficient pricing and output decisions.

The concept of natural monopoly was embraced by successive governments after 1945 and helped to change state policy in significant ways. The nationalization of large sections of British industry, and the commitment to public service by the post-war Labour and Conservative governments, were key instruments of industrial and labour market regulation that gave substance to the concept of the 'mixed' economy. They also provided spurs to national collective bargaining, the growth of trade unions in key sectors (coal, steel, railways, port transport and the utilities), and the socialization of health and education provision. The effects on workers lives in the largest industries and services of the British economy are incalculable.

Externalities surface as a significant issue if goods and services are 'non-rival' or cannot be provided on a 'non-excludable' basis. Cutting through the jargon, this means that the consumption of a good by one person does not reduce its availability to another. The cost of provision and payment for street lighting is a classic example. If, as is clearly the case, street lighting cannot be rendered on a personal (excludable) basis, 'free rider' problems and market failure make the case for state intervention. Security is another example. Why pay towards the provision of security when one can 'benefit' from protection without personal cost? In the employment sphere, why join a trade union when the gains in terms and conditions secured by a union (better health, safety, sickness and holiday provision) may benefit all workers without direct cost? Historically, and partially, the choice to abstain from union membership and free-ride on union services was curtailed by the institution of the 'closed shop', now prevented by law.

Is economic analysis able to explain the state's existence and deep involvement in managing, constructing and regulating markets in key industries, firms, and public services such as local government, health, and education? Can it account for the sudden and decisive shift in the character of state policy in the 1980s – nowhere more dramatic than in the UK – when large sections of the public sector were privatized and subject to a new regime of light touch regulation? Do the concepts of natural monopoly and externalities explain the recent and dramatic attempts by governments – most remarkably in the US – to inhibit a global economic crisis by nationalizing the banks, building societies, investment and insurance companies?

Economic analysis is theoretically and conceptually ill-equipped to illuminate the fundamental issues of the nature, form and functions of the state in modern capitalism. To be sure new sub-branches of theory were elaborated to interpret and provide optimal conditions and rules of regulation to catch up with the new political steer in public policy after 1980. But the basic issues concerning the political and class character of state intervention were, as before, side-stepped, treated as if they lay outside the purview of economic reasoning. Beyond economics, state theory is at once more developed and contentious, but also in crucial respects more inconclusive.

Pluralism once gave a lead but the departure point of pluralist analysis – the belief that power is dispersed and that the state is a benign force – seemed to lose purchase in the last quarter of the 20th century. State offensives against organized labour, the unemployed and the poor increasingly provided the primary spur to the restructuring of workplaces, labour markets and the organization and management of capital. These were the years of the rise of 'neo-liberalism' as ideology and practice. Established notions of state support (tolerance at minimum) for collective bargaining, union engagement with public policy and progressive social policy were eroded, derailed and disappeared. The state no longer acted as if, or pretended that, it was a neutral force.

Neo-liberalism is the leitmotif invoked by many scholars to capture the shift in the character and content of government policy in Western economies in the last quarter of the 20th century. The term is deployed to signify either the wholesale abandonment of, or more usually partial withdrawal by governments from, the policies that underpinned the Keynesian Welfare State. The term is not without problems (for a discussion, see Harvey 2005). The withdrawal of states from the provision of established social welfare, care and benefit systems coincided with a significant extension of state dirigisme in the leading capitalist economies (see Crouch, this volume). Withdrawal from intervention was the last thing that guided the actions of the Thatcher governments of the 1980s, as they set about the task of dismantling coal mining, steel, port transport and car production in the heartlands of British heavy industry. The restructuring of the British economy required more not less state intervention, more laws to regulate and limit the rights of labour, more intervention to promote the access of private capital to areas of economic activity previously governed by notions of public service (broadcasting is a good example), and more use of state agencies, such as the police, to maintain public order in a period of heightened industrial, social and economic upheaval.

The state as a proactive force for the restructuring of capital–labour relations is well established in the Marxist literature. Does the state act in the 'interests' of capital, certain sections of capital (elites), or does it intervene to guarantee the reproduction of the structure of wage–labour relations in general, which may involve intervening on behalf of labour to protect the long-term stability of the status quo ex ante? Marxist analysis has struggled with these competing positions for decades without resolution, yet there has been much illumination in the process. Few contemporary scholars, for example, would feel at ease with the notion that the state mobilizes to secure the interests of capital, whatever those interests might be. Nor would the more insightful accounts advocate the idea that elites dominate state apparatuses to the extent of dictating the objectives and forms of state intervention. Attention must instead be given to the dialectical interplay of structure and agency if the nuances and complexities of state theatre are to be grasped.

Globalization, Politics and the Nation State

Have national governments' economic and social policies been transformed to accommodate shifts in the character of capitalist economies? Have governments responded in similar ways and has there has been a convergence in the policies pursued? 'Globalization' – at best an ill-defined concept – is frequently regarded as the most fundamental cause of change. Some commentators depict an essentially 'borderless' world economy in which goods, capital, labour power and information are able to be harnessed from different regions of the world with few restrictions. Ohmae (1990, 1995), for example, has argued that the unleashing of global market forces has resulted in new, 'naturally' occurring 'regional states' composed of economic activities that may be organized across national frontiers or at sub-national level rendering irrelevant the nation as a unit of economic analysis. Others are more sceptical. Hay (2006) argues that recent European experience has been one of 'de-globalization', with European integration leading to an increase in the relative importance of intra-European trade and foreign direct investment (FDI).

The globalization debate has served to focus attention on labour standards and social protection in both the developed and developing economies. In the case of developing economies, views have differed on the extent to which the liberalization of barriers to trade and investment should be accompanied by a strengthening of labour standards. While advocates of market forces have argued that increased trade will inevitably result in economic growth and an improvement in working conditions, others have pointed to evidence of growing inequality in countries, such as China and Chile, that have reduced trade barriers and have emphasized the need for political action to be taken to defend labour standards for example social clauses in trade agreements (Elliott and Freeman 2003).

The key question in respect of the developed economies is whether established forms of social and employment protection are sustainable in the face of new economic challenges. Greater economic openness and capital mobility are said to be encouraging governments to weaken welfare and employment protection in an effort to attract and retain capital (Yeates 2001). Cerny (1995: 620) claims that the welfare states of the developed economies are transforming into 'competition states' in which the focus of public policy becomes 'the proactive promotion of economic activities, whether at home or abroad, that will make firms and sectors located within the territory of the state competitive in international markets'. Governments have thus become increasingly concerned with factors such as skills, research and development, infrastructure and the 'maintenance of a public policy environment favourable to investment (and profit making)'. The last of these implies a weakening of protections in the areas of employment, labour rights and social welfare. Furthermore, Cerny alleges that the pressures exerted by global economic forces have greatly reduced the scope for variation in the nature of interventions by national governments. The implication is that governments in developed economies are likely to seek to weaken employment and labour market protections while simultaneously attempting to boost the supply of skills as part of a broader strategy designed to reposition and strengthen capital.

A general and substantial erosion of the welfare state would have significant implications for industrial relations to the extent that social insurance ensures that the reproduction of labour power can occur irrespective of whether or not workers receive a wage (Burawoy 1985). A reduction in the value or availability of welfare benefits would imply an increase in the potency of the threat of dismissal, an intensification of labour's subordination to capital and a probable increase in workers' willingness to make concessions to employers. Evidence for the undermining of the welfare state is, however, mixed (Navarro *et al.* 2004). Hay's (2006) analysis suggests that while state benefits have diminished in a number of countries, they have increased in others (markedly so in the case of the Nordic countries). Conversely, evidence of increased spending may in part reflect demographic changes (for example, ageing populations) and it is also the case that many governments have sought to refashion the relationship between paid work and welfare by restricting entitlements to benefits and making those entitlements conditional on participation in the labour market.

Whether one regards globalization as a reality, an emerging reality or a myth, it is clear that the post-1997 Labour government has frequently invoked global-ization in attempting to justify its minimalist approach to employment rights and enthusiasm for market forces (Watson and Hay 2003). In Hay's (2006) view the government has overstated the extent of globalization. The prominence of refer-ences to globalization in New Labour's policy discourse is a reflection of a mis-taken acceptance of the reality of economic globalization and a consequent belief in the necessity of pursuing 'neo-liberal' policies. The influence of globalization on policy is therefore not rooted in economic developments, but rather in ideas about those developments. Yet as Coates (2001) argues, Hay does not explain why New Labour has been led to a (supposedly) mistaken belief that globalization has greatly reduced the scope for political choices. Hay's analysis, according to Coates, underestimates the extent to which the internationalization of manufacturing and finance and the UK's entrenched position as a low-wage, low-investment economy have acted as structural constraints and reduced the space for 'politi-cal projects committed to improving the industrial and social rights of workers' (Coates 2001: 304).

New Labour and Varieties of Capitalism

The extent to which New Labour's economic and social policies have differed from those pursued by the Conservative governments of the 1980s and early 1990s has been a much debated subject (for example, Freeden 1999; Hay 1999; Hopkin and Wincott 2006). There has certainly been considerable continuity. For example, New Labour accepted much of the macroeconomic analysis that had informed the policies of the preceding government, particularly the belief that demand man-agement could not deliver high and stable levels of employment, and thus followed the Conservatives in abandoning Keynesianism, prioritizing the maintenance of low inflation and focusing on reforming the supply-side of the economy (Kitson and Wilkinson 2007). However, Labour's prescriptions for boosting productivity placed less emphasis on the removal of labour market 'rigidities' than had been the case under Thatcher. Inspired by post-neo-classical endogenous growth theories (Romer 1990, Sachs and Larrain 1993), Labour's proposals for achieving economic growth stressed the importance of skill formation, knowledge, innovation and entrepreneurialism.

A comparatively high rate of job creation in the USA during the early 1990s also convinced the Labour Party leadership of the benefits of weakly regulated labour markets and the contribution that workfare could make in tackling unemployment (Deacon 1999). Soon after taking office, Labour introduced its own version of workfare in the form of 'New Deal' measures designed to encourage the unemployed and other welfare recipients to find work. These measures combined tighter restrictions on benefit entitlements with incentives in the form of tax credits and a national minimum wage (see Grimshaw and Rubery, this volume). The latter policy, which had been an election manifesto commitment, fell far short of trade union expectations when it was implemented and was an early example of the government's concern to ensure that new individual and collective employment rights should not damage competitiveness and job creation. In practice, this has meant that the government has frequently been willing to dilute proposals in response to pressure from employers (Coates 2005: 85). The minimalist nature of the resulting regulations has been well documented (Colling, this volume; Pollert 2007; Smith and Morton 2006).

The continuity between Conservative and New Labour government policies is largely consistent with the predictions of the 'varieties of capitalism' (VoC) analysis associated with Hall and Soskice (2001). In brief, Hall and Soskice seek to distinguish differences in the way firms attempt to resolve 'coordination problems' in the spheres of industrial relations, vocational training, corporate governance, inter-firm relations, and the day-to-day management of the employment relationship. They distinguish between 'liberal market economies'(such as the UK), in which coordination is achieved through formal contracting and market-mediated exchanges, and 'coordinated market economies' in which economic activity is coordinated through institutions and networks that facilitate access to information, skills and other resources. According to Hall and Soskice (2001: 57), the increased mobility of capital facilitated by international liberalization has enhanced the ability of firms in 'liberal market economies' to pressure governments to deregulate markets and weaken trade unions (see the discussion by Brown, this volume, on the factors promoting the decline of collective bargaining). Weaker regulation is assumed to be of benefit 'since firms that coordinate their endeavours primarily through the market can improve their competencies by sharpening its edges' (ibid.).

Hall and Soskice's analysis has proved highly influential, yet their approach suffers from a number of weaknesses. It is increasingly recognized that many European governments have adopted 'hybrid' economic and social policies that correspond to neither of the two capitalist varieties described by Hall and Soskice (Ferrera and Hemerijck 2003; see also Hyman, this volume). For example, Hall and Soskice associate Ireland with the 'liberal market economy' variety of capitalism, yet since the late 1980s Ireland has developed new institutions to coordinate economic and social policy and has involved employers, trade unions and other civil society organizations in national social dialogue and the negotiation of national-level partnership agreements. These developments do not fit comfortably with the path-dependent development trajectories predicted by the varieties of capitalism approach.

The analytical framework provided by Hall and Soskice is ill-equipped to explain significant departures from established policies and practices. Echoing neo-classical economists, Hall and Soskice's explanation for change in 'national systems' emphasizes the importance of 'external shocks' in technology and tastes, which 'unsettle the equilibria on which economic actors have been coordinating and challenge the existing practices of firms' (op. cit.: 62). In the absence of such external shocks actors will behave in ways that reflect and serve to reproduce institutional structures. Governments will respond positively to pressures exerted by firms anxious to maintain established sources of comparative advantage.

Applying Hall and Soskice's analytical approach to the UK, the Conservative government's antipathy to trade unions and employment protections, and New Labour's concern with maintaining labour market flexibility, could be explained in terms of successful efforts by firms to preserve comparative advantages associated with market-based forms of coordination. While the business lobby has undoubtedly exerted substantial influence over government policy since 1997 and won many concessions, an adequate account of New Labour's record in government would need to recognize the role that structural constraints, ideas about the nature of those constraints and the strategies of political actors have played in shaping the policy agenda. Long-standing weaknesses in the British economy, financial market liberalization and increased capital mobility have shaped the parameters of policy interventions and encouraged the retention of a number of core Conservative policies, particularly in the area of macroeconomic policy (Coates 2001). The reforms of the Labour Party's decision-making structures that had been initiated in the 1980s, coupled with the weakened condition of the trade union movement, strengthened the hand of the 'modernizing' Labour leadership, increasing its ability to abandon long-standing policy commitments and impose a new agenda on the Party.

This agenda represented a continuation of many of the policies inaugurated by Thatcher after 1979, although the analytical perspective offered by New Labour differed from that of the Conservatives in certain respects. For example, in contrast to the Conservative Party's assertion that the state should avoid intervening in the 'private sphere', New Labour emphasized the need for the state to play an 'enabling role' in relation to the economy and society (Smith 2004), a view that was consistent with its adoption of policy goals influenced by endogenous growth theory. As noted, the Conservative Party's official ideology of withdrawal was not mirrored in its actions during the Thatcher years, but this should not serve to distract attention from differences between Thatcherism and New Labour. Some of New Labour's goals, including its commitments to increased public expenditure, poverty alleviation and the achievement of full employment, had a social democratic hue. The government's resistance to calls for stronger employment rights was, to an extent, a result of its concern that an increased 'regulatory burden' on business would have damaging consequences for its employment and welfare policy, which relied on the use of incentives (e.g. New Deal subsidies) to encourage private sector cooperation with government objectives.

Such attempts to achieve mildly social democratic objectives by working with the grain of the market distinguished New Labour from Thatcherism. Yet not only was New Labour's faith in the market's ability to deliver greater social justice misplaced, but elements of its project, including its concern to maintain labour market flexibility, its lack of support for collective bargaining and its unwillingness to address increasing income inequality, militated against the achievement of this goal. The consequences of the tensions and contradictions embedded in the government's strategy, and the role that credit has played in allowing consumption to expand despite rising inequality and continued poverty, have recently become glaringly apparent.

The State, Governance and Labour Relations

The continued influence of highly restrictive state economic policy can also be observed in the area of public administration (see Bach, this volume). Over the past 30 years, Conservative and New Labour governments have attempted to remodel public administration along private sector lines and to that end have adopted measures associated with the 'New Public Management' (NPM). The central principle of NPM is that systems of public administration can be strengthened through the adoption of micro-management practices associated with the private sector. The NPM agenda includes a greater emphasis on measuring the performance of government departments and non-departmental public bodies (NDPBs) through setting targets and evaluating outcomes, improved accountability and coordinated policy development and service delivery. The prescriptions associated with the NPM have been propagated by international organizations, including the OECD, World Bank and IMF, which have presented the 'NPM as *the* globally applicable formula for building modern government and administration' (Wollmann 2001: 152).

NPM reforms have affected the processes through which policies are developed and the mechanisms by which they are implemented (for an overview, see Evans 2009). The reform process began in the early 1980s with the introduction of performance measurement, market testing and the delegation of service-delivery responsibilities to executive agencies, which were headed by chief executives and supposed to operate as businesses (Jordan and O'Toole 1995). New Labour came to power in 1997 equally convinced of the merits of private sector management practices and their applicability in a public service context. In an effort to ensure that that policy formation and service delivery are target driven, the government has required that departmental budgets be linked to measurable objectives enshrined in public service agreements (PSA).

The government has also encouraged civil servants to engage in 'evidence-based' policy making (Sanderson 2002). The expectation is that new initiatives should be grounded in reliable, clear and comprehensive research evidence, that ministries should calculate the anticipated impact of proposed policies and use this information when selecting from a range of possible alternatives, and that policies and programmes should be subjected to rigorous processes of evaluation. Government departments are thus required to conduct regulatory impact analyses, through which the potential consequences of policy reforms for the competitiveness of the national economy and specific sectors are identified and assessed. As a result of British influence, a similar evaluation model was recently adopted by the European Commission (Pollert 2007: 116).

In practice, there have been tensions between the model of strategic, evidence-based policy making envisaged by the government and 'the powerful political forces of inertia, expediency, ideology and finance' (Walker 2000). The government has downplayed, suppressed or ignored evidence when it has been politically expedient to do so. An example is provided by the national minimum wage regulations. Since its first report (Low Pay Commission 1998), the Low Pay Commission (LPC) has consistently recommended that workers aged 21 be entitled to the full adult minimum wage rate. In making this recommendation, the LPC has been able to point to evidence that most employers pay full adult wages to 21-year-old employees. Nevertheless, the government has doggedly refused to extend the coverage of the full adult minimum wage to include 21-year-old workers.

Despite the government's penchant for setting targets and its rhetoric concerning the importance of manager–worker cooperation in bringing about the 'modernization' of the workplace, it has tended to be reluctant to set anything other than very broad objectives for policies relating to industrial relations. Two reasons can be given for this absence. First, relationships between industrial relations phenomena and performance outcomes are complex and, moreover, disputed (see Edwards and Sengupta, this volume). Second, precise targets relating to industrial relations have the potential to be highly controversial, given differences in the interests of employers and trade unions. However, in Ireland the setting of performance indicators for industrial relations has been more extensive and strategic objectives that explicitly link competitiveness to industrial relations measures have sometimes been established (DETE 2003: 67). It is possible that the maintenance of national social dialogue in Ireland has provided the 'political space' to set objectives that link industrial relations to economic performance. The continued lack of social dialogue in the UK may in part explain the absence of similar objectives from the strategic targets set by the British government.

From government to multi-level governance?

NPM has been identified as one facet of a wider shift that is alleged to have taken place from a hierarchical and bureaucratic model of government to a new model of policy formation and service delivery, encapsulated by the term 'governance'. While governance can be defined in a number of different ways (Treib *et al.* 2007), over the past two decades many researchers have employed the term when referring to a reduced role for the state in the determination of public policy and delivery of public services, an increase in the involvement of non-state actors and the development of methods of policy implementation that rely on networks as opposed to hierarchies.

A particularly influential account of the alleged shift from government to governance is that of Rhodes (1996), who argues that the privatization of public services, more extensive involvement of non-departmental public bodies (NDPBs) and executive agencies in the delivery of public services, the transfer of decision-making powers to the European Union institutions, and the rise of the new public management have resulted in a fragmentation of the core executive and a 'hollowing out' of the state. At the same time, a more extensive involvement of non-governmental organizations, including firms, voluntary groups and agencies, in policy implementation and service delivery has resulted in the formation of 'self-governing interorganizational networks' that are resistant to direction by central government. The state, according to this argument, is no longer sovereign, central government has become but one of a number of levels of government and the boundary between the state and civil society has been substantially eroded.

A number of Rhodes' assumptions, in particular the claim that a process of state 'hollowing out' has occurred, have been echoed by researchers attempting to understand the relationship between national governments and supranational agencies, particularly the institutions of the European Union. The concept of *multi-level* governance, which Peters and Pierre (2001) define as 'negotiated, non-hierarchical exchanges between institutions at the transnational, national, regional and local levels', has become extremely influential in the field of European Union research. Its emergence reflects the dissatisfaction of some researchers with state-centric analyses that focus on the relationship between European-level institutions and EU member states and that treat the two levels as alternative sources of authority (Jordan 2001). Proponents of multi-level governance, by contrast, argue that authority has ebbed away from national governments to actors at both sub-national and supranational (e.g. EU) levels, resulting in the creation of multiple centres of power and a consequent need to study linkages between the various levels at which power is exercised (Hyman, this volume; Marks 1996; Hooghe and Marks 2001).

Is the state being 'hollowed out'?

The concepts of governance and multi-level governance are increasingly being employed by researchers seeking to map and understand sub-national, national and supranational regulatory influences on industrial relations within the EU (see, for example, Marginson and Sisson 2004; Regalia 2007). However, industrial relations research has yet to provide a critical engagement with a number of the core assumptions associated with the governance literature, including the claim that markets and networks have replaced hierarchies as the principal methods of governance, that a substantial transfer of power from central governments to supra- and sub-national levels has occurred, that power has become more diffuse and that the state has been 'hollowed out' to such an extent that it is no longer the dominant actor in the development and delivery of public policy.

To what extent do changes in the institutional forms and practices associated with labour administration in the UK substantiate the view that the state has been 'hollowed out' and that the core executive has become more fragmented? When the formal roles of government departments are considered, it certainly appears that responsibility for policy areas relating to industrial relations has become more widely dispersed, particularly since the mid-1990s. In 1995, the Department of Employment (originally the Ministry of Labour), which had been responsible for matters relating to employment, health and safety and industrial relations, was merged with the Department for Education to create a new Department for

Education and Employment (DfEE). Responsibility for industrial relations was transferred to the Department of Trade and Industry (DTI) (now the Department for Business, Innovation and Skills (BIS)) while responsibility for health and safety was assumed by the Department of the Environment (subsequently retitled the Department of the Environment, Transport and the Regions (DETR)). Further major changes occurred following the 2001 general election when responsibility for employment policy was shifted to a new department – the Department for Work and Pensions (DWP) – which also took on responsibility for social security and (in 2008) health and safety. The education and training responsibilities of the DfEE were reallocated across two new departments, the Department for Innovation, Universities and Skills (DIUS) and the Department for Children, Schools and Families. In 2009, responsibility for the policy areas covered by DIUS was transferred to a new Department for Business, Innovation and Skills.

Fragmentation is also evident in relation to the labour inspection activities performed by the state. In contrast to many other countries within and outside Europe, the UK lacks a unified labour inspectorate (see Colling, this volume). Responsibilities for labour inspection are divided between the Gangmasters' Licensing Authority, which issues licences to labour suppliers in the agriculture, horticulture, shellfish gathering and food processing sectors and reports to the Department of the Environment, Food and Rural Affairs, the Employment Agencies Standards Inspectorate, which is part of the Employment Relations Directorate of BERR, the Health and Safety Executive, which reports to the Department of Work and Pensions, and HM Revenue and Customs, which is responsible for enforcing the national minimum wage.

Fragmentation does not signify the erosion of the capacity and power of the core executive. It is certainly the case that the complex nature of the UK's system of labour administration has created substantial policy coordination challenges for the government and encouraged the development of various initiatives designed to bring about 'joined-up' policy making (Heyes 2001). A recent example is the creation of a Fair Employment Enforcement Board to promote collaboration between the various bodies with responsibilities relating to labour inspection. Yet there is also evidence that the power of the core has increased since the election of the Labour government in 1997, with policy development and implementation processes being driven by the Prime Minister's office and the Treasury to an unprecedented extent (Kavanagh and Seldon 2000; Richards and Smith 2004).

The allocation of responsibilities across Whitehall is largely a consequence of attempts by the government to find effective ways of pursuing particular policy goals. For example, the creation of the Department of Work and Pensions, and the associated merger of two Executive Agencies – the Employment Service and Benefits Agency – to create JobCentre Plus, was intended to support the government's policy of linking the payment of welfare benefits to participation in the labour market. The demise of the Department of Employment, which occurred in the face of TUC opposition, reflected the (then) Conservative government's determination to ensure that existing and proposed employment rights be evaluated primarily in terms of their potential impact on economic performance (the assumption being that any strengthening of employment rights would damage the economy).

What of the claim that civil society actors have achieved a more prominent role in the governance of the economy and society? In the 1980s and early 1990s, the period during which the participation of non-governmental actors is said to have increased, opportunities for the CBI and (particularly) the TUC to partici-pate in governance were substantially reduced. The Conservatives disbanded the Manpower Services Commission and the National Economic Development Committee, which had previously provided employers and unions with a role in labour administration and a limited voice in policy deliberations. The practice of including trade union leaders on government inquiry panels and committees was also suspended and trade union leaders were typically only consulted on issues that were deemed to be of direct concern to them (Crouch 1995). Contact, where it did occur, tended to be initiated by the unions and occurred at a lower level than had previously been the case (McIlroy 1995: 201; Mitchell 1987; Marsh 1992). The CBI, which was on occasion critical of the government, was also viewed with a certain amount of suspicion. The government was more sympathetic to the right-wing Institute of Directors, which was openly supportive of the supply-side measures introduced by the Conservative administrations. During this period, the DTI was reorganized so to reduce 'the closeness of the links between trade association and units within the department. Civil servants were encouraged to talk directly to companies and not to use trade associations or the CBI as interme-diaries' (Budge and McKay 1993: 48).

The current Labour government has displayed a greater willingness than its predecessor to involve trade unions and employer organizations in the develop-ment and delivery of public policy relating to industrial relations, employment and social protection. The most notable development has been the creation of the Low Pay Commission (LPC), the body charged with making recommendations on the level and coverage of the national minimum wage. The LPC is composed of an equal number of employer and trade union representatives (plus three independent experts) and thus provides employers and unions with an oppor-tunity to influence a key area of labour market policy. Employers and trade unions have also been granted representation on a variety of advisory groups. For example, they participate in the Illegal Working Group, which is composed of representatives of various civil society organizations and has a remit to tackle illegal migrant working. In addition, unions and employers have contributed to various 'taskforces' that have been established to discuss policy proposals and provide advice on implementation in relation to issues such as flexible work-ing for parents, the development of a national skills strategy and reforms of the Employment Tribunal system.

Opportunities for unions and employers to participate in labour administra-tion have therefore increased, although their involvement remains less extensive than in some other EU economies and is typically restricted to participation in consultation exercises or the provision of advice. Furthermore, the opportunities extended to trade unions remain more limited than those offered to employers. Business representatives have taken most of the key advisory positions offered by the government (Barratt Brown 2001; Taylor 2000: 267) and dominate a number of those NDPBs that have service delivery responsibilities, particularly those concerned with vocational education and training (the Learning and Skills Council, the Sector Skills Councils and the recently established UK Commission for Employment and Skills).

The government has also tended to be more sympathetic to the interests of employers than organized labour when consulting the two sides on issues of common concern (Coates 2005). The consultation process that preceded the introduction of the 1999 Employment Rights Act (ERA) provides a significant illustration. Prior to the introduction of the ERA, the government had encouraged the TUC and CBI to hold talks aimed at establishing a jointly agreed position on the operation of a new statutory trade union recognition procedure. The talks were held, but broke down following disagreements over the size of bargaining units and the procedure for determining support for recognition. The government sided with the CBI while making limited concessions to trade unions in other areas (such as the right of the individual to union representation in grievance situations). The CBI also objected to a government proposal, contained in the *Fairness at Work* white paper, that training should automatically be a matter for collective bargaining in workplace where trade unions were recognized. The proposal was subsequently dropped.

The relationship between national and European levels of decision making has been one of the main concerns of the multi-level governance literature. Power and authority are said to have flowed away from national governments to the supranational level, thereby contributing to the hollowing out of the state. The importance of the European level of decision making for industrial relations is undeniable: European directives have placed new obligations upon employers, the single market has facilitated the mobility of capital and the Stability and Growth Pact has resulted in downward pressure on public expenditure and consequent cuts in welfare spending (Bouget 2003). However, do these developments represent strong evidence in support of the argument that the authority of national governments has been substantially weakened? There are a number of reasons for thinking otherwise.

First, national governments play an important role in shaping EU policy. The Labour government, for example, has been an active champion of economic and social reform at the European level. It was one of the principal advocates for the adoption of the Lisbon agenda and used its 2005 presidency of the EU as an opportunity to promote the concept of flexicurity, arguing that excessive employment protection had acted in many European economies as a fetter on structural adjustment and growth and contributed to unemployment. Second, the adoption of the Open Method of Coordination (OMC) means that the achievement of the EU's economic and social policy goals is largely dependent on the voluntary efforts of national governments (see Trubek and Mosher 2003). However, it appears that one of the EU's principal social policy coordinating mechanisms – the European Employment Strategy – has had an uneven influence on the policies of national governments and very little influence on those of the UK (Mailand 2008). Third, the EC has itself promoted the idea of multi-level governance to the extent that its policy pronouncements have emphasized the importance of extensive 'social dialogue'. However, the ability of the social partners to affect change through inter-professional and sectoral social dialogue at the European level is extremely limited while the extent of social dialogue within member states continues to be largely determined by national politics and the strength of employer and union organizations (Gold *et al.* 2007; Hamann and Kelly 2003; Hyman, this volume; de la Porte and Nanz 2004). Perhaps unsurprisingly, the EC's exhortations have had little impact on the British government's propensity to involve employers and unions in governance processes (Mailand 2008).

Social capital

A number of the central themes of the governance debate are also to be found in the burgeoning literature devoted to the concept of social capital. Examples include the relationship between the state and 'civil society', transfers of responsibility from government to non-governmental actors, the development of networks and their role in shaping economic and social outcomes.

Interest in the concept of social capital has spread rapidly across the social sciences over the past decade and it has had a considerable impact on the research agendas of several disciplines and fields of study, including sociology, social policy, education and economics. Robert Putnam, one of the three key proponents of the concept (the others being the sociologists Pierre Bourdieu and (separately) James Coleman) has defined social capital as 'features of social organisations, such as networks, norms and trust that facilitate co-ordination and co-operation for mutual benefit' (Putnam 1993: 41). Early studies of social capital, such as those of Coleman (1988), Bourdieu (1986) and Putnam (1993), depicted social capital as a resource that individuals might access through participation in networks. Over time, however, the focus of research on social capital has expanded to include the contribution that institutions and high-trust relationships might make to social and economic development. Interest in this issue has not been confined to academia: from the late 1990s the concept of social capital had a profound influence on the work of the World Bank and its analysis of appropriate policies for stimulating economic development. The 'post-Washington consensus' regarded the creation of social capital as an important means by which governments could address market imperfections (Fine 2001).

While the concept of social capital has infiltrated the social sciences to a remarkable extent, industrial relations researchers have so far paid it little attention. This is perhaps surprising, given that a number of industrial relations topics, including the emerging interest in 'new actors' (Heery and Frege 2006), community unionism and social mobilization, could be analysed through the conceptual lens of social capital. Indeed, trade unions, as voluntary associations, could be viewed as a manifestation of social capital, as could collective bargaining, social dialogue and participation by employers and unions in labour administration. However, it is possible that the absence of a rush to embrace the concept of social capital is a reflection of researchers' scepticism about its analytical value. A fundamental weakness of the concept is that its meaning is open to numerous competing interpretations (Portes 1998; Johnston and Percy-Smith 2003). It remains unclear whether social capital refers to resources (e.g. shared values and mutual trust) that are *created* through participation in networks or the *presence* of such networks and resources. Is it something that individuals or groups may acquire, or something that social actors might create yet be unable to appropriate?

More important, as far as the focus of this chapter is concerned, is the failure of the governance and social capital literatures to problematize the nature of the state. The state is viewed as a benign force composed of multiple sites of authority none of which is dominant. It acts to create institutions and networks that facilitate information sharing, innovative behaviours, coordination and joint problem solving by social actors. The state and its relationship to society are thus conceived of in pluralist terms (Smith 2006). Yet pluralism lacks a clear theory of the state, certainly lacks a theory of the *capitalist* state and therefore fails to problematize the nature of the state's relationship to capital and labour. A social capital perspective on the state's role in industrial relations might therefore experience difficulties in attempting to account for the unwillingness of the government to promote social dialogue, delegate responsibilities for labour administration to employers and trade unions, strengthen rights to participation and representation at workplace and company levels and introduce other measures designed to encourage high-trust industrial relations.

Conclusion

Engagement with state theory remains relatively uncommon in the industrial relations research literature. However, it is possible that the developing interest in multi-level governance will encourage researchers to pay greater attention to theoretical perspectives on the form and functions of the state and its relationships with other social agencies. Taking forward the multi-level governance research agenda will require more than an investigation of actors, institutions and rules that operate at, and link, the national, sub- and supranational levels. It will also require an explicit engagement with the pluralist assumptions associated with the concept of multi-level governance, including the belief that the state no longer plays a central role in regulating the economy. The current economic crisis is, in any case, likely to encourage a reassessment of this view.

The policy agenda is currently in a state of flux. Theories, concepts and prescribed courses of action that have dominated the policy discourse for the past 30 years have been questioned and even abandoned as policy makers and analysts have struggled to understand and tackle the most severe economic crisis in 80 years. The disruptions of the 1930s eventually led to the widespread acceptance of new ideas concerning the state's role in the management of the economy. Social unrest also encouraged the emergence of new accommodations between the state and organized labour as reflected in, for example, the United States' New Deal measures. Could we be reaching a similar turning point? The economic hardships that have to date mainly affected the private sector will almost certainly be experienced in due course by the public sector as cuts in state expenditure feed through to jobs and pay. To what extent will industrial action and social protest increase in the face of threats to living standards? Will we witness a renewed interest in the 'political exchanges' associated with 1970s corporatism? As economic and social circumstances change, will space be created for the adoption of policies more favourable to labour than those that have been pursued during the past 30 years? In what ways will domestic and international business interests and supranational agencies attempt to influence government policy? Whatever happens, the state will play a central role in shaping the course of events.

References

Barratt Brown, M. 2001: *The Captive Party*. Nottingham: Spokesmen Books.

Bouget, D. 2003: Convergence in the social welfare systems in Europe: from goal to reality. *Social Policy & Administration*, 37 (6), 674–693.

Bourdieu, P. 1986: The forms of capital. In Richardson, J. (ed.) *Handbook of Theory and Research for the Sociology of Education*. New York: Greenwood.

Budge, I. and McKay, D. 1993: *The Developing British Political System: The 1990s*. London: Longman.

Burawoy, M. 1985: *The Politics of Production: Factory Regimes under Capitalism and Socialism*. London: Verso.

Cerny, P.G. 1995: Globalization and the changing logic of collective action. *International Organization*, 49 (4), 595–625.

Coates, D. 2001: Capitalist models and social democracy: the case of New Labour. *British Journal of Politics and International Relations*, 3 (3), 284–307.

Coates, D. 2005: *Prolonged Labour: The Slow Birth of New Labour Britain*. Basingstoke: Palgrave Macmillan.

Coleman, J. 1988: Social capital in the creation of human capital. *American Journal of Sociology*, 94 (Supplement): S95–S121.

Crouch, C. 1995: The state: economic management and incomes policy. In Edwards, P.K. (ed.) *Industrial Relations in Britain*. Oxford: Basil Blackwell.

De la Porte, C. and Nanz, P. 2004: The OMC – a deliberative-democratic mode of governance? The cases of employment and pensions. *Journal of European Public Policy*, 11 (2), 267–288.

Deacon, A. 1999: Learning from the US? The influence of American ideas upon 'new labour' thinking on welfare reform. *Policy & Politics*, 28 (1), 5–18.

Department of Enterprise Trade and Employment (DETE) 2003: *Statement of Strategy 2003–2005*. Dublin: DETE.

Elliott, K.A. and Freeman, R.B. 2003: *Can Labor Standards Improve under Globalization?* Washington DC: Institute for International Economics.

Evans, M. 2009: Gordon Brown and public management reform – a project in search of a 'big idea'. *Policy Studies*, 30 (1), 33–51.

Ferrera, M. and Hemerjick, A. 2003: Recalibrating Europe's welfare regimes. In Zeitline, J. and Trubeck, D.M. (eds) *Governing Work and Welfare in a New Economy: European and American Experiments*. Oxford: Oxford University Press.

Fine, B. 2001: *Social Capital Versus Social Theory: Political Economy and Social Science at the Turn of the Millennium*. Oxon: Routledge.

Freeden, M. 1999: The ideology of New Labour. *Political Quarterly*, 70 (1), 42–51.

Gold, M., Cressey, P. and Leonard, E. 2007: Whatever happened to social dialogue? From partnership to managerialism in the EU employment agenda. *European Journal of Industrial Relations*, 13 (1), 7–25.

Hall, P.A. and Soskice, D. (eds) 2001: *Varieties of Capitalism: The Institutional Foundations of Comparative Advantage*. Oxford: Oxford University Press.

Hamann, K. and Kelly, J. 2003: The domestic sources of differences in labour market policies. *British Journal of Industrial Relations*, 41 (4), 639–664.

Harvey, D. 2005: *A Brief History of Neoliberalism*. Oxford: Oxford University Press.

Hay, C. 1999: *The Political Economy of New Labour: Labouring under False Pretences*. Manchester University Press.

Hay, C. 2006: What's globalization got to do with it? Economic interdependence and the future of European welfare states. *Government and Opposition*, 41 (1), 1–22.

Heery, E. and Frege, C. 2006: New actors in industrial relations. *British Journal of Industrial Relations*, 44 (4), 601–604.

Heyes, J. 2001: *Labour Administration in the United Kingdom*. Geneva: International Labour Organization.

Hooghe, L. and Marks, G. 2001: *Multi-level Governance and European Integration*. Rowman and Littlefield.

Hopkin, J. and Wincott, D. 2006: New Labour, economic reform and the European social model. *BJPIR*, 8: 50–68.

Johnston, G. and Percy-Smith, J. 2003: In search of social capital. *Policy & Politics*, 31 (3), 321–34.

Jordan, A. 2001: The European Union: an evolving system of multi-level governance . . . or government? *Policy & Politics*, 29 (2), 193–208.

Jordon, G. and O'Toole, B.J. 1995: The next steps: origins and destinations. In O'Toole, B.J. and Jordan, G. (eds) *Next Steps: Improving Management in Government*. Aldershot: Dartmouth.

Kavanagh, D. and Seldon, A. 2000: *The Powers behind the Prime Minister: The Hidden Influence of Number Ten*. HarperCollins.

Kitson, M. and Wilkinson, F. 2007: The economics of New Labour: policy and performance. *Cambridge Journal of Economics*, 31, 805–816.

Low Pay Commission 1998: *The National Minimum Wage: The First Report of the Low Pay Commission*. London: The Stationery Office.

McIlroy, J. 1995: *Trade Unions in Britain Today*. Manchester: Manchester University Press.

Mailand, M. 2008: The uneven impact of the European Employment Strategy on member states' employment policies: a comparative analysis. *Journal of European Social Policy*, 18 (4), 353–365.

Marginson, P. and Sisson, K. 2004: *European Integration and Industrial Relations*. Basingstoke: Palgrave Macmillan.

Marks, G. 1996: An actor-centred approach to multi-level governance. In Jeffery, C. (ed.) *The Regional Dimension of the EU*. London: Frank Cass.

Marsh, D. 1992: *The New Politics of British Trade Unionism*. Basingstoke: Macmillan.

Mitchell, N. 1987: Changing pressure group politics: the case of the TUC, 1976–1984. *British Journal of Political Science*, 17, 509–517.

Navarro, V., Schmitt, J. and Astudillo, J. 2004: Is globalisation undermining the welfare state? *Cambridge Journal of Economics*, 28, 133–152.

Ohmae, K. 1990: *The Borderless World: Power and Strategy in the Interlinked Economy*. HarperCollins.

Ohmae, K. 1995: *The End of the Nation State: The Rise of Regional Economies*. Free Press.

Peters, B.G. and Pierre, J. 2001: Development in intergovernmental relations: towards multi-level governance. *Policy & Politics*, 29 (2), 131–135.

Pollert, A. 2007: Britain and individual employment rights: 'paper tigers, fierce in appearance but missing in tooth and claw'. *Economic and Industrial Democracy*, 28 (1), 100–139.

Portes, A. 1998: Social capital: its origins and applications in modern sociology. *Annual Review of Sociology*, 24, 1–24.

Putnam, R. 1993: *Making Democracy Work: Civic Traditions in Modern Italy*. Princeton: Princeton University Press.

Regalia, I. 2007: Towards multi-level governance in industrial relations: mapping the field. Paper presented to the European Conference of the IIRA, Manchester, 13–17 September 2007.

Rhodes, R.A.W. 1996: The new governance: governing without government. *Political Studies*, XLIV: 652–667.

Richards, D. and Smith, M.J. 2004: The 'hybrid state': Labour's response to the challenge of governance. In Ludlum, S. and Smith, M.J. (eds) *Governing as New Labour: Policy and Politics under Blair*. Basingstoke: Palgrave Macmillan.

Romer, P.M. 1990: Human capital and growth: theory and evidence. *Carnegie-Rochester Conference Series on Public Policy*, 32, 251–286.

Sachs, J. and Larrain, F. 1993: *Macroeconomics in the Global Economy*. Englewood Cliffs, NJ: Prentice-Hall.

Sanderson, I. 2002: Evaluation, policy learning and evidence-based policy making. *Public Administration*, 80 (1), 1–22.

Smith, M.J. 2004: Conclusion: defining New Labour. In Ludlum, S. and Smith, M.J. (eds) *Governing as New Labour: Policy and Politics under Blair*. Basingstoke: Palgrave Macmillan.

Smith, M. 2006: Pluralism. In Hay, C., Lister, M. and Marsh, D. (eds) *The State: Theories and Issues*. Basingstoke: Palgrave Macmillan.

Smith, P. and Morton, G. 2006: Nine years of New Labour: neoliberalism and workers' rights. *British Journal of Industrial Relations*, 44 (3), 401–420.

Taylor, R. 2000: *The TUC: From the General Strike to New Unionism*. Basingstoke: Palgrave.

Treib, O., Bahr, H. and Falkner, G. 2007: Modes of governance: towards a conceptual clarification. *Journal of European Public Policy*, 14 (1), 1–20.

Trubek, D.M. and Mosher, J.S. 2003: New governance, employment policy and the European social model. In Zeitlin, J. and Trubek, D.M. (eds) *Governing Work and Welfare in a New Economy: European and American Experiments*. Oxford: Oxford University Press.

Walker, R. 2000: Learning if people will work: the case of New Deal for disabled people. *Policy Studies*, 21 (4), 313–331.

Watson, M. and Hay, C. 2003: The discourse of globalisation and the logic of no alternative: rendering the contingent necessary in the political economy of New Labour. *Policy & Politics*, 31 (3), 289–305.

Wollmann, H. 2001: Germany's trajectory of public sector modernisation: continuities and discontinuities. *Policy & Politics*, 29 (2), 151–170.

Yeates, N. 2001: *Globalization and Social Policy*. London: Sage.State, Capital And Labour Relations In Crisis

6

TRADE UNIONS: POWER AND INFLUENCE IN A CHANGED CONTEXT

MELANIE SIMMS AND ANDY CHARLWOOD

Introduction

The primary function of trade unions is to represent the interests of their members. Beneath this relatively simple statement lies a raft of complex, and sometimes contradictory, ideas. The purpose of this chapter is to establish what unions seek to achieve, how they have tried to secure their objectives in the UK context, and what future options and strategies are open to them. The main objectives are to describe and analyse the continued decline of unions in the UK and to examine and evaluate strategies proposed as routes to renewal. Before doing this, it is necessary to locate these developments in a broader analytical context. First, we explore the *rationale* for the existence of trade unions. Then we develop the concept of *workers' interests* as central to understanding the nature and purpose of unions. Third, the determinants and expression of union *power* are explored as unions seek to protect and advance the interests of those they represent.

We take as our starting point that there is a fundamental imbalance of power in the employment relationship between employers and individual workers (see Colling and Terry, this volume). This has political implications as the interests of workers may be seen as less legitimate or important than the interests of businesses, property owners, shareholders or 'the market'. The right of workers to form and join collective organizations (trade unions) is a common response to these power imbalances. This fundamental right has long been accepted in most democratic industrialized economies and the right to join a trade union is enshrined both in the legal codes of many nation states and in instruments such as the United Nations Universal Declaration of Human Rights. Despite this, political acceptance of the legitimacy of unions was challenged and significantly weakened in the UK in the 1980s and 1990s and this is discussed later.

The ways in which unions have pursued the collective interests of workers vary from country to country (Hyman 2001 develops a conceptual analysis). In the UK, union representation structures are complex with a mixture of large general unions with members in the public and private sectors (such as Unite and the GMB), unions largely representing public sector workers, but where some members are located in the private sector (Unison and Public and Commercial Services (PCS) are examples), large unions representing professionals, predominantly in the public sector (the Royal College of Nursing (RCN), National Union of Teachers (NUT) and British Medical Association (BMA)) and small occupationally or sector-specific unions in both the public and private sectors (University and Colleges Union (UCU), or the RMT representing staff in transport). Unions often compete with each other for members and an employer may recognize the legitimacy of more than one union to represent workers.

The primary mechanism through which UK unions have represented their members' views to employers is through collective bargaining; the formally institutionalized process of negotiating that takes place between trade unions and employers (see Brown, this volume). While the incidence and coverage of bargaining are shrinking (Brown, this volume; Charlwood 2007), it remains the primary mechanism through which collective interests are formally expressed. As the incidence, coverage and influence of collective bargaining have shrunk, unions have sought other means of influencing employment relations, notably enforcement of legal rights and obligations, but workplace representation and negotiation remain critical to such strategies (see Colling; Terry, both this volume).

The ways in which unions define their objectives raises two important questions. First, how do unions identify and advance particular workers' interests? Second, what are the sources of power and influence they use to advance those interests and how do they mobilize power resources? The argument here rests on understanding that the collective interests of workers that are given voice by trade unions are a social construct. In other words, those collective interests do not simply 'exist'. Individual workers have – and always have had – different interests; some of which coincide with those of other workers and some of which are more individual, or specific to smaller groups. Unions have always faced the challenge of trying to identify issues and interests which affect as many workers as possible. This process of social construction has, in the past, for example, created strong incentives for unions to promote and reinforce the idea that there is a working class that shares core interests that are most effectively pursued by unions (see Hyman 1999 for a more lengthy discussion of this point). This was both feasible and important while there was a large group in society that faced, daily, vulnerability in their employment relationship, and while the societal conditions in which they lived helped reinforce the idea that 'ordinary workers' shared interests that were far more deep-seated than any differences (Cronin 1984).

Over the past 30 years, British unions have declined in power and influence on every measure. The argument in this chapter is that this is partly because of the social, political and economic changes which have come together to make it even more difficult than in earlier periods to identify, construct and promote a single, coherent set of collective interests amongst workers. While legal and political changes in the 1980s were undoubtedly important in undermining the power of unions, in comparison to the mid-20th century, society has now changed so profoundly that efforts by unions to renew themselves show little evidence of success and are unlikely to do so. As discussed below, different prescriptions for renewal emerge from different analyses of the challenges facing unions, but we are pessimistic about the opportunities for any sustained reversal of fortunes because of the challenges in constructing a broad-based understanding of collective interests in contemporary society. We argue that these difficulties, combined with the legislative, political and economic legacies of the 1980s, make it hard for unions to re-establish a role as the legitimate representatives of workers in most workplaces. This weakens their ability to use coercive power through industrial action, creating a vicious circle which, we argue, largely explains the failure of renewal efforts throughout the 1990s and 2000s. Our argument here is that the decline of trade unionism in the UK is a function of the complex interaction of these factors; political challenges, economic restructuring, and some profound changes to how people work and live have all made it difficult for unions to organize and represent working people in the ways that they have previously.

Before we develop this argument, it is necessary to summarize two key ideas that are central to our analysis; workers' interests and union power. We want to be clear about how we conceptualize these ideas before considering some of the measures to evaluate union power. This is important because understanding how unions obtain and use power has links to how and why they prioritize particular interests over others. The main part of this chapter reviews some of the explanations of the decline in union power before considering the efforts unions have made to renew themselves in recent years. Although our analysis has a pessimistic tone, we agree with Hyman (1999) that it is, at least theoretically, possible for unions to 'reimagine' these collective solidarities and interests within contemporary society. In practice, however, we see little evidence of this and argue that it remains unlikely that unions will be able to re-establish their role as the legitimate representatives of workers' interests on a wide scale.

Workers' Interests

The notion of being an organization that represents the *interests* of workers is central to what a union is. This raises questions about what workers' interests are, how they come to define them, and how unions decide which interests to represent from the array of competing interests. Worker interests are socially constructed (Fox 1971; Edwards and Wajcman 2005). What workers think and feel about their employment relationship reflects their norms and expectations, acquired through, amongst other things, education, family, friends, community, the media, managers and co-workers. Unions as collective organizations have to decide which interests are the most important to represent and how they will be represented. In turn, these decisions give *legitimacy* to the interests chosen above others.

Because unions are democratic organizations, with objectives decided by members who participate in decisions, they have tended to prioritize the interests of full-time male employees, because they traditionally made up the majority of members (Bain and Price 1980). Leaders and officials also exert influence on which interests unions represent. As informed and experienced professionals who are often seeking to expand membership and bring in less well-represented groups, union leaders can have an important role in shaping members' conceptions of their interests through argument and debate (Kelly and Heery 1989). Leaders can help shape members' perceptions of what their interests are and what can be done to advance them (Kelly 1998). These competing objectives mean that there are frequently tensions within unions between a desire to prioritize the narrow economic interests of the largest group of members, and a desire to take a more expansive, solidaristic perspective. Allan Flanders (1970: 15) famously argued that unions have two faces: one advancing 'vested interests', the other acting as a 'sword of justice'. While the dynamics of these processes are complex and often contested, the decisions about which interests unions should pursue are the consequence of different views and interests accommodated through negotiation and compromise. The outcome of that process can create or reinforce ideas about which interests are *legitimate*. This idea of legitimacy is an important one and one that we will return to because it relates directly to how unions gain and use power.

Union Power

The ability of workers and their unions to advance their interests is critically dependent on the power resources that they have at their disposal because without power, unions will struggle to persuade employers to make changes which advance members' interests. We can think of unions (and employers) having two types of power resource at their disposal (French and Raven 1968). First, *coercive power* is the power to force someone to do something because they fear the consequences of not doing it. Second, *legitimacy power* is the power that unions have because employers accept the legitimacy of unions' representation and bargaining roles, often because the government signals to employers that unions should be recognized and engaged with.

In line with Kelly (1998) we argue that workers act collectively to use the coercive power at their disposal when they have both a group identity that binds them together and ideological resources, for example doctrines of Marxism or socialism, that promote collective action. Ideology is important because it provides frameworks that shape the way that workers think about their employment relationship. If workers possess a group identity and are equipped with ideological frameworks that predispose them towards collective action, then a critical influence on their chances of success is their labour market position (Marshall 1910). Airline pilots are a good example of a group of workers that enjoy favourable conditions: labour costs are a comparatively small proportion of the total costs of running an airline, and pilots cannot easily be replaced because it takes time to train them and there is no readily available pool of unemployed but trained pilots waiting to step in. Textile workers, on the other hand, have an unfavourable labour market position: demand for textiles is highly price sensitive, labour costs are a large proportion of a firm's costs, and competition from firms paying lower wages can destroy the jobs of workers who are successful in bargaining up their wages. This helps explain why unions have often been more effective at supporting workers who already enjoy some degree of labour market power. A secondary influence on the coercive power of workers is how the state deploys the coercive power at its disposal. If the state sides with employers, and uses its power against workers and unions, workers may be less inclined to try to use their own coercive power for fear of facing costly defeat.

Legitimacy power reflects the extent to which unions are taken to be the legitimate representatives of workers by employers and by the state, the latter reflected in the messages that governments send about the role of unions. The Conservative governments of the 1980s sought fundamentally to undermine union legitimacy through, for example, their exclusion from social and economic policy-making processes (Heyes and Nolan, this volume). State policies to involve or exclude unions are important in sending a message to employers about whether or not they should engage with unions. What employers do is also a source of legitimacy power. If a company recognizes a trade union for collective bargaining, the legitimacy power of the union is established and institutionalized. By bargaining with the union, the company accepts the union as the representative voice of workers.

So, the concept of union power has two aspects: coercive and legitimacy. In this chapter, we are focusing on British unions, but this way of thinking about power and interests can also be helpful in other contexts. Legitimacy and coercive powers interact in different ways in different contexts and by using this distinction, we can explain why union power has declined so profoundly in Britain over the past 30 years and why unions are struggling to renew themselves. But before we do that, we need evaluate union power.

Evaluating union power

Union membership density (the proportion of employees who are union members) is one of the most widely used proxies for union power. The proportion of union members as a percentage of the national workforce, of the workforce in particular sectors or industries, of the workforce in individual companies, and of the workforce in specific workplaces are all important measures of the combined legitimacy and coercive powers of unions. As a crude proxy measure of power, membership density is a reasonable starting point. But the power of a union may exceed, or be far less than, density figures indicate. For example, a union which has bargaining rights to represent clerical workers in a hospital may be setting the terms and conditions of employment for all clerical staff in that workplace, even though membership density may be low. Similarly, a union which negotiates on a wide range of employment issues is likely to be more influential on workers' lives than one that negotiates on only a few. Thus, the coverage and scope of collective bargaining and the influence of the outcome of the union's bargaining would be far more influential within the hospital than low membership density would indicate. However, union power in this context comes from the legitimacy power that management bestows through formally recognizing the right of that union to represent a group of workers. If a union has relatively low membership density, it will be much harder – if not impossible – to get members to deploy coercive power through effective collective action.

Many economists would measure the effectiveness or the influence of a union in more quantitative terms and would evaluate the impact of unions on the labour market (Booth 1995). Specifically, economists focus on the extent to which unions can negotiate a proportion of a firm or industry's profits (or rents) to benefit workers through higher wages. A key question is whether union members earn more than equivalent non-members. If workers in workplaces where unions are recognized for collective bargaining are paid more than workers in equivalent non-union workplaces, this is known as the 'union wage mark-up'. Blanchflower and Bryson (2004) found evidence that the mark-up has declined in Britain since the early 1980s, suggesting a loss of union power. A further method for estimating union power and influence on the labour market is to look at the impact of unions on wage dispersion or inequality because unions tend to pursue wage bargaining strategies that reduce wage differentials while employers may have an interest in maintaining or increasing them. The evidence here (Card *et al.* 2003; Addison *et al.* 2006) also suggests that wage dispersion has increased at the same time as union power has declined in the unionized sector since the 1980s.

A final measure of union power that we consider here is the influence of unions on policy makers. British unions established the Labour Party in order to pursue their political (as opposed to economic) objectives (Minkin 1991). This relationship, although changing, remains important (Ludlum and Taylor 2003) and typically means that during periods of Labour governments, unions have greater access to influencing public policy than when the Conservative Party is in power. Influence can be seen in policy making such as the seats allocated to union representatives on the Low Pay Commission which is responsible for recommending the rate of the national minimum wage (Brown 2000) and bodies responsible for running local policy issues (see also Keep *et al.* on training bodies, this volume). But it would be wrong to imagine that unions have no political influence during periods of Conservative governments. For example, during the 1980s and early 1990s, the powerful voice of unions within the National Health Service had an influence over the speed and the extent of changes there (Bach and Winchester 1994), showing that when unions are recognized as the legitimate voice of workers' interests they can exercise important influence.

Union Decline

Having outlined how we conceptualize and evaluate union power, it is important to note that on all of the measures above, the power of trade unions in the UK has declined persistently since the late 1970s. Membership density has fallen (Charlwood and Metcalf 2005) at almost all levels of analysis, and collective bargaining coverage has declined (Charlwood 2007). Unions bargain over a narrower range

of issues (Kersley *et al.* 2006; Brown *et al.* 2000) and strike action is at a historical low point (Charlwood 2004). The union wage mark-up has become smaller
(Blanchflower and Bryson 2004) and wage dispersion amongst union workers
has increased (Card *et al.* 2003; Addison *et al.* 2006). Much has been written about
the sustained decline in collective organization and representation since the election
of Margaret Thatcher in 1979 and a brief overview of the figures highlights the
extent and nature of that decline (see Figure 6.1).

There are now around 7.1 million employees in union membership in Britain
(Mercer and Notley 2008). This is still a very large number, but fewer than the
13.3 million members in 1979 (Charlwood and Metcalf 2005). During this period,
the number of workers in the UK workforce has also changed and so the aggregate
density across the workforce becomes important. In 1979, around 57% of workers
were union members (Charlwood and Metcalf 2005), but in 2007 that had declined
to 28% (Mercer and Notley 2008). This is a big change, but it illustrates that union
membership is still relatively common and is in line with the EU average and above,
for example, density figures in the USA (Visser 2006). However, these aggregate
figures mask differences between the public and private sectors. In 2007, in the
public sector, where around one in five workers is employed, union density is
58.8%, while in the private sector it is 16% (Mercer and Notley 2008).

Most unions have experienced membership decline but the degree and extent
of that decline varies considerably. Unions that have been most successful in recent
years, often bucking the trend of membership decline, have been those, such as

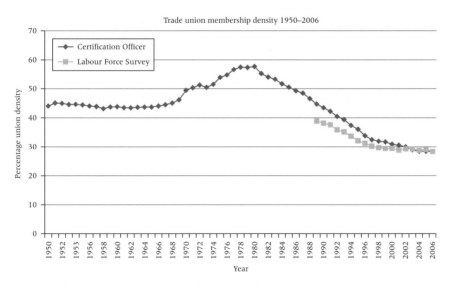

Figure 6.1   Trade union membership density 1950–2006

Source: Certification Officer: The numerator is the number of members of trade unions headquartered
in the United Kingdom, as supplied by the trade unions to the Certification Officer. Note that these
data contain a number of irregularities – see Charlwood and Metcalf (2005) for further discussion.
The denominator is employee jobs. Note that this may bias estimates of union density downwards
as some employees have more than one job. The density figures from the Labour Force Survey are
more accurate, but only go back as far as 1989.

the Royal College of Nursing and the teaching unions, which organize professionals in the public sector. Membership of this type of union has increased for several inter-related reasons. Since 1999, employment in public sector professions has risen as spending on public services has increased (see Bach, this volume; Hicks *et al.* 2005). These unions have expanded their job territories by organizing new and growing occupational groups such as teaching assistants. They have also increased membership density by offering legal and insurance services, which protect their members against the risk of being sued for negligence.

On the measure of the political influence of unions, there have also been significant changes since the 1980s. Prior to the election of the Conservative government in 1979, the working political assumption by parties of both the Left and the Right was that unions were a powerful voice of workers that were a useful and legitimate way of expressing interests at different levels of society: community groups, councils, regional and national decision-making structures. By contrast, over the 1980s, there were concerted efforts to remove union influence from these structures. That is not to say that no trade unionists sat on these bodies; many politicians and community activists are members of trade unions. But the reflex of involving unions in their own right in political decision making reduced. Although there has been some change since the election of the Labour government in 1997, unions do not enjoy the kind of close relationship with policy makers that they once had (Dorey 1995).

Explaining union decline

A fundamental question to consider is why unions have declined on so many measures of power over the past 30 years. Union decline has been a feature of all advanced industrial economies over this period, in part because of widespread changes in technology and economic organization (Blanchflower 2007; Ebbinghaus and Visser 1999). However, union decline has been greater in Britain than in any country other than the USA (Blanchflower 2007). This is partly because, between 1979 and 1997, successive Conservative governments took a series of decisions which weakened unions. These decisions were taken within the context of a political programme designed to decollectivize the British economy and society (Gamble 1994). Union decline in the UK can largely be explained by the interaction of economic, political, legal and social changes. Secular changes to economic organization influenced labour markets partly as a result of changing trade patterns and partly as a result of technological change. Political and legal changes delegitimized trade unions, stripped them of ideological resources, and made workers pessimistic about the possibility of effective collective action while exposing unions to the full force of wider economic changes. Alongside these developments, British society changed. The Conservative governments of 1979–1997 had a central role in bringing about all of these changes, and as a consequence both coercive and legitimacy powers of unions were profoundly undermined. But it is important that we do not apportion blame entirely to the external environment; unions must surely share some of the responsibility and we therefore look at each of these factors in more detail.

Economic and social change   Increasing global trade, both between developed countries (in the case of Britain, particularly increased trade with the EU), and between developed and developing countries, combined with rapid technological change, for example improvements in information and communications technologies, have had important impacts in countries like Britain. Disentangling the relative importance of growing trade and technological change is a difficult and controversial task that is beyond the scope of this chapter (but see Freeman 1995 for a discussion). Whether these changes are attributed to trade or technology, the impacts on labour markets, and by extension trade unions, have been considerable. In particular, internationally, manufacturing capacity expanded both as a result of industrialization in countries like China, India and Brazil, and technological changes that mean firms can make more with less.

This has had effects for British trade unions. First, increasingly competitive product markets can present challenges to unions; it can be harder for unions to win concessions from employers and the costs of unionization and collective action may be higher (Brown *et al.* 1997). Second, technological change has made it easier and cheaper for firms to replace labour with capital. These technological changes have impacted disproportionately on workers performing routine but skilled or semi-skilled jobs (Autor *et al.* 2003; Goos and Manning 2007), for example machinists in the engineering and textiles industries, who have been replaced by computer-controlled robots, and possibly lower skilled workers (Machin 2001). The impact of these changes has been disastrous for British unions because it was these workers who once formed the core of the labour movement. Their labour market position gave them comparatively hard to replace skills and the apprenticeship system restricted entry to these jobs at the same time as promoting a collective identity.

These changes intensified the pace of social changes that were already under way by the mid-20th century. In comparison to the early 21st century, working people 50 years ago were much more likely to live closer to work and closer to each other. This shared geography, lifestyle and community was challenged by social change and economic restructuring in the latter part of the 20th century (Putnam 2000; Phelps Brown 1990). At the same time, experiences of work have become more heterogeneous as manufacturing employment has declined. Together, these changing geographies and changing experiences of work mean that an increasing diversity of interests compete for attention and it is more difficult to use ties outside work, of class and of community, to build collectivism. In this context, identifying and bargaining around one particular set of interests becomes more difficult for unions. We would stress that these long run social changes are not the primary causes of union decline, but they do make the task of reimagining and rebuilding unions in the 21st century more difficult.

The rapid decline of British manufacturing over the 1980s led to structural economic change. Jobs moved from manufacturing to service work and unions found it difficult to establish themselves in these new workplaces (Beaumont and Harris 1990). Many workers were unable to retrain to take on the new jobs. Long-term unemployment amongst workers previously employed in manufacturing became a feature of many UK towns and cities. Since the mid-1980s, the economy has restructured so that the majority of UK workers are now in service sector employment (see Arrowsmith, this volume). But it took a decade or more of adjustment, during which time trade unions suffered badly from an inability to respond quickly enough to these economic and social shocks. Alongside these changes, women have also entered the labour market in far larger numbers (see Dean and Liff, this volume). This reflects wider social changes particularly the rise of the women's movement in the 1960s and 1970s, the growing importance of dual-income families, and changes in expectations that women will continue to work after marriage and/or having children. The consequences for trade unions are significant; not only are workers now doing different jobs than in the past, the people who work are more diverse than previously and their experiences of work vary more. Taken together these help explain why unions declined so dramatically over the 1980s and why they are struggling to re-establish themselves as the representatives of workers' interests. But these changes, which were common to most advanced industrial economies, are only part of the story. They were underpinned and reinforced by political and legal developments which were deliberately implemented by Conservative Party governments between 1979 and 1997.

Political and legal change   Union decline was initially triggered by the global recession of 1980 (Disney and Carruth 1988). This had a more severe effect on Britain than on other industrial nations because of the way the Conservative government managed the economy. Monetarist policies, which tried to control inflation through higher interest rates, added to other pressures leading to the closure of large parts of British manufacturing industry (Keegan 1984). As these manufacturing jobs were lost, many trade union members either moved into alternative service sector jobs, or into unemployment.

Changes to the way in which the public sector was managed also impacted negatively on unions (see Bach, this volume). The public sector shrank as a result of budget cuts, and compulsory competitive tendering and privatization led to redundancies, the erosion of terms and conditions and work intensification. When workers resisted these changes through industrial action, the government resolved to face down demands in order to deter other groups of workers from striking. Significant numbers of public sector workers were taken out of collective bargaining as pay review bodies and individual contracts were introduced. Consequently, by the 1990s there were fewer public sector workers and union members, and unions were less able to secure gains for members. In common with other sectors, union attempts to mobilize workers in support of collective grievances became fewer, leading to the erosion of the social custom of membership, with the result that there was less incentive to join. Despite these changes, public sector union membership is still significantly higher than in the private sector, partly due to the recognition by employers that unions are the legitimate representatives of workers.

The Conservatives also changed the ideological context. Ideas based on collectivism and social democracy were attacked and discredited. In their place came a neo-liberal consensus which deprived workers and their unions of the ideological resources to challenge management. Mobilization theory posits that workers will only be willing to act collectively if they possess the ideological resources that allow them to frame issues of grievance in a way that promotes collective action (Kelly 1998). The triumph of neo-liberal ideas disempowered workers because 'attributions for injustice which focus on impersonal forces such as "the market" or "global competition" are disabling (regardless of their validity)' (Badigannavar and Kelly 2005: 520).

Political change challenged the legitimacy power of unions throughout the 1980s. This was a deliberate policy pursued by the Conservative governments of the 1980s and 1990s. It was explicitly driven by a view that trade unions had become too powerful during the post-1945 era, that they had misused their coercive powers to promote interests and policies that were disadvantageous to the British economy, and that the 'free market' is a more effective and legitimate way to determine the price of labour than collective bargaining. This view rejects the idea that workers need protection in the inherently unequal employment relationship and reinforces the view that seeking such protection is an illegitimate activity. To further these political objectives, the governments of that period also enacted a series of laws that constrained and undermined the ability of unions to use their coercive power through industrial action (see Dickens and Hall, this volume.)

The determination with which the Conservative Party pursued these legal and political changes signalled the degree of hostility towards unions and was, at least in part, responsible for their considerable success in challenging both the legitimacy and coercive powers of British unions. Combined with the economic changes happening on a global and national level during the 1980s, the effect was to weaken the power of unions. We argue later that this also explains why efforts at union renewal since the late 1990s have generated relatively little response. But before we move on to look at the contemporary context, we need to reflect on what unions were doing during this period.

Union behaviour   We are not suggesting that union decline is *only* a function of the external context. If we look back to the formation of the trade union movement in the UK (Webb and Webb 1920) or to the continued existence of trade unions in difficult socio-economic contexts we see that unions are sometimes capable of reacting and responding to difficult environments; evolving new forms of unionism better adapted to changed conditions. To a large degree, the ability of unions to overcome these challenges rests on developing sufficient legitimacy power and being able to mobilize coercive power where needed. So what did unions do during the 1980s and 1990s, and why did these actions fail to stop the decline in power?

The first point is that UK unions, unlike many in continental Europe, are largely dependent on their members for their income, so as unions lost membership their income declined. Union officers then had to make decisions about how to continue to run the union as income fell. Typically this meant cutting services, or prioritizing the representation of existing members rather than expanding into new areas. This lack of expansionist organizing activity can become a vicious circle; if unions focus on their core constituencies when those constituencies are shrinking, membership decline can only worsen, and income declines still further. Worse, when unions attempted to organize new workplaces in the 1980s, as many as 80% of campaigns ended in failure (Beaumont and Harris 1990). Many of the new service sector jobs were in smaller workplaces which are resource-intensive for unions to target for organizing activity. Equally, many new jobs were in sectors where workers lack any significant labour market power; the retail and hospitality sectors, for example. Better union tactics may have delivered better results, but given the scale of new organizing needed to make up for lost members, and unions' declining resource base, it is difficult to see what they could have done to bring about their own revival.

At the same time, as we have already stressed, the workforce was changing very profoundly. The increasing diversity of workers, the move to service work, changing patterns of employment, changing lifestyle habits such as working further from home, the increased use of technology, the changing skills base of the workforce and many other factors all interacted to create a context within which not only was the legitimacy of the role of unions in representing the collective interests of workers questioned but the process of identifying collective interests became more difficult. Confronted with profound challenges to both legitimacy and coercive power, unions needed to reimagine alternative forms of legitimacy (Hyman 1999). But the social, economic, political and legislative changes of the 1980s made that extremely difficult. During the 1990s, TUC General Secretary John Monks tried to create new sources of legitimacy power for unions by promoting the idea of a more European style of 'partnership' industrial relations (Heery 1998). But this vision failed to find sufficient support amongst politicians and policy makers to make any substantial impact on union fortunes. Equally, many employers were reluctant to engage with unions in this way, and many activists were suspicious, if not overtly hostile, to the idea.

Thus, our argument is not that unions were simply victims of changing circumstances but that, as reflective actors within that context, their opportunities for action were limited. Previous authors have argued for the relative importance of external factors (Bain and Elsheikh 1976) or internal factors (Undy *et al.* 1981) or a combination of each (Metcalf 1991) in influencing union growth and decline. Our view is that the external context explains much of what happened. And although unions are able to renew themselves by responding to a changing external context, when the external context is threatening to unions, as it was during the years of Conservative government during the 1980s and 1990s, their capacity to respond diminishes (Charlwood 2004). In 1997, however, the political context in the UK changed and the New Labour government, led by Tony Blair, won its first election for 18 years. On face value, it may have seemed that this was the opportunity for British unions to re-establish themselves, but while things have undoubtedly become easier, we have seen relatively little reassertion of union power. We therefore examine some of the continuities and changes that the subsequent period of New Labour administration has brought.

New Labour and the Changing Environment

Although unions were optimistic that the election of New Labour would create a less hostile context, it was clear by 1997 that there would be no repeal of the Conservative industrial relations legislation. Indeed, it was a deliberate, and highly contested, electoral strategy of the Labour Party to rebrand itself 'New Labour' and to accept many of the policies of the Conservatives. Specifically, there was a commitment to keeping public spending in the early years within the constraints planned by the Conservative Party, to retaining the legislation constraining industrial action, and to keeping the flexible labour market policies that gave comparatively few rights to British workers. Further, where the UK was obliged to implement workers' rights – often as a result of EU legislation – these were implemented in such a way as to minimize their impact. Nonetheless, there was also a clear commitment to providing a national minimum wage, to developing a system for statutory trade union recognition (see Dickens and Hall, this volume), and to sign the Social Chapter of the Treaty of Maastricht which granted British workers a number of new rights including the right to European Works Councils, working time protections, parental leave, family leave, etc. This combination of a continuity of Thatcherite policies, combined with a strengthening of minimum rights for workers at the lower end of the labour market was central to the much-discussed 'Third Way' (Howell 2004).

The economy was also considerably healthier between the mid-1990s and 2007, with steady economic growth, falling unemployment and low inflation. One reading of the economic data would suggest that this was a comparatively benign environment for unions (Heery *et al.* 2003). However, while unemployment was low, there was still considerable 'hidden' unemployment (Faggio and Nickell 2003). For example, in 1979 21% of working age men were economically inactive. By 2007, at the peak of the last economic boom, the percentage of economically inactive working age men had risen to 29% (www.statistics.gov.uk). At the same time and as many as half of the new jobs created since 1997 have gone to migrant workers (Statistics Commission 2007). During this period, low inflation and strong real wage growth have been achieved largely without collective bargaining meaning that many workers have little incentive to unionize. In short, the secular economic changes which so undermined the unions in the 1980s were not reversed in the 1990s. Nevertheless, the political environment has been less hostile than in the 1980s and unions have been able to make some moves towards attempted renewal. The different renewal responses reflect a slightly different analysis of the underlying cause of union decline. We examine each of the main approaches before trying to explain why all of them have been relatively unsuccessful in achieving a renewal of union power.

Union Renewal Efforts

There has been much debate around the issue of union renewal. Typically, the three most common union renewal strategies are summarized as (1) developing partnerships with employers, (2) organizing new members and (3) providing better services to union members. A fourth approach is to merge with other unions. While this is not technically an effort at renewal, union officers often argue that the proposed benefits of a larger union (primarily opportunities to reduce duplication of effort and save money on administration) may free up resources to allow for investment in renewal. It can, undoubtedly, be rather simplistic to lump together many complex organizational responses to decline in this way, and these approaches are certainly not mutually exclusive. Nonetheless, they are a useful tool for analysis as they emerge from different analyses of the causes of union decline. We argued previously that over the course of the 1980s and 1990s, unions lost both legitimacy power and coercive power. And we can see that different strategies and tactics for renewal have been focused, albeit with different emphases, in trying to regain both forms of power.

Partnership with employers

During the 1980s, unions' legitimacy power declined in the eyes of both government and many employers. In an effort to renew that legitimacy, attention has been paid to the potential for mutual gains for both employers and employees that could derive from unions and employers working in partnership with each other (Kochan and Osterman 1994; Terry, this volume). Although the notion of partnership is not well defined, it includes ideas of mutual acceptance of the legitimacy of each partner (here unions and managers), cooperation, and joint decision making (Haynes and Allen 2001).

Kelly (2004) differentiates between three kinds of partnership agreement. The first wave of agreements involved a single union agreeing to forego aspects of its coercive power by, for example, signing agreements that it would not take industrial action. These agreements were often with foreign companies setting up large new factories (Sony and Sanyo are examples). There were never many of these agreements and they have not been in evidence since the late 1980s. Nonetheless, they received a great deal of attention and, conceptually, they were an effort to establish legitimacy power, largely ignoring any coercive power unions may have had. More recent second wave agreements have been signed in organizations experiencing substantial restructuring (NatWest bank, Thames Water, Diageo) or where there has been a previous hostility which has prompted an effort to try to re-establish industrial relations on a more cooperative basis (Barclays Bank, Tesco). Since 1999, a third wave of agreements has taken advantage of the statutory recognition legislation to establish union recognition in organizations and workplaces where there was previous resistance (Carillion Services, Eurotunnel). In essence, this third kind of deal consists of union recognition agreements which include a commitment by the union to work in a cooperative manner.

In all of these cases, we see that by getting employers to accept the right and legitimacy of the union to express the collective interests of workers, the unions hope to use this as a platform from which to convince workers that their voices will be listened to. But this approach has been strongly criticized (Kelly 1996, 2004). There is a danger that workers may think that because the union works cooperatively with managers it is not an independent body that represents their interests. Equally, the union may lose the ability to put the workers' point of view effectively because it lacks or is unwilling to use its coercive power. Further, Kelly (2004) demonstrates that there have been few of the wider benefits discussed as potential gains for workers and their unions; increased job security, benefits in wages, terms and conditions, increased union density, etc. Contrary to Kelly, Oxenbridge and Brown (2002, 2004) argue that partnership has delivered benefits to unions and workers, although they find that these are in the form of intangibles such as improved informal cooperation and greater trust. They also argue that, ultimately, the robustness and survival of partnership rests on employer choices, and for partnership to work, employers need to remain committed. Partnership can only, therefore, be a viable renewal strategy if large numbers of employers are committed to it. This employer support has been conspicuous by its absence (Terry 2003). In practice, partnership remains an important rhetoric for British unions to re-establish their legitimacy, but rarely produces consistently positive effects or renewal (Stuart and Martinez Lucio 2005).

Organizing new workers

Partly in response to some of the problems identified with partnership (Kelly 1996, 2004), and partly in response to developments in the USA (Bronfenbrenner *et al.* 1998), in the mid-1990s British unions started focusing on organizing new workers. 'Organizing' can mean many different things. It can mean recruiting workers who are not members in workplaces where the union has a recognition agreement. It can mean recruiting workers where there is no union recognition agreement in the hope that the employer can be persuaded or legally forced to recognize the union. Or it can mean an approach to trade unionism which emphasizes the involvement of ordinary members in decision making. In all of these meanings there is more emphasis on responding to the interests of workers (both members and non-members) than in the partnership approach. This has led some academics (Heery 2002) to contrast 'partnership' and 'organizing' as potentially opposing strategies for unions to try to renew themselves.

Some unions have focused on trying to rebuild coercive power through assertive organizing tactics. The union *Community*, for example, tries to organize workers in workplaces where there has not previously been a union. It does this by emphasizing the different interests of workers and managers, and by showing how workers can pursue their interests by acting collectively. *Unite* union takes a similar approach and has done some innovative work with low-paid cleaners in London, building local networks and tapping into local activism (Wills 2005).

This approach has been influenced by ideas from America (Bronfenbrenner *et al.* 1998) and by mobilization theory (Kelly 1998). It rests on the notion that the collective power of workers will force the employer to listen to them and take their interests seriously. But it is difficult to do this in the current social context and within the considerable legal constraints on unions using their coercive power. Many studies of organizing campaigns (Gall 2003, 2006) highlight the challenges; it is often expensive and time consuming, successful outcomes are far from certain, and there is a risk that the employer may counter-mobilize. Although there are examples of success and unions have secured new recognition agreements either through the statutory processes (Kwik-Fit, Network Rail, Royal Shakespeare Company) or through a voluntary agreement (ISS Mediclean, Intertissue), the impact on overall union membership is weak (Gall 2004, 2007). Aggregate membership has stabilized (although, arguably, decline could have been worse without investment in organizing), and even where recognition deals are secured, there is little evidence of a concerted effort to expand into new territories.

It should also be noted that some employers are hostile to union involvement and have resisted organizing campaigns. Gall (2003) highlights examples of companies, such as the printing firm Printworks, that have resisted organizing efforts by challenging their legal basis on each point of the statutory recognition process; by organizing letters from workers resigning their union membership; and by dismissing activists and representatives. While such anti-union behaviour is not the norm in the UK (Heery and Simms 2003), it is sufficiently common to mean that organizing is a potentially risky and expensive activity for unions. Drawing on a case study of Seacat ferry service, Wills (2003) identifies the problems of finding common interest between different parts of the workforce. In her case study, workers on the ferries were reasonably easy to organize as they worked closely together as a team in often difficult and potentially hazardous working conditions. However, organizing the staff in the call centres that take bookings for the ferries was far more difficult as they tended to work more individually, in a comparatively comfortable environment, and had a far higher labour turnover than their sea-going colleagues. Finding collective interests shared by *both* ferry workers and call centre staff was even more difficult, showing how challenging organizing can be in practice.

Once the union is established in a workplace, it still faces challenges. Activists need to continue to recruit colleagues and identify issues that are important. Often their time gets channelled into ensuring that members with problems have sufficient support and representation, which is essential but may distract attention from organizing work. Simms (2006) also shows how a union that is ineffective at securing collective bargaining outcomes on issues that workers feel are important can lose membership quickly. Using a case study of a call centre that was successfully unionized, she shows how difficult it is to strike the balance between enthusing workplace activists, and making sure that bargaining is done by professional and experienced officers. If officers try to take too much control of bargaining and representation, workplace activists can feel excluded and irrelevant. On the other hand, activists may not have the necessary time, skills and expertise to undertake this complex work.

The main point here is that organizing is difficult and success can be fragile. This is largely because of the difficulties presented by the external context (the opportunities for employers to resist unionization, challenge the legitimacy of the union, and place barriers in the way of unions using coercive power) and the difficulties in building collective interest between workers. Nonetheless, many unions see organizing as a more robust response to the decline of the 1980s and 1990s because it appeals to *workers' interests* rather than *managerial interests*.

Providing services to members

Unions must, ultimately, do something effective in order for workers to want to join. There is plenty of evidence that workers either do not join or leave if they think their union is ineffective at defending and promoting their interests (Charlwood 2002; Waddington and Whitston 1997). Unions have often, therefore, reflected on how they can better provide services. During the long decline of the 1980s and 1990s, many unions expanded the range of services they provided in the hope this would attract new members. Examples include providing credit cards, or discounts on insurance. These incentives were largely ineffective and not a priority for workers (Waddington and Whitson 1997), but although the precise nature of the services being offered may have been new, the idea that unions provide members with services is certainly not. Looking to the past, we see that from the very early days, unions offered a range of financial services such as forms of life assurance, or assistance with funeral costs as these have always been of concern to working people.

The issue here is that unions must provide some services to their members. If they are unable to defend and promote their members' interests, they will lose membership. What the experiments of the 1990s showed was that the essential service of protecting members both individually and collectively was central to what members want from their unions. So the issue is to establish the legitimacy and coercive powers to be able to do that effectively. This highlights the fact that these three renewal approaches are not mutually exclusive. Many unions have pursued all three simultaneously either because they have targeted different employers or groups of workers with different approaches (for example, agreeing to work in partnership with less hostile employers but organizing in a more assertive manner with more reluctant employers), or because they argue that it is important to provide effective services alongside either organizing or partnership approaches. Nonetheless, we see important tensions in union renewal efforts relating not to the different renewal approaches, but to the more fundamental question about whose interests unions seek to represent, how they represent those interests, and how they involve members – and perhaps even non-members – in those processes. We will return to these in a moment, but it is also necessary to comment on union mergers as a response to the difficult conditions faced in the 1980s and 1990s.

Union mergers

A fourth organizational response to declining membership has been mergers between unions. We do not see merger as inherently involving renewal efforts. But merger does offers unions a way of mitigating the worst effects of decline by offering opportunities to restructure, to make cost savings and to refocus activities. For example, in 2007, Unite was formed as the largest UK union. It brought together two large unions; Amicus and the TGWU. Amicus was itself the product of recent mergers between unions in engineering (the AEEU), financial services (MSF and Unifi) and printing (the GPMU). Most of the large, generalist unions in the UK have been the product of mergers at some point, although the outcomes have been far more complex than foreseen, advantages have been harder to secure than anticipated, and have not always resulted in the level of cost saving envisaged (Undy 2008). Arguably, growth of conglomerate unions presents problems because the representative and administrative functions of unions can become decoupled, with the union leadership a greater distance from the members that they are supposed to represent (Willman 2004). Despite this, merger is often the only sensible option open to a union with declining membership and income.

Tensions in union renewal efforts

At the heart of our argument in this section is the view that there was little unions could have done to change the external context that they faced during the 1980s and 1990s; much of the economic and labour market change was beyond their control. Similarly, the political and legal contexts are outside their immediate control. During the period of Conservative governments between 1979 and 1997, the only effective action that unions could take to change that broader context was to campaign for the election of a Labour government and welcome the introduction of social legislation from European Union level. That is not, however, to argue that unions did nothing. They campaigned and lobbied against legislation restricting their activity; they took test cases in the hope of challenging legislative constraints; they campaigned around issues of social justice; and they continued to fight changes in social policy which adversely affected their members (McIlroy 1995 summarizes many of the campaigns run over this time). But in the face of concerted opposition, successes were small and with relatively minimal impact.

What they could do was to focus on the internal processes. Whatever position one takes on the argument about the relative importance of external and internal factors in influencing union power, it is empirically accurate to say that there has been a relatively limited range of options adopted by unions in an effort to renew themselves. Central to understanding the behaviour of unions in responding to the changes and pressures discussed above is an understanding of how workers come to form and express their collective interests. This notion is at the core of what a union 'is', what it 'does' and what it seeks to be 'for'. To restate our argument, we start from the view that these collective interests do not simply 'exist'. Their development and expression is a socially constructed process and unions play an active role in that process. Studies of union campaigns in workplaces as diverse as Seacat (Wills 2003), the not-for-profit sector (Simms 2007a) and food factories (Holgate 2006) show how skilled unions are at doing this. However, despite these efforts, British unions have been relatively unsuccessful in organizing workers in the non-union sector. In large part, this failure is the result of the external environment, for reasons outlined above. But we also argue that there has been a central tension within union renewal efforts; between encouraging participation of members and activists, while also ensuring that the union is providing effective bargaining outcomes and representation.

In other words, union renewal activity needs to encourage both *participation* (Fairbrother 2000) and needs to be *coordinated* by a central union leadership or bureaucracy (Simms 2007b). While one or the other may dominate different strategies (organizing, for example, tends to emphasize participation, whereas provision of effective membership services requires more emphasis on coordination) both are necessary. The tensions between participation and coordination (or between administrative efficiency and representational efficiency, in the language of Willman 2004) can be traced to efforts by unions to seek an effective way to construct the interests they now need to represent. Without legitimacy in the eyes of workers, unions cannot develop participation. At the same time, within the current legislative environment, coordination is essential to deploy effective and lawful coercive power; industrial action can no longer lawfully take place as a spontaneous assertion of dissatisfaction. Both participation and coordination require a clear vision of the collective interests being represented and building those interests amongst an increasingly heterogeneous workforce is extremely difficult – especially with the lack of ideological resources available. We have seen in the examples above that building collective interests can depend on factors such as how closely workers work together, whether or not they see their job as long term, and how difficult or dangerous their work is (Wills 2003). All union renewal efforts show tensions between building participation to include and represent a diverse a set of interests, and needing to prioritize some interests over others in order to coordinate union activity effectively. These tensions further help explain why the responses of unions have been so ineffective over the past decade.

Conclusions

We are by no means the first authors to argue that unions are facing seemingly insurmountable challenges (see, *inter alia*, Gospel 2005; Howell 2005; Metcalf 2005; Willman 2005). Our analysis attempts to understand the sources of power available to unions, and why changes over the past 30 years or so have made it difficult for unions to re-establish both legitimacy and coercive power. Notwithstanding the historical successes of unions in improving working conditions and living standards, the continuing impact of the union 'sword of justice' (Flanders 1970; Metcalf *et al.* 2001) in bringing fairness to the labour market, and the conventions that enshrine the rights of workers to organize in international law, we see little prospect for a revival in union fortunes. Our analysis rests on four factors. First, the environment has remained inhospitable: although unemployment fell, considerable hidden unemployment remained, evidenced by the rising rate of economic inactivity amongst working age men, and is likely to rise again. Low inflation and strong real wage growth meant workers had little incentive to unionize. Technological change and increasing global trade ended the ability of most unions to gain coercive power through the control of labour markets, as technology removed routine but skilled jobs and increasing trade intensified product market competition. Despite the election of New Labour in 1997, the main aspects of the Conservative anti-union legislation, particularly restrictions on the right to strike, remained. New Labour also did little to revive the legitimacy power of trade unions, arguing that while 'partnership' between employers and workforce was desirable, unions were not necessary for partnership. Further, they took little action to impel employers towards a partnership approach.

Second, long run social changes, linked to the increasingly heterogeneous experience of work, the break-up of occupational communities and the privatization of social life have made it harder for unions to construct and articulate collective interests. Third, the ideological resources available to unions have diminished, as neo-liberal ideas became part of the conventional wisdom of policy makers and socialist ideologies became discredited and seen as impractical. Finally, despite extensive experiments with a number of strategies for renewal, unions have not succeeded in creating new forms of unionism adapted to the changed economic, social and political circumstances. The way in which unions organize themselves, particularly the tensions between encouraging participation and coordination, control and resource allocation in an environment where union resources are diminishing, is a barrier to the success of these experiments.

Of course, it is impossible to foresee the full consequences of the economic crisis that erupted in 2008 and it seems probable that some of the aspects of the wider economic context are likely to change profoundly. And despite difficulties, around one in three British workers are still members of unions. But we see no immediate reason to imagine that working people are likely to turn to trade unions to develop collective responses. Nor do we feel it likely that the underlying trends of increasingly competitive markets, a heterogeneous labour force, and fundamental tensions within the responses developed by unions are likely to reverse any time soon. Thus, while there clearly remains an important role for unions in some workplaces, we see little reason to imagine that there will be a resurgence of union power in the current context. In short, while Hyman (1999) is theoretically optimistic about the opportunities for unions to 'reimagine' collective interests that can rebuild forms of solidarity, we see little basis for such optimism in practice; such renewal would take a leap of imagination that is not, in our view, currently evident within the British trade union movement. Thus, opportunities to build legitimacy in the eyes of workers, employers and the state will remain severely constrained.

References

Addison, J., Bailey, R. and Siebert, S. 2006: The impact of deunionisation on earnings dispersion revisited. *Research in Labor Economics*, vol. 26, 337–364.

Autor, D., Levy, F. and Murnane, R. 2003: The skill content of recent technical change: an empirical investigation. *Quarterly Journal of Economics*, 118 (1), 273–333.

Bach, S. and Winchester, D. 1994: Opting out of pay devolution? The prospects for local pay bargaining in UK public services. *British Journal of Industrial Relations*, 32 (2), 263–282.

Badigannavar, V. and Kelly, J. 2005: Why are some organising campaigns more successful than others? *British Journal of Industrial Relations*, 43 (3), 513–535.

Bain, G.S. and Elsheikh, F. 1976: *Union Growth and the Business Cycle*. Oxford: Blackwell.

Bain, G.S. and Price, R. 1980: *Profiles of Union Growth*. Oxford: Oxford University Press.

Beaumont, P. and Harris, R. 1990: Union recruitment and organizing attempts in Britain in the 1980s. *Industrial Relations Journal*, 21 (4), 274–286.

Blanchflower, D.G. 2007: International patterns of union membership. *British Journal of Industrial Relations*, 45 (1), 1–28.

Blanchflower, D. and Bryson, A. 2004: Union relative wage effects in the United States and the United Kingdom. *Proceedings of the 56th Annual Meeting of the Industrial Relations Research Association*, 133–140.

Booth, A. 1995: *The Economics of the Trade Union*. Cambridge: Cambridge University Press.

Bronfenbrenner, K., Friedman, S., Hurd, R.W., Oswald, R.A. and Seeber, R.L. 1998: *Organizing to Win: New Research on Union Strategies*. Ithaca, New York: ILR Cornell University Press.

Brown, W. 2000: Putting partnership into practice in Britain. *British Journal of Industrial Relations*, 38:2.

Brown, W., Deakin, S. and Ryan, P. 1997: The effects of British industrial relations legislation 1979–97. *National Institute Economic Review*, 161 (April), 69–83.

Brown, W., Deakin, S., Nash, D. and Oxenbridge, S. 2000: The employment contract: from collective procedures to individual rights. *British Journal of Industrial Relations*, 38:4.

Card, D., Lemieux, T. and Riddell, W.C. 2003: Unionization and wage inequality: a comparative study of the US, the UK and Canada. NBER Working Paper 9473, Boston: NBER.

Charlwood, A. 2002: Why do non-union employees want to unionize? *British Journal of Industrial Relations*, 40 (3), 463–492.

Charlwood, A. 2004: Influences on trade union organising effectiveness. *British Journal of Industrial Relations*, 42 (1), 69–94.

Charlwood, A. 2007: The de-collectivization of pay determination in British establishments 1990–1998: incidents, determinants and impact. *Industrial Relations Journal*, 38 (1), 33–50.

Charlwood, A. and Metcalf, D. 2005: Appendix: union membership. In Metcalf, D. and Fernie, S. (eds) *British Unions: Resurgence or Perdition?* London: Routledge, pp. 231–239.

Cronin, J. 1984: *Labour and Society in Britain 1918–1979*. London: Batsford.

Disney, R. and Carruth, A. 1988: Where have two million trade union members gone? *Economica*, 55 (1), 1–19.

Dorey, P. 1995: *British Politics Since 1945*. Oxford: Blackwell.

Ebbinghaus, B. and Visser, J. 1999: When institutions matter: union growth and decline in Western Europe. *European Sociological Review*, 15 (2), 135–158.

Edwards, P. and Wajcman, J. 2005: *The Politics of Working Life*. Oxford: Oxford University Press.

Faggio, G. and Nickell, S. 2003: The rise of inactivity among adult men. In Dickens, R., Gregg, P. and Wadsworth, J. (eds) *The Labour Market under New Labour: The State of Working Britain II*. London: Palgrave Macmillan.

Fairbrother, P. 2000: *Trade Unions at the Crossroads*. London: Mansell.

Flanders, A. 1970: *Management and Unions: The Theory and Reform of Industrial Relations*. London: Faber.

Fox, A. 1971: *A Sociology of Work in Industry*. London: Macmillan.

Freeman R. 1995: Are your wages set in Beijing? *The Journal of Economic Perspectives*, 9 (3), 15–32.

French, J.R.P. and Raven, B. 1968: The bases of social power. In Cartwright, D. and Zander, A. (eds) *Group Dynamics*. New York: Harper and Row, pp. 259–269.

Gall, G. 2003: Employer opposition to union recognition. In Gall, G. (ed.) *Union Organizing: Campaigning for Trade Union Recognition*. London: Routledge.

Gall, G. 2004: Trade union recognition in Britain 1995–2002: turning a corner? *Industrial Relations Journal*, 35 (3), 249–270.

Gall, G. 2006 (ed.): *Union Recognition: Organising and Bargaining Outcomes*. London: Routledge.

Gall, G. 2007: Trade union recognition in Britain: an emerging crisis for trade unions? *Economic and Industrial Democracy*, 28 (1), 7–109.

Gamble, A. 1994: *The Free Economy and the Strong State: The Politics of Thatcherism*. London: Macmillan.

Goos, M. and Manning, A. 2007: Lousy and lovely jobs: polarization of work in Britain. *Review of Economics and Statistics*, 89 (1), 118–133.

Gospel, H. 2005: Markets, firms and unions: a historical-institutionalist perspective on the future of unions in Britain. In Fernie, S. and Metcalf, D. (eds) *Trade Unions: Resurgence or Demise?* London: Routledge.

Haynes, P. and Allen, M. 2001: Partnership as union strategy: a preliminary evaluation. *Employee Relations*, 23 (2), 164–187.

Heery, E. 1998: The re-launch of the Trades Union Congress. *British Journal of Industrial Relations*, 36 (3), 339–350.

Heery, E. 2002: Partnership versus organising: alternative futures for British trade unionism. *Industrial Relations Journal*, 33 (1), 20–35.

Heery, E. and Simms, M. 2003: *Bargain or Bust? Employer Responses to Union Organising*. New Unionism Pamphlet. Trades Union Congress, London.

Heery, E., Delbridge, R., Simms, M., Salmon, J. and Simpson, D. 2003: Organising for renewal: a case study of the TUC's Organising Academy. In Cornfield, D. and McCammon, H. (eds) *Labor Revitalization. Research in the Sociology of Work*. New York, JAI Press.

Hicks, S., Lindsay, C., Livesey, D., Barford, N. and Williams, R. 2005: *Public Sector Employment*. London: Office for National Statistics.

Holgate, J. 2006: Union recognition in Asian workplaces: springboard to further organising and recognition campaigns? In Gall, G. (ed.) *Union Recognition: Organising and Bargaining Outcomes*. Routledge, pp. 134–150.

Howell, C. 2004: Is there a third way in industrial relations? *British Journal of Industrial Relations*, 42 (1), 1–22.

Howell, C. 2005: *Trade Unions and the State: The Construction of Industrial Relations in Britain 1890–2000*. Princeton: Princeton University Press.

Hyman, R. 1999: Imagined solidarities: can trade unions resist globalisation? In Leisink, P. (ed.) *Globalization and Labour Relations*. Cheltenham: Edward Elgar.

Hyman, R. 2001: *Understanding European Trade Unionism: Between Market, Class and Society*. London: Sage.

Keegan, W. 1984: *Mrs Thatcher's Economic Experiment*. London: Allen Lane.

Kelly, J. 1996: Union militancy and social partnership. In Ackers, P., Smith, C. and Smith, P. (eds) *The New Workplace and Trade Unionism*. London: Routledge, pp. 77–109.

Kelly, J. 1998: *Rethinking Industrial Relations: Mobilization, Collectivism and Long Waves*. London: Routledge.

Kelly, J. 2004: Social partnership agreements in Britain: Labor cooperation and compliance. *Industrial Relations*, 43 (1), 267–292.

Kelly, J. and Heery, E. 1989: Full-time officer and trade union recruitment. *British Journal of Industrial Relations*, 27 (2), 196–213.

Kersley, B., Bryson, A., Forth, J., Alpin, C. and Bewley, H. 2006: *Inside the Workplace: Findings from the 2004 Workplace Employment Relations Survey*. London: Routledge.

Kochan, T. and Osterman, P. 1994: *The Mutual Gains Enterprise: Forging a Winning Partnership among Labor, Management and Government*. Boston, MA: Harvard Business School Press.

Ludlum, S. and Taylor, A. 2003: The political representation of labour in Britain. *British Journal of Industrial Relations*, 41 (4), 727–749.

Machin, S. 2001: The labour market consequences of technological and structural change. *Oxford Bulletin of Economics and Statistics*, 63 (5), 753–766.

Marshall, A. 1910: *Principles of Economics*. Cambridge: Cambridge University Press.

McIlroy, J. 1995: *Trade Unions in Britain Today*. Manchester: Manchester University Press.

Mercer, S. and Notley, R. 2008: *Trade Union Membership 2007*. London: National Statistics.

Metcalf, D. 1991: British unions: dissolution or resurgence? *Oxford Review of Economic Policy*, 7 (1), 18–32.

Metcalf, D. 2005: Trade unions: resurgence or perdition? An economic analysis. In Fernie, S. and Metcalf, D. (eds) *Trade Unions: Resurgence or Demise?* London: Routledge.

Metcalf, D., Hansen, K. and Charlwood, A. 2001: Unions and the sword of justice: unions and pay systems, pay inequality, pay discrimination and low pay. *National Institute Economic Review*, 176, 61–75.

Minkin, L. 1991: *The Contentious Alliance: Trade Unions and the Labour Party*. Edinburgh: Edinburgh University Press.

Oxenbridge, S. and Brown, W. 2002: The two faces of partnership? An assessment of partnership and co-operative employer/trade union relationships. *Employee Relations*, 24 (3), 262–276.

Oxenbridge, S. and Brown, W. 2004: Achieving a new equilibrium? The stability of co-operative employer-union relationships. *Industrial Relations Journal*, 35 (5), 388–402.

Phelps Brown, E.H. 1990: The counter-revolution of our time. *Industrial Relations*, 29 (1), 1–14.

Putnam, R. 2000: *Bowling Alone*. New York: Simon Schuster.

Simms, M. 2006: The transition from organizing to recognition: a case study. In Gall, G. (ed.) *Union Recognition: Organising and Bargaining Outcomes*. London: Routledge, pp. 167–180.

Simms, M. 2007a: Interest formation in greenfield organising campaigns. *Industrial Relations Journal*, 38 (5), 434–454.

Simms, M. 2007b: Managed activism: two union organising campaigns in the not-for-profit sector. *Industrial Relations Journal*, 38 (2), 119–135.

Statistics Commission 2007: Foreign workers in the UK, a briefing note. Downloaded from: http://www.statscom.org.uk/C_1238.aspx

Stuart, M. and Martinez Lucio, M. (eds) 2005: *Partnership and Modernization in Employment Relations*. London: Routledge.

Terry, M.A. 2003: Can partnership reverse the decline of British trade unions. *Work, Employment and Society*, 17 (3), 459–472.

Undy, R. 2008: *Trade Union Merger Strategies: Purpose, Process and Performance*. Oxford: Oxford University Press.

Undy, R., Ellis, V., McCarthy, W.E.J. and Halmos, A.M. 1981: *Change in Trade Unions*. London: Hutchinson.

Visser, J. 2006: Union membership statistics in 24 countries. *Monthly Labor Review*, 129 (1), 38–49.

Waddington, J. and Whiston, C. 1997: Why do people join unions in a period of membership decline? *British Journal of Industrial Relations*, 35 (4), 515–546.

Webb, S. and Webb, B. 1920: *The History of Trade Unionism*. London: Longman.

Willman, P. 2004: Structuring union: the administrative rationality of collective action. In Kelly, J. and Willman, P. (eds) *Union Organisation and Activity*. London: Routledge.

Willman, P. 2005: Circling the wagons: endogeneity in union decline. In Fernie, S. and Metcalf, D. (eds) *Trade Unions: Resurgence or Demise?* London: Routledge.

Wills, J. 2003: Organizing in transport and travel: learning lessons from TSSA's Seacat campaign. In Gall, G. (ed.) *Union Organizing: Campaigning for Trade Union Recognition.* London: Routledge, pp. 133–152.

Wills, J. 2005: The geography of union organising in the low-paid service industries in the UK: lessons from the T&G's campaign to unionise the Dorchester Hotel, London. *Andipode*, 37 (1), 139–159.

SECTION THREE

CONTEXTS

7

PUBLIC SECTOR INDUSTRIAL RELATIONS: THE CHALLENGE OF MODERNIZATION

STEPHEN BACH

Introduction

For more than a quarter of a century Britain has been in the vanguard of public sector reform intended to boost efficiency and effectiveness. Starting in 1979, when Mrs Thatcher's Conservative government was elected on a mandate to reduce public expenditure and shrink the state, the size and scope of the public sector were reduced. Established patterns of public service industrial relations were destabilized as trade union power diminished but attempts to embed managerialism and marketization within core public services had a more limited impact. Inheriting this uneven legacy, successive Labour governments repositioned these reforms and attempted to steer a 'third way' in their philosophy and delivery of public services (Giddens 2000). They acknowledged the limitations of paternalistic state provision, favoured by previous Labour governments, and identified public service modernization as pivotal in responding to the competitive challenge of globalization.

Measures have been taken to adapt the managerial and market-based model of Conservative governments to develop a fairer and more user-centred public sector. The Labour government used many of the same managerial recipes as their predecessors, but recalibrated them, emphasizing collaboration as much as competition and highlighting the importance of service quality alongside cost minimization. Nonetheless, by 1999, Prime Minister Tony Blair expressed frustration at public sector resistance to change, contrasting the dynamism of the private sector with the difficulties of 'getting change in the public sector ... I bear the scars on my back after two years in government' (Blair 1999).

This chapter examines the role of the public sector as an employer and the consequences of the modernization agenda. It traces the process of public service reform over recent decades before examining the implications for public sector employment and pay determination. It concludes by drawing out the consequences of the modernization agenda and examines the apparent paradox that since 1997, the public sector has grown in terms of staff numbers and their earnings, but these changes have been accompanied by workforce dissatisfaction with the reform agenda. This is attributed to the prominence of a centralized and directive target regime that has disempowered the public sector workforce.

The State as Employer

Despite more than two decades of reform many of the characteristics of public service employment still derive from the unique role of the state as employer. The need for governments to be sensitive to their electoral constituency and to reconcile the interests of multiple stakeholders (or 'political contingency' in Ferner's term (1988)) remains a prominent conditioning feature. The state has also continued to use its authority to be a 'model employer' highlighting effective employment relations practice (Fredman and Morris 1989). What is considered 'best practice' has changed, influenced by trends in employment relations and by the political priorities of the government. In the 1980s, the Conservative government promoted anti-unionism by abolishing collective bargaining machinery for teachers and instructing 4000 workers at GCHQ (Government Communications Headquarters) that they could no longer retain their trade union membership. By contrast, after 1997, the Labour government promoted forms of social partnership with trade unions and highlighted the importance of gender and race equality.

The state is also accountable for public expenditure that is derived mainly from taxation. Comparative measures of public spending as a proportion of GDP vary considerably and highlight the UK's designation as a *liberal market economy* with a relatively restricted state sector (Hall and Soskice 2001). The range runs from 26% in Australia to 36% in the USA and around 54% in France and Sweden; the comparable figure for the UK is 42% (cited in Julius 2008). A substantial proportion of public expenditure is accounted for by salary costs and citizens expect transparency and accountability in the use of public funds. This encouraged the development of standardized employment practices to demonstrate that personnel practice was based on objective criteria rather than patronage. Managerial authority was traditionally codified in detailed personnel rules, but this led to concerns that public sector employment rules were inflexible and stifled innovation. The emergence of a 'new public management' (Hood 1991) did not remove the public expectation that the state should be accountable as an employer, but it shifted the forms of accountability from adhering to standardized process-orientated rules towards an emphasis on accountability for results.

Finally, the distinctive role of the state and the character of employment relations are shaped by the composition of the workforce which differs significantly from the private sector. As Table 7.1 indicates, the state employs a high proportion of women in services such as education, health and social services and in the UK 65% of employees are women compared to 41% in the private sector. These gender characteristics also contribute to high levels of part-time working in the sector. One consequence is that public sector employers have been more

Table 7.1   Proportions employed within the UK public and private sectors by key characteristic in 2006 (%)

	Public	Private
Men	34.8	58.9
Women	65.2	41.1
Age: 18–24	5.8	13.8
Age: 50+	29.8	26.0
Ethnicity: white	92.2	91.9
Ethnicity: non-white	7.8	8.1
Full-time	70.7	75.5
Part-time	29.3	24.5
Job tenure more than 10 years (all ages)	40.2	27.9
Trade union member	59.5	15.8
Professional occupations	22.5	10.3
Degree level or equivalent	32.4	19.2

Source: Millard and Machin (2007)

receptive to equal employment policies, but also more vulnerable to equal pay claims, pursued with assistance from public sector trade unions and law firms (see Colling; Liff and Dean, both this volume). The workforce also contains a high proportion of professional staff reflected in levels of educational attainment. The employment relations challenge of managing professions, often characterized as resistant to change, has been one of the key drivers of reform. The public sector workforce is also ageing rapidly with many countries confronting a looming retirement wave. This will not only lead to a loss of experienced staff, but it has also directed attention at the relatively generous and growing burden that public sector pensions places on public expenditure (OECD 2007). Finally, as Table 7.1 indicates, the workforce is highly unionized, density is three times the level of the private sector and the gap has widened over the last two decades. Overall, although new public management reforms have been premised on the assumption that employment relations practices used in the private sector can be applied with the same outcomes in the public services, the distinctive features of state employment caution against such an interpretation (Bordogna 2008).

Public sector reform and the model employer tradition

From 1945 onwards, public sector employment in health, education and social services grew rapidly as part of the development of the welfare state. For Fredman and Morris (1989) the state was a 'model employer' setting an example to the private sector by endorsing principles of fairness, involvement and equity in its treatment of its workforce. These principles were associated with the encouragement of trade union membership, support for centralized systems of collective bargaining and other forms of workforce participation which encouraged the expression and resolution of grievances. Repeated Labour government attempts to bear down on wage inflation during the 1970s disproportionately impacted on the living standards of public sector workers and led to increased strike action. Widespread disruption of public services during the 1978–79 'winter of discontent' created public antipathy towards the trade union movement and the Labour government and led to a lengthy period of Conservative government (Winchester 1983). After 1979, Conservative governments departed radically from this tradition for a mixture of ideological and economic reasons.

The Conservative legacy

The Conservative government of Mrs Thatcher was elected on a wave of anti-union sentiment and began a programme of public sector reform that continued until 1997. The main aim was to reduce the size of the state sector and embed market principles within the remaining core public services. Thatcherism had two distinctive 'market' and 'managerial' strands (Jenkins 2007). The first ideological element increased the role of the private sector and market principles in public service delivery, and attacked collective non-market institutions, including the trade unions and the professions. Consequent reluctance to invest in public services exacerbated staff shortages and led to a questioning of the unspoken assumption that public expenditure automatically entailed service delivery by the state (Glennerster 2004: 238). Instead the Conservative government started to encourage more diverse service provision mainly from the private sector but also from the voluntary sector.

The most visible component of this agenda was a far-reaching programme of privatization. Nationalized industries and utilities such as gas, water and electricity were privatized on a scale not seen elsewhere in Europe, undermining trade union influence in these sectors and the broader economy (Arrowsmith, this volume; Pendleton 1997). The remaining public services were subject to processes of market testing. The initial emphasis on cleaning and refuse collection was extended to incorporate white-collar 'back-office' functions such as IT and payroll services. Regardless of whether a service was retained in-house or outsourced, this policy led to substantial reductions in the workforce and accompanying payroll savings. Women were particularly hard hit and their employment tended to decline more than men's, especially as job losses were greatest amongst part-time workers (Escott and Whitfield 1995). Managers had an incentive to alter working practices, erode national terms and conditions and enhance the monitoring of service standards. Government pressure to accept the lowest cost tender also led to serious concerns about service standards (Colling 1999). By contrast, professional groups such as doctors challenged the government's market-style reforms and ensured they were implemented in modified forms which only partially undermined their control over the organization of work (Kirkpatrick *et al.* 2005).

The second strand of Thatcherism was managerial and involved an unprecedented degree of centralized control and intervention. Paradoxically, it was only by strengthening the role of the state that Mrs Thatcher could impose her vision of a market society, reinforcing the hand of management to implement reforms. Organizational change contributed to this process with the establishment of autonomous, commercially orientated enterprises, exemplified by the establishment of civil service agencies, NHS trusts and grant-maintained schools. The influence of senior managers was strengthened and formal responsibility to shape human resource management practice increased, placing pressure on professional staff to deliver more customer-focused services. In practice, however, managerial authority remained constrained by frequent political intervention and the resistance of highly organized professional groups. Conservative governments therefore made large strides in altering the organizational and managerial principles governing the sector, but it remained an unfinished revolution, in terms of the transformation of employment practices.

Labour government modernization   At the end of this period, lack of investment was reflected in decaying infrastructure and widespread staff shortages amongst professional groups such as nurses, teachers and social workers. The Labour government elected in 1997 embarked upon a modernization agenda stemming from the third way philosophy developed by Giddens (2000). At its core was an assumption that intensifying global competition required effective public services to enhance national competitiveness. Modernization entailed an active but altered role for the state. Intervention was required to invest in skills to enable individuals to thrive (see Lloyd *et al.*, this volume) and to develop community cohesion. But its broader role shifted to one of regulation rather than direct provision, defining and monitoring standards to be met by a plurality of service providers and employers.

Unprecedented investment in public services from 2000 was underpinned by a buoyant economy and public concern at the state of public services. Following an initial two year period in which the preceding government's spending restrictions were retained, investment in the NHS increased in real terms by nearly 90% to 2007 and the equivalent in education and transport was 60% (HM Treasury 2007a). In health, expenditure increased from £40 billion to £100 billion up to 1997 (HM Treasury 2008a). These increases permitted rapid expansion of the workforce but by 2006–07 rapidly deteriorating economic circumstances and a concern about the effectiveness of increased investment led the government to develop far less generous public spending commitments for the period 2008–11, inevitably placing downward pressure on public sector pay settlements.

The narrow efficiency objectives prioritized by previous governments were extended by the modernization agenda. The Labour government adapted the market and managerial strands and added a third strand, 'mobilization', intended to engage users, professionals and communities in service improvements. These policy concerns became particularly prominent in recent years as continued marketization fostered a diverse range of private and third sector providers. This was based on the belief that competition would drive up standards and encourage innovation but this was rooted more in pragmatic than ideological support for the private sector. Such distinctions though failed to convince the trade union movement, provoking bitter criticism of the government's 'creeping privatization' agenda (Whitfield 2006).

One of the most controversial forms of private sector involvement has been the Private Finance Initiative (PFI) in which a private consortium is contracted by the state, or a state agency, to finance, build and operate public service facilities (e.g. new hospitals, roads, prisons, or schools) in exchange for an agreed annual payment for the duration of the contract (usually 25–35 years). PFI became the dominant method of procuring major new assets in the public sector and in 2008 the Treasury was tracking 628 signed PFI deals with a capital value of £58.6 billion; virtually all new hospitals have been procured under PFI and school refurbishment is dominated by PFI schemes (HM Treasury 2008b).

Public service trade unions opposed PFI as a form of privatization, arguing that it provided poor value for money and benefited shareholders rather than service users. The Treasury's intention was to transfer the risk of construction delays and cost escalation to the private sector, but this aspiration became even less likely as PFI deals faltered during the credit crunch. Employees transferring from the public to the private sector under such deals have their employment contracts legally protected by the Transfer of Undertakings (Protection of Employment) Regulations (TUPE) but unions argued strongly that new staff should have the same pay and conditions as the protected employees to avoid the creation of a 'two-tier' workforce. Trade unions have also been concerned that TUPE regulations do not protect transferred workers' advantageous public sector pensions (Bach and Givan 2005).

Government sensitivity to charges that they were privatizing public services, effective union mobilization on the two-tier workforce, and the government's desire to stifle opposition to PFI led to a series of concessions on pay and pensions. New sector-specific arrangements specified that new recruits are entitled to 'terms and conditions no less favourable' than those of transferred local government and health service staff. Terms and conditions for outsourced workers in health were boosted following conclusion of the new pay system (*Agenda for Change*), when the government required contractors to apply those terms and conditions across outsourced contracts. Funding difficulties has often complicated implementation at local level (Bewley 2006; Unison 2008) but trade unions have had some success in extending public sector wage agreements to the private sector. The irony for unions, however, is that employment protection policies such as TUPE provide some reassurance to transferred staff, facilitating the expansion of the private and third sector in the public domain (Julius 2008: 38–39). The upshot is that a third of all public services are delivered by the private and third sectors and the UK spends a larger share of its GDP on outsourced services than any OECD country except Sweden and Australia (ibid.).

Managerial innovation was also enthusiastically continued by the Labour government which intensified the focus on performance management. National targets were emphasized especially in health and education and failure to attain key targets usually led to top managers being removed from their posts. In hospitals key clinical targets related to maximum waiting times in accident and emergency departments (4 hours), maximum waiting times for admission for elective surgery and ambulance response times. The use of targets has proved contentious but has the benefit of indicating the commitment of politicians to achieving results in an accountable manner (Chapman 2007). The government suggested that targets have raised performance and these benefits are reflected in large reductions in NHS waiting times (Wanless *et al.* 2007). Public service professionals have grudgingly acknowledged that top-down performance management has stimulated change that had not been forthcoming before (Levenson *et al.* 2008).

Doubts, however, have been expressed about the distortions and perverse incentives introduced by targets (Givan 2005; Flanagan 2008). Chapman (2007: 122) notes that they encourage staff to concentrate on satisfying the requirements of central government, rather than meeting the needs of service users. This difficulty is exacerbated because the workforce has not been sufficiently involved in establishing targets and the Audit Commission (2002: 22) pinpointed the paperwork associated with targets as the most important reason why public sector workers left their jobs. Lack of staff involvement encourages 'gaming' because of the financial and managerial consequences that arise from failure. For example, NHS staff redesignated corridors as 'pre-admission units' to circumvent waiting time targets for accident and emergency care (Public Administration Select Committee 2003). In many cases there have been significant discrepancies between officially reported levels of performance and the lower levels of service experienced by patients (Bevan and Hood 2006: 528–529). More fundamentally public service professionals have seen targets as signalling a lack of trust in their judgment and an attempt to strengthen the role of managers, as the custodians of improvement at organizational level.

The government increasingly acknowledged the validity of these criticisms: 'persisting with too many top-down targets can be counterproductive; we know services must value professionals if we are to foster innovation and excellence' (Cabinet Office 2008: 11). Consequently, more emphasis has been placed on mobilizing staff, service users and providers across organizational boundaries to deliver 'joined up' government. Labour governments since 1997 have recognized the importance of the workforce. They have sought to reinvent the model employer tradition, promoting diversity, to ensure that the workforce is more attuned to the needs of service users (Corby 2007). This support was qualified, however, by concerns that the workforce remained insufficiently committed to developing user-centred services. In principle the government was willing to view public sector workers as altruistic 'knights' rather than self-serving 'knaves' (see Le Grand 2003) but, in practice, many prescriptive employment practices (e.g. new contracts for consultant medical staff) signalled a lack of trust in public service professionals, contributing to a growing sense of unease with the modernization agenda (Gleeson and Knights 2006; Lawson 2007).

Government therefore sought to re-engage the public service workforce, using the language of 'new professionalism' (Cabinet Office 2008). This term is designed to acknowledge the ethos and contribution of a wide range of staff, extending beyond the traditional professions, but is also intended to link rewards to 'excellence'. These changes are connected to more user-centred services in which users have been provided with a range of information online, frequently compiled into league tables, intended to enhance choice and improve service delivery. The mobilization of users is being extended through an emphasis on personalization, with stronger one to one support developed for those who need most targeted assistance at school or in the community. In social care, personal budgets have been piloted enabling individuals to have greater influence over service provision. These changes have substantial implications for work organization as organizational boundaries are redrawn. In the civil service, for example, this led to the creation of Jobcentre Plus; a one stop shop for benefit recipients establishing a single gateway to a range of services. Usually accessible by telephone or online, such a service not only requires different skill sets, with employees having to deal with a wide range of queries, but it has often been provided by call centres, in a new type of working environment. Developing these forms of service delivery has resulted in staff transfers across organizational boundaries, for example between health and social care, with attendant complications in terms of differing employment conditions and occupational cultures.

Public Sector Employment

Public sector employment has fluctuated in response to these organizational and managerial reforms. In 1981, 29% of employees worked in the public sector and this fell sharply during the 1980s and continued to decline in the 1990s (Pearson 1994). As Table 7.2 indicates, at the end of the 1990s the Labour government started to increase public expenditure substantially and this resulted in an increase in public employment, peaking at just over 20% of the workforce in 2005 before declining fractionally to employ just under 5.8 million employees in 2008 (Hicks and Lindsey 2005; ONS 2008). It is conventional to differentiate between three main subsectors (Table 7.2).

First, 2.5 million staff are employed by central government. This category includes all administrative departments of government and non-departmental

Table 7.2   UK public sector employment by sector; headcount (000s)

	Central government	Local government	Total general government	Total public corporations	Total public sector	of which: civil service
1991	2306	3072	5378	600	5978	589
1993	2274	2788	5062	531	5593	598
1995	2156	2758	4914	454	5368	552
1997	2079	2728	4807	368	5175	513
1999	2115	2735	4850	352	5202	504
2001	2232	2771	5003	373	5376	522
2003	2434	2832	5266	373	5639	560
2005	2564	2923	5487	367	5854	570
2007	2505	2941	5446	339	5785	539

Source: Hicks and Lindsay (2005); ONS (2008).

public bodies (NDPBs). The latter are organizations which have a role in national government, but operate at arm's length from ministers. The largest component of central government is the NHS and it also includes most of the civil service and HM Forces. Second, 2.9 million staff are employed by local authorities covering a specific geographical location. These are organizations with elected leaders who have the power to raise funds through charges and local taxes and have some power to control their own affairs, within a framework established by central government. They are responsible for the provision of school education (which comprises the largest component of their workforce); social services; police; fire and other local services such as libraries and refuse collection. Third, around 330 000 staff are employed in public corporations controlled by government, which nevertheless have substantial freedom to conduct their activities along commercial lines. Royal Mail is the most significant employer in this category. Finally, because civil servants can be classified to central government or public corporations, they are shown as a separate category in Table 7.2.

Aggregate employment data disguise considerable variation in relative growth in employment since 1997. The most concentrated growth has been in health, education and amongst the police (see Table 7.3). All are services with a high political profile, which had previously confronted staff shortages and which were central to the Labour government's commitment to deliver world class public services. The NHS has been a key beneficiary and targeted increases in medical and nursing staff encouraged the migration of health professionals to the UK.

A second important change in the public sector workforce relates to its composition, partly as a consequence of the modernization agenda mentioned above. Across the public services, the role of professionals as the dominant service provider has been supplemented by the establishment of new practitioner roles and enhanced responsibilities of existing jobs such as health care assistants. Within schools, there has been a huge increase in the number of teaching assistants (Table 7.3) and also a variety of new roles to support pupils such as learning mentors. Similar developments have occurred in the police service with a prominent role assigned to a growing cadre of civilian Community Police Support Officers (Gash 2008). There is also the prospect in social care of substantial growth in personal assistants, a casualized workforce that may be outside the scope of public sector employment regulation (Yeandle and Stiell 2007).

Finally, there has been much analysis of the quality of public service employment. Critics of the modernization agenda have suggested that the use of targets in conjunction with more flexible and Taylorist forms of work organization have eroded professional influence and been used to intensify work, leading to characterizations of 'New' Labour's restructuring as 'hard labour' (Law and Mooney 2007). Staff surveys indicate workforce concerns about work pressures and difficulties in reconciling work and home life. Of the 155 000 staff who responded to the 2007 NHS staff survey, more than four in ten felt that they could not meet all the conflicting demands on their time at work (42%) or did not have time to carry out all their work (47%). These figures were unchanged in 2005 and 2006 despite increased NHS staff levels (Healthcare Commission 2008). In a smaller

Table 7.3 UK public sector workforce in the UK headcount

	1997	2006	% change
1997–2006			
National Health Service	1 190 000	1 522 000	+28%
Of which:			
Doctors (England)	89 619	126 251	+41%
Nurses (England)	318 856	398 335	+25%
Education	1 131 000	1 397 000	+24%
Of which:			
Teachers (England & Wales)	437 980	476 940	+9%
Teaching assistants (England)	68 074	199 331	+193%
Police	230 000	275 000	+20%
Public administration	1 139 000	1 245 000	+9%
Of which:			
Civil service	516 000	558 000	+8%
Other public sector	708 000	733 000	+4%
HM Forces	220 000	204 000	–7%
Other health and social work	436 000	385 000	–12%
Construction	124 000	65 000	–48%
All public sector	**5 178 000**	**5 826 000**	**+13%**

Source: Various cited in IFS (2008), page 161.

survey of senior civil servants, only 48% agreed that they were able to strike the right balance between work and home life, a result that compared unfavourably with respondents from other organizations (ORC International 2006). Despite the wider availability of flexible working than in the private sector (Bach *et al.* 2009), staff are not satisfied with their work–life balance. Consequently, some professional staff such as nurses and social workers have abandoned permanent employment for the increased flexibility and discretion available as agency workers (de Rutyer *et al.* 2008; Tailby 2005).

Reforms of Pay Determination

Reforms of pay determination have been at the core of the government's modernization agenda, intended to address gender inequality, strengthen the link with performance and encourage greater flexibility (White and Hatchett 2003). In comparison with trade union exclusion during the period of Conservative government, traditional collective bargaining was reinvented as a less adversarial 'social partnership', designed to reach accord on service redesign and the more flexible utilization of labour. To achieve these strategic goals from around 2000 there has been a trend towards long-term (usually three year) pay deals intended to spread the cost and difficulties associated with complex new pay systems. More recently long-term pay deals are being sought to avoid industrial action in the public sector, which is much more prevalent than in the private sector, until after the general election expected in 2010 (IDS 2008a).

The government was also influenced by the Conservative legacy of decentralized pay determination in which managerial reform encouraged employers to link pay arrangements to their local circumstances. Workplace employment relations survey data indicates a dramatic increase from 36% in 1990 to 59% in 1998 in the proportion of employee relations managers responsible for pay and conditions. Formal responsibility for pay and conditions, however, did not always translate into local managerial authority over decision making. There were significant variations between subsectors with decentralization progressing furthest in education (Kirkpatrick and Hoque 2005). Overall, in 2004, 92% of local public sector managers had to follow policy on pay rates set elsewhere in the organization (Bach *et al.* 2009). The most marked retreat from local pay bargaining occurred in the NHS in the 1990s. Managerial reluctance to antagonize the workforce in a context of forceful union opposition, alongside limited managerial skills and severe financial constraints stymied local pay (Bach and Winchester 1994). When delegated pay determination occurred, as in the civil service, wide pay disparities appeared between civil servants undertaking the same work and on the same pay grade, but who worked in different departments (IDS 2007).

Across the public services forms of pay decentralization exposed the extent to which pay systems did not comply with equal pay legislation and in conjunction with the Labour government's predilection for centralized control resulted in less fervent support for decentralization. Employers, however, opposed a return to prescriptive national agreements and demanded greater flexibility within integrated national pay systems. An important dimension of pay modernization has been the expansion of the system of independent pay review to address staff shortages and high workloads, often utilizing forms of social partnership, while retaining strong indirect control over pay.

Pay review bodies

The pay review body system covers 1.8 million employees with an annual paybill in excess of £56 billion (OME 2008). Separate bodies exist for each professional group, including doctors and dentists, nurses, senior civil servants and judges, teachers and the armed forces. All of the review bodies have a small group of members appointed by the government and are serviced by an independent civil service secretariat. Each year they invite written and oral evidence from interested parties, visit workplaces to meet managers and employees, and commission their own research. On this basis they make recommendations on pay increases – and other matters identified in their terms of reference – which are not binding on the government.

The extension of the pay review system has attracted little comment but it marks an important departure from previous Labour governments' ambivalent attitude towards independent pay review, which undoubtedly reflected trade union concerns about the loss of formal bargaining rights. In 2001 a pay review body for the prison service was established; the first review body ever created by a Labour government. The review body for nurses was extended to cover all NHS staff except doctors, dentists and top managers and renamed the NHS Pay Review Body (NHSPRB) to safeguard the integrity of the pay structure and the principle of equal pay. In comparison with traditional forms of national pay bargaining, the review body process has encouraged a more systematic analysis of a wider range of issues relating to affordability, recruitment and retention, morale, workload and job roles. Partly for these reasons the pay review process seems to offer a more acceptable mechanism for determining public service pay than those that preceded it.

For government independent review distances ministers from direct pay negotiations with trade unions while enabling it to exert a very powerful influence by establishing the terms of reference or remit of each review body and coordinating evidence to them via the Public Sector Pay Committee. The remit process has been expanded. The Labour government instructed the review bodies to have regard for affordability, stressing its 2.5% inflation target and has added other priorities such as promoting greater regional variation in pay settlements (IDS 2006). Government influence is also exerted by its authority to accept, stage or reject the recommendations of each review body, allowing it to retain ultimate control over the cost of review body recommendations as occurred in 2007–08. The risk is that considerable political capital is expended when review body recommendations are not accepted in full and the credibility of *independent* pay review is jeopardized if they are viewed as susceptible to Treasury control.

Independent pay review has also proved attractive to government because it has discouraged industrial action. This is an important consideration because strike action is concentrated in the public sector (Hale 2007) and can have unpredictable political consequences. The establishment of the prison service review body was accompanied by a voluntary agreement precluding strike action, reinforcing a pattern of trading off industrial action against the granting of independent pay review. An official review confirmed that 'the history of the pay review body system as a whole shows that it is associated with improved industrial relations where previously they were poor' (Booth 2007: ix). In addition, the occupational structure of independent pay review and the autonomy of each review body have enabled differential awards, allowing targeted pay increases to key occupational groups rather than more costly sector-wide pay increases which arise from national collective bargaining. Paradoxically extending the scope of the nurses' pay review body to encompass most NHS staff may diminish its ability to target pay increases at specific occupational groups employed within different labour markets.

Equal pay

Alongside institutional change, a second goal of pay modernization has been to address equal pay concerns. In the last two decades it has become clear that complex and unreformed pay systems did not comply with equal pay legislation.

Key issues included: the use of length of service as a criterion for pay differentials (which can discriminate indirectly against women taking career breaks for child care); access to bonus payments (which can exclude some groups); comparability between jobs on separate pay structures within the same service or organization; and developing the use of formal job evaluation to assess equal pay for work of equal value (IDS 2000).

Public service employers faced litigation but the length of time involved in bringing cases, reflected in the notorious 14 year long *Enderby* case in the NHS, and the cost of gender-proofing public sector pay systems delayed government action until recently. New pay systems, notably in the NHS, have been underpinned by equal value principles and the growth of job evaluation, which increased in usage from 18% to 44% of public sector workplaces between 1984 and 2004 (Bach *et al.* 2009). Significant barriers remained, however, to gender proofing pay systems, including the effects of outsourcing and the cost of implementing new pay systems. This has preserved the vulnerability of local authorities, for example, to equal pay litigation often driven by no-win, no-fee lawyers (see Colling and Dickens, this volume).

Performance pay

Aligning rewards to performance has provided the third dimension of the modernization of pay determination. Conservative governments focused on the establishment of individual performance-related pay (PRP) which provoked strong trade union opposition and limited support from managers who mainly used it to increase work effort (Marsden 2004). The Labour administration adopted a much broader approach to rewards in which a variety of incentives, including non-pay incentives, were to be used to motivate good performance and encourage retention. In the civil service, the influential Makinson (2000) report recommended that team-based performance bonuses should replace individual PRP schemes, but set at a group level that would be more meaningful for employees. This encouraged experimentation with team-based rewards in Jobcentre Plus and the Inland Revenue linked to achieving operational targets.

A major change has been to move away from pay progression based on virtually automatic increments towards some form of performance-based progression (Marsden 2007). The aim is to reduce the cost of automatic progression, remove a plethora of costly allowances and enhance managerial control. Across the sector the language has been softened to make it more acceptable to the workforce, with performance pay reframed as contribution- or competency-based pay, usually involving a mixture of skill acquisition and demonstrating competence (IDS 2008b). These forms of progression can coexist with more long-standing forms of individual performance pay, which in the civil service have been extended beyond the confines of senior management. Bonuses have become a feature of recent civil service pay deals but are not consolidated into base salaries because they relate only to recent performance. Individuals who attain top appraisal ratings are eligible for bonus payments, but these are quite small, typically less than £500 for lower grades and up to £3000 for more senior staff (IDS 2008c: 7).

Social partnership

Finally, there is the manner in which these changes have been secured, with a shift towards cooperative approaches manifest in social partnership agreements. Government has aimed to secure union support for new pay systems that facilitate service redesign, exchanging employer requirements for flexible working and cooperative employment relations with union priorities of job security and improved employment standards, such as reduced working hours. A tripartite Public Services Forum was established at national level to strengthen dialogue between government, trade unions and employers but the most important developments have occurred at sectoral level; permitting major reforms of pay and working conditions in health and education and providing some impetus to the stalled single status agreement in local government (Kessler and Dickens 2008). Overall, an estimated one third of public sector employees are covered by partnership agreements and it has been suggested that because of high levels of union density, public sector unions gain more from partnership than their private sector counterparts (Bacon and Samuel 2007).

There is scepticism within unions, however, about the meaning and benefits of social partnership. Some are concerned that the term has been devalued by labelling any discussions with the workforce, however superficial, a form of social partnership. In addition, government and employer impatience with trade union opposition has surfaced quickly and led to the imposition of change. For example, the second consecutive imposed pay award in the Maritime and Coastguard Agency prompted staff to take strike action for the first time in their history (IDS 2008d: 16). Where change has demonstrably benefited the majority of the workforce, partnership working has proved more straightforward, as under *Agenda for Change* in the NHS. This can be contrasted with the recently more confrontational context in 2008 when below-inflation settlements were proposed to curb inflation and maintain tight control over public expenditure. This encouraged a more assertive stance amongst nursing, midwifery and prison officer unions and the Police Federation, and a reappraisal of their acquiescence or active support for 'no-strike' agreements (IDS 2008e).

Pay Modernization and Workforce Reform: Sectoral Variation

Although pay modernization has been underpinned by similar principles, analysis of attempts to modernize pay systems considers separately developments in the civil service, the NHS and local authorities because of variations in outcomes between different parts of the public services.

Civil service

The reform of pay determination arrangements have been more comprehensive in the civil service, mainly because government ministers have been able to exercise more direct control than elsewhere. Following the creation of semi-autonomous executive agencies, the Treasury delegated its direct responsibility for negotiating pay and conditions to individual departments and agencies. This was followed in 1996 by the abolition of civil service-wide pay, except for the 4000 most senior civil servants whose pay is determined by a system of independent pay review. In place of a handful of national agreements over 150 new bargaining units were created as each department and executive agency established its own pay and grading structures, leading to variation in pay structures (Kessler *et al.* 2006). Despite this process of delegation, the bargaining process is tightly controlled by the Treasury. It issues guidance to departments and approves the planned pay awards under the so-called remit process. Treasury 'guidance' severely constrains departmental autonomy; for example in 2007–08, it stated bluntly 'Basic awards will be no more than 2%' (HM Treasury 2007b: para. 6.1.3).

The Public and Commercial Services Union (PCS), the main civil service trade union representing lower graded staff, has called for a return to national collective bargaining. Although opposed to national bargaining, the Treasury has supported other elements of this 'coherence agenda', for example encouraging departments to raise minimum starting salaries to reduce inequalities and pay dispersion. In tight public expenditure contexts funding for such initiatives has been squeezed. Nonetheless with some caveats, the civil service is making progress in implementing the Gender Equality Duty (Business, Enterprise and Regulatory Reform Committee 2008: 31). At the same time the government is keen to point out the value of 'total rewards' for public servants, stressing in particular that 'Public service pensions are a key benefit of public service employment and should be celebrated as such' (Cabinet Office nd: 9).

Partnership as a basis for implementation is less apparent here than in schools and hospitals. A major source of conflict arose from the review of efficiency across the civil service by Sir Peter Gershon. Without prior notification to its social partners, the government announced that between April 2004 and 2008, there would be gross reductions of 70 600 posts after some reallocation of staff to the front line. The largest decrease (30 000) was planned in the Department of Work and Pensions (Gershon 2004: 31) and the 2007 Comprehensive Spending Review followed up with a 5% annual reduction in administrative budgets in real terms (HM Treasury 2007a: 4). In conjunction with privatization and the imposition of pay awards, this process has resulted in ongoing disputes in the civil service over recent years.

Two other factors are significant. First, the remit process is disempowering for trade unions making it difficult to work in partnership. Treasury advice states that 'Departments should not enter into formal negotiations with Trade Unions until their Remit has been agreed' (HM Treasury 2007b: 5.1.6). After the remit has been approved, however, there is only limited scope for meaningful negotiations on the pay award. Second, PCS strategy under its forceful general secretary, Mark Serwotka, has been crucial. The union is not affiliated to the Labour Party and has been a highly vocal critic of government policy, showing a marked willingness to involve members in campaigning and industrial action (Serwotka 2007). This strategy has proved effective, not least in reaching a national agreement with the Cabinet Office in 2008 to avoid compulsory redundancies for civil servants (Cabinet Office and CCSU 2008).

National Health Service

After the failure of previous experiments with local pay, the incoming Labour government outlined in 1999 the case for a comprehensive modernization of NHS pay systems. The *Agenda for Change* (AfC) proposals were agreed in November 2002, replacing almost 650 staff grades and numerous complex allowances and working arrangements with harmonized terms and conditions and better career progression. This pay structure was designed to address unequal pay; provide rewards based on skill acquisition and responsibility rather than length of service; and to encourage innovative working practices (Department of Health 1999). A single pay spine is divided into a series of pay bands underpinned by an NHS-wide job evaluation scheme. Staff are allocated to a pay band on the basis of 'job weight' matched with nationally agreed job profiles or determined by job evaluation locally. Notionally, pay progression is no longer based exclusively on automatic service-based increments but is linked at key points to a competency-based assessment of knowledge and skills, the Knowledge and Skills Framework (KSF). The KSF process was also expected to establish a new culture of career development and work redesign, providing opportunities for low-paid staff in particular to progress. AfC covered all staff with the exception of doctors and dentists and some top managers who have separate contracts.

The ambitious nature of *Agenda for Change* has resulted in a mixed evaluation of its effects. Buchan and Evans (2007) point to poor value for money and little evidence that productivity has increased. A major criticism relates to the implementation of the KSF which has lagged other elements of pay modernization. The 2007 NHS national staff survey indicated that only 61% of respondents had received an appraisal or performance development review in the previous 12 months, a slight improvement on 2006 (58%). The NHS Pay Review Body (2008: 74) also expressed disappointment at the slow implementation of the KSF. Managers suggest that it is too complicated and time consuming; in practice salary increments remain virtually automatic, making the KSF irrelevant. There are other misgivings amongst employers, however, especially about the scope for local flexibility. NHS employers expressed concern that *Agenda for Change* was a compliance issue, another target to achieve, rather than a basis for changes in working practices and improved productivity (NHS Employers 2006).

Critics, however, do not sufficiently acknowledge the urgent need to address equal pay problems and the level of dissatisfaction amongst managers and staff with the previous structure of NHS pay determination (Bach 2004). The main beneficiaries of reform have been low paid, often female, manual workers such as cleaners. The skills escalator concept has also encouraged some modest improvements in skills acquisition for ancillary staff and health care assistants (Cox 2007) and the partnership benefits of the negotiation and implementation process have been considerable (National Audit Office 2009). AfC was developed at national level and implemented locally, bolstering forms of cooperative working in the NHS. These benefits will be harder to sustain after the government staged the implementation of NHS pay awards in England during 2007 and in a context of severe financial constraint from 2008 onwards.

Pay modernization was also extended to general practitioners (family doctors) and the most senior, consultant medical staff. Although the details of the consultant and GP contract are very different, what unites their implementation is that the government achieved the unusual feat of substantially boosting earnings while antagonizing the medical profession to an unprecedented degree. In 2005–06 the average pay of consultants was £109 974, an increase of 27% in three years (National Audit Office 2007) while for GPs, pre-tax take-home pay in England increased by 58% from £72 011 in 2002–03 to £113 614 in 2005–06 (National Audit Office 2008). The degree of antipathy by the medical profession towards the government stems in part from their criticisms of the target culture but more specifically arises from a concern that new contractual arrangements are based on a low-trust model in which doctors have to account for their time and activities, damaging medical professionalism (Levenson *et al.* 2008: 24–25). Irrespective of the merits of these grievances, the government confronts difficulties in achieving its reform agenda with a disengaged medical profession.

Local government

The 1997 'single status' agreement was greeted by employers and trade unions as a major turning-point for employment relations in local government. A national pay spine, based on a jointly agreed job evaluation scheme, was designed to provide a framework within which each local authority could seek local agreement on a grading structure covering all staff. Alongside the harmonization of basic conditions such as working time and holidays, the agreement greatly increased the prospect of equality of employment between men and women, as well as between manual and white-collar staff. Over the last decade, however, progress on the local implementation of the agreement has been slow; less than half of local authorities achieved the deadline of 31 March 2007 for the implementation of equality proofed local pay and grading structures (IDS 2008b).

Overall, the obstacles that have delayed the implementation of the local government agreement reveal the scope and complexity of pay modernization and the continuing vulnerability of many public sector employers to equal pay claims. Additional funding from central government to meet the cost of moving to single-status pay and conditions has not been forthcoming, reflecting the less generous public financing of core local government in comparison to the higher priority assigned to health and education (HM Treasury 2007a: 12). Measures proposed by some local authorities to offset the costs of single status – for example, to increase productivity or reduce allowances – invariably were resisted by employees and union representatives. This opposition was exacerbated by the anxieties of some groups of white-collar employees who expected to gain nothing from assimilation onto a single pay spine, and the fears of manual workers that they would lose their bonus payments and allowances, prompting industrial action in a few authorities (IDS 2008f). By early 2008, almost half of local authorities had completed pay reviews at an estimated cost of £2.8 billion, incorporating many features of the modernization agenda.

By contrast, the government has celebrated the success of the reforms of the school workforce. The School Teachers' Review Body (STRB), in response to union pressure, played an important role in highlighting key issues of teacher shortages and unsustainable workloads, providing the impetus for government action. The proposed solution known as *Remodelling the School Workforce* resulted in a national agreement in 2003 between the government, employers and school workforce unions, except the National Union of Teachers (NUT), to reform the school workforce (DfES 2003). It agreed reductions in teachers' workload, enabling them to focus on teaching and learning. A key element of the agreement was to increase the role of support staff, especially teaching assistants, but also technicians and bursars, to undertake work usually done by teachers. The national agreement outlined a three year phased process of implementation which included the removal of 24 administrative tasks from teachers, a maximum 38 hour annual limit for covering for absent teachers and guaranteed planning, preparation and assessment time amounting to 10% of normal timetabled teaching time.

The outcomes in 32 pilot sites identified that teachers reported a reduction in working hours, work was transferred to other staff and in general staff were positive about the reforms (Gunter and Rayner 2007). These findings have been reiterated by detailed case studies that highlight the contribution of teaching assistants and the increased scope, albeit from a low base, for development in their role (Bach *et al.* 2006). Concerns have been raised, however, that the government's agenda is designed to substitute other staff for teachers; a form of 'deprofessionalization' rather than the 'new professionalism' of government rhetoric (Stevenson 2007). Abuses in the utilization of teaching assistants led the Workforce Agreement Monitoring Group (WAMG) to issue new guidance on the appropriate deployment of support staff (WAMG 2008).

The workforce agreement has been the trigger for further reforms of the school workforce with all schools required to review their staffing structures. These initiatives built on earlier contentious reforms which linked pay to performance. Teachers were given the opportunity to apply to pass through a performance threshold, and if successful, which most teachers were, gain access to a higher pay scale, resulting in an immediate £2000 pay increase. The School Teachers' Review Body (STRB) also supported plans for an excellent teachers' scheme and the abolition of management allowances with proposals developed on a partnership basis. Teachers can gain additional income either by taking on extra responsibilities that result in high-quality teaching (termed responsibility payments) or by demonstrating excellent results. The implementation of these proposals has not been straightforward and in May 2007 only 34 Excellent Teachers (ETs) were in post. The STRB (2008) remained concerned about the implementation of the ET scheme and frustrated by the unwillingness of schools to utilize their existing pay flexibilities to address local priorities.

A few conclusions arise from the experience of pay modernization. First, despite variations between sectors the government has been successful in ensuring that the principles of equal pay, rewards for contribution, partnership working and altered roles underpin reformed pay structures, reflecting a return to a more centralized control of pay determination. However, effective implementation of comprehensive pay reforms in sectors with a heterogeneous workforce (e.g. local authorities and the NHS) requires a large investment of management time and resources, a high degree of inter-union agreement and additional funding from central government. In the absence of one or more of these conditions, incremental and piecemeal reform can be introduced, but it often leads to poor implementation, creating new workforce grievances. Second, most innovations in pay systems – for example, competency-based pay or major changes in salary structures – have a relatively brief shelf-life and require frequent amendment or fine-tuning. Finally, cyclical changes in labour market conditions and public expenditure constraints can rapidly alter the climate of employment relations in the public services and undermine the initial rationale of pay reforms or their later impact.

Discussion: The Challenge of Modernization

Changing organizational structures, accompanied by enhanced competitive and performance pressures, have altered employment relations in the public services for each of the main actors; unions, employers and the government.

At first sight, the state of public service trade unionism appears robust. They dominate the trade union movement (Table 7.4); of the 14 trade unions with more than 100 000 members, the majority organize mainly in the public service sector (Certification Office 2008). Yet although increased public sector employment has permitted some membership growth, overall trade union density declined from 84% in 1980 to 57% in 2004 (Bach *et al.* 2009). This is a major concern because it erodes the credibility of trade unions and reduces their effectiveness as workplace union organization becomes more limited.

The modernization agenda has reinforced these difficulties. The fragmentation and outsourcing of public services has required that unions follow their members into the private sector, to maintain membership levels. This is not straightforward as unions have to deal with a proliferation of employers and bargaining units and local activists need to be assisted to gain union recognition, undertake local negotiations and ensure that national agreements are implemented. Existing workplace union representatives are often hostile or indifferent to outsourced workers and this may reinforce the impression amongst potential members that these unions are not welcoming to private sector employees (Bach and Givan 2005). To overcome these challenges, Unison, the largest public service trade union, established the Private Contractors Unit (PCU), to provide a coordinated approach to organizing in the private sector. It has identified a number of target companies such as Capita, Initial, Serco and Sodexho with the goal of developing recruitment and organization in the private sector (Bach and Givan 2008).

Organizing is now the main priority of public service trade unions, involving the development of durable workplace organization and encouraging an active and informed membership. PCS has established a dedicated national organizing department with over 20 national organizers, agreed a national organizing

Table 7.4   Membership of UK trade unions with more than 100 000 members in 2007

	Male	Female	Total
Unite	1 505 800	446 426	1 952 226
Unison	403 200	940 800	1 344 000
GMB	326 037	264 088	590 125
Royal College of Nursing[a]	35 075	358 790	393 865
National Union of Teachers	89 670	284 500	374 170
Union of Shop, Distributive & Allied Workers	150 374	205 672	356 046
National Association of Schoolmasters/ Union of Women Teachers	89 327	224 023	313 350
Public and Commercial Services Union	120 428	184 401	304 829
Communication Workers Union	189 133	47 546	236 679
Association of Teachers and Lecturers	52 732	155 836	208 568
British Medical Association	78 711	59 648	138 359
Union of Construction Allied Trades and Technicians	127 106	1959	129 065
University and College Union[b]	61 684	55 293	116 977
Prospect	79 764	22 931	102 695

(a) Figures for year ended 31/03/08
(b) Figures for 15 months ended 31/08/07
Source: Certification Officer AR21 Returns

strategy which tracks membership levels by civil service department, identifies priority areas for action, and sets targets for membership growth (PCSU 2008). The changing composition of the workforce has led unions to broaden their membership base and encourage into membership occupational groups that were previously excluded or had a low priority. For example, both Unison and the Royal College of Nursing are focusing more attention on the recruitment of health care assistants. The Secondary Heads Association has extended its membership from head teachers to incorporate the leadership group in schools, including non-teachers such as bursars, within the reconstituted Association of School and College Leaders. These developments indicate that unions have strengthened their management processes to direct union efforts at critical organizational goals (Heery 2006).

Trade unions have remained important national institutional actors and have been able to articulate membership concerns around sensitive political issues relating to privatization, but their capacity to regulate terms and conditions of employment and influence managerial decision making has diminished significantly. This stems from the introduction of competitive pressures, mirroring the economic impact of product market pressure in the private sector. Furthermore, increased diversity of public service provision has made the government less politically exposed to industrial action; disputes become more localized as they occur within separate employers and are less subject to media scrutiny.

Amongst employers, the focus on traditional bargaining machinery has been supplemented by a stronger workplace orientation, and by an emphasis on employee engagement and voice. The views of the workforce are canvassed regularly in staff opinion surveys and opportunities are available to question top managers at staff forums. More emphasis has been placed on the needs of individual workers with a focus on work–life balance policies and a commitment to diversity and equality. Formal organizational practice indicates that the public sector has embraced policies associated with the 'model employer' to a far greater extent than the private sector. For employers the difficulty is that the immediate work experience of most public sector staff has been shaped primarily by the priority assigned to key government targets, reinforcing a sense of disempowerment and making staff unreceptive to measures that reinvent the model employer tradition. Employer difficulties are reinforced by a lack of confidence in those managers tasked with implementing a complex modernization agenda. In the civil service, the capability reviews – which assess each department's capability in the core areas of leadership, strategy and delivery – identify serious weaknesses, which reinforce wider concerns about leadership capability (Lodge 2006). Similarly, in the NHS poor leadership has been identified as compromising improvements in care (Health Committee 2008) and these shortcomings have fostered a preoccupation with developing public service leaders.

Part of the difficulty stems from incongruence between the objectives of governments and those of employers. Sensitive to concerns about fairness and equality, governments have focused on lifting remuneration for lower paid workers, reinforcing internal equity within national pay structures. Employers, however, have been more concerned with the recruitment and retention of professional and specialist staff with a greater focus on their external worth. Employers also express disquiet about the compression of pay structures and limited scope to reward contribution (CBI 2006), accentuated in a period of very low pay settlements. Employers have also been ambivalent about the return to more centralized forms of pay determination because public service provision is becoming more fragmented and employers are seeking greater flexibility to respond to diverse local circumstances.

The main challenge for the Labour government has been to fulfil electoral mandates to invest in and improve public services and to address public concerns about a public sector 'in crisis'. These expectations were partly met by substantial additional resources intended to address recruitment and retention problems for key groups of public sector employees, improving service standards. Results, however, were achieved by embracing and intensifying Conservative government policies of managerialism and marketization. These approaches were far more straightforward to impose on staff than more complex forms of user and workforce mobilization which straddle organizational boundaries and embed new ways of working. Consequently, the transformation of employment relations remained incomplete and the Labour government continued to express concern that: 'Too many services are still designed around the needs of the service provider rather than the service user' (Cabinet Office 2008: 12).

Despite common principles that underpin the modernization agenda, its application has varied resulting in a less uniform model of public service employment and differing outcomes between subsectors. The NHS Pay Review Body (2008: 74) reported a decline in morale and only a quarter of staff report that their trust valued their work (Healthcare Commission 2008). Research on 'what matters to staff in the NHS' reported that many staff 'see the NHS serving a business agenda driven by financial considerations and irrelevant targets. This frustration, it appears, is driving a feeling of alienation' (DH 2008: 22). A comparison with the education sector highlights the difficulties in health. First, the pace of reform in education has been less frenetic than in health. Second, the reform agenda has been more consistent than the uncertainties and confusion in relation to the contribution of markets in the health sector. Overall, there has been less emphasis on private sector involvement in education, which has served to create distrust of government in health. Third, the managers (such as head teachers) charged with reform in education share the same background and basic values as those they manage, while in health there is a great deal of distrust between managers and clinical staff which is reinforced by the larger scale of hospitals as employers (Brooks *et al.* 2007; Lawson 2007).

Irrespective of the party in government, the limitations of a highly centralized and directive approach are encouraging a reform agenda characterized by attempts to re-engage professional staff and develop leadership capacity, initiatives to bolster user involvement, measures to strengthen the role of the third sector and attempts to devolve more responsibility for employment relations practice to local providers. The prospects for the modernization agenda, however, remain highly uncertain. From autumn 2008 the UK economy entered a severe recession with far-reaching consequences for public expenditure and employment. The public sector workforce confront many years of retrenchment following a period of unprecedented investment. Valued aspects of the model employer tradition, especially generous pension provision, are certain to be subject to renewed scrutiny. The irony is that the last decade has witnessed unprecedented investment in public services and its workforce; it may, however, only be in the coming period of public expenditure austerity that the public service workforce grudgingly acknowledge that they have benefited substantially from the modernization agenda developed since 1997.

References

Audit Commission 2002: *Recruitment and Retention: A Public Service Workforce for the Twenty-first Century*. London: Audit Commission. www.audit-commission.gov.uk/.

Bach, S. 2004: *Employment Relations in the NHS: The Management of Reforms*. London: Routledge.

Bach, S. and Givan, R. 2005: Union responses to public-private partnerships in the National Health Service. In Fernie, S. and Metcalf, D. (eds) *British Unions: Resurgence or Decline*. London: Routledge, pp. 118–137.

Bach, S. and Givan, R. 2008: Public service modernization and trade union reform: towards managerial led renewal? *Public Administration*, 86 (2), 523–539.

Bach, S. and Winchester, D. 1994: Opting out of pay devolution? Prospects for local pay bargaining in UK public services. *British Journal of Industrial Relations*, 32 (2), 263–282.

Bach, S., Givan, R. and Forth, J. 2009: The public sector in transition. In Brown, W., Bryson, A., Forth, J. and Whitfield, K. (eds) *A Quarter Century of Change in British Employment Relations*. Cambridge: Cambridge University Press.

Bach, S., Kessler, I. and Heron, P. 2006: Changing job boundaries and workforce reform: the case of teaching assistants. *Industrial Relations Journal*, 37 (1), 2–21.

Bacon, N. and Samuel, P. 2007: Partnership agreement adoption and survival in the British private and public sectors. Paper presented at the IIRA European Congress Manchester, September.

Bevan, G. and Hood, C. 2006: What's measured is what matters: targets in the English public health care system. *Public Administration*, 84 (3), 517–538.

Bewley, H. 2006: Raising the standard? The regulation of employment and public sector employment policy. *British Journal of Industrial Relations*, 44 (2), 351–372.

Blair, T. 1999: Speech to Venture Capitalist Association, London.

Booth, C. 2007: Determining pay in the police service: the second part of a review of police service pay arrangements. http://police.homeoffice.gov.uk/publications/policereform/Booth_Review_Second_Report.pdf

Bordogna. L. 2008: Moral hazard, transaction costs and the reform of public service employment relations. *European Journal of Industrial Relations*, 14 (4), 381–400.

Brooks *et al.* 2007: *Public Services at the Crossroads*. London: IPPR. http://www.ippr.org.uk/members/download.asp?f=%2Fecomm%2Ffiles%2Fcrossroads%5Fsummary%5Ffor%5Fweb%5F2%2Epdf

Buchan, J. and Evans, D. 2007: *Realising the Benefits? Assessing the Implementation of Agenda for Change*. London: King's Fund. http://www.kingsfund.org.uk/publications/kings_fund_publications/realising_the.html

Business, Enterprise and Regulatory Reform Committee 2008: *Jobs for the Girls: Two Years On*. London: House of Commons. http://www.publications.parliament.uk/pa/cm200708/cmselect/cmberr/634/634.pdf

Cabinet Office nd: *Civil Service Reward Principles*. London: Cabinet Office.

Cabinet Office 2008: *Excellence and Fairness: Achieving World Class Public Services*. London: Cabinet Office. http://www.cabinetoffice.gov.uk/~/media/assets/www.cabinetoffice.gov.uk/strategy/publications/world_class_public_services%20pdf.ashx

Cabinet Office and Council of Civil Service Unions 2008: *Protocol for Handling Surplus Staff Situations*. London: Cabinet Office. http://www.civilservice.gov.uk/documents/doc/strengthening_protocols.doc

CBI 2006: *For What it's Worth. Managing Public Sector Reward 2008–2011*. London: CBI.

Certification Office 2008: Annual Report of the Certification Officer 2007–2008. www.certoffice.org

Chapman, J. 2007: Living in the machine: New Labour and public services. In Hassan, G. (ed.) *After Blair: Politics After the New Labour Decade*. London: Lawrence and Wishart.

Colling, T. 1999: Tendering and Outsourcing: Working in the Contract State. In Corby, S. and White, G. (eds) *Employee Relations in the Public Services*. London: Routledge.

Corby, S. 2007: Equality and diversity. In Dibben, P., James, P. and Roper, I. (eds) *Modernising Work in Public Services*. Basingstoke: Palgrave.

Cox, A. 2007: Re-visiting the NVQ debate: 'bad' qualifications, expansive learning environments and prospects for upskilling workers. SKOPE Research Paper No. 71. www.skop.ox.ac.uk

DfES. 2003: *Raising Standards and Tackling Workload: A National Agreement*. London: DFES. http://www.tda.gov.uk/upload/resources/na_standards_workload.pdf

Department of Health 1999: *Agenda for Change: Modernising the NHS Pay System*. London: The Stationery Office. www.dh.gov.uk/PolicyAndGuidance/HumanResourcesAndTraining/ModernisingPay/AgendaForChange/fs

Department of Health 2008: What matters to staff in the NHS. http://www.dh.gov.uk/en/Publicationsandstatistics/Publications/DH_085536

De Ruyter, A., Kirkpatrick, I., Hoque, K., Lonsdale, C. and Malan, J. 2008: Agency working and the degradation of public service employment: the case of nurses and social workers. *International Journal of Human Resource Management*, 19 (3), 432–445.

Escott K. and Whitfield, D. 1995: *The Gender Impact of CCT in Local Government*. Manchester: EOC.

Ferner, A. 1988: *Government, Managers and Industrial Relations*. Oxford: Blackwell.

Flanagan, R. 2008: Independent review of policing by Sir Ronnie Flanagan – final report. http://police.homeoffice.gov.uk/publications/police-reform/Review_of_policing_final_report/

Fredman, S. and Morris, G. 1989: *The State as Employer: Labour Law in the Public Services*. London: Mansell.

Gash, T. 2008: *The New Bill: Modernising the Police Workforce*. London: IPPR. http://www.ippr.org.uk/publicationsandreports/publications.asp?title=the+new+bill&author=&pubdate=&theme=&search=search

Gershon, P. 2004: Releasing resources to the frontline: independent review of public sector efficiency. http://www.hm-treasury.gov.uk/media/C/A/efficiency_review120704.pdf

Giddens, A. 2000: *The Third Way and its Critics*. Cambridge: Polity.

Givan, R. 2005: Seeing stars: human resources indicators in the National Health Service. *Personnel Review*, 34 (6), 634–647.

Gleeson, D. and Knights, D. 2006: Challenging dualism: public professionalism in troubled times. *Sociology*, 40, 277–295.

Glennerster, H. 2004: Mrs Thatcher's legacy: getting it in perspective. In Ellison, N., Bauld, L. and Powell, M. (eds) *Social Policy Review 16*. Bristol: Policy Press.

Gunter, H. and Rayner S. 2007: Modernizing the school workforce in England: challenging transformation and leadership. *Leadership*, 3(1): 47–64.

Hale, D. 2007: Labour disputes in 2006. *Economic and Labour Market Review*, 1 (6), 25–36. http://www.statistics.gov.uk/elmr/06_08/downloads/elmr_jun08_hale.pdf

Hall, P. and Soskice, D. (eds) 2001: *Varieties of Capitalism: The Institutional Foundations of Comparative Advantage*. Oxford: Oxford University Press.

Health Committee 2008: *NHS Next Stage Review*. Volume 1 HC53-I. http://www.publications.parliament.uk/pa/cm200809/cmselect/cmhealth/53/53i.pdf

Healthcare Commission 2008: National NHS staff survey 2007: summary of key findings. http://www.healthcarecommission.org.uk/healthcareproviders/nationalfindings/surveys/healthcareproviders/surveysofnhsstaff/2007.cfm

Heery, E. 2006: Union workers, union work: a profile of paid union officers in the United Kingdom. *British Journal of Industrial Relations*, 44 (3), 445–471.

Hicks, S. and Lindsey, C. 2005: Public sector employment. *Labour Market Trends*, April, 139–147.

HM Treasury 2007a: *Meeting the Aspirations of the British People: 2007 Pre-Budget Report and Comprehensive Spending Review, Cm 7227*. London: The Stationery Office. http://www.hm-treasury.gov.uk/pbr_csr07_repindex.cfm

HM Treasury 2007b: *Civil Service Pay Guidance 2007–08*. London: The Stationery Office. http://www.civilservice.gov.uk/documents/doc/pay_reward/CSPayGuidance2007–08.doc

HM Treasury 2008a: *Public Expenditure: Statistical Analyses 2008, HC 489*. London: The Stationary Office. http://www.hm-treasury.gov.uk/economic_data_and_tools/finance_spending_statistics/pes_publications/pespub_index.cfm

HM Treasury 2008b: *The Private Finance Initiative (PFI): Signed Projects List*. London: The StationeryOffice.http://www.hm-treasury.gov.uk/documents/public_private_partnerships/ppp_PFI_stats.cfm

Hood, C. 1991: A public management for all seasons. *Public Administration*, 69 (1), 3–19.

Incomes Data Services 2000: Equal pay. *IDS Pay Report*, No. 805, 10–13.

Incomes Data Services 2006: Understanding reward. *IDS Pay Report*, No. 957, 14–15.

Incomes Data Services 2007: Pay in the civil service. *IDS Pay Report*, No. 972, 12–20.

Incomes Data Services 2008a: Pay rises under long-term deals. *IDS Pay Report*, No. 1003, 10–12.

Incomes Data Services 2008b: Local government pay benchmarking survey. *IDS Pay Report*, No. 995, 7–17.

Incomes Data Services 2008c: Understanding reward: bonus schemes. *IDS Pay Report*, No. 1001, 6–7.

Incomes Data Services 2008d: Civil service pay. *IDS Pay Report*, 15–16.

Incomes Data Services 2008e: Industrial relations: are 'no-strike' demands a good way to resolve disputes? *IDS Pay Report*, No. 1003, 13–15.

Incomes Data Services 2008f: Strike at Birmingham City Council over pay and grading. *IDS Pay Report*, No. 995, 5.

Institute of Fiscal Studies 2008: The IFS Green Budget 2008. http://www.ifs.org.uk/publications/4112

Jenkins, S. 2007: *Thatcher and Sons: A Revolution in Three Acts*. London: Penguin.

Julius, D. 2008: *Public Services Industry Review*. London: BERR. http://www.berr.gov.uk/files/file46965.pdf

Kessler, I. and Dickens, L. 2008: Dispute resolution and the modernization of the public services in Britain: the case of the Local Government Pay Commission. *Journal of Industrial Relations*, 50 (4), 612–629.

Kessler, I., Heron, P. and Gagnon, S. 2006: The fragmentation of pay determination in the British civil service: a union member perspective. *Personnel Review*, 35 (1), 6–28.

Kirkpatrick, I. and Hoque, K. 2005: The decentralisation of employment relations in the British public sector. *Industrial Relations Journal*, 36 (2), 100–120.

Kirkpatrick, I., Ackroyd, S. and Walker, R. 2005: *The New Managerialism and Public Service Professions*. Palgrave: London.

Law, A. and Mooney, G. 2007: Strenuous welfarism: restructuring the welfare labour process. In Mooney, G. and Law, A. (eds) *New Labour/Hard Labour? Restructuring and Resistance inside the Welfare Industry*. Bristol: Policy Press.

Lawson, N. 2007: *Machines, Markets and Morals*. London: Compass. http://clients.squareeye.com/uploads/compass/documents/MachinesMarketsandMorals.pdf

Le Grand, J. 2003: *Motivation, Agency, and Public Policy: Of Knights and Knaves, Pawns and Queens*. Oxford: Oxford University Press.

Levenson, R., Dewar, S. and Shepherd, S. 2008: *Understanding Doctors: Harnessing Professionalism*. London: King's Fund. http://www.kingsfund.org.uk/media/doctors_feel_there.html

Lodge, G. 2006: *Is Whitehall Fit for Purpose?* London: IPPR. http://www.ippr.org.uk/members/download.asp?f=%2Fecomm%2Ffiles%2FIs%5Fwhitehall%5Ffit%2Epdf

Makinson, J. 2000: *Incentives for Change: Rewarding Performance in National Government*. London: Treasury.

Marsden, D. 2004: The role of performance-related pay in renegotiating the 'effort bargain': the case of the British public sector. *Industrial and Labor Relations Review*, 57 (3), 350–370.

Marsden, D. 2007: Pay and rewards in public services: fairness and equity. In Dibben, P., James, P. and Roper, I. (eds) *Modernising Work in Public Services*. Basingstoke: Palgrave.

Millard, B. and Machin, A. 2007: Characteristics of public sector workers. *Economic and Labour Market Review*, 1 (5), 46–55. http://www.statistics.gov.uk/elmr/05_07/downloads/ELMR_0507Millard_Machin.pdf

National Audit Office 2007: *Pay Modernisation: A New Contract for NHS Consultants in England*. London: National Audit Office.

National Audit Office 2008: *NHS Pay Modernisation: New Contracts for General Practice Services in England, HC 307*. London: National Audit Office.

National Audit Office 2009: *NHS Pay Modernisation in England: Agenda for Change*. London: National Audit Office.

NHS Employers 2006: Agenda for Change: From Pay Reform to System Improvement: Briefing June 2006. http://www.nhsemployers.org/restricted/downloads/download.asp?ref=1498&hash=22843ed65b0193e60b793ba1a4f9de73&itemplate=e_pay_conditions_3col_agenda-for-change

NHS Pay Review Body 2008: Twenty-Third Report 2008. http://www.ome.uk.com/downloads/NHS%20PRB%202008%20Report.pdf

OECD (Organization for Economic Co-operation and Development) 2007: Public sector pensions and the challenge of an ageing workforce. OECD Working Papers on Public Governance, 2007/2. Paris: OECD.

OME 2008: About us. http://www.ome.uk.com/about.cfm

ONS 2008: Public sector employment Q2 2008. http://www.statistics.gov.uk/pdfdir/pse0908.pdf

ORC International 2006: *Senior Civil Service Overall Highlights Report*. ORC International.

Pearson, N. 1994: Employment in the public and private sectors. *Economic Trends*, 483 (January), 92–98.

Pendleton, A. 1997: What impact has privatisation had on pay and employment? A review of the UK experience. *Relations Industrielles*, 52 (3), 554–579.

Public Administration Select Committee 2003: *On Target? Government by Measurement, Fifth Report of Session 2002–03, HC 62-I*. London: House of Commons. http://www.publications.parliament.uk/pa/cm200203/cmselect/cmpubadm/1264/126402.htm

Public and Commercial Services Union 2008: National organising strategy 2008. http://www.pcs.org.uk

School Teachers' Review Body 2008: Seventeenth Report – Part One, Cm 7252. http://www.ome.uk.com/downloads/11768%20STRB%20Web.pdf

Serwotka, M. 2007: The future of public services under Labour. University of Hertfordshire Business School, Working Paper 3. https://uhra.herts.ac.uk/dspace/bitstream/2299/1408/1/S77.pdf

Stevenson, H. 2007: Restructuring teachers' work and trade union responses in England: bargaining for change? *American Educational Research Journal*, 44 (2), 224–251.

Tailby, S. 2005: Agency and bank nursing in the UK National Health Service. *Work Employment and Society*, 19 (2), 369–389.

Unison 2008: Tackling the two tier workforce: problems and issues. http://www.unison.org.uk/acrobat/PP040308.pdf

WAMG 2008: WAMG Note 22: The appropriate deployment of support staff in schools. http://www.socialpartnership.org/wamg_notes.aspx

Wanless, D., Appleby, J., Harrison, A. and Patel, D. 2007: *Our Future Health Secured? A Review of NHS Funding and Performance*. London: King's Fund.

White, G. and Hatchett, A. 2003: The pay review bodies in Britain under the Labour government. *Public Money and Management*, 23 (4), 237–244.

Whitfield, D. 2006: *New Labour's Attack on Public Services*. Nottingham: Spokesman.

Winchester, D. 1983: Industrial relations in the public sector. In Bain, G. (ed.) *Industrial Relations in Britain*. Oxford: Blackwell.

Yeandle, S. and Stiell, B. 2007: Issues in the development of the Direct Payments Scheme for older people in England. In Ungerson, C. and Yeandle, S. (eds) *Cash for Care in Developed Welfare States*. Basingstoke: Palgrave Macmillan.

8

INDUSTRIAL RELATIONS IN THE PRIVATE SECTOR

JAMES ARROWSMITH

Introduction

This chapter is concerned with describing and analysing strategies and policies for the management of the employment relationship in the private sector. It emphasizes the importance of the concept of the *sector* for our understanding of these approaches. Though there are common structural and other characteristics that differentiate the private from the public, it is necessary to further subdivide the private sector. The distinction between manufacturing and services has long been recognized and is deployed here, but to these a third is added – the privatized sector – which has its own peculiar characteristics and management traditions. An important factor in all three groups is the profile of collective bargaining, which has generally reduced with implications for broader patterns of employment and industrial relations. The chapter begins with a definition of the private sector and a brief consideration of the characteristics that set it apart from the public (see Bach, this volume). After noting the changing composition of private-sector employment, the next section outlines why a sector framework is useful to industrial relations analysis. Subsequent sections explore developments in the privatized sectors; manufacturing and private services, respectively. The concluding section discusses the demise of formal industrial relations across much of the private sector.

Defining the Private Sector

The private sector consists of a huge range of firms and activities that have in common the pursuit of profit in more or less competitive markets. This explicit focus on competitiveness and its results has particular implications for the management of employees, notwithstanding the size of firm, its ownership structure or economic sector of activity. First, the employment context is inherently unstable. Underperforming firms have to rationalize, restructure or reinvent themselves if they are to remain viable; successful firms often achieve their position by investment and innovation in new markets or technologies that also directly impact on employment levels and the organization of work. Second, the need to return a profit (or at least avoid recurring losses) tends to render the tensions involved in the employment relationship particularly visible and acute (see Sisson and Purcell, this volume). On the one hand, workers are valued productive 'assets' for their employers and both parties share a common interest in the commercial success of the firm. On the other, workers are also a cost, and represent 'assets' that may need to be intensively exploited, or even disposed of, for economic gain.

Employment in the private sector is particularly turbulent (Hijzen *et al.* 2007). Tensions are evident in the public sector too (see Bach, this volume), as a result of competitive and public expenditure pressures, but public employment has been relatively sheltered. While the governance of public-sector organizations involves a more or less institutionalized role for different groups of 'stakeholders', including workers and their representatives, firms in the private sector are fundamentally accountable to shareholders or other private owners. Decision making is responsive to market change and the imperative of attracting and retaining investment. Employment change tends to be immediate, dynamic and extensive, especially in so-called *liberal market economies* or LMEs (Hall and Soskice 2001). Here, investors tend to focus on short-term financial performance and corporate governance gives them influence over management strategy, under threat of investment withdrawals (see Sisson and Purcell, this volume). Firms listed on the stock market need to prioritize 'shareholder value', which involves returning dividends and, especially, maintaining the share price in order to defend against company takeovers. Crucially, finance directors believe the share price to be strongly influenced by reported current earnings and accounting profits over short cycles (Grinyer *et al.* 1998). By contrast, countervailing protections for workforces, endowed by law or by representative institutions, tend to be weak (see Crouch; Dickens and Hall; and Terry, all this volume). In the absence of such coordinating mechanisms, market pressures are felt in full and at the level of individual organizations.

Institutional environments of this kind explain the particularly deep and sustained patterns of restructuring apparent in the UK private sector. Long-term shifts away from primary (extractive) and secondary (manufacturing) industries towards the service sector are evident in all developed economies, a process referred to usually as 'tertiarization' (see Brook 2008). But decline in the UK has been so steep that it is often termed 'deindustrialization' (Brady and Denniston 2006). Employment in retail, distribution, hotels and catering grew by a third (32%) in the 30 years between 1978 and 2007, and the workforce in finance and business services by 132% (Table 8.1). In the same period, manufacturing employment declined by more than half (55%), and energy and water supply, which became privately owned in the late 1980s, by nearly three quarters (73%).

Table 8.1 Workforce jobs by industry (000s), 1978–2007

	All Jobs	Agriculture & fishing	Energy & water	Manufacturing	Construction	Retail, distribution, hotels & restaurants	Transport & comms	Finance & business services	Public admin, education & health	Other services
1978	27146	639	680	7128	1898	5458	1710	2856	5655	1121
1987	27599	659	446	5245	2082	5947	1577	3859	6361	1423
1997	28780	584	222	4533	1847	6656	1605	5103	6571	1658
2007	31620	451	183	3172	2208	7117	1854	6651	7991	1992

Source: ONS, Economic and Labour Market Review, June 2008.
Notes: Workforce jobs includes self-employment. Standard Industrial Classification (1992); Figures are for UK, seasonally adjusted, December.

The Importance of Sector Context

The central argument advanced in this chapter is that the dynamics of employment relations are structured by sector-specific factors (Arrowsmith and Sisson 1999, 2001). In comparison to other European countries, these do not stem from industry level governance of employment specifically. Industry bargaining has always been relatively weak in the UK and imploded almost entirely in recent memory, with important exceptions such as printing, construction and agriculture (see Brown, this volume). However, drawing on the work of Hollingsworth and Streeck and their colleagues, it is argued that a focus on formal institutions is only part of the picture. This is because the sector must be understood in three ways, each of which has implications for management and employee relations.

The first is in terms of activities. For Hollingsworth *et al.* (1994: 8), 'a sector is simply a population of firms producing a specified range of potentially or actually competing products', a definition which extends to supplier firms and others with a specialist or dependent interest in the generation and sale of the end-product. This is the basis for official statistical classifications of the sector, which group together businesses under increasingly specified codes according to the nature of their product or service offered. This has strong intuitive appeal, and it is not difficult to observe similarities within groups of analogous companies, such as banks, supermarkets, call centres or car factories. But, why do employment practices and industrial relations outcomes look so similar between firms in a given sector when employers are at once disorganized and ascendant in LMEs?

In part, the answer is structural. Management practices and employment relations strategies are strongly influenced by the intrinsic dynamics of sectoral 'social systems of production' (Hollingsworth and Boyer 1997), informing what practices are realistically open to actors to choose (Streeck and Schmitter 1985; Hollingsworth *et al.* 1994; Hollingsworth and Boyer 1997). Firms within a sector face similar pressures and options in the organization of work and labour relations by virtue of common activities and constraints such as the nature of the external labour market, patterns of demand, and technology and capital requirements. To take working time, for example, the extensive use of part-time work across private services is structured by patterns of demand that are highly variable yet predictable; the immediacy of the customer; a relatively high labour intensity; and lower skills and training requirements which facilitate larger-volume recruitment.

The second dimension of the sector is identity. This refers to the actors' awareness of sector dynamics and is likely to be related to historical contingencies (such as state approaches to regulation) as well as to the intrinsic cohesion and integration of the sector environment. For example, sector identity is likely to positively correlate to the concentration of the sector (i.e. the degree to which it is dominated by a relatively small number of firms), and inversely relate to the level of differentiation in the nature of the product or service offered. Hence, employers in a sector such as energy supply will have a high degree of collective identity and associational ties since it is oligopolistic, fairly homogeneous and regulated by the state. But even a 'dispersed' sector such as temporary agency work (TAW), which in the UK is largely comprised of small firms, can develop a sectoral self-identity (Arrowsmith 2009). This is partly linked to sector growth but also to the development of self-organization for the purposes of promoting industry standards and public policy lobbying.

This leads us to the third feature of the sector, which is the organization of employers and trade unions into sector-level associations. As already observed, the formal articulation of industrial relations is basically non-existent at sector level in the UK. However, employers are usually well-organized in business and trade associations if not employers' associations (which engage in collective bargaining), and trade unions maintain sector groups even where mergers have seen many industry unions become absorbed into larger general organizations (see Marginson and Meardi, this volume). The 'social partners' may also maintain informal relationships at sector level and liaise more actively around issues such as training or health and safety policy, which is to some extent organized by state institutions such as sector skills councils (see Keep *et al.*, this volume).

In short, even without formal coordination of industrial relations, the common activities of business sectors help shape common patterns and outcomes through cultural and cognitive mechanisms (DiMaggio 1997), as well as through more deliberate processes of mimicry such as benchmarking and pattern bargaining. The tacit and informal influence of the sector pressures on firm-level actors has been demonstrated in case study work, notably in Smith *et al.*'s (1990) development of a 'firm-in-sector' approach to the analysis of strategic change in Cadbury (see also Pollert 1995).

Of course, this does not necessarily mean that individual firms within a sector must always resemble each other. There is much diversity in the principal business activities and strategies of firms, and this is arguably increasing as a result of enhanced managerial discretion and more varied responses to competition (Dølvik 2001). But a focus on the sector does help explain differences *within* national employment systems (Hollingsworth *et al.* 1994), which has been relatively neglected in the 'varieties of capitalism' framework (Hall and Soskice 2001).

Distinguishing Private Sectors

The remainder of this chapter examines private-sector employment and industrial relations practice within a sector context, under the umbrella categories of privatized firms, private industry and private services. It is of course impossible to cover all aspects of private-sector industrial relations but reference is made to management strategy, trade unions and collective bargaining, and key outcomes in terms of pay, working time and work organization. To set the scene, it is useful to outline very briefly the distinguishing characteristics of the three broad 'sectors', while acknowledging that there will be major differences between organizations and individual sectors within these categories.

First, privatized firms share a common heritage of former state ownership, which contributes to relatively high levels of union membership. They are generally large employers, with a mix of blue- and white-collar labour. Many have pursued a strategy of restructuring and workforce fragmentation in different parts of their operations such as production, retail, customer services and call centres. Most of these firms provide essential public services such as energy, transport or communications; political visibility is therefore high, as is the disruptive capacity of trade unions. Second, manufacturing and industrial firms normally face high levels of competition, often internationally from within the enlarged EU and from developing countries such as India and China. New manufacturing systems are geared towards continued quality improvement and short-term customer responsiveness. Trade union organization is concentrated in the larger firms and workplaces, with only one in five workplaces (two in five employees) now covered by collective bargaining (Kersley *et al.* 2006: 180). Capital mobility, restructuring and rationalization mean that manufacturing trade unions were increasingly defensive even before the beginnings of recession in 2008. Third, private services are also competitive sectors, with a wider range of small and large firms. Workplace fragmentation and labour turnover mean that trade union organization is difficult and membership very low in sectors like retailing, 'horeca' (hotels, restaurants and catering), and leisure and tourism. In terms of union density, retail banking forms the exceptional case, partly due to a strong legacy of staff associations that were largely transformed into a sector trade union, now part of the union Unite.

Industrial Relations in the Privatized Sectors

Privatization involves the sale of state assets to private-sector organizations and individuals, and was a core policy of the Conservative governments led by Margaret Thatcher (1979–90) and John Major (1990–97). In their Hayekian worldview, the growth of the public sector had 'crowded out' productive investment in the economy and stifled entrepreneurialism; insufficient competition and 'producer capture' by vested interests also meant that public-sector organizations were overstaffed and insufficiently focused on customer satisfaction and value for money to the taxpayer.

Consequently, privatization was expected by its advocates to deliver improvements in service quality while maintaining better control of costs. Organizations would not only be freed from political interference but disciplined by shareholders and commercial competition. New regulatory bodies were introduced in industries such as rail transport, energy and telecommunications where competition was limited by market concentration; these were intended to simulate competitive pressures through mechanisms such as price control. Hence, industrial relations and employment issues were to the fore in the privatization agenda. Managers would be compelled to drive changes to employment levels, work organization, and terms and conditions of employment in order to satisfy shareholders and the regulatory authorities.

The most important privatizations, whether in terms of revenues generated or numbers of workers involved, occurred in the communications, energy and transport sectors. The most significant early privatizations, British Telecom (BT) in 1984 and British Gas in 1986, were presented as extending 'shareholding democracy' amongst employees, citizens and consumers but ownership soon passed largely into the hands of institutional investors. Later utility privatizations included the water industry in 1989 and electricity generation and supply between 1990 and 1991. In the transport sectors, the bus and coach network was progressively liberalized and privatized through the 1980s; the ports privatized in 1983–84; British Airways (BA) and the British Airports Authority were sold in 1987; and the railway network was broken up and sold off between 1995 and 1996. In addition, a series of state-owned manufacturing and engineering companies were also placed in the private sector, sometimes in stages, including British Petroleum, British Aerospace, Cable and Wireless, Jaguar, British Shipbuilders, Rolls Royce, British Airways, Rover (formerly British Leyland) and British Steel.

Perhaps the most symbolic triumph of the Thatcherite privatization process was paradoxically one of the least generally noticed. The nationalization of the coal industry in 1946 had been a major victory for the miners' union and a defining moment for the broader labour movement which had just secured its first majority Labour government. However, the victory of the miners' strikes over pay in 1972 and 1974 exercised the Conservative imagination. The Thatcher government was well prepared for the 1984 strike, and the miners were defeated after a stoppage that lasted for a year. The privatization of British Coal followed in 1994, a ten-year period in which the mining workforce fell from over 180 000 employed in 170 collieries to a rump of 10 000 working just 16 pits.

The story of the coal industry is emblematic for economic as well as political reasons: 'symptomatic, but in a very extreme form, of the deindustrialization of the UK economy' (Glyn and Machin 1997: 197). The collapse of employment in the mines occurred because of a loss of markets, due to the availability of North Sea gas, international competition and technological innovations that accelerated productivity growth.

This was also the story, albeit less dramatically, elsewhere; employment usually fell following privatization but the causes were often more complicated than the change in ownership alone. In BT, a reduction in employment from 238 000 at privatization to 124 700 15 years later was linked to a shift from cable and mechanical networks to optical fibres and wireless-based technologies. Similarly, in British Gas, automation contributed to a reduction in headcount from 92 000 at privatization to 70 000 by 1994. However, this was not a universal trend – for example, employment in the water industry actually rose from nearly 46 000 in 1990–91 to over 58 000 two years later (Parker 2004) – nor could it be sustained. Arguably more significant to management goals of improving productivity over the longer term was a widespread decentralization and individualization of employment relations (Colling and Ferner 1995). In the electricity sector, for example, in the course of just a few years four sets of occupationally based central negotiations were replaced by around 20 company agreements and subsequently around 60 sets of business-level negotiations.

Decentralization served to assert local managerial control and stretched union resources at a time of significant overall membership decline. It also facilitated the introduction of 'human resource management' (HRM) practices such as employee involvement, direct communication, teamworking and performance management techniques such as employee appraisal and variable pay. An important example concerns pay setting in the electricity, gas and water companies (IRS 2003). There were 56 pay settlements in 1990 covering over 334 000 workers. None had any merit-pay component except for very senior managerial staff. By 1995 the number of collective agreements had grown to 78 (but now covering only 174 000 workers), with 10% of employees in receipt of merit pay. In 2002 there were 85 collective agreements, covering 130 000 workers, and merit pay applied to one in five; estimates for 2003 suggested a further dramatic jump in merit pay to over one in three employees. Furthermore, many agreements contained only broad guidelines regulating how merit pay would be administered and distributed at local level. This trend towards decentralization and HRM in the privatized utilities has been linked to continuous business re-engineering and the introduction of managerial 'account-ability' through performance targets and tight budgetary control (Mulholland 2002; Ogden *et al.* 2006).

Notwithstanding membership decline and the rise of HRM, union density generally remained relatively high in privatized firms and there was even a sign of some revitalization of local activism in response to decentralization (Fairbrother 1994; Dundon 1997). The resilience of trade unions also reflects the disruptive capacity of organized labour, however localized, in sectors like the utilities and rail or air-passenger transport. With privatization, relatively small stoppages now had major impacts, not just on service provision but on profits and the company brand, and could attract additional penalties imposed by any industry regulators for failure to meet service targets. Thus, on the one hand, privatization served to weaken trade unions by increasing the transaction costs of representing a declining membership base in a fragmented institutional context. The withdrawal of state support to ailing industries or firms facing intense competition, such as in motor manufacturing and steel production, also severely reduced the capacity of trade unions to resist rationalization. This was most especially the case when firms were acquired by multinational companies (MNCs) that took an international view of their investment and production portfolios. On the other hand, privatization in many cases enhanced the potency of industrial action now that these organizations were competing for customers in the marketplace, answerable to shareholders for financial performance and, in the case of the railways and utilities, monitored by state regulators over their service standards.

Hence, privatized firms have generally been inclined to manage often quite radical change in ways that engage trade unions, or at least minimize antago-nism from them. This pattern varies, of course, between industries according to such features as competitive pressures and company profitability but, overall, industrial relations institutions were reformed rather than abandoned after pri-vatization, and conflict avoidance has been more evident than displays of 'macho management'. In broad terms, four patterns may be identified. At one end of the spectrum are the utilities companies which operate in fairly stable and highly profitable markets. Many of these were at the forefront of the development of 'partnership' agreements with trade unions as they sought to reconfigure industrial relations away from the public-sector past (Terry 1999). Employment reductions were usually managed by offering relatively generous 'voluntary' redundancy terms, and above-average pay settlements were made to remaining employees (Arrowsmith 2003). Pay in the utilities continues to be significantly higher than for the private sector overall, though with production workers faring better than retail and administrative groups (IRS 2007; Sharp 2008).

On the railways, where the unions remained strong but the prospects for employers were less benign, a different pattern emerged. Industrial disputes over pay and working conditions have become relatively common but are usually settled without recourse to strike action. When strikes do occur, they tend to be relatively short and localized. This is in large part a measure of union strength rather than weakness. Local bargaining has increased the prospect for industrial action because of the scope for 'pattern bargaining', as unions seek to upwardly harmonize terms across companies, and it is also easier for the unions to mobilize for localized action. This can have a serious financial impact on a train operating company (TOC) because of performance penalties as well as lost revenues incurred. A successful ballot for industrial action is therefore of itself an effective bargaining lever. This strategy was most successfully pursued by the drivers' union Aslef to achieve a 35-hour week and higher consolidated pay, though the RMT (which represents on-board crew, platform staff and maintenance workers) also had some success in maintaining relative pay (IDS 2007). Employers varied in their response to such union pressures. For example, whereas GNER chose a 'partnership' approach with RMT, Connex became well known for an aggressive management style; ultimately, however, the industrial disputes that this provoked led to the early termination of its south central franchise in 2000 and its southeastern operation in 2003. This concentrated the minds of other poorly performing TOCs which might have been tempted to pursue a harder, cost-driven approach to industrial relations. First Great Western, for example, the worst-performing operator in 2007 and which RMT general secretary Bob Crow described as having a 'confrontational style of management', quickly reached agreement with Aslef and RMT in 2008 after both unions successfully balloted for strike action over use of managers as on-board crew.

The third group consists of employers that pursued a more sustained and successful strategy of union marginalization. Confrontational management was perhaps most immediately and extensively observed following privatization in the ports (Turnbull 1993) and in shipbuilding (McKinlay and Taylor 1994). Both industries faced somewhat exceptional circumstances of depressed markets and an urgently perceived need to rapidly implement work flexibility and intensification. In the coal industry, RJB Mining has pursued a less belligerent approach than its predecessor British Coal, but the company has reinforced the marginalization of two unions through HRM techniques such as direct communication, share schemes and incentive pay (Parry *et al.* 1997).

Finally, two major companies experienced 'oscillating patterns of industrial relations' (Ferner and Colling 1991: 407) after privatization. Both BT and BA are large firms operating in competitive sectors and the varying balance between quality and cost in their business strategies has had different implications for industrial relations. In BT, deteriorating relations with the union culminated in a national engineers' strike in 1987, after which senior management decided to focus on changing corporate culture through techniques such as total quality management, and to pursue a more constructive approach to organizational restructuring with the union. This paved the way for a form of partnership agreement with the Communications Workers' Union in 1991 (Stoney 2002). The most significant dispute since, involving call-centre workers in 1999, was settled after a one-day strike by management concessions over workloads and the use of agency workers. In BA, business and HR strategies were still more uncertain between service and price (Turnbull *et al.* 2004). The more aggressive approach introduced in the mid-1990s resulted in the débâcle of the cabin crew dispute in 1997, when 300 strikers were joined by more than 2000 colleagues absenting themselves due to sickness. The company sought closer working relations subsequently with the TGWU, and introduced local partnership agreements with other unions (e.g. in the world cargo division, in its former subsidiary Go, and with the pilot workforce). Compared to the 1990s, strikes are now sporadic and specific. An unofficial strike by customer service staff in 2003 was settled by management assuring workers that a new system for recording working time would not be used to impose split shifts or annualized hours. A two-day walkout by Heathrow baggage handlers, also unofficial, occurred in 2005. The action was a protest in support of sacked workers at the catering sub-contractor Gate Gourmet, and cost the airline an estimated £42 million.

Thus, though there is much variation between particular companies, two things stand out about industrial relations in the privatized sectors. First, union influence has diminished due to the fragmentation of industrial relations institutions and the individualization associated with the introduction of HRM practices designed to generate a commercial outlook on the part of employees. Traditional-style industrial relations arrangements now coexist with new methods of employee involvement and the growth of variable pay, which is often not determined by collective bargaining (Pendleton 1999). Second, however, union density remains relatively high and collective bargaining is still extensive. This has largely helped contain conflict even when employers have driven major revisions to employment levels and working practices. In the utilities, the ordering of industrial relations is linked to a company's ability to 'buy out' change over time, in a context of stable and profitable markets, but also to the differentiation of collective bargaining between divisions and profit centres which dilutes trade union strength. In the railways, it is a product of a curious privatization structure that introduced little real competition while fragmenting operations between companies. This provided a fertile context for well-organized unions to pursue coordinated bargaining strategies and defend their members' pay and conditions. With ticket prices capped, and infrastructure, energy and leasing costs largely fixed, employment costs were the main variable cost under the TOCs' control. However, as employers soon discovered, the potential impact of industrial action is intensified by privatization. This is because it affects all three company goals: revenue and profit generation; maintaining brand image; and avoiding the censure of the regulatory bodies. In contrast, unions are weaker in privatized firms operating in declining and/or intensely competitive markets, such as motor manufacturing, steel production and shipbuilding. Here, the priority is enterprise survival, especially in the case of multinational owners operating internal markets for investment and production. BT and BA fall in between; both operate in competitive markets, but from a position of leadership, which makes constructive industrial relations and the minimization of disputes both attractive and perhaps more feasible than in struggling companies.

Industrial Relations in the Manufacturing Sectors

The recent history of UK manufacturing at best makes for very mixed reading. While employment has shrunk dramatically, and manufacturing is relatively less important to gross domestic product (GDP) than it once was, output has continued to increase and the UK remains the sixth-largest manufacturer in the world. In 25 years from 1979, the overall share of GDP accounted for by manufacturing fell from 27% to 14%, and employment halved to around 3.5 million – though perhaps up to 20% of this decline is accounted for by externalizing support and service operations to 'service-sector' contractors (Oxford Economics 2007). At the same time, there was very strong productivity growth resulting from investment in new technologies and forms of work organization, together with the closure of less productive plants (Disney *et al.* 2003).

There is also much variation of experience between different sectors, not least due to the different effects of 'globalization'. The rapid rise of the so-called 'BRIC' economies of Brazil, Russia, India and China has presented new markets for manufacturers of high value-added, knowledge-based industrial goods, though their markets for consumer products remain relatively limited. Conversely, traditional manufacturers of standardized products have been hit by a combination of low-wage competition from overseas, falling costs of international transportation and relatively high sterling exchange rates, until very recently. Hence, whereas output in textiles halved between 1980 and 2006, for example, output in pharmaceuticals more than quadrupled, and aerospace doubled (Oxford Economics 2007).

Chemicals, pharmaceuticals and aerospace are the 'high fliers' of UK manufacturing but much of the sector is characterized by a 'low-skills equilibrium', centred on cost competition in the product market and the exploitation of a plentiful supply of relatively cheap, low-skilled labour (Finegold and Soskice, 1988; see Keep *et al.*, this volume). Yet every part of manufacturing experienced significant employment decline in the last decade (Table 8.2). In the eight years from 1998 (when the classification system changed) to 2006 (the most recent available data), manufacturing employment declined by 29%. The textile and leather workforce collapsed, and major reductions also occurred in the electrical equipment and machinery manufacturing sectors. According to ONS, by 2006 employment in manufacturing was at its lowest since records began in 1841. The largest manufacturing sector in terms of employment is now food and drink production and processing, where proximity to market is important, followed

Table 8.2   Manufacturing employment, 1998–2006

	1998	2006	% change
All manufacturing	4416	3141	−28.9
Food products; beverages and tobacco	538	445	−20.9
Textiles and textile products	342	116	−66.1
Leather and leather products	34	11	−67.6
Wood and wood products	91	85	−6.6
Pulp, paper and paper products; publishing and printing	507	403	−20.5
Coke, refined petroleum products and nuclear fuel	27	24	−11.1
Chemicals, chemical products and man-made fibres	274	212	−22.6
Rubber and plastic products	271	208	−23.2
Other non-metallic mineral products	150	113	−24.7
Basic metals and fabricated metal products	560	406	−27.5
Machinery and equipment not elsewhere classified	406	278	−31.5
Electrical and optical equipment	545	327	−40.0
Transport equipment	430	326	−24.2
Manufacture not elsewhere classified	240	188	−25.8

SIC 2003; average yearly total.

Source: ABI, ONS, June 2008.

by the broad collection of businesses classified under paper manufacturing, publishing and printing.

Nevertheless, when in a context of overall economic growth, policy makers were generally less agitated about numbers employed in the sector than they were concerned with productivity and skills (see e.g. BERR/Department for Innovation, Universities and Skills 2008). In particular, 'high-performance' work systems (HPWS) were promoted as a means to close the productivity gap with international competitors while improving job quality through the development and involvement of employees (DTI 2002). In contrast to Taylorist forms of work design and control, HPWS are associated with teamwork and flexible job design; an emphasis on training, learning and employee commitment; extensive communication systems; employee involvement and responsibility in decision making; performance management and appraisal; and employers' commitment to job security. As such, HPWS represents both a form of strategic HRM based on 'bundles' of integrated labour policies and practices (MacDuffie 1995), while also closely resembling the TUC notion of partnership (Danford *et al.* 2005).

The concept of HPWS also has had a wide appeal to policy makers and practitioners (EEF/CIPD 2003; TUC 2006) but there is little evidence for its extensive adoption in UK manufacturing (Wood 1999; Guest *et al.* 2003). The association between HPWS practices and performance outcomes is also generally weak (Edwards and Sengupta, this volume; Ramsay *et al.* 2000). Initiatives such as teamwork and employee participation are insufficiently 'deep' to challenge existing attitudes and the fundamentals of job design (Edwards *et al.* 2002). Indeed, the superficial introduction of HPWS can be seen as a means to intensify work and assert managerial control, not through the direct methods associated with Taylorism (which structures conflict and is less appropriate to complex production systems), but by more subtle techniques such as peer surveillance, multitasking and working-time flexibility (Godard 2004).

The limited adoption of HPWS in part reflects the challenges posed by competition to the manufacturing sector. It is difficult to commit to ongoing training when resources are tight, or to job security when the reality is organizational restructuring and 'downsizing'. Yet it is also indicative of the more fundamental features of corporate governance within the UK indicated at the beginning of this chapter. The ability to pursue HPWS is limited by a systemic short-term and cost-centred focus within UK firms (see also Sisson and Purcell, this volume). Modern techniques of cost accounting and budgetary control, together with the extensive use of management performance targets based on unit labour costs, reinforce the structure of short-termism within the firm (Armstrong 2000). Tight financial discipline is an important reason why most UK manufacturing firms have relatively low investment rates, even when economic conditions and interest rates are favourable (Wilkes *et al.* 1996). The situation is compounded by the highly internationalized nature of UK manufacturing. Nearly half (46%) of MNCs in the UK are manufacturing firms, and foreign-owned MNCs alone account for nearly a fifth (18%) of the manufacturing workforce (Edwards *et al.* 2007). 'Coercive comparisons' of performance are a feature of industrial relations in international manufacturing firms as a means to discipline local management and labour (Mueller and Purcell 1992). Importantly, such comparisons need not actually result in disinvestment; the collection and comparison of performance data may be enough by itself (Arrowsmith and Marginson 2006).

Thus, in the 'Anglo-Saxon' model most manufacturing companies are structurally averse to HPWS forms of employment. Instead, firms tend to adapt low-skilled labour to new techniques such as just-in-time and cellular production, since this enables them to respond to increased variability in demand and requirements for product customization without fundamentally altering the nature of workplace relations (Ackroyd and Procter 1998). Even in the R&D-intensive sectors such as pharmaceuticals, engine manufacture and defence, employers are generally unwilling or unable to adopt radically new forms of work organization or industrial relations based on meaningful worker involvement. A study of the pharmaceutical and aerospace industries, for example, found that employee consultation and participation were limited by short-term cost considerations (Lloyd 2000), irrespective of whether the work was highly skilled or the workforce strongly unionized (Lloyd 1999; Lloyd and Newell, 2001). Commercial exigencies undermine HPWS in practice (Danford *et al.* 2007).

Elsewhere, in the 'low road' parts of manufacturing, unions are largely absent and managers show little interest in practices such as formal employee involvement. This is particularly the case in small firms in sectors like food manufacturing, where workers generally possess limited skills and have little work autonomy; they also receive low pay and benefits and have very few opportunities for promotion (Sengupta *et al.* 2009). At the same time, case-study research identifies compensatory factors such as relative employment security, sociable work relations and limited work intensity (Edwards *et al.* 2009). Other studies of low pay and marginal work indicate that there are far fewer signs of labour exploitation found in manufacturing than in parts of the service sectors (Palmer *et al.* 2008; CoVE 2008; Low Pay Commission 2008).

As economic recession develops, the potential for industrial conflict may well increase, over pensions and redundancy as well as pay and collective bargaining rights. Yet, in practice, industrial action remains rare; only 22 strikes were recorded across all manufacturing sectors in 2007 (Hale 2008). Indeed, with the global as well as domestic economy entering recession, and as the lack of liquidity hits investment as well as demand, the prospects for manufacturing unions appear bleak. Job losses in unionized firms reduce membership levels and make unions appear impotent in the face of rationalization. The appeal of trade unions to workers, and their recognition and involvement by employers, is thereby diminished across both organized and unorganized firms, with the latter a significant cause of earlier decline (Machin 2000). Their fundamental problem, now more acute with recession, is that 'no one can be bothered to join an ineffective union and managers see no need to deal with a weak one' (Terry 2003b: 459).

Industrial Relations in the Service Sectors

The UK service sector accounts for most private-sector employment. It is large and heterogeneous, comprising a diverse range of activities with great variation in markets, firm size and competitive strategies. It can, however, be differentiated into consumer, business and social services. Consumer services employ the largest number of people. These include retailing, which now employs around the same number of workers as manufacturing, at 3.1 million; wholesale and distribution, with 1.8 million employees; and hotel and catering with 1.9 million (Brook 2008). Other large consumer service sectors include leisure and tourism (723 000 employees), real estate (498 000); machinery hire (175 000); personal services such as child care and hairdressing (365 000); and retail banking (543 000). The business service sector comprises firms that provide creative, technical and support services to other firms. These also employ large numbers: the Annual Business Inquiry (ABI) records nearly 4 million workers in business services including 918 000 in legal and accounting firms, 737 000 in labour recruitment, 585 000 in computer services firms, 426 000 in industrial cleaning, 354 000 in architecture and engineering services, 284 000 in business and management consulting and 101 000 in research and development services (DTI 2007). Finally, private firms in sectors such as health and social services employ 1.2 million people, with another 1.4 million involved in other community-based personal services.

Notwithstanding this diversity, a number of employment features unite much service-sector work and differentiate it from manufacturing. For example, there are a larger number of small firms and a higher proportion of low paid, female and part-time employment. Outside of banking and insurance, trade union representation is almost universally low. Many jobs also have an emphasis on 'soft' as well as technical skills given the direct and immediate relationship with the customer, raising the peculiar issue of 'emotional labour'. There are also concerns of the extent of 'vulnerable work' in many service-sector occupations. These themes are explored below.

Firm size

Small and medium sized enterprises (SMEs) are strongly represented in the service sectors due to relatively low barriers to entry (see Ram and Edwards, this volume). In business services as a whole, average employment is eight staff and only accountancy and research and development demonstrate market concentration (DTI 2007: 20). Over a third of retail firms, two in five hotel and catering businesses and more than half of private-sector firms engaged in health and social work activities, had fewer than 50 employees in 2007. This compares to less than one in five (18.7%) manufacturing firms. At the same time, large firms are prominent in sectors such as banking and retailing, some of which have been amongst the biggest and most profitable private-sector employers in the UK. Food retailing is another sector with enormous concentration. The supermarket giant Tesco now employs over 280 000 staff, and returned a pre-tax profit of over £2 billion in 2008.

Flexible employment

The service sector is characterized by widespread use of 'flexible' patterns of work, especially part-time employment, whatever the size of firm (Grimshaw and Rubery, this volume). In particular, approaching a third (30.6%) of workers in the retail and hotel and catering sectors were either part-time or temporary in 2006, compared to 4.7% in manufacturing, according to the Labour Force Survey (LFS). There are a number of inter-related demand- and supply-side explanations for this. First, service-sector firms such as hotels, restaurants, shops and banks experience cycles of demand that vary according to season, days of the week and parts of the working day. The planned use of part-time and temporary work is a cost-effective way to meet peak demand, and offer extended trading hours, without hoarding labour over slack times. Second, many service-sector firms are labour rather than capital intensive and are thus keen to minimize staffing since a relatively high proportion of costs are related to employment. According to ABI (2007) data, employment costs in horeca are 27.7% of sector turnover, compared to 17.4% in manufacturing and 6.7% in electricity, gas and water supply. The use of part-time work also offers a broader population of employees from which to arrange cover for absence, which has a bigger impact where staffing is minimized. Third, part-time and temporary work can sustain productivity and service quality in jobs that can be both fast-paced and monotonous. Processing customers while ensuring attentive personal service can be demanding in jobs like checkout operating, waiting on tables, or in call centres, and may be better delivered over shorter time periods. The extensive use of part-time and temporary employment is also enabled by the elementary nature of much service-sector work. Though many occupations require technical skills, and most rely heavily on undervalued 'soft' interpersonal skills, a large number of frontline service positions require few formal qualifications or extended periods of training. This serves to widen the pool of available recruits, depress wage rates and reduce the duplication and disposal costs of training associated with part-time and temporary employment. Finally, these so-called 'atypical' forms of employment also help employers draw more easily on groups such as students, care-givers and older workers who need or choose to work shorter hours. A majority (56%) of working-age women with dependent children work part-time, and a third of all men in employment after state retirement age also work part-time (Smeaton and McKay 2003). According to the NatWest Student Living Index 2008, three quarters of a million undergraduates (42% of the UK student population) will be in part-time employment at the start of the 2008/09 academic year. Such workers may have fewer demands for career development and may be more tolerant of lower pay as the price of working-time flexibility, especially where the job is viewed as interim or providing supplementary income (Walsh 1990; Arrowsmith and McGoldrick 1996).

Hence, employment patterns in services are related to the segmented demography of the workforce and wider societal conditions. Education and child care costs, for example, contribute to low pay, low skills and low working time. As Rubery (2005: 276) puts it, 'employers take into account the segmentation of the labour market in shaping their employment systems'.

Trade unions

A further factor relevant to low pay is a lack of trade union organization. The sectors with the lowest average rates of pay, according to the Annual Survey of Hours and Earnings (ASHE), are hotels and restaurants and retail. Average gross weekly pay for full-time workers in hotel and catering was £187 in 2006, and in retailing £198; these are less than half the rates prevailing in the more well-organized and male-dominated sectors such as manufacturing (£431) and energy and water (£530). According to WERS data (Kersley et al. 2006: 180), only 9% of workplaces in wholesale and retail had any collective bargaining over pay, and just 2% of hotels and restaurants; elsewhere, the figure for business services was 10%, with financial services the exceptional outlier with 63% coverage. In terms of union density, the LFS reports figures of 5.6% for hotels and restaurants; 10% in business services; 11.1%, wholesale and retail; 20.3%, other services; and 24.3% in financial intermediation (Grainger and Crowther 2007: 18). This compares to 22.2% in manufacturing, 41.2% in transport, storage and communication and 49.3% in electricity, gas and water supply.

Unions have been energetic for some time in trying to engage the service-sector workforce (Waddington and Dølvik 2002) but the combination of employer apathy and hostility with the intrinsic difficulties of organizing a workforce that is twice dispersed has provided durable obstacles. Workers are scattered across a large number of often small workplaces; these problems of spatial dispersion are compounded by a temporal fragmentation of working hours (part-time work) and employee turnover. In addition, demand for union membership is often attenuated by three considerations: fear, reflecting indi-vidual employee vulnerability (Poynter 2000); ignorance, with immigrant and young workers in particular often never having encountered a trade union (Haynes *et al.* 2005); and calculations of cost relative to anticipated benefits (Galenson 1994; Visser 2002).

Even where trade unions are recognized, they often have limited influence (Marchington and Parker 1990). For example, a significant proportion of service-sector union members work in retail or banking, which have both experienced increased competition and major technological changes resulting in pressure on pay and employment. In food retailing, the arrival of the discounters in the early 1990s reintroduced aggressive price competition to an increasingly oligopolistic sector in which the market leaders had been promoting a differentiation strategy based on product quality and customer service. At the same time, increased trad-ing times resulting from the deregulation of opening hours added to pressures on costs. Employer strategies focused both on reducing total labour hours, through more sophisticated scheduling and part-time work and on reducing labour costs per hour, through the removal of hours premia and allowances. They met with active union resistance only in the distribution depots (Waddington 2001). The shopworkers' union USDAW estimates it has to recruit some 70 000 workers a year just to maintain its membership levels, making it highly dependent on its relationships with the large employers such as Tesco, where it has a partnership agreement.

Similarly, in the financial services sector, the intense competition that followed deregulation in the late 1980s was followed by major changes associated with the introduction of new technology in the 1990s. Computerization of data processing enabled the banks to centralize and separate 'back office' work from the branch network, which now became focused more explicitly on selling. This process was associated with work intensification, branch closures and a reduction in full-time employment. Perhaps not surprisingly, union membership density held up in the face of this transformation in the experience of work, and the large banks have maintained trade union recognition agreements. Collective bargaining encour-aged the banks to follow an approach to rationalization that avoided compulsory redundancies, though this commitment began to look fragile as thousands of job losses were announced at the beginning of 2009. However, it also came at a price; even in the era of super-profits, pay growth was limited and increasingly directed away from base earnings to variable payments systems outside the remit of collective bargaining (Arrowsmith *et al.* 2008).

Work organization and the experience of work

Trade union weakness is both a symptom and a cause of the individualization and informality of employee relations observed in much of the service sector (Ram *et al.* 2001). The employment relationship in services is also distinguished by its triangular nature, whereby workers have direct contact with, and are normally visible to, the customer. This has implications for managerial approaches to motivation and control. On the one hand, the direct relationship that frontline workers have with the customer might promote a more progressive management style based on employee job satisfaction and commitment. On the other hand, much of the literature suggests that the customer relationship is yet another device with which to subjugate labour. This is said to occur in three main ways. First, the immediate nature of the customer relationship, which is shared by management and staff, reinforces the unitarist assumptions of management and the use of customer service as an ideological notion to assert 'normative and cultural' control over workers' attitudes (van den Broek 2004). Second, the customer participates as an agent of managerial control via the potential sanction of complaints (Leidner 1996). Third, the presence of the customer draws attention to the construction and presentation of the self, or what Hochschild (1983) termed the performance of 'emotional labour', encouraging workers to be self-disciplined in meeting customer (i.e. employer) expectations in subjective terms as well as in getting tasks done.

However, forms of control are mediated by context and contingencies such as market conditions and management strategies. As Boxall observes (2003: 15), the customer–employee interface means that 'the match, or fit, between competitive strategy and HR strategy is greater in services than it is in manufacturing', but how this is exercised depends on the nature of the business and its differentiating strategy. Where the strategy is based on innovation or service quality then forms of 'soft' HRM may be observed that emphasize employee involvement and 'empowerment'; where the essential focus is on cost reduction then 'hard' HRM may be to the fore (Schuler and Jackson 1987). Cost competition around fairly standardized service offerings (as in fast-food retailing) is more likely to involve a Taylorist labour process involving close supervision and target-driven, low-discretion work but even here, unhappy employees are likely to be bad for business. Furthermore, the world of work offers scope for employee resistance, whether individual and informal or organized and explicit. That employment is necessarily a 'contested terrain' only adds to the diversity observed in management strategy and style, which can be seen even in three sectors that seem to typify a 'hard' approach to the management of labour. Call centres have become of increasing interest because of their rapid growth and the opportunities that technology provides for the close supervision of staff. Fast-food retailing is an equally large sector, with McDonald's usually served up as the paradigm case of a highly Taylorized organization of work. Hotels are also seen to offer scope for autocratic management exercised through personal forms of control. However, as will be briefly suggested below, there is also variation within each sector that reflects contingencies such as labour market conditions and employee turnover; the type of business, or product market niche; and a firm's financial and management resources.

Employment in call centres, or customer contact centres, has grown rapidly due to advances in computer technology. In 1995 there were 143 900 workers in around 2500 call centres; by 2003 there were 790 000 (half a million of whom were customer service representatives, or CSRs) employed in over 5320 centres (DTI 2004). Notwithstanding the 'offshoring' of call-centre work, the sector has continued a steady growth, with industry estimates of nearly 650 000 CSRs and 6000 centres in 2007. Most call-centre work involves operators processing a succession of remote customer requests or problems via telephone enquiries, though some are also engaged in 'outward' calls to sell or market products. Early research likened call centres to 'white-collar factories' or 'electronic sweatshops', where work was subjectively experienced as an 'assembly line in the head' (Taylor and Bain 1999). This was because much of the work was routine, highly scripted and intense. Management was able to closely monitor and therefore discipline employees by using customer-processing data and listening to customer interactions. Fernie and Metcalf (1998) likened this to an all-seeing but unseen 'electronic panopticon'. The result for workers was 'emotional exhaustion' owing to a high volume of customer interactions and a lack of variety of tasks (Deery *et al.* 2002).

However, not all call centres are the same. Some work requires staff to have a high level of product knowledge or confers a degree of discretion because it involves problem solving and customization (Lankshear *et al.* 2001). In these circumstances, there is some evidence of employee involvement, teamwork, a commitment to training, better and more stable pay and choice over working time, all of which have fewer deleterious implications for workers' well-being (Hutchinson *et al.* 2000; Holman 2004). Furthermore, surveillance is not just used as a control mechanism and sanction against 'poor performers'. It can also be used to reward effective performance, support employees via training, and offer them protection in their interactions with customers (Austrin and West 2005). Recruitment and retention problems (often exacerbated by the clustering of call centres within regional development areas) also provided an incentive for management to ameliorate some of the worst aspects of call-centre work (Halliden and Monks 2005; Kinnie *et al.* 2000). Finally, workers also have available to them various forms of individual and collective resistance, including manipulation of workloads, quit threats and peer pressure against 'rate-busters', as management try to reconcile cost and efficiency targets with quality of service (Bain and Taylor 2000). Indeed, the managerial rhetoric of quality customer service also becomes a potential resource for workers to mobilize protest and influence managerial and customer expectations (Rosenthal 2004).

The fast-food sector is commonly seen as the closest approximation of service-sector work to the Taylorist manufacturing paradigm. Customer demand is for low priced, standardized products; production is high volume, low margin and delivered 'just-in-time'; and the work, which is repetitive and closely supervised, involves limited skill or discretion. Pay and benefits are relatively low, reflecting labour substitutability (Royle 1999). Job satisfaction is also limited because there is little scope for any meaningful engagement with customers. Yet, even in such a highly structured work environment there is large variation in management style, workplace culture and the experience of work (Newman 2007). This is related to the relatively small size of these workplaces which makes the personalities and views of individual managers (and franchise-holders) particularly significant to business strategy and management style; some will be autocrats but others will prefer to be benevolent paternalists. This observation also applies to the broader hotel and catering sector, where it has been argued that cost-control generates an 'extreme' or 'ruthless' approach to employee relations manifested in authoritarian management, close employee monitoring and ready use of dismissal (Head and Lucas 2004: 707). However, firms may employ a differentiated approach to staff, with 'softer' methods designed to attract and retain scarce and higher-skilled employees such as cooks; equally, hotels operating in the higher-quality end of the market are more likely to have in place HR strategies and practices predicated on a connection between customer service and staff training, communication, responsibility and job satisfaction (Hoque 1999). Again, the immediacy of the customer relationship means that firms have to reconcile a tension between cost control and the qualitative dimensions of service delivered by frontline staff (Korczynski 2001).

This is not to deny, however, that a significant part of service sector employment is characterized by routine, unsatisfying work which is governed unilaterally by hard-line management. The TUC's Commission on Vulnerable Employment identified a 'vulnerable workforce' of 2 million people in the UK, employed mainly in care homes, hotels and restaurants, hairdressing and beauty businesses, and cleaning and security firms. Vulnerable work is defined as 'precarious work that places people at risk of continuing poverty and injustice resulting from an imbalance of power in the employer–worker relationship' (CoVE 2008: 12). It is insecure and often 'informal' labour (particularly in the case of migrant workers) in which little real protection is available from arbitrary management either collectively, from trade unions, or in practice from the law. It is also the case that private services account for most low-paid jobs. Labour Force Survey data shows that 70% of workers in hotel and catering and 55% in retail and wholesale were paid less than £7 per hour in 2007, compared to 21% in manufacturing (Palmer *et al.* 2008: 77). Seven of the Low Pay Commission's ten low-paying sectors are private services (the remainder are agriculture, food processing and clothing), and nearly two thirds (64%) of minimum-wage jobs are held by women (LPC 2008: 7–8). This has particular implications for gender pay equality given the extent of female employment in the service sector and their under-representation in trade unions; a mere 13.1% of female private-sector workers are members, compared to nearly two in ten (19.3%) for men.

Discussion and Conclusions

Two things stand out from this review of the key features of employment and industrial relations in the UK private sector. The first is the demise of formal, institutional, industrial relations. Most firms do not deal with trade unions and where they do, unions generally lack influence. The exceptions are likely to be found in privatized firms. This draws attention to a second point, that sector is an important shaper of, and constraint on, 'strategic choice'. There are differences within sectors according to competitive strategy and other contingencies, but also clear differences between sectors in terms of employment patterns and the regulation of work.

The demise of private sector industrial relations

The conventional notion of 'industrial relations' barely applies across much of the private sector. First, employment regulation is in large part de-collectivized and subject to unilateral management control. At firm level, trade union membership, recognition and collective bargaining are now low, not only historically and relative to the public sector, but in absolute terms. Organized conflict is rare, and usually confined to ex-public-sector firms. Only 13% of days lost to strike action occur in the private sector, even though this accounts for around 80% of jobs (Hale 2008).

Second, where collective bargaining occurs, management is more than ever in the driving seat, utilizing unions as 'partners' in 'productivity coalitions' where it suits (Hyman 1996; Terry 2003b), or incorporating and effectively marginalizing them through 'negotiations' that are narrowly focused and often ritualistic (Forth and Millward 2002; Brown et al. 1998). It is increasingly difficult to demonstrate trade union effectiveness in manufacturing or private services, whether in terms of collective bargaining or the recruitment and mobilization of workers. Somewhat ironically, unions are more likely to be effective at the individual level, for example by sponsoring claims to Employment Tribunals (Colling 2006).

Third, non-union forms of collective representation are also exceptional (Charlwood and Terry 2007; see also Terry, this volume) and, where they do develop, generally constitute feeble mechanisms for channelling employee voice (Lloyd 2001; Gollan 2001, 2002; Butler 2005). Recent research suggests that little has changed following the introduction of the Information and Consultation of Employees (ICE) Regulations 2004 (Hall et al. 2007; Terry this volume).

The decline of private-sector trade unions began in the Thatcher era with the demise of large-scale manufacturing, the expansion of private services and a series of legal restrictions on their ability to function effectively (Metcalf 2004). The intensification and internationalization of competition in the 1990s, and the organizational restructuring that ensued, rendered their situation 'close to critical' by the turn of the decade (Terry 2003b: 459). But more than a decade of Labour government has made little difference. Despite the reintroduction of a statutory union recognition procedure, UK workers have relatively limited countervailing power, either in law (Gourevitch and Shinn 2005) or from independent organization. Across much of the growing service sectors, it is difficult to recruit, retain and organize workers due to the atomization of workplaces and fragmented patterns of labour use. In manufacturing and industry, heightened competitive pressures and employment decline have also contributed to trade union weakness. In some cases, the integration of production into rapid-response 'lean' systems has increased the potential power of workers, but the union membership has been largely well disciplined by the internationalization of competition and the threat or actualization of relocation, outsourcing and other forms of organizational restructuring.

Private-sector unions have responded to these challenges in three main ways. The first is essentially defensive, and involves consolidating the existing membership and resources by a series of mergers. The general union Unite, which was formed by a merger between the TGWU and Amicus in 2007, is by far the largest in the private sector, with a total membership of around 2 million. Amicus was itself the product of a merger between MSF and AEEU in 2002, and in 2004 absorbed the finance union Unifi and print union GPMU. The second response is also basically defensive, and involves making the case for trade union representation to employers in the language of 'partnership' (Terry 2003a; see also Terry, this volume). These arrangements offer reassurances to trade unions concerning workforce access and representation rights. The quid pro quo is that unions emphasize their commitment to business goals and aversion to industrial action. The upshot, according to some studies, is that unions cede greater control to management over the pace and organization of work (Upchurch *et al.* 2008). 'Partnership' can thus be seen as the product, and even a further cause of trade union weakness (Kelly 2004). The third response involves experimenting with various servicing and, increasingly, organizing initiatives in order to increase membership levels, but this has been difficult to sustain against widespread employer opposition (Heery and Simms 2007; Simms and Charlwood, this volume).

Overall, none of this has done more than arrest the rate of membership decline. A couple of generations ago, when Mrs Thatcher took office, most private-sector workers were union members. By 1995 the figure was one in five (21.6%) and in 2006 just 16.6% (Grainger and Crowther 2007: 4). Of private-sector workplaces with ten or more employees in 2004, 86% had no arrangements for collective bargaining and more than three quarters (77%) had no union members at all (Kersley *et al.* 2006: 112).

The (tacit) significance of sector

Beneath these general observations, however, lie important nuances at the level of sector. Privatized firms, manufacturing companies and service sector firms are each distinct categories, and further patterns of variation were identified within them. Whereas employers' power resources are intrinsic to their role as recruiters and managers of labour and reflect their relative wealth, the power resources available to labour are much more likely to vary. Crucially, they depend on the ability 'to impose sanctions, directly or indirectly, on the employer' (Batstone 1988: 223). This has two dimensions; first, it is a product of the organization of the production system, i.e. the disruptive capacity of labour; second, it reflects scarcity value in the labour market, which is related to skill and substitutability. Of course, the presence and mobilization ability of trade unions is also very important for these workers' resources to have any purposeful effect.

It is evident that not only do the power resources available to labour vary between sectors, they have generally diminished over time (Simms and Charlwood, this volume). In most privatized firms workers remain highly organized with high disruptive capacity and moderate to high scarcity value; this is attenuated, however, in firms operating in competitive sectors where the exercise of power may be self-damaging. International competition has generally diminished workers' power resources across manufacturing, compounding the effects of structural short-termism to retard implementation of such employment innovations associated with 'high performance working'. The power resources available to workers are generally weakest in private services, and more closely linked to individual scarcity value in the labour market. Trade unions are largely absent and conflict is likely to be informal and individualized (Edwards 1988).

A future agenda for industrial relations research could be to analyse this 'frontier of control' (Batstone 1988) further, incorporating the cognitive dimensions identified in organizational sociology. Empirical research is necessary to investigate how far similarities in employment practices within sectors, and differences between them, are maintained by structural features relating to sector *activities*, including technologies, patterns of demand and, in some cases, regulation; and how far *identities* and *networks* play a part even in the absence of formal articulation and coordination by employers' associations and trade unions, which is now the case in most private sectors. In the meantime, the vicious circle of diminishing power resources and trade union organization is likely to continue across the private sector for some time.

References

Ackroyd, S. and Procter, S. 1998: British manufacturing organization and workplace industrial relations: some attributes of the new flexible firm. *British Journal of Industrial Relations*, 36 (2), 163–183.

Armstrong, P. 2000: Accounting for insecurity. *Critical Perspectives on Accounting*, 11, 383–406.

Arrowsmith, J. 2003: Post-privatisation industrial relations in the UK rail and electricity industries. *Industrial Relations Journal*, 34 (3), 150–163.

Arrowsmith, J. 2009: *Temporary Agency Work and Collective Bargaining*. Dublin: European Foundation.

Arrowsmith, J. and Marginson, P. 2006: The European cross-border dimension to collective bargaining in multi-national companies. *European Journal of Industrial Relations*, 12 (3), 245–266.

Arrowsmith, J. and McGoldrick, A. 1996: HRM service practices: flexibility, quality and employee strategy. *International Journal of Service Industries Management*, July, 7 (3), 46–62.

Arrowsmith, J. and Sisson, K. 2001: International competition and pay, working time and employment: exploring the processes of adjustment. *Industrial Relations Journal*, 32 (2), 136–153.

Arrowsmith, J. and Sisson, K. 1999: Pay and working time: towards organisation based systems? *British Journal of Industrial Relations*, 37 (1), 51–75.

Arrowsmith, J., Nicholaisen, H., Bechter, B. and Nonell, R. 2008: The management of variable pay in banking: forms and rationale in four European countries. *Bulletin of Comparative Labour Relations*, 67, 201–240.

Austrin, T. and West, J. 2005: Skills and surveillance in casino gaming: work, consumption and regulation. *Work, Employment and Society*, 19 (2), 305–326.

Bain, P. and Taylor, P. 2000: Entrapped by the 'electronic panoptican'? Worker resistance in the call centre. *New Technology, Work and Employment*, 15 (1), 2–18.

Batstone, E. 1988: The frontier of control. In Gallie, D. (ed.) *Employment in Britain*. Oxford: Basil Blackwell, pp. 218–247.

BERR/Department for Innovation, Universities and Skills 2008: *Manufacturing: New Challenges, New Opportunities*. London: BERR.

Brady, D. and Denniston, R. 2006: Economic globalization, industrialization and de-industrialization in affluent democracies. *Social Forces*, 85 (1), 297–327.

Brook, K. 2008: Developments in measuring the UK service industries, 1990 to 2006. *Economic and Labour Market Review*, 2 (1), 18–29.

Boxall, P. 2003: HR strategy and competitive advantage in the service sector. *Human Resource Management Journal*, 13 (3), 5–20.

Brown, W., Deakin, S., Hudson, M., Pratten, C. and Ryan, P. 1998: *The Individualisation of Employment Contracts in Britain*. Department of Trade and Industry Employment Relations Research Series 4, London: HMSO.

Butler, P. 2005: Non-union employee representation: exploring the efficacy of the voice process. *Employee Relations*, 27 (3), 272–288.

Charlwood, A. and Terry, M. 2007: Twenty-first-century models of employee representation: structures, processes and outcomes. *Industrial Relations Journal*, 38 (4), 320–337.

Colling, T. 2006: What space for unions on the floor of rights? Trade unions and the enforcement of statutory individual employment rights. *Industrial Law Journal*, 35 (2), 140–160.

Colling, T. and Ferner, A. 1995: Privatisation and marketization. In Edwards, P. (ed.) *Industrial Relations*. Oxford: Blackwell, pp. 491–514.

CoVE 2008: *Hard Work, Hidden Lives*. London: TUC Commission on Vulnerable Employment (CoVE). http://www.vulnerableworkers.org.uk/files/CoVE_full_report.pdf

Danford, A., Richardson, M., Stewart, P., Tailby, S. and Upchurch, M. 2005: *Partnership and the High Performance Workplace – Work and Employment Relations in the Aerospace Industry*. Basingstoke, UK: Palgrave Macmillan.

Danford, A., Richardson, M., Stewart, P., Tailby, S. and Upchurch, M. 2007: Capital mobility, job loss, and union strategy: the case of the UK aerospace industry. *Labor Studies Journal*, 32 (3), 298–318.

Deery, S., Iverson, R. and Walsh, J. 2002: Work relationships in telephone call centres: understanding emotional exhaustion and employee withdrawal. *Journal of Management Studies*, 39 (4), 471–496.

Disney, R., Haskel, J. and Heden, Y. 2003: Restructuring and productivity growth in UK manufacturing. *The Economic Journal*, 113 (July), 666–694.

DiMaggio, P. 1997: Culture and cognition. *Annual Review of Sociology*, 23, 263–287.

Dølvik, J.-E. 2001: Determinants of service employment: an overview. In Dølvik, J.-E. (ed.) *At Your Service? Comparative Perspectives on Employment and Labour Relations in the European Private Sector Services*. Brussels: P.I.E. Lang, pp. 17–52.

DTI 2002: *High-Performance Workplaces: The Role of Employee Involvement in a Modern Economy*. London: DTI.

DTI 2004: *The UK Contact Centre Industry: A Study*. London: Department of Trade and Industry (DTI).

DTI 2007: Business services and globalization. *Economic Papers, no. 19*. London: DTI.

Dundon, T. 1997: Post-privatised shop steward organisation and union renewal at Girobank. *Industrial Relations Journal*, 29 (2), 126–136.

Edwards, P. 1988: Patterns of conflict and accommodation. In Gallie, D. (ed.) *Employment in Britain*. Oxford: Basil Blackwell, pp. 187–217.

Edwards, P., Edwards, T., Ferner, A., Marginson, P. and Tregaskis, O. with Adam, D. and Meyer, M. 2007: *Employment Practices of MNCs in Organisational Context: A Large-Scale Survey*, report of main survey, June. http://www2.warwick.ac.uk/fac/soc/wbs/projects/mncemployment/conference_papers/full_report_july.pdf

Edwards, P., Geary, J. and Sisson, K. 2002: New forms of work organization in the workplace. In Murray, G., Bélanger, J., Giles, A. and Lapointe, P.-A. (eds) *Work and Employment Relations in the High Performance Workplace*. London: Continuum, pp. 72–119.

Edwards, P., Sengupta, S. and Tsai, C.-J. 2009: Manufacturing low-skill workers: a study of small UK food manufacturing firms. *Human Resource Management Journal*, 19 (1), 40–58.

EEF/CIPD 2003: *Maximising Employee Potential and Business Performance: The Role of High-Performance Working*. London: CIPD.

Fairbrother, P. 1994: Privatisation and local trade unionism. *Work, Employment and Society*, 8 (3), 339–356.

Ferner, A. and Colling, T. 1991: Privatization, regulation and industrial relations. *British Journal of Industrial Relations*, 29 (3), 391–409.

Fernie, S. and Metcalf, D. 1998: *(Not) Hanging on the Telephone: Payments Systems in the New Sweatshops*. Centre for Economic Performance, London School of Economics.

Finegold, D. and Soskice, D. 1988: The failure of training in Britain: analysis and prescription. *Oxford Review of Economic Policy*, 4 (3), 21–53.

Forth, J. and Millward, N. 2002: Pay settlements in Britain. *NIESR Discussion Paper173*. London: National Institute of Economic and Social Research.

Galenson, W. 1994: *Trade Union Growth and Decline: An International Study*. Westport, CT: Praeger Publishers.

Glyn, A. and Machin, S. 1997: Colliery closures and the decline of the UK coal industry. *British Journal of Industrial Relations*, 35 (2), 197–214.

Godard, J. 2004: A critical assessment of the high-performance paradigm. *British Journal of Industrial Relations*, 42 (2), 349–378.

Gollan, P. 2001: Tunnel vision: non-union representation at Eurotunnel. *Employee Relations*, 23 (4/5), 376–400.

Gollan, P. 2002: So what's the news? Management strategies towards non-union employee representation at News International. *Industrial Relations Journal*, 33 (4), 316–331.

Gourevitch, P. and Shinn, J. 2005: *Political Power and Corporate Control: The New Global Politics of Corporate Governance*. Princeton, NJ: Princeton University Press.

Grainger, H. and Crowther, M. 2007: *Trade Union Membership 2006*. London: DTI.

Grinyer, J., Russell, A. and Collinson, D. 1998: Evidence of managerial short-termism in the UK. *British Journal of Management*, 9, 13–22.

Guest, D., Michie, J., Conway, N. and Sheehan, M. 2003: Human resource management and corporate performance in the UK. *British Journal of Industrial Relations*, 41, 291–314.

Hale, D. 2008: Labour disputes in 2007. *Economic and Labour Market Review*, 2 (6), 18–29.

Hall, M., Hutchinson, S., Parker, J., Purcell, J. and Terry, M. 2007: *Implementing information and consultation: early experience under the ICE Regulations*. Employment Relations Research Series No. 88, London: Department for Business, Enterprise and Regulatory Reform (BERR).

Hall, P. and Soskice, D. 2001: An introduction to varieties of capitalism. In Hall, P. and Soskice, D. (eds) *Varieties of Capitalism: The Institutional Foundations of Comparative Advantage*. Oxford: Oxford University Press, pp. 1–68.

Halliden, B. and Monks, K. 2005: Employee-centred management in a call centre. *Personnel Review*, 34 (3), 370–383.

Haynes, P., Vowles, J. and Boxall, P. 2005: Explaining the younger–older worker union density gap: evidence from New Zealand. *British Journal of Industrial Relations*, 43 (1), 93–116.

Head, J. and Lucas, R. 2004: Employee relations in the non-union hotel industry: a case of 'determined opportunism'? *Personnel Review*, 33 (5/6), 693–710.

Heery, E. and Simms, M. 2007: Employer responses to union organizing in the United Kingdom. *Cardiff Human Resource Management Working Papers H2007/5*, October.

Hijzen, A., Upward, R. and Wright, P. 2007: Job creation, job destruction and the role of small firms: firm-level evidence from the UK. *Research paper 2007/01*, University of Nottingham, Leverhulme Centre for Research on Globalisation and Economic Policy.

Hochschild, A. 1983: *The Managed Heart: Commercialization of Human Feeling*. Berkeley, California: University of California Press.

Hollingsworth, J. R. and Boyer, R. (eds) 1997: *Contemporary Capitalism: The Embeddedness of Institutions*. Cambridge and New York: Cambridge University Press.

Hollingsworth, J., Schmitter, P. and Streeck, W. 1994: Capitalism, sectors, institutions and performance. In Hollingsworth, J., Streeck, W. and Schmitter, P. (eds) *Governing Capitalist Economies: Performance and Control of Economic Sectors*. Oxford: Oxford University Press.

Holman, D. 2004: Employee well-being in call centres. In Deery, S. and Kinnie, N. (eds) *Call Centres and Human Resource Management*. Basingstoke: Palgrave, pp. 223–244.

Hoque, K. 1999: New approaches to HRM in the UK hotel industry. *Human Resource Management Journal*, 9 (2), 54–76.

Hutchinson, S., Purcell, J. and Kinnie, N. 2000: Evolving high commitment management and the experience of the RAC call centre. *Human Resource Management Journal*, 10 (1), 63–78.

Hyman, R. 1996: Changing union identities in Europe. In Leisink, P., Van Leemput, J. and Vilrokx, J. (eds) *The Challenges to Trade Unions in Europe: Innovation or Adaptation*. Cheltenham: Edward Elgar, pp. 53–73.

Incomes Data Services (IDS) 2007: Pay on the railways. *IDS Pay Report*, 981, 7–12.

IRS 2003: Pay in the utilities sector: between a rock and a hard place. *IRS Employment Review*, 782, August.

IRS 2007: Electricity, gas and water: bargaining pace picks up. *IRS Employment Review*, 883, November.

Kelly, J. 2004: Social partnership agreements in Britain: Labor cooperation and compliance. *Industrial Relations*, January, 43 (1), 267–292.

Kersley, B., Alpin, C., Forth, J., Bryson, A., Bewley, H., Dix, G. and Oxenbridge, S. 2006: *Inside the Workplace*. London: Routledge.

Kinnie, N., Hutchinson, S. and Purcell, J. 2000: Fun and surveillance: the paradox of high commitment management in call centres. *International Journal of Human Resource Management*, 11 (5), 967–985.

Korczynski, M. 2001: The contradictions of service work: call centre as customer-oriented bureaucracy. In Sturdy, A., Grugalis, I. and Wilmott, H. (eds) *Customer Service: Empowerment and Entrapment*. London: Palgrave, pp. 79–101.

Lankshear, G., Cook, P., Mason, D., Coates, S. and Button, G. 2001: Call centre employees' responses to electronic monitoring: some research findings. *Work, Employment and Society*, 15 (3), 595–605.

Leidner, R. 1996: Rethinking questions of control: lessons from McDonald's. In Macdonald, C. and Sirianni, C. (eds) *Working in the Service Society*. Philadelphia: Temple University Press.

Lloyd, C. 1999: Regulating employment: implications for skill development in the aerospace industry. *European Journal of Industrial Relations*, 5 (2), 163–185.

Lloyd, C. 2000: Managing employees in high-skill sectors. Dublin: European Foundation, http://www.eurofound.europa.eu/eiro/2000/08/feature/uk0008186f.htm

Lloyd, C. 2001: What do employee councils do? The impact of non-union forms of representation on trade union organization. *Industrial Relations Journal*, 32 (4), 313–327.

Lloyd, C. and Newell, H. 2001: Changing management–union relations: consultation in the UK pharmaceutical industry. *Economic and Industrial Democracy*, 22 (3), 357–382.

Low Pay Commission (LPC) 2008: *National Minimum Wage: Low Pay Commission Report 2008*, cm 7333. London: TSO.

MacDuffie, J. 1995: Human resource bundles and manufacturing performance. *Industrial and Labor Relations Review*, 48, 197–221.

Machin, S. 2000: Union decline in Britain. *British Journal of Industrial Relations*, 38 (4), 631–645.

Marchington, M. and Parker, P. 1990: *Changing Patterns of Employee Relations*. London: Harvester.

McKinlay, A. and Taylor, P. 1994: Privatisation and industrial relations in British shipbuilding. *Industrial Relations Journal*, 25 (4), 293–304.

Metcalf, D. 2004: British unions: resurgence or perdition? September. http://www.psi.org.uk/docs/2005/davidmetcalf-seminar-paper.pdf

Mueller, F. and Purcell, J. 1992: The Europeanization of manufacturing and the decentralization of bargaining: multinational management strategies in the European automobile industry. *The International Journal of Human Resource Management*, 3 (1), 15–34.

Mulholland, K. 2002: Managers and managerialism in the post-privatised utilities. *Capital and Class*, Summer, Issue 77, 53–87.

Newman, J. 2007: *My Secret Life on the McJob: Lessons from Behind the Counter Guaranteed to Supersize Any Management Style*. New York: McGraw-Hill.

Ogden, S., Laister, K. and Marginson, D. 2006: Empowerment and accountability: evidence from the UK privatized water industry. *Journal of Management Studies*, 43 (3), 521–555.

Oxford Economics 2007: Is manufacturing in terminal decline? *Economic Outlook*, January, 9–13.

Palmer, G., MacInnes, T. and Kenway, P. 2008: Monitoring poverty and social exclusion 2008. York: Joseph Rowntree Foundation.

Parker, D. 2004: Editorial: lessons from privatization. *IEA Economic Affairs*, September, volume 24, 2–8.

Parry, D., Waddington, D. and Crichter, C. 1997: Industrial relations in the privatized mining industry. *British Journal of Industrial Relations*, 35 (2), 197–214.

Pendleton, A. 1999: Ownership or competition? An evaluation of the effects of privatisation on industrial relations institutions, processes and outcomes. *Public Administration*, 77 (4), 769–791.

Pollert, A. 1995: A Sectoral approach: A mode of overcoming invisibilities of employment. In Èrbes-Seguin, S. (ed.) *Beschaftigung und Arbeit: Eine Diskussion Zwischen Ökonomie und Soziologie*. Berlin: edition Sigma, rainer bohn verlag.

Poynter, G. 2000: *Restructuring in the Service Industries: Management Reform and Workplace Relations in the UK Service Sector*. London: Cassell.

Ram, M., Edwards, P., Gilman, M. and Arrowsmith, J. 2001: The dynamics of informality: employment relations in small firms and the effects of regulatory change. *Work, Employment and Society*, 15 (4), 845–861.

Ramsay, H., Scholarios, D. and Harley, B. 2000: Employees and high performance work systems: testing inside the black box. *British Journal of Industrial Relations*, 38 (4), 502–531.

Rosenthal, P. 2004: Management control as an employee resource: the case of front-line service workers. *Journal of Management Studies*, 41 (4), 601–622.

Royle, T. 1999: Recruiting the acquiescent workforce: a comparative analysis of McDonald's in Germany and the UK. *Employee Relations*, 21 (6), 540–555.

Rubery, J. 2005: The shaping of work and working time in the service sector: a segmentation approach. In Bosch, G. and Lehndorff, S. (eds) *Working in the Service Sector: A Tale from Different Worlds*. London: Routledge, pp. 261–288.

Schuler, R. and Jackson, S. 1987: Linking competitive strategy with human resource management practices. *Academy of Management Executive*, 3, 207–219.

Sengupta, S., Edwards, P. and Tsai, C.-J. 2009: The good, the bad and the ordinary: work identities in 'good' and 'bad' jobs in the UK. *Work and Occupations*, 36 (1), 26–55.

Sharp, R. 2008: Pay awards fall back to 3.2%. *IRS Employment Review*, 897, May.

Smeaton, D. and McKay, S. 2003: *Working after State Pension Age: Quantitative Analysis*, research report no. 182, London: DWP.

Smith, C., Child, J. and Rowlinson, M. 1990: *Reshaping Work: The Cadbury Experience*. Cambridge: Cambridge University Press.

Stoney, C. 2002: *Is it Good to Talk? Examining the Process and Outcomes of Social Partnership at British Telecommunications plc*, School of Public Policy and Administration, Carleton University, Ottawa, working paper 54.

Streeck, W. and Schmitter, P. 1985: Community, market, state – and associations? The prospective contribution of interest governance to social order. In Streeck, W. and Schmitter, P. (eds) *Private Interest Governance*. London: Sage.

Taylor, P. and Bain, P. 1999: 'An assembly line in the head': work and employee relations in the call centre. *Industrial Relations Journal*, 30 (2), 101–117.

Terry, M. 1999: Assessing the significance of partnership agreements. *Eironline*, July. http://www.eurofound.europa.eu/eiro/1999/07/feature/uk9907214f.htm

Terry, M. 2003a: Partnership and the future of trade unions in the UK. *Economic and Industrial Democracy*, 24 (4), 485–507.

Terry, M. 2003b: Can 'partnership' reverse the decline of British trade unions? *Work, Employment and Society*, 17, 459–472.

TUC 2006: High performance workplaces – impact of union presence and training arrangements. http://www.unionlearn.org.uk/policy/learn-956-f0.cfm

Turnbull, P. 1993: Docks. In Pendleton, A. and Winterton, J. (eds) *Public Enterprise in Transition: Industrial Relations in State and Privatised Corporations*. London: Routledge.

Turnbull, P., Blyton, P. and Harvey, G. 2004: Cleared for take-off? Management-labour partnership in the European civil aviation industry. *European Journal of Industrial Relations*, 10 (3), 287–307.

Upchurch, M., Danford, A., Tailby, S. and Richardson, M. 2008: *The Realities of Partnership at work*. Basingstoke: Palgrave Macmillan.

Van den Broek, D. 2004: 'We have the values': customers, control and corporate ideology in call centre operations. *New Technology, Work and Employment*, 19, 2–13.

Visser, J. 2002: Why fewer workers join unions in Europe: a social custom explanation of membership trends. *British Journal of Industrial Relations*, 40 (3), 403–430.

Waddington, J. 2001: United Kingdom: restructuring services with a deregulated regime. In Dølvik, J.-E. (ed.) *At Your Service? Comparative Perspectives on Employment and Labour Relations in the European Private Sector Services*. Brussels: P.I.E. Lang, pp. 103–143.

Waddington, J. and Dølvik, J.-E. 2002: Private sector services: challenges to European trade unions. *Transfer*, 3 (2), 356–376.

Walsh, T. 1990: Flexible labour utilisation in the private service sector. *Work, Employment and Society*, 4 (4), 517–530.

Wilkes, F., Samuels, J. and Greenfield, S. 1996: Investment decision making in UK manufacturing industry. *Management Decision*, 34 (4), 62–71.

Wood, S. 1999: Human resource management and performance. *International Management Review*, 1, 367–413.

9

MULTINATIONAL COMPANIES: TRANSFORMING NATIONAL INDUSTRIAL RELATIONS?

PAUL MARGINSON AND GUGLIELMO MEARDI

Introduction

In the 1990s and 2000s debates on social and economic issues have been dominated by the issue of 'globalization'. In the employment sphere, the role of multinational companies (MNCs) has become the most visible and disputed issue. Do MNCs disseminate global 'best practices' worldwide, leading to global convergence? Or do they rather exploit different national comparative advantages, driving divergent trends? Are they guilty of 'regime shopping' and a 'race to the bottom' in labour standards, or are they engines of social development? Are they footloose organizations, too powerful to be controlled and prone to relocate from one country to another, or can they be constrained by law and joint regulation through collective negotiations?

Overall, MNCs are a crucial agent in the transformation of national industrial relations. United Nations figures demonstrate the speed of MNCs' recent expansion. In 2007, new investments by companies in operations overseas, known as 'foreign direct investment' (FDI), reached $1833 billion, ten times the 1990 value, and there were estimated to be 79 000 multinationals worldwide, more than double the 1990 total. Multinationals employ increasing numbers of workers: employment in their overseas operations totalled 82 million in 2007, up from 25 million in 1990 (UNCTAD 2008). Amongst the OECD (advanced industrialized) countries, one in five employees directly works for an MNC and a further one in five is employed in companies supplying MNCs (Marginson 2000).

The chapter examines the impact of MNCs on industrial relations principally, but not exclusively, through the prism of the UK. Britain serves as an instructive country case for three main reasons. First, it is a large, internationally open economy characterized by significant inward (from overseas-owned firms) and outwards (from UK-based companies) flows of FDI over a sustained period. Second, the UK economy has become progressively integrated with those of the other member states of the European Union, and its associated and applicant countries, as the process of European economic integration and enlargement has been driven forward over the past quarter century (Hay 2004). Within this regional economic bloc, MNCs increasingly organize their production and market servicing on a Europe-wide basis undergoing in the process substantial restructuring as their operations are reconfigured (Marginson and Sisson 2004/2006: 30–34). Third, as a major 'liberal market economy' (Hall and Soskice 2001), the UK is characterized by comparative institutional permissiveness in industrial relations, when compared to the main 'coordinated market economies' of continental Europe. This provides companies with scope for choice over structures and practices and therefore innovation and, in the context of MNCs, inwards diffusion of practice from companies' home country operations or those in third countries. The UK, however, is also a particular case: its distinctive political economy (see Crouch, this volume) compared to other established and newly industrialized countries, especially those across the enlarged EU, continually informs MNC decisions as to which kinds of business activity to locate in Britain.

The chapter first presents a profile of MNCs' operations, and reviews the impact of overseas-owned companies on employment practice, in Britain. The decisions of MNCs on where to locate their different activities – routinized production, knowledge-intensive activity, research and development, headquarters functions – shape the international division of labour and with it the employment structure of national and local economies. We then examine the impact of these decisions for industrial relations, along with the influence of the industrial relations system of the parent country in which companies are headquartered. MNCs' impact also derives from the international integration of their activities which creates potential for practices to be transferred from one country to another, for workforce costs and performance to be compared across borders, and for implementation of common cross-border policies. Finally, the chapter addresses trade union responses to the impact of MNCs, which have varied widely, and the development of transnational industrial relations structures and regulation.

Multinational Britain

Profile

Already the most internationally open of Europe's large economies, and significantly more so than the USA, Britain's economy has become even more internationalized over the past two decades with a further expansion of MNC activity to the fore. The sustained increase in FDI flows across the world economy has been particularly marked in the UK. Much of this has been due to merger and acquisition, which has accounted for around three quarters of FDI into and out of Britain over the period since 1990 (Edwards and Walsh 2009). As a result, the UK remains second only to the USA, the world's largest economy, in its share of the global stock of FDI and accounts for over 10% of both inward and outward FDI (UNCTAD 2008).

The UK's stock of inward FDI stood at $1348 billion in 2007, six times more than in 1990, and represents the activities of over 13 500 overseas-owned companies in the UK. These overseas-owned firms accounted for 27% of UK manufacturing employment in 2005, up from 19% in 2000 (OECD 2007). No figures are available for services, although overseas ownership is prominent in sectors such as financial and business services, retailing and hotels and catering. As government procurement policies increasingly encourage private sector involvement, MNCs are moving into public service provision in areas such as health and education (see Bach, this volume). In both manufacturing and services, workers employed in locally owned firms that supply these MNCs account for a further proportion of UK employment.

The outward stock of FDI, by UK companies overseas, has risen even more rapidly. In 2006 it stood at $1486 billion, up by a factor of more than six since 1990, when it stood at some $230 billion. The 2006 total comprised the overseas activities of 2360 UK parent companies. Although the USA represents the single most important destination for outwards FDI by UK companies, the proportion of the overall total going elsewhere in the EU has been growing (Hay 2004). A regional concentration of overseas assets and sales is a widespread feature amongst MNCs from all the main industrialized economies (Rugman 2005). One quarter of the worldwide employment of UK-based multinationals is located overseas. At the same time, these companies have a substantial presence in the domestic economy, accounting for an estimated 45% of manufacturing employment (Marginson 2000). Again no equivalent data are available for services, albeit that UK-based service sector companies have a substantial international presence. Overall, the proportion of Britain's workforce employed by MNCs, both overseas and home owned, is almost certainly higher than in any of the other large industrialized economies (Edwards and Walsh 2009).

The profile of MNCs operating in the UK can be elaborated by drawing from a major survey of 302 medium- and larger-sized multinationals with operations in the UK (Edwards *et al.* 2006, 2007). Amongst overseas-owned MNCs, the most prominent country of origin was the USA, which accounted for approaching one half of the overseas-owned total. Companies headquartered elsewhere in Europe, i.e. outside of the UK, accounted for over one third of the same total (most represented are those based in France, Germany and Sweden). Japanese-based MNCs accounted for a further 7% of the overall total, leaving less than 10% of the overseas total based in the rest of the world. Overall, as with the broader global picture (UNCTAD 2008), UK inwards FDI is dominated by multinationals based in the countries of the so-called 'Triad' of North America, Europe and Japan and East Asia.

Reflecting the global acceleration in FDI in the service sectors, MNCs in services (48% of the total) marginally outnumbered those in manufacturing (45%), with a smaller proportion in non-manufacturing production such as the utilities and construction (6%). The international scale of the multinational of which the UK operations were a part varied considerably in terms of size and geographic spread.

How long overseas-owned MNCs have had operations in the UK provides a rough indicator of the extent to which they might be influenced by local industrial relations traditions (see below). Longer-established, mature operations are more likely to have become embedded, and to have adapted to prevailing practice. Approaching two thirds of the overseas-owned companies had had a UK presence for ten or more years, including almost 30% with a presence dating back at least 25 years. Yet the indicator is an imperfect one, as the 13% of MNCs reporting a UK presence of less than five years could have entered through the acquisition of an indigenous business and with it a local industrial relations tradition. Indeed, four out of every five of these recent 'arrivals' also reported being involved in recent acquisition activity. Of the UK-owned companies, almost three quarters had had an overseas presence for at least ten years.

Forward and backwards linkages in terms of international business integration, which is likely to increase the scope for cross-border influences, are widespread amongst overseas-owned MNCs, with over 60% reporting that sites in the UK supplied those in other countries, almost 80% reporting that sites in other countries supplied those in the UK, and about one half reporting two-way flows. The main products and services of three quarters of the MNCs were standardized either across a global region or globally. UK operations often play a 'strategic' role in the wider MNC through either the assignation of international responsibility, or a 'mandate', for a product or service to local operations (almost one half of the overseas-owned companies) or significant research and development activity (around one third of overseas-owned MNCs).

Impact on industrial relations

The permissive nature of the UK's institutional arrangements for industrial relations offers MNCs scope for choice over their industrial relations practice. For overseas-owned companies, this choice includes, but is not confined to, the alternatives of conforming to local practice and transferring into the UK established practice from the home country.

Reviewing the evidence on the practice of overseas-owned MNCs from major surveys of workplace industrial relations practices and company-level industrial relations policy undertaken during the first half of the 1980s, Edwards and Walsh (2009) identify a mix of features which conform with local conventions and others which are distinctive, and therefore consistent with inwards transfer of practice from the home country. There was little difference between overseas- and UK-owned firms in propensity to recognize trade unions and the incidence of joint consultative structures, suggesting conformity with local conventions. However, in an era when multi-employer bargaining arrangements still covered parts of the private sector, overseas-owned companies were markedly more likely to engage in single-employer (i.e. company- or establishment-based bargaining) than were UK-owned firms. Overseas-owned MNCs were also noticeably more likely to embrace direct forms of employee communication and involvement than UK firms. And there were distinct differences in the resources and profile of the human resource function. Those in overseas-owned firms had greater resources, in terms of staff, than had UK-owned firms (see Sisson and Purcell, this volume). And amongst multi-site organizations, policy making in the human resource function was more likely to be centralized in overseas-owned than

British-owned firms. These findings suggest that 20 years ago overseas-owned MNCs had gone further in developing organization-specific employment systems than had domestic firms. Indeed, they were more likely to report that they had an overall philosophy towards the management of employees, which was formally communicated to employees. A further survey of company industrial relations policy undertaken in the early 1990s differentiated between locally owned firms which were themselves multinational and those which were solely domestic in scope, and found that internationalized UK companies more closely resembled their overseas-owned counterparts than did those whose operations remained domestic in scope (Marginson *et al.* 1993). This suggests the presence of a 'multi-national' as distinct from an 'overseas-owned' effect on industrial relations.

By 2004, the workplaces of overseas-owned companies had become rather less distinctive, relative to those of UK-owned firms 20 years previously (Edwards and Walsh 2009). Comparing findings from the 2004 Workplace Employment Relations Survey (WERS) with those of the 1984 survey, and controlling for other factors that may have changed in the intervening period such as sector and size of workplace, there remained little difference between overseas- and locally owned workplaces in the incidence of union recognition and arrangements for joint consultation. But by 2004 bargaining arrangements in the workplaces of overseas-owned firms were less distinctive, largely because most UK-owned workplaces were now also covered by single-employer arrangements. The widespread take-up of a range of employee communication and involvement practices by UK-owned workplaces also meant that overseas-owned workplaces had become less distinctive. Specialist human resource managers were, however, still more widespread in overseas- than UK-owned workplaces. But by 2004, the human resource function at higher levels was more, not less, likely to be involved in policy making in UK-owned multi-site as compared with overseas-owned firms. Data from the 2006 survey of MNCs with operations in the UK (Edwards *et al.* 2007) enables a comparison between overseas- and UK-owned multinationals that broadly confirms the picture. UK-owned multinationals were as likely to use an extensive range of employee involvement and communication practices as their overseas-owned counterparts, and also to have similar numbers of human resource specialists controlling for the size of the UK operation (own calculations).

In sum, although the pressure for local conformity has probably eased as a result of politico-economic changes in the UK over the past 20 years, the distinctiveness of overseas-owned MNCs' practice appears to have diminished. This could be because of convergence between overseas-owned and indigenous firms towards common business requirements.

The Contingencies Shaping MNCs' Practice

MNCs' industrial relations practice varies, being shaped by a range of influences, or 'contingencies', and interactions between these. These include the motivation for locating FDI in a given country; the nature of the national business, and associated industrial relations, systems in both MNCs' country of origin and the host country;

the mode by which MNCs established operations (new, 'greenfield' investment or acquisition); and the degree to which MNCs' business operations are internationalized (Edwards and Ferner 2002: Marginson and Meardi 2006). These key influences are considered in turn below.

Motivation for FDI

A key distinction is between FDI which is motivated by securing a presence in national and local product markets, termed 'market seeking', and that which is motivated by attaining more favourable production conditions, termed 'efficiency seeking'. Securing competitive advantage in labour costs and/or labour quality and/ or labour productivity through reducing unit labour costs of production is an important consideration underlying the second type. 'Efficiency-seeking' motives have increasingly featured in manufacturing sectors, while a 'market-seeking' rationale tends to remain more prominent in the service sectors.

In general, FDI which is primarily motivated by market access tends to result in long-term commitments (with implications for security of employment). Further, such companies are likely to be concerned that they should be viewed by local consumers as a good employer, and possibly, therefore, will be more likely to conform to local conventions in employment practice rather than engage in inwards transfer of home-country practice. In a study of US manufacturing MNCs' decisions on where to locate overseas operations covering 22, mainly OECD, countries, Bognanno *et al.* (2005: 171) found that host country market size was 'by far the main determinant of MNC location decisions', although wage levels and the industrial relations environment were also identified as significant influences (see below). For the UK, the relative size of its national market was historically an important attraction for FDI by overseas-owned MNCs. But with the progress of European economic and market integration, there is less impetus for companies to have production operations in each national market. In manufacturing sectors, MNCs have reorganized to supply a European-wide market from a few centralized locations. An efficiency-seeking calculus has become increasingly prominent.

The impact of efficiency-seeking FDI on industrial relations practice is more variable. To the extent that it is prompted by specific national conditions in terms of the configuration of labour costs, quality and productivity then MNCs may tend to conform to local conventions. In contrast, where MNCs' operations are highly integrated across borders, and potentially mobile as the balance of comparative advantage shifts, then inwards transfer of practices from operations in other countries becomes more likely. This variability also reflects the impact of a further distinction between efficiency-seeking FDI which is labour intensive in nature, where considerations of labour costs and productivity via intensive working are to the fore, and that which is more capital intensive in nature, where considerations of labour quality and productivity via smarter working are prominent. There is some tendency for FDI in labour intensive activities to be attracted to lower-cost industrializing countries. Yet, the dominant flows of FDI continue to be between advanced industrialized economies (UNCTAD 2008). Despite significantly lower labour costs, and industrial relations systems that placed fewer constraints on employer flexibility, low-wage/low-skill industrializing economies attract significantly lower volumes of FDI because of even larger differentials in relative productivity (Cooke and Noble 1998).

For an industrialized economy such as the UK, therefore, how it compares with alternative destinations, primarily within the EU, in terms of wage costs, labour quality, productivity and (less straightforwardly) industrial relations, is a crucial determinant of the capacity to attract and retain efficiency-seeking FDI. Since the 1980s, both Conservative and Labour governments have partly attributed the UK's comparative success to the policies which initially created, through a programme of labour market deregulation during the 1980s, and subsequently sustained a relatively lightly regulated or 'flexible' labour market (see HM Treasury, 2003). An influential example supporting this view was Nissan, which selected a northern English site for its new European factory in the late 1980s, because of the possibility of a no-strike collective agreement allowing flexible wages, something that the more rigid wage determination structures and more entrenched strike rights in continental Europe precluded (Garrahan and Stewart 1992).

These policies have tended to attract a particular type of efficiency-seeking investment, arising from 'institutional arbitrage' (Hall and Soskice 2001) as MNCs locate different operations in different countries in order to exploit their comparative institutional strengths. In European terms, the UK occupies an intermediate position in terms of configuration of unit labour costs (Marginson and Sisson 2004/2006: Ch. 9). Costs are lower, but so too are labour quality and labour productivity, than in France, Germany, Benelux and the Nordic countries. As a result, the UK is not a favoured European destination for FDI in knowledge-intensive or high-technology sectors, which continues to flow to the higher-wage, more densely regulated economies of its continental neighbours. The UK's advantage has been in sectors characterized by semi-skilled, routinized operations (Barrell and Pain 1997), but is now being eroded by the more favourable configuration of unit labour costs (lower labour costs but equivalent flexibility and productivity) in the EU's central east European member states. Moreover, the UK's 'flexible' labour market has a double-edged character: it is easy for MNCs to exit as well as to enter, a feature apparent in recent international restructurings in internationally integrated sectors such as automotive.

Country of origin

MNC preferences are widely seen to be shaped by the institutions and conventions governing industrial relations in their home environments: institutions which form part of an interlocking set which variously define the specific characteristics of different 'national business systems' (Whitley 1999). Extensive attention has been paid to these 'country of origin' effects (Ferner 1997), which are considered here through the specific lens of arrangements for employee representation and the articulation of employee voice, through either direct or indirect (representative-based) channels.

Studies of the UK operations of MNCs headquartered in different countries of origin have established their different preferences over representation and voice arrangements. US-based MNCs are associated with hostility to unions in their foreign operations, confirmed by the comparatively high incidence of non-unionism amongst their operations in Britain reported in a number of surveys (see Ferner *et al.* 2005). Reflecting the American system, where there is little scope for non-union forms of representation, US multinationals also display a distinct preference for direct forms of employee involvement. Yet amongst the operations of US-based MNCs in Britain, Colling *et al.* (2006) detect a measure of pragmatism: union recognition being widely accepted in the longer-established, manufacturing operations they studied. Japanese-owned MNCs prefer some form of enterprise union or company council, reflecting the company union model that prevails in Japan. In the UK, union recognition has taken the particular form of a single union agreement. Also, they tend to pursue a dual track approach to consultative voice, embracing both non-union-based consultative forums and direct forms such as team briefings and quality circles (Guest and Hoque 1996; Wilkinson *et al.* 1993). Not all Japanese-owned MNCs follow this pattern, with some preferring non-unionism and little scope for consultative voice (Elger and Smith 2005). The German model is associated with extensive indirect consultation and codetermination. In a major survey of the operations of German-based MNCs in Britain, Tüselmann *et al.* (2008) identify the emergence of a modified German model which combines newer, direct consultation practices with established ones of indirect consultation. In the UK context, union recognition is combined with widespread take-up of direct consultation practices. Ferner and Varul (2000) draw attention to non-unionism in the UK operations of some German-owned MNCs, as a result of devolution of IR policy responsibility to subsidiary managers.

UK-based MNCs have been found to be more likely to recognize trade unions in their UK operations than their overseas-owned counterparts, but less likely to embrace direct forms of employee voice (Marginson *et al.* 1993). There was no difference in the incidence of indirect (representative-based) consultative voice. A recent study of the European operations (including Britain) of 25 UK-based MNCs found that only one in six had union-based representative arrangements, and that one third had no representative arrangements whatsoever, relying solely on direct forms of consultative voice (Wood and Fenton-O'Creevy 2005). Although the two surveys are not directly comparable, the findings of the second suggest that practice amongst UK-based MNCs might have shifted since the first was undertaken.

Examining the representation and voice practice in the UK operations of MNCs from a range of home countries, Marginson *et al.* (2010) confirm the preference of US-based multinationals for non-unionism, more generally for non-representation, and to emphasize direct forms of consultative voice. German- and UK-based multinationals are significantly more likely to have union-based representation than their American counterparts, but as likely to emphasize direct consultative voice mechanisms. Japanese-owned companies are not significantly more likely to recognize unions, but are more likely to emphasize representative-based consultative voice. UK-based MNCs are additionally distinctive in being significantly more likely to have hybrid arrangements, embracing union representation at some sites and non-union representative structures at others. These country-of-origin effects were complemented by significant sector and mode of entry influences, confirming the presence of variation within national 'models' (Almond and Ferner 2006).

Nature of the host country

Account needs also be taken of the institutions and conventions governing industrial relations in the host economy (see Colling; Dickens and Hall, this volume). The UK is characterized by a relatively lightly regulated labour market and permissive institutional environment, open to inwards transfer of practice. Country of origin effects are likely to be more marked than in the more densely regulated labour markets of continental western and Nordic Europe. Yet, MNCs operating in the UK are not unconstrained. For example, the survey of multinationals found that a significant minority of multinationals has established new employee representative arrangements in the previous three years, in order to comply with the UK's 2005 Information and Consultation of Employee Regulations (Marginson *et al.* 2010; Terry, this volume).

A further consideration is the degree of difference between the business system and industrial relations institutions of an MNC's home country and that of the host environment. A German-based company will face challenges of a different order in adapting to local practice in the UK than a US-based one, because the UK's business system and industrial relations environment more closely resembles that of the USA than of Germany. At the same time, MNCs headquartered in Germany and other coordinated market economies may see the establishment of operations in the UK as an opportunity to experiment with Anglo-American practices and subsequently transfer them back to operations in the home country (Ferner and Varul 2000).

Mode of entry and age of UK operation

MNCs can establish a presence in a given host country through two main, alternative modes of entry – investing in a new or 'greenfield' operation and acquiring a local company. Greenfield sites have been seen as offering considerable scope for the inwards transfer of employment practices, a phenomenon that was widely associated with the rapid growth of FDI by Japanese MNCs from the mid-1980s to the mid-1990s (Oliver and Wilkinson 1992). In contrast, acquisition entails inheriting a legacy of established industrial relations practice, and is therefore more likely to be associated with conforming to local conventions – or even with 'reverse diffusion' of effective practices back to home country operations. The contrast between modes of entry is not, however, clear cut: greenfield sites are frequently less distinctive in their employment practice than is commonly supposed (Newell 2000) and there are instances where practice changes considerably following acquisition. The influence of the duration over which MNCs have had a presence in the UK is partly confounded by mode of entry, since the majority of recently arrived companies established their presence in the UK through acquisition, and therefore inherited industrial relations practices (Edwards *et al.* 2007). Even so, longer established companies which may have implemented distinctive practices on first arriving in the UK may, over the course of time, have become constrained – for example, by union pressure – to conform to local practice (Colling *et al.* 2006). Longer established firms might also engage in 'double breasting' (Beaumont and Harris 1992), entailing a mix of union and non-union arrangements and associated practices at, respectively, older and newer sites.

International integration

The nature and extent of the international integration of operations within MNCs further shapes how far companies conform to local practice or adopt practices which are utilized elsewhere in companies' operations. Where MNCs are highly diversified, comprising businesses which operate in different markets, then the rationale for inwards transfer of employment practices will be weak or absent, and conformity with local conventions likely. Amongst the larger number of MNCs where there are operational linkages across countries, two features are important: the nature of operational integration and the degree of product standardization (Edwards 2007; Meardi *et al.* 2009). Operational integration takes two main forms: 'vertical segmentation', where there is continuous transfer of semi-products and information between sites which are solely responsible for one element of an integrated process; and 'horizontal segmentation', where sites compete with each other for mandates for different products from the parent company. Under vertical segmentation, impetus towards common industrial relations practice flows from the consequences of poor performance, or even disputes, at one site having repercussions at others, although this is attenuated by the differences in the nature of work, occupational mix and strategic role of subsidiaries (Birkinshaw 2000), at sites undertaking different operations within the integrated process. With horizontal segmentation, operational integration is weaker and the impetus towards common industrial relations practice across sites correspondingly less. An alternative logic is standardization, which involves production of a standardized product at a series of locations which are comparable to each other, perhaps driven by considerations of market access or proximity (where transport costs are high or products need to be delivered at the point of consumption). The impetus to adopt common industrial relations practices under standardization will be greater than under either form of segmentation. Reviewing the limited evidence available from a range of international sources, Edwards (2007) concludes that the practice of MNCs from several different sectors is consistent with these differing possibilities.

The International Dimension to MNCs' Practices: Two Interlinked Processes

Growing internationalization of markets and international integration of production, globally as well as within the EU, has stimulated the deepening of international forms of management coordination and organization within MNCs. The role of the traditional organizational building block of the MNC, the national subsidiary, has been progressively downgraded. The survey of the UK operations of MNCs (Edwards *et al.* 2007) found that virtually all had one or more international axes of internal management organization, including international business divisions, regional organizations and/or global business functions. National subsidiaries continued to be present in over half of companies, but in only 6% were they reported to be the most important level of internal management organization (own calculations).

These international management structures have brought a growing capacity to develop transnational, i.e. cross-border, approaches – either 'centralized' or 'decentralized' – to industrial relations and human resource practice, under-pinned by a burgeoning 'international architecture' (Waechter *et al.* 2006) within the HR function. Under a centralized approach common policies are explicitly promulgated across borders, whereas under a decentralized approach the pursuit of common policies is secured through coordinating a series of local decisions, underpinned by benchmarking processes which involve a combination of mecha-nisms to diffuse 'best practices' and the compilation of 'coercive' comparisons of performance across locations and countries.

The potential for the elaboration of centralized, transnational industrial rela-tions and human resource policies is signalled by the 53% of multinationals operating in the UK with a worldwide committee with responsibility for framing international HR policies (Edwards *et al.* 2007). A significant part of their activity is likely to relate to managerial employees. Common policies for non-managerial employees are less widespread, and tend to cover employee training and development, employee involvement and communication, equal opportunities, data protection, privacy and use of intra-net and e-mail, and remuneration systems, including financial participation. They are found amongst multinationals in international-ized sectors such as automotive, food and drink manufacture, pharmaceuticals and financial services. Although centralized in origin, these policies frequently take the form of frameworks or 'global footprints', which lay down the main principles and parameters, but leave detailed implementation to the individual businesses and countries in the light of local regulation, conventions and practice. The frameworks may be mandatory, but they can also take on a 'softer' advisory or 'recommended' character for individual countries and businesses (Marginson and Sisson 2004/2006: Ch. 8).

One impetus towards the promulgation of common, transnational policies stems from the mounting pressures on MNCs to demonstrate their 'corporate social responsibility'. Rising numbers of MNCs, including prominent UK-owned multinationals, have adopted codes of conduct governing their worldwide opera-tions, and those of the local firms which constitute their supply chains. Many of these address basic individual and collective employment rights, including prohi-bition of child and forced labour, health and safety standards, anti-discrimination, minimum wages, freedom of association and the right to collective bargaining. An OECD inventory of 246 codes of conduct found that 148 addressed aspects of labour management and/or labour standards (OECD 2000).

MNCs' pursuit of common, cross-border practices through a decentralized approach rests on processes of cross-border benchmarking. There are two sides, or faces, to these benchmarking processes, which interact with, and mutually reinforce, each other, invoking both 'regime coordination' across and 'regime competition' between locations in different countries. The first is mechanisms to identify and internationally diffuse those employment and work practices which are deemed to be 'best'; the second is the deployment by international management of coercive comparisons of performance between locations, bringing pressure to bear on local management and local workforces to make flexibility-enhancing and/or cost-saving changes to local employment and work practices, including the adoption of 'best' practices from elsewhere in the MNC. Earlier studies of cross-border diffusion of 'best' practices were largely preoccupied with forward diffusion from the home country operations of MNCs based in dominant economies to those overseas, whether by US MNCs in the 1960s and 1970s or Japanese MNCs in the 1980s. From the 1990s onwards, as MNCs have become increasingly internationalized in their management organization, and as their operations have become ever more internationally integrated, forms of reverse diffusion – involving practices either flowing between the overseas operations or moving from them back to the home country – have become increasingly prominent (Edwards and Ferner 2004).

In order to promote the diffusion of examples of best employment and work practices across different countries, many MNCs have put in place management systems to foster and steer the process. Such systems include the regular convening of meetings of production and HR managers from sites in different countries – in order to share ideas and compare initiatives, rotation of managerial staff across countries from one location to another – both to champion the diffusion of particular initiatives and to learn about others, and the assignment of a corporate management taskforce with a specific remit to identify, document and diffuse examples of best practice (Coller 1996; Edwards *et al.* 1999). The extent of such networking is indicated by the close to two thirds of MNCs operating in the UK which report that HR managers from different countries are brought together systematically through such mechanisms as regular meetings, international conferences and task forces (Edwards *et al.* 2007). For local management, the emphasis is on implementing practices which are tailored to local business conditions and requirements, selected from a menu which contains a range of best practice examples. Their successful realization is conditioned by both structural and micro-political factors (Edwards and Ferner 2004).

International management looks to reinforce best practice benchmarking processes through international systems of performance control. Based on the collection and processing of systematic data on labour, as well as financial and market, indicators, these enable international management to compare the performance of workforces across countries. The routine collection of data on aspects of workforce performance is widespread and extensive amongst MNCs operating in the UK (Edwards *et al.* 2007). Indeed, labour performance comparisons would seem to be very much on the agenda of the cross-border meetings of, and networking amongst, local HR managers referred to above. The outcome of these comparisons is deployed by international management to place pressure on local management to improve site performance, and to implement working and employment practices which have been deemed 'best' within the MNC (Coller 1996; Edwards *et al.* 1999).

In this way, sites performing poorly come under threat of loss of production mandates, disinvestment and ultimately rundown and closure. Local management utilize the outcome of these 'coercive' comparisons to drive through concessions in employment and work practices from workforces. In contrast, strongly performing sites are rewarded with new production mandates and fresh investment, while workforces are continually reminded of the need to remain competitive in terms of their performance.

The management perspective underpinning these benchmarking processes is transnational, yet any negotiation over the implementation of working practices deemed 'best', and/or concessions in terms of flexibility-enhancing or cost-saving measures, remains largely local or national. The dynamics are well illustrated by the changes in working time arrangements that were effected through a sequence of local negotiations across the west European, including UK, operations of General Motors in 1997–98, in a cross-border round of local concession bargaining as sites strove to demonstrate their competitiveness, and thereby secure current production and future investment, in the face of overcapacity (Hancké 2000). An increasingly pervasive element of the discourse of such local negotiations is management threats to relocate production, intended to have the effect of inducing concessions from the workforce. There are no reliable estimates of the scale of such threats. Research on German works councils has, however, demonstrated that threats to relocate are more widespread in more open sectors in terms of international trade and investment flows, and that the 'bark' from such threats has a widespread 'biting' effect in prompting workforce concessions in company-level negotiations (Raess and Burgoon 2006). Meardi *et al.* (2009) found the occurrence of relocation threats in automotive components – a sector where investment flows in the enlarged EU are driven by efficiency considerations – to be associated with the degree and nature of integration of MNCs' operations across borders. In similar vein, MNCs in internationally integrated production sectors, such as auto manufacture, hold out the 'promise' of new investment in order to prompt 'beauty contests' in which countries, and localities within them, are invited to engage. Labour costs, flexibility, skills, reliability and regulation are prominent factors in these contests (Meardi 2006).

The credibility of relocation threats rests on the periodic occurrence of actual incidents. In contrast to the pervasiveness of threats, actual incidents of relocation – when productive activity is transferred from a location in one country to that in another – seem relatively uncommon. Of the 2 300 780 job losses arising from company restructurings across Europe documented by the European Restructuring Monitor over the period from 2004 until the end of 2008, only 5.9% were attributed to relocation. The UK figure was above the average, at 7.2%, reflecting a combination of relatively high labour costs in the context of the enlarged EU and relatively weak regulatory constraints on restructuring. The figures probably greatly underestimate the overall volume of restructuring activity (because of their reliance on press reports as the primary data source) but the proportion of those involving cross-border relocation is unlikely to be larger, as these tend to be the cases which attract media interest. According to the same data, the sectors in the UK most affected by cross-border relocations were financial services, engineering, motor manufacture and food manufacture. Relocations affecting financial services were rarer elsewhere in the EU, where manufacturing sectors accounted for most instances. The higher exposure of UK financial services probably reflects both weaker regulatory constraints and the availability of highly qualified, English-speaking workforces in lower labour cost locations in countries such as India, where large finance companies including Barclays, Lloyds, Prudential, Experian and Norwich Union have relocated 'offshore' processing and customer service operations from the UK in recent years.

Overall, pervasive threats to relocate, as well as periodic instances of relocation, reinforce and amplify the cross-border regime competition within MNCs which the deployment of coercive comparisons entails.

Labour's Response

Trade unions have long been aware that their action can only be effective if they match the geographic spread of employers, who otherwise can easily bypass them by relocating elsewhere; in other words, their action needs to cover the extension of product markets. Therefore, while trade unions were not concerned by the primary sector's multinationals that dominated most of the first half of the 20th century (extractive industries, coffee and tobacco do not put British workers in competition with foreign counterparts), they have been increasingly concerned by the emergence of multinationals as global producers. Though unions have cooperated internationally since their beginnings in the 19th century, they have grown into principally national organizations operating at the industrial or plant level in specific country contexts – which do not correspond to the main level of decision making in MNCs.

Charles Levinson (1972) had identified three gradual steps trade unions could make in MNCs. First, they could support each other internationally when a union in one country took industrial action, e.g. by sending messages of solidarity, organizing solidarity demonstration, distributing information, and even, if possible, solidarity strikes. A second step could be the coordination of collective bargaining, timing national negotiations together and proceeding together. The final stage should be true transnational collective negotiations and agreements, harmonizing, if not wages, at least working conditions. Decades after it was elaborated, it appears that trade unions have only been able to make, in the best cases, the first step in this ambitious plan.

After a number of mostly failed attempts at creating 'World Works Councils' in the 1960–70s, cross-border union organization in MNCs has become a more important concern since the early 1990s, especially in integrated markets such as NAFTA and the European Union. In 1996, the US company Hoover sent a worrying warning message to European trade unions when it relocated production from France to Scotland because in the latter trade unions had consented to a pay freeze and a no-strike deal. A year later, Renault's European factories were the scene of the first so-called 'Euro-strike' organized against job cuts. Although ultimately unsuccessful on job defence, the strike had major effects both on the interpretation of European Works Councils' prerogatives (see next section) and, as a powerful symbol, on political perceptions of labour's capacities.

These organization efforts led to attempts at negotiating with multinational employers, and notably to the signing, by Global Union Federations (sector-level international union organizations) of over 60 International Framework Agreements (IFA) in MNCs (see next section). Some of them (a dozen so far) included the creation of World Works Councils that, unlike the failed unilateral attempts of the 1960–70s, are now recognized by management as interlocutor, and benefit from some company resources for their activity.

Union responses to MNCs still meet major obstacles, which foster three kinds of reason to be pessimistic relating to actors, institutions and contexts (Ramsay 1999). At the actor level, workers can face powerful opposition from their employers; limited organizational and financial resources in their unions; and difficulties in establishing shared interests with foreign counterparts in far away countries, who are easily perceived as competitors rather than colleagues. Institutionally, there is still no legal basis for transnational union action (see next section), and industrial relations regulations vary significantly country by country (see Colling, this volume), especially on the crucial aspects of union rights, collective bargaining and the right to strike. In most countries, critically, it is forbidden to organize a strike in solidarity with foreign employees. Finally, the global context makes it difficult to secure union solidarity amongst countries of different socio-economic levels, where employees may have very different concerns; dominant free-market ideology and governments' dependence on – and therefore submissiveness to – foreign capital are also seen as obstacles.

While these obstacles are still serious, recently more optimistic perspectives have emerged. Erne (2008) has analysed conditions within the EU under which trade unions promote European rather than national action. This has occurred in 'democratic' forms (organizing and protesting) as well as in more 'technocratic' ways, using institutional and legal resources. Outside the EU, the latter option is much less realistic given the lack of transnational institutions: as a consequence, in North America or Asia organizing campaigns are more frequent (Bronfrenbrenner 2007; Lévesque and Murray 2010). More researchers are looking at trade union action not from a formal industrial relations perspective, which would focus on the enduring lack of institutional bases for transnational action, but from network and social movement perspectives, pointing at increased communication across borders and at innovative campaigns with broader social movements, e.g. against Coca-Cola (Thomas 2008).

The contingent factors described earlier in this chapter affect not only management practices, but also trade union responses (Meardi et al. 2009). The country of origin effect is visible in the fact that Global Work Councils have developed mostly in continental Europe, with a pre-existent history of works councils and/ or strong trade union recognition in the workplace. This contrasts with very few such solutions in British and especially US-based or Asian companies. However, American origin may also have unexpected effects. In fact, the most important cases of transnational union mobilization in Europe occurred at two American companies, General Motors and Ford. In these cases, European trade unions found it easier to cooperate against a common, external opponent, than against companies from one of the member states, as risks were more equally dispersed amongst all locations (Fetzer 2008). Also, social movement campaigns have been targeting principally British (e.g. Shell) and especially American companies (e.g. Nike, Coca-Cola). Host countries are also clearly important, with mobilization easier in some countries than in others; in particular, in companies with important operations in low-wage or authoritarian countries such as China, the competitive pressure for trade unions in the advanced industrialized countries is much stronger and transnational reaction more difficult to achieve. The objectives underpinning FDI affect the degree of trade union concern: in services, for instance, even when employees are affected by major global restructuring, trade unions are less interested in cooperating internationally as different country operations are rarely in direct competition with each other. Mode of entry and age are similarly important: greenfield sites are rarely unionized, but over time may be targeted by local unions, which especially in poorer countries see major pay-offs (in terms of potential gains and publicity) in organizing foreign companies. Finally, international integration affects the nature of cross-national networks. Internationally integrated production fosters the development of cross-border employee networks, which – as Erne (2008) showed in the ABB-Alstom Power case – may translate into collective action capacity. By contrast, in geographically segmented companies, trade unions may be more inclined toward national-level strategies; local political exchange, production strategies or mobilization may be more likely to succeed (at least in the short to medium term) than audacious, risky transnational action. The nature of transnational operation varies mostly by sector, explaining why cross-border company-level trade unionism is strongest in large metalworking companies (Anner *et al.* 2006). But it also varies according to the production process; in labour intensive production, cross-border cooperation is a more compelling necessity for employee organizations.

Within this broader picture the UK occupies a particular position in two respects. First, in the manufacturing sector, British unions have tended to be less prone to initiating, or participating in, cross-border mobilizations than their counterparts in western continental Europe. Erne (2008), for example, notes that the British unions did not mobilize for the key Euro demonstration over the merger and restructuring of ABB-Alstom Power, nor did the British workforce participate in the subsequent protest strike. The reasons are various. Institutionally, until introduced under recent EU directives, the UK had no statutory rights to employee information and consultation (see Dickens and Hall; Terry, this volume). Unions therefore tend to lack the advanced information necessary to frame strategic actions in response, for example, to international restructuring. At company level, unions also lack the resources and access to expertise available to their counterparts elsewhere in western Europe. The consequences were well illustrated at the former Rover group, where following its acquisition by BMW, the British unions relied on advance information on plans for the UK operation made available to their German counterparts under German co-determination legislation (Whittall 2000). Moreover, the restrictions on strikes introduced in the 1980s (Dickens and Hall, this volume) place particular obstacles in the way of participating in international action. Ideologically, although British trade unions reversed their former opposition to the EU in the late 1980s, a residue of scepticism persists, evident in union ambivalence towards the recent EU treaty reforms. By contrast, affinities with the USA are suggested by the signing of an international alliance and merger project between Amicus-T&G (now Unite) and United Steelworkers (USW) in 2007, which includes the aim of developing common approaches to collective bargaining in MNCs. Second, in the service sector – which is particularly prominent in the UK – the offshoring of call centres and back-office processing is primarily an Anglophone phenomenon. Faced with the prospect of substantial numbers of jobs being relocated overseas, British unions have been amongst the first to react. Responses have included the conclusion of innovative collective agreements which anticipate the consequences of offshoring with major companies such as Barclays, BT and HSBC, along with international action, including growing cooperation with trade unions in India (Taylor and Bain, 2008).

Transnational Structures and Regulation

Growing internationalization of MNCs' operations and management structures has given rise to pressures for the establishment of transnational industrial relations regulation, particularly marked within the European Union. Conventions, codes of conduct and recommendations have been issued by international institutions, including the United Nations' Global Compact, the International Labour Organization's Tripartite Declaration on Multinational Enterprises and the OECD's Guidelines on Multinational Enterprises (Seifert 2008). These documents each include clauses upholding freedom of association and collective bargaining, but their implementation has been variously limited by being either voluntary in nature (Global Compact), rejected by some countries (the ILO Declaration) or covering only MNCs from developed countries (OECD Guidelines). Relatively few cases have been successfully remedied under the provisions of these documents, largely being confined to instances of significant political and/or media interest. None of these documents has introduced transnational industrial relations structures.

More progress has been made at the regional level. In North and South America, the North American Agreement on Labour Conditions and the Social Labour declaration of Mercosur, while not introducing any transnational structures for multinational companies, have addressed labour rights (including the right to strike for Mercosur) and complaint procedures, which have been used for cross-national union grievances and disputes at companies including GE and McDonald's.

But the most important institutional experiment in transnational industrial relations in MNCs has occurred in the European Union. Recognition of the growing deficit in employee rights to information and consultation within MNCs, over decisions that simultaneously affect workers in two or more countries, lay behind the adoption by the EU of the European Works Councils (EWCs) Directive in 1994 (Hyman, this volume). Hitherto, workforces and their representatives had not had any rights to access transnational management decision-making structures.

Originally adopted by eleven of the then 12 member states, the UK having opted out, the directive's coverage was extended to the UK in 1997 (following a change of government) and now covers all 27 member states of the enlarged EU. The directive requires 'Community-scale' companies, defined as having 1000 or more employees in the EU and operations employing at least 150 in at least two member states, to establish European-level representative structures (EWCs) for the purposes of information and consultation on matters of a transnational nature affecting employees' interests. A second EU measure, adopted in 2001, accompanies the EU legislation giving effect to the European Company Statute (ECS) with a supplementary directive on employee participation in a Societas Europea (SE), i.e. European company. By mid-2007, only 28 SEs which actually employ numbers of workers had been established since the ECS came into force in 2004 (Keller and Werner 2008), of which none were headquartered in the UK although ten have UK operations. Experience of the practice of the employee participation provisions has yet to accumulate. The present focus is therefore on the longer-established EWCs.

Some 2300 MNCs are estimated to be covered by the EWCs directive, of which EWCs have been established in around 830, representing just over one third of the total (ETUI-REHS 2008). The EWCs concerned are in multinationals which together have over 14 million European employees, and involve an estimated 15 000 employee representatives (European Commission 2008a). Both totals increased tangibly with the 2004 and 2007 EU enlargements: one quarter of existing EWCs are estimated to now include representatives from one or more of the new member states (ETUI-REHS 2008). The multinationals covered include not only those headquartered in the EU but also those based elsewhere, including the USA and Japan, because of the scale of their European operations. EWCs have been established in 110 UK-owned MNCs, out of a total of 260 covered. Also the UK operations of a substantial number of overseas-owned MNCs are covered by the EWC structures of the parent company. Of the overseas-owned MNCs surveyed in 2006 (Edwards *et al.* 2007) nearly one in three reported being covered by an EWC (own calculation). The scope of the potential influence of these European-level structures within the UK is therefore considerable.

The potential effectiveness of EWCs to advance employee interests at transnational level has been repeatedly questioned, and is one of the factors that prompted the revision of the directive in 2009. Streeck (1997: 329) notably observed that EWCs' formal consultation rights are defined only as 'dialogue' or an 'exchange of views'; there is no obligation to consult in the sense that management act only after employee representatives 'have had an opportunity to present a considered opinion' and no requirement for co-determination on any matters (as is the case for Works Councils in Germany and some other countries). Studies of the actual practice of EWCs, in terms of information and consultation, present a varied picture. Surveys of managers with experience of EWCs (reviewed by Hall and Marginson 2005), undertaken in UK-, US- and Japanese-owned MNCs, found managerial perceptions to be positive in overall terms in most cases. Amongst the benefits identified were the role of EWCs as a two-way channel for providing information and eliciting employee views and their capacity to foster cooperation and to involve employee representatives more fully in the business. In addition to the resource costs involved, a principal management concern was that EWCs might raise employee expectations of influence on business decisions. Managerial perceptions of the impact of EWCs on transnational business decisions are that they are, in all but a few instances, marginal.

In surveys of employee opinion, Waddington (2003, 2006) highlights widespread dissatisfaction among EWC representatives from a subset of EU countries. These relate to the scope of the agenda, the timing and quality of information provision and the occurrence and nature of any consultation. The extent of this dissatisfaction varies. EWC representatives from the UK and Ireland, where there is little tradition of mandatory employee information and consultation structures, tend to be less negative. Those from Germany, the Netherlands and the Nordic countries, who have experience from long-established domestic traditions, tend to be more critical. MNCs' country of origin is a second feature underpinning variation. Employee representatives reported the agenda to be more restricted, the quality of information provision poorer and consultation less likely to occur in multinationals headquartered in the Anglophone countries, including the UK and the USA, as compared with those headquartered in continental Europe.

Investigations of the actual practice of EWCs identify considerable diversity in their functioning and impact on management decisions (Lecher *et al.* 2001; Marginson *et al.* 2004), ranging from 'symbolic EWCs', involving a low level of information provision and no consultation, little or no contact between employee representatives between (usually) annual meetings, and no ongoing liaison with management, and various forms of 'active EWC' (Lecher *et al.* 2001). Active EWCs are characterized by regular contact and networking amongst employee representatives, including exchange of information, and ongoing liaison with management. Some develop common positions and/or systematize information exchange in the form, for example, of surveys of working conditions. A few have built the capacity to secure formalized consultation over transnational business decisions which have major implications for the workforce. Accordingly, the impact of EWCs on management decision making also varies considerably. In a study of UK- and US-based MNCs, Marginson *et al.* (2004) found that EWCs were as likely to have no impact as they were to have some. Moreover, any impact rarely influenced the substance of the business decisions; it was more likely to affect the way in which decisions were implemented, for example successfully pressing for measures to reduce redundancies or to change their distribution across countries so that 'pain is shared'. The emergence of transnational negotiations amongst a minority of EWCs is a sign of their potential as a source of international regulation. In the majority of cases to date, the outcome is a joint text which addresses principles or particular aspects of MNCs' employment policy. In a few cases, however, framework agreements for handling European-wide restructuring have been concluded. Assessing this emerging phenomenon, the European Commission (2008b) identified 88 such joint texts and framework agreements concluded in 42 MNCs, almost all of which were headquartered in continental or Nordic Europe.

As noted earlier, growing pressures on MNCs to demonstrate their 'corporate social responsibility' by ensuring that their operations worldwide, and those of their local suppliers, conform to internationally recognized labour standards, has led to the emergence of autonomous international regulation in the shape of International Framework Agreements (IFAs). Concluded between MNCs and, most commonly, global federations of trade unions, IFAs not only address basic employment rights but in many cases provide for mechanisms to monitor and enforce their implementation. Current estimates are that IFAs have been concluded in some 65 MNCs, the great majority of which are headquartered in continental and Nordic Europe (just one UK-owned multinational has concluded an IFA), covering about 3.5 million workers (Schoemann *et al.* 2008). They are largely found amongst MNCs which are inserted into producer-driven supply chains; few have been concluded by multinationals controlling buying-driven supply chains. Accordingly, IFAs are concentrated in particular sectors, including construction, energy, food manufacturing and metalworking (Hammer 2008). Several IFAs try to deal with a crucial difficulty: that of covering not just the direct employees of MNCs, but also the workforce of local suppliers – where scrutiny is weaker and working conditions often much worse.

Conclusions

This chapter has highlighted the emergence of MNCs as distinctive actors in industrial relations. While their impact is sometimes magnified in public debates, especially on the issue of relocations, there is no doubting the growth in their size and influence. It has documented their specificity as employers, especially through their capacities to engage in cross-border diffusion of employment practices and cross-border performance and cost comparisons which frame the context for local negotiations and management decisions. As the chapter has shown, these phenomena are particularly visible in an open economy such as the UK, characterized by integration in the European single market, a sizeable national market, openness to foreign acquisitions and relatively permissive industrial relations institutions. At the same time, and in response to the growing impact of MNCs on industrial relations, specific local, national and international trade union responses have developed. Reflecting the international scale of MNC decision making, and its impact, the period since 1990 has also seen the emergence of transnational regulations and industrial relations, from European Works Councils to International Framework Agreements.

Research on the implications of the growing international reach of MNCs for industrial relations has flourished in recent years. This has served to enhance understanding of the dynamics at play, which involve interactions and tensions between local and global pressures, the exercise of choices and institutionally framed constraints, and between management at different levels, from different functions and in different countries, as well as conflicts with workforces and communities. Drawing on this research, the chapter has underlined the importance of a range of factors – in particular sector, country of origin, investment motivation, mode of entry and international integration – in the dynamics at play, and their role in shaping variation the employment practice of multinationals. It has shown that there are partial and contingent answers to the questions posed at the outset. The activities of MNCs are not leading to a widespread global convergence in employment practice; at the same time there are bounds to the local divergences that are arising from the tendency to exploit different national comparative advantages. Regime competition is increasingly pervasive, and brings significant pressures to bear on local industrial relations actors to implement cost-reducing and flexibility-enhancing reforms. Yet, actual relocations, and any evidence of a 'race to the bottom' in labour standards, are confined to rather specific circumstances. What is certain is the increased relevance of MNCs for the ongoing transformation of national industrial relations systems.

Acknowledgement

Sections of this chapter draw extensively on the findings of the large-scale, 2006 survey of employment in multinational companies operating in the UK jointly undertaken by one of the authors (Marginson) with Paul Edwards (Warwick), Tony Edwards (Kings College, London), Anthony Ferner and Olga Tregaskis (both De Montfort University). The survey was funded by ESRC (award RES-000–23–0305).

References

Almond, P. and Ferner, A. 2006: *American Multinationals in Europe*. Oxford: OUP.

Anner, M., Greer, I., Hauptmeier, M., Lillie, N. and Winchester, N. 2006: The industrial determinants of transnational solidarity: global interunion politics in three sectors. *European Journal of Industrial Relations*, 12 (1), 7–27.

Barrell, R. and Pain, N. 1997: The growth of foreign direct investment in Europe. *National Institute Economic Review*, No. 160 (April), 63–75.

Beaumont, P. and Harris, R. 1992: Double-breasted recognition arrangements in Britain. *International Journal of Human Resource Management*, 18 (7), 1246–1262.

Birkinshaw, J. 2000: *Entrepreneurship in the Global Firm*. London: Sage.

Bognanno, M., Keane, M. and Donghoon, Y. 2005: The influence of wages and industrial relations environments on the production location decisions of US multinational corporations. *Industrial and Labor Relations Review*, 58 (2), 171–200.

Bronfrenbrenner, K. (ed.) 2007: *Global Unions: Challenging Transnational Capital Through Cross-Border Campaigns*. Cornell: ILR Press.

Coller, X. 1996: Managing flexibility in the food industry. *European Journal of Industrial Relations*, 2 (2), 153–172.

Colling, T., Gunnigle, P., Quintanilla, J. and Tempel, A. 2006: Collective representation and participation. In Almond, P. and Ferner, A. (eds) *American Multinationals in Europe* Oxford: OUP.

Cooke, W. and Noble 1998: Industrial relations systems and US foreign direct investment abroad. *British Journal of Industrial Relations*, 36 (4), 581–609.

Edwards, P., Edwards, T., Ferner, A., Marginson, P. and Tregaskis, O. 2006: *Employment Practices of MNCs in Organisational Context: Report of Telephone Screening Survey*. Available at: http://www2.warwick.ac.uk/fac/soc/wbs/projects/mncemployment/conference_papers/telephone_screening_survey_report_20-06-2007.pdf

Edwards, P., Edwards, T., Ferner, A., Marginson, P. and Tregaskis, O. 2007: *Employment Practices of MNCs in Organisational Context: Report of Main Survey*. Available at: http://www2.warwick.ac.uk/fac/soc/wbs/projects/mncemployment/conference_papers/full_report_july.pdf

Edwards, T. 2007: The nature of international integration and HR policies in multinational companies. Paper presented to the 2007 British Academy of Management HR conference, London, May.

Edwards, T. and Ferner, A. 2002: The renewed 'American challenge': a review of employment practice in US multinationals. *Industrial Relations Journal*, 33 (2), 94–111.

Edwards, T. and Ferner, A. 2004: Multinationals, reverse diffusion and national business systems. *Management International Review*, 44 (1), 49–79.

Edwards, T. and Walsh, J. 2009: Foreign ownership and industrial relations in the UK. In Brown, W., Bryson, A., Forth, J. and Whitfield, K. (eds) *The Evolution of the Modern Workplace*. Cambridge: CUP.

Edwards, T., Rees, C. and Coller, X. 1999: Structure, politics and the diffusion of employment practices in multinationals. *European Journal of Industrial Relations*, 5 (3), 286–306.

Elger, T. and Smith, C. 2005: *Assembling Work: Remaking Factory Regimes in Japanese Multinationals in Britain*. Oxford: OUP.

Erne, R. 2008: *European Unions. Labor's Quest for a Transnational Democracy*. Cornell: ILR Press.

ETUI-REHS, 2008: The database on European Works Council Agreements. www.ewcdb.eu (accessed March and July).

European Commission 2008a: *Commission invites social partners to negotiate about European works councils*. DE Employment, Social Affairs and Equal Opportunities, IP1081265, Brussels.

European Commission 2008b: *Mapping of transnational texts negotiated at corporate level*. DE Employment, Social Affairs and Equal Opportunities, EMPL F2 EP/bp 2008 (D) 14511, Brussels.

Ferner, A. 1997: Country of origin effects and HRM in multinational companies. *Human Resource Management Journal*, 7 (1), 19–37.

Ferner, A. and Varul, M. 2000: 'Vanguard' subsidiaries and the diffusion of new practices. *British Journal of Industrial Relations*, 38 (1), 115–140.

Ferner, A., Almond, P., Colling, T. and Edwards, T. 2005: Policies on union representation in US multinationals in the UK. *British Journal of Industrial Relations*, 43 (4), 703–728.

Fetzer, T. 2008: European Works Councils as risk communities: the case of General Motors. *European Journal of Industrial Relations*, 14 (3), 289–308.

Garrahan, P. and Stewart, P. 1992: *The Nissan Enigma. Flexibility at Work in a Local Economy*. London: Mansell.

Guest, D. and Hoque, K. 1996: National ownership and HR practices in UK greenfield sites. *Human Resource Management Journal*, 6 (4), 50–74.

Hall, M. and Marginson, P. 2005: Trojan horses or paper tigers? In Harley, B., Hyman, J. and Thompson, P. (eds) *Participation and Democracy at Work*. Basingstoke: Palgrave Macmillan.

Hall, P. and Soskice, D. (eds) 2001: *Varieties of Capitalism*. Oxford: OUP.

Hammer, N. 2008: International framework agreements in the context of global production. In Papadakis, K. (ed.) *Cross-Border Social Dialogue and Agreements*. Geneva: International Institute for Labour Studies/International Labour Organization.

Hancké, B. 2000: European Works Councils and industrial restructuring in the European motor industry. *European Journal of Industrial Relations*, 6 (1), 35–59.

Hay, C. 2004: Common trajectories, variable paces, divergent outcomes? Models of European capitalism under conditions of complex economic interdependence. *Review of International Political Economy*, 11 (2), 231–262.

HM Treasury 2003: UK membership of the single currency: an assessment of the five economic tests. *HM Treasury*, Cm. 5776.

Keller, B. and Werner, F. 2008: The establishment of the European company. *European Journal of Industrial Relations*, 14 (2), 153–175.

Lecher, W., Platzer, H.-P., Rüb, S. and Weiner, K.-P. 2001: *European Works Councils: Developments, Types, Networking*. Aldershot: Gower.

Lévesque, C. and Murray, G. 2010: Cross-border trade union alliances within multinational companies. *Industrial Relations Journal*, 41 (forthcoming).

Levinson, C. 1972: *International Trade Unionism*. London: Allen and Unwin.

Marginson, P. 2000: Multinational companies: innovators or adaptors? In Rainbird, H. (ed.) *Training in the Workplace*. Basingstoke: Macmillan.

Marginson, P. and Meardi, G. 2006: EU enlargement and the FDI channel of industrial relations transfer. *Industrial Relations Journal*, 37 (2), 92–110.

Marginson, P. and Sisson, K. 2004/2006: *European Integration and Industrial Relations*. Basingstoke: Palgrave Macmillan.

Marginson, P., Armstrong, P., Edwards, P., Purcell, J. with Hubbard, N. 1993: The control of industrial relations in large companies. *Warwick Papers in Industrial Relations* No. 43, Coventry: IRRU.

Marginson, P., Edwards, P., Edwards, T., Ferner, A. and Tregaskis, O. 2010: Employee representation and consultative voice in multinational companies. *British Journal of Industrial Relations*, 48 (forthcoming).

Marginson, P., Hall, M., Hoffmann, A. and Müller, T. 2004: The impact of European Works Councils on management decision-making in UK- and US-based multinationals. *British Journal of Industrial Relations*, 40 (2), 209–233.

Meardi, G. 2006: Multinationals heaven? Uncovering and understanding worker responses to multinational companies in post-communist central Europe. *International Journal of Human Resource Management*, 17 (8), 1366–1378.

Meardi, G., Marginson, P., Fichter, M., Frybes, M., Stanojevic, M. and Toth, A. 2009: The complexity of relocation and the diversity of trade union responses. *European Journal of Industrial Relations*, 15 (1), 27–47.

Newell, H. 2000: Training in greenfield sites. In Rainbird, H. (ed.) *Training in the Workplace*. Basingstoke: Macmillan.

OECD 2000: *Codes of Conduct: An Expanded Review of Their Contents*. TD/TC/WP99(56)/Final. Paris: OECD.

OECD 2007: *Measuring Globalisation: Activities of Multinationals*. Vol. 1: Manufacturing, 2000–04, Paris: OECD.

Oliver, N. and Wilkinson, B. 1992: *The Japanisation of British Industry*. 2nd edition, Oxford: Blackwell.

Raess, D. and Burgoon, B. 2006: The dogs that sometimes bark. *European Journal of Industrial Relations*, 12 (3), 287–309.

Ramsay, H. 1999: In search of international union theory. In Waddington, J. (ed.) *Globalization and Patterns of Labour Resistance*. London/New York: Mansell, pp. 192–239.

Rugman, A. 2005: *The Regional Multinationals*. Cambridge: CUP.

Schoemann, I., Sobczak, A., Voss, E. and Wilke, P. 2008: *Codes of Conduct and International Framework Agreements*. Luxembourg: Office for the Official Publications of the European

Communities/European Foundation for the Improvement of Living and Working Conditions.

Seifert, A. 2008: Global employee information and consultation procedures in worldwide enterprises. *International Journal of Comparative Labour Law and Industrial Relations*, 24, 327–348.

Streeck, W. 1997: Neither European nor works councils. *Economic and Industrial Democracy*, 18 (2), 325–337.

Taylor, P. and Bain, P. 2008: United by a common language? Trade union responses in the UK and India to call centre offshoring. *Antipode*, 40 (1), 131–154.

Thomas, M. 2008: *Belching Out the Devil: Global Adventures with Coca-Cola*. London: Ebury Press.

Tüselmann, H.-J., Heise, A., McDonald, F., Allen, M. and Voronkova, S. 2008: *Employee Relations in Foreign-Owned Subsidiaries. German Multinational Companies in the UK*. London: Palgrave.

UNCTAD 2008: *World Investment Report 2008*. Geneva: UNCTAD.

Waddington, J. 2003: What do representatives think of the practices of European Works Councils? *European Journal of Industrial Relations*, 9 (3), 303–325.

Waddington, J. 2006: Contesting the development of European Works Councils in the chemicals sector. *European Journal of Industrial Relations*, 12 (3), 329–352.

Waechter, H., Peters, R., Ferner, A., Gunnigle, P. and Quintanilla, J. 2006: The role of the international personnel function. In Almond, P. and Ferner, A. (eds) *American Multinationals in Europe*. Oxford: OUP, pp. 248–270.

Whitley, R. (ed.) 1999: *European Business Systems*. London: Sage.

Whittall, M. 2000: The BMW European Works Council. *European Journal of Industrial Relations*, 6 (1), 61–83.

Wilkinson, B., Morris, J. and Munday, M. 1993: Japan in Wales: a new industrial relations. *Industrial Relations Journal*, 24 (4), 273–283.

Wood, S. and Fenton-O'Creevy, M. 2005: Direct involvement, representation and employee voice in UK multinationals in Europe. *European Journal of Industrial Relations*, 11 (1), 27–50.

10

INDUSTRIAL RELATIONS IN SMALL FIRMS

MONDER RAM AND PAUL EDWARDS

Introduction

There is no shortage of reasons to justify a focus on the management of people in small firms. Numerical significance is an obvious starting point. There were an estimated 4.7 million private sector enterprises in the UK at the start of 2007. Small and medium sized enterprises (SMEs) together account for 99.9% of all enterprises and 59% of private sector employment.[1] SMEs 're-emerged' after the 1980s (Greene and Mole 2006), increasing from 2.4 million in 1980 to the current position of nearer 5 million. They have played a pivotal role in post-Fordist restructuring (Scase 2003). Hence, technological change and 'descaling' have allowed small firms to enter sectors previously closed to them; the fragmentation of large firms has created space for subsidiaries, franchise operations and new forms of subcontracting relationships (Shutt and Whittington 1987); and the service sector has increased in importance, generating opportunities for high-tech and 'knowledge-intensive' firms that are emblematic of the 'new economy' (Ackroyd 2002). Small firms also occupy a particularly important place in a variety of policy domains. Successive governments have been wedded to an imperative to encourage business start-ups (Greene and Mole 2006), often despite countervailing empirical evidence (Parker 2006; Storey 2005). Importantly, small firms have figured prominently in policy-oriented discourses on the 'burden of regulations'. For example, there remains a strong business-lobby inspired view that the national minimum wage (NMW) and other employment regulations are contributing to increased informal working (Lea 2003), despite research evidence pointing to its small effects on aggregate employment and pay differentials (Dickens and Manning 2003). This theme, to which we will return, highlights the often contradictory depictions of small firms as engines for growth, and at the same time as enterprises particularly susceptible to regulation. How are employment relations actually managed in such a context?

Before addressing this core question, it is worth reflecting briefly upon the state of both industrial relations (IR) and small firms as 'disciplines'. Serious questions have been raised over the preoccupation of IR research with collective institutions and the workplace (Ackers and Wilkinson 2005). According to Ackers (2002: 4), 'the current problem of order is not centred on the internal life of the workplace, but on the troublesome linkage between employment and society'. Small firms have also lain outside the mainstream preoccupations of IR such as collective bargaining, so that IR's irrelevance might be particularly marked here.

The field of small business and entrepreneurship has witnessed its own version of this debate. For example, the level of analysis remains stubbornly focused on the individual (Davidsson and Wiklund 2001), often detached from wider societal developments. Viewing the entrepreneur as an 'individual' falls into the trap of thinking in terms of the 'self-identities of such entities rather than the less obvious working interactions which constitute and support them' (Chia 1995: 596). The people who actually work in small firms – often critical to the process of entrepreneurship – rarely figure within prevailing discourses (Ogbor 2000). Inconclusive debate on the extent to which small business and entrepreneurship can be considered a distinctive 'domain' has prompted one leading commentator to observe, 'I am not sure that the entrepreneurship field has reached some sort of theoretical clarity during the past decade' (Gartner 2001: 28). Such scepticism is compounded by the relative youth of the field, and means that this subject too jostles for acceptability within the academic mainstream (Gartner *et al.* 2006).

Although such challenges have elements of accuracy, they are far too sweeping. Work on employment relations in small firms has made important headway on at least two fronts. First, IR studies have applied the core tenets of employment relations – conflict, tension and contradiction – to small firms and demonstrated considerable analytical leverage (Marlow 2005; Ram and Edwards 2003). This conceptual contribution has also helped to illuminate policy-oriented debates on key issues, notably in relation to the 'impact' of regulation on small firms (Edwards *et al.* 2004). Second, through its interaction with the milieu of the small enterprise, employment relations have been infused with a sensitivity to family, community and households – concepts and processes that traditional IR has often ignored (Ackers 2002). For example, small firms are saturated with the ideology of the family (Ram and Holliday 1993); recent work has demonstrated how gender and familial relationships react back onto the employment relationship (Baines and Wheelock 1998a; Ram 2001). These processes are often central to the 'beliefs, ideologies and taken-for-granted assumptions' (Edwards 2003: 14) that constitute employment relations in small enterprises.

This chapter examines the intersection of employment relations and small firms, focusing in particular on developments in three areas. First, the various contexts in which small firms are embedded are outlined. Research has developed considerably from size-essentialist explanations that view working life in small firms as inevitably harmonious or necessarily bleak (Marlow 2005).

Empirical progress is the second element to be addressed. In addition to shedding light on key issues such as the dynamics of informality, recent work has added weight to a particular strength of British IR research, that is, 'the development of research that offers genuinely explanatory accounts derived from context-sensitive analysis' (Edwards 2005: 265). This has involved parts of the economy that have been little studied, for example the informal sector and high-tech and professional service firms. This progress allows light to be shed on one key issue: the nature of the employment relationship together with employee responses to it. An outstanding fact from the 2004 Workplace Employment Relations Survey was that workers in small firms expressed greater satisfaction with their jobs than did large-firm workers (Forth *et al.* 2006). The reasons for this fact have often been in dispute; recent work explains it, and also gives some grounding as to what it means.

Finally, a framework (Edwards *et al.* 2006) is presented that advances recent calls for 'integrated' approaches to employment relations that are 'embedded in the totality of the firm's economic relations' (Barrett and Rainnie 2002: 427). The framework builds upon the case study tradition of small firms research, but offers, in addition, a more systematic means of examining how sets of causal influences combine.

Contextualizing Small Firm Industrial Relations

Debates on what actually constitutes a 'small firm' have been characterized by a 'great deal of agonising' (Curran *et al.* 1986: 3) and ultimately have proved inconclusive. The heterogeneity of the small firm sector militates against a single uniformly acceptable definition (Storey 2005). Some studies include organizations with as many as 500 workers (Wagar 1998). A rough indication of the importance of small firms comes from official UK statistics which give the distribution of private sector employment in 2005 as follows (SBS 2006):

- Small firms (0–49 employees): 47%
- Medium-sized firms (50–249 employees): 12%
- Large firms (250 employees or more): 41%

These categories are those used in European Union statistics, which sometimes also identify a 'micro' category (0–9 employees) within the small-firm group. The pattern is similar in many EU countries, though in such countries as Italy and Greece the importance of small firms is even greater (EIRO 2006). Our focus is mainly on 'small', that is, firms with fewer than 50 employees.

The meaning of 'smallness' will vary from sector to sector. An engineering firm with 80 employees might be considered small; a similar size enterprise would probably be regarded as a large firm in parts of the professional service sector. The context-dependent nature of firm size is captured in Curran *et al.*'s (1986) advocacy of a 'grounded' approach to defining small firms, embracing legal independence, types of activity, organizational patterns and economic activities. In part, this is recognition that the legal form of the company is often an unreliable guide to the operation of the business. Indeed, Taylor (1999: 16) refers to the legal vehicle as a 'stylized shell' that provides 'only partial insight into the processes of enterprise that create, operate and perpetuate it'. In Ackroyd's (1995) account of small 'dynamic' UK-based information technology firms, the distinctive and functioning organization often had no legal identity at all. These firms customarily operated as part of an 'informal affiliation' comprising self-employed consultants, separate companies, and even divisions of larger enterprises; they came together to form a team-based 'operating unit'. An integral feature of these units was the capacity of firms to 'draw in more staff from outside the organization, to use sub-contract workers, and to move people around within the organization itself' (Ackroyd 1995: 149). In such settings, the *language* of IR is unfamiliar, even though the underlying processes are still going on (Edwards 2003).

Economic context

The manner in which economic location shapes practices within the firm is a key consideration. Curran and Stanworth (1981) underlined the importance of sector, demonstrating that workers in two sectors – electronics and printing – often had more in common with large-firm workers from the same sector than with employees of similarly sized firms in different sectors. Scott *et al.* (1989) developed this approach by identifying four broad sectoral groups: traditional manufacturing, hi-tech manufacturing, traditional services (e.g. hotels) and hi-tech services. Kitching's (1997) examination of labour regulation in different small service sector enterprises continues the theme. The study focused upon three contrasting sectors: computer services, employment and secretarial services, and free houses and restaurants. A different employment 'culture' was found to exist in the three sectors. These cultures, referred to as 'work', 'money' and 'sociability' types, gave meaning to employment and to the relationship between owner-managers and employees.

More theoretically oriented statements of the importance of economic context have also been a feature of recent work. For instance, Rainnie (1989; see Barrett and Rainnie 2002 for an updated statement) argued against an undue focus upon dynamics within the workplace, and maintained that small firms are shaped primarily by relations of power with large firms. This may have exaggerated the extent of dependence and placed primary explanatory emphasis on large firms rather than small-firm responses, but it nonetheless strongly underlined not only the importance of the market but also the fact that it is a structure of power (Edwards and Ram 2006). Shutt and Whittington's (1987) 'fragmentation thesis' takes this further. The revival of small businesses owes much to large firms' propensity to reconfigure their enterprise activities into subsidiaries and franchised operations. Hence, it is the increasingly widespread large-firm strategies of outsourcing, unbundling and subcontracting that generate opportunities for small firms. But '[w]hat appear to be small businesses often are not. Many of them are owned and often affiliated to very large businesses' (Ackroyd 2002: 136).

From the field of urban studies, Rath and Kloosterman (2000) stress the interplay between the social, economic and institutional contexts. The authors are critical of research that underplays the importance of market conditions,

> as if bakers, car-repair, ice-cream parlors, garment factories and bureaus for intercultural communication operate under more or less identical market conditions, have to deal with the same set regulations and of institutions and thus demand similar entrepreneurial skills and produce similar results. (Rath and Kloosterman 2000: 668)

Drawing on this perspective, Jones and Ram (2007: 451) argue that 'sectoral location can often be the key to explaining many otherwise mysterious features of ethnic entrepreneurship'. However, the influence of sector on small firms is rarely homogeneous, even within quite narrow market niches (for a broader discussion of the importance of sector, see Arrowsmith, this volume). There is often ample scope for within-sector variation. This reflects the highly specific circumstances of firms operating in ostensibly similar market circumstances, combined with the 'entrepreneurial effect of different levels of management expertise, experience, strategies and access to capital' (Arrowsmith *et al.* 2003: 438). The manner in which clothing firms have adapted to changes in the regulatory environment occasioned by the relaxation of the Multi-Fibre Arrangement (which had previously restricted imports to the UK) and the 'shock' of the national minimum wage is a case in point (Arrowsmith *et al.* 2003). The modal response was one of retrenchment, as employers desperately tried to cut costs and manage production. This has often been accompanied by closer monitoring of employees and work intensification. But other firms had been pushed into the grey market or out of the market altogether. A small minority managed, through identifying a suitable niche together with an element of good fortune, to secure a foothold in higher value activities. This example illuminates the diverse ways in which relations between small and large firms actually work, and the role that the state (through regulation) plays in shaping employer responses. The form that the outcomes of these relationships take is discussed below.

The mixed embeddedness perspective also recognizes that business owners and workers are located in particular cities, spaces and neighbourhoods; and that this spatial configuration will have a bearing upon the types of businesses that they start and in which they participate. Rekers and van Kempen's (2000) framework explicitly highlights the role of the urban space economy in the shaping of such businesses. The framework is drawn on by Ram *et al.* (2002) to throw light on the way in which the urban setting itself helps to create a continually changing mix of opportunities and constraints for racialized minority entrepreneurs; and the way in which the success and failure of individual firms is influenced by entrepreneurial adaptation to this environment. The influence of locality on work relations has rarely been acknowledged in studies of employment relations in small firms. It is necessary to delve into the industrial sociology literature to gain an insight into the manner in which locality impinges upon social relations at work. For example, drawing on evidence of social relations in a Northern Ireland telecommunications plant, Maguire (1988: 72) notes:

> It is the interaction between *work* and *non-work* which is important. In the study of social control in the workplace it is neither solely the external environment nor the 'internal state' of the workplace which requires examination, but the inter-penetration of the two.

More recently, Felstead *et al.* (2005) examined the nature of work in three different socio-spatial contexts: offices, home and on the move. Accordingly, they distinguish between 'work stations' (the site where work takes place), 'work places' (buildings designated for work) and 'work scapes' (the total network of places). Such studies begin to draw attention to the 'spatiality of everyday life' (Ward 2007: 267), although considerable scope remains for further explicating the geographical dimension and its impact on work and employment (Herod *et al.* 2007).

Familial networks

A defining feature of many small firms is their ability to call on the labour of family members. Almost three quarters of the US business households investigated by Heck *et al.* (1999) had at least two residential household members working in the business; and 27% utilized non-household relatives as unpaid workers. Baines and Wheelock's (1998a) study of UK micro-businesses found that 40% of respondents were 'family businesses' in the sense that they formally involved family members as co-owners or employees. Evidence from mainland Europe (EIRO 2006) reports a similarly high incidence of family-owned small enterprises.

Ackers' (2002: 5) trenchant critique of the limited terrain of traditional industrial relations (IR) is at its most forceful, and perhaps persuasive, on the issue of the family: the 'neglect of work-and-family relations is perhaps the most striking single instance of the anti-social character of traditional IR'. In contrast, the fields of industrial sociology and small firms have many examples of the inextricable link between work and employment. Sociologically informed accounts of 'family strategies' (Roberts 1994) and the 'micro-business household' (Baines and Wheelock 1998a) suggest that individual behaviour is the product of complex interactions within the household and the enterprise; moreover, it is fundamentally shaped by status, gender and generational issues. Moen and Wetherington (1992) use the term 'family adaptive strategy' as a metaphor to convey the household as a site of negotiation and as a flexible, decision-making unit that actively chooses various patterns of behaviour. Family strategies are needed to adapt to the 'constraining economic, institutional, and social realities in the larger opportunity structure' (p. 234). For example, in their study of service sector businesses, Baines and Wheelock (1998b) found that survival was predicated upon family members' willingness to adjust their daily lives to accommodate the unpredictable workload of the small enterprise.

Recent writings on 'entrepreneurship' have sought to draw on these insights, and further attest to the centrality of family dynamics to all forms of organization (Aldrich and Cliff 2003; Dyer 2003: Hoy 2003). Aldrich and Cliff (2003) acknowledge Moen's (1998) 'life-course' approach in setting out their 'family embeddedness' perspective; this attempts to capture the causal processes linking family systems and entrepreneurial activity. A central feature of the framework is the recognition that 'the norms, attitudes, and values held by entrepreneurial family members likely influence . . . founding strategies, processes and structures' (p. 590). Equally, the interdependent nature of this relationship is such that the entrepreneurial process is likely to contribute to changes within the family system.

Baines and Wheelock (1998a) look specifically at the ways in which work and employment practices in the small firms are embedded in the household and the family. They stress the negotiation of tensions that are inherent in managing 'partially decommodified' relations within the firm. This applies even when new, non-family, workers are brought into the firm. Difficulties can ensue in the process of inculcating recruits to the expectations and idiosyncrasies of life in the family enterprise. Often, employers were 'struggling to create understandings and establish a way for doing things' (p. 591). The theme recurs in a recent study examining the issue of employment regulations and small firms (Edwards *et al.* 2004). It was not uncommon for management (usually family) to absorb the additional work that ensued as a result of changes arising directly or indirectly from employment regulations. In one case, a care home, the advent of the national minimum wage had made it more difficult to recruit experienced staff. Management had to 'put in more hours', to train the younger and more inexperienced workers that were now being recruited. Further, management spoke of the constant 'juggling' and 'arm-twisting' involved in trying to arrange cover at short notice. Arranging cover for night staff was 'one of the major issues' that she has faced over the last month, 'because they don't want to work at minimum wage'. This difficulty often resulted in family members covering for night staff.

As these examples illustrate, embeddedness in family and community ties is often thrown into sharp relief in the context of small firms. It would, however, be wrong to see this as a unique small-firm characteristic. Several celebrated industrial relations events, notably the miners' strike of 1984–85, reflected the linkage of work, family and community. The relevant links may be more frequent in small firms, but these firms are not a different species from large ones.

Important though these contributions are in asserting the importance of household relations and family labour to the workplace, attention needs to be accorded to the way in which such processes operate in different types of small (and indeed large) firms. The influence of family does not operate in a homogeneous manner in all small businesses. For instance, a husband and wife-owned consultancy is very different from a family-run restaurant. The resource, moreover, is not fixed for all time; for example, changing expectations of the gender division of labour in the home will affect the nature of the supply of labour available in the economic sphere (Edwards and Ram 2006). Dynamics are thus crucial. As Ackers (2002: 4) himself argues, much of the social analysis pertaining to family and community 'lacks a firm anchor in the employment relationship'.

Empirical progress

The growing recognition that small firms are embedded in a web of social and economic relationships has been an important feature of research over the last decade or so. This has put paid to a number of stylized views. First, the generic models of harmony and autocracy have been found wanting. Conceptually, the trend has been towards the recognition that small firm employee relations are characterized by complexity and heterogeneity. There is also growing acknowledgement of the importance of informal regulation in the workplace, individualized negotiation, and the distinctive nature of labour and product market arrangements (Marlow 2005; Ram and Edwards 2003; Edwards and Ram 2006). This has been borne out by detailed case study work that demonstrates the complex, contested and conflictual nature of employment relations in small firms (Holliday 1995; Ram 1994; Ram *et al.* 2001; Moule 1998). In such accounts, the 'whip of the market' is particularly severe given that the setting is often highly competitive in sectors like clothing and the restaurant trade. However, it is often mediated by 'employee skill, scarcity value and the extent to which there are fraternal or familial relationships within a firm' (Gilman *et al.* 2002: 54). For example, Moule's (1998) study of a button manufacturer that was largely dependent on a single customer is instructive. Management tolerated shopfloor fiddles and unpredictable worker behaviour because they were reliant on employees to meet exacting customer schedules. This created space for workers to reinterpret, or modify, control through the process of negotiation.

Second, the longstanding stereotype of 'informal' small firms versus 'formal' large ones has been challenged. The fact that large firms, as much as small ones, are shaped by their context has been established through the firm-in-sector approach (Smith *et al.* 1990). The 2004 Workplace Employment Relations Survey (WERS) (Forth *et al.* 2006) departed from the practice of previous years by including firms with as few as five employees. It found that some employment practices, for example communication with staff, equal opportunity policies and discipline procedures, were widely established in small firms. Formality therefore is present in small firms too. Nonetheless, WERS also shows that workplaces owned by small firms are indeed relatively non-formalized. Hence, there is a 'size effect' which stems from the fact that because capital is personified in one (or more) individual(s), employment systems and relationships tends to be 'informal' (Arrowsmith *et al.* 2003). Informality is a matter of degree rather than kind; and it is more prevalent in some aspects of employment relations than others.

The treatment of informality in small firms has also changed quite markedly, with the erroneous conflating of informal with harmonious work relations, evident in some early accounts (e.g. Bolton Committee 1971), being shown to have little theoretical or empirical justification. Informality cannot eliminate the power relations that shape the management process. Indeed, informality and the invocation of familial ideologies can mask highly exploitative work regimes (Holliday 1995). Rather, informality is structured by external influences relating to the nature of the product market and the characteristics of the available and existing labour force. It is also shaped by the demands and constraints imposed by existing modes of work organization and technology. There is real scope for management choice, but within certain limits, and as circumstances change the nature and extent of informality adapts (Ram *et al.* 2001).

Research has sought to demonstrate how sets of causal influences combine to structure the character of informality in small firms (Arrowsmith *et al.* 2003; Kitching 1997; Marlow 2003; Ram 2001). The context for many of these studies has been how small firms accommodate to employment regulations that have been introduced by the Labour government since 1997. The findings show that 'informality' is a dynamic process; employment regulations have to be seen against the backcloth of continually changing product and labour market conditions. Many firms are constrained by their market situations, as we saw with clothing manufacturers who 'retrenched' their operations as a response to competitive pressures and regulatory change. But a minority use such regulations as an opportunity to move up-market, that is, focus on more value-added products or services (rather than price competition). Internal and external factors are interconnected. These observations apply to the informal economy as much as they do to small firms considered to be in the 'mainstream' economy (Jones *et al.* 2006; Ram *et al.* 2007; Williams 2006).

The informal economy[2]

It is worth dwelling on the informal economy for both empirical and conceptual reasons. Empirically, the informal economy has rarely attracted attention within the fields of IR and small business and entrepreneurship. Hence, an activity that contributes anything between 1 and 34% of GDP in different countries (with 6.8% being the average guesstimate, Williams 2004), and is seen as an intrinsic feature of advanced economies (Sassen 1991) is effectively ignored by these domains. Extant theorizing on the informal economy tends to be sharply polarized between the stances of neo-liberals and proponents of the 'marginalization' thesis. The former explain informalization as a consequence of state over-regulation that drives small firms underground. The latter see it as an unavoidable expression of the uneven development inherent in late capitalism; it is a site filled by the exploited. The shortcomings of these homogenizing perspectives are outlined by Williams (2006); he emphasizes the heterogeneity of the sector and explains its emergence by recourse to a complex set of economic, political, cultural and urban forces rather than a single cause.

An employment relations perspective that is sensitive to a shifting economic context as well as family community relationships is uniquely placed to examine the dynamics of the informal economy. It can also address the policy question relating to the extent to which employment regulations are driving entrepreneurs into the underground economy. Ram *et al.* (2007) examined firms from the clothing and restaurant trade. The key finding was that informal employers remained largely immune to the NMW. In some of the firms, even the highest wages were below the NMW level. Most employers evaded the NMW by underdeclaring of the number of hours worked by employees. Employers largely shared the view expressed by one respondent that the NMW had 'no influence at all. It's just another level of bureaucracy we have to deal with.'

There were two main processes leading to these results. First, firms were under product market pressure to contain costs. Restaurateurs made repeated reference to the clustering of rival firms, commenting on the 'cut-throat' nature of the competition and 'trying to outdo one another'. For nearly all clothing employers, survival rested upon price-cutting, sourcing cheap imports and a retreat from manufacturing. Second, the labour market continues to supply workers willing to work for extremely low wages. The reluctance of workers to challenge non-compliant employers has to be seen in the context of the paternalistic bargain prevailing in such firms; this bargain had its roots in familial and community links. Though this harmonious equilibrium is profoundly unstable, it is constantly being remade, as for example with the use of new groups of workers to plug recruitment gaps. This informal status quo is further reinforced by the absence of any truly effective external deterrence from the state.

Firms that complied with the NMW did so mainly because they occupied distinct niches that enabled them to pay relatively high wages. They were assisted in this by being connected to business networks that suggested potential routes out of very competitive low-wage activities. Unhappily for advocates of assimilating informal enterprises into the mainstream, it would take a great deal more than simple exhortation to get others to follow the example of these role models. Quite simply, the typical 'informal' employer shares neither their market advantages nor their mindset.

Professional firms

Research has also begun to address another (sharply contrasting) sector, that of high-tech and professional service firms (Gilman and Edwards 2008; Ram 2001; Davis and Scase 2000). Interpersonal relations here are quite different from those of the small firms which have, to date, dominated research on employment relations in small firms. For example, market relations, or 'demand-side networks' (Bryson *et al.* 1993) are thought to be particularly distinctive in professional service firms because of the importance of 'reputation' and personal contacts (Clark 1995), the significance attached to 'managing' the interface with clients (Alvesson 1993), and the role the customers play in configuring the delivery of work (Goffee and Scase 1995). Ram (2001) undertook a detailed case study of a management consultancy in order to assess the nature of employment relations in such a context. The study drew upon Mintzberg's concept of 'mutual adjustment', but augmented it with a conflict perspective that drew attention to pressures arising from the employment relationship; the dynamics of maintaining market relations; and the control of autonomous workers. The emphasis upon tension was important, and was evident in the insecure nature of the consultancy process, in which consultants (and clients) struggle to achieve a degree of control in their relationship (Sturdy 1997); the potentially costly eventuality of becoming 'locked' into relationships with particular clients; and the pressure to deliver 'marketable' outputs. Moreover, even 'high-trust' relationships came under strain during times of heightened market uncertainty, as was demonstrated during the course of the year-long study. References to 'being mates' and 'trusting each other' may have been suggestive of harmony and stability in the case study firm; but a harsh edge soon developed when the firm faced a difficult time in the market.

Bearing in mind earlier comments on the importance of family to small firms, the case was also noteworthy because the company was owned by a husband and wife team. Hence a theme that emerged during the course of the study was the particular ways in which credentialized and highly skilled employees operating in this consultancy business coped with family dynamics. As one consultant pointed out, this was a fact of life in the business: 'I think it's a family business. It's a family business sort of masquerading as a professional company . . . The fact that both of [the owners] are working in the company is one of the defining characteristics, certainly of working life.'

There was an uneasy coexistence of professional and familial norms, which was a source of significant tension in the company. Baines and Wheelock (1998a: 596) suggest that such findings are not likely to be unusual: 'Family . . . emerges as a salient feature of work and employment in this sector, a sector which is not normally associated either with tradition or with the family.'

Methodological underpinnings

Many of these studies have adopted a case study approach or other intensive methods of investigation. This has been fundamental to elucidating the lived experience of employment relations in small firms and the subtle forms of control at play in such settings.

A particular strength of such approaches is that they facilitate a more rounded consideration of espoused policies and practices than can be achieved by relying on one-off employer statements. They also have the capacity to cast light on the actual 'meaning' of employment practices. For example, Taylor's (2006) case studies of four small firms highlighted that kinship links were still important to the recruitment process despite management's advocacy of formal methods. Ostensibly formal procedures still had to be 'filtered through managerial politics, individual preferences and prejudices, organizational or local cultures and instrumental demands' (Taylor 2006: 4). Similarly, Marlow (2002) found that although respondents in her firms did indeed have formal, written policies on all aspect of human resources, they were rarely utilized by management. Even when problems arose, the preference was for personalized and informal action rather than recourse to formal procedures. The designation of 'Investor in People' in Ram's (2001) study of three professional service firms had little substantive impact on training, other than to generate additional paperwork for compliance purposes. Hence proprietary control in small firms will colour the deployment of formal practices; the personalized and informal nature of the workplace will shape the operation of formality.

Developing a Framework

Empirical research has, then, illuminated the dynamics of small firms, and demonstrated how a range of factors interact to shape behaviour at work. However, attempts to move beyond such accounts towards a more systematic framework of causal analysis are rare. Two longstanding attempts at classification are often drawn upon: Rainnie (1989) and Goss (1991). The product market was the central feature of Rainnie's model, while Goss focused upon the dependence of employers and employees on the other party. Although the models are useful insofar as they contribute towards a framework, they have certain limitations (Kitching 1997), two of which are germane to the present discussion. First, each model is deterministic in the sense that they assume that internal features are effectively prescribed by external conditions. Second, they concentrate on the economic position of firms, and say nothing about familial and other contexts (Ram and Edwards 2003).

The framework

Edwards *et al.* (2006) have developed a framework that builds upon product and labour market conditions by explicitly incorporating family (and other) resources available to small firms. In addition, it identifies three relatively action- or process-oriented variables. The first is the degree of conscious strategic choice exercised by the firm: firms may respond to markets by developing strategies for new products, or react relatively passively to events. Second, firms have internal rules and routines which may be formalized and universalistic, or alternatively based on more *ad hoc* and individual preferences (particularism). Third, regardless of espoused policy, managers may apply rules in an authoritarian or democratic fashion. These last two aspects are important in characterizing the regime of a firm. A final addition to the model is the firm's embeddedness in external institutions such as business associations and public support bodies. The point here is that a strongly integrated firm is more likely than an isolated one to learn and adopt new ideas (Bacon and Hoque 2005; Hendry *et al.* 1995; Huggins and Williams 2007).

This framework has three purposes. First, it is possible to identify various ideal typical cases that act as models or benchmarks. Goss (1991) offered four of these such as the sweatshop and the 'fraternal' firm based on a sense of equality between owner and worker, the standard example being a construction company where the boss had risen from the ranks and continued to work at the trade. But the new framework identifies others such as the traditional family firm. Second, it also places weight on choice and strategy, as opposed to the structurally driven model of Goss, and it recognizes that out of choice and negotiation emerge multi-faceted relationships. The work of Moule (1998), for example, underlined the fact that workers can share a sense of purpose with managers and feel a degree of personal obligation, while also being capable of bargaining in their own interests. Such a picture is hard to derive from earlier models.

Third, the framework can be used to chart the dimensions of real firms. Two sets of examples are illustrative, for they come from types of firm rarely studied in the employment relations tradition; they are discussed after the dimensions are explained.

Each of the now seven dimensions is dichotomized for analytical purposes as follows.

Product market: highly *competitive*, or under a degree of *control* by the firm. Competitive conditions mean that firms have little control of prices; the more that a firm operates in a distinct niche, the more will it be able to exert some influence over the market. In the latter case, the environment is shaped by firms as well as the reverse (Child 1997); Ackroyd (1995) has demonstrated empirically how small high-tech firms can enact their environment rather than simply adapting to markets.

Labour market: the firm recruits *openly* for labour of a given kind, or it operates in a *restricted* pool defined by ethnicity or other factors. The further a firm is towards the latter condition, the more the elements of particularism creep in, with recruitment turning on friendship or family ties rather than instrumental rationality. The interaction of product and labour market influences underlies Goss's (1991) model.

Resources: a firm's stock of human and social capital may be a *positive* aid in responding to market pressures or a *negative* constraint on flexibility. Resources may have both features at the same time – for example, where family labour can be called on at short notice but also lacks skills – but for simplicity they are distinguished analytically.

Strategic choice: the firm has a clear *strategy* as to its business direction, or it is passive and largely *reactive* to events. This dimension is a reasonably formal one, and the general literature has been able to identify types of strategy. Note that a firm may make a conscious choice to shift down market (see cases in Ram *et al.* 2001), as well as the more commonly discussed effort to strengthen its market position.

Rules and routines: these are either *universalistic* and formalized, or *particularistic*, unwritten and informal. The more a firm lies towards the latter category, the more it will allow privileges to some workers, based on kinship or length of service, that it does not avail to others. This distinction is widely made in the general management and sociological literatures.

Management style: Scase (2003) speaks of authoritarian and egalitarian styles. The framework utilizes the dichotomy of *authoritarian* or *democratic*. The former is based on the power of the manager and it can entail the arbitrary use of sanctions. It is a core feature of Richard Edwards' (1979) 'simple control'. The 'democratic' form embraces the degree to which there is a degree of discussion and the flow of opinions up as well as down the hierarchy.

Networks: small firms use networks to gain knowledge of their customer markets and access to various material, financial and human resources for doing business (Hendry *et al.* 1995). Linkages to relevant networks can be conducive to the uptake of human resource practices (Bacon and Hoque 2005) and the promotion of competitiveness (Huggins and Williams 2007). In the present context, a firm that is linked into business support networks can be expected to have access to knowledge that would otherwise be lacking.

Illustrations

First, Gilman and Edwards (2008) studied four hi-tech firms. They found that the structural dimension of product market position helped to explain variations between them; for example, the firms in the stronger positions tended to have more developed employment relations systems. But there were also differences that reflected choice. It is a commonplace in small firms research that individual managers make distinct choices, often on highly idiosyncratic grounds (Bishop 2006). An extreme example from one study was a hotel and restaurant owner who, when the national minimum wage was about to be introduced, paid his staff well above the minimum, partly because he could afford to do so and partly because of his interpretation of the advice that he had received from local contacts; he thus paid more than other establishments a few yards away (Arrowsmith *et al.* 2003). In the hi-tech firms, personal choice determined whether or not complex recruitment and selection systems were used. It also pointed to an important tension: though the firms had formal employment systems, the owners saw the firms as their own property and would intervene in the setting of pay in ways which undermined ideas of formal pay structures. Using the framework can help to characterize such behaviour: it reflected a tension between, on the one hand, the 'formality' of the product market and the firm's resources and, on the other, the 'informality' of management style and rules and routines.

Our second set of examples comes from the creative and media (C&M) sector. Table 10.1 gives the dimensions of the framework, organized in terms of structural and industry-level features followed by processual and more firm-level dimensions. It characterizes the sector and then two firms within it.[3]

To start with the sector as a whole, in the product market, maintaining relationships with customers was essential, in that the business turned on winning a series of commissions, and reputation was an important asset. A key difference from hi-tech firms as studied by Gilman and Edwards (2008), however, was that lateral relationships with other firms were important, and there was a much stronger sense of networking within a shared community. Business associations were relatively strong, at local and national levels. The reason for this was that there was something of a shared community in that firms dealt with the same customers and also fished in the same labour market pool for technical personnel. Hi-tech firms, by contrast, tend to have highly specialized products that differ from those of other firms, and to relate most directly with their individual customers. In the C&M sector, there is much more movement between firms as commissions start and end; and over half the sector's workforce is estimated to be employed on a freelance basis. In this context, firms had an interest in regulating the labour market, which they did in two ways: using national standards for basic pay and conditions; and relying on personal networks to judge the value of job applicants.

The C&M firms, like their hi-tech counterparts, were often run by an owner-manager but the family played less of a role than it did in the more traditional small firm. These were modern businesses, though, as we will see, they had not abandoned all of their personal particularism. In terms of strategy, they relied heavily on their ability to identify a distinct competitive product. The difference was that the product was less tangible, and more based in reputation and style. This reinforced the need for networking in the industry, as opposed to relying on a specific technological niche.

Employment practices, captured in Table 10.1 under the heading of rules, were on the face of it formalized. Recruitment was open. Pay was set according to industry benchmarks, albeit with variation according to the specific skills of individuals and the nature of the commission. Performance appraisals were common. One important conclusion is that there was indeed a clear employment relationship. C&M firms are sometimes seen as being based on equality and employee autonomy,

Table 10.1 Dimensions of an organization: the sector and the firm

	Product market	Labour market	Networks	Resources	Strategy	Rules	Style
Sector							
Media	Competition within collaboration	Open within a shared space	Local associations & supply chain	Network & business skills of owners, outside investors	Growth, or strength in a niche	Formal, but with degree of fraternalism	n/a
Firm							
Mediaco	High value niche product, market leader	Moderate reliance on local labour; also draws on national talent	Strong embeddedness in local networks	Majority owned by one person, plus venture capital funding	Strong strategic intent to grow	Standard procedures, formal accreditation	Flat structure; degree of abdication from detailed control
Televisionco	Variety of high value products; market leader	Moderate reliance on local labour; actively supports its development	Strong embeddedness in local networks	Majority owned by two partners; venture capital funding	Strong strategic intent to grow and lead in terms of technology	Standard ind. guidelines, some informality in their application	Close control of creative side, some operational autonomy

with the implication that they have transcended the concerns of an employment relations view (Scase 2005). In fact, manager–worker division was evident. It was recognized explicitly by managers and by workers. And it was reflected in the use of appraisals and the like, for a genuine community of equals would not need these. It was also reflected in the reward system, with there being virtually no profit sharing or financial participation: profits were the reward of ownership. Pay, moreover, was low compared to other professional occupations, not least because work loads fluctuated and most workers were paid only for work done; fringe benefits were also largely absent. That said, the relationship had distinctive features. There was a high level of professional autonomy in the conduct of the job itself. The small-firm environment also created a sense of informality that would be absent in larger firms. This informality moderated some of the formal rules, but it also made management control a matter of personal judgment rather than the application of rules which left space for personal particularism.

We can now illustrate variation within the sector by examining two companies that were very similar in many respects and yet had differences which the framework helps us to understand. They were both relatively new, 'Televisionco' being founded ten years before the date of the study (2005) and 'Mediaco' four. They had about 40 and 20 permanent employees, respectively. They had each won numerous awards for their work, and were generally regarded as industry leaders. In terms of product market relations, both firms had established a niche position, producing distinctive work that helps them to build relationships with customers. In the labour market, the firms offered considerable opportunities for career development to their permanent employees. At Mediaco, for example, the career development was formalized under a 'moving up' scheme whereby the employees could move up the ladder by undertaking formal training. Both firms also followed the industry practice of using large numbers of freelance workers. But these workers are not seen as cheap hired help or as peripheral. As a member of the senior management team at Televisionco put it, 'even the freelance professionals are here over a long term on short term contracts, and we like to contribute to their growth and development'. The firm provided assistance to new independent production companies in the form of production facilities and even recommended its freelance professionals to other independent production companies in order to protect the freelance community.

Despite structural similarities, the companies differed in their degree of formality. In essence, Televisionco, though the larger (with twice as many employees as Mediaco) and longer established, was the more informal. This can be grasped through our framework in terms of management style. Managers at Televisionco placed a relatively strong emphasis on informal working relationships. Most human resources processes were not formally documented, and there was strong reliance on personal recommendations while recruiting new staff (for example, the new financial assistant is the girlfriend of the auditor). Pay rises were shaped by perceptions of senior managers regarding the competence of employees, and there was a lack of agreed channels of communication. At Mediaco, all human resource policies were fully documented and the policies were made known to the employees through their contract of employment and an employee handbook.

An annual formal review was conducted combined with regular feedback, and there was a clear job description for all the employees.

These differences in style appear to reflect strategic choice. Mediaco wished to succeed through a formal business model. Financial control is one of its key assets, with a professional finance director playing a central role. Televisionco has been able to retain rather more of its small firm informality.

Revisiting 'satisfaction'

These results allow us to return to the issue of apparent high levels of satisfaction in small firms. First, across all small firms there are benefits to employees in face-to-face relationships. This certainly does not mean that there is a wholly shared view of the firm or that workers naively accept managerial authority. It means that they work closely with these managers and can deal with issues in an immediate and informal way. This removes some of the distance and anonymity of large firms, and enables workers to appreciate the efforts made by managers. Second, workers have realistic expectations and know that they may be paid less than those in larger firms. Third, in particular sectors there are implicit negotiations of the wage–effort bargain. In the C&M firms, professional autonomy and systematic training was balanced by poor pay and the absence of a career structure. In lower-paying small firms, low pay goes along with only limited Taylorization and rationalization of work (Tsai *et al.* 2007). Fourth, in some small firms family relationships reduce overt worker–management conflict. In others, employees, though not direct relations of owners, may be recruited through kinship ties or other networks (as, for example, where they originate from the same village or region in, say, India). In yet others, family-like mutual obligations remain significant.

These factors do not inherently mean that work in small firms is 'better' than that in large ones. They mean, rather, that there is a particular balance of relationships that tends to make employees relatively content with their lot. On some criteria, jobs in small firms tend, on average, to be 'worse' than jobs in large firms, pay levels being the clearest case. But workers evaluate jobs on a range of criteria, and in doing so they are realistic. High levels of satisfaction do not mean deep moral loyalty to the owner. They reflect an assessment of a set of features that go together to make up a job.

Conclusion

Conventional employment relations seems strangely dislocated from institutions, notably the family, that are often central to small firms; small firms research is often individual-centric, hidebound by managerial imperatives and unitarist assumptions, and weak in its grasp of the actual conduct of the employment relationship. Research on employment relations in small firms has provided an important bridging function which has led to a heightened sensitivity to the various contexts in which small firms are embedded, empirical development in neglected areas of the economy and an inductively derived framework capable of capturing causal influences.

By drawing on the core employment relations concept of negotiation, studies of small firms have questioned longstanding stereotypes and offered a more nuanced account of work in small firms. The effect has been to provide a measure of 'discipline and structure' (Chua *et al.* 2003) to a field of study characterized by complexity, heterogeneity and a dearth of explanatory frameworks. Such borrowing from established fields can accelerate theoretical development because the concepts in question have already been subject to close scrutiny. In effect, the openness of small firms and entrepreneurship render it a 'border zone' (Steyaert 2005) for the imaginative application of ideas from other domains. Evidently though, the reverse should also be true. That is, the study of small firms can usefully inform the field of employment relations. Instructive here, for example, is the stream of work that has demonstrated how negotiation and trade-offs in households and families are of material importance to relations at work. This begins to address Ackers' (2002) concern that employment relations should be studied in conjunction with social relationships, problems and institutions. Importantly, the aim should be to assess how such institutions give effect to the conduct of the employment relationship (Sisson 2007) and not independently from workplace dynamics.

Empirical studies of work in small firms have served to broaden the traditional landscape of employment relations. Although 'low value added' mainstream small firms continue to be studied, neglected areas such as high-tech enterprises and the informal economy have increasingly attracted interest. The latter context in particular demonstrates the enduring value of an employment relations perspective. The qualitative and, in many cases, ethnographic character of much of this research has been instrumental in illuminating the subtle, informal and contradictory patterns of control in small firms. This has contributed towards the dismantling of stereotypical depictions of 'harmony' and 'autocracy', as well as explaining the variable impacts of policy interventions of the kind we have seen in the sphere of employment regulations (Edwards *et al.* 2004). Hence, recent small firm studies have demonstrated in either particular cases (e.g. Moule 1998) or comparisons across sectors (Arrowsmith *et al.* 2003) how sets of causal influences combine. This is of critical importance in assessing the impact of policy interventions, notably employment regulations. As the studies above demonstrate, variety of responses is possible, even in firms operating in a comparatively narrow segment of the market. The variation in patterns of response owes much to the external context as well as the particular 'informal' characteristics of employment relations in the small firms. Employment regulations do not have impacts on small firms that are easily predictable in advance; they are mediated not just by the different external environments in which the firms operate but also by the often opaque and complex internal dynamics within the 'black box' (Ram and Edwards 2003).

We have analysed small firms in terms of the playing out of generic features of the employment relationship within a specific small-firm context. This approach moves beyond the treatment of small firms as inherently different from large ones. As noted above, links between the firms and the wider community also occur in large firms; and 'irrationality' and informality, often seen as features of small firms, are common in large ones. Analysis has moved beyond 'size essentialism' to address how employment relationships are structured in given contexts.

Notwithstanding this progress, there is still considerable scope to strengthen the explanatory potential of case study-based research. For instance, Edwards (2005) argues that a more explicit grounding of studies within a critical realist ontology would be valuable illuminating the process that cases are seeking to explain, and may also provide lessons for broader issues. Such instincts informed Edwards *et al.*'s (2006) framework on employment relations in different kinds of small firms.

Notes

1 http://stats.berr.gov.uk/ed/sme/smestats2007-ukspr.pdf
2 The term 'informal economy' is bedevilled by a whole range of competing labels and interpretations (Williams 2004). For present purposes we define it as the remunerated production of goods and services perfectly legal in themselves, but hidden from the state for tax and welfare purposes.
3 The following discussion is based on a research project conducted jointly with Sukanya Sengupta and Chib-ju Tsai.

References

Ackers, P. 2002: Reframing employment relations: the case for neo-pluralism. *Industrial Relations Journal*, 33 (1), 2–19.

Ackers, P. and Wilkinson, A. 2005: British industrial relations paradigm: a critical outline history and prognosis. *Journal of Industrial Relations*, 47 (4), 443–456.

Ackroyd, S. 1995: On the structure and dynamics of some small, UK-based information technology firms. *Journal of Management Studies*, 32 (2), 142–161.

Ackroyd, S. 2002: *The Organization of Business*. Oxford: OUP.

Aldrich, H.E. and Cliff, J.E. 2003: The pervasive effects of family on entrepreneurship: toward a family embeddedness perspective. *Journal of Business Venturing*, 18 (4), 573–596.

Alvesson, M. 1993: Organizations as rhetoric: knowledge-intensive firms and the struggle with amibiguity. *Journal of Management Studies*, 30 (6), 997–1015.

Arrowsmith, J., Gilman, M., Edwards, P. and Ram, M. 2003: The impact of the National Minimum Wage in small firms. *British Journal of Industrial Relations*, 41 (3), 435–456.

Bacon, N. and Hoque, K. 2005: HRM in the SME sector: valuable employees and coercive networks. *International Journal of Human Resource Management*, 16 (11), 1976–1999.

Baines, S. and Wheelock, J. 1998a: Reinventing traditional solutions: job creation, gender and the micro-business household. *Work, Employment and Society*, 12 (4), 579–601.

Baines, S. and Wheelock, J. 1998b: Working for each other: gender, the household and micro-business survival and growth. *International Small Business Journal*, 17 (1), 16–35.

Barrett, R. and Rainnie, A. 2002: What's so special about small firms? *Work, Employment and Society*, 16 (3), 415–432.

Bishop, D. 2006: The small firm in the training market. Research Paper 67, SKOPE. www.skope.ox.ac.uk

Bryson, J., Keeble, D. and Wood, P. 1993: The creation and growth of small business service firms in post-industrial Britain. *Small Business Economics*, 9 (3), 345–360.

Chia, R. 1995: From modern to postmodern organizational analysis. *Organization Studies*, 16 (4), 579–604.

Child, J. 1997: Strategic choice in the analysis of action, structure, organizations and environment. *Organization Studies*, 18 (1), 43–77.

Chua, J.H., Chrisman, J.L. and Steier, L.P. 2003: Extending the theoretical horizons of family business research. *Entrepreneurship Theory and Practice*, 27 (3), 331–338.

Clark, T. 1995: *Managing Consultants: Consultancy as the Management of Impressions*. Buckingham: Open University Press.

Curran, J. and Stanworth, J. 1981: A new look at job satisfaction in the small firm. *Human Relations*, 34 (3), 343–365.

Curran, J., Stanworth, J. and Watkins, D. 1986: *The Survival of the Small Firm 1 – The Economics of Survival and Entrepreneurship*. Aldershot: Gower.

Davidsson, P. and Wiklund, J. 2001: Levels of analysis in entrepreneurship research: current research practice and suggestions for the future. *Entrepreneurship Theory and Practice*, 25 (4), 81–100.

Davis, H. and Scase, R. 2000: *Managing Creativity: The Dynamics of Work and Organizations*. Milton Keynes: Open University Press.

Dickens, R. and Manning, A. 2003: Minimum wage, minimum impact. In Dickens, R., Gregg, P. and Wadsworth, J. (eds) *The Labour Market under New Labour*. Basingstoke: Palgrave.

Dyer, W.G. 2003: The family: the missing variable in organizational research. *Entrepreneurship Theory and Practice*, 27 (4), 401–416.

Edwards, P. 2003: The employment relationship and the field of industrial relations. in Edwards, P. (ed.) *Industrial Relations* 2nd edition. Oxford: Blackwell.

Edwards, P. 2005: The challenging but promising future of industrial relations: developing theory and method in context-sensitive research. *Industrial Relations Journal*, 36 (4), 264–282.

Edwards, P. and Ram, M. 2006: Surviving on the margins of the economy: working relationships in small, low wage firms, the modern economy. *Journal of Management Studies*, 43 (4), 895–916.

Edwards, P., Ram, M. and Black, J. 2004: Why does employment legislation not damage small firms? *Journal of Law and Society*, 31 (2), 245–265.

Edwards, P., Ram, M., Sengupta, S. and Tsai, C. 2006: Institutionalized action without institutions: negotiated meanings in small firms. *Organization*, 13 (5), 701–724.

Edwards, R. 1979: *Contested Terrain*. London: Heinemann.

EIRO (European Industrial Relations Observatory) 2006: Employment relations in SMEs. www.eiro.eurofound.eu.int/2006/02/study/tn060201s

Felstead, A. Jewson, N. and Walters, S. 2005: *Changing Places of Work*. Basingstoke: Palgrave.

Forth, J., Bewley, H. and Bryson, A. 2006: *Small and Medium-sized Enterprises: Findings from the 2004 Workplace Employment Relations Survey*. London: Department of Trade and Industry.

Gartner, W. 2001: Is there an elephant in entrepreneurship? Blind assumptions in theory development. *Entrepreneurship Theory and Practice*, 25 (4), 27–39.

Gartner, W., Davidsson, P. and Zahra, S. 2006: Are you talking to me? The nature of community in entrepreneurship scholarship. *Entrepreneurship Theory and Practice*, 30 (2), 321–331.

Gilman, M. and Edwards, P.K. 2008: Testing a framework of the organization of small firms: fast-growth, high-tech SMEs. *International Small Business Journal*, 26 (5), 531–558.

Gilman, M., Edwards, P., Ram, M. and Arrowsmith, J. 2002: Pay determination in small firms in the UK. *Industrial Relations Journal*, 33 (1), 52–67.

Goffee, R. and Scase, R. 1995: *Corporate Realities: The Dynamics of Large and Small Organisations*. London: Routledge.

Goss, D. 1991: In search of small firm industrial relations. In Burrows, R. (ed.) *Deciphering the Enterprise Culture*. London: Routledge.

Greene, F. and Mole, K. 2006: Defining and measuring the small business. In Carter, S. and Jones Evans, D. (eds) *Enterprise and Small Business*. London: Prentice Hall.

Heck, R., Trent, E. and Kaye, K. 1999: The prevalence of family business from a household sample. *Family Business Review*, 12 (3), 209–228.

Hendry, C., Arthur, M.B. and Jones, A.M. 1995: *Strategy through People: Adaptation and Learning in the Small-Medium Enterprise*. London: Routledge.

Herod, A., Rainnie, A. and McGrath-Champ, S. 2007: Working space; why incorporating the geographical is central to theorizing work and employment practices. *Work, Employment and Society*, 21 (2), 247–264.

Holliday, R. 1995: *Investigating Small Firms – Nice Work?* London: Routledge.

Hoy, F. 2003: Legitimizing family business scholarship in organizational research and education. *Entrepreneurship Theory and Practice*, 27 (4), 417–422.

Huggins, R. and Williams, N. 2007: Enterprise and public policy. University of Sheffield Management School, Discussion paper 2007,03.

Jones, T. and Ram, M. 2007: Re-embedding the ethnic business agenda. *Work, Employment and Society*, 21 (3), 439–457.

Jones, T., Ram, M. and Edwards, P. 2006: Shades of grey in the informal economy. *International Journal of Sociology and Social Policy*, 26 (9/10), 357–373.

Kitching, J. 1997: *Labour Regulation in the Small Service Sector Enterprise*. Unpublished PhD thesis, Small Business Research Centre, Kingston University.

Lea, R. 2003: *Red Tape in the Workplace: The Reregulation of the Workplace II – The Sequel*. London: Institute of Directors.

Maguire, M. 1988: Work, locality and social control. *Work, Employment and Society*, 2 (1), 71–87.

Marlow, S. 2002: Regulating labour management in small firms. *Human Resource Management Journal*, 12 (3), 285–295.

Marlow, S. 2003: Formality and informality in employment relations. *Environment and Planning C: Government and Policy*, 21 (4), 531–547.

Marlow, S. 2005: Introduction. In Marlow, S., Patton, D. and Ram, M. (eds) *Managing Labour in Small Firms*. Abingdon: Routledge, pp. 1–17.

Moen, P. 1998: A lifecourse approach to the entrepreneurial family. In Heck, R. (ed.) *The Entrepreneurial Family*. Boston: Family Business Resources Inc.

Moen, P. and Wetherington, E. 1992: The concept of family adaptive strategies. *Annual Review of Sociology*, 18, 233–251.

Moule, C. 1998: Regulation of work in small firms. *Work, Employment and Society*, 12 (4), 635–653.

Ogbor, J. 2000: Mythicizing and reification in entrepreneurial discourse: ideology-critique of entrepreneurial studies. *Journal of Management Studies*,37 (5), 605–635.

Parker, S. 2006: *The Economics of Self-Employment and Entrepreneurship*. Cambridge: Cambridge University Press.

Rainnie, A. 1989: *Industrial Relations in Small Firms*. London: Routledge.

Ram, M. 1994: *Managing to Survive*. Oxford: Blackwell.

Ram, M. 2001: Family dynamics in a small consultancy firm: a case study. *Human Relations*, 54 (4), 395–418.

Ram, M. and Edwards, P. 2003: Praising Caesar not burying him: what we know about employment relations in small firms. *Work, Employment and Society*, 17 (4), 719–730.

Ram, M. and Holliday, R. 1993: Relative merits: family culture and kinship in small firms. *Sociology*, 27 (4), 629–648.

Ram, M., Edwards, P., Gilman, M. and Arrowsmith, J. 2001: The dynamics of informality: employment relations in small firms and the effects of regulatory change. *Work, Employment and Society*, 15 (4), 845–861.

Ram, M., Edwards, P. and Jones, T. 2007: Staying underground: informal work, small firms and employment regulation in the UK. *Work and Occupations*, 34 (3), 318–344.

Ram, M., Jones, T., Abbas, T. and Sanghera, B. 2002: Ethnic minority enterprise in its urban context: South Asian restaurants in Birmingham. *International Journal of Urban and Regional Research*, 26 (1), 24–40.

Rath, J. and Kloosterman, R. 2000: Outsiders' business: a critical review of research on immigrant entrepreneurship. *International Migration Review*, 34 (4), 657–681.

Rekers, A. and van Kempen, R. 2000: Location matters: ethnic entrepreneurs and the spatial context. In Rath, J. (ed.) *Immigrant Businesses: The Economic, Political and Social Environment*. London: Macmillan.

Roberts, B. 1994: Informal economy and family strategies. *International Journal of Urban and Regional Research*, 18 (1), 6–22.

Sassen, S. 1991: *The Global City*. Princeton: Princeton UP.

Scase, R. 2003: Employment relations in small firms. In Edwards, P. (ed.) *Industrial Relations*. 2nd edition. Oxford: Blackwell.

Scase, R. 2005: Managerial strategies in small firms. in Marlow, S. *et al.* (eds) *Managing Labour in Small Firms*. Abingdon: Routledge.

Scott, M., Roberts, I., Holroyd, G. and Sawbridge, D. 1989: Management and industrial relations in small firms. Department of Employment Research Paper 70. London: DE.

Shutt, J. and Whittington, R. 1987: Fragmentation strategies and the rise of small units: cases from the North West. *Regional Studies*, 21 (1), 13–23.

Sisson, K. 2007: Revitalizing industrial relations: making the most of the 'institutional turn'. *Warwick Papers in Industrial Relations*, 85, Industrial Relations Research Unit, University of Warwick.

Small Business Service (SBS) 2006: *Small Business Statistics 2005*. Available at http://www.sbs.gov.uk/sbsgov/action.

Smith, C., Child, J. and Rowlinson, M. 1990: *Reshaping Work*. Cambridge: CUP.

Steyaert, C. 2005: Entrepreneurship: in between what? On the 'frontier' as a discourse of entrepreneurship research. *International Journal of Entrepreneurship and Small Business*, 2 (1), 2–16.

Storey, D.J. 2005: *Understanding the Small Business Sector*. London: International Thomson.

Sturdy, A. 1997: The consultancy process – an insecure business? *Journal of Management Studies*, 34 (3), 389–413.

Taylor, M. 1999: The small firm as a temporary coalition. *Entrepreneurship and Regional Development*, 11 (1), 1–19.

Taylor, S. 2006: Acquaintance, meritocracy and critical realism: researching recruitment and selection processes in smaller and growth organizations. *Human Resource Management Review*, 16 (4), 478–489.

Tsai, C.-J., Sengupta, S. and Edwards, P. 2007: When and why is small beautiful? The experience of work in the small firm. *Human Relations*, 60 (12), 1779–1808.

Wagar, T. 1998: Determinants of human resource management practices in small firms: some evidence from Atlantic Canada. *Journal of Small Business Management*, 36 (2), 13–23.

Williams, C.C. 2004: *Cash-in-Hand Work: The Underground Sector and the Hidden Economy of Favours*. Basingstoke: Palgrave.

Williams, C.C. 2006: *The Hidden Enterprise Culture*. Cheltenham: Edward Elgar.

SECTION FOUR

PROCESSES

11
NEGOTIATION AND COLLECTIVE BARGAINING

WILLIAM BROWN

Introduction

Negotiation permeates the relationship between employer and workers. For all but the most transitory of jobs, both sides have some degree of discretion over what they give to the relationship, and what they take from it. Whether it is the employer's discretion over discipline, pay, or working arrangements, or the worker's discretion over effort levels, cooperation, or customer relations, there is the potential for bargaining. Employment is, by its nature, an open and usually long-term transaction. It is intrinsically difficult to specify the detail of tasks, to monitor work, or to predict the future content and stability of requirements. Bargaining is central to how employers and workers cope with this transactional uncertainty. However stacked against the worker it may be, some degree of bargaining establishes the norms and expectations on which work is conducted.

What is true for individual workers has much greater force when they think and act collectively, whether or not they are unionized. If workers do not have a clear collective understanding of what they should expect, and of what is expected of them, the consequent uncertainty is likely to be deeply demotivating. It is not just a matter of knowing what is expected of one's work; it is also one of having a basis for believing that there is some degree of equity of expectations across the workforce.

Consistency of treatment consequently lies at the heart of good employment relations. A common, collective understanding comes in many forms. It may be expressed through, for example, shared norms, job descriptions, pay scales, works rules and collective agreements. All these may be negotiable. But the extent of such negotiation depends in large part upon workers' organizational strength and management's freedom to manoeuvre. How much pressure are workers able to put on their employer? And what scope is there for an employer to make concessions regarding organizational, legal and market constraints?

The term 'collective bargaining' is used when trade unions are involved in negotiation about the employment relationship. The outcomes become, in effect, contractual terms of employment. But the constituency of workers across whom consistency matters will vary with the aspect of employment in question. The competence of conduct of a particular task may matter mainly to one's immediate workmates, but the rate at which it is paid may be relevant to everyone in the building and the associated pension arrangements may be relevant to everyone in the company. As a result, different aspects of the employment relationship are typically negotiated at different organizational levels, from the place of work itself, up through corporate or industrial levels, even as high (in the case of a statutory minimum wage) as a national 'social partnership'.

This chapter discusses negotiation in industrial relations. It starts with the changing part played by collective bargaining in recent years. It then looks closer at the nature of the bargaining process and of the procedures that shape collective bargaining; procedures that are intended to cope with its intrinsic conflict. It concludes with a broader discussion of the political character of employment in which negotiation is placed.

The Rise and Retreat of Collective Bargaining

Employers have been bargaining with their workers as collective groups since employment began, at least in informal ways. But it was not until the mid-19th century that it developed in Britain in a way that became more formally acceptable. After a number of false starts, a compromise emerged under which labour disputes were to be handled by employers' associations and trade unions and thereby kept out of the courts. By the start of the 20th century, although only about one in ten workers was in a trade union, a template for collective bargaining had been established. It would be conducted around broadly defined product markets – ship-building, cotton-spinning, carpet-making, or whatever – initially on a regional but increasingly on a national basis.

So satisfactory did this form of, in effect, sectoral self-governance seem that, by the early 20th century, it was receiving strong encouragement from government. With little party-political controversy, a number of what were generally called 'national joint industrial councils' were set up. Hitherto relatively unorganized industries thereby acquired an institution for negotiating collective agreements that would fix basic pay rates, hours of work and other important details to permit the consistent treatment of workers.

The First World War consolidated these institutions and saw their counterparts develop in the public sector. For some low-paying industries where union organization was absent, the government established legally enforceable statutory minimum wages, initially intended to be temporary measures until proper collective bargaining arrangements could develop. These sectoral minima were fixed by what were called 'wages councils', established from 1909 onwards and abolished for all but agriculture in 1993.

Although the inter-war economic depression caused a substantial setback to trade union membership, especially in the private sector, the template of industrial collective agreements continued to prevail. During and immediately after the

Second World War, under governments that were particularly sympathetic to trade unions, it was extended and consolidated. By 1950 collective bargaining covered almost all public sector workers, but it also covered over half of private sector workers.

Figure 11.1 provides an approximate picture of changes in the proportion of private sector employees covered by different pay fixing arrangements from 1940 until 2004. These are, it should be emphasized, estimates derived from a number of different sources. The chart distinguishes between three main categories. First, there are 'multi-employer agreements', which is another way of describing the sectoral or industrial agreements reached between associations of employers and trade unions mentioned earlier. Second, there are 'single-employer agreements' reached at the level of individual enterprises, or of some part within them such as a division or site. Third, there are wages council statutory minimum rates.

The structure of collective bargaining arrangements in place by the mid-20th century was widely seen to provide a basis for regulating employment that was both stable and largely comprehensive of the employed workforce (Flanders and Clegg 1954). It was to prove uncontroversial in party-political terms until the 1980s. That might have been partly because it was superficially very similar to the systems of sectoral collective bargaining that had been established or consolidated in most continental western European countries since the war. But there was one crucial difference. Unlike those systems, it had no legal reinforcement. British collective agreements were not intended to be enforced in the courts of law (Colling; Dickens and Hall, this volume). And while the assumption was that

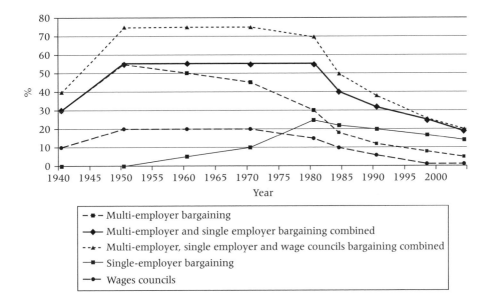

Based on estimates derived from various sources: *Ministry of Labour Handbook*, Flanders and Clegg (1954), Milner (1995) and successive WIRS and WERS surveys.

Figure 11.1   The approximate coverage of principal pay fixing arrangements for private sector employees in Great Britain, 1940–2004

agreements were negotiated between employers' association officials and national trade union officers, there was no legal barrier to their being supplemented by, for example, relatively lowly works managers, in deals with local union officials, or even with workplace union activists such as shop stewards.

By the 1960s, it had become clear that this was what was happening. The tight labour markets of the 1950s had encouraged local managements to fudge pay increases in an effort to attract and retain scarce labour. Piecework incentive systems, merit rates, overtime payments and the like were bargained over at workplace level to raise wages, which consequently 'drifted' (as it was described at the time) higher than sectoral collective agreements had allowed. Faced with increasingly ineffective agreements, and encouraged by the diagnosis of the Donovan Royal Commission in 1968, employers began to pull out of multi-employer arrangements and to bargain on their own.

The growth of this single-employer bargaining, especially in the 1970s, is evident in Figure 11.1. Sectoral (multi-employer) agreements were by now in steady decline. Single-employer bargaining was to overtake multi-employer bargaining in terms of its coverage in the private sector around 1980, but then was to join it in decline. Collective bargaining has continued to be overwhelmingly important in the British public sector. But in the private sector, by the early 21st century, the coverage of collective bargaining had diminished to no more than one worker in five. For the great majority of private sector workers, the only cushion against the vagaries of an open labour market has been provided by the state. The introduction, in 1999, of the national minimum wage (see Grimshaw and Rubery, this volume), provided a statutory safety net that was both broader and stronger than that provided by the old wages councils.

The Causes of Collapse

What is the explanation of this sustained collapse of collective bargaining in the British private sector since the early 1980s? Can it be attributed to changes in industrial structure, with the contraction of traditionally highly unionized industries and the demise of large manufacturing workplaces? Is it the consequence of the legislative attacks on trade unions of Conservative governments between 1979 and 1997? Or is there a more far-reaching explanation, less tied to place and time? It has been possible to investigate these questions in considerable detail by analysis of the series of five Workplace Employment Relations Surveys (WERS) that were carried out between 1980 and 2004 (Brown *et al.* 2009).

We can dismiss the view that we are witnessing the consequence of the decline of the industrial heartlands of collective bargaining with their long union traditions and large workforces, such as engineering, docks, steel and textiles. If one makes the artificial statistical assumption that industrial distribution and workforce size remained constant, it is possible to test, by multivariate analysis, how far the outcome would have been different. The answer is that only one tenth of the decline in the workplace incidence of collective bargaining in the private sector between 1984 and 2004 can be attributed to change in workplace size and industrial composition (Blanchflower and Bryson 2009: 30). Something far more powerful and pervasive was at play.

Nor can the collapse of collective bargaining be attributed directly to anti-union legislation during the 1980s. There is no doubt that the legislation increased the difficulty and cost of trade union organization in general and of strike activity in particular (Dickens and Hall, this volume). It was designed to that end. This made it easier for employers to withdraw from collective bargaining arrangements but it was not a sufficient condition for them to do so. The withdrawal from collective bargaining was uneven both between and within industries (Brown *et al.* 1998). This is particularly marked in the contrast between public and private sectors. In 2007 it was estimated from the Labour Force Survey that collective agreements affected 72% of public sector employees – a figure that would be much higher if we consider the Pay Review Bodies to be a proxy for collective bargaining (see Bach, this volume). But they only affected 20% of private sector employees (Mercer and Notley 2008: 41). Within the private sector, there have been marked differences in experience, with collective bargaining coverage holding up in, for example, electricity, railways, theatre and chemical refining, but withering away in, for example, construction, buses, food manufacture and printing (see Arrowsmith, this volume). Legislation may have had a catalytic effect, but it varied greatly between employment environments.

Furthermore, however damaging the legislation of the 1980s, there is evidence that the decline of collective bargaining was already well under way by then. It is the older workplaces in the private sector that are more likely to use collective bargaining, even when account is taken of the industries they are in. Thus, in 1998, WERS suggest that 45% of workplaces set up in the 1940s still had collective bargaining; compared with 23% of those set up in the 1960s; and compared with 12% of those set up in the 1980s. By 2004, 32% of workplaces set up in the 1960s were still using collective bargaining; compared with 13% of those set up in the 1970s (Brown *et al.* 2009: 29). If we assume that the decision to rely on collective bargaining is taken relatively early in the life of a workplace, this suggests that employers setting up workplaces more recently were either less likely to use collective bargaining, or established it in a less durable form, or both. If there was a 'golden age' of collective bargaining, this implies that it was just after the Second World War, and that things have been going downhill since then.

Nor is it evident that a change of government had a substantial impact on the contraction of collective bargaining. The Conservative governments of the 1980s and early 1990s displayed overt hostility to collective bargaining. This was in sharp contrast to the generally supportive, if 'arm's length' stance of New Labour, which introduced a statutory procedure for achieving trade union recognition in 1999 as well as rights, such as those to accompany workers in grievance procedures, which might have been expected to consolidate local union strength. The decline in trade union membership, so marked in the 1980s, levelled out from the late 1990s but this did not happen to the coverage of collective bargaining. It continued to diminish into the 21st century at an annual rate, taking other factors into account, that was little different between 1998 and 2004 than it had been between 1990 and 1998 (op. cit.: 31). Government policy, legislative or otherwise, does not appear to have been the prime cause of collective bargaining's retreat.

The Pressure of Competition

It is the changing environment of competition that has irrevocably damaged collective bargaining (see also Sisson and Purcell, this volume). Trade unions were best able to gain a bargaining purchase on a share of profits for their members working in the market for a given product when they could organize all the employers within that market, and if that market was, in the economic sense, imperfect. Each employer would then be able to pay a little more to their employees so long as they were all obliged to do it, and to pass on the cost to the consumer in higher prices. Wages were, in the time-honoured phrase, 'taken out of competition' between employers because all those employers agreed to pay according to the same multi-employer wage scales. So long as product markets were roughly confined to single countries, or their subregions, that was the basis of the relative stability of multi-employer collective bargaining in Europe for much of the 20th century. But in recent decades product markets have become extended far beyond national frontiers. Whether or not they are less imperfect, they generally cannot be organized by trade unions operating within a single country.

The most obvious force stretching product markets beyond the reach of collective bargaining arrangements has been the steady growth in international trade – which for some decades has been at roughly twice the annual rate of growth of world income (see Marginson and Meardi, this volume). This is obvious to most people at the level of the supermarket. International retail chains such as Wal-mart, Tesco and Aldi, which stock their shelves from the cheapest sources they can find in the world, have grown steadily, assisted by falling costs of freight and improved monitoring of suppliers. But it applies just as much for intermediate goods and services. Overall, British imports of manufactures, expressed as a percentage of home demand for manufactures, rose from 25% in 1980 to 62% in 2005 (Annual Abstract of Statistics 2008: 319).

Less immediately obvious is the effect of the increasing internationalization of capital markets and thereby of the ownership of domestic employers. A British-based firm that has an international presence may find it easy to circumvent a collective agreement in Britain by sourcing a component or service from one of its subsidiaries in a country with cheaper labour. Companies with British roots have increased their foreign direct investment substantially in recent years – the average annual level roughly doubled between the 1990s and 2000s. No less important, the ownership of British-based firms has become more international. The proportion of shares listed on the London Stock Exchange which are owned by investors outside Britain rose from 4% in 1981 to 40% in 2006 (National Statistical Office: StatBase/Product.asp?vlnk+930). Whether or not a firm is engaged in foreign trade itself, the internationalization of capital markets increases the competitive pressure on employers; it diminishes their national loyalties; and it increases the mobility of their capital to cheap labour sources abroad.

There is ample evidence that tightening competition has eroded collective bargaining. The WERS asked firms about the number of competitors they faced. Throughout the period from 1984 to 2004, collective bargaining was more likely to be used in firms that claimed that they 'dominated' their market than those where they reported up to five competitors. They, in turn, were more likely to use collective bargaining than those with six or more competitors. By 2004, firms that dominated their markets were twice as likely to have collective bargaining as those that reported 'many' competitors. The change over the period underlines this. Use of collective bargaining fell by 35% in companies that dominated their market, but fell by 62% where they had up to five competitors and by 70% where they had six or more (Brown *et al.* 2009: 38). Collective bargaining survives best in markets where monopoly elements are more evident because they offer more scope for the sharing of profits with the workforce.

Another way of assessing how changes in collective bargaining are affected by competition is to see whether they are associated with the profitability of industries. It was possible to divide the WERS sample workplaces into four categories, according to in which quartile of the distribution of profitability their industrial sector was. This showed clearly that collective bargaining was, for the whole 20 years, more likely for those in the top quartile of profitability than the others. It also showed that the percentage decline in use of collective bargaining between 1984 and 2004 was substantially less for those in the top quartile than for the others.

What about a change in relative profits? Another test using the same data was to see how collective bargaining fared in industries with different relative experience of profitability over the 20 years. The industries that enjoyed profitability above the median at the start and finish of the period had both the highest incidence of, and the least fall in, collective bargaining. They included financial intermediation, and food and drink manufacture. Those that were below the median at start and finish, such as construction, and those that started below but ended above, such as retail, had a similar experience of seeing their collective bargaining coverage halved. But it was those industries that saw profits tumble from being above the median in 1984 to below the median in 2004 that saw the greatest, five-fold average decline in use of collective bargaining (ibid.: 40). These were the industries – examples were hospitality and electrical machinery manufacture – where trade unions had least to bargain a share of and where employers could least afford to make concessions. Collective bargaining has retreated farthest and fastest where profitability has been hardest hit.

What happened, then, when privatization suddenly exposed state monopolies to the open market? Overall, use of collective bargaining fell back towards levels more comparable with the established private sector (see Arrowsmith, this volume). But the impact was very uneven. There were some operations, such as buses, waste disposal, research laboratories and catering, where collective bargaining declined dramatically. But in parts of other industries, collective bargaining continued to be the main way of fixing pay; gas, water, electricity, telecommunications and rail provide examples. The reason for this diversity is that privatization does not by any means imply the creation of perfect markets. Naturally monopolistic conditions may be enjoyed by train drivers, sewage workers, telephone engineers, and power station operators whether privatized or not – the existence of official regulatory bodies such as Ofrail, Ofwat, Ofcom and Ofgem reflects this. But where such protection from full exposure to product market competition was not available, coverage of collective bargaining continued to decline for some years after privatization, a decline that ceased, but was not reversed, with the arrival of New Labour in 1997 (ibid.: 44).

The underlying cause of the collapse of collective bargaining was, in summary, increasing product market competition. Legislative restraints on trade unions may have accelerated the process, but it was tougher competitive environments that reduced the share of profits that they could win for their members. Competitive pressure on unit costs forced managements to tighten controls over employment and thereby to reduce the scope for union influence. Or it encouraged them to shift the work overseas and beyond trade union reach.

This is not to say, it should be added, that there is an iron law whereby tighter competition denies employers choice as to whether to use collective bargaining. There are many sectors, from cosmetics to construction and from banking to baking, where competition has become tougher but where many successful firms still choose to grant trade unions full collective bargaining rights as a key component of an inclusive employee relations strategy. But changing competitive circumstances have made this less likely. They have eroded multi-employer bargaining from being the dominant default position to one of quirky rarity. They have made it harder for unions to win bargaining rights through the mobilization of collective strength. One can see in retrospect that what had once permitted collective bargaining to flourish, as a system of industrial governance in which trade unions played so substantial a part, was the comparatively imperfect and local product markets that had prevailed in the mid-20th century.

The Changing Character of Collective Bargaining

Before discussing the processes involved, we should note the varied depth of union involvement in collective bargaining. At one extreme, it may be intense, with few aspects of pay, hours and the organization of work not subject to close joint regulation with unions. This was the case 30 years ago in, for example, the coal and commercial television industries. It remains the case in, for example, the public prison service and some airlines. At the other extreme, the degree of union involvement may be slight, intruding no more than by providing an agreement setting out basic pay scales, as may be found today in, for example, much of construction and many universities.

It should also be emphasized that it is not only the coverage of collective bargaining that has diminished substantially, but also its influence where it is still to be found. Some indication of this comes from comparable responses to successive workplace surveys that asked managers about the issues on which they negotiated. If we take responses from workplaces with 25 or more employees where trade unions were recognized at the time, in 1980 the proportion of managers saying that they negotiated with union representatives at the workplace was 43% on recruitment, 64% on internal redeployment, and 49% on manning levels (Daniel and Millward 1983: 197). By 1998, comparable responses had tumbled. Managers said they negotiated with the union representative in only 3% of cases for recruitment and selection, and only 6% for staffing or manpower planning (Brown *et al.* 2000: 617). In 2004, responses to comparable questions remained at much the same low level. The proportion reporting negotiation was 5% for recruitment and selection, and 6% for staffing and manpower planning (Brown and Nash 2008: 99). Union influence over the organization of work, even in those places where collective bargaining was active at workplace level, had collapsed over the 1980s and 1990s. Negotiation over work organization is no longer commonplace – particularly in the private sector, where it is now rare.

As its influence has diminished in the private sector, collective bargaining has tended to be more consultative (see Terry, this volume). In the 2004 survey, in those workplaces with union representatives, they and their managers were in broad agreement that, averaged across the main issues on which they interacted, the relationship was twice as likely to be characterized by consultation and information rather than negotiation (Brown and Nash 2008: 101). Trade unions' dealings with management have always been a blend of cooperation and confrontation. In recent years the cooperative aspect has been in the ascendancy. But two decades or more earlier, when strike threats were credible, confrontation was the more conspicuous aspect of collective bargaining. Bargaining was backed, to a greater or lesser extent, by a constant, latent threat of sanctions.

The bargaining process

The context of the power relationship in collective bargaining was and is distinctive. It differs from commercial relationships between customers and suppliers partly because it is so close and continuous. Employers and employees are heavily dependent on each other. Shedding a workforce is as unpalatable to an employer as losing a job is for an employee. However bitter the dispute of the day, both sides know that, in the near future, they will have to pick up the bits and make amends. Bargainers on both sides are usually acutely anxious to avoid the mutual damage of strike action. They strive to take into account changing market conditions in making their claims and offers. A shrewd understanding of each other's market position and organizational strength, and a lurking awareness of an implicit strike threat, can lead to a shift in the balance of advantage being reflected in the agreed settlement without any strike action being necessary. In John Hicks' seminal theoretical analysis, should the two sides have perfect information about each other's strengths, weaknesses and preferences, agreement would be reached without the occurrence of strikes (Hicks 1932).

But when the two sides have different evaluations of their relative market and organizational strength, a strike may be precipitated. The employer may call what they believe to be the union's bluff. Or the union may believe that the employer has not appreciated how the union's strength has increased, perhaps as a result of raised employee aspirations. In either case, the open fighting out of a strike can be a worthwhile investment for whichever side emerges as the winner, with consequences lasting well beyond the current bargaining period. Bargaining reputations endure. Examples of long-lasting union victories were those of the coalminers in 1974, the fire-fighters in 1978 and the water-workers in 1981. Enduring union defeats include those of the coalminers in 1985, the seamen in 1988 and the fire-fighters in 2003.

Whether or not a given negotiation involves a strike, the outcome may carry heavy implications for the survival of the business as well as for the continuing relationship between employer and their employees' union. As a result, the negotiating process tends to have considerable complexity. Effective collective bargaining requires sophistication on the part of those involved and the commitment of time and money, deemed worthwhile if it avoids damaging disputes or results in the more efficient management of change. The most serviceable analysis of the complexities of collective bargaining is that by Walton and McKersie (1965). They identified, from a substantial number of observed negotiations in the USA, four distinct processes that can be found at work in parallel with each other.

The first process, which fits the popular conception, is what they called 'distributive bargaining'. This is a 'zero-sum' bargain over how the 'cake' should be divided up, typical of simple annual pay claims. In terms of behaviour, it is characterized by a rather formal process, for which opposing parties meet round a table, make (often confrontational) statements for the record and edge towards compromise by means of a series of adjournments. Distributive bargaining was a dominant feature of the more confrontational form of collective bargaining that has, as we have noted, diminished so markedly in the British private sector since the 1980s.

The second is 'integrative bargaining'. This is a 'positive-sum' or 'win-win' process that is characterized by both sides taking a problem-solving approach. Confrontation is minimized and informality emphasized. Such bargaining is usually carried out away from the normal place of work, perhaps in a weekend retreat in a country hotel. The objective is to encourage both sides to adopt lateral thinking and flexible attitudes in order to facilitate concessions and improved ways of working. In Britain it became a feature of the 'workplace partnership' agreements that flourished, with government and TUC encouragement, at the end of the 1990s. Although the 'partnership' word quickly fell from favour, an emphasis on integrative bargaining continues to be a feature of the more consultative and cooperative style of collective bargaining in the British private sector of the 2000s as, indeed, it always has been in the public sector (Oxenbridge and Brown 2004).

But negotiators do not operate in a vacuum: Walton and McKersie (ibid.) identify two further complementary processes. First is the way the negotiators tackle the attitudes and preferences of the organizations on whose behalf they negotiate; this they described as 'intra-organizational bargaining'. Informal networking, report-back meetings and statements to the media are important in this. The other, described as 'attitudinal structuring', is a more diffuse process whereby they seek to influence the wider climate of opinion and expectation, not least of the opposing side. It is sometimes called 'framing' attitudes, and can summon up a strategic approach similar to that of propagandists in wartime.

Before considering further the context within which these parallel processes interact, we need to reflect on two further crucial aspects. The first concerns the internal politics of each side – their intra-organizational efficiency. The second is the relationship between the individual bargaining agents who confront each other. Both of these contribute towards the necessary conditions for effective negotiation.

Intra-organizational efficiency

An important determinant of the effectiveness of a negotiation arises from the intra-organizational complexity of the two opposing parties. Whether trade unions or employers, they often comprise uneasy coalitions of interests. The greater their heterogeneity, the bigger the task of intra-organizational bargaining whereby divergent interests can be reconciled and agreement reached on a compromise set of priorities and bargaining objectives. Failure can lead to paralysis. Much depends upon the clarity of the coalition's decision-making constitution and the skill and sensitivity of the officers who have to administer it.

Taking the employers' side first, this was an important issue for employers' associations involved in multi-employer bargaining. Forming a united front against the unions was bound to be difficult for employers who were in direct competition with each other in their product market. It was especially so where employers differed substantially: in size; in the extent to which their sales were in specialized niches; or in the extent to which they relied upon export markets. Such heterogeneity creates substantial constitutional challenges for the maintenance of unity. Thus, for example, in both 1979 and 1989, the most historically important private sector employers' association, the Engineering Employers' Federation, ended up making substantial concessions in the face of strike action in union campaigns for the reduction of the length of the working week. The strategic failure of the Federation's constitution to cope with conflicting pressures within its membership effectively killed it as a bargaining institution. Currently, in the public sector, the large employer federations that manage collective bargaining for local authorities, the police and the fire and emergency services all struggle to achieve efficient but representative bargaining outcomes with heterogeneous, geographically defined memberships, which have a patchwork of local party political allegiance to add complexity.

The challenge of maintaining a united front is a different one for trade unions. Unions often have to mobilize a credible threat of collective action. At very least they have to mobilize consent to an eventual agreement, often across a diversity of markets, skill levels and occupational interests (see Simms and Charlwood, this volume). In support of this, the union movement has developed a substantial rhetoric of egalitarianism and solidarity, often best seen as functional rather than ideological. Unions place, of necessity, great emphasis on constitutional rectitude and democratic procedures. Joint union negotiating committees typically have carefully balanced representative membership and precise standing orders to ensure clear legitimation of decisions. They usually are required to ratify provisional pay bargaining settlements through a final democratic consultation with the rank-and-file. When constitutional rectitude within the union side breaks down, settlement with the employers can become all but impossible. The national mineworkers' strike of 1984/85 finally ended without agreement partly because the dispute had been allowed to develop without proper adherence to internal union procedures to secure a democratic mandate for the action. No constitutional basis remained for negotiating an agreement. This resulted in the union splitting, a partial strike and a deadlock that lasted a year. It was terminally disastrous for both the union and its industry.

Failures of internal decision making within the opposing bargaining parties arise from ambiguous authorization procedures, from inadequate means of disseminating information and explanation, and from inconclusive mechanisms of internal debate. The more complex is the process of establishing a bargaining mandate, of reference back and of ratification, the more constraints are placed on the negotiating committee. This, then, is a first condition for effective negotiation: an efficient and clear constitutional arrangement for decision making within each of the opposing bargaining parties. The greater are the intra-organizational constraints under which the individual negotiators are obliged to operate, the less is their chance for success in the side-deals, trade-offs, face-savers and compromises which will ease the way to agreement. We shall now focus on this relationship between the opposing negotiators.

The bargaining relationship between negotiators

A key determinant of the effectiveness of a negotiation is the quality of the bargaining relationship between the opposing negotiators. This is to do with the efficiency with which they exchange information. The bargaining relationship can be defined as the extent to which the negotiators are able to make each other aware of the constraints under which they operate and of the likely reactions of one organization to actions by the other. The better the bargaining relationship is, the better is the information exchange and the more accurate (and less costly) the anticipation of responses to fresh developments (Brown 1973: 134).

With a strong bargaining relationship, the negotiators have a much greater freedom of action and manoeuvre than when it is weak. They can informally float possible solutions in a way that is without prejudice and will not be held against them should their suggestions sink. They can allow the other side to put on a public show of strength or outrage without over-reacting, aware that such a show was aimed at placating intra-organizational pressures behind the negotiators putting it on, not at antagonizing the negotiators they face. They can provide their opposing negotiators with insights into the underlying priorities of the side they are representing, and of the strength of feeling on different bargaining issues of their constituents. They can help their opposing negotiators manage their respective organizations by arranging credit for small victories and avoiding their humiliation (Batstone *et al.* 1977: 171, 264).

This is not to say that, at times, even negotiators with excellent bargaining relationships may not see advantage in tactical ploys that increase the uncertainty confronting their opponents. Schelling (1960) wrote the classic game-theoretic analysis of the many tricks used by negotiators. They include making themselves unavailable at key phases of negotiations, and unexpectedly making apparently binding commitments. An ability to ride out each other's bargaining tactics without damaging the bargaining relationship is a sign of professionalism. But in the long run, the power relationship will be managed most efficiently, and with least use of costly sanctions, if the bargaining relationship is strong.

One way of describing a strong bargaining relationship is that it has a high level of trust. It is a reciprocal business relationship between professional negotiators. It may, or may not, involve affective friendship. But it frequently does, not least because informal chats in pubs lead on to mutual moans about intractably awkward bosses and cloud cuckoo-land constituents, and on from there. Indeed, close but professional friendships are a feature of some of the most productive bargaining relationships.

There are, of course, inherent dangers if the professional negotiating teams become too close. Any strong bargaining relationship can mutate into a self-serving stitch-up between consenting professionals if they are not exposed to some sort of democratic or managerial accountability. The more isolated the negotiators, the greater the danger of this. The history of trade unionism is littered with negotiators who were considered to have 'sold out' by developing too close a relationship with management. It is, perhaps, a particular problem when the individuals in question become too far separated from the day-to-day running of their organizations. It is a hazard when career paths potentially lead on to higher things beyond the organization. Again, labour movement history has many examples of negotiators whose migration into management, Parliament and peerages was accompanied by a reputation for betrayal.

This, then, is a second precondition for efficient negotiation: a close, but professional bargaining relationship between the key negotiators. The negotiating skills touched on here, which still feature in some management and trade union training courses, used to be widely diffused across British industry. Much of that expertise has been lost, as a consequence of the decline of collective bargaining and the contracting-out of many personnel management functions. Examples of more recent high-profile disputes that might have been avoided had this not happened include the dispute at Heathrow around the Gate Gourmet catering workers in 2005 and the dispute over pensions at the Grangemouth oil refinery in 2008. But even with the best intra-organizational constitutions, and the subtlest of bargaining relationships between the negotiators, agreement is sometimes elusive. At this point it may help to bring in an outsider, and the way that role works sheds further light on the bargaining process.

Active conciliation

Third party intervention has long provided a safety-net for collective bargaining. Most countries have some sort of state-sponsored conciliation and arbitration service. It is state-sponsored because a service paid for by the disputants usually has its independence challenged. Some countries have had legal requirements to use such interventions – Canada's compulsory conciliation and Australia's compulsory arbitration endured for most of the 20th century. Britain's Ministry of Labour provided a conciliation service from the 1890s until it was replaced by the Advisory, Conciliation and Arbitration Service (ACAS) in 1976.

ACAS is run at arm's length from government by a council constituted on a 'social partnership' basis, with equal numbers of representatives from union and employer backgrounds. This constitution ensures that ACAS remains broadly sympathetic towards collective bargaining, even though the explicit duty to encourage its extension was removed from ACAS' statutory duties in 1993 (Sisson and Taylor 2006). It currently employs about 500 full-time conciliators whose main task is dealing with over a hundred thousand complaints per year by individual employees against employers about unfair dismissal, discrimination, underpayment, denial of parental leave, or some other statutory employee entitlement (see Dickens and Hall; Colling, this volume). But the conciliators also process about a thousand collective disputes per year, between employers and trade unions, of which pay-related issues are the most numerous. The great bulk of these are settled through conciliation, but about 5% are passed on to a panel of part-time arbitrators, most of them being dealt with by a single arbitrator. Although arbitrated awards are not legally binding, there has been no case of an award being rejected or contravened since ACAS was established.

There is a spectrum of third party interventions, from conciliation to arbitration. At one extreme, conciliation may amount simply to facilitating information exchange between the disputing parties. At the other, arbitration is a quasi-judicial process in which a formal hearing leads to an 'award' that is binding on the disputants. But in practice there is a range of more-or-less active interventions between these extremes, some of which may be referred to as mediation.

One part of the conciliator's role is the relatively passive one of transmitting perceptions and proposals between the disputing parties, who are usually kept in separate rooms. But in practice such a role quickly becomes more active. An important first step is, perhaps surprisingly, to get the parties to agree on what they are in disagreement about. This can take time as they often have different perceptions of both what is in dispute and what issues underlie it. Getting agreed understanding of the issue, and getting agreement to put aside tangential controversies over causes and motives, often paves the way to getting a settlement. Many an arbitration has been averted because the process of agreeing the terms of reference has led to a voluntary settlement.

Effective conciliation can call on a variety of skills. The disputing parties have often become so bogged down in particular ways of looking at the issues in contention that the fresh eye of the conciliator may allow them to be repacked in novel and more acceptable ways. An important early part of the conciliator's task is getting each party, independently and alone, to describe and analyse the issues, testing and rephrasing and probing ambiguities in order to clarify the disputing parties' thinking. The conciliator's fresh eye and genuinely naïve questions may help the parties to avoid worn pathways of thought. Lateral thinking is always helpful.

Another phase may be one of getting the parties, again in isolation from each other, to discuss the worst possible outcome of a failure to agree, and to reflect aloud about its more unpleasant implications. If done before an adjournment, when they can brood on it, this may improve the acceptability of hitherto unacceptable compromises. Both sides are, metaphorically, made to look over the precipices down which they could drop if agreement is not reached. A successful conciliator is far from passive. He or she may have to make the opposing parties extremely uncomfortable during the course of the process. Eventual agreement typically comes not through rational argument and sweet reason, but through the painful adjustment of expectations to a more realistic appreciation of the options and the costs.

Preventing loss of face by the negotiators is often important in a third party intervention. This applies at both the personal and the public level. Negotiators who have been stuck in each other's company through long meetings will place considerable store in emerging with their mutual respect and self-esteem intact. But during the negotiations they may have used some fairly outrageous, possibly moralistic and tendentious arguments. They may have conceded some passionately defended positions. The conciliator will know that they will reach agreement easier if both sides can envisage a dignified exit in each other's eyes. Considerable store is thus placed on devising what is often called a 'silken ladder' down which those who have to make major concessions can climb. It may involve the puffing up of a minor favourable concession, subordinate to the main issue at stake, to look like a major one. It may require a robust (but actually unenforceable) agreed statement of intent about the future. If the bargaining relationship is good, the negotiators will protect each other's self-esteem.

At the public level, it is important to ensure if possible that neither negotiator should have reason to fear that they might be humiliated either by the media or in the eyes of their respective organizations. An old adage of American union negotiators was 'mourn in victory; cheer in defeat' – meaning that it was foolish in terms of long-term relations for the perceived winner to emerge triumphant. Settlements are often followed by soundbites in televised interviews about the courage and toughness of the opposition, and statements of the sort: 'a victory not for either side but for common-sense'.

It usually helps to have a number of variables in play, around which concessions can be traded. It particularly helps if the two sides differ slightly in the priority they place on these, or in their perception of the importance ascribed to them by their respective organizations. At one extreme, a settlement of technical complexity can often be 'sold' relatively easily to each organization because different aspects of it can be stressed to the different audiences. But a single-issue dispute is more difficult. A conciliator may be able to create negotiating space by, in effect, breaking down a single-issue bargain into separate items. Each side may be able to soften the unpopular aspects of the settlement with their respective constituencies by choosing which aspects to emphasize.

Arbitration

During the course of a conciliation process, it may come about that the two sides are unwilling to be seen to be accepting a settlement that they both can see is the only one that is feasible. The appropriate action may then be for the conciliator formally to propose it as the settlement, and for the two sides to accept it with public protests of reluctance. This process, which is sometimes called mediation, or 'med-arb', leaves the two sides free to 'blame' the conciliator for what they have, in the interest of settlement, gone along with. This function is more evident in a straightforward arbitration – the arbitrator is there to be blamed for his or her 'award', and will normally have no further contact with the organization that was in dispute. The prime objective of the arbitration is to protect the continuing relationship between the opposing parties from the consequences of their clash. The relationship with the arbitrator *per se* is as expendable as a car's inflatable air-bag.

Labour arbitrations have many functions. One function is simply to be there as an option, as a threat to encourage a negotiated outcome: 'If you do not settle it between yourselves, you are at the mercy of an outsider – some random professor!' One function of the prospect of an arbitration is to make the parties analyse their dispute by forcing them to work out and agree terms of reference, as already mentioned. This is itself a negotiation, because good terms of reference have to set sufficiently tight limits to constrain the damage that an incompetent arbitrator might inflict.

Another function of arbitration is to provide either side with the chance to kick an embarrassment into touch so it will not sour their wider relationship. One typical example would be where a middle manager has made a mistake, perhaps by neglecting some informal arrangement to which the workforce felt entitled by custom and practice. The senior management may not want to be seen to be climbing down, but they are content to have the manager's hapless decision reversed by an arbitrator. Another common example these days is when management and the local union negotiators have concluded a deal which is seen to be sensible if not generous, only to have it rejected in a ballot of the members. The restoration of something like the lost deal by an arbitrator will set relations back on course. Arbitrators are accustomed to, in effect, being used tacitly to protect an otherwise functional collective bargaining arrangement.

The actual procedure of arbitration can also have intrinsic utility. A basic rule is that nothing that the arbitrator reads is not also read, and can be challenged, by the other side. Nothing the arbitrator hears is not heard, and can be challenged, by the other side. The arbitrator's questioning, always with both sides present, usually uncovers issues neither side has articulated, and often allows the competing cases to be set out with stark clarity that exposes any weaknesses. There is often an institutional therapeutic value, quite irrespective of the final award, in the arbitration hearing process. Each side has to listen while the other sets out its case and has it probed by an independent person. Each side has an opportunity to challenge the other side's case, in what is almost always a calm and positive atmosphere.

The arbitrator's written award augments this process. Usually under a thousand words in length, it sets out the background to the dispute, and then summarizes the two sides' arguments as concisely and as strongly as possible. The objective at this stage is to make each side feel not only that their case has been understood, but that they have put forward their arguments effectively. Then the arbitrator writes what are called 'general considerations', which is a terse statement of the points that appear to be relevant to deciding the award, usually put in such a way that suggests that neither side is wholly right or wrong. Relevant arguments might relate to existing agreements, special circumstances, agreed custom and practice, and reasonable expectations. The words of the actual award stick very closely to those of the initial terms of reference in order to minimize the chance that unforeseen precedents might be set. There is no right of appeal because it is not a judicial process. As was mentioned earlier, ACAS-arbitrated awards have, over the past 30 years, always been adhered to by both sides.

The possibility of arbitration plays an important role in the breaking of deadlocks in collective bargaining. But arbitration is best seen as supporting conciliation rather than the other way round. The conciliator's objective is to facilitate independent collective bargaining, and the possibility of arbitration provides the conciliator with a form of sanction. Used sparingly, it may be unavoidable, but neither arbitration nor the conciliation it supports provides a substitute for a strong embedded bargaining procedure.

Conclusions: Collective Bargaining and Society

This account started with the observation that negotiation permeates the relationship between employer and workers. For much of the past century, and for much of the British workforce, this has been conducted within a framework of collective bargaining. But in recent years this framework has collapsed for the private sector. It has been argued here that the prime reason for that collapse has been the changing competitive environment in which increasing numbers of people work. If correct, this implies that the collapse is largely irreversible. Setting aside a convulsion in the world economy on a scale that would have far wider implications, there is little prospect of traditional collective bargaining regaining the central position it once occupied in the governance of private sector employment.

This does not mean that certain forms of collective bargaining may not continue to flourish. The particular circumstances of the public sector will continue to be conducive to it, albeit constrained by managerial techniques for cultivating pseudo-competition such as performance league tables, competitive tendering and threats of privatization. Any occupation that can win the protection of some sort of state licence to operate for safety and quality reasons should be also able to function as an effective collective and bargain accordingly; examples are accountants, architects, lawyers, vets, Hackney cab drivers and civil engineers. New technologies will bring new forms of industrial action. For example, trade unions with members working in internationally traded goods and services may be able to use consumer campaigns to combat competition that relies on demonstrably exploited labour, following the contours of international product markets by mobilizing purchasing power through the worldwide web. But for most less-skilled employees in the private sector, the prospects for collective bargaining are bleak.

It could be argued that this is just where the state has been stepping in to provide protections. During the past 30 or so years, encouraged by membership of the European Union, Britain has created many statutory individual employment rights. These range from protections against unfair dismissal and disability discrimination to rights to minimum holidays and minimum wages. Some of these have been developed from a 'social dialogue' process involving negotiations between the CBI and TUC. In the case of the national minimum wage, there is, in effect, an annual negotiation between the 'social partners' within the Low Pay Commission (Brown 2009).

It can, however, be questioned how far these rights have provided a substitute for the substance of collective bargaining (see Colling, this volume). As national minima, they reflect the lowest common level, rather than what different sectors can, in some sense, afford. Many have been aimed at maximizing an economically effective workforce as a government objective, rather than achieving a more secure workforce as union members might have voted (Davies and Freedland 2007). Furthermore, unlike other European countries, apart from for the minimum wage and for health and safety at work, Britain does not have a labour inspectorate or other proactive enforcement agency for employment rights. As a result, these are 'self-service' rights that may be hard to access for the unorganized employees who need them most. It has been demonstrated that the absence of collective bargaining at a workplace places the workers employed there at a disadvantage with regard to both access to and improvement on statutory rights (Brown *et al.* 2000: 627). Employment rights activated by the individual employee are a poor substitute for an agreement enforced at the place of work.

The loss of the process of collective bargaining is at least as serious as the loss of its substantive outcomes. Collective bargaining provides a more-or-less democratic structure of representation at the workplace. The WERS evidence suggests that a union presence is associated with a wider range of means of communicating between employer and worker, both direct and indirect, than where there is no union presence (Willman *et al.* 2009). It also suggests that, where trade unions are present, employee trust in management tends to be higher where unions are relatively strong (Bryson 2001: 102). More generally, the process of collective bargaining is at the heart of a pluralist approach to employment, one that expects management to make a case for changing workers' lives, and for those workers to have some opportunity to argue about it. Its decline is likely to diminish popular experience of the exercise of citizenship at the place of work and to reduce the capacity to achieve negotiated adjustments to change.

There are wider implications of collective bargaining for employers and civil society. Trade unions may not always represent the most liberal views about society, because they speak on behalf of their members, but they do at least represent those members. This means that they provide a political structure that is open to negotiation. When truck drivers, upset about fuel tax, paralysed the British road transport system in September 2000, and when refinery construction workers threatened something similar in opposition to immigrant workers in February 2009, the main problem confronting both employers and the government was the absence of any authorized representatives with whom to negotiate. Mobile phones and the internet provided impressive organizational tools, but it takes some sort of democratic structure to provide the representatives who can negotiate and legitimate a deal. The earlier discussion of bargaining emphasized the sophistication of intra-organizational structures that is necessary for the management of conflict. Effective representation is necessary for the protection of pluralism when markets change.

In the comparatively brief history of liberal democracies of the past couple of centuries, trade unions have played an important part. They have founded and nurtured parliamentary political parties. They were amongst the first institutions to be attacked by the totalitarian regimes of the 1930s, and amongst the first, for the same reason, to be restored, with greater protections, with peace in the late 1940s. They were the prime movers in the birth of democracy in South Africa and in Poland in the 1980s. It is not obvious that new representative, as opposed to mobilizing, structures are emerging in the internet and blogosphere. At time of writing, as the world economy tips into its worst crisis since the 1930s, that is a cause for concern for the prospects of a tolerant society.

Acknowledgements

The author is grateful for the suggestions of Jon Trevor and the editors.

References

Annual Abstract of Statistics. 2008: London: Office of National Statistics.

Batstone, E., Boraston, I. and Frenkel, S. 1977: *Shop Stewards in Action*. Oxford: Blackwell.

Blanchflower, D.G. and Bryson, A. 2009: Trade union decline and the economics of the workplace. In Brown, W.A., Bryson, A., Forth, J. and Whitfield, K. (eds) (2009) *The Evolution of the Modern Workplace*. Cambridge: CUP.

Brown, W. 1973: *Piecework Bargaining*. Oxford: Blackwell.

Brown, W. 2009: The process of fixing the British National Minimum Wage, 1997–2007. *British Journal of Industrial Relations*, 47 (2), 430–444.

Brown, W. and Nash, D. 2008: What has been happening to collective bargaining under New Labour? Interpreting WERS 2004. *Industrial Relations Journal*, 39 (2), 91–103.

Brown, W., Bryson, A., Forth, J. and Whitfield, K. (eds) 2009: *The Evolution of the Modern Workplace*. Cambridge: CUP.

Brown, W., Deakin, S., Hudson, M., Pratten, C. and Ryan, P. 1998: *The Individualisation of Employment Contracts in Britain*. London: DTI.

Brown, W., Deakin, S., Nash, D. and Oxenbridge, S. 2000: The employment contract: from collective procedures to individual rights. *British Journal of Industrial Relations*, 38 (4), 611–630.

Bryson, A. 2001: The foundation of 'partnership'? Union effects on employee trust in management. *National Institute Economic Review*, 176, 91–104.

Daniel, W.W. and Millward, N. 1983: *Workplace Industrial Relations in Britain*. London: Heinemann.

Davies, P. and Freedland, M. 2007: *Towards a Flexible Labour Market: Labour Legislation and Regulation since the 1990s*. Oxford: OUP.

Flanders, A. and Clegg, H.A. 1954: *The System of Industrial Relations in Great Britain*. Oxford: Blackwell.

Hicks, J.R. 1932: *The Theory of Wages*. London: Macmillan.

Mercer, S. and Notley, R. 2008: *Trade Union Membership 2007*. London: BERR.

Milner, S. 1995: The coverage of collective pay setting institutions in Britain 1895–1990. *British Journal of Industrial Relations*, 33, 69–92.

Oxenbridge, S. and Brown, W. 2004: Achieving a new equilibrium? The stability of co-operative employer-union relationships. *Industrial Relations Journal*, 35 (5), 388–402.

Schelling, T.C. 1960: *The Strategy of Conflict*. New York: Galaxy, OUP.

Sisson, K. and Taylor, J. 2006: The Advisory, Conciliation and Arbitration Service. In Dickens, L. and Neal, A.C. (eds) *The Changing Institutional Face of British Employment Relations*. Alphen aan der Rijn: Kluwer Law International.

Walton, R.E. and McKersie, R.B. 1965: *A Behavioral Theory of Labor Negotiations*. New York: McGraw-Hill.

Willman, P., Gomez, R. and Bryson, A. 2009: Voice at the workplace: where do we find it, why is it there and where is it going? In Brown, W.A., Bryson, A., Forth, J. and Whitfield, K. (eds) (2009) *The Evolution of the Modern Workplace*. Cambridge: CUP.

12
EMPLOYEE REPRESENTATION

MICHAEL TERRY

Introduction

The largely decentralized character of UK industrial relations institutions and processes has meant that much of the debate concerning employee representation over the last 20 years or more deals principally with the enterprise and workplace levels. Thus it pays particular attention to the representation of employees in their relationships with their own employer; that is to say with *single-employer* relationships at single workplaces or, where the enterprise involves several workplaces, at multiple workplaces and/or at enterprise level. This is a significant contrast with many continental European systems of employee representation which may involve representation at the industry or sector (multi-employer) level as well as single-employer activity. Within the UK the public sector remains a partial exception where, despite significant decentralization in recent decades with consequent growth in the importance of local employee representation, national-level arrangements continue to be important (see Bach, this volume). This concentration at enterprise and workplace levels gives employee representation in the UK unique structural characteristics. 'Dual channel' representation, involving union activity (collective bargaining) at sectoral level and enterprise-level activities based around works councils, of the kind found in many continental European countries, is largely absent from the UK where the 'single channel' of union representation at all organizational levels has long been the dominant model.

Two very different debates revolve around the subject of employee representation within the workplace. The first, with a longer history and located within a clear industrial relations framework, concerns the political and industrial rights of employees to be represented, if they wish, by strong independent interest organizations as a counterweight to the power of the employer in regulating the terms and conditions of employment. Such representation rights can be conferred through legal rights to employee representation, as found in the 'Works Council' legislation of many northern European countries, through independent trade union organization or a mix of the two. This debate derives from pluralist or radical/ Marxist perspectives on the employment relationship that argue, in different ways, that individual employees are at a significant power disadvantage in their dealings with employers and hence have a right to offset this imbalance through collective organization and/or legal rights. The decentralized nature of UK industrial relations processes and institutions means that many debates concerning the nature, power and activities of trade unions revolve around workplace activity and in particular the activity of workplace union representatives. In recent years, given the long-term decline of trade unionism, this has also meant that many strategies for the renewal of trade unionism have focused on workplace activities (see Simms and Charlwood, this volume). Viewing employee representation from this perspective focuses on factors such as: trade union organization; membership density; the representativeness of employee representatives; the independence of employee organization from management; the centrality of bargaining; and the nature and effectiveness of legal rights for employee and/or trade union representation within the workplace. Outcomes often used to assess the effectiveness of such representation include both procedural and substantive issues: the former include appropriate machinery for negotiation and consultation with employers and systems of grievance and disciplinary procedures that provide a fair hearing and procedural justice; the latter are issues such as pay, working hours and other aspects of working conditions, health and safety issues, etc.

The other, vastly different, approach to employee representation in the workplace derives in large part from approaches that might be labelled 'soft HRM'. This is a more recent argument that employee involvement may act as a management tool, producing benefits in the form of improved organizational performance obtained through the involvement of employees in decisions affecting them. Much of the HRM literature on change management extols the virtues of employee engagement as a means of gaining employee acceptance of the need for change and of reducing any potential resistance. The underlying perspective of this approach is unitarist, in that it suggests that congruence of interest between employer and employee may be achieved by sharing information and listening to and taking account of voiced concerns. Much of this literature is silent on the issue of trade unions. Indeed, unions may be presented as incompatible with this approach insofar as they may represent a competing loyalty within the workplace, although some accounts concede a role for what is sometimes termed 'responsible' trade unionism. The emphasis here is on processes of information dissemination and consultation, in particular dealing with problems and challenges facing the organization, and on seeking employee endorsement of managerial proposals. This approach sometimes treats *indirect* participation through the involvement of employee representatives, whether union based or not, and *direct* participation (teamworking, briefings, newsletters, etc.) as functionally equivalent, a perspective that would not be shared by the earlier approach or by authoritative academic analysis (Marchington and Wilkinson 2000).

The items dealt with through such forms of participation may include anything from the improvement of work organization to the company's financial prospects, but items such as pay and the terms and conditions of employment may often not feature so strongly on the agenda. The common element tends to be that they are managerial concerns and the approach taken is one of problem solving, not negotiation. Typical 'outputs' expected from such processes are improved employee morale and performance (the 'psychological contract'), and reduced absenteeism and turnover – ultimately contributing to improved organizational performance.

Two important further ideas flow from these distinct approaches to our understanding of employee representation. The first is that, given the centrality of the workplace to many aspects of industrial relations and human resource management in the UK, it has been the focus of much activity and analysis in recent years. Unions concerned with how to regenerate and redefine their own position and activity have paid a great deal of attention to workplace structures and processes; indeed, the extent and quality of workplace representation are critical building blocks in the so-called 'organizing model' of union renewal (see Simms and Charlwood, this volume). Workplace representation has been the subject of recent legislative intervention, mostly emanating from European Union law, designed to provide employees with a floor of representative rights. Employers, looking to improve productivity and competitiveness, for example through the complex of activities referred to as 'High Performance Work Systems' have sometimes identified employee representation as one of the central building blocks in managing change and 'modernization'. Second, considerable attention has been paid to examining whether the two different logics of action lead to mutually incompatible structures and activities and a great deal has been written as to whether, notwithstanding their very different perspectives and implications, systems of workplace representation can simultaneously serve both purposes: that of enhancing employee rights and influence; and of contributing to competitive advantage. This discussion, which has often taken place under the broad heading of 'partnership', will be examined in a later section.

Workplace Representation – The Current State of Play

In the United Kingdom, as in most other so-called 'voluntarist' IR systems (see Dickens and Hall; Colling, this volume, for explanation), employee rights to representation have been traditionally exerted through trade union membership. Inevitably this meant that, even at the height of trade union influence in the 1970s, not all employees had access to representative rights. Workers in sectors and workplaces where unionism was absent – in particular large parts of the private service sector and small firms – were in effect denied access to effective representation (in 1980 at the height of union presence only 28% of private service workplaces reported a shop steward present, compared to 55% in manufacturing and 77% in the public sector (Charlwood and Forth 2009)). Even where unions were present and recognized by employers the quality of representation provided was uneven and restricted; uneven in that, for example, the priorities of trade unions and their representatives often reflected the interests of male, full-time employees, and restricted in that the terrain of engagement with employees was largely limited to the terms and conditions of employment and, in some workplaces, to the detailed organization and performance of work. This picture began to change in the 1970s as more women became active in unions, particularly in the public sector, and unions responded to growing criticism of their lack of representativeness.

In the United Kingdom, with its strongly decentralized system of industrial relations, representation for the majority of unionized employees was discharged through workplace-based structures of representation where 'shop stewards' – locally elected or appointed union representatives – provided both individual and collective representation to employers on behalf of members.[1]

As employee representation has until recently been overwhelmingly provided by trade unions it is not surprising to find that representation has declined heavily and continuously since the middle 1980s, mirroring the decline in trade union membership over the period (see Simms and Charlwood, this volume). The story of representative decline has been presented in earlier editions of this book (Terry 2003) and more recently has been dealt with in detail in an analysis of the Workplace Employee Relations Surveys and their predecessors over a 25 year period (Charlwood and Forth 2009). This summary relies heavily on the latter work and on the WERS2004 data (Kersley et al. 2006). Charlwood and Forth estimate that in 2004 there were 128 000 trade union representatives in the UK, down from a peak of 335 000 in 1984. By 2004 well over half were found in the public sector, reflecting the lesser decline in that sector compared to the private. By 2004 only 23% of all workplaces of 25 employees or more contained a representative of a recognized trade union, compared with 55% at their peak presence in 1984. The decline was most marked in the private sector – both manufacturing and services – and less so in the public sector, mirroring the uneven picture of union decline. Where trade unions were recognized a majority of workplaces had at least one union representative, but the size of this majority had again reduced – from 83% to 62% over the same period. In other words, by 2004 38% of workplaces where trade unions were recognized had no workplace representative; a statistic whose significance lies in the argument that the vitality of UK trade unionism is rooted in the contact between members and local representatives. Against that needs to be set the fact that 53% of all employees work in establishments where there is at least some form of local representation (including non-union representation).

By 2004 senior union representatives were more likely to be female than in 1980, in part reflecting the change in the gender composition of the workforce. However, senior representatives were more likely than earlier to be older than their constituents (in 2004 78% were aged 40 or more compared with 60% of union members) and very few senior representatives came from ethnic minorities (3% in 2004). Collection and analysis of such data reflects the importance attached by unions to seek demographic identity between representatives and represented following arguments developed from the 1970s onwards that, for example, women's interests tended to be better represented by women than by men.

While attention has traditionally been focused on union representatives, the decline of union presence and of employer interest in the potential benefits of employee participation have led to growth in non-union forms of indirect employee representation (see Moore et al. 2008; Terry 1999). Charlwood and Forth (2009) report the remarkable finding that by 2004 non-union representatives were as numerous as union representatives although they represented a significantly smaller proportion of the workforce (around 17% compared with 37% for union representatives) reflecting the greater likelihood of union presence in large workplaces. Given that prior to 2004 there was no legal right to permanent representation (with the exception of health and safety representatives) it can be concluded that virtually all non-union representatives exist as a consequence of managerial decision, either as a consequence of a union avoidance or exclusion strategy or as evidence of commitment to the organizational benefits of employee participation or both. Yet managerial enthusiasm for such forms of representation should not be exaggerated; between 1998 and 2004 the incidence of joint consultative committees – often the preferred vehicle for non-union representative engagement – declined. Non-union representatives tend to be younger than their union counterparts, more likely to be female, and to have been in post for a shorter period. Importantly, they are less likely to have been selected through a process of employee election, virtually universal for union representatives (see Moore *et al.* 2008). Less than 40% of non-union representatives are elected into the position by members, suggesting that the remainder either emerge through informal processes of self-selection or, more likely, are selected or appointed by management (Moore *et al.* 2008: 12); a process that appears to be at odds with one of the fundamental principles of representative democracy. This may in turn contribute to the findings that while union representatives appear to be valued by their members, non-unionists show no such appreciation of the value of non-union representatives (Charlwood and Forth, 2009) and that non-union representatives show greater trust in management than do their union counterparts (Moore *et al.* 2008: 2).

However, it is clear that union and non-union arrangements are not inevitably independent of each other; they may interact. Willman and his colleagues (2007: 1321) have shown through an analysis of WERS between 1984 and 1998 that while union-only systems declined, as reported above, and non-union systems grew, arrangements involving both union and non-union mechanisms remained relatively stable, certainly a great deal more stable than union-only structures.[2] The potential importance of such hybrid structures (see also Charlwood and Terry 2007) for the future of employee representation is explored in a later section.

As the decline in trade union representative presence has reflected that of trade unions more widely in the UK economy, so too has their influence. For much of the period after the Second World War into the early 1980s the dominant feature of UK industrial relations, initially in the private manufacturing sector and then in the public, was that of decentralized collective bargaining, at workplace or establishment level, between union representatives and managers. Such 'single-employer bargaining' over pay and other issues became a central feature of UK industrial relations, in contrast to the continued dominance of multi-employer (industrial or sectoral) bargaining structures characteristic of most other European countries in the same period (see Brown, this volume).

A succession of analyses confirms the declining significance of negotiation (joint regulation) as the dominant mode of interaction between union representatives and employers and its replacement by consultation or the simple provision of information. The 2004 WERS shows that pay, the traditional focus of workplace bargaining, was reported to be a subject of negotiation by 48% of senior union representatives (Kersley *et al.* 2006: 153); the remaining 52% of cases stating that it was subject to consultation, or information provision, or to no process of interaction at all. Other issues were less frequently the subject of negotiation and more often of what have been seen as less effective modes of collective interaction. This is of particular significance given the importance traditionally attached to the concept of 'joint regulation' – the negotiation of agreed rules between unions and employers on both substantive and procedural matters – which was held to form the bedrock of 'voluntarist' UK industrial relations. Charlwood and Forth (2009), examining both survey and case study data over the last two or three decades, conclude:

> The picture that emerges from this . . . evidence on the activities of union representatives suggests that there has been a substantial diminution of their role within the workplace. In some cases, workplace trade unionism became a hollow shell, where union representatives enjoyed little substantive or procedural role. In others the procedural role . . . was preserved but their influence declined markedly as they spent less time on collective bargaining and more time on representing individual members.

Importantly, the same authors note that the role of non-union representatives in the bargaining of the terms and conditions of employment is negligible (see also Kersley *et al.* 2006: 168–175).

This summary indicates a continuation of the decline in union representative coverage discussed elsewhere. However, decline is not necessarily to be equated with inactivity and, as discussed below, representation within the workplace has arguably been the subject of more initiatives over the last decade than in the preceding three. Some of these are dealt with below. Before that it is useful to make a few comments on the concept of consultation, which is central to several of the more significant initiatives.

Consultation and the implications for employee representation

The recent shift away from negotiation and towards consultation has been widely noted in both the language and the practice of workplace industrial relations (Cully *et al.* 1999; Brown *et al.* 2000). Negotiation is characterized as bargaining in which the bargaining parties may deploy economic sanctions (strikes, lockouts) as well as arguments in order to obtain their objectives. It is a process characterized by the exercise or threat of coercive power. Eventual agreement represents acceptance by both parties and hence can be characterized as a shared decision or, as characterized by Flanders, 'joint regulation'. In this sense therefore negotiation constitutes a replacement of managerial prerogative by a commitment to joint regulation of the employment relationship. The characteristic subjects of such negotiation have been pay and conditions (working time and so on). In this process the job of the employee (union) representative is to seek and codify member interests and aspirations, present them to the employer and, if necessary, organize the mobilization of support for those interests.

Consultation differs from negotiation in several important respects. First, it is a process that retains the managerial right to take the final decision. Thus consultation, although it indicates the need for such decision to take into account employee views, is ultimately a process of unilateral regulation. Second, it is typically characterized as a process involving the exchange of ideas, opinions and suggestions within which the use or threat of sanctions is considered inappropriate. (Indeed in countries such as Germany, where works councils have a legal right to engage in consultation, the use of strike or other sanctions is expressly denied to the works council.) For both these reasons it is often characterized in the UK as a weaker form of collective engagement than negotiation. Third, it often involves a range of issues different from and wider than those handled through negotiation. In European countries where consultation is embedded into the enterprise-level IR framework, it may involve dealing with issues of organizational restructuring, productivity and competitiveness, investment strategies and other broad company activities at the macro-level and with a list of micro-organizational issues such as teamworking; job rotation; multiskilling and many other issues linked to the concept of high performance working (see Edwards and Sengupta, this volume). Indeed, in some countries wage issues are explicitly excluded from consultation processes and are reserved to distinct actors and processes, often external to the individual company or workplace, handled at industrial or sectoral level. Effective representative activity in consultation involves seeking the views of employees but beyond that requires the deployment of forms of professional expertise, both in handling the issues presented for consultation and in marshalling and presenting arguments on behalf of employees. This is a very different process from negotiation, essentially one of advocacy, requiring a different set of skills from those associated with traditional bargaining.

Thus consultation does have important behavioural and structural implications for unions and their representatives different from those associated with negotiation. Success in consultation is perceived to rely on force of argument and technical competence rather than on 'muscle'. This expertise may be provided by the employee representatives themselves through appropriate training and, as in the case of Germany (by law) and Italy (in some collective agreements), by external experts appointed by the unions to consultative bodies. A powerful case can be made that employee representative expertise with regard to a range of technical matters is a precondition of effective consultation. Such expertise in turn may have implications for representatives' relationships with their members, since it may be necessary for representatives to acquire professional and technical skills different from those available to those they represent. This can in turn have implications for internal processes of representative democracy and accountability as the acquisition of technical skills may make representatives appear irreplaceable and hence immune from electoral challenge.

The issue is further complicated by the broader agenda of issues referred to above, characteristically seen as appropriate for consultation as opposed to negotiation. In the negotiation of pay and conditions the essential union demand was uncomplicatedly for more, better, or both. In this traditional situation the interests of the membership are, *prima facie*, relatively easy to define. But with many of the issues currently assumed to be on the union agenda in consultation this appears less clear-cut. How, for example, is it best to characterize employee interests with regard to the macro- and micro-level issues identified above? To understand the implications of these issues for UK employee representatives it is worth looking at the experience of other countries where consultation processes over such issues are more fully developed. In northern European countries such as Sweden and Germany, for example, trade unions, directly or indirectly through works councils, have devoted considerable amounts of money to the development of detailed and sophisticated proposals or counter-proposals dealing with the organization, nature and intensity of work as part of the process of consultation with employers.

Leaving aside the essentially political argument as to whether unions *should* become engaged in such managerial issues, many British trade unions and their representatives as currently staffed and funded would struggle to provide the resources or expertise for analogous exercises, or the necessary skills for their local promulgation (a partial exception might be made for the public sector where more vertically integrated unions and a longer tradition of consultation have facilitated some imaginative union engagement). Nevertheless, without such resources it is very difficult to see how much 'consultative' workplace unionism can be anything more than an acceptance of managerial proposals, for lack of an armoury of appropriate responses, amongst other reasons. The subjects of union–employer engagement are as important as the methods. For all these reasons consultation should not simply be seen as an attenuated form of 'real' bargaining (negotiation); it must be presented as a qualitatively different process drawing on different resources, techniques and structures.

The significance of consultation as a challenge for employee representatives, whether union or non-union, derives both from an apparent managerial preference for consultation, as opposed to negotiation, and from the centrality of consultation as the key process specified in recent legislative interventions into structures and processes of workplace unionism. The former will be examined later under the broad heading of 'partnership' but first it is necessary to examine some of the more significant legal initiatives in greater detail.

The Growth of a Statutory System of Employee Representation

As the coverage and activity of the traditional voluntary union-based system have declined, a development novel to the United Kingdom has emerged, namely the burgeoning of *legal* rules designed to provide employees with statutory rights to consultation and information. In a recent discussion paper Podro and Suff (nd) identified 15 specific areas of workplace activity for which some legal rights and protections are provided by law, both UK and EU. Legal protection is limited and variable and not all workplaces will have, or be entitled to have, all of them. In many cases these functions and rights may be combined in one or a few representatives with a multiplicity of roles. But the role of law in underpinning local representative functions has changed dramatically over three decades. Not all these functions are discussed in this chapter although some, such as Union Learning Representatives, are described later.

Arguably of still greater significance, however, is the growing importance of legal frameworks providing support for the development of workplace representative structures (as opposed to rights and functions). Virtually all of these have emerged as a direct consequence of the UK's membership of the European Union. In many other countries much of this legislation has passed relatively unnoticed, since it adds little to existing domestic legislation providing similar (or stronger) rights. The main exception to this has been the European Works Council, a genuinely novel development in all countries which is discussed later. But first this chapter will look at the emerging legislative framework for national systems of domestic (workplace and enterprise) representation.

European Union legislative intervention: a consultative model

European Union legislation dealing with issues of information and consultation generally confers rights on employees rather than on trade unions and hence fits uneasily into a country where unions and their members have traditionally enjoyed a monopoly of representation rights. In line with this 'single channel' tradition the transposition of early EU directives, those dealing with consultation rights in situations of collective redundancies and business transfers (transfers of undertakings), into UK legislation confined the consultation right to representatives of recognized trade unions, thus retaining the unions' longstanding monopoly and in doing so excluding employees who were not members of recognized unions.

But in 1994, decisions at the European Court of Justice required the extension of consultation rights to workers where unions are not recognized (Hall 1996). As a consequence the Collective Redundancies and Transfer of Undertakings (Protection of Employment) (Amendment) Regulations 1995 made provision for 'the designation of employee representatives for the purposes of information and consultation . . . in situations where there are no recognized unions' (Hall 1996: 17). The Conservative government that introduced these regulations did so in a manner seen by some commentators to be negating their potential for underpinning stable and effective representation structures (O'Hara 1996: 26–27) as well as by taking the opportunity to reduce consultation by increasing the threshold number of redundancies that would require mandatory consultation. The Labour government has since strengthened the Regulations, in particular by insisting that where a union is recognized it must be consulted over redundancies (the earlier Regulations had allowed employers to bypass such recognized unions, although this rarely happened (Hall and Edwards 1999)) and by strengthening the election requirements for non-union representatives. This represented the first clear set of legal provisions that anticipated the possibility of representation of employees who were not union members through a structure of non-union workplace representation.

More recent legislative initiatives have developed the rights available through non-union representation. The 1996 Health and Safety (Consultation with

Employees) Regulations extended consultation rights in this area from union members to all employees, providing a statutory basis to a form of non-union representation for the first time, and in doing so provoking the Association of British Chambers of Commerce into expressing the fear that this would 'introduce works councils through the back door' (cited in James 1996: 13). UK employers and their organizations have resisted every effort to introduce or strengthen such consultation and information rights, usually on the grounds that they would prove costly and likely to reduce flexibility and competitiveness.

In the late 1990s the Working Time Regulations 1998, introducing into the UK the provisions of the EU Working Time Directive, and Regulations implementing the EU Parental Leave Directive in 1999, introduced the novel (for the UK) concept of so-called 'workforce agreements' on these matters (see Dickens and Hall, this volume) to cover all or part of a workforce not represented by a union in collective bargaining. The precise mechanisms for such workforce agreements are not clearly specified, and there is no evidence yet of their widespread adoption, but in conforming to the EU norm that rights to engagement with such issues extend to all employees, not just those represented by a union, they prefigured potential systems of non-union representation, operating on a statutory basis. Important though these are, they deal only with specific issues and do not necessarily imply stable, permanent mechanisms of employee representation, rather than bodies established on a temporary basis to deal with a specific issue, such as redundancy.

The Information and Consultation of Employees Regulations: 'works councils' for the UK?   Potentially far more radical and far-reaching than any of the above was the enactment in June 2001 of an EU directive on national information and consultation that would require 'all undertakings with at least 50 employees . . . to consult employee representatives about a range of business, employment and work organization issues' (Hall 2000: 107). Longstanding UK government opposition to the directive was eventually withdrawn early in 2001, in part facilitated by European agreement to allow countries such as the UK, with no 'general, permanent and statutory' system of information and consultation, or of workplace representation, to phase in its introduction. The arrangements were that undertakings with at least 150 employees would be covered as from April 2005, from April 2007 for undertakings with 100 employees or more and from April 2008 for undertakings with 50 or more.

The implications of the Information and Consultation of Employees Regulations 2004 (the ICE Regulations) are potentially far-reaching in that they confer formal rights on the great majority of UK employees. However, it is critically important to understand that the Regulations are formulated in such a way that nothing happens under the legal procedures unless employees (or the employer) take steps to 'trigger' the procedures laid down in the Regulations. There is no obligation on employers to do anything unless employees decide to operate this 'trigger' (for details see Dickens and Hall, this volume). It can be plausibly hypothesized that employees will in many cases not act in this way, because of ignorance of the existence of the Regulations, fear of employer opposition, satisfaction with existing processes or indifference. Hall (2003) has characterized the approach taken to the implementation of the EU into UK law as one of 'legislatively prompted voluntarism' in which the existence of legal provision encourages employers, employees and trade unions to seek voluntary agreement on appropriate information and consultation arrangements without needing to invoke the legal provisions directly, leaving them to act as a fall-back in the event of failure to reach voluntary agreement (see also Hall and Terry 2004).

The Regulations provide employees, not trade unions, with rights to information from and consultation with employers, thus distinguishing them from earlier trade union-based arrangements in two respects: first, that rights to representation can be provided without the presence of trade unions; and second, that the dominant mechanism, as with all EU-derived legislation in this field, is one of consultation rather than negotiation. The difference is potentially a crucial one; as already noted, consultation presumes an exchange of opinions and ideas but retains the right of employers to make any final decision. The characteristic objective of trade union recognition, by contrast, implies shared responsibility for decisions after a process of bargaining, possibly accompanied by the use of sanctions. As noted above, trade unions in the UK have viewed consultation as a relatively weaker form of engagement and thus have far less experience of it than many continental European counterparts. For both these reasons British trade unions, while formally welcoming the ICE Regulations, have responded to them with some uncertainty.

It is important to bear in mind that the Regulations, although providing a statutory framework for employee rights, also provide mechanisms through which access to statutory enforcement mechanisms may be pre-empted. In particular, voluntary, so-called pre-existing arrangements (i.e. existing mechanisms that satisfy the Regulations' criteria in providing systems of information and consultation for all employees) do not provide access to statutory enforcement. Only 'negotiated agreements' or the enforcement of the Regulations' 'default procedures' in cases of failure to reach agreement after a legitimate employee request provide such access. As Barnard and Deakin have noted (2000: 341, cited in Hall *et al.* 2007: 7) the Regulations have been designed in such a way as to 'underpin and encourage autonomous processes of adjustment' between employers and employees.

Research data on the impact of the ICE Regulations are limited but intriguing. First, the WERS 2004 data, collected shortly before the implementation of the first phase of the Regulations, showed that overall the incidence of joint consultation had fallen since 1998. There is thus no suggestion that UK employers were seeking to anticipate or pre-empt the Regulations by introducing their own systems. A more recent survey of UK-based multinational companies (Marginson *et al.* forthcoming) shows that a significant proportion have amended or updated their consultative arrangements, most probably as a consequence of the legislation. These are large organizations with existing consultative arrangements and with a high level of union recognition for which coming into conformity with the new regulatory requirements was in line with existing practice and did not indicate significant innovation. Nevertheless the survey data currently available do suggest a clear but limited legislative impact.

The first detailed case study data of private sector companies that appear to have responded to the promptings of the ICE Regulations provide some further insights (Hall *et al.* 2007). These results suggest that organizational initiatives to come into conformity with the Regulations are overwhelmingly taken and driven forward by management, with employees and unions playing at best a minor role. Characteristically, such companies tend already to have an existing system of employee representation, union or non-union, and are developing or extending it to come into legal conformity. The implications for trade union-based representation are mixed. While in most organizations with an established union presence managements were prepared to guarantee existing union rights with respect to collective bargaining enabling them to coexist alongside structures providing representation for all employees with regard to information and consultation provision, doubt persists as to the long-term stability of such formal 'structural dualism'. On the other hand, some organizations that were hostile to trade union recognition were using newly established non-union representative structures as part of their union avoidance strategy.

One of the most important consequences of the ICE Regulations (and indeed of much other EU legislation transposed into UK law) is the extension of representative rights to non-union members in companies where a degree of union representation already exists. The most usual outcome in such cases is a consultative body containing both union representatives acting on behalf of groups for whom unions are already recognized for collective bargaining and representatives elected by and from employees in unrecognized groups, who of course are significantly less likely to be union members. Before looking in greater detail at the implications of such 'hybrid representation' it is necessary first to examine briefly the other major change in employee representation introduced as a consequence of EU intervention, the European Works Council.

The European Works Council   The European Works Councils Directive was passed in 1994 but only implemented in the UK in 2000. Briefly, its objective is to promote the establishment of EWCs (European Works Councils) or other information and consultation procedures in 'Community-scale' undertakings or groups with at least 1000 employees within the territorial scope of the directive, including at least 150 in each of two or more member states. In the late 1990s it was estimated that some 230 UK-based multinationals were subject to the EWCs Directive. By the early 2000s it was estimated that EWCs had been established in approximately 40% of these (Waddington and Kerckhofs 2003, cited in Hall and Marginson 2005: 209) slightly above the average for affected countries, but still only a minority.

A recent overview of the considerable research that has been undertaken into EWCs (Hall and Marginson 2005) reveals a number of findings relevant to our understanding of employee representation in the UK (see also Marginson and Meardi, this volume). EWCs in UK-based multinationals are overwhelmingly joint (management–employee representative) bodies, reflecting UK national practice, rather than employee-only bodies characteristic of some other EU countries. On the whole British managers in companies with EWCs saw them as playing a useful role but principally as a corporate communications mechanism rather than a means of effective consultation. By contrast employee opinion tends to be more negative, reflecting EWCs' limited role, although British employee representatives are more positive than their continental counterparts (Waddington 2003), a finding that the author suggests may reflect the limited information characteristically made available to employee representatives in the UK through workplace procedures. A further intriguing finding, entirely consistent with the particular characteristics of UK workplace representation, is that even in UK-based companies (or companies where the UK workforce was the largest in the multinational) UK employee representatives frequently allowed representatives from other countries to take the lead role. As Hall and Marginson (2005) argue, this almost certainly reflects the lack of familiarity in the UK with institutions and processes of this kind, in particular consultation with senior management on issues of corporate strategy, an activity almost entirely absent from the UK until very recently.

Despite the enormous potential impact of these developments the long-term implications for structures of UK representation are still far from clear. A generally positive evaluation of EWCs by the European Commission indicated that some problems persisted nevertheless, amongst them the 'very low level of transnational information and consultation provided by some agreements' and the need for 'efficient information and consultation systems to exist at national level and for an effective flow of information between Community and national levels of worker representation' (EWCB 2000: 5). This latter point is particularly likely to pose problems within the UK, given the uneven and fragmented nature of many existing systems of national representation, as described above. In addition, recent cases have suggested that, the careful wording notwithstanding, the new rights are weaker than seemed. In the wake of the announcement during 2000 of large-scale redundancy fears at both Rover and Vauxhall, major motor vehicle companies, concern was expressed about 'the adequacy of the UK's legal framework for employee information and consultation' (Hall 2001) leading to calls for government strengthening of the rights.

Legal rights, universal representation and 'hybrid' structures There is longstanding debate within the UK concerning the implications for trade unions of these new universalistic legal rights going back at least to an influential debate between Kelly (1996) and Hyman (1996). On the one hand, there is concern that the new structures may be 'captured' by management and used, in effect, as tools of managerial influence and control, especially where trade unions are weak, a not uncommon situation in many private sector organizations, as argued above. On the other, it is argued that a framework of legal rights is a necessary buttress against further decline and, more optimistically, that unions may be able to use 'works council' structures as a vehicle for advancing their own organizations. To a certain extent the argument is coloured by the vagaries of the European experience; those fearful of the negative consequences for unions point to the French *comités d'enterprise*, introduced in the 1980s, and allegedly largely controlled by management, while the optimists point to the German unions' success (at least amongst manual workers) in dominating elections to works councils. Brewster *et al.* (2007: 70) have more recently argued that the European evidence suggests that works councils and collective bargaining tend to coexist and the effect of that may be either to expand the union role or to undermine it according to local circumstances. That the potential exists for British employers, if they choose, to use the new framework provided by the ICE Regulations as a means of 'union avoidance' is undeniable, but whether unions could be successfully excluded in this way at a time when their legal position is being strengthened and in a country where there is still a widespread belief in many workplaces that unions are more influential and powerful than union-free representation, remains to be seen.

One point that will be of the greatest significance for the effectiveness of these employee-based statutory mechanisms will be the practical, and eventually the judicial, interpretation of the concept of consultation. In traditional UK usage it has, as noted above, connotations of ineffectiveness and weakness, since it allows unilateral managerial action notwithstanding the views expressed by employees or their representatives. In any case, as argued above, it seems to prefigure a new and problematic mode of collective interaction between employee representatives and employers. Both the EWC Directive and the ICE Regulations define consultation as 'the exchange of views and establishment of dialogue' between employee representatives and management, a process clearly distinct from negotiation. However, some EU legislative provision gives the concept additional reinforcement by speaking of 'consultation with a view to reaching agreement', a form of words found in both the Collective Redundancies Directive and the fall-back provisions of the ICE Regulations. Precisely what this means in practice in the UK context remains unclear.

As noted above, the conferral on employees of legal rights to information and consultation has contributed to the growth of a 'hybrid' system of employee representation involving both union and non-union representatives sitting on the same body engaged in information and consultation activities. While these are not new (see, for example, Charlwood and Forth, 2009) and a small proportion of workplaces have for some time contained consultative committees formed on this basis, it is arguable that their presence may be given a boost by the ICE Regulations. One significant feature of such hybrids is that they may provide a test of the viability and potential of both union and non-union forms of representation. On the one hand, unionized employees may come to feel that equivalent rights are available without the costs of union membership and this may contribute to a further decline in union membership and activity. On the other, it may provide union representatives the opportunity to demonstrate to both non-union representatives and non-members as well as to management the benefits of union membership as a support to effective consultation through, for example, access to union resources of expert advice, legal support and training facilities. Early research (Hall *et al.* 2007) does not indicate trends in either direction but does provide examples of effective cooperation between union and non-union representatives, a development whose significance may be strengthened by the fact that the latter often represent managerial and other professional groups of employees, whose expertise may provide a resource that workplace union representatives alone had previously lacked.

Of at least equal significance is the observation (see Willman *et al.* 2007) of the greater robustness of hybrid structures than either their 'pure' union or non-union counterparts (i.e. they appear to be longer-lasting than the others; see also Charlwood and Terry 2007). Indeed, there appears to be growing evidence that union representation combined with other forms of representation, either in hybrid form or in conjunction with forms of 'direct' employee representation is both more stable and from certain perspectives more effective than representation based solely on unions. Several reasons can be speculatively advanced for this of which one must be that the legitimacy of structures covering all employees is less open to the challenge of lack of representativeness than union-based systems where only a small proportion of the workforce is in union membership. As noted above, the long-term stability of such combinations may be open to question but for the moment they represent an important development.

It is clear that the terrain of workplace unionism and the job of the union representative will for the foreseeable future be increasingly informed by legal rights and statutorily based structures (see Colling; Dickens and Hall, this volume). For union representatives the issues are twofold: first are the problems of reconciling traditional representative structures based on the 'single channel' of unionism with the new universalistic rights. Shopfloor unions and representatives may have to take on the role of electoral machines for the new structures and, once elected, assume the responsibility of speaking for all constituents; they may also have to accept the idea, once anathema, of working together with non-union representatives. Second, unions and both union and non-union representatives will have a greater range of legal rights at their disposal, to set alongside, or perhaps to compensate for the loss of, traditional tactics. This may require the development of new expertise, and of new language and tactics in dealing with employers. Significant change may be near.

It is of the greatest importance, however, to recognize that these developments, in providing legal rights to a form of representation for all employees, irrespective of union membership, represent a challenge as well as an opportunity for trade union-based representation. While they may seek to use the new rights to buttress their position and legitimacy, unions are acutely aware that the same rights provide employees with access to information and consultation without the need for union membership. As recent research on the implementation of the ICE Regulations has demonstrated (Hall *et al.* 2007) this can provide the basis for the emergence of non-union representative structures, in some cases as part of an explicit managerial preference for union avoidance. The crucial question is whether such rights can be effectively articulated on a continuing basis in the absence of a strong trade union presence. There is some evidence from continental Europe that they cannot (Terry 1994: 234–235).

UK developments: the law, union initiatives and the role of the representative

The role of employee representatives, and in particular of union representatives, has typically been characterized as the representative of collective interests, involved above all in negotiations with employers. Given the decline in the significance of collective bargaining it is not surprising that recent surveys have revealed a significant increase in the time dedicated by such representatives to individual casework, supporting members in discipline and grievance issues and a host of other matters (Charlwood and Forth 2009). It is indeed arguable that such activities have always been of much greater significance than often believed, both in terms of the amount of time dedicated to them and of the value attached to them by employees – this may well be true of non-union as much as union representatives. With this in mind, and alongside recognition of the great range of issues that may be addressed in the modern workplace, increasing attention has been paid to the potential for developing cadres of specialist representatives dealing with specific areas of employee concern. It has also been hoped that such developments may prove attractive in recruiting into representative roles employees not keen to take on the traditional role of negotiation and thus broaden the potential pool of volunteers to take on such a role. The case of specialist health and safety representatives in both union and non-union workplaces has a history going back to 1974 (see Terry 1999 for a brief summary). More recently, trade unions have been working to develop the role of the Union Learning Representative (ULR) with specific responsibility for developing training programmes for employees (see Keep *et al.*, this volume). Given statutory recognition and backing in the Employment Act 2002 including a right to time off for appropriate activities, this is a clear example of a union proposal broadly accepted by government for the development of union representative structures dealing with an area – training – long seen as one in which unions and employers share the same broad objectives and hence, in principle at least, as non-conflictual. Indeed, significant amounts of government funding have been pumped into this activity through the state-supported Union Learning Fund (Hollinrake *et al.* 2008: 393). The impact of this initiative appears mixed. The TUC has claimed that by 2007 some 18 000 union members had received training as ULRs and that as a consequence some 150 000 employees have been helped to access training courses and there has been a growth in so-called 'training partnerships' often facilitated by ULRs (Wallis and Stuart 2007; Rainbird 2005). On the other hand, a Unionlearn survey suggested that the age, sex and ethnicity profile of ULRs was similar to that for existing union representatives, although there were signs that the proportion of women and ethnic minority unionists in this role was growing (Unionlearn 2006: 2). For the present it remains unclear whether this initiative has succeeded in drawing previously non-participating union members into activism. The Unionlearn survey shows that some two-thirds of ULRs also perform other union duties, suggesting that in many cases the specific training responsibility has been added to the list of activities performed by existing representatives.

Along similar lines trade unions have been looking to develop the role of equality representative, in the hope of stimulating interest in these roles amongst certain groups; in particular women and ethnic minorities have not always been adequately represented in existing representative structures and perhaps are not keen to take on traditional roles. Evidence on the success of this initiative is so far limited. A TUC survey in 2007 found 19 affiliated unions with equality representatives and identified a number of initiatives to foster the idea. Union efforts to persuade government to provide statutory rights to such representatives as for ULRs have so far proved unsuccessful, although the government has indicated general support for the initiative. Unions have also been looking to develop both equal pay representatives and 'workplace disability champions' and have started to provide dedicated training courses for both. There has also been discussion concerning the designation of environment representatives with specific responsibilities for the 'green' agenda within the workplace. These efforts share two features: first, they hope to identify areas of activity which some employees might be enthusiastic to work in outside the traditional focus of union activities, and second, they are areas where it might be expected that employee and employer interests might converge such that representatives working in such areas might not become involved in potentially uncomfortable disagreement and conflict. They also reflect the multiplicity of interests employees bring with them to the workplace (see Simms and Charlwood, this volume) not all of which have been captured by unions' traditional emphasis on their role as negotiators of pay and conditions. It is too early to predict whether they will succeed in enhancing workplace representative capacity, although ULRs at least have succeeded in establishing a stable base in some workplaces.

Employee Participation and Organizational Change: Partnership and 'Mutual Gains'

During the 1990s, but most particularly since the election of the 1997 Labour government, a new expression entered the UK industrial relations lexicon. 'Partnership', sometimes preceded by the qualifier 'social', derives from northern European experience (Germany, Austria, the Netherlands and, with some difference of emphasis, Scandinavia). In those countries, to simplify greatly, it refers to the interlocking systems of collective relationships between unions, their confederations and employers' associations at national, sectoral and workplace level that make up their characteristic industrial relations systems. These usually include structures for the negotiation of wages and other terms and conditions of employment, often largely at sector or industry level, and within that sphere recognizes and allows for conflict and its expression. But the approach also makes explicit provision for the development of collaborative, consensual processes between the social partners, both at the macro-level (economic and social policy, training, environmental protection) and at the workplace. At the latter level its most sophisticated expression is probably the 'consensual' German works council, which is explicitly forbidden from bargaining and which has the responsibility of handling structural change (technological innovation, organizational change) within a framework that recognizes the commitment of all parties to the commercial success of the enterprise. Almost always buttressed by legal rights and restrictions far more extensive than anything presently envisaged in the United Kingdom, the continental European works council model (and the social partnership approach more generally) is claimed by its supporters to have enabled successful adjustment to structural change without conflict and without damaging the employment and working lives of employees (see Jacobi *et al.* 1992). Central to an understanding of the consensual workplace relationships are the strong legal protections for the works council and its members, the legally backed guarantees of security and stability for workers at times of economic restructuring, and the handling of wage-bargaining at sectoral level. The premise is one of 'mutual gains', delivering benefits both for employees and for the employing organization.

The application of the concept of partnership to the United Kingdom is problematic, since virtually none of the infrastructural elements above the level of the workplace, essential for the integration of the whole concept, obtain in this country. But the term has been advanced as embodying the New Labour government's early approach to industrial relations, and has been strongly endorsed by them, by many national trade unions, and by some employers (Brown 2000: 305; for thorough discussion of the concept see Oxenbridge and Brown 2004). Essentially, they consist of agreements in which the 'partners' – employers and employees (usually represented by workplace unions) – strike an agreement that characteristically commits all parties to work for the commercial success of the enterprise and in particular seek to provide undertakings of employment security for workers and their union representatives in exchange for their acceptance of the need for organizational change and flexibility. Characteristically, they also provide an enhanced consultative role for trade unions, usually over matters relating to the economic and commercial performance of the organization and training and development opportunities for employees. These characteristics reveal the debt to the continental model. The emphasis is again on consultation rather than negotiation and on persuading employers of the value of employee representation. Indeed, it might be described as an approach that stresses 'the business case for effective employee representation'.

Although the concept of partnership as initially promulgated by the TUC and some affiliated unions naturally stressed the role of workplace trade unions, its subsequent endorsement by the Labour government in the late 1990s made clear that in their view unions were not necessary conditions for effective partnership; it could equally be developed in non-union workplaces and, indeed, on the basis of employee participation through direct, as opposed to indirect, mechanisms. However, since all research has revealed that partnership agreements were overwhelmingly struck in workplaces with recognized trade unions and paid particular attention to the role of workplace unions (Terry and Smith 2003; Oxenbridge and Brown 2004) the following discussion will focus on the implications for union-based representation (see also Simms and Charlwood, this volume).

As Brown notes, the partnership agenda, which most unions and stewards would have rejected two decades ago as hopelessly collaborationist, is 'in part, a symptom of a weakened union movement' (2000: 307). In practical terms the managerial interpretation of such partnership arrangements tends to be that unions will take formal account of commercial considerations in formulating pay claims and will actively cooperate in the introduction of organizational change seen as necessary to commercial success. This leads directly to a second central feature; unions' active participation in the achievement of measures to promote flexibility. Here the traditional union response of caution and resistance should be replaced by the co-management of change. For some union activists this goes too far in giving management *carte blanche* in day-to-day workforce management.

Of particular significance for this chapter are the implications of partnership agreements for the survival of workplace union representation. Partnerships may be seen as involving an implicit exchange between greater managerial recognition of union rights in exchange for union concession on substantive issues. This, for some commentators, is the key consideration. After decades of being marginalized, watching from the sidelines, the problem for unions was 'not . . . whether to fight or collaborate, but [how to] get a foot in the door and begin to advance their *institutional centrality* . . . social partnership presents itself as such a strategy' (Ackers and Payne 1998: 546, emphasis added).

Yet social partnership presents acute challenges for the traditional shopfloor representative model. First, both the language and the practice of partnership seem to shift local union representatives to a position closer to that of management than to the independent representation of members' interests. The balance between the two, noted by Greene *et al.* (2000) as central to the health of workplace unionism, may be fundamentally compromised. Second, the emphasis on consultation, corporate success and the other elements identified above indicates a union input based more on expertise and professionalism than on claims backed up by collective interest.

Opinion in the United Kingdom on the implications for unions is divided. Ackers and Payne (1998: 544–545) argue that partnership 'marks out a favourable industrial relations terrain, in which unions can regain the initiative and work to rebuild their institutional presence in British society'. Kelly, by contrast, argues that it will further demobilize and debilitate union representative organization, through embracing a managerial agenda that will distance stewards from their members and the effective representation of their interests (Kelly 1996).

Where to from Here?

It can be plausibly suggested that the subject of workplace representation has received greater attention during the last five years than at any time since the heyday of debates about the role and nature of shop stewards in the late 1960s and 1970s. The nature of that attention is, however, vastly different. The debate no longer concentrates on such issues as pay bargaining, strikes and job controls but instead deals with mechanisms for the expression of employees' burgeoning legal rights and with the contribution workplace representation can make to economic development. Evidence of the former is discussed at length above. The latter can be witnessed most clearly in responses to the government's 2007 consultation exercise on workplace representatives (DTI 2007). These responses, endorsed by the government, suggest that 'workplace representatives bring an identifiable range of benefits worth £476 million up to £1333 million annually, (Podro and Suff nd: 12). Additional benefits are estimated to derive from the activities of Union Learning Representatives and productivity gains tentatively but plausibly attributed to effective employee representation are estimated by government as being anything up to an astonishing £3.4 billion (Podro and Suff nd: 12; see also DTI 2007). These figures recently led the government to declare formally that it recognizes the valuable role played by workplace representatives, both union and non-union, and formally declare that it 'considers that more should be done to re-affirm the importance of modern trade unions and the contribution their representatives make at the workplace' (BERR 2007: 5). It acknowledged the role played by non-union representatives while noting that it was more limited and narrower than that provided by union representation (ibid.: 14). However, while happy to make such supportive statements the government remained opposed to further legal intervention and argued that ultimately it remains up to employers and employees to decide on appropriate representation arrangements within the existing statutory framework.

However, despite this evidence and the battery of legal and other initiatives described above, all directed at providing effective employee representation, the extent and impact of employee representation continues to decline in the UK. As a result of EU legislative intervention and in particular the ICE Regulations, British employees enjoy more extensive legal rights to representation than at any time in their previous history. But the structures they have prompted appear less effective at delivering benefits for employees than in the past and appear less robust than those provided by analogous legislation in many continental European countries. Explanations include the continuing decline of trade unionism, historically the dominant basis of workplace representation, and the weak forms in which EU directives have been transposed into UK legislation. The legal rights, albeit greater than what went before, are difficult to articulate and enforce. They provide at best an uncertain basis for trade union organization and give employers considerable flexibility of interpretation. Legal rights, as Koukiadaki has recently shown (2008), are insufficient guarantees of effective employee rights if employee representatives lack the capacity to articulate and guarantee those rights. Such capacity may be provided by more effective mechanisms of legal enforcement, strong trade union development, or a managerial preparedness both to invest the necessary resource for effective consultation and to engage in meaningful consultation.

Analyses of union and legal weakness need to be located within a framework of continued managerial indifference to employee representation and a preference for unilateral managerial action. Unconstrained by powerful trade unions or strong laws this managerial preference appears as a dominant explanation of the continued decline in effective representation (see Brown, this volume). There is no evidence to suggest that many managers and employers accept the implications of the financial benefits arguments outlined above despite their endorsement by government. Were they to have done so there should have been greater growth in the incidence of employee representation than is identified above. Nevertheless, employer strategy is key to understanding what is happening to employee representation. As noted above, where representative systems do exist, managers, according to the 2004 WERS, express a preference for non-union over union representatives and for representatives appointed by managers rather than elected by employees. Managers are largely responsible for the rise of non-union representative systems, either out of a belief in the business benefits of such arrangements or as a result of a union avoidance strategy (see Hall *et al.* 2007), but such evidence as we have suggests that without union input representative systems lack vitality and sustainability (see also Terry 1999). The growing body of evidence indicating the greater long-term viability and effectiveness of 'hybrid' systems of representation (Charlwood and Terry 2007) – combining both union and non-union forms of representation – indicates one possible line of development, but as yet the implications for the longer term remain unclear.

As unions continue to decline legal provision and management attitudes have become increasingly important factors determining the existence, nature and activity of employee representative systems. Given the relative weakness of legal provision and the fickleness of management adherence to the 'business case' for employee representation it is difficult to be optimistic about the prospects for its future. But it remains a subject of continuing interest to practitioners and policy makers that the concept of employee representation as a basic legal right in democratic societies is more firmly entrenched than ever and it would be unwise to predict its demise.

Notes

1 While the traditional term 'shop steward' is still found, most especially to refer to union representatives of manual workers in manufacturing industry, it is being increasingly replaced by the term 'union representative' and sometimes 'employee representative' although the latter fails to distinguish between union and non-union representatives.

2 It is important to remember that Willman *et al.*'s data for non-union systems includes so-called 'direct representation' mechanisms such as briefing groups and problem-solving groups and thus reports a much higher incidence than analyses that look only at indirect (representative) systems. However, this does not invalidate the general point above.

References

Ackers, P. and Payne, J. 1998: British trade unions and social partnership: rhetoric, reality and strategy. *The International Journal of Human Resource Management*, 9 (3), 529–550.

BERR 2007: *Workplace Representatives: A Review of their Facilities and Facility Time. Government Response to Public Consultation*. London: Department of Business, Enterprise and Regulatory Reform.

Brewster, C., Wood, G., Croucher, R. and Brookes, M. 2007: Are works councils and joint consultative committees a threat to trade unions? *Economic and Industrial Democracy*, 28 (49), 49–76.

Brown, W. 2000: Putting partnership into practice in Britain. *British Journal of Industrial Relations*, 38 (9), 299–316.

Brown, W., Deakin, S., Nash, D. and Oxenbridge, S. 2000: The employment contract: from collective procedures to individual rights. *British Journal of Industrial Relations*, 38(4), 611–629.

Charlwood, A. and Forth, J. 2009: Employee representation. In Brown, W., Bryson, A., Forth, J. and Whitfield, K. (eds) *The Evolution of the Modern Workplace*. Cambridge: Cambridge University Press.

Charlwood, A. and Terry, M. 2007: 21st-century models of employee representation: structures, processes and outcomes. *Industrial Relations Journal*, 38 (4), 320–337.

Cully, M., Woodland, S., O'Reilly, A. and Dix, G. 1999: *Britain at Work*. London: Routledge.

DTI 2007: *Consultation on Workplace Representatives: A Review of their Facilities and Facility Time*. London: Department of Trade and Industry.

EWCB 2000: Commission assesses implementation of EWCs Directive. *European Works Council Bulletin*, 28 (July/August), 4–6.

Greene, A.M., Black, J. and Ackers, P. 2000: The union makes us strong? A study of the dynamics of workplace leadership at two UK manufacturing plants. *British Journal of Industrial Relations*, 38 (1), 75–93.

Hall, M. 1996: Beyond recognition? Employee representation and EU law. *Industrial Law Journal*, 25 (1), 15–27.

Hall, M. 2000: Assessing the information and consultation of employees' regulations. *Industrial Law Journal*, 34 (2), 103–126.

Hall, M. 2001: Government launches review of redundancy consultation laws. *EIROnline*, January. www.eiro.eurofound.ie

Hall, M. 2003: Draft information and consultation legislation published. *European Industrial Relations Observatory*. http://www.eiro.eurofound.eu.int/2003/07/feature/uk0307106f.html

Hall, M. and Edwards, P. 1999: Reforming the statutory redundancy consultation procedure. *Industrial Law Journal*, 28 (4), 299–318.

Hall, M. and Marginson, P. 2005: Trojan horses or paper tigers? Assessing the significance of European Works Councils. In Harley, B., Hyman, J. and Thompson, P. (eds) *Participation and Democracy at Work*. Basingstoke: Palgrave Macmillan.

Hall, M. and Terry, M. 2004: The emerging system of statutory worker representation. In Healy, G., Heery, E., Taylor, P. and Brown, W. (eds) *The Future of Worker Representation*. Basingstoke: Palgrave Macmillan.

Hall, M. and others 2007: Implementing information and consultation: early experience under the ICE Regulations. *Employment Relations Series*, No. 88, London: Department for Business, Enterprise and Regulatory Reform.

Hollinrake, A., Antcliff, V. and Saundry, R. 2008: Explaining activity and exploring experience – findings from a survey of union learning representatives. *Industrial Relations Journal*, 39 (5), 392–410.

Hyman, R. 1996: Is there a case for statutory works councils in Britain? In McColgan, A. (ed.) *The Future of Labour Law*. London: Cassell.

Jacobi, O., Keller, B. and Müller-Jentsch, W. 1992: Germany: codetermining the future? In Ferner, A. and Hyman, R. (eds) *Industrial Relations in the New Europe*. Oxford: Blackwell.

James, P. 1996: Mixed responses to new safety consultation rights. *IRS Employment Review*, 607: Health and Safety Bulletin, 245 (May), 13–14.

Kelly, J. 1996: Works councils: union advance or marginalisation? In McColgan, A. (ed.) *The Future of Labour Law*. London: Cassell.

Kersley, B. and others 2006: *Inside the Workplace: Findings from the 2004 Workplace Employment Relations Survey*. Abingdon: Routledge.

Koukiadaki, A. 2008: Reflexive regulation and the development of capabilities: the impact of the 2002/14/EC Directive on information and consultation of employees in the UK. Unpublished PhD thesis, University of Warwick.

Marchington, M. and Wilkinson, A. 2000: Direct participation. In Bach, S. and Sisson, K. (eds) *Personnel Management*. Oxford: Blackwell, pp. 340–364.

Marginson, P., Edwards, P., Edwards, T., Ferner, A. and Tregaskis, O. forthcoming: Employee representation and consultative voice in multinational companies. *British Journal of Industrial Relations*, forthcoming.

Moore, S., Tasiran, A. and Jefferys, S. 2008: The impact of employee representation upon workplace industrial relations outcomes. *Employment Relations Research Series*, No. 87, Department for Business, Enterprise and Regulatory Reform.

O'Hara, J. 1996: *Worker Participation and Collective Bargaining in Britain: The Influence of European Law*. London: Institute of Employment Rights.

Oxenbridge, S. and Brown, W. 2004: A poisoned chalice? Trade union representatives in partnership and co-operative employer-union relationships. In Healy, G. and others (eds) *The Future of Worker Representation*. Basingstoke: Palgrave Macmillan, pp. 187–206.

Podro, S. and Suff, R. nd: Employee representatives: challenges and changes in the workplace. *Acas Policy Discussion Papers*. London: Acas.

Rainbird, H. 2005: Assessing partnership approaches to lifelong learning: a new and modern role for trade unions? In Stuart, M. and Martinez Lucio, M. (eds) *Partnership and Modernisation in Employment Relations*. London: Routledge, pp. 26–62.

Terry, M. 1994: Workplace unionism: redefining structures and objectives. In Hyman, R. and Ferner, A. (eds) *New Frontiers in European Industrial Relations*. Oxford: Blackwell.

Terry, M. 1999: Systems of collective employee representation in non-union firms in the UK. *Industrial Relations Journal*, 30 (1), 16–30.

Terry, M. 2003: Employee representation: shop stewards and the new legal framework. In Edwards, P. (ed.) *Industrial Relations: Theory and Practice*. 2nd edition. Oxford: Blackwell.

Terry, M. and Smith, J. 2003: Evaluation of the Partnership at Work Fund. *DTI Employment Relations Research Series*, No. 17. London: Department of Trade and Industry.

Unionlearn 2006: *Making a Real Difference*. London: Unionlearn.

Waddington, J. 2003: What do representatives think of the practices of European Works Councils? Views from six countries. *European Journal of Industrial Relations*, 9 (3), 303–325.

Wallis, E. and Stuart, M. 2007: A collective learning culture: a qualitative study of workplace learning arrangements. *Unionlearn Research Papers*, No. 3. London: Unionlearn.

Willman, P., Bryson, A. and Gomez, R. 2007: The long goodbye: new establishments and the fall of union voice in Britain. *International Journal of Human Resource Management*, 18 (7), 1318–1334.

13

THE CHANGING LEGAL FRAMEWORK OF EMPLOYMENT RELATIONS

LINDA DICKENS AND MARK HALL

Introduction

This chapter describes the current framework of British labour law and analyses its nature and rationale in the light of major legislative changes made by Conservative governments in the period 1979–97 and by Labour governments since 1997. It highlights how European Union law increasingly has shaped national labour law and charts the demise of the 'voluntarist' tradition and the increasing 'juridification' of industrial relations in Britain.

Voluntarism and the Growth of Legal Intervention

The period up to the 1960s

In Britain, for most of the 20th century, regulation of the employment relationship was by means of collective bargaining between employers and unions (and, where absent, by employers acting unilaterally). This was far more important than legal regulation through Acts of Parliament (statute law). 'Voluntarism', as this approach is termed, was supported by unions who saw the main role of legislation as preventing hostile intervention by the courts in industrial disputes, and by employers keen to avoid legislation that constrained their freedom to manage. Where statute law intervened it sought to support and extend collective bargaining and to plug gaps in its coverage and protections. Thus, voluntarism did not mean a complete absence of statutory intervention but, rather, a system of 'collective laissez-faire' (on which see Davies and Freedland 1993) resting on autonomous self-regulation.

Legislation had been required in the late 19th and early 20th centuries to legalize trade union activity, notably to provide 'immunity' in order for unions to organize industrial action during disputes with employers, which would otherwise be unlawful under common (judge-made) law (see Colling, this volume). It was used to encourage and support voluntary collective bargaining with *auxiliary* measures (e.g. the provision of conciliation and arbitration machinery to aid dispute settlement), and *regulatory* measures (e.g. governing the terms and conditions of employment for certain groups, notably those not covered by collective bargaining). These gap-filling measures were seen as supplementing rather than challenging collective organization as the main source of worker protection. They included legally binding minimum wage rates set by Wages Councils in sectors where collective bargaining was underdeveloped; the statutory regulation of the working hours of women and young workers; and health and safety laws covering various occupations and industries.

Nevertheless, compared with other industrialized countries, the crucial and distinguishing characteristic of British employment law (outside wartime provisions) from 1870 to the 1960s was its limited role. In 1954 a leading academic lawyer commented:

> There is, perhaps, no major country in the world in which the law has played a less significant role in the shaping of industrial relations than in Great Britain and in which today the law and legal profession have less to do with labour relations. (Kahn-Freund 1954: 44)

1960s and 1970s: pressure for reform

The 1950s proved to be the heyday of voluntarism. By the end of the decade greater legal intervention was increasingly advocated to achieve a range of labour market and industrial relations objectives. Early examples of a shift towards greater legal regulation included legislation in the mid-1960s which introduced minimum periods of notice of termination of employment and written particulars of terms and conditions of employment, and provided for compensation to be paid to workers losing their jobs for economic reasons. Such 'redundancy payments' were an instrument of economic policy to encourage labour mobility. However, a Royal Commission established in 1965 in response to growing pressure for the greater legal regulation of industrial relations, particularly strikes, reaffirmed voluntarism, arguing against 'destroying the British tradition of keeping industrial relations out of the courts' (Royal Commission on Trade Unions and Employers' Associations 1968: 47). It saw some role for increased legal intervention (for example, in protecting workers against unfair dismissal) but its emphasis was on the reform of collective bargaining which was to remain the main regulatory mechanism.

Despite this, however, both the then Labour government and the subsequent Conservative government accorded a central role to legal intervention in the reform of industrial relations. The Conservatives' Industrial Relations Act 1971, in particular, represented an ambitious, but ultimately unsuccessful and short-lived attempt at the comprehensive legal regulation of industrial relations (Weekes *et al.* 1975).

The remainder of the 1970s, under the Labour governments of 1974–79, saw further legislation but of a kind which could be seen as a return to a modified, supplemented form of voluntarism. The 1971 Act's abandonment of the traditional system of immunities for industrial action was reversed and various auxiliary measures to support collective bargaining were enacted. Piecemeal legislation in the area of health and safety gave way to the more comprehensive Health and Safety at Work Act 1974, which emphasized self-regulation within a framework of state inspection and enforcement, and associated 1977 Regulations provided for union safety representatives. Anti-discrimination legislation was enacted covering sex and race, and equality commissions were established. The Employment Protection Act 1975 restructured much of the institutional framework of the industrial relations and employment law system, providing a statutory basis for the activities of the Advisory, Conciliation and Arbitration Service (ACAS), which took over dispute settlement functions from the government, and establishing the Central Arbitration Committee (CAC). It also introduced important new individual employment rights and strengthened others. The previous gap-filling role of the law gave way to a more 'universal' approach. Davies and Freedland (1984: 347) argue that the 1975 Act 'accomplished the crucial transition from a statutory floor of rights concerned primarily with the termination of employment to [one] concerned with the content of the employment relationship'.

1979–97: the decisive break with voluntarism

Although voluntarism came under challenge in the 1960s, and the 1970s saw an increase in the *extent* of legal regulation, it was the *nature* of the employment law reforms introduced by Conservative governments between 1979 and 1997 which constituted a decisive shift away from the longstanding view that collective bargaining was the best way of conducting industrial relations. Law was used to curb union strength and to restrict and reduce regulation through collective bargaining, but not to replace it with legal regulation. The scope of individual legal rights was curtailed, employer freedom of action enhanced and union autonomy reduced.

Conservative governments in the 1980s and 1990s made extensive use of the law with the aim of radically redressing the balance between employers and trade unions, between individual liberty and collective interests and between managerial prerogative and employee rights – in each case tilting the balance towards the former. The legislative agenda was strongly influenced by the government's neoliberal economic and social objectives, with law being seen as a key instrument facilitating labour market restructuring. The major elements of the Conservatives' employment law programme were the legal restriction of industrial action; the eradication of compulsory union membership; the regulation of internal union government; the dismantling of statutory supports for collective bargaining; the removal of statutory floors to wages; and the curtailment of individual employment rights.

This deregulation of the UK labour market and labour law conflicted with the approach being taken at European level. As a member of the European Union, the UK is required to conform to EU requirements. Particularly from the 1980s onwards, legal intervention in the employment relationship reflected not only national concerns but also this growing supra-national influence (see Hyman, this volume). European legal instruments (usually legally binding directives) sought to address disparities between levels and costs of employment protection legislation across the member states, and to develop the 'social dimension' of the single European market. The significance of EU regulation in shaping or constraining the domestic legislative agenda will be seen at various points in the discussion that follows.

Key aspects of the industrial relations agenda pursued by the Conservative governments of the 1980s and 1990s – especially the restriction of the freedom to take industrial action and the statutory regulation of trade union government – were unaffected by EU requirements (although they breached other, non-enforceable, international standards). But the need to conform to EU law limited the extent to which they were able to pursue their deregulatory ambitions in other areas. In a succession of instances, the government was forced – by EU directives and rulings of the European Court of Justice (ECJ) – to take legislative steps it would rather have avoided (for example, relating to gender pay equity, discrimination and employees' rights when business ownership was transferred). It complied with a self-confessed 'remarkable lack of enthusiasm' (Davies and Freedland 1993: 577), adopting a minimalist response often coupled with other deregulatory measures (Deakin 1990).

The mismatch that clearly existed between the Conservatives' domestic labour market policies and the EU social agenda reflected different regulatory traditions: the legal regulation of employment and industrial relations has been embedded more deeply in most continental European countries than it has in Britain (see Colling, this volume). But it reflected also a clash between competing philosophies of liberalism and collectivism in labour market regulation – that is, whether regulation promotes or detracts from efficiency, employment creation and growth. The Conservatives attempted to exempt the UK from EU employment regulation. In 1989, the UK government refused to sign the Community Charter of the Fundamental Social Rights of Workers (the 'social charter') and more significantly, in 1991, it negotiated an 'opt-out' from the 'social chapter' of the Maastricht Treaty on European Union, fearing that it would further erode the UK's ability to block legislation it opposed (Hall 1994). Nevertheless, EU measures originating before the 'opt-out' continued to impact on the domestic labour law agenda.

Post 1997: New Labour – change and continuity

By the time a Labour government was returned to office in 1997, the debate was no longer about *whether* the law should play a role in British industrial relations but about *what* role it should play. The New Labour government accepted large parts of the previous Conservative administrations' industrial relations legislation, notably restrictions on industrial action and the regulation of union governance, while in other areas such as the minimum wage both the Labour party and trade unions had come to favour legal intervention.

Retention of the existing laws on strikes was strongly emphasized by the party's 1997 election manifesto and was seen as central to the 'business-friendly' credentials of New Labour. The emphasis on the desirability of a flexible labour market remained also but, in contrast to the previous Conservative governments, Labour sought to balance employers' flexibility with minimum standards of 'fairness at work' (Dickens and Hall 2006). This change of emphasis and the reversal of the UK opt-out from the EU social chapter resulted in significant legislative development. By signing up to the Maastricht social chapter, the 1997 Labour government demonstrated a major change in policy from that of its predecessors, and significant aspects of the current legislative framework flowed from this decision.

However, there was no return to the public policy that prevailed up to the 1970s of encouraging and supporting collective bargaining as the best method of conducting industrial relations. Although, as Wedderburn noted, the Labour government's white paper, *Fairness at Work* (with its proposal for a new statutory procedure for securing trade union recognition), was 'the first major government document since 1981 to recognize and promote instruments of collective industrial relations' (1998: 254), there is an apparent reluctance to privilege collective bargaining and collective voice over more individualized methods of conducting employment relations. The current legal framework is one which reflects the individualization (de-collectivization) of employment relations which took place during the 1990s.

The following sections look in more detail at the current legal framework, discussing the measures enacted since 1997 against the background of what preceded them. We first explore the rationale, nature and impact of individual employment rights and then turn to collective rights (relating to union organization, collective bargaining and representation and industrial action).

Individual Rights: Managerial Prerogative and Worker Protection

Rationales for action: justice, efficiency and competitiveness

The individual employee's position is one of subordination, though the asymmetry in power between employer and employee is clothed 'by that indispensable figment of the legal mind known as the contract of employment' (Kahn-Freund 1983: 18). Statutory regulation that constrains the freedom of the contracting parties and impinges on managerial prerogative may be justified, therefore, because it counteracts the inequality of bargaining power inherent in the employment relationship (Colling and Terry, this volume).

As we have noted, under the voluntarist system collective bargaining was seen as the primary method of addressing this inequality and the regulatory function of law was limited. In the 1960s and 1970s, however, there was a marked increase in the extent to which the law sought to restrict managerial prerogative in handling the employment relationship, particularly in the areas of recruitment (through discrimination law) and job termination. Importantly, however, individual rights legislation was seen also as a means of promoting efficient management, reducing industrial conflict and promoting the development of 'orderly' industrial relations for example, the redundancy payments and unfair dismissal legislation (Anderman 1986: 433; Dickens 1994).

In a significant change of approach, Conservative governments from 1979 to 1997 aimed to reduce or remove workers' statutory employment rights in order, it was argued, to promote employment and enhance the flexibility seen as crucial to competitive success (e.g. DE 1989). There was a shift towards an increasingly 'contractualist' approach which, in the writings of the 'new right', treated freedom of contract as if it were a social reality rather than a legal concept. Workers' statutory protections impose costs on employers which, it was argued, worked to the disadvantage of job creation. The Conservatives also believed that downward pressure on wages would stimulate employment. Measures (whether in labour law or social security) which acted to provide a floor to wages were seen as undesirable. Thus, for example, the long-established Wages Councils were first restricted and then abolished.

At the end of the Conservatives' period of deregulation the framework of individual employment rights remained largely intact, but their substantive content had been weakened and – importantly – coverage of these rights substantially reduced. For example, increasing the length of service required to qualify for many employment rights deprived many workers of protection. Deregulation removed certain legal protections from those least likely to be in unions, particularly those in 'non-standard' employment. Also, changes to substantive law and enforcement procedures made it harder for those who were covered by the legislation to pursue their legal rights and to succeed, and the available remedies deteriorated.

As noted, partly as a result of the incoming Labour government's more positive attitude to Europe, and partly through domestically driven policies, the importance of legislation as a source of employment rights in Britain increased significantly following the 1997 election. Whereas the Conservatives had promoted flexibility at the expense of security, Labour sought to develop a 'flexible labour market underpinned by fair, minimum standards'. Labour ministers were prepared to articulate rationales for legal intervention based on notions of social justice and fairness. But there was a continuing concern not to overburden employers (e.g. DTI 1998: para. 1.13). Employer concerns about 'burdens on business' meant that the shift towards worker protection under the 1997–2001 Labour government was less extensive than originally heralded.

Finally, in terms of rationales for legal intervention, it is worth noting that some legislative changes (notably those concerning maternity and parental leave and the right of parents and carers to request flexible working) were presented as 'family-friendly' measures rather than as labour rights. This linked them to different policy debates, concerning family policy and work–life balance rather than labour relations, with which New Labour may have felt more comfortable (Simpson 1998). This discourse arguably also served to make overt employer resistance more difficult, not least since such measures were presented as helping parents 'balance the needs of their work and their children so that they may contribute fully to the competitiveness and productivity of the modern economy' (DTI 2000).

Individual employment rights: nature and scope

At the time of the change of government in 1997, the legal framework included statutory rights for employees to:

- a minimum period of notice of termination;
- a statement of the principal terms and conditions of the contract of employment and of discipline and dismissal procedures;
- an itemized pay statement;
- a statement of the reason for dismissal;
- protection against unfair dismissal;
- protection against discrimination on grounds of race, sex and disability;
- time off work for antenatal care;
- maternity leave and pay;
- return to work after leave for childbirth;
- time off work for various public and trade union duties;
- equal pay and other contractual terms as between men and women;
- redundancy payments;
- protection against dismissal or action short of dismissal on grounds of trade union membership, non-membership or union activity; and
- *preservation of acquired rights on the transfer of undertakings.*

Since 1997, a range of new rights and protections have been enacted, notably:

- the national minimum wage (NMW);
- protection against dismissal or detriment for 'whistleblowing';
- the right to be accompanied in grievance and disciplinary hearings;
- *statutory limits on working time;*
- *paid annual leave*
- *parental leave;*
- *time off for family emergencies;*
- the right to request flexible working;
- paternity leave and pay;
- adoption leave and pay;
- *equal treatment for part-time workers;*
- *protection for fixed-term employees;* and
- *protection against discrimination on grounds of age, religion or belief and sexual orientation.*

(The measures appearing in italics implemented EU directives.)

The implementation of the EU Working Time Directive in 1998 and the introduction of the NMW in 1999 represented the most significant development of employment rights in the UK, constituting for the first time the general regulation of pay and working time through basic universal minimum standards (see Grimshaw and Rubery, this volume).

Historically, in keeping with the voluntarist tradition, there had been no general legal regulation of working time in the UK. Moreover, in the 1980s and 1990s,

Conservative governments repealed legislation which had served to regulate the working hours of particular groups (Hall and Sisson 1997) while seeking to block the EU Working Time Directive (unsuccessfully challenging its legal basis). The Working Time Regulations introduced by the Labour government in 1998 provided for the first time in the UK a comprehensive statutory framework regulating a broad range of working time issues, including a 48 hour limit on average weekly working hours, minimum daily rest periods, rest breaks, restrictions on night and shift work and the provision of paid annual leave (see Hall *et al.* 1998). However, reflecting the directive, the working time standards specified by the Regulations were subject to a complex set of exceptions and 'derogations' (conditional scope for the adoption of lower standards). More generally, the flexible application of some of the Regulations' standards was possible not only through agreements with trade unions (who provide some countervailing power) but also through 'workforce agreements' with elected employee representatives where there is no recognized union. Also – and crucially for the impact of the legislation, discussed below – the Regulations provided that individual employees could agree to opt out of the 48 hour limit on average weekly working hours.

Whereas the Working Time Regulations implemented an EU directive, the NMW was part of the government's domestic agenda and in the view of one commentator was arguably 'the most radical and far reaching reform of employment rights made by the 1997 Labour government' (Simpson 1999: 1). Legislation had been used in the past to protect particularly vulnerable workers against abusive practices by employers relating to the level of pay, and to regulate deductions from pay and methods of payment, and legislation concerning gender pay equality was enacted in the 1970s and 1980s. But the NMW brought in the principle of a universal floor for pay.

In addition to enacting additional rights for workers vis-à-vis their employers, the 1997 Labour government reversed the narrowing of the coverage of existing protections which had occurred under its Conservative predecessors and improved the remedies. The service qualification period which applied to unfair dismissal rights was halved to one year, and clauses in fixed-term contracts whereby people could be asked to waive their right to claim unfair dismissal were no longer allowed. The remedies for unfair dismissal were improved by raising and index linking the maximum compensation limit. (There is no maximum limit for compensation in discrimination cases; European law required the maximum in discrimination cases to be removed in the 1990s.)

In an important recognition of the diverse (and at times disguised) nature of subordinate labour, and the changing UK labour market, the Labour government proposed bringing more 'non-standard' workers within the scope of employment protections (see Colling, this volume for further discussion). Some new legislation, for example on working time and the NMW, applied to the broader category of 'workers' and not just 'employees', thus including those who may have difficulties establishing a particular employment status. But this was not done consistently. More systematic moves to widen the scope of legislative protection were envisaged, and consultations undertaken, but no steps taken.

In common with its predecessors, New Labour has been concerned to reduce the number of cases coming to Employment Tribunals (the forum for determining individual employment rights). In 2004 it introduced statutory minimum dispute resolution procedures which set out basic standards for handling disciplinary and grievance cases in all workplaces. The purported intention was to encourage workplace resolution of individual disputes but in practice these procedures reduced access to rights enforcement and had a number of adverse consequences for employers also, leading to their repeal in 2009 and replacement by a new ACAS code of practice on disciplinary and grievance procedures.

Some 'family-friendly' employment rights (such as paid maternity leave) pre-dated the 1997 Labour government. Again, the post-1997 reforms reflected both EU law and 'home-grown' policy objectives. New statutory entitlements to paren-tal leave and to time off work for family emergencies, required by EU Parental Leave Directive, were introduced in 1999, alongside improvements to existing maternity leave provision. Provisions introduced in 2003 entitled working par-ents of children under six years of age or disabled children up to the age of 18 to request flexible working and to have their request considered by their employer. This right was extended to carers of elderly or sick partners or relatives in 2007 and further extensions were proposed in 2008. The Employment Act 2002 also lengthened the period for which maternity leave is paid, increased statutory maternity pay, and introduced paid paternity leave for fathers.

In the area of equality, post-1997 Labour governments, prompted by an EU directive, introduced regulations preventing employment discrimination on grounds of sexual orientation, religion or belief and age, adding to the established body of anti-discrimination legislation covering sex, race and disability (see Dean and Liff, this volume). Disability discrimination legislation dating from 1995 was progressively extended to all employers. A Disability Rights Commission was set up in 2000 on the same footing as the existing equality commissions (covering sex and race) before all three commissions were subsumed into a new single body in 2007 – the Equality and Human Rights Commission (EHRC). This was part of a broader overhaul of the UK's equalities framework, which will include a new single Equality Act, proposed to simplify and strengthen the current framework of anti-discrimination legislation (Dickens 2007), although at the time of writing the emphasis appears to be more on the former. An important development in this area has been the imposition on public authorities of statutory duties to promote equality in the areas of sex, race and disability. These will be consolidated into a single equality duty and extended to include other strands. These duties – although limited to the public sector – mark an important conceptual shift in policy towards regulating to promote equality, rather than simply to outlaw discrimination.

Impact of individual rights

In broad terms, employees have benefited from the enactment of individual employment rights in that many seek redress at Employment Tribunals in circumstances where previously none would have been available. As regards the longer-standing employment rights, the unfair dismissal legislation has had the effect of curbing arbitrary 'hire and fire' approaches to discipline and promoting the formalization and standardization of workplace procedures in line with the legal provisions and associated codes of practice. However, the law does not go far in challenging managerial prerogative and has afforded only limited job protection for employees.

Anti-discrimination legislation has curbed the most overt discriminatory practices, especially in recruitment; has indicated how less overt, taken for granted, practices can be discriminatory; and has encouraged the development of equal opportunities policies. Pay structures have been revised, with the use and threat of equal pay actions providing a lever to reform, and the gender pay gap has narrowed, although the broader picture is still one of continuing labour market disadvantage for women, ethnic minorities and other social groups (see also Dean and Liff, this volume). 'Family-friendly' rights help facilitate interaction with the labour market, lessening the penalties arising from unequal division of paid and unpaid work and caring responsibilities within households, but they can be double-edged. For example, taking time away from work for child care continues to have an adverse impact on women's career progression. There is evidence that individual statutory rights have provided a floor for collectively bargained improvements (though there are also indications that the 'floor' may form a 'ceiling', with employer provision restricted to that required by legislation).

The nature of the individual employment rights enacted since 1997 and their extended coverage potentially benefit disadvantaged labour market groups who predominate in non-standard employment. For example, women constitute over 80% of part-time workers. They also are more likely than men to have short service in their current job and are less likely to work in unionized sectors. The continuing emphasis on an individualized 'victim complains' approach to rights enforcement, however, means the potential of legal rights to offer protection to disadvantaged groups in the labour market may not be fully realized (Pollert 2005).

Amongst the main legislative initiatives pursued by the post-1997 Labour governments, the NMW affected about 1.1 million workers when first introduced, with subsequent up-ratings affecting similar numbers. Around two thirds of beneficiaries have been women. According to the Low Pay Commission (LPC), the NMW has had a significant impact on narrowing the gender pay gap at the bottom of the earnings distribution (LPC 1998, 2003). Despite dire predictions from employers, adverse employment effects have been small, though the relatively buoyant state of the labour market was important in moderating any negative impact (Dickens and Manning 2003).

The impact of the Working Time Regulations has been less clear-cut (see also Grimshaw and Rubery, this volume). The 2004 Workplace Employment Relations Survey (WERS 2004) showed that 11% of employees usually worked more than 48 hours a week (Kersley *et al.* 2006). Employers have ensured that employees make extensive use of the individual opt-out from the 48 hour limit. The CBI's (2007) employment trends survey, for example, showed an average of 32% of employees had signed an individual opt-out, although the proportion of employees who in practice worked more than 48 hours per week was lower at 13%. According to Barnard *et al.* (2003a, 2003b), the Regulations have not stimulated widespread changes to the way working time is organized. Reliance on the individual opt-out has been the key route to flexibility, with little evidence of the flexible application of the statutory working time standards by collective or workforce agreements.

In terms of Labour's 'family-friendly' employment legislation, WERS 2004 showed increased and extra-statutory provision. For example, in 5% of private and 84% of public sector workplaces at least some portion of maternity leave is on full pay. It also found marked increases in the availability of paid paternity leave and emergency paid leave since 1998. However, some employers are still not providing the statutory minima (Kersley *et al.* 2006) and the employee survey undertaken as part of WERS 2004 suggests that the availability of flexible arrangements which – in some circumstances – could assist in work–life balance may be ad hoc and individualized rather than embedded in workplace policy and practice. The CBI (2007) reported employers' 'positive' experience of the operation of the statutory right for employees to request flexible working arrangements for child care purposes noting that when requests were made, the vast majority (94%) had been accepted by employers.

The impact of the post-1997 Labour governments' equality measures is discussed more extensively in Dean and Liff (this volume). Legislative influence, however, is indicated in WERS 2004 findings that employers were now more likely to have equal opportunities policies (EOPs) and also for them to cover discrimination on the 'new' grounds of sexual orientation, religion or belief and age. Although practices associated with fair treatment are more likely to exist where there is a formal EOP, WERS 2004 revealed a continuing gap between the existence of a policy and action likely to give it practical effect. It also indicated a continuing neglect of pay within EOPs with only 7% of workplaces in the 2004 survey reviewing relative pay rates as between men and women; even fewer review by other characteristics. The lack of attention to pay – where the aggregate data show continuing gender and racial pay gaps – needs to be seen in the context of the lack of any mandatory requirement for employers to undertake equality pay audits or to take positive action to remedy disadvantage. In both cases this can be seen as an example of workplace practice reflecting the limitations of the legislation as well as its positive aspects (Dickens 2006). The WERS 2004 survey provided some discouraging findings of relevance to the race equality duty (the earliest of the public sector equality duties) suggesting that 'the statutory duty had not fed through to employer practice' (Kersley *et al.* 2006: 310).

Collective Rights: Collective Bargaining, Employee Representation and Industrial Action

The process of 're-regulation' by the post-1997 Labour governments was not simply a question of enacting additional individual employment rights. In the name of promoting 'partnership', the Labour government introduced important new statutory provisions affecting collective bargaining, employee representation and information and consultation, while largely retaining its predecessors' legislation restricting industrial action and regulating unions' internal procedures.

Statutory trade union recognition

The Employment Relations Act 1999 fulfilled one of Labour's major manifesto commitments by providing a statutory procedure through which a union could seek an enforceable award from an independent body – the CAC – that an employer recognize it for collective bargaining in respect of pay, hours and holidays. The recognition procedure clearly demarcated the New Labour government's approach to industrial relations from that of its Conservative predecessors. In its detail, however, the procedure fell short of the statutory assistance that unions had hoped for, and in its final form it incorporated most of what the employers lobbied for rather than union demands (Wood and Godard 1999). A government review of the provisions initiated in 2003 resulted only in 'fine tuning'. Firms with fewer than 21 workers are excluded and the applicant union(s) needs a threshold membership of 10% of the workers for whom it wishes to bargain (its proposed bargaining unit) plus the majority of workers likely to support it, in order to have its application accepted by the CAC. Where there is already a recognition agreement applying to workers in the proposed bargaining unit, the application cannot be accepted. This is so even if this agreement is with a union which is not independent of the employer, or does not cover pay. The CAC has to determine whether the union-proposed bargaining unit is appropriate, where this is not agreed between the employer and union, paying particular regard to the need for it to be 'compatible with effective management' and avoiding fragmentation. The CAC can declare the union recognized without holding a ballot if more than 50% of the workers in the bargaining unit are members of the union but it will not do this if it considers a ballot would be in the interests of good industrial relations, or where there is credible evidence that employees do not want the union to conduct collective bargaining on their behalf. Where the CAC calls for a ballot, recognition will be granted if a majority of those voting, and at least 40% of the workers in the bargaining unit, vote in favour. This majoritarian principle contrasts with the approach of the recognition legislation of the 1970s which was concerned more with whether there was sufficient support to sustain collective bargaining, acknowledging the 'virtuous circle' effect, whereby union membership increases following employer recognition.

Following a declaration of recognition the parties are required to agree a method of bargaining and, if they do not, the CAC will impose a procedure which is legally binding unless the parties agree otherwise. Where one party does not abide by the procedure the other may apply to the courts for an order that the party act as required (specific performance). Failure to abide by an order for specific performance could (in theory) lead to quasi-criminal sanctions for contempt of court, although the circumstances in which a court would order this remedy and its willingness to do so in this area are uncertain (Hepple 2000). This final sanction has not had to be tested.

Various statutory rights apply within unionized workplaces, and so flow from recognition. These include the right to paid time off work for union learning representatives introduced under the Employment Act 2002.

A right to representation

British legislation protects both positive and negative freedom of association (the right of an individual to join or not to join a trade union). The Employment Relations Act 1999 enabled regulations to ban employer blacklists of union activists – a power ministers did not seek to use until 2009 – and, in 2004, the ability of employers to offer inducements to their employees not to belong to a trade union or not to have their terms and conditions of employment determined by collective agreement was constrained. But, outside the limited provisions within the statutory recognition procedure, the law provides no right for trade unions to organize.

There is, however, an individual employment right with considerable potential significance in collective industrial relations terms – a statutory right for workers to be accompanied by a trade union official or fellow worker at workplace disciplinary and grievance hearings even where the union is not recognized by the employer and irrespective of the size of the organization. These statutory provisions, introduced in the 1999 Act, fell short of providing a fully-fledged 'right to representation', as they limited the scope for the accompanying person to intervene in the proceedings (subsequently expanded to include responding on the worker's behalf to views expressed at the hearing). At the time of its introduction, however, it was suggested that the operation of this right might boost unions' organizing efforts by enabling them to gain access to the workplace and demonstrate the value of their role in supporting workers. There is some evidence that union officers have sought to encourage use of this right in conjunction with union recruitment campaigns (Oxenbridge *et al.* 2003).

Statutory information and consultation provisions

Driven primarily by EU requirements, there has been a growth in statutory provisions requiring employers to inform and consult employee representatives, irrespective of union recognition. Most notably, the Information and Consultation of Employees (ICE) Regulations 2004 represent a highly significant development in employment law terms, taking the UK further away from its voluntarist traditions.

EU requirements for consultation over collective redundancies and business transfers were transposed into UK law in 1975 and 1981, respectively, but the original UK legislation confined the right to be consulted to representatives of trade unions recognized by the employers concerned, providing no mechanism for consulting employee representatives in the absence of union recognition. In 1994, this approach was found to be inadequate by the ECJ, prompting the then Conservative government to amend the law to require consultation on these issues either with representatives of recognized unions or with other representatives elected by employees. The Labour government further amended the law in 1999 to prioritize consultation via the representatives of recognized unions, and provide that consultation should otherwise take place with appropriate existing elected employee representatives (for example, a consultative committee) or representatives specially elected by employees under regulated balloting procedures. In public policy terms, these reforms were of considerable significance as they overturned the tradition that recognized unions constituted the 'single channel' through which collective statutory employment rights were applied. For the first time, UK law introduced issue-specific employee representation mechanisms in the absence of representation via recognized unions, though research into the operation of the amended redundancy consultation legislation suggested that some employers found the organization of elections for *ad hoc* employee representatives difficult or uncomfortable (Hall and Edwards 1999).

Other issue-specific employee representation mechanisms followed. The ECJ ruling led to the introduction of health and safety regulations in 1996 which required employers to consult employees who were not covered by union-appointed safety representatives, but gave them the discretion to consult employees directly or through elected representatives (James and Walters 1997). The Working Time Regulations 1998 made provision for the (voluntary) conclusion of 'workforce agreements' regulating working time issues with elected employee representatives in respect of groups of employees not covered by collective bargaining (Hall *et al.* 1998), and the concept of workforce agreements also featured in the Maternity and Parental Leave Regulations 1999 as a vehicle for company-specific parental leave arrangements differing from the legislation's model scheme. The capacity of unorganized workers effectively to negotiate such agreements, however, has to be questioned and in practice they are rare.

More general and systematic information and consultation obligations were contained in further EU directives but applied on a transnational basis within companies operating in more than one EU country (see Hyman, this volume). The European Works Councils (EWCs) Directive was eventually transposed into UK law in 1999 as a consequence of the reversal of the UK's social policy opt-out, followed by the implementation of the Employee Involvement Directive linked to the European Company Statute in 2004.

However, from a domestic point of view, potentially the most far-reaching EU legislation in this area was the 2002 Information and Consultation Directive, resulting in the ICE Regulations. These established for the first time in the UK a general statutory framework giving employees the right to be informed and consulted by their employers on a range of key business, employment and restructuring issues. The legislation allowed employers considerable flexibility of response, both procedurally and substantively. Under the Regulations, employers need not act unless 10% of their employees trigger statutory procedures intended to lead to negotiated agreements. Moreover, voluntary, 'pre-existing agreements' (PEAs) may effectively pre-empt the use of the Regulations' procedures. Under either route there is considerable latitude to agree enterprise-specific information and consultation arrangements. Only in the event that the Regulations' procedures are triggered but no agreement is reached are 'standard' or default information and consultation provisions enforceable (see Terry, this volume for further discussion).

Significantly, under these default requirements (like those of the earlier EWCs regulations), information and consultation representatives must be elected by employees in a ballot, irrespective of any existing trade union structures within the undertaking. While this represented a notable departure from the 'union priority' (Davies and Freedland 2007: 147) or 'supplemented single channel' approach of the 1999 legislation, there was strong employer pressure – and a government preference – for the principle of all-employee ballots and for keeping consultation arrangements structurally separate from trade union recognition and collective bargaining in the Regulations' prescriptive or default provisions.

Impact of the recognition and ICE procedures

The statutory trade union recognition procedure which began operation in 2000 helped produce a significant growth in union recognition agreements both in anticipation of its enactment and subsequently. Gall (2004a) reported 2331 recognition agreements since 1995, covering 725 787 workers, and a reduction in the extent of 'de-recognition'. As of September 2008 the CAC had received 680 applications. Researchers concur that the direct effect of the law in terms of recognition achieved through use of the legislation has been less important than the 'shadow of law' and symbolic effect. The changed context has encouraged voluntary (and pre-emptive) agreements and change in (some) employers' attitudes to trade unions. Other factors have also been at work, including an increased union emphasis on organizing, the preparedness of some unions to enter into particular 'partnership' arrangements and, possibly, some employer recognition of efficiency benefits in recognizing unions to provide effective collective voice, possibly enhanced in the context of ICE requirements. Surveys of union officials indicate that union campaigns have met with positive responses from employers more than adversarial or oppositional responses (Heery and Simms 2005; see also Gall 2004b).

Nevertheless, the overall decline in the level of union recognition has continued (see Simms and Charlwood, this volume). WERS 2004 showed 27% of workplaces (accounting for 48% of employees) recognized trade unions for the purposes of negotiating pay and conditions for at least some of their workforce, compared with 33% (covering 53% of employees) in 1998. However, most of the decline since 1998 occurred amongst smaller workplaces (employing fewer than 25); the incidence of recognition in workplaces with 25 or more employees remained broadly stable (39% in 2004 compared to 41% in 1998).

In terms of workers covered, in-filling (building on areas of traditional union presence) and close expansion have been more prevalent than expansion into new areas. Bargaining units have been relatively small in statutory recognition claims and union campaigns (CAC 2008: 7; Moore et al. 2005).

In terms of the quality of resultant union–management relationships where recognition is agreed or awarded, findings so far (e.g. Moore et al. 2002, 2005) present a mixed picture as to whether the existence of statutory recognition has led to adversarial or cooperative employment relations, with no single dominant approach or outcome. The evidence suggests that, particularly outside manual and craft areas, a weak form of recognition may result (at least initially), with failure to conclude collective agreements in some cases. However, in the majority of cases where the law has been used to help achieve recognition, bargaining relationships have been established in that negotiations have taken place since recognition.

Statutory intervention has encouraged the formalization of recognition and collective agreements (now more often in writing) but research indicates that the content of agreements is fairly limited in breadth and depth. For example, one in five new voluntary agreements analysed by Moore *et al.* (2005) limited the scope to 'pay, hours and holidays' (the scope of statutory recognition) and where equal opportunities, training or pensions were mentioned in agreements it is more often in the context of specifically excluding these topics. Collective agreements in the UK, however, traditionally rest more on procedural than substantive content, and the effect of recognition on employee–employer relations may be felt through the provision and impact of employee voice and not simply in relation to substantive outcomes of negotiations on terms and conditions.

To date, there has been little systematic evidence on how employers, employees and trade unions have responded to the ICE Regulations. Prior to their commencement in 2005, it was suggested that their main impact was likely to be 'legislatively-prompted voluntarism' (Hall and Terry 2004: 226), with the new legislation driving the diffusion of organization-specific information and consultation arrangements. The findings of WERS 2004 showed that the prospect of the ICE Regulations had not resulted in an upturn in the proportion of workplaces covered by joint consultative committees; on the contrary, the previous downward trend had continued (Kersley *et al.* 2006). Subsequently, however, a number of smaller surveys suggested that the Regulations had prompted increases in the incidence of formal consultation arrangements (CBI 2006) and modifications to existing arrangements (IRS 2006; LRD 2006), particularly in the UK operations of multinational companies (Marginson *et al.* forthcoming).

Other research also suggested considerable employer-led activity in terms of reviewing, modifying and introducing information and consultation arrangements (Hall 2006), but currently no data are available of the incidence of 'pre-existing agreements' or 'negotiated agreements' as defined by the Regulations. An assessment one year after the commencement of the Regulations noted that relatively few companies were reported to have put formal PEAs in place, despite the protection they offer against the Regulations' statutory procedures being invoked by employees, and that negotiated agreements appeared to be extremely rare (Hall 2006). Trade unions generally have adopted a defensive approach to the Regulations, reflecting concern that the introduction of workforce-wide information and consultation arrangements could potentially undermine or marginalize union recognition where it exists. While little litigation has arisen under the Regulations, the leading case, *Amicus and Macmillan Publishers Ltd* (UKEAT/0185/07/RN) demonstrates the scope for employees and unions to use the law effectively against defaulting employers.

The legal regulation of industrial disputes

The freedom to take industrial action has traditionally been seen as offering the prospect of some kind of countervailing social power for employees via effective trade unionism, recognizing the disparity between the bargaining position of individual employees and that of their employer. In Britain, there is no *right* to strike as such and industrial action is always in breach of the individual contract of employment. The freedom to take industrial action has been conferred by granting trade unions, their officials and representatives statutory protections or 'immunities' from common law liabilities which would otherwise make their action unlawful. Without these, the organizers of industrial action would be liable for civil wrongs (torts), including that of inducing breach of employment contracts, and would thus be exposed to court injunctions (orders) and claims for damages. The system of immunities was developed in the late 19th and early 20th century, culminating in the Trade Disputes Act 1906, and remains the cornerstone of the contemporary statutory framework for industrial action.

One problem with relying on immunities is that their effectiveness has at various points been undermined by the development by the courts of new common law liabilities that outflanked the scope of the existing statutory protections. Amending legislation has been required (for example, in the 1960s and 1970s) to widen the scope of the statutory immunities in response to judicial creativity. Moreover, despite the immunities being the functional equivalent of the positive right to strike enjoyed by workers in other countries, their legal form enabled politicians and commentators on the political right increasingly to characterize them as 'unique privileges' which put trade unions 'above the law – terminology designed to create an impression of unwarranted legal status' (Fredman 1992: 26). Such arguments accompanied successive changes to the law introduced by the Conservative governments of the 1980s and 1990s to narrow the scope and application of the immunities and thus tighten the legal restrictions on industrial action. By the end of the period of Conservative government in 1997 the freedom to strike still existed in the UK but 'a host of cumulative, interlocked limitations ensure[d] it [was] more circumscribed than at any time since 1906' (McIlroy 1999: 523) and it has been adjudged to fall below the minimum international standards (e.g. Deakin and Morris 2005: 1087).

The current position can be summarized as follows. Trade unions organizing industrial action have immunity from liability for inducing or threatening to induce breach of a contract or interference with its performance where they are acting 'in contemplation or furtherance of a trade dispute'. This is defined as a dispute between workers and their own employer which relates wholly or mainly to a range of issues including their pay and conditions, dismissal, allocation of work, discipline, negotiating rights and machinery, etc. The restrictive definition of a trade dispute sits uneasily with the increasing complex structures of employing organizations: it may be problematic, for example, where workers are employed through an intermediary company. There is no protection for solidarity action (that taken on behalf of other workers) or that taken predominantly for 'political' ends. Particular problems may arise here for public service workers who may wish to protest about government policies, for example on privatization, which will affect their terms and conditions of employment. Immunity for unions is dependent on gaining majority support in a postal ballot of the members concerned and giving due notice to an employer about the ballot and commencement of industrial action. The legal requirements concerning industrial action ballots were simplified somewhat in 2005 but there are still significant procedural hurdles (Gall 2006). Government codes of practice on picketing and balloting procedures contain further 'practical guidance' which can be – and on occasion has been – taken into account in relevant court proceedings (Davies and Freedland 1993: 461). However, certain provisions of the codes are more restrictive than the legislation they purport to amplify, e.g. limiting the number of pickets to six. This is widely thought to be a statutory requirement but in fact is guidance in the code of practice on picketing.

It is open to employers or any party to a contract broken or interfered with by unlawful industrial action to take legal action against the union or individual organizers concerned. The range of potential litigants in cases of unlawful industrial action was widened in the late 1980s and the early 1990s to include union members and citizens deprived of goods and services. Legal action normally takes the form of seeking an injunction (court order) requiring named organizations and individuals to cease organizing unlawful industrial action. Unions are liable for unlawful action they have authorized or endorsed, including unofficial action if not 'repudiated'. Non-compliance with an injunction is a contempt of court and could lead to the imposition of fines and the sequestration of union assets. An injunction is technically an interim measure prior to the full trial of an action for damages, but normally the employer's aim is to stop industrial action rather than obtain damages.

The 1997 Labour government reduced the scope for the lawful dismissal of employees involved in industrial action. The Employment Relations Act 1999 made it unfair to dismiss an employee for taking part in lawfully organized industrial action unless the action lasted for more than eight weeks and the employer had taken reasonable procedural steps to resolve the dispute. This protection was extended to 12 weeks in 2005. It remains unfair to dismiss some of those taking lawful industrial action but not others at the same establishment, though selective re-engagement is permitted after three months. Since 1990, those dismissed in the course of unofficial industrial action may not claim unfair dismissal.

The effects of the restrictive legal framework for industrial action established by the Conservative governments were seen in a number of developments. During the 1980s, particularly after the law exposed unions to damages claims for unlawful industrial action and made strike ballots a legal requirement, a rise in the level of legal action by employers against unions was observed, though this appears to have been temporary, declining as unions learnt to live with the new legal constraints. Although legal action by employers had a profound impact in several key disputes during the 1980s in terms of weakening the position of the unions involved (Dickens and Hall 1995: 283; McIlroy 1999), litigation during disputes remains exceptional.

The legal changes prompted the overhaul of union procedures for handling industrial action. Unions tended to become more cautious in the tactics they adopted during disputes and to strengthen central union control over how and when industrial action was called and who should be empowered to authorize it. In particular, the use of strike ballots rapidly became the norm. In terms of the implications for collective bargaining, it was widely perceived that the use of ballots often helped strengthen the union's negotiating position (Elgar and Simpson 1993). The outcome of the great majority of strike ballots is a vote in favour of industrial action, but in most cases this leads to the settlement of the dispute without a strike occurring (Hale 2007), suggesting that, where they are confident of securing support, unions may treat balloting as part of the negotiation process.

The scope for lawful industrial action was considerably restricted by the legislation introduced over the 1980s and 1990s. The extent to which this has been a factor in the recent, historically low levels of industrial action in the UK, however, is difficult to assess. Some econometric studies suggested a correlation between restrictive legislation and a fall in the level of industrial action (Dunn and Metcalf 1996: 86–87). But other social, economic and political factors are clearly likely to have been influential. The safest conclusion is that the legal changes were part of a much wider range of developments affecting strike activity. It is unlikely that the specific legal reforms had a direct effect on the number of strikes, but they certainly symbolized a determination to act against what was perceived as the inappropriate use of industrial power, and the numerous legal restrictions made the use of industrial action a more considered move than it had been in the 1970s.

The legal regulation of internal union affairs

A key element of the traditional voluntarist framework of British industrial relations was the limited statutory regulation of internal trade union affairs. In Kahn-Freund's words (1983: 274), it had, 'on the whole, been common ground that in [the] dilemma between imposing standards of democracy and protecting union autonomy the law must come down on the side of autonomy'. With the exception of statutory requirements governing the administration of unions' political funds and union amalgamations, unions were generally free to devise their own rules and procedures without statutory regulation (although at times the common law intruded, as in the miners' strike in 1984–85). The position, however, was altered radically by the Conservative governments of the 1980s and 1990s through a series of measures regulating unions' internal affairs which reflected a highly individualistic conception of the rights and obligations associated with trade union membership (McKendrick 1988: 141). The main focus of these was to require the use of secret ballots by unions in internal elections and before taking industrial action. The stated rationales for this policy concerned both its internal and external impacts (Auerbach 1990: 118). The basic internal justification for intervention was to make unions more democratic and responsive to the wishes of their members. This in turn was expected to have important external effects: more representative (and, implicit in the Conservatives' analysis, more moderate) union leaderships and the use of strike ballots were expected to help restrain industrial action.

Unions are required to hold five-yearly ballots for election of union executive committees, presidents and general secretaries. As already noted above, industrial action not preceded by an independently scrutinized postal ballot is unlawful, and union members have the statutory right to seek court orders to restrain non-balloted industrial action. Unions' political funds, which are necessary to finance party-political affiliation and political campaigning activities, are subject to ten-yearly review ballots. Although trade unions opposed the introduction of this legislation, the balloting practices it required became accepted as a fact of union life. The electoral systems of many unions were transformed by the legal requirements, but in few cases did this result in significant change in the political complexion of the union leadership. Similarly, against initial expectations, union political funds have in every case been maintained.

The law also provides individual union members with a range of statutory rights enforceable against their union, amongst them the right not to be unjustifiably disciplined, including for refusing to take part in industrial action. The Conservative government appointed a public official in 1988 to assist union members in legal action against their unions. Little use was made of this institution and it was abolished by the Labour government in 1999 with its main responsibilities being subsumed into the remit of the Certification Officer who has a range of administrative and regulatory functions relating to trade unions (Cockburn 2006).

Conclusion: The Demise of Voluntarism

From the 1960s onwards, and particularly since the end of the 1970s, British employment law has undergone rapid and far-reaching changes. Although differing legal strategies have been pursued by Labour and Conservative governments, both have furthered the trend towards the legal regulation of industrial relations and the 'juridification' of the employment relationship, whereby management policy is increasingly shaped by law, and legal norms and values permeate industrial relations practice.

It is not simply a question of there being 'more law'. The nature and scope of legal regulation has also shifted decisively, going to the heart of the employment relationship. At the time of the 1997 election, central elements of British industrial relations still remained largely outside the scope of statutory regulation. Key elements of Labour's employment law programme – principally, the legislation introduced on the NMW, working time, trade union recognition and information and consultation – not only represented a marked change in policy from that of its Conservative predecessors but also extended legal regulation into areas of the employment relationship which previously had been largely a matter for voluntary determination. It is now possible to argue that 'British labour law has reached the stage where it can be said that we now have a comprehensive labour code', albeit one concerned primarily with minimum standards (Ewing 2003:150).

Voluntarism is dead. Primacy is no longer afforded to regulation through collective bargaining, supported by public policy. Protection at work relies increasingly on legal rights not collective organization. Legal regulation of employment relations now plays a central role within the context of considerably weakened collective regulation.

This process has been accompanied by growing expressions of concern on the part of employers' groups over the volume and cumulative administrative impact on businesses of employment regulation, even if key (domestically driven) measures such as the NMW and the right to request flexible working have in practice met with considerable employer acceptance. Trade unions too, while continuing to advocate more robust legal protections for employees, have increasingly voiced resentment at Labour's retention of the Conservative legislation restricting industrial action and regulating internal union procedures. Amongst the aims of the (unsuccessful) union-sponsored Trade Union Freedom Bill is to 'reduce regulatory burdens, which frustrate the ability of unions to give effect to their members' democratic wishes and to act in their members' interests' (TUC 2008: 15).

In view of employer opposition or scepticism towards key elements of the post-1997 legislative agenda – and despite the absence of a tradition of 'social partnership' in the UK – the government has on a range of issues gone beyond its standard public consultation procedures and directly involved employer and union representatives in the formulation of legislative proposals. Employer and union representation on commissions and task forces or agreements with or between the CBI and TUC have been used to produce what are considered to be workable (or at least acceptable) outcomes on issues such as the statutory union recognition procedure, NMW, right to request flexible working and the ICE Regulations. Ministers have also shown considerable responsiveness to employer lobbying in the framing of legislation, as well as in specific deregulatory moves (such as amendments to the Working Time Regulations to reduce the record-keeping requirements on employers). More generally, the government has made repeated commitments to 'better regulation' and to reducing the complexity and compliance costs for businesses of employment legislation.

Relatedly, and notwithstanding the overall trend towards the juridification of employment relations, the post-1997 Labour governments have pursued what Davies and Freedland (2007: 241) have labelled a 'light regulation' approach, involving a range of techniques of labour market regulation that enable the flexible application statutory rights. Such an approach not only reflects the New Labour policy of fairness *and* flexibility but is also intended to play well with the employers' lobby. It involves, for example, building into legislation the scope for agreed outcomes that may depart from statutory standards, or relying on employees to trigger or request the implementation of their rights. Arguably, such an approach is consistent with the notion of 'reflexive' employment law whereby 'the preferred mode of intervention is for the law to underpin and encourage autonomous processes of adjustment' by the parties to the employment relationship (Barnard and Deakin 2000: 341). The ICE Regulations are a prime example: employers need take no action unless employees trigger statutory procedures, and the Regulations encourage organization-specific outcomes while specifying (minimalist) 'default' information and consultation arrangements as a fallback. The legislation giving working parents and carers 'the right to request' flexible working represents the most 'business-friendly' variant of Labour's light regulation approach, in which the granting of flexible working is entirely contingent on whether the desired working pattern can be accommodated within the needs of the business, as assessed by the employer.

A theme in this chapter has been the extent to which successive governments' employment legislation has been shaped by EU requirements. The 1997 Labour government's symbolic reversal of the UK 'opt-out' from the social chapter of the Maastricht treaty meant that the UK became subject to the parental leave and EWCs Directives and was party to the negotiation of subsequent EU social policy measures including the directives on part-time and fixed-term work and information and consultation. It did not imply, however, that the new Labour government wholeheartedly embraced the evolving EU social policy agenda. It initially opposed the adoption of the directive on information and consultation (on the grounds of protecting the UK 'voluntarism' in this area), as well as those on agency workers and the revision of the Working Time Directive (on the grounds of protecting labour market flexibility). But the logic of majority voting within the EU council of ministers resulted in each case in the UK ultimately having to accept these directives – albeit having negotiated significant concessions – with direct consequences for the UK's domestic employment law agenda. At the same time, the nature of the current generation of EU directives, providing minimum standards and the scope for agreed derogations, has influenced and facilitated New Labour's 'light regulation' techniques. Nevertheless, in 2007, under pressure from employers' groups, the Labour government sought and secured its own opt-out – this time from the legal enforceability given to the Charter of Fundamental Rights under the Lisbon treaty. With employment law principally in mind, the aim of the opt-out was to ensure that the charter cannot be used to challenge current UK legislation in the courts or to introduce new rights in UK law.

For its part, the Conservative Party has produced proposals for an aggressive approach to deregulation which, in the absence of extensive deregulation at EU level, would involve seeking further UK opt-outs from 'all [EU] employment and social regulation', including extricating the UK from existing directives (see Hall 2007). Both the TUC and, more circumspectly, the CBI have questioned the practicality of this and it remains to be seen whether the party leadership commits itself to such a policy. It remains likely that regulation emanating from the EU, which has been such a major contributor to the growing juridification of UK employment relations, will continue to be a significant influence on the UK legal framework in the future.

References

Anderman, S. 1986: Unfair dismissals and redundancy. In Lewis, R. (ed.) *Labour Law in Britain*. Oxford: Blackwell.

Auerbach, S. 1990: *Legislating for Conflict*. Oxford: Clarendon Press.

Barnard, C. and Deakin, S. 2000: In search of coherence: social policy, the single market and fundamental rights. *Industrial Relations Journal*, 31 (4), 331–345.

Barnard, C., Deakin, S. and Hobbs, R. 2003a: Fog in the channel, continent isolated: Britain as a model for EU social and economic policy? *Industrial Relations Journal*, 34 (5), 461–476.

Barnard, C., Deakin, S. and Hobbs, R. 2003b: Opting out of the 48-hour week: employer necessity or individual choice? *Industrial Law Journal*, 32 (4), 223–252.

CAC 2008: *Central Arbitration Committee Annual Report 2007–08*. London: CAC.

CBI 2006: Employment Trends Survey, London, CBI.

CBI 2007: Employment Trends Survey, London, CBI.

Cockburn, D. 2006: The Certification Officer. In Dickens, L. and Neal, A. (eds) *The Changing Institutional Face of British Employment Relations*. Kluwer Law International.

Davies, P. and Freedland, M. 1984: *Labour Law: Text and Materials*. 2nd edition. London: Weidenfeld and Nicolson.

Davies, P. and Freedland, M. 1993: *Labour Legislation and Public Policy*. Oxford: Clarendon Press.

Davies, P. and Freedland, M. 2007: *Towards a Flexible Labour Market: Labour Legislation and Regulation since the 1990s*. Oxford: Oxford University Press.

DE (Department of Employment) 1989: *Removing Barriers to Employment*. London: HMSO.

Deakin, S. 1990: Equality under a market order: the Employment Act 1989. *Industrial Law Journal*, 19 (1), 1–19.

Deakin, S. and Morris, G. 2005: *Labour Law*. 4th edition. Oxford: Hart Publishing.

Dickens, L. 1994: Deregulation and employment rights in Great Britain. In Rogowski, R. and Wilthagen, T. (eds) *Reflexive Labour Law*. Deventer: Kluwer.

Dickens, L. 2006: Equality and work-life balance: what's happening at the workplace? *Industrial Law Journal*, 35, 445–449.

Dickens, L. 2007: The road is long. Thirty years of equality legislation in Britain. *British Journal of Industrial Relations*, 45, 463–494.

Dickens, L. and Hall, M. 1995: The state, labour law and industrial relations. In Edwards, P. (ed.) *Industrial Relations: Theory and Practice in Britain*. Oxford: Blackwell.

Dickens, L. and Hall, M. 2006: Fairness – up to a point. Assessing the impact of New Labour's employment legislation. *Human Resource Management Journal*, 16, 338–356.

Dickens, R. and Manning, A. 2003: Minimum wage, minimum impact. In Dickens, R. *et al.* (eds) *The Labour Market under New Labour*. Basingstoke: Palgrave.

DTI (Department of Trade and Industry) 1998: *Fairness at Work*. Cm 2968. London: HMSO.

DTI 2000: Press release.

Dunn, S. and Metcalf, D. 1996: Trade union law since 1979. In Beardwell, I. (ed.) *Contemporary Industrial Relations*. Oxford: Oxford University Press.

Elgar, J. and Simpson, B. 1993: *Union Negotiators, Industrial Action and the Law*. Mimeo. London School of Economics.

Ewing, K. 2003: Labour law and industrial relations. In Ackers, P. and Wilkinson, A. (eds) *Understanding Work and Employment*. Oxford: OUP.

Fredman, S. 1992: The new right: labour law and ideology in the Thatcher years. *Oxford Journal of Legal Studies*, 12 (1), 24–44.

Gall, G. 2004a: Trade union recognition in Britain, 1995–2002: turning a corner? *Industrial Relations Journal*, 35 (3), 249–270.

Gall, G. 2004b: British employer resistance to trade union recognition. *Human Resource Management Journal*, 14 (2), 36–54.

Gall, G. 2006: Research note: injunctions as a legal weapon in industrial disputes in Britain, 1995–2005. *British Journal of Industrial Relations*, 44, 327–349.

Hale, D. 2007: Labour disputes in 2006. *Economic and Labour Market Review*, 1 (6), 25–36.

Hall, M. 1994: Industrial relations and the social dimension of European integration: before and after Maastricht. In Hyman, R. and Ferner, A. (eds) *New Frontiers in European Industrial Relations*. Oxford: Blackwell.

Hall, M. 2006: A cool response to the ICE Regulations? Employer and trade union approaches to the new legal framework for information and consultation. *Industrial Relations Journal*, 37, 456–472.

Hall, M. 2007: Unions criticise opposition party's deregulation proposals. *European Industrial Relations Observatory*.http://www.eurofound.europa.eu/eiro/2007/09/articles/uk0709019i.htm

Hall, M. and Edwards, P. 1999: Reforming the statutory redundancy consultation procedure. *Industrial Law Journal*, 28 (4), 299–319.

Hall, M. and Sisson, K. 1997: *Time for Change? Coming to Terms with the EU Working Time Directive*. London and Coventry: IRS and IRRU.

Hall, M. and Terry, M. 2004: The emerging system of statutory worker representation. In Healy, G., Heery, E., Taylor, P. and Brown, W. (eds) *The Future of Worker Representation*. Basingstoke: Palgrave Macmillan.

Hall, M., Lister R. and Sisson, K. 1998: *The New Law on Working Time: Managing the Implications of the 1998 Working Time Regulations*. London and Coventry: IRS and IRRU.

Heery, E. and Simms, M. 2005: Union organising under certification law in the United Kingdom. In Gall, G. (ed.) *Union Recognition: Organising and Bargaining Outcomes*. London: Routledge.

Hepple, B. 2000: Supporting collective bargaining: some comparative reflections. In Towers, B. and Brown, W. (eds) *Employment Relations in Britain. 25 Years of the Advisory Conciliation and Arbitration Service*. Oxford: Blackwell.

Industrial Relations Services (IRS) 2006: A two-way process: informing and consulting employees. *IRS Employment Review*, 859, 8–15.

James, P. and Walters, D. 1997: Non-union rights of involvement: the case of health and safety at work. *Industrial Law Journal*, 26 (1), 35–50.

Kahn-Freund, O. 1954: Legal framework. In Flanders, A. and Clegg, H.A. (eds) *The System of Industrial Relations in Great Britain*. Oxford: Blackwell.

Kahn-Freund, O. 1983: *Labour and the Law*. 3rd edition (Davies, P.L. and Freedland, M. (eds)). London: Stevens.

Kersley, B., Alpin, C., Forth, J., Bryson, A., Bewley, H., Dix, G. and Oxenbridge, S. 2006: *Inside the Workplace: First Findings from the 2004 Workplace Employment Relations Survey*. London: Routledge.

Low Pay Commission 1998: *First Report of the Low Pay Commission*. London: HMSO.

Low Pay Commission 2003: *The National Minimum Wage: Building on Success*. London: HMSO.

Labour Research Department (LRD) 2006: Information and consultation regulations make their mark. *Workplace Report*, 35, 15–17.

Marginson. P., Edwards, P., Edwards, T., Ferner, A. and Tregaskis, O. 2010: Employee representation and consultative voice in multinational companies operating in Britain. *British Journal of Industrial Relations*, forthcoming.

McIlroy, J. 1999: Unfinished business: the reform of strike legislation in Britain. *Employee Relations*, 21 (6), 521–539.

McKendrick, E. 1988: The rights of trade union members: Part 1 of the Employment Act 1988. *Industrial Law Journal*, 17 (3), 141–161.

Moore, S., McKay, S. and Bewley, H. 2002: *The Content of New Voluntary Trade Union Recognition Agreements 1998–2002: Volume One – An Analysis of New Agreements and Case Studies*. Employment Relations Research Series, No. 26. London: DTI.

Moore, S., McKay, S. and Bewley, H. 2005: *The Content of New Voluntary Trade Union Recognition Agreements 1998–2002. Volume Two – Findings from the Survey of Employers*. Employment Relations Research Series, No. 43. London: DTI.

Oxenbridge S., Brown W., Deakin, S. and Pratten, C. 2003: Initial responses to the statutory recognition provisions of the Employment Relations Act 1999. *British Journal of Industrial Relations*, 41 (2), 315–334.

Pollert, A. 2005: The unorganised worker: the decline in collectivism and new hurdles to individual employment rights. *Industrial Law Journal*, 34 (3), 217–238.

Royal Commission on Trade Unions and Employers' Associations 1968: Report. Cmnd 3623. London: HMSO.

Simpson, B. 1998: Fairness at work. *Industrial Law Journal*, 27 (3), 245–253.

Simpson, B. 1999: Implementing the national minimum wage: the 1999 Regulations. *Industrial Law Journal*, 28 (2), 171–182.

Trades Union Congress (TUC) 2008: *General Council Report to Congress 2008*. http://www.tuc.org.uk/congress/tuc-15225-f0.pdf

Wedderburn, K.W. (Lord) 1998: A British duty to bargain: a footnote on the end-game. *Industrial Law Journal*, 27 (3), 253.

Weekes, B., Mellish, M., Dickens, L. and Lloyd, J. 1975: *Industrial Relations and the Limits of Law*. Oxford: Blackwell.

Wood, S. and Godard, J. 1999: The statutory union recognition procedure in the employment relations bill: a comparative analysis. *British Journal of Industrial Relations*, 37 (2), 203–244.

14

LEGAL INSTITUTIONS AND THE REGULATION OF WORKPLACES

TREVOR COLLING

Introduction

The principal objective of this chapter is to explore questions about the relationship between law and the behaviour of actors within the employment relationship. These are important in a context where the nature of employment regulation is changing. Just two decades ago collective bargaining between unions and employers determined the formal terms and conditions of employment for nearly three quarters of the workforce in Britain (see Brown, this volume) and the law played an auxiliary and relatively marginal role. The preceding chapter (Dickens and Hall, this volume) outlined the recent growth of statutory intervention in the employment relationship and the variety of mechanisms through which legal standards are enforced, much of this process being driven by policy making at European level (Hyman, this volume). In the context of declining coverage of collective bargaining and workplace representation (Brown; Terry, this volume), these legal institutions have assumed much more prominent roles in the regulation of employment than has been the case previously. Evidence discussed below suggests that, while important change is apparent, these coinciding processes have not delivered clear improvements in workplace justice and, as Edwards has noted (2007: 10), 'there is remarkably little by way of sustained public discussion as to how to improve this situation'.

In this chapter, problems are located in the structure of the law and the nature of legal institutions in Britain. A broad definition of legal institutions is used, 'as systems of rules that provide frameworks for social action within larger rule-governed settings' (Ruiter 1997: 358). This offers scope to consider the operation of legal rules alongside those emanating from other important sources, such as collective bargaining. The central argument is that all legal systems are vulnerable to failures in legal standards, because actors do not understand the law or find space beyond its reach to avoid its requirements. In *liberal market economies*, like the UK, this space is preserved by the principal role in economic coordination afforded to markets and market rationales (see Hall and Soskice 2001: 8). Legal institutions in such circumstances prioritize the discretion of contracting parties to form bargains subject to the circumstances they face, including employers and their workers. Such regulatory principles and institutions might therefore be described as porous. While permitting valuable flexibility, they also create complexity in legal provision and uncertainty in enforcement.

This argument proceeds through four main sections. First, the growth of legal regulation and its effectiveness is reviewed, highlighting evidence that increasingly dense legislative structures have not created directly compliant behaviour in workplaces. Literature from the sociology of law is drawn upon to highlight circumstances in which conformity is more or less likely. This line of analysis is applied to legal institutions in the second section, which considers the properties of differently constituted systems, those based predominantly on common and civil law, respectively. These are linked to models of *liberal* and *coordinated market economies*, raising the argument about the porosity of the former. This discussion helps to isolate three factors influencing the effectiveness of legal regulation which are then applied to Britain in the penultimate section. Here it is argued that fragmented law making and enforcement and the weak articulation of social and legal regulation limit the reach of the law, providing gaps in coverage and compliance. Finally, the conclusions argue that greater attention should be paid to ensuring that rights are easily understandable and enforceable by a broader range of employment relations actors than is possible presently.

The Growth and Impact of Legal Regulation

Recent years have witnessed significant growth in the reach of 'Law's Empire' (Hillyard 2007: 273–274). The legislative programmes of recent governments have been increasingly dense; in just ten years between 1997 and 2007 over 400 Acts of Parliament containing over 23 000 sections were introduced, along with approximately 32 000 Statutory Instruments. In the employment sphere, these trends are apparent cross-nationally, particularly in so-called *liberal market economies* such as the USA and Britain, where they have been strongly associated with declining collective bargaining. Colvin notes (2006: 74), 'at the same time as organized labour's strength has weakened, legal protections of individual employment rights have been expanded in many countries', while Piore and Safford (2006: 300) identify the development in the USA of, 'a regime of substantive employment rights specified in law, judicial opinions, and administrative rulings'. This section explores the effectiveness of legal regulation in ensuring basic standards of fairness in Britain's workplaces.

Several new rights have been introduced in Britain with explicitly stated objectives of delivering changes in workplace culture, for example by ensuring fairness, improving work–life balance, and promoting high-performance workplaces. Government commissioned reviews have provided pictures of good jobs, growing real wages and employment security and identify 'successful labour market policies' as key contributory factors (Fitzner 2005: 9). The significance of the shift towards a set of minimum employment standards specified in statute is not in doubt, and it is equally certain that this has fundamentally altered the context in which employment relations develop (see Grimshaw and Rubery, this volume). Yet many observers remain sceptical about the potential to achieve significant workplace change through legal regulation. In an important series of essays published by the Work Foundation, Coats (2005; and with Lekhi 2008) and Edwards (2007) share a cautious approach towards the impact of law: 'A mix of regulatory and non-regulatory interventions will be required, *simply because it is not possible to legislate for high quality employment or high trust workplace relationships*' (Coats and Lekhi 2008: 8, emphasis added).

Certainly, trust in management is not universal at present: only around half the workforce is prepared to say that managers always keep their promises (Kaur 2003: 23). A similar proportion (42%) report experiencing problems at work (Casebourne *et al.* 2006: 98), while 1.6 million workers (7% of the workforce) report discrimination against them on grounds of age, race, sex, etc. (Grainger and Fitzner 2007: 8). The most common problems, affecting 22% of all respondents, were associated with pay. Others indicated difficulties ensuring even the simpler elements of statutory employment rights, particularly those 'associated with receiving a contract or written statement of the terms and conditions of the job; taking rest breaks at work; and the number of hours or days required to work; all of which were reported by 13 per cent of all respondents' (Casebourne *et al.* 2006: 5). Significantly, the evidence suggests that problems are part of the common fabric of some employment relationships, rather than isolated incidents. Those reporting problems indicated an average of 2.8 different issues in the previous five years (ibid.). Some groups are markedly more likely than average to face difficulties. The majority (60%) of 16–24 year olds had experienced a problem at work. Incidence was reportedly 22% higher in the private sector and problems appear particularly entrenched in parts of the service sector (see Pollert 2009 for discussion of critical cases).

If this suggests difficulties in ensuring *substantive* employment standards, that the outcome required by law is not materializing, there is evidence also of variation in the use of *procedures* required by law. It is widely acknowledged, for example, that growing legal requirements in relation to discipline and dismissal have prompted the growth of formally expressed workplace procedures (see Dickens and Hall, this volume). Recent findings (Kersley *et al.* 2006: 216–220) that 88% of workplaces have a grievance procedure of some sort is not surprising, but significantly these did not all comply with the three stages encouraged at the time by codes of practice. Nearly half did not always require the employee to put the grievance in writing, one quarter did not necessarily require a formal meeting to discuss the grievance and a small number (3%) did not explicitly provide an appeal stage. Overall, only 43% of workplaces reported that all three of these stages were always used.

Should we be surprised to find that significant numbers of workers receive treatment that falls short of statutory employment standards? Two reasons may be advanced as to why we should. First, in democratic societies, rule making through the law is designed to command legitimacy and compliance, and involves input from elected representatives to this end. Second, surely economic actors will agree to be bound by established sets of rules, since they provide a basis for predictability in social relations.

A brief acquaintance with the sociology of law provides correctives to such mechanistic conceptualization, since the critical central lesson is that the enactment of particular legislation does not lead straightforwardly to altered behaviour.

> What an institution proscribes is not just translated into identical behaviour by the actor, be it by socialisation, respect for authority or what not. What the actor does, on the other hand, is to *orient* his or her behaviour to an institution: this is something quite different from mechanically following what the rules lay down. The actor may not know what the rules say; he or she may misunderstand them; or he or she may decide not to follow the law. (Swedberg 2004: 76)

Where the law conspicuously serves the interests of one group over another, for example, it is unlikely to secure universal observance, or to do so for very long at any rate. The law played a vital, partisan and often brutal role through the process of industrialization in enforcing the development of capitalist relations. As one prominent industrial historian put it, the British working class, 'was not allowed to grow as in a sunny garden, it was forged over a fire by the powerful blows of a hammer' (Pollard in Aherling and Deakin 2007). But the law cannot be always and universally unfair. As E.P. Thompson wrote eloquently,

> If the law is evidently partial and unjust, then it will mask nothing, legitimise nothing, contribute nothing to any class's hegemony. The essential precondition for the effectiveness of law, in its function as ideology, is that it shall display an independence from gross manipulation and shall seem to be just. It cannot seem to be so without upholding its own criteria and logic of equity; indeed, on occasion, by actually being just. (Thompson, E.P. 1975 in Thompson, D. 2001: 436)

This posits the law as a site of tension, an arena in which groups vie to secure their interests by mobilizing through the legislative and litigation processes. It is a dynamic and multidimensional view of the law that goes beyond the elementary conception of a body of systematic constraints imposed mechanically upon actors. Rules may take different forms and be enforced to differing degrees: 'how the law is put into effect is clearly as important as its content' (Cotterrell 1992: 56). Some law is *purposive* and is implemented likewise. The provisions of criminal law relating to assault, battery and homicide are diffused widely, generally understood and policed and prosecuted with determination. Other dimensions of law might have different functions. *Educative legislation* is an attempt to alter perceptions and calculations of legitimacy in the hope that behaviour will gradually begin to change through extra-legal routes. Enforcement mechanisms remain vague or absent until the underlying principles are accepted. These may be developed through *soft law*, such as policy recommendations and *codes of practice*, rather than the formal specification of sanctions but these at least provide levers to affected groups in their attempts to alter behaviour. *Symbolic legislation*, on the other hand, is largely instrumental. That is, there is a need to legislate on a matter, perhaps to satisfy powerful interest groups, but there is no sustained intention that enforcement should make the legislation a reality.

Effective law then cannot and does not function in isolation; compliance depends upon interaction with other institutions, with economic pressures and with prevailing beliefs and ideologies. Influence therefore does not flow inexorably in one direction, from legislators to actors. Actors subject to the law can play decisive roles in its interpretation and can even influence calculations about the form in which legislation is expressed. Table 14.1 sketches a range of possible responses to the development of standards of behaviour and links them with the extent to which legislative requirements mesh with ideological beliefs. In this simple presentation, (+) indicates acceptance of a particular principle in either its ideological or its legislative form and (–) its rejection. In combination these lead to one or other kind of adaptive behaviour. The final behaviour, *rebellion*, indicates circumstances where prevailing legal and ideological beliefs are questioned so intensely as to lead to fundamental change, such as in revolutionary contexts. Focus here will be on the first four behaviours which are more common, from conformity to retreatism.

Conformity with the law can be expected where legislative requirements are more or less congruent with prevailing ideological presumptions. For Merton, this was the normal condition of healthy societies because, 'were this not so, the stability and continuity of the society could not be maintained' (Merton 1938: 677). Important examples of such mutually reinforcing standards come easily to mind. The relatively rare incidence of homicide must be due to some extent to the purposeful prosecution of offences but the fact that the law is shaped and amplified by still more prominent religious and ethical norms surely is the decisive factor. Such moral certainty is not apparent in every aspect of social life, however; principles of justice and fairness in the employment sphere are often contested, reflecting the fundamental tension at the heart of the employment relationship (see Colling and Terry, this volume). Ensuring connections between ideological and legislative mechanisms will turn therefore on the extent to which the law is mediated through social institutions, such as collective bargaining.

Table 14.1   Mapping responses to legislation

	Ideological beliefs	*Legislative requirements*
Conformity	+	+
Innovation	+	–
Ritualism	–	+
Retreatism	–	–
Rebellion	*	*

Adapted from Merton (1938: 676).

Compliance is less likely where these connections between different rule-making systems are weakened or absent. Actors then may move to alter or avoid the rules of the game. *Innovation* in legal systems is likely where legal rules are seen to lag behind changing ideological norms. Thus there may be demands for legislation to govern emerging social concerns, such as equal opportunities in employment (see Dean and Liff, this volume). Conversely, where the law is seen to impose new norms that are out of step with predominant values or pressures, responses are likely to be characterized by *ritualism*: a tendency to comply instrumentally with the formal letter of the law without the action necessary to carry forward its spirit. Where requirements are unsupported by ideological norms or by effective enforcement mechanisms, actors are likely to respond by *retreating*: by avoiding them actively (through explicit opposition) or passively (by simply ignoring them).

The next section develops these analytical themes by thinking about differences between legal systems and their implications for the strategies adopted by economic actors within them, for our purposes employers, workers and unions as their representatives. The central argument is that regulatory systems in *liberal market economies* like the UK provide room for opportunistic behaviour by actors, and by employers in particular.

Varieties of Legal Institutions

Legal scholarship has long recognized structural differences between legal institutions in different national settings, manifest in attempts to identify legal 'families', groups of countries sharing similar approaches to legal regulation and enforcement (Florkowski 2006; Glenn 2006; De Cruz 1999). Families can be collated on different criteria and in varying numbers of groups but these tend often to be collapsed into just two broader groups; those characterized by predominantly civil law approaches and others principally dependent on the common law. There is congruence here with another influential binary model, the literature on *Varieties of Capitalism* (Hall and Soskice 2001). *Coordinated market economies* (including France, Germany, Italy and Spain) tend to have civil law systems while *liberal market economies* (Britain, Australia, USA and New Zealand) rely more upon judge-made common law (see Colling and Terry; Crouch, this volume).

The key distinction between civil and common law systems lies at the root in the systematized and codified nature of the latter, in the underlying 'desire for one common statement of a nation's law in a rational and coherent form, intelligible to the ordinary man (*sic*)' (Stein 1982: 12). That is, these systems are driven by the objectives of providing clear roles and mandates for courts and transparent legal rules for those subject to them. Once established, these broad principles are applied universally and take precedence over the independent wishes of contracting parties. The state plays a prominent and direct role in articulating the law through the development of statute and legal codes but principles of universality are extended by the way that the courts treat extra-legal norms. Collective agreements in many civil law systems operate under *erga omnes* principles, which means that their terms are taken to cover all those in employment within signatory firms, regardless, for example, of trade union membership. This basis for generalization is given legal force by the relatively straightforward integration of collective agreements and legal norms: agreements are often legally enforceable and legal principles, such as the obligation to act in *good faith*, can be inserted into them by the courts.

Consequently, courts play important roles in diffusing general principles into the variety of contractual arrangements that come before them: 'civil law judges have considerable power to shape the terms of contractual relationships through the application of open-ended general clauses, such as the principle of good faith, in ways that have no equivalent in the common law' (Aherling and Deakin 2007). These far-reaching mechanisms come to structure commercial and inter-firm relationships. Deviation from generally applied business conventions is frowned upon with the consequence that, for example, 'German businesses rarely attempt to vary the terms of standard form agreements, and it is doubtful whether they have the power to contract out of many of the obligations of good faith which are implied into commercial agreements as a matter of law' (Deakin and Wilkinson 1997: 156). And it is not just the *substantive* content of the employment contract that is affected in this way; civil law systems reserve considerable *procedural* powers to courts and state agencies. Attempts in France to provide derogations from general principles, and thereby more flexible forms of contracting for particular labour market groups, have been fiercely resisted by and through the courts (Freedland and Kountouris 2008). More generally, social actors find it hard in civil law systems to avoid the jurisdiction of the courts and to deploy alternative approaches such as private arbitration (Finkin 2008).

By contrast, common law systems are not as transparent and the development and application of legal principle is mediated much more by judges. The idea of 'common law' developed in opposition to approaches in the royal and ecclesiastical court systems. It was intended to be flexible and to reflect the concerns of ordinary citizens. Consequently, where civil law is aimed at expressing the authority of the state in clear and consistent terms, common law prioritizes the freedom of social actors to reach contracts of whichever kind they wish: 'in civil law, the tendency is for freedom of contract to be socially conditioned when, in common law systems, it is, formally, unconstrained' (Aherling and Deakin 2007). The state assumes relatively muted roles in establishing legal norms. The theme of homicide, referred to above, provides a possibly startling illustration in the British context. Though the *punishment* of murder is set out in statute, *defining* the offence itself is a matter of common law, established by 'common sense' judge-made principles, developed in case law since the 18th century (Gillespie 2007: 12). Cotterrell (1992: 17) describes these processes colourfully:

> Law grows like coral through the slow accumulation of minutiae over the centuries, the encrustation of precedent. The rational strength of legal doctrine comes not from any systematic overall structure but from the accumulated wisdom of the judges preserved in the thousands of recorded cases which make up this coral kingdom.

It is not that statute law is irrelevant; judges are obliged to apply the formal content of the law and to consider when reaching their decisions the intention of legislators. But such factors will be considered alongside those emerging from extant case precedent which is not inevitably displaced by a wave of the legislator's pen. Critically too, in contractual matters, common law precedent is applied through fragmented and often individualized mechanisms. It is generally more difficult to extend contractual norms from collective bargaining into the employment contract, for example. This can happen where incorporation is expressly permitted in the agreement, or where it might be implied from prevailing custom and practice, but the principle is not automatic and can be contested. In Britain, 'the theory of incorporation of collectively bargained norms is an essentially selective one which ensures that collective bargaining remains as an exogenous source of terms of the contracts of employment rather than as an endogenous component of the contract itself' (Freedland and Kountouris 2008: 61). Since extension of norms and legal principles through the contract of employment is a more qualified process, legal adjudication of disputes tends to be a matter for the individual parties to the contract rather than groups or collective agencies: 'inspired by the belief in the equality (real or fictitious) of individuals; it operates between individuals and not otherwise' (Davies and Freedland in Collins *et al.* 2002: 27).

This affords judges wide discretion in interpreting the law and applying it to particular circumstances, subject to the facts of the case. If the benefit of common law systems is the flexibility they provide and the sensitivity of judgments to specific circumstances, the other side of that coin is unpredictability. Cases with quite similar facts can give rise to opposing judgments as a consequence of argument in the court room and the selection and interpretation of precedent. The relatively opaque nature of the law also provides the possibility that actors will misunderstand regulations or contest their interpretation when challenged. Actors have opportunities to raise wide-ranging arguments in defence of their alleged breach, arguing even that the particular facts of their case justify their actions. As important, decisions arising from litigation are usually applicable only to the applicants in question, with limited possibilities of extending outcomes to other affected groups.

At this stage it is necessary to enter a number of caveats to this broad line of argument. First and foremost, there is no intention to suggest that civil law systems are havens of *conformity* with the law. Even if common law systems provide particularly fertile ground for *ritualism* and *retreatism*, opportunistic behaviour is possible everywhere. Gonzalez Menendez and Almond (2006), for example, explore the development in civil law systems like Spain of parallel spheres of informal employment beyond the relatively closely regulated formal one. While valuing the analytical purchase of these broad comparisons, for the underlying characteristics and dynamics highlighted, it is also important not to reduce complex institutional systems to one binary divide. Just as models from the *Varieties of Capitalism* literature, 'constitute ideal types at the poles of a spectrum along which many nations can be arrayed' (Hall and Soskice 2001: 8), it should be acknowledged that legal institutions develop and interact in complex ways. In national systems that are increasingly integrated internationally, elements of legal principle and reasoning transfer across borders: 'the boundaries of legal tradition are fuzzy [. . .] The information at the heart of every legal tradition will be complemented [. . .] by information from other legal traditions' (Glenn 2006: 425). This is particularly the case within economic regions such as Europe, where reasoning and precedent in British courts are influenced inevitably by the senior European courts (see Hyman, this volume). There are also important differences between systems of similar types, depending upon the formation and expression of the law and the degree to which legal rule making is geared with social structures. For example, Britain and the USA are conventionally grouped closely as *liberal market economies* and they share a number of characteristics, including common law systems. Yet those legal institutions differ in terms of the legal status of collective agreements; the extent and costs of litigation faced by employers; and the potential for litigants to join cases in group or class actions (see Kagan 2007; Colvin 2006; Nielsen 1999). The argument so far simply is that the impact of the law depends not just upon its content, which by common consent is now considerable in Britain, but also upon its operation and enforcement. There is considerable variation in these *legal institutions*; in the way that they relate to other sources of rule making; and in the way that social actors respond to them.

Legal Institutions in *Liberal Market* Britain

If we have been witnessing a shift in the nature of regulation in Britain, in the Webbs' terms from collective bargaining towards legal enactment (Wedderburn 2000), it has not been overseen by any guiding strategic vision and there has been no 'clean break' from the past. Particular legal rights have evolved separately from each other and pragmatically for the most part, often in a reactive way to accommodate specific domestic or European pressures. The structure and mandate of state agencies responsible for enforcement have changed haltingly, subject to unresolved conflicts in policy, between reducing 'burdens' on business while extending employment protections, for example. Many of the outcomes were unintended: escalating financial costs to the Exchequer of the Employment Tribunal infrastructure have been particularly unwelcome. Most important, while antagonism towards trade unions and social regulation has been less marked in recent government policy, no positive case has been made systematically for it either and there has been reluctance to address the institutional fissures between social and legal regulation. While the state now provides employment rights that once were exclusively the preserve of collective bargaining, the two sources of rule making in the employment relationship remain largely separate, with important consequences for diffusion and enforcement of standards. Building on the themes outlined above, this section reviews the fragmented character of legal institutions and rule making in Britain.

Fragmented law and law making

The way that the law is expressed affects the behaviour of actors by easing or obstructing their comprehension of the main requirements. The residues of common law regulation continue to resonate strongly in Britain. Even while extending the reach of law into previously untouched areas of the employment relationship, legislators have acted to preserve the widest possible discretion for actors and to employers in particular. Where possible, they have allowed firms time to adapt to regulations by staging their implementation (e.g. the Information and Consultation of Employees Regulations); to provide derogations to allow firms to tailor regulations to their needs (e.g. the Working Time Regulations). Such instincts have been reinforced repeatedly by employers, who have provided arguments against wide-ranging or detailed statutory prescription. As many have observed (e.g. Dickens *et al.* 2006), this tension between *fairness* and *flexibility* in employment policy has resulted in a patchwork of compromise solutions to specific problems reached at different times without subsequent integration.

The problem of employment status provides illuminating illustration of tensions in policy making. Though the range of employment rights has increased dramatically in recent years, their coverage is very far from universal. In order to ensure protection, workers need to have a contractual relationship with the firm and in most cases that must be an employment contract, rather than a contract for services offered to self-employed workers. This limits the scope of statutory employment protections, particularly where the form and expression of contracts vary widely, as in common law systems like Britain. From their series of interviews with workers Burchell *et al.* (1999: 6) calculated that nearly one third of the workforce had an employment status that was unclear or expressed equivocally:

> They were made up of two groups: those defining themselves as self-employed, but who were not directors or partners in their own business, and who did not employ others; and those defining themselves as employees who had some type of non-standard working pattern or classified their jobs as non-permanent.

Governments since 1997 acted to extend the scope of many new protections to all 'workers' and reserved powers to systematize the availability of all employment rights. Examples of new rights with wide scope include the national minimum wage and working time protections; rights to be accompanied to disciplinary hearings; and protections for 'whistleblowers' making public interest disclosures. As with the discrimination jurisdictions, which also apply broadly, their wide coverage is justified by the fundamental protections they bestow. Others, however, are considered more contingent and access to them is more selective. Rights still accorded only to employees include: unfair dismissal protection; redundancy compensation; minimum notice upon termination; guaranteed pay; maternity, parental and adoption rights; and rights to time off for trade union learning representatives. The scope for misunderstanding becomes consequential when workers seek to rely upon protections they presume they have as employees, often in the context of claims against arbitrary dismissal, only to find them denied on examination of their employment status. Courts have become more purposive in dismissing 'sham' contracts designed to obscure or deny basic rights (see

Protectacoat Firthglow Ltd v. Szilagyi [2009] EWCA Civ. 98; [2009] WLR (D) 67), but there have been ongoing demands for expanded and clarified statutory definition.

In 2002, the government initiated consultation on proposals to extend a broader range of employment protections to all workers. However, the approach was characteristically guarded, with prominent invitations to express concerns about over-regulation and barriers to flexibility: for example, whether 'extending certain rights may reduce employers' willingness to offer atypical working arrangements', or 'increase administrative burdens on business' (DTI 2002: 28). Four years elapsed before the government announced an outcome to the process; it was determined that the prevailing structure of rights should be retained, since 'the present legal framework reflects the wide diversity of working arrangements and the different levels of responsibility and rights in different employment relationships' (DTI 2006: 17). The conclusions rested substantially on evidence provided by employers:

> Businesses suggested that any regulatory extension of many or all employment rights to workers would mean additional costs and administrative burdens for them, especially individual businesses making extensive use of atypical arrangements and those industries where there are established traditions of atypical work. (ibid.)

At the time of writing, it appears that government has been forced into qualifying this broad preference quite significantly following adoption of the Directive on Temporary Agency Work (2008/104/EC) requiring equal treatment in basic terms and conditions of employment with employees of the end-user (BERR 2009). New rights will apply to an important constituency of agency workers, comprising about 2% of the British workforce (Kersley *et al.* 2006: 103), whose entitlements to basic protections have been subject to particular confusion under competing case precedents (see Wynn and Leighton 2008). However, this episode illustrates further the fragmented and highly pragmatic nature of policy making in the employment sphere. It follows a protracted six year period in which the British government systematically blocked progress towards the directive in terms almost exactly congruent to the employment status review. Subsequent agreement was wrought under some pressure, following the unexpected progress through the British parliament of a private members bill on the topic. Even now opportunities to address entitlements to rights in a conclusive and systematic way have been eschewed. The law relating to the similarly uncertain circumstances of those broader groups of workers identified by Burchell *et al.* (op. cit.) remains unreformed and unclear. These include the increasing proportion of the workforce, around 13%, who now consider themselves to be self-employed (*Economic and Labour Market Review*, January 2009) and the one million people working from their own homes (Holden 2006: 4) to provide products and services to 6% of workplaces (Kersley *et al.* 2006: 105).

Fragmented enforcement

Enforcement influences the behaviour of actors by signalling the intended force of the law and affecting the calculation of risks associated with non-compliant behaviour. Evidence from the USA suggests that, even where the meaning of law is unclear or contested, actors may develop compliant behaviour where there are high risks of regulatory intervention or of effective private litigation.

> Ambiguous federal laws could produce compliance activities among organisations uncertain of what is required of them. Ambiguity in legislation leads firms to invent compliance measures on their own, to be tested by the courts. (Kelly and Dobbin 1999: 458)

In the UK, though, a fragmented body of law is enforced through similarly fragmented institutions. Agency enforcement is apparent but powers vary and are constrained. By far the most important method of enforcement is individual complaint to the Employment Tribunal system and from there into the courts, but the incidence and impact of private litigation are generally low.

Agency enforcement   There is no general labour standards inspectorate in Britain, of the kind found in many civil law systems. Legislatively set standards are overseen by a range of bodies including the Advisory Conciliation and Arbitration Service (ACAS); the Equalities and Human Rights Commission (EHRC); the Employment Agencies Standards Inspectorate (EASI); the Gangmasters Licensing Authority (GLA); the Health and Safety Executive (HSE); and Her Majesty's Revenue and Customs (HMRC). While the scope of the law has grown in recent years, there are clear limits on the capacity of these agencies to influence systematically and coherently the day-to-day management of employment.

Agencies in Britain vary significantly in the roles they have been given and the strategies they have adopted for their specific tasks. Consequently, they can be positioned differently on the continuum from *purposive* to *educative* approaches to enforcement. Responsibility for the national minimum wage, for example, necessarily involves offering protection to relatively vulnerable workers in circumstances where pay details may be unclear and disputed. Agency enforcement duties lie with the HMRC which has wide ranging powers to access pay records; to support individual complaints; and to initiate prosecutions in its own name. Such approaches are seen as critical in securing relatively high rates of compliance (see Grimshaw and Rubery, this volume) and this has led some commentators to argue that it provides a model to be followed for employment rights more broadly (Brown 2006). Other agencies, however, have been given markedly different roles requiring approaches that are more *educative* in nature. The enforcement role given to ACAS, for example, is broader and derived from duties in the resolution of individual and collective disputes and the identification and encouragement of best practice. ACAS has statutory conciliation duties in relation to applications to Employment Tribunals, where officers are required to explore the possibilities of resolving disputes outside formal hearings. The body also produces *Codes of Practice*, in relation to disciplinary and grievance procedures, for example, and fields enquiries about employment rights from employers and workers. All of this requires a non-partisan, 'problem-solving' role rather than *purposive* direct enforcement. Rather than threatening the 'stick' of formal sanctions, change is attempted through the 'carrot' of advice and persuasion behind the scenes.

This fragmentation and variation in roles has attracted considerable criticism. Disadvantage in the labour market rarely has one single source and effective action requires the flexibility to move across jurisdictions.

> Employers who flout the law usually commit multiple breaches. It is therefore deeply unhelpful that, for example, HMRC inspectors do not tell HSE about suspected breaches of health and safety law or local authority environmental health departments about accommodation that is overcrowded or unfit for human habitation, even though they have checked if the accommodation offset to the minimum wage has been correctly used in such a case. (TUC 2007a: 16)

Pressure to integrate these various regulatory functions has grown in recent years. Business groups increasingly ask for greater coordination of environmental, financial and commercial regulation, and the Citizens Advice Bureaux have called repeatedly for a single Fair Employment Commission (FEC), a labour inspectorate in effect (see also Burkitt 2003). Elements of this agenda have been pursued with some energy, signalled in the rebranding of the Department of Trade and Industry to focus on Business, Enterprise and *Regulatory Reform* (emphasis added) (see Heyes and Nolan). Agencies have gradually been merged, the creation of the EHRC to oversee all aspects of discrimination being the most prominent example to date (see Dean and Liff, this volume; Hepple 2006; Mabbett 2008). Where merger has not yet been possible, there have been attempts to increase inter-agency working and cooperation, overseen by a new Fair Employment Enforcement Board (BERR 2008). Real and substantial barriers to information sharing across agencies remain but there has been some progress on increasing project-based coordination on issues like migrant working (HSE 2008).

These initiatives have the potential to deepen coherence and consistency in approaches to regulation, but fundamental tensions in the overall approach potentially inhibit the scope for *purposive* enforcement. First, there has been sustained pressure on resources, though the reasons for this have changed. Active enforcement requires an adequate body of staff and potentially the capacity to conduct inspections and pursue litigation, both of which are expensive. Government during the 1980s and 1990s, with strong beliefs in limiting the role of the state, abolished some public bodies and cut the budgets of others. This ideological climate changed somewhat in 1997 and agency funding increased but this has been in a context of exponential expansion in the range of statutory rights and the duties placed on agencies. The new EHRC, for example, accrued duties additional to those of its predecessor bodies (Hepple 2006) but the merger resulted in rationalization of employment structures to a total of 500 posts in the new organization (Niven 2008: 24).

Second, the new reform agenda has been strongly influenced by an abiding preference for 'light touch' regulation (see Munday 2008). Expressed concerns amongst policy makers to enhance and augment enforcement capacity have been tempered by broader government objectives of freeing business from gratuitous intervention. For example, regulatory reform is driven forward by the Better Regulation Executive, with a proclaimed aim of 'helping to take the pressure off and make life easier for businesses, charities, and public sector organisations, which is especially important in the more challenging economic environment we now face' (BRE 2008: 1). The Hampton Review (2005) of inspection and enforcement was commissioned by the Treasury and adopted a principal focus, explicit in the title of its final report, on *Reducing Administrative Burdens*. That review advocated a decisive shift amongst agencies towards *educative* approaches: 'The review believes that, by eliminating unnecessary inspection, *more resources could be directed to advice*' (Hampton 2005: 5, emphasis added). A complementary review of the sanctions available to regulators (Macrory 2006), identified a general over-reliance on litigation-based approaches, seen as inflexible and expensive, and recommended expanding a range of administrative sanctions available without recourse to the law. Overall, this resource and policy context has encouraged selectivity in agency inspection and litigation strategies.

Finally, while there is broad consensus that persuasion and partnership working between agencies and business is critically important, there are a number of concerns about how this can be achieved in the current context. In a largely decentralized system of employment regulation (see Sisson and Purcell; Brown, this volume), there has been a tendency for agencies to focus at the level of the firm. Even when these are selected to ensure the maximum impact, action of this kind often fails to diffuse effective good practice across industries, hence the demand from some observers for sector-wide mechanisms for discussing and extending good practice (Edwards 2007). Second, though agencies explicitly seek to engage worker representatives wherever possible, and there are particularly notable examples of coordinated anti-discrimination work with unions, this carries challenges in the current context of declining worker representation (see Terry, this volume). As Callaghan (2007: 4) has noted, the Health and Safety Executive has attempted to augment its traditional work with trade union accredited safety representatives by developing links with non-union employee representatives, 'but these are entirely at the discretion of the employer. We have no data on the numbers of employee representatives of safety. I suspect that there are very few.' Paucity in employee representation means that partnerships between agencies and business can take on a distinctly partial and fragmented character, links with workers becoming reliant upon websites and telephone helplines rather than organized structures. Evidence suggests activity of this kind has unclear impacts in practice. While the demand for advice from ACAS has increased dramatically in recent years, workers appear still to rely predominantly on sources within their workplace. Casebourne *et al.* (2006: 109–144) found only small numbers in their sample approaching ACAS, well behind managers, trade union representatives, work colleagues and even voluntary bodies such as the Citizens Advice Bureaux.

Employment Tribunals   In the absence of systematic agency action, private litigation by individuals is the predominant form of rights enforcement. The first step on this ladder is adjudication by an Employment Tribunal from where there is a right of appeal to the Employment Appeal Tribunal and on into the senior court system.

Employment Tribunals developed through pragmatic necessity in the 1970s; small existing roles were extended following the Donovan Commission in the hope that allowing them to adjudicate unfair dismissal claims might stem the growth of informal industrial action. Their role and reach has grown substantially since then; tribunals now oversee around 80 jurisdictions, many contributed since 1997 (see Dickens and Hall, this volume). Applications doubled over the course of the 1990s and, as noted above, the rate of increase has hardly abated since. Increasing complexity of cases is as much of a problem as increasing incidence. Many applications are now multi-jurisdictional, meaning, for example, that claims are submitted for unfair dismissal and discrimination together. The most intractable cases are for equal pay concerning multiple litigants mainly from the health and local government sectors and this has created a substantial backlog of outstanding cases.

These growing pressures have stimulated public debate around the role played by tribunals and a series of reviews of their role (e.g. Gibbons 2007). Some change has been evident, designed principally to deflect the demand for tribunal hearings or to streamline case management. Incremental changes have included some easing of the burden of proof in discrimination cases; the availability of an arbitration alternative to an Employment Tribunal hearing; and changes to the rules of procedure allowing multiple cases to be heard together. But these have not produced any strategic reorientation of the legal system or of its relationship with the broader system of employment regulation.

Problems with the operation of the system are too complex to explore in depth here. Observers have pointed to growing delays in the system, formalization of legal argument and problems of representation (see *inter alia* Colling 2004; Dickens 2007; Hammersley *et al.* 2007; Pollert 2005). Four factors are particularly relevant to the concerns developed here. First, workers often are not in a position to enforce their employment rights through litigation. The vast majority of employers will never face a formal tribunal claim: annual rates of application proceed currently at around 2.2 per 1000 workers and affect only 8% of employers (Kersley *et al.* 2006: 227). Only small minorities of workers initiate tribunal proceedings, estimated by government research at around 15–25% of 'justiciable' disputes (DTI 2001: 25). Instead, workers are dependent upon managers to articulate the law effectively within workplaces. Yet awareness of the law amongst managers varies significantly, according to the sector, workforce characteristics, company size and associated factors such as the presence or not of specialist personnel/human resources functions. Amongst small firms, for example, 'most, if not all, employers address individual employment rights (IERs) and their detail on a need to know basis. Only when employers have to address IERs in relation to *their* enterprise will they do so' (Blackburn and Hart 2002: xiv; see also Saridakis *et al.* 2008).

Second, where formal claims are made the chances of success are limited. An obvious response is to suggest that this is because claims are frivolous in the first place, but this is not supported by the evidence. Tribunals have powers in pre-hearing procedures to pick out weak claims and to dissuade litigants from proceeding. In 2007, only around 8% of all submitted claims were rejected initially and one third of these were accepted on subsequent resubmission (ETS Annual Statistics 2006–07). Conversely, there is strong evidence that potentially actionable complaints are withdrawn by applicants because of fears about cost and the technical and adversarial nature of litigation (see Fawcett Society 2007; Hayward *et al.* 2004). Of those proceeding, nevertheless, only 12% overall were successful at a full hearing. This masks significant variation between jurisdictions; while nearly one third of those seeking redundancy payments are successful, win rates are around 2–3% in most discrimination cases (ETS Annual Statistics 2006–07).

Third, even where success is secured, the outcome is usually compensatory rather than remedial. In other words, the prevailing approach to enforcing employment rights is to provide *post-hoc* financial relief when they have been breached, rather than proactive initiatives to prevent or repair breaches. It is technically possible to order reinstatement in unfair dismissal cases, but such orders have never featured prominently and occur in tiny minorities of cases now. Likewise, in discrimination cases it is possible to deliver Action Recommendations, requiring employers to consider the implications of individual cases for broader groups of workers and amend policies as necessary. This too has been used rarely (Dickens 2007) though the current Equality Bill promises scope for this power to be developed and applied more widely.

Financial sanctions may have an effect where there is a perception that they may be severe, as is often the case in the USA (Kagan 2007). Such potential is now available in Britain following the lifting in the 1990s of statutory maxima in discrimination cases and subsequent increases in the awards available to those unfairly dismissed. In practice, however, most awards remain relatively meagre. In 2007, the median award for unfair dismissal was £3800 and only slightly higher awards were in evidence in race (£7000) and sex discrimination (£6724) cases (ETS Annual Statistics 2006–07).

Fourth, outcomes are confined to the individual case and cannot usually be extended to groups of workers or across workplaces. Fragmented and narrow judgments leave scope for fragmented and narrow responses. Evidence from the *Workplace Employment Relations Survey* suggests that litigation does not necessarily lead to changed behaviour in workplaces (Kersley *et al.* 2006: 228). Overall, 56% of companies facing a challenge made no changes to procedures subsequently. Of those indicating some change, the majority (52%) had acted merely to ensure that existing procedures were followed more effectively. Only 27% of those moved to change procedures had introduced new policies and a similar proportion had made changes to terms and conditions of employment.

Weak articulation of legal and social enforcement

Argument so far has established that *conformity* with the law is likely to be fostered where standards are articulated clearly and extended reciprocally through legal and social regulation involving collective bargaining. Active, informed and well-resourced systems of employee representation have the potential to review and develop legal standards, diffusing knowledge of them and mediating their interpretation. Certainly that has been the experience in those parts of the UK still characterized by robust collective bargaining. There is less recourse to formal disciplinary sanctions in unionized environments and basic statutory requirements (such as provision of contractual details) are observed most widely there. Unions also use statutory standards as a floor from which to bargain upwards provisions relating to paternity leave, sick pay, pensions, holidays and health and safety (Brown *et al.* 2000; DTI 2001; McKay 2001; Saundry and Antcliff 2006). It follows that the virtual collapse of employee representation in workplaces substantially impedes or retards the effectiveness of legal standards, leaving workers reliant on the prevailing individualized private law model of enforcement. This weakens the reach of legal regulation by providing only limited roles for trade unions and some powerful disincentives to their involvement in litigation-based enforcement.

Management is now the principal actor in dispute resolution in Britain. Only two in ten workers experiencing difficulties are able to approach trade union representatives for advice (Casebourne *et al.* 2006: 107). Nearly half overall (47%) do not seek any advice at all to resolve the issue (ibid.). The split between public and private sectors is particularly striking here; while more than two thirds (70%) of public sector employees sought advice on their problems, less than half of those in the private sector did so (46%). Managers are the most common source of advice and are the principal actors in addressing workplace issues irrespective of whether advice is sought (Casebourne *et al.* 2006: 133). Yet it should be noted that significantly fewer employees were happy with the advice they received from managers (42%) and personnel/HR advisors (41%), compared to the independent advice received from solicitors (100% satisfaction) and trade union officers (59%) (ibid.: 113).

For many observers, absent or weak workplace representation is linked directly to the rising demand for external advice (from agencies) and adjudication (by tribunals) noted earlier. Yet opportunities to strengthen the connections between legal and social regulation through workforce representatives have been missed. Until 1986, an intermediary role was afforded to the Central Arbitration Committee in remedying discrimination in pay structures at the request of trade unions or employers: 'the CAC – at the time a standing arbitration body handling collective industrial relations disputes and enforcing certain legal rights granted to trade unions – was arguably an institution better suited to handling polycentric disputes (those where an individual case can affect many others) and dealing with workplace and labour market realities, than the tribunals' (Dickens 2007: 482). Calls from the statutory equality bodies (now merged to form the EHRC) for such a role to be reinstated have not been heeded.

Similarly, there has been growing pressure on government to concede a role for trade unions and agencies in developing *representative actions* through the tribunal system. This would introduce the possibility of litigation strategies similar to those available through class actions in the USA, with a critical difference. Pivotal roles in class actions are taken often by entrepreneurial or social-action-oriented law firms, who offer to bring together individual litigants. Representative actions are taken rather by bodies with representative standing of some kind, meaning agencies or trade unions usually in the British context. To this extent, permission to take such actions would reintegrate social and legal regulation, allowing unions to protect vulnerable individuals from the exigencies of litigation and to seek coherent collective resolution to complex problems (e.g. see TUC 2007b).

There has been movement towards collective litigation models in other civil courts, most notably under consumer law jurisdictions, but this has not been mirrored in the employment sphere where mechanisms are available merely for the grouping of similar cases. Proposals for reform have received extensive consideration under a series of reviews, most notably the Discrimination Law Review and the Gibbons Review of dispute resolution and feature at present in debates around a new Single Equality Bill. Employer opposition, however, has been expressed vociferously throughout. The CBI, for example, strongly opposed any extension of representative actions to the Equalities and Human Rights Commission (because it would undermine partnerships with employers, who would avoid seeking advice for fear of prosecution) and to unions (because of the claim that collective litigation in the USA has promoted adversarial and legalistic employment relations). They insist that multiple claims should continue to be derived from individual claims, each of which must have been subject to grievance or disciplinary procedures.

Unions nevertheless are involved in the litigation of individual disputes (see Armstrong and Coats 2007; Colling 2006; Colling and Dickens 1998, 2001; Gilbert and Secker 1995). This is necessary in order to meet growing demand from individual members for legal services but may also be important for broader policy or collective reasons (LRD 2005; Thompsons 2008). For example, legal challenges may be mounted in order to get definitive court judgments on government or employer initiatives and action on individual rights ultimately may generate collective benefits (Welch 2000). For example, equal pay litigation coordinated by public sector unions was instrumental in bringing about new pay structures and collective agreements in the NHS and local government (see *Enderby v. Frenchay Health Authority*; *Ratcliffe v. North Yorkshire County Council*).

Practical experience of this kind, however, can diminish these incentives where they do not remove them altogether. UNISON, for example, 'brought equal pay claims on behalf of 17 000 female members who were not permitted to join their employers' pension schemes owing to their part-time status' (UNISON 2007: 5).

> Various test cases grew out of this litigation, resulting in members' claims being struck out, claims being stayed, and some cases being settled. The claims were lodged in 1993 and are still being litigated. In that time, the members on whose behalf we have litigated have not seen the justice they set out to achieve, but are still embroiled in litigation. This process is not only frustrating for our members, but the costs to UNISON will run into millions of pounds. (ibid.: 5)

Investment of scarce union resources on this scale may be justified where the benefits are identifiable and secure but litigation rarely provides such certainty (see Colling 2009). It is not that the law does not deliver judgments favourable to unions. Rather, case authority does not guarantee any particular response from those from whom compliance is sought and the foundations it provides for bargaining strategies beyond the workers immediately involved are inherently subject to challenge.

Consider further the issues faced by those unions campaigning for equal pay in the public sector. After several years of litigation and negotiation, a *Single Status* agreement for local government workers was concluded in 1997, prompting unions to agree a moratorium on further cases. Funding problems proved intractable, however, and local negotiations to implement the equal pay principles were still ongoing a decade later. It was in this context that some groups of workers began to vent their frustration by turning legal reasoning against their own unions. In *Allen and Ors v. GMB* (for fuller discussion, see Dean and Liff, this volume) a group of women workers challenged the bargaining strategies used by their union, paradoxically securing a finding of indirect discrimination against them at the Court of Appeal. It is not merely that the outcome was adverse for unions, the tone in which it was expressed at the initial Employment Tribunal was hostile and it is worth quoting in some detail:

> It is clear from the facts that the Council were procrastinating in making lame excuses *which no Union would normally tolerate. The least the Union should, and normally would, have done was to issue proceedings* . . . to establish an early date for the calculation of back pay and then if necessary to agree to stay that claim pending the single status job evaluation. [. . .] The Union [. . .] refused to support litigation *in our judgment because it did not want to 'rock the boat' and offend the Council* so that progression to single status would be delayed or impeded. (Employment Tribunal judgment quoted by Maurice Kay LJ, in *Allen* at para. 11. Emphasis added)

There are dangers, it seems, that far from encouraging identification with union objectives, the law may be substituted for them. Far from strengthening relations between unions and their members, the insinuation of law and legal process may undermine them. Far from the legal standards meshing with systems of workplace representation, the two systems may actually be brought into conflict.

Conclusions

As collective bargaining has declined, the law has begun to play a much more important role in the regulation of employment in Britain. Key employment standards once established by employers and trade unions (as representatives of the relevant workforces) are now set by government through statute law. The form and role of *legal institutions* becomes critical in this context, since they assume wider responsibility for interpreting, diffusing and enforcing employment standards.

Increasingly dense nets of employment law in Britain do not in themselves ensure workplace justice. Significant proportions of the workforce report problems in establishing effective employment standards in workplaces. This empirical finding has been explored here through consideration of the factors likely to promote or inhibit compliance with the law. Rather than seeing the law as constraints placed straightforwardly upon actors by those in government, a more differentiated and dynamic view is preferred. Aspects of the law may be differentiated in the sense that they may be expressed and enforced in different ways. And the law is dynamic because actors play powerful roles in its development. To the extent that they perceive the force of the law, they will conform to its requirements where they mesh with prevailing beliefs; where they judge that they do not prevent effective operation in the circumstances that they face; or where the risks of non-compliance are severe. Calculations of this kind are especially likely in the employment sphere, where ethical and moral standards are less clear-cut and subject to contestation.

Distinctions become relevant between civil and common law systems. There are important variations in each kind of model but civil law systems share an underlying dynamic to establish legal requirements unambiguously and extend their reach by inserting common clauses into contracts. The development of common law, conversely, tends to be more dependent on the accumulated decisions of judges, which prioritize the formal freedom of actors to contract with each other as they choose. Attempts to obviate the law are apparent everywhere in different forms but common law systems leave particular scope for discretion by actors because the law is not always clear, because it is not closely geared to structures of social regulation (like collective bargaining), and because there is ample scope to contest and defeat claims, thereby obviating sanctions.

Critically, change in the role and status of legal institutions has not been accompanied by any strategic reorientation in their operation. Expanded influence over the employment relationship has developed by default, as a consequence of perceived weaknesses in the system of collective bargaining and the pragmatic and separate development of particular legal provisions. As a consequence, Britain has begun to take on by accretion the trappings of a civil law system, in terms of the scope of legal provision, without the clear codification and institutional infrastructure required to give it systematic force across the economy. Most important, supports for collective bargaining and employee representation remain relatively weak in Britain undermining the scope for those systems to diffuse and augment legal standards. Paradoxically, the impact of legal regulation in the future will depend critically on the health of social regulation through collective bargaining and the development of mechanisms connecting the two.

Acknowledgement

Elements of the argument raised here have developed from engaged discussions with Tim Claydon, Linda Dickens, Anthony Ferner and students of employment relations at De Montfort University Leicester and Warwick Business School. Any errors of interpretation or fact are my responsibility.

References

Ahlering, B. and Deakin, S. 2007: Labour regulation, corporate governance, and legal origin: a case of institutional complementarity? *Law Society Review*, 41 (4), 865–884.

Armstrong, K. and Coats, D. 2007: The costs and benefits of Employment Tribunal cases for employers and claimants. *Employment Relations Research Series No. 83.* London: Department for Business, Employment and Regulatory Reform.

Better Regulation Executive 2008: *Making it Simple: Annual Review 2008.* London: HM Government.

BERR 2008: *Vulnerable Worker Enforcement Forum – Final Report and Government Conclusions.* London: Department for Business, Enterprise and Regulatory Reform.

BERR 2009: Directive 2008/104/EC on Temporary Agency Work (the 'Agency Workers Directive – AWD'). At http://www.berr.gov.uk/whatwedo/employment/employment-agencies/consultation-2002/page30034.html, consulted 5th February 2009.

Blackburn, R. and Hart, M. 2002: Small firms' awareness and knowledge of individual employment rights. *EMAR Research Series.* London: Department of Trade and Industry.

Brown, W. 2006: The Low Pay Commission. In Dickens, L. and Neal, A. (eds) *The Changing Institutional Face of British Employment Relations.* Alphen aan den Rijn: Kluwer Law International, pp. 63–79.

Brown, W., Deakin, S., Nash, D. and Oxenbridge, S. 2000: The employment contract: from collective procedures to individual rights. *British Journal of Industrial Relations*, 38 (4), 611–629.

Burchell, B., Deakin, S. and Honey, S. 1999: The employment status of individuals in non-standard employment. *EMAR Employment Relations Research Series No. 6.* London: Department of Trade and Industry.

Burkitt, N. 2003: Achieving quality job for all: new policy instruments. In Burkitt, N. (ed.) *A Life's Work: Achieving Full and Fulfilling Employment.* London: Institute for Public Policy Research, pp. 162–181.

Callaghan, B. 2007: Employment relations: the heart of health and safety. *Warwick Papers in Industrial Relations*, 84, May.

Casebourne, J., Regan, J., Neathey, F. and Tuohy, S. 2006: Employment Rights at Work: Survey of Employees 2005. *Employment Relations Research Series.* London: Department of Trade and Industry.

Coats, D. 2005: *An Agenda for Work: The Work Foundation's Challenge for Policy Makers.* London: The Work Foundation.

Coats, D. and Lekhi, R. 2008: *'Good Work': Job Quality in a Changing Economy.* London: The Work Foundation.

Colling, T. 2004: No claim, no pain? The privatisation of dispute resolution in Britain. *Economic and Industrial Democracy*, 25, 555–579.

Colling, T. 2006: What space for unions on the floor of rights? Trade unions and the enforcement of statutory individual employment rights. *Industrial Law Journal*, 35, 140–160.

Colling, T. 2009: Court in a trap? Legal mobilisation by trade unions in the United Kingdom. *Warwick Papers in Industrial Relations.* Coventry, Industrial Relations Research Unit.

Colling, T. and Dickens, L. 1998: Selling the case for gender equality: deregulation and equality bargaining. *British Journal of Industrial Relations*, 36 (3), 389–411.

Colling, T. and Dickens, L. 2001: Gender equality and trade unions: a new basis for mobilisation? In Noon, M. and Ogbonna, E. (eds) *Equality, Diversity and Disadvantage in Employment.* Basingstoke: Palgrave, pp. 136–156.

Collins, H., Ewing, K. and McColgan, A. 2002: *Labour Law: Text and Materials.* Oxford: Hart Publishing.

Colvin, A. 2006: Flexibility and fairness in liberal market economies: the comparative impact of the legal environment and high performance work systems. *British Journal of Industrial Relations*, 44 (1), 73–97.

Cotterrell, R. 1992: *The Sociology of Law: An Introduction*. London: Butterworths.

De Cruz, P. 1999: *Comparative Law in a Changing World*. London: Cavendish Publishing.

Deakin, S. and Wilkinson, F. 1997: What makes markets work? *New Economy*, 155–158.

Department of Trade and Industry (DTI) 2001: *Routes to Resolution: Improving Dispute Resolution in Britain*. London: Department of Trade and Industry.

Department of Trade and Industry (DTI) 2002: *Discussion Document on Employment Status in Relation to Statutory Employment Rights*. London: Department of Trade and Industry.

Department of Trade and Industry (DTI) 2006: *Employment Status Review: Summary of Responses*. London: Department of Trade and Industry.

Dickens, L, 2007: The road is long: thirty years of equality legislation in Britain. *British Journal of Industrial Relations*, 45 (3), 463–494.

Dickens, L., Hall, M. and Wood, S. 2006: Review of research into the impact of employment relations legislation. *Employment Relations Research Series*. London: Department of Trade and Industry.

Edwards, P. 2007: Justice in the workplace: why it is important and why a new public policy initiative is needed. *Provocation Series*, 2, 3. London: The Work Foundation.

Fawcett Society 2007: Response to: 'Framework for Fairness: Proposals for a Single Equality Bill for Great Britain'. September.

Finkin, M. 2008: Privatisation of wrongful dismissal protection in comparative perspective. *Industrial Law Journal*, 37 (2), 149–168.

Fitzner, G. 2005: How have employees fared? Recent UK trends. *Employment Relations Research Series*. London: Department of Trade and Industry.

Florkowski, G. 2006: *Managing Global Legal Systems*. Abingdon: Routledge.

Freedland, M. and Kountouris, N. 2008: Toward a comparative theory of the contractual construction of personal work relations in Europe. *Industrial Law Journal*, 37 (1), 49–74.

Gilbert, K. and Secker, J. 1995: Generating equality? Equal pay, decentralisation, and the electricity supply industry. *British Journal of Industrial Relations*, 33, 190–207.

Gibbons, M. 2007: *Better Dispute Resolution: A Review of Dispute Resolution in Britain*. London: Department of Trade and Industry.

Gillespie, A. 2007: *The English Legal System*. Oxford: Oxford University Press.

Glenn, H.P. 2006: Comparative legal families and comparative legal traditions. In Reimann, M. and Zimmerman, R. (eds) *The Oxford Handbook of Comparative Law*. Oxford: Oxford University Press, pp. 421–441.

Gonzalez Menendez, M. and Almond, P. 2006: Varieties of capitalism and employer opportunism. Paper prepared for the *14th World Congress of the International Industrial Relations Association*, Lima, Peru. 11–14 September.

Grainger, H. and Fitzner, G. 2007: The First Fair Treatment at Work Survey: executive summary. *Employment Relations Research Series*. London: Department of Trade and Industry.

Hall, P. and Soskice, D. 2001: An introduction to varieties of capitalism. In Hall, P. and Soskice, D. (eds) *Varieties of Capitalism: The Institutional Foundations of Comparative Advantage*. Oxford: Oxford University Press.

Hammersley, G., Johnson, J. and Morris, D. 2007: The influence of legal representation at employment tribunals on case outcome. *Employment Relations Research Series*, No. 84. London: Department for Business, Enterprise and Regulatory Reform.

Hampton, P. 2005: *Reducing Administrative Burdens: Effective Inspection and Enforcement*. London: HM Treasury.

Hayward, B., Peters, M., Rousseau, N. and Seeds, K. 2004: *Findings from the Survey of Employment Tribunal Applications 2003*. London: Department of Trade and Industry.

Health and Safety Executive 2008: *Migrant Working – Topic Inspection Pack*. London: HSE.

Hepple, B. 2006: The equality commissions and the future Commission for Equality and Human Rights. In Dickens, L. and Neal, A. (eds) *The Changing Institutional Face of British Employment Relations*. Alphen aan den Rijn: Kluwer Law International, pp. 1010–1115.

Hillyard, P. 2007: Law's empire: socio-legal empirical research in the twenty first century. *Journal of Law and Society*, 34 (2), 266–279.

Holden, N. 2006: *Equal Rights = Equal Employment Rights: Report on Employment Rights*. Leeds: National Group on Homeworking.

Kagan, R. 2007: Globalisation and legal change: the 'Americanisation' of European law? *Regulation and Governance*, 1 (1), 99–120.

Kaur, H. 2003: Employee attitudes: main findings from the British Social Attitudes Survey 2003. *Employment Relations Research Series*. London: Department of Trade and Industry.

Kelly, E. and Dobbin, F. 1999: Civil rights law at work: sex discrimination and the rise of maternity leave policies. *The American Journal of Sociology*, 105 (2), 455–492.

Kersley, B., Alpin, C., Forth, J., Bryson, A., Bewley, H., Dix, G. and Oxenbridge, S. 2006: *Inside the Workplace: Findings from the 2004 Workplace Employment Relations Survey*. London: Routledge.

Labour Research Department (LRD) 2005: Win or no-win union legal services are no fee. *Labour Research*, 14–16.

Mabbett, D. 2008: Aspirational legalism and the role of the Equality and Human Rights Commission in Equality Policy. *Political Quarterly*, 79 (1), 45–52.

Macrory, R. 2006: *Regulatory Justice: Making Sanctions Effective*. London, Better Regulation Executive.

McKay, S. 2001: Between flexibility and regulation: rights, equality, and protection at work. *British Journal of Industrial Relations*, 39 (2), 285–303.

Merton, R. 1938: Social structure and anomie. *American Sociological Review*, 3 (5), 672–680.

Munday, R. 2008: In the wake of good governance: impact assessments and the politicisation of statutory interpretation. *Modern Law Review*, 71 (3), 385–412.

Nielsen, L. 1999: Paying workers or paying lawyers? Employee termination practices in the United States and Canada. *Law and Policy*, 2 (3), 247–282.

Niven, B. 2008: The EHRC: transformational, progressively incremental, or a disappointment? *The Political Quarterly*, 79 (1), 17–26.

Piore, M. and Safford, S. 2006: Changing regimes of workplace governance, shifting axes of social mobilisation, and the challenge to industrial relations theory. *Industrial Relations*, 45 (3), 299–325.

Pollert, A. 2005: The unorganised worker: the decline in collectivism and new hurdles to individual employment rights. *Industrial Law Journal*, 34 (3), 217–238.

Pollert, A. 2009: The reality of vulnerability amongst Britain's non-unionised workers with problems at work. In Bolton, S. and Houlihan, M. (eds) *Work Matters: Critical Reflections on Contemporary Work*. Basingstoke: Palgrave Macmillan.

Ruiter, D. 1997: A basic classification of legal institutions. *Ratio Juris*, 10 (4), 357–371.

Saridakis, G., Sen-Gupta, S., Edwards, P. and Storey, D. 2008: The impact of enterprise size on employment tribunal incidence and outcomes: evidence from Britain. *British Journal of Industrial Relations*, 46 (3), 469–499.

Saundry, R. and Antcliff, V. 2006: Employee representation in grievance and disciplinary matters – making a difference? *Employment Relations Research Series, Number 69*. London: Department of Trade and Industry.

Stein, P. 1982: Fundamental legal institutions. *Legal Studies*, 2 (1), 1–13.

Swedberg, R. 2004: On legal institutions and their role in the economy. In Dobbin, F. (ed.) *The Sociology of the Economy*. New York: Russel Sage Foundation, pp. 74–93.

Thompson, D. (ed.) 2008: *The Essential E.P. Thompson*. New York: The New Press.

Thompsons 2008: *Labour and European Law Review*. London: Thompsons Solicitors.

Trades Union Congress (TUC) 2007a: *Low Pay Commission 2007: The TUC Evidence*. London: TUC.

Trades Union Congress (TUC) 2007b: *National Minimum Wage Penalties, Fair Arrears and Employment Agencies Standards*. London: TUC.

UNISON 2007: *Discrimination Law Review: UNISON Response to the Green Paper*. London: UNISON. August.

Wedderburn, P.L. 2000: Collective bargaining or legal enactment: the 1999 Act and union recognition. *Industrial Law Journal*, 29 (1), 1–42.

Welch, R. 2000: Into the twenty first century – the continuing indispensability of collective bargaining as a regulator of the employment relation. In Collins, H., Davies, P. and Rideout, R. (eds) *Legal Regulations of the Employment Relation*. London: Hart Publishing, 615–63.

Wynn, M. and Leighton, P. 2008: Will the real employer please stand up? Agencies, client companies, and the employment status of the temporary agency worker. *Industrial Law Journal*, 35, 301–320.

SECTION FIVE

OUTCOMES

15

PAY AND WORKING TIME: SHIFTING CONTOURS OF THE EMPLOYMENT RELATIONSHIP

DAMIAN GRIMSHAW AND JILL RUBERY

Introduction

Pay and working time are fundamental components of the wage–effort bargain that underpins the employment relationship, the focus of industrial relations (IR) enquiry. Because labour is a 'peculiar commodity', the wage–effort bargain reflects not only economic attributes, but also a range of social, political and historical conditions (Polanyi 1957). These diverse conditions often conflict, and IR research has done much to reveal the indeterminacy of pay, thereby calling into question mainstream economic notions of a 'market rate' or an 'equilibrium wage'. From an IR perspective, the determination of pay is a contested issue. Changes in supply and demand of labour matter, but so too does conflict – over what value employers and citizens attach to particular jobs and occupations, over norms about what size of pay differentials between the rich and poor are fair, or over the use of seniority and merit-based principles for payment systems. Working time defines the period of time for which labour is rewarded and sets a boundary between work time and personal time. The establishment of a working time norm has long been at the heart of what is considered a 'standard' employment relationship (Thompson 1967). In recent years, working time standards have increasingly also become contested terrain. On the one hand, there have been challenges to customary expectations about the length of a full-time week and an erosion of pay premiums for additional and unsocial hours worked. On the other hand, there have been trade union campaigns and legal efforts to harmonize conditions for part-time work with the standard employment relationship. Here, more than in any other area of IR research, there is a direct connection between the employment sphere and the organization of the day-to-day lives of individuals in households and families. Traditionally, the reconciliation between work and family responsibilities was achieved through women providing support in the home and not participating in employment, except on a casual basis. Now with the widespread trend towards dual earner households, coupled with the changing patterns of working time at the workplace, there is a need to find new ways of reconciling work and family and personal life (see Dean and Liff, this volume). This embracing of issues relating to family and household organization within the field of IR is part of a general trend within IR theory and analysis, to engage more with and to borrow ideas from other disciplines and spheres of analysis (Ackers and Wilkinson 2003).

The main goal of this chapter is to review and interpret key developments in pay and working time in the UK. Recent years have witnessed rapid changes towards more flexible and 'individualized' systems of pay and working time. Comparative research suggests such trends are not unique to the UK. But unlike its European neighbours, the UK's IR system has become increasingly exclusive, with a majority of workers falling outside the protection of union membership or joint regulation of employment conditions (see Brown, this volume). Moreover, there is only limited legal intervention to compensate for the limited coverage of collective regulation (see Dickens and Hall; Colling, this volume). As a result, it is employers, not the state or unions, who tend to drive changes in pay and working time. There are, however, two areas where government intervention has increased: first in wage-setting through the national minimum wage and second in the area of work–life balance through leave entitlements and legislation to support flexible working hours (as an employee right to request more flexible work and an employer duty to consider such requests). These developments reflect policy concerns over low pay and the need to develop new ways of balancing work and life now that women's participation in the labour market has become a social norm.

The chapter begins by considering pay, with a review of developments concerning joint regulation, low pay, gender inequalities and variable pay. The discussion then considers working time, with a focus on recent general trends, developments in full-time and part-time work and trends in flexible working. The analysis concludes with some observations concerning interactions between pay and working time.

Pay

Pay is central to the theory and practice of industrial relations. The receipt of a wage in return for an employee's labour under guidance of an employer's authority is the conventional definition of an employment relationship. Pay is also the cause of many IR disputes, both during periods of economic growth when unions seek to win a fair reward for workers' economic contribution and during recessionary periods, when below-inflation pay settlements may cut into individuals' real earnings.

Despite its centrality to IR as a field of study and practice, however, there is no universally accepted theory of what determines pay, or of what types of pay practices or payment systems are most appropriate for a given set of conditions. This is not to say there have been no theoretical developments. Within the field of IR, thinking on pay has evolved through a combination of detailed critique of theoretical claims; borrowing of ideas from other disciplines (especially labour economics and sociology of work); and, perhaps most importantly, analytical insight from detailed empirical enquiry, especially case studies and workplace surveys.

IR research on pay reflects a schism in academic thinking between those influenced by neo-classical economic models of pay, on the one hand, and those inspired by institutionalist and sociological approaches, on the other. Economic models suggest pay primarily operates as a price signal in the labour market and as a payoff to human capital investment. As a price signal, pay is said to adjust automatically to balance supply and demand, rising to attract labour when demand is high and declining in response to increasing unemployment. Using measures of human capital (such as education and work experience), the related argument is that the allocative function of pay also ensures an appropriate reward to a worker's contribution to the value of the service delivered or output produced. Policy conclusions from such a framework are conservative and support a laissez faire approach to pay-setting. These include the general view that 'distortions' to the labour market ought to be minimized, especially government wage regulation and union involvement in pay. Recommendations on how to eliminate pay differentials amongst worker groups (disaggregated by sex, race or ethnicity) emphasize the supply side by pointing to differences in acquisition of human capital. And recommendations regarding how to improve the effectiveness of pay practices within workplaces encourage principles that directly reward individual worker output.

In contrast to human capital theory, institutionalist theorists consider that when it comes to pay it is not only the productivity of the individual that matters, as in human capital theory, but also the productivity of the organization in which they work. Organizations enjoy different levels of economic rents, reflective of differences in product markets by sector but also of differences in the firm's own comparative advantage within the market. At the level of the organization, bargaining over pay may focus on the sharing of economic rents, but pay is also influenced by much wider institutional factors. Indeed, institutionalist theorists regard pay as an outcome of competing interests – between the principal social actors, unions, government and employers, as well as between the organized and the unorganized, the skilled and the less skilled, the qualified and the unqualified, and so on. The emphasis is on the role of institutions, formal and informal, as a fundamental component that shapes the long-run trajectory of pay. For example, governments may legislate for minimum wages, for the extension of collective bargaining agreements, or for equal pay between men and women. The impact of employers and unions on pay depends very much on their degree of organization – do they act in a coordinated or fragmented manner and is pay negotiated within local workplaces or at a more centralized level? But it also varies according to the particular strategies adopted by unions and employers towards pay, such as, for example, whether or not there is a focus on improving opportunities for pay progression, reducing wage inequalities, rewarding performance or skill acquisition and defending pay premiums for overtime and unsocial hours working.

Rather than envisage pay as a market price, with the connotation of a single price for a piece of work, an institutionalist approach conceptualizes pay as a rule. This rule consists of a particular classification system that guides the determination of pay and that varies by workforce group, by workplace, sector and country. For example, pay may be aligned with a mix of any of the following attributes – skill, qualification, seniority, responsibility, experience or directly measured performance. And comparative research underlines the enormous variation and changing trends in rules for setting pay, with a close association between qualification and pay in German firms, high use of employee share ownership schemes in the USA and changes in the balance of seniority and merit-related pay in Japanese firms, for example (Brown *et al.* 1997; Jackson 2007; Kruse *et al.* 2009; Rubery 1998a).

Ideas on pay from a sociological perspective suggest it ought to be theorized as one part of an employment relationship that is socially constructed. Pay is a signal of social status, or class, and as such is shaped by the prevailing societal norms about the value of work. These norms are influenced by a wide range of changing beliefs and rules, especially those related to fairness. Examples include norms related to a decent wage, a living wage and a family wage, as well as the legal entitlement to equal pay for equal work. Research also demonstrates that socially constructed norms governing pay are strongly gendered and establish and reinforce what men and women do and how they live (Figart *et al.* 2002). Conditions of the wider societal system also influence pay: societies organised around a male breadwinner household model may provide higher pay for men than for women; rules of corporate governance shape what is possible at the top end of the wage structure to reward high earners; and government intervention shapes what is acceptable as a low wage, through setting tax credits, unemployment benefits and a minimum wage.

Because pay serves a variety of functions (Rubery 1997), ideas from each of these approaches are required to understand the key trends and patterns of pay in the UK. It not only acts as a market signal to allocate labour but is also a key aspect of an organization's competitive strategy, forming both a major element in total costs but also a major motivator of the employment relationship and labour productivity. At the same time pay structures and system are both influenced by and influential in shaping dominant social norms. The importance of one function over another is likely to depend on the particular circumstances – especially the economic conditions, the industrial relations environment, the workforce group and the sector. These contextual issues are illuminated in the following discussion of four dimensions of pay and their development within the UK in recent years: the decline of joint regulation; the regulation of low pay; gender pay issues; and the use of variable pay schemes.

The decline of joint regulation

In the 1960s and 1970s, estimates suggest around four in five UK workplaces had pay set by collective bargaining (see Brown, this volume). This customary approach to pay-setting changed radically after the mid-1980s with the withdrawal of many employers from joint agreements and the collapse of industry level agreements.

By 1990, just 54% of workplaces were covered by collective bargaining (Brown *et al.* 2003: Table 8.1). Findings from WERS show that this continued to fall – to 38% in 1998 and 35% in 2004 (Kersley *et al.* 2006: Table 7.6).[1]

Analysis of WERS data suggests certain workplace characteristics are associated with collective bargaining. The most obvious is union recognition. Almost nine in ten workplaces where one or more unions are recognized use collective bargaining to set pay for some employees, compared to just 2% of those where no union is recognized (Kersley *et al.* 2006: Table 7.1). The problem, however, is that rates of union membership have declined – from 33% in 1995 to 28% in 2006 (Grainger and Crowther 2007: Table 1). Workplace size is also strongly associated with collective bargaining, with one in five small workplaces (10–24 employees) using collective bargaining compared to approximately two in three large workplaces (500 or more employees) (Kersley *et al.* 2006: Table 7.1). Other factors positively associated with collective bargaining include the type of sector (with high coverage in the public services, transport and communication, utilities and financial services sectors), absence of a controlling family ownership and foreign ownership (op. cit.).

The reality for the vast majority of private sector employees in the UK is that management sets their pay, not trade unions. The situation is different in the public sector, which accounts for around one fifth of UK employment, where the incidence of collective bargaining has remained relatively stable since the late 1990s; in 2004 nearly eight in ten public sector workplaces used any collective bargaining and 32% used the consultative, tri-partite pay review bodies. Table 15.1 shows clearly that the decline in collective bargaining has been much more dramatic in the private sector than in the public sector (see Arrowsmith, this

Table 15.1   Pay determination in UK workplaces, 1998–2004

	1998			2004		
	Public sector	Private sector	All	Public sector	Private sector	All
Any collective bargaining	79%	17%	30%	77%	11%	22%
Any set by management	21%	81%	69%	28%	79%	70%
Any individual negotiations	1%	16%	13%	2%	15%	13%
Any other methods	39%	8%	14%	32%	2%	7%
Pay Review Body	–	–	–	(32%)	(0)	(6%)

Note: Sample limited to workplaces with ten or more employees.

Source: Adapted from Kersley *et al.* (2006: Table 7.4).

volume). In 2004, the most common form of wage-setting amongst private sector workplaces was unilateral determination by management, either at the workplace or at a higher level.

Pay determination for the bulk of UK workplaces is thus exclusive in nature, meaning that most workers fall outside the scope of joint regulation and collective solidarity amongst workers is low (see Simms and Charlwood, this volume). This raises concerns for both fairness at work and organizational performance. With low levels of union membership and collective bargaining coverage, many individual workers will be unlikely to address problems about pay or other workplace issues because of a weak bargaining position; the time and effort required; or a fear of damaging their reputation (Pollert and Charlwood 2009). Moreover, it is conceivable that employers will lose out from not hearing worker views, which, once resolved, might contribute to improved staff retention or to innovations in work organization.

Regulation of low pay

The UK's exclusive system of collective pay determination is an important factor in explaining the country's stubbornly high incidence of low wage work, despite more than a decade of sustained economic growth from the mid-1990s to 2007. Estimates from earnings data (NES Panel Dataset) point to a steady and significant rise in the share of employees in low paid jobs (defined as pay less than two thirds of the median for all employees) between 1977 and 2001, from around 12% to slightly more than one in five employees (Mason *et al.* 2008: Figure 1.1), precisely the period that saw a shrinkage of collective bargaining coverage and falling levels of union membership. More recently, there has been a small fall in the share of low wage work (by around one percentage point), but with 21% of employees still in low wage work[2] the UK has much to do to shake off its international reputation as a low pay economy. Moreover, the continued high share of low wage work is puzzling to many observers who point to the anticipated positive wage effects of new technologies; the increased share of graduates in the labour market; and the offshoring of low wage jobs in manufacturing and services (Keep *et al.*, this volume).

The issue of low pay has not gone unnoticed. The last decade or so has witnessed trade union campaigns, living wage movements and public debates related to government policy reforms, as well as a proliferation of academic research seeking to understand the factors shaping pay at the bottom end of the labour market. The key manifestation of interest in low pay was the introduction of a statutory national minimum wage in 1999, with the explicit purpose of improving pay at the bottom of the wage structure, coupled with the establishment in 1997 of the Low Pay Commission, a tri-partite, advisory body given permanent status in 2001 (Dickens and Hall, this volume). Table 15.2 lists the rates.[3] One of the key questions therefore is what effect has the minimum wage had on low wage work?

One issue is that low pay may persist despite a minimum wage because it is not properly enforced (see Colling; Heyes and Nolan, this volume). However, the evidence for the UK suggests a high level of compliance, although the Low Pay

Table 15.2 Listing of national minimum wage rates

	Age 22 and over	Age 18–21	Age 16–17
April 1999	£3.60	£3.00	–
June 2000	£3.60	£3.20	–
October 2000	£3.70	£3.20	–
October 2001	£4.10	£3.50	–
October 2002	£4.20	£3.60	–
October 2003	£4.50	£3.80	–
October 2004	£4.85	£4.10	£3.00
October 2005	£5.05	£4.25	£3.00
October 2006	£5.35	£4.45	£3.30
October 2007	£5.52	£4.60	£3.40
October 2008	£5.73	£4.77	£3.53
October 2009	£5.80	£4.83	£3.57

Source: Low Pay Commission reports (2006, 2007, 2008, 2009).

Commission recognizes problems with respect to employers of migrant workers and others operating in the informal sector (LPC 2008: 116–126; see also Ram and Edwards, this volume). There is a dual system for enforcing the minimum wage: workers can take their case to an Employment Tribunal or a civil court, or the government department – HM Revenue and Customs (HMRC) – can take action either by responding to a worker's complaints or proactively investigating a suspect employer following a risk assessment.[4] Problems of non-compliance are clearly greater in the informal sectors of the economy, but there is some evidence to suggest the minimum wage has acted as a catalyst to government action to root out exploitation. In 2005, the government launched a three year pilot in the East Midlands to establish closer cooperation between the UK immigration service; HMRC; the then Department for Trade and Industry; the Department of Work and Pensions; the Health and Safety Executive; and the Gangmasters Licensing Authority. Also, in an effort to tackle exploitation by employers of migrant workers, each month the HMRC selects a random sample of 15 employers from around the country using information from the Workers' Registration Scheme; between November 2004 and December 2006, 20% of employers were found to be non-compliant, with pay arrears identified for 1171 workers (LPC 2007: 224–225).

A further possible reason for the limited effect of a minimum wage is that it is set at a low level and/or it does not increase above growth in median earnings. Evidence for the UK's minimum wage is mixed. It was initially set at a relatively low level (Burkitt *et al.* 1999; Thornley and Coffey 1999), but subsequently witnessed above-average growth albeit in an inconsistent fashion. During 1999–2002, it increased from £3.60 to £4.20, an average of 4.6% each year. The Low Pay Commission's cautious approach reflected uncertainty about the impact a new minimum wage would have on job growth (Bain 1999). However, during 2003–06, the LPC explicitly sought to increase the relative level of the minimum, evidenced by a series of higher rises, averaging more than 6% per year. The change of stance responded in part to revelations that earnings data used to calculate the initial level of the minimum wage were flawed and in fact only around half the number of workers estimated were shown to be covered (Dickens and Manning 2003; LPC 2003). During this period, the minimum wage increased significantly from 36 to 40% of the average wage (or from 48 to 53% of the median wage) (Figure 15.1).

Since 2006, the LPC has adopted a different stance, reverting to a more cautious approach. This responded both to lobbying from the CBI,[5] which since 2005 has repeatedly called for alignment with average earnings growth, and a worsening of labour market conditions. In its spring 2006 report, the LPC made the following clear statement:

> We do, however, consider that the phase in which the Commission is committed to increases in the minimum wage above average earnings is complete and looking forward, the Commission will start with no presumption that further increases above average earnings are required. . . . [The 2003–2006 increases represent] an appropriate upward adjustment from the cautious level at which the minimum wage was originally set, but the Commission has always recognised that the minimum wage cannot increase faster than average earnings indefinitely. (LPC 2006: vi)

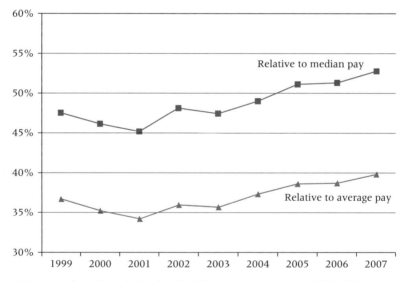

Figure 15.1   Trends in the relative level of the minimum wage, 1999–2007

Note: Earnings refer to average gross hourly pay for adults excluding overtime payments. Data for median and average pay cover all full-time and part-time, male and female employees.

Source: National Statistics Office ASHE data; own calculations.

Thus, while low wage workers enjoyed a short period of relatively generous hikes in the minimum wage, it is very likely that the coming years will witness a levelling relative to average pay, despite the fact that it only just registered at 40% of the average wage in 2007; OECD data for 2005 placed the UK seventh out of 13 advanced countries used for comparison by the Low Pay Commission (Low Pay Commission 2007). But even during the period of above-average growth in the minimum, it is notable that there was little change in the incidence of low wage work.[6]

So what are the features of the UK's employment system that seem to lock in a high share of workers in low wage work? One is the absence of an inclusive system of collective bargaining for diffusing statutory increases at the bottom of the wage structure further up the chain (Grimshaw 2008). In its absence, the evidence suggests firms may use one of three tactics: use the minimum wage not as a floor to pay rates but as the going rate for many occupations (IDS 2004)[7]; respond to increases in the minimum by eliminating pay scales and using single spot rates instead (ibid.); or avoid restoring pay differentials (Denvir and Loukas 2007). In many UK workplaces, therefore, workers are in a weak position to negotiate a pay rise with their manager and are more likely to experience erosion of pay differentials with lower paid colleagues.

A second feature is the system of in-work benefits (Working Tax Credits) and other means-tested welfare payments paid to low wage workers. Although research evidence is lacking, it is possible that where an employee receives tax credits and housing benefits, the employer, on the one hand, may be disinclined to raise wages in response to rising living costs and the employee, on the other hand, has weaker incentives to bargain for higher wages, especially where there is a high clawback of benefits for every additional pound of earnings. The problem faced by government is that tax credits risk keeping afloat 'parasitic employers' (Figart et al. 2002) by removing their need to pay for the social costs of their workforce. And UK trade unions face the challenge of how to promote wage bargaining amongst the low paid where workers face high effective marginal tax rates.

Gender pay issues

International comparisons demonstrate that gender discrimination is strongly entrenched in pay practices in the UK, as evidenced by the size of the gender pay gap, the concentration of women in low paid part-time jobs and the apparent undervaluation of many jobs where women workers are over-represented (Dean and Liff, this volume). The last two decades have seen a slow convergence of male and female employees' average pay (Figure 15.2). Relative to male full-timers' average hourly pay (overtime included), pay for all female employees (full-time and part-time) increased from 66% in 1984 to 78% in 2006. The trend has been rather unsteady and is marked by two periods of catch-up: 1987–92 and 2002–05. During what we might call the lost decade of 1992–2002, women's average relative pay improved by just one and a half percentage points, from 70.5% to 72.0%. This process of slow and unsteady convergence mirrors that of the 1970s when,

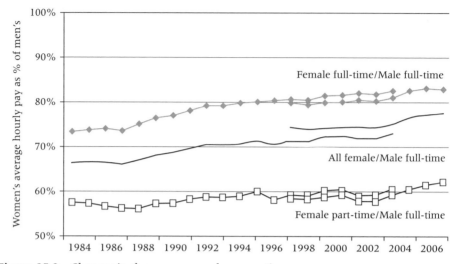

Figure 15.2   Changes in the average gender pay ratio

Note: Average gross hourly earnings, including overtime, for employees on adult rates whose pay for the survey period was not affected by absence. Average pay for all female employees for 1984–2003 are calculated using employment figures for full-time and part-time employees from the Labour Force Survey to improve the accuracy of New Earnings Survey data which under-represent female part-time workers.

Source: New Earnings survey (1984 to 2003) and Annual Survey of Hours and Earnings (1997 to 2006).

following the introduction of the Equal Pay and Sex Discrimination Acts (1970 and 1975), there was a rapid and significant improvement in women's earnings up to around 1977 and subsequently no or very little improvement until the late 1980s (Harkness 1996).

Trends in women's hourly pay for full-time and part-time workers are quite distinct. Comparing both groups to male full-timers (as a wage standard), women in full-time work experienced an increase in relative hourly pay of close to ten percentage points, whereas women in part-time work saw an improvement of less than five percentage points. What we see over this period, therefore, is a growing pay gap between women in full-time and part-time work. Average hourly earnings for female part-timers were 78% of female full-timers in 1984, but dropped to 75% in 2006. As we explore in more detail below in the section on working time, the problem of part-time pay is largely caused by the concentration of women in low paid part-time jobs, a problem not found in other countries such as the Netherlands where part-time work is more evenly distributed across occupations. For example, while around one in four jobs is represented by women in part-time work, amongst minimum wage jobs this rises to nearly half (47%) (LPC 2007: Figure 2.8).[8]

The other problem is that of undervaluation of many jobs, full-time and part-time, that are associated with female labour. This phenomenon is complex and is the outcome of inter-related social, economic and institutional conditions (Grimshaw and Rubery 2007). One important feature relates to evidence that pay is shaped by the degree of sex segregation at the workplace. After adjusting for human capital variables, as well as occupational, sectoral and job characteristics, Forth and Millward (2000) find that working in an all-female workplace in the private sector reduces the pay by 7%, compared to a premium of 6% in an all-male workplace. The effect is more extreme amongst low skilled workers; working in an all-female workplace carries an 18% pay penalty compared to an all-male workplace (Forth and Millward 2001: Table 4.3).

A second feature that reinforces undervaluation of women's work relates to gender bias in job grading systems. The more informal the system, the more scope there is for discrimination to influence the level of pay. Also, monitoring for equality is facilitated by transparency of the principles underlying the reward structure (Hastings 2003; Shaw and Clark 2000). But a problem that is particularly acute in the UK relates to the ability of employers to construct separate pay hierarchies related to different kinds of jobs. For example, an employer may design an extended pay scale with opportunities for performance-related pay for some families of jobs and a flat pay scale with no merit pay for other jobs. Research from the early 1990s found that such practices carry the risk that separate pay hierarchies are associated with female-dominated and male-dominated families of jobs, even within the same workplace (Bevan and Thompson 1992). This problem has been largely remedied in some parts of the public sector (local authorities and the National Health Service), following the introduction of new harmonized job grading and pay structures (Bach, this volume), but in many workplaces it remains.

Policy developments with respect to gender pay issues were keenly anticipated with the publication of the Women and Work Commission's 2006 report (WWC 2006). The Commission made several positive recommendations, followed up by a government action plan and a report monitoring progress 12 months on. Ongoing policy initiatives cover a wide range of areas from improving girl's career choices while at school and removing barriers to mothers returning to work, to improving the quality of part-time work and supporting women with business start-ups. However, many of the programmes are rather patchy (such as the £500 000 investment to improve the quality of part-time jobs), or reliant on voluntary initiatives (such as the network of 1000 women to support female entrepreneurs in selected areas). Moreover, the WWC failed to reach a consensus on the important policy issue of whether or not to require organizations to complete an annual equal pay review; it therefore did not make a recommendation in its 2006 report. Instead, in its summing up of the pros and cons of making reviews compulsory, the WWC made a strong case for the government, as public sector employer, to lead the way. It recommended the Treasury 'should ask public sector employers to account for their progress on equal pay during the Comprehensive Spending Review' and argued the proposed Public Sector Pay Committee should ensure all new pay systems are 'at the forefront of good practice on equal pay' (WWC 2006: 89–90, 92). But it is not self-evident that practice in the public sector will have any significant impact on the private sector. There has been limited success of a voluntary approach to pay reviews in the private sector. Despite campaigns by government and trade unions during 2001–02, by 2005 only 34% of large companies in the private sector had completed a review (Adams *et al.* 2006). Further progress in closing the gender pay gap is therefore uncertain.

Use of variable pay schemes

Variable pay schemes are used to reward individual or collective worker effort or performance through incentive-based payments. The rise of variable pay schemes in the UK, such as performance-related pay, share-ownership schemes and profit-related pay, represents a direct contrast to traditional pay rules that set a standard rate for the job. At the same time, growth in incentive pay schemes has occurred both in unionized and non-unionized workplaces (for example, incentive pay schemes are more common in unionized manufacturing workplaces than in non-unionized workplaces – Kersley *et al.* 2006: 190). Thus while the design and outcomes of variable pay schemes ought to be interpreted in the context of weakened joint regulation over wage-setting, their use is not necessarily associated with a decline in collective bargaining.

WERS data again provide the best source of information on the incidence of variable pay schemes amongst UK workplaces, distinguishing between performance-related pay, share ownership and profit-related pay (Table 15.3). Performance-related pay schemes were the most common form of variable pay scheme in 2004, present in two in five workplaces. Objective schemes were more common than subjective schemes, the majority of workplaces (56%) applied the scheme to both managerial and non-managerial employees and the schemes were twice as likely to be used in the private sector as in the public sector (Kersley *et al.* 2006: 190). Various forms of share ownership schemes were used in approximately one in five workplaces, with a greater likelihood of extension

Table 15.3 Incidence of variable pay schemes, 2004

Type of pay schemes	% of workplaces
Performance-related pay schemes	40%
– only payment by results (objective measure)	23%
– only merit-based system (subjective assessment)	9%
– both schemes	7%
Share ownership schemes	21%
– Save as you earn	13%
– Share incentive plan	8%
– Company Share Option plans	6%
– Other scheme	4%
Profit-related payments	30%

Source: Adapted from text in Kersley et al. (2006: 189–192).

to non-managerial employees (85%) compared to performance-related pay. Such schemes are especially prevalent in the financial services sector (82% of workplaces) and amongst foreign-owned firms. Amongst large organizations (more than 1000 employees), they are also more likely to be used in unionized workplaces than in non-unionized workplaces. Finally, profit-related pay schemes were utilized in three out of ten workplaces. Similar factors to those explaining the higher incidence of share schemes apply to profit sharing schemes, albeit limited to the trading sectors (op. cit.: 191–193).

While often treated as an innovation in pay practices in much of the HRM literature (despite a long tradition applied to blue-collar work in the UK), the actual effects of variable pay schemes on worker effort, recruitment and retention and organizational performance are still not adequately understood and certainly do not produce universal positive outcomes. Many of the UK studies derive their analytical approach from a mix of labour economics and psychology theories. From economics, agency theory suggests employees respond to higher pay with higher effort, in a context where performance measures are sufficiently reliable and reputable (Lazear 1995; Milgrom and Roberts 1992). From psychology, expectancy theory (Vroom 1964; Lawler 1971) suggests employees will work at a specified level of effort according to the desirability of the reward for working at that level and the subjective probability that the reward will follow from working at that level; that is, it is the employee's perception of the satisfaction to be derived that is important, not some objective measure of reward. Other relevant approaches from psychology include goal-setting theory. This stresses the motivating power of defining appropriate work goals (their difficulty and specificity) and engaging employee commitment to them (Locke and Latham 1990). The emphasis here is on dialogue between line managers and employees.

A particularly striking set of findings for the UK derive from studies of the public services sector. On the one hand, research suggests strong evidence of employee disenchantment with performance-related pay (Marsden and French 1998; Marsden and Richardson 1994), despite a high level of sophistication of the developed schemes (e.g. with review mechanisms, information sharing, etc.). Moreover, only a small share of employees believes variable pay schemes provide an incentive to work beyond their job requirements or to take more initiative. In line with earlier research (Kessler and Purcell 1992), public sector workers often perceive variable pay schemes to be divisive and line managers report that they undermine cooperation amongst staff, especially problematic amongst professional teams. On the other hand, Marsden's (2004) research suggests certain factors may improve perceptions. These include the design of effective appraisals, setting of clear targets, increased scope to improve performance and use of group schemes. The detailed case studies and survey data point to an important finding (Gilman 2004; Marsden 2004), that the effectiveness of variable pay schemes depends less on their effect on motivation than on their direct association with a radical change in performance norms and renegotiation of job design and work rules; lessons from industrial relations (e.g. Hyman and Brough's (1975) 'negotiated order') rather than psychology would therefore appear to be more relevant to further research.

Working Time

Working time arrangements take on significance in industrial relations for two main reasons. First, it is a fundamental element in the wage–effort bargain that underpins the employment relationship; changes to working time arrangements may have significance beyond the pattern or length of working hours (Rubery *et al.* 2005). Second, it represents the interface between work and personal life and family life, an interface that is increasingly contested as working time becomes more variable and as the society moves from single to dual earner households (Crompton *et al.* 2007).

Control over working time has also in some countries been directly connected to policies to reduce the threat of long-term unemployment, if working time is not reduced in line with productivity gains. However, the linkage between macro-economic issues such as unemployment and working time policy has been less strong in the UK than in many European countries; for example, in France one of the main planks of socialist governments – in 1982 and again in 1998 – has been to reduce working hours (Erhel and Zajdela 2004), with strong support from trade unions. Also in Germany there has been more of a tradition of trade unions negotiating over reducing working hours as a means of avoiding lay-offs, as in a famous agreement at VW in 1994, when hours were reduced to 28.8 hours to avoid lay-offs. While these policies of the 1990s have been in part reversed in the 2000s, both in respect to the VW policy (EIRO 2006) and the French shorter working week (EIRO 2008), there has not been a developed debate on the linkages between working time and employment in the UK in either decade.

In the UK, working time policies have always been closely linked to the wage–effort bargain at the workplace. Time has traditionally been the numeraire for determining pay. Under the traditional or standard employment relationship it is labour time that is sold, primarily in continuous daily blocks under open-ended contracts, and it is up to the employer to extract the anticipated labour power through the management of work organization and employee effort and performance. Industrial relations in the UK traditionally focused on collective bargaining over the length of the working week and on the definition of standard daily working hours. These were two key elements in the traditional wage–effort bargain as they not only set a limit to employers' control of labour time but also determined the point at which additional pay should be made available for overtime work.

The survival of a standard hours-based employment relationship is being challenged by a number of developments. These include the effective disappearance in the private sector of sector level collective agreements that set standard working weeks and other provisions for a whole sector (Rubery 1998b); now most collective bargaining over working time tends to be conducted at the organization level. Changes in the employment arrangements are also occurring that decouple the link between time and pay: for example, by making pay depend upon output or performance measures, or by requiring workers to work until the task is completed, part of the responsibility (and the risks and reward) for work organization and performance is shifted onto employees. These new approaches to performance and reward have been associated with the prevalence of long working hours based on unpaid overtime. High performance work systems have been found, for example, to impinge on work–life balance for staff as performance is given higher priority than the maintenance of a clear divide between work and personal time (White *et al.* 2003).

A second but rather different challenge to the standard full-time employment relationship is found in the growth of more flexible and fragmented time schedules, principally associated with the development of part-time work. This approach enables employers to seek performance improvements and/or cost reductions by ensuring that work time is only paid for when employees can be expected to be working above a minimum level of effort; that is, paid 'on the job inactivity' (Supiot 2001: 65), due to interruptions of, or slowdowns in, work flow, is reduced. This fragmentation is particularly important in services where work cannot be stored but involves co-production of services with the customer. It is also potentially significant in any just-in-time production system, to match customer demands to paid labour hours.

Another element of the standard working hours notion that is under challenge is the right to additional payments for either working longer than standard hours or working outside the standard 8 (or 9) to 5 Monday to Friday routine. Several factors account for this challenge. First, there has been the growth of extended operating and service hours, sometimes called the rise of the 24/7 economy. Second, the growth of part-time work has been associated with the development of more flexible working time patterns and arrangements that enable organizations to cover non-standard hours without paying overtime or unsocial hours premia (Rubery 1998c). Third, the increase in employment participation of women, and indeed students, has provided some increased demand for different patterns of working time. Over time organizations have tended to extend definitions of normal working hours, where no premium is payable (including some organizations determining that no premia are to be paid for the whole 24/7 period). Flexible scheduling of work has also been extended from part-timers to full-timers to meet varying demands over the day, week or year without the payment of overtime premia (IDS 2006). This normalization of non-standard and flexible working has reduced the distinction between work time and personal time. These boundaries have been further blurred by the development of new forms of technology such as email and mobile communications. These technologies facilitate a more flexible organization of work around domestic requirements and the avoidance of commuting time but at the same time may create a context where an employee may not be actually working but may be expected to be available to work.

The debate over changes to working time and their implications for the future of the employment relationship started primarily in the 1990s and is continuing today. However, as we will see below, many of the recent contributions have suggested that there has been a reversal of some of the changes and trends observed in the 1990s and that the 2000s have seen not only a stabilization of working time arrangements but also a greater recognition of work–life balance conflicts than was found in the early 1990s. There is even some evidence of a reduction in the work intensification and long hours working that sparked the debate in the 1990s. We thus review the most recent evidence on trends in working time patterns and arrangements, placing these more recent developments in the patterns of developments since the beginning of the 1990s and with reference to prevailing practices in the USA and other parts of Europe. This review of trends and practices is then used to inform the final section where we return to consider the implications of the developments we have uncovered in both pay and working time for the changing employment relationship.

Recent trends and practices in working time arrangements

During the 1980s and 1990s the UK came to be known as the EU country renowned both for its long and for its short hours of work – or in other words for its deviation from standard full-time working.

The reputation for long hours working was built on three factors. First, the absence of national regulation of total working hours at least until 1998 when the EU's Working Time Directive was implemented, when a 48 hour limit was introduced but with options for employers to ask employees to agree to voluntary opt-outs from the directive (Hyman, this volume). Second, the high share of full-time workers recording long hours of work compared to other EU15 countries. And third, the strong upward trend in long hours working for male and female full-timers in the 1990s, associated with a growth in unpaid overtime.

At the other end of the spectrum the UK not only has a high share of employees working only part-time hours but also a high share of the part-time jobs offering only relatively short hours per week, a characteristic associated with poor job quality.

The wide spectrum of working hours in the UK from the short to the long has been presented by UK governments as evidence of a high level of individual choice over working hours in Britain and thus as a contribution to work–life balance.

> However, it is important to note that there is no 'standard' working week in the UK. It is this diversity that provides people with the choice of work to suit their individual needs and circumstances. This flexibility is particularly important for women. 44% of all women in work take advantage of opportunities for part-time employment because they choose to, not because they cannot find a job (but just 9% of male employment). Only 6% of women said they worked part-time because they could not find a full-time job. (UK National Action Plan on Employment 2002: 39)

Alternative interpretations have contrasted high pressures towards long hours working, associated with the culture of 'presenteeism' where working longer is more important than working smarter. Likewise the decision to work in short part-time jobs may be regarded as a choice but influenced by the constraints of limited and expensive childcare and other support for mothers in employment.

These characteristics of both high levels of long hours working and short hours part-time jobs are still prominent in the UK labour market but the last decade has seen a stabilization and attenuation of these trends. For some commentators this reversal of trends towards more standard working hours and more work–life balance options across a wider spectrum of jobs signals an end to the worst excesses of the flexible labour market and an indication that diversity of working hours can be combined with some reference to the needs of employees and citizens.

However, it is important not only to assess the trends but also the desirability of current working time arrangements. Furthermore, as the favourable trends have emerged during tight labour markets, it is also important to consider the mechanisms and processes in place that protect employees in this important dimension to the employment relationship as the UK economy heads back towards high levels of unemployment.

Working hours for full-timers: a return to standard employment?

As Table 15.4 indicates, there was a slight upward trend in average working hours during the 1990s for full-time workers followed by a slight downturn in the late 1990s and 2000s. This has applied for men and women separately. Here we consider all employees; that is, we exclude the self-employed who are more able to determine the length of their own working hours but include both full-timers and part-timers in the numeraire. For men, the share working more than 45 hours

Table 15.4   Usual weekly hours worked, by percentage share of employees, 1992–2008

	1992	1996	2000	2004	2008
All persons					
Less than 6	1.6	1.8	1.4	1.2	1.1
6–15	8.4	8.3	7.7	7.4	6.5
16–30	13.6	15.2	16.1	17.6	18.0
31–45	55.3	51.3	52.3	54.3	55.5
More than 45	21.1	23.5	22.5	19.6	18.8
Men					
Less than 6	0.7	0.8	0.6	0.5	0.6
6–15	2.4	2.9	3.0	3.2	3.1
16–30	3.1	4.2	4.9	6.2	6.9
31–45	60.6	55.1	56.8	60.4	61.4
More than 45	33.3	37.0	34.7	29.7	28.0
Women					
Less than 6	2.6	2.9	2.3	1.9	1.7
6–15	14.9	13.9	12.7	11.7	10.1
16–30	25.1	26.9	28.2	29.6	29.7
31–45	49.6	47.1	47.5	47.9	49.4
More than 45	7.7	9.2	9.3	8.9	9.1

Source: Labour Force Survey (March–May data for each year).

on a usual basis rose from around 33% in 1992, hitting a high of 37% by 1996 but then fell steadily to 28% by 2007. In contrast the share of women working more than 45 hours rose from 7.7% in 1992 to over 9% at the end of 1990s. It then fell below 9% in the early 2000s but by 2008 had reached 9.1% again.

This trend decline in long hours working for men is also confirmed by the third work–life balance survey (WLB3) in two respects. First of all there was a marked increase in the share reporting that their employment contract included a set number of contracted hours – 83% in 2006 compared to 79% in the second work–life balance survey (WLB2) in 2003 (Hooker *et al.* 2007). Those without contracted hours could be expected to be particularly likely to be subject to pressures towards long hours and in both surveys the number without set contracted hours is certainly significant, even if the share declined from over a fifth to around one sixth of the workforce. Further evidence of reduced pressure to work long hours is found in the changing share of those working overtime hours; in WLB2 in 2003 only 33% of respondents worked no overtime while that share rose to 49% in WLB3 in 2006 (Table 15.5) (Hooker *et al.* 2007). The decline was fairly evenly shared between paid forms of overtime and unpaid forms of overtime, and opportunities for time off in lieu for unpaid overtime remained fairly constant, with around 56% of those working unpaid overtime never being offered time off to compensate. On these figures around 15% of employees work unpaid overtime without compensation.

It is clear from a number of different sources that the main factor promoting long hours work from the point of view of the individuals is the demands of the job and not the opportunity for additional earnings. The WLB3 survey found 44% citing 'too much work to finish in normal office hours' compared to 42% in WLB2, while the share saying the main reason for working overtime was to make more money declined from 21 to 19% (Hooker *et al.* 2007). The findings chime with those of the Working in Britain survey in 2000 which found that of those working long hours, 83% did so because of pressures to meet deadlines and 75% because it was a job requirement, compared to just 39% who worked long hours to earn extra money (White *et al.* 2003). Such reasons nevertheless differ by occupational group (Table 15.6), with manual workers, skilled and less

Table 15.5   The incidence of paid and unpaid overtime in WLB2 and WLB3

	WLB2 % 2003	WLB3 % 2006
Paid overtime only	29	21
Unpaid overtime only	29	22
Both paid and unpaid	9	9
No overtime	33	49
Unweighted base	2003	2081

Source: Hooker et al. (2007: Table 2.2).

Table 15.6   Reasons for working long hours, % of employees
by occupational group

	Job requirement %	Deadlines %	Money %	Work satisfaction %
Higher level professionals/ managers	68	90	14	66
Lower level professionals/ managers	71	80	19	58
Higher admin/ clerical/sales	58	81	42	58
Lower admin/ clerical/sales	66	53	50	47
Technicians/ supervisors	76	77	47	45
Skilled manual	59	77	81	28
Semi- and unskilled manual	66	65	70	43

Source: Employment in Britain survey 2000 (White *et al.* 2004).

skilled, citing making more money as the main reason (81% and 70%). But even amongst this group around three fifths and up to four fifths also cited job requirements and deadlines as a reason for the long hours of work. In contrast under a fifth of managers, even lower level managers, worked long hours for additional money.

To complement the evidence on actual hours of work, there is also evidence of a decline in the number of workplaces where non-managerial staff were working longer than the 48 hours allowed for in the working time regulations introduced in 1998 to comply with the European directive on working time. The UK in implementing the directive has made use of the possibility for a voluntary individual opt-out from the regulations, a feature that it has fought hard to retain throughout ongoing political negotiations over whether the opt-out will remain when the directive is revised (Hyman, this volume). In 2006, 21% of workplaces reported having some managerial staff actually working in excess of 48 hours, but only 9% reported having someone below managerial level working more than 48 hours in the past 12 months, down from 15% in 2003. The shares of workplaces where there was actual reported use of the opt-out was lower still with only 6% reporting any managerial employees opting out and only 5% any non-managerial employees (Hayward *et al.* 2007).

These trends can be interpreted through either a glass half full or a glass half empty lens. From a half full perspective they certainly represent a more favourable trajectory than might have been anticipated in the mid-1990s. The share of workplaces operating Monday to Friday only has remained fairly constant at around 46% between 2003 and 2007, with around 54% open for business six or seven days a week. Moreover, the share working overtime has declined significantly and there has been no further increase in the share working unpaid as opposed to paid overtime. All of this suggests a marked attenuation of the trends towards a results-based employment culture and a return to a time-based or standard employment contract.

However, the argument for a glass half empty perspective is stronger; in 2007 the UK still had the longest working hours in the EU25 for full-time employees, exceeded only by the new accession countries, Bulgaria and Romania (EIRO 2007), and the retention of the individual opt-out from the directive still means there is no effective maximum working time in place. It should be remembered that in 2000 the Working in Britain survey found that the greatest decline in job satisfaction during 1992–2000 occurred because of the hours people are now required to work (White *et al.* 2003); levels of satisfaction with hours worked dropped from 35% to 20% amongst men and from 51% to 29% amongst women. Improvements to working time arrangements were thus long overdue and are unlikely yet to have been sufficient to have made good the deterioration in the 1990s. Moreover, there are few grounds for believing that these trends will continue if economic growth slows. The move to a 24/7 economy continues with one third of workplaces now open for business seven days a week, up from 29% in 2003. Employers are continuing to increase effort levels with spillover effects to working time as two thirds of workplaces in the 2007 WLB3 considered that workloads for managers and professionals had increased and overtime, where worked, is increasingly oriented to getting the work done rather than improving earnings (Hayward *et al.* 2007). The continued decline in union recognition means that there is ever more limited protection from pressure to work long hours; moreover, research suggests that working long hours is a very important factor in securing promotion opportunities (Francesconi 2001).

The consequences of these working time developments are felt amongst staff at different points of the skill and pay structure. A government-commissioned survey of IT employees found that 11% worked more than 10 hours per day, with no gender difference in this pattern (Flexecutive 2004). Advances in technologies make it possible for these employees to be available to work 24 hours a day, to join the 'always-on workforce'. Nearly three in four long hours workers said they did not have full control over their working hours and three in four of those working long hours said they did not get involved with their family as much as they would like (op. cit.). For low wage workers, the motivation to work long hours is often to earn a decent wage. In Toynbee's (2003) portrayal of low wage Britain, a care assistant earning a little above the minimum wage regularly worked more than 48 hours per week, with only a 15 minute break for each 6 hour shift during Monday–Friday and gruelling 12 hour shifts at weekends. The work was physically hard and low paid, but the care assistant stayed because it gave her the chance to earn extra money when she needed it. In Toynbee's words:

> For reasons neither she nor I could understand, she got no overtime rate, no time-and-a-half or double-time for these terrible extra weekend hours. But at least here she could always work as many hours as she wanted when she needed to earn more, which is one reason some employers get away with low pay. [The care assistant] said she often thought of leaving, but the trouble was that many jobs that paid more per hour . . . didn't offer enough hours' work to match her present total wage. (Toynbee 2003: 202)

Long hours may therefore in some contexts be preferable to jobs offering only limited and fragmented hours of work, the issue to which we now turn.

Part-time work and the employment relationship

Part-time work is widely available in the UK but tends to be concentrated in lower paid jobs in the service sector. This contrasts with the situation in some other European countries with high part-time rates such as the Netherlands and Sweden where part-time working opportunities are more available throughout the job hierarchy. In the Netherlands hours for full-timers are relatively short and strongly regulated and people have the right to request to work part-time – and to return to full-time working (Fagan *et al.* 2006). In Sweden much part-time work relates to mothers or fathers exercising the right to reduced hours working when their children are below the age of eight (and often receiving some income compensation for the reduced hours (Kosseck and Lambert 2005)). In contrast in the UK most mothers until recently were not necessarily able to stay in their job after childbirth unless they were willing to work full-time; many, in a context of limited child care, chose to change jobs and take up a part-time job, often below their previous occupational level. There is now a policy concern to increase options to work part-time through the job hierarchy and parents of young children (extended to those with older children from April 2009) are allowed to request the right to work part-time and their employers are required to take the request seriously and provide reasons for turning down any such request. Nevertheless, this remains a weaker right than in the Netherlands and Sweden. Further obstacles to the spread of part-time work into higher level jobs are found in the expected long hours of work amongst full-timers; when working weeks are open ended and long, it is difficult to incorporate someone on a fixed hours basis as implied by a part-time contract.

Part-time work in Britain so far remains concentrated amongst the low paid and low skill occupational groups, reflecting, on the one hand, problems of sex segregation and sex discrimination and, on the other hand, obstacles to the development of quality part-time jobs caused by general restructuring of time at work. Part-time workers in the UK account for one in four of all workers (42.6% of women and 10.6% of men – 2006 data (CEC 2007)). The share of men in part-time work has been rising but from a low level, from 7.8% in 2000 to 10.6% in 2006, while the share of women has been stable at around 44% over the past decade until declining slightly in 2005 and 2006 to around 42.6% (CEC 2007).

Table 15.4 shows that although most short hours working is in long part-time jobs (16–30 hours), 11.8% of all women in employment are still in 'mini-jobs', that is, working under 16 hours per week, compared to 3.7% of men.

Part-time work is often associated with accommodating the needs of mothers or students to their outside commitments, and as such is seen to provide enhanced work–life balance. However, part-time jobs are often organized and designed to maximize employer flexibility, to meet fluctuations in customer demand or to provide for cover for sickness and holidays. There is thus strong potential for conflict between the flexibility requirements of employers and those of employees. While many part-timers do obtain jobs that fit their family requirements others may be left to juggle their family arrangements as their employers in turn juggle their working time often at short notice to fit changing demands. The outcome may be that part-timers have to be available for work for a larger share of the week than is the case for those on standard contracts. For example, in a recent study of part-time working, one employer in discussing scheduling of part-time work of 20 to 30 hours a week expected staff to fit with shift arrangements anywhere between 10 am and 8 pm at night, Monday to Friday (Grant *et al.* 2005).

Availability of flexible work options

There is a much wider range of flexible work options than part-time work. One of the major changes over recent years has been the increase in at least the formal availability of flexible work options, as revealed by both data from the WERS survey (see Table 15.7) and the three WLB surveys (see Figure 15.3). The latter surveys show, however, that although there has been a strong growth in availability of options the actual take-up rate has grown much more slowly (Figure 15.3). For example, the availability of flexitime options has increased from 32 to 53% between 2001 and 2006 but the take-up of the option has only increased by three percentage points up to 27% from 24%. One explanation for the low take-up is the fairly widespread recognition amongst employees – even those who have chosen to take up one of the options – that there are disadvantages attached. For example, the 2006 WLB3 employees' survey (Hooker *et al.* 2007) found that 42% of those who had worked one of the flexible options felt that they had suffered some detriment, 29% financial and 13% a reduced work–life balance. This finding underscores the fact that not all flexible work options contribute to work–life balance. Working from home, working compressed working weeks and working annualized hours are particularly likely to lead to deteriorating work–life balance, according to this survey.

Annualized hours is one form of working time arrangements that was anticipated to spread as a consequence of the growth of the 24/7 economy and the desire on the part of employers to reduce the costs of non-standard working. The system provides for stable monthly or weekly earnings even though the actual schedule of hours may vary by week, month or season. This provides employees with potentially higher guaranteed earnings and offers to employers opportunities to reduce the costs of additional hours or overtime working. There are many factors that may discourage the introduction of annualized hours, in particular

Table 15.7 Flexible working and leave arrangements for non-managerial employees in continuing workplaces, 1998 and 2004

	% of continuing workplaces	
	1998	*2004*
Flexible working arrangement		
Switching from full-time to part-time hours	46	64
Flexitime	19	26
Job-sharing	31	41
Homeworking	16	28
Term-time only	14	28
Annualized hours	8	13
Zero hours contracts	3	5
Leave arrangement		
Parental leave	38	73
Paid paternity/discretionary leave for fathers	48	92
Special paid leave in emergencies	24	31

Base: All continuing workplaces with ten or more employees in 1998 and 2004. Figures are weighted and based on responses from at least 847 managers.
Source: Kersley et al. 2006.

problems of staff shortage (McBride 2003) and unpredictability of demand, but Arrowsmith (2007) points to another fact that may have inhibited its spread compared to other European countries; the absence of collective bargaining in much of the private sector. The complexities of such schemes and the potential for winners and losers means that these new arrangements are more acceptable when employees are reassured by trade unions that their interests are being taken care of. In short, annualized hours may be a possible outcome of a process of integrative bargaining but UK employers are not engaged in processes of joint problem solving.

Pay and Working Time: Some Interactions

This chapter has focused on trends in both pay and working time as outcomes of the changing patterns of industrial and employment relations in the UK. In this final section we focus on some interactions between pay and working time arrangements. First of all, if we consider the incidence of working long hours we find that it is higher paid workers (professionals and managers) who have the greatest tendency to work overtime hours (Hooker *et al.* 2007). By and large, these extra hours are not directly paid for, only indirectly in the rising pay levels

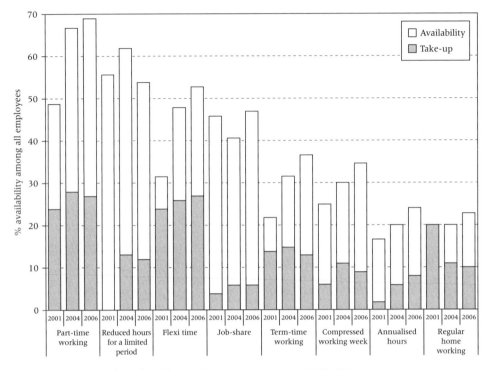

Figure 15.3   Trends in flexible working arrangements, 2001–06

Source: Hooker *et al.* (2007) Tables 3.3 and 3.4.

for higher level staff over recent years. Male manual workers also tend to work overtime, but less frequently than higher level staff and usually for additional pay. In general, however, the rising inequality in earnings in the UK has been associated with a concentration of both the volume of work and of earned income in the upper part of the pay distribution. At the other end of the distribution, low hourly pay is concentrated amongst part-time workers, thereby exacerbating inequalities in weekly or annual earnings.

There are particular issues as to how working time interacts with earnings and earnings potential over the life course. Part-time work has a range of negative impacts on potential lifetime earnings (see EOC 2005 for a review). First of all part-time workers miss out on skill development opportunities, receiving 40% less training than their full-time counterparts (Francesconi and Gosling 2005). Moreover, for each year of part-time employment, hourly wages decrease by 1%, compared to an annual increase of 3% for full-time workers (Olsen and Walby 2004). Indeed, there is a large penalty on lifetime earnings amongst women who always remain in part-time work, and even those who switch to full-time work after just one year in part-time work suffer a 10% earnings penalty after 15 years in employment compared to a similar worker in continuous full-time work (Francesconi and Gosling 2005).

Part-timers are more likely than full-timers to be in insecure jobs, that is, hired on fixed-term, seasonal or casual contracts (Francesconi and Gosling 2005) and they are less likely to be protected by trade unions: 21% of part-timers are trade union members compared to 32% of full-timers (Hicks and Palmer 2004). Moreover, case studies (Grant *et al.* 2005) and survey results (Darton and Hurrell 2005) suggest that four in five part-time workers are working below their potential, either because they have held previous jobs where required qualifications or skills were higher, or because they are employed in jobs that do not use their latent potential. Finally, part-time workers are less likely to have access to occupational pensions than full-timers and even when they do, the move towards defined contribution/stock market-based pensions is likely to further disadvantage those on part-time work in their early prime years as under these schemes it is early investment that is likely to lead to higher pensions.

These illustrations of interaction effects underline the strong inter-relationship between pay and working time at the core of the employment relationship. For working-age people, pay is still the most important (often the only) form of income and working time is the principal indicator of labour market participation. Despite their centrality to living standards and social and economic well-being, however, pay and working time outcomes are largely left to the market in the UK. As we described above, the industrial relations system is exclusive, meaning that most workers fall outside of the protection offered by independent representative bodies such as trade unions. This contrasts with the inclusive industrial relations systems found in most European countries where collective bargaining shapes the conditions of pay and working time for the bulk of the workforce. Outside the few pockets of joint regulation in the UK, particularly the public sector, protection of pay and working time conditions rests on new legislation such as the statutory minimum wage and support for flexible working hours. Therefore, the challenge for the UK is whether or not employers are able and willing to adapt conditions of pay and working time in line with the rapid changes in social, cultural and economic conditions that are changing the needs and aspirations of individuals and families in the UK. The evidence above suggests there are several issues for concern, especially the high share of workers in low wage jobs and the limited take-up of flexible working arrangements to sustain a satisfactory work–life balance. Given past trends, it is unlikely that further minor legal reforms will improve matters significantly simply because in the context of an exclusive industrial relations system new entrants to the labour market as well as experienced workers are in a weak position to negotiate the contested terrain of pay and working time to their benefit.

Notes

1   Note that the data are not comparable over time since the WERS data for 1998 and 2004 cover workplaces with ten or more employees whereas earlier data refer to workplaces with 25 or more employees. This means that the recent drop in coverage is overstated since restricting the 1998 and 2004 data to larger workplaces would increase coverage rates. In 2004, the coverage rate amongst workplaces with fewer than 25 employees is just 19% (Kersley *et al.* 2006: 179).

2   Hourly earnings data for 2008 from the Annual Survey of Hours and Earnings show that 21% of all employees (full-time and part-time, male and female) earned less than two thirds of the median hourly pay, excluding overtime, for all employees (own calculations) (National Statistics online).

3   Initially, young people aged under 18 were exempt from the legislation. However, in response to evidence that employers were offering young people jobs at very low wages with no training provision, the LPC recommended in 2004 that a new rate be set for 16–17 year olds to prevent exploitation.

4   For example, in 2005–06 2100 complaints of underpayment were made to the HMRC. Also the HMRC completed around 4900 investigations into minimum wage underpayment. The incidence of non-compliance detected from investigations was 32% and the value of underpayments estimated at £3.3 million (LPC 2007: 220–221).

5   In its website on the national minimum wage, the CBI in fact claims that it was 'instrumental' in persuading the Commission to adopt this new position (see link from the page http://www.cbi.org.uk/ndbs/, accessed November 2007).

6   Mason *et al.* (2008: Figure 1.1) in fact show a decline amongst women but a corresponding rise amongst men, so that the overall level was relatively stable during 1995–2005.

7   For example, the IDS found that the median starting rate for a nursery assistant in 2001 and again in 2003 was the exact equivalent of the minimum wage (£4.10 in 2001 and £4.50 in 2003). Three quarters of pubs and restaurants surveyed paid new recruits the minimum wage. Also, at half of the hotels surveyed in 2003 the starting rate was the minimum wage.

8   Minimum wage jobs refer to adults aged 22+ paid £5.25 or less in April 2006, youths aged 18–21 paid £4.40 or less and youths aged 16–17 paid £3.25 or less (see LPC 2007 for methodology).

References

Ackers, P. and Wilkinson, A. (eds) 2003: *Understanding Work and Employment: Industrial Relations in Transition*. Oxford: OUP.

Adams, L., Carter, K. and Schäfer, S. 2006: Equal pay reviews survey 2005. EOC Working Paper Series No. 42.

Arrowsmith, J. 2007: Why is there not more 'annualised hours' working in Britain? *Industrial Relations Journal*, 38 (5), 423–438.

Bain, G. 1999: The National Minimum Wage: further reflections. *Employee Relations*, 21 (1).

Bevan, S. and Thompson, M. 1992: *Merit Pay, Performance Appraisal and Attitudes to Women's Work*. IMS Report No. 234 for the Equal Opportunities Commission. Brighton: Institute of Manpower Studies.

Brown, W., Marginson, P. and Walsh, J. 2003: The management of pay as the influence of collective bargaining diminishes. In Edwards, P. (ed.) *Industrial Relations: Theory and Practice*. Oxford: Blackwell.

Brown, C., Nakata, Y., Reich, M. and Ulman, L. 1997: *Work and Pay in the US and Japan*. Oxford: OUP.

Burkitt, N., O'Donnell, C. and Patel, B. 1999: George Bain and a 'mechanistic formula': the purposes and politics of £3.60. *Industrial Relations Journal*, 30 (3), 178–183.

CEC 2007: *Employment in Europe*. Commission of the European Communities: Luxembourg.

Crompton, R., Lewis, S. and Lyonette, C. 2007: *Women, Men, Work and Family in Europe*. London: Palgrave.

Darton, D. and Hurrell, K. 2005: People working part-time below their potential. (September) Manchester: EOC.

Denvir, A. and Loukas, G. 2007: The impact of the National Minimum Wage: pay differentials and workplace change. Prepared for the Low Pay Commission by the Institute for Employment Studies. www.lowpay.gov.uk/lowpay/research/pdf/0394_lpc final_layout.pdf (accessed March 2008).

Dickens, R. and Manning, A. 2003: Minimum wage, minimum impact. In Dickens, R., Gregg, P. and Wadsworth, J. (eds) *The Labour Market under New Labour: The State of Working Britain*. London: Palgrave.

EIRO (European Industrial Relations Observatory) 2006: Union agrees to more working hours to safeguard jobs at Volkswagen. European Foundation for the Improvement of Living and Working Conditions. http://www.eurofound.europa.eu/eiro/2006/10/articles/ de0610039i.htmn

EIRO (European Industrial Relations Observatory) 2007: Working time developments. European Foundation for the Improvement of Living and Working Conditions. http://www.eurofound.europa.eu/eiro/studies/tn0804029s/tn0804029s.htm#hd4

EIRO (European Industrial Relations Observatory) 2008: New rules for union representativeness and working time. European Foundation for the Improvement of Living and Working Conditions. http://www.eurofound.europa.eu/eiro/2008/08/articles/fr0808039i.htm

EOC 2005: *Part-time is no Crime – So Why the Penalty?* Interim Report of the EOC's Investigation into Flexible and Part-time Working, and Questions for Consultation. Manchester: EOC.

Erhel, C. and Zajdela, H. 2004: The dynamics of social and labour market policies in France and the United Kingdom: between path dependence and convergence. *Journal of European Social Policy*, 14, 125–142.

Fagan, C., Hegewisch, A. and Pillinger, J. 2006: *Out of Time – Why Britain Needs a New Approach to Working-time Flexibility*. London: Trades Union Congress. www.tuc.org.uk

Flexecutive 2004: *Flexible Working in the IT Industry: Long-hours Cultures and Work Life–Balance at the Margins?* Report for the Department for Trade and Industry. http://www.berr.gov.uk/files/file11416.pdf

Figart, D., Mutari, E. and Power, M. 2002: *Living Wages, Equal Wages: Gender and Labor Market Policies in the US*. New York: Routledge.

Forth, J. and Millward, N. 2000: *The Determinants of Pay Levels and Fringe Benefit Provision in Britain*. NIESR Discussion Paper No. 171. London: National Institute of Economic and Social Research.

Forth, J. and Millward, N. 2001: *The Low-Paid Worker and the Low-Paying Employer: Characteristics Using WERS98*. NIESR Discussion Paper No. 179. London: National Institute of Economic and Social Research.

Francesconi, M. 2001: Determinants and consequences of promotions in Britain. *Oxford Bulletin of Economics and Statistics*, 63 (3), 279–310.

Francesconi, M. and Gosling, A. 2005: Career paths of part-time workers. EOC Working Paper Series No. 19. Manchester: EOC.

Gilman, M. 2004: The puzzle of performance-related pay? Canterbury Business School Working Paper Series, No. 58. http://www.kent.ac.uk/KBS/pdf/Gilman-No-58.pdf, accessed July 2008.

Grainger, H. and Crowther, M. 2007: *Trade Union Membership 2006*. London: DTI. Available at www.berr.gov.UK/files/file39006.pdf.

Grant, L., Buckner, L., Escott, K., Fisher, P., Suokas, A., Tang, N. and Yeandle, S. 2005: Low paid part-time work: why do women work in jobs below their potential? EOC Working Paper Series. Manchester: EOC.

Grimshaw, D. 2008: The UK: developing a progressive minimum wage in a liberal market economy. In Vaughan-Whitehead, D. (ed.) *The Minimum Wage Revisited in the Enlarged EU*. Geneva: ILO.

Grimshaw, D. and Rubery, J. 2007: *Undervaluing Women's Work*. Equal Opportunities Commission Working Paper Series No. 53.

Harkness, S. 1996: The gender earnings gap: evidence from the UK. *Fiscal Studies*, 17 (2), 1–36.

Hastings, S. 2003: Grading systems and estimating value. In White, G. and Druker, J. (eds) *Reward Management: A Critical Text*. London: Routledge.

Hayward, B., Fong, B. and Thornton, A. 2007: *The Third Work–Life Balance Employer Survey: Main Findings*. BMRB Social Research for the Department for Business, Enterprise and Regulatory Reform Employment Relations Research Series No. 86.

Hicks, S. and Palmer, T. 2004: Trade union membership: estimates from the autumn 2003 Labour Force Survey. *Labour Market Trends*, March: 99–101.

Hooker, H., Neathey, F., Caseborne, J. and Munro, M. 2007: *The Third Work–Life Balance Employee Survey: Main Findings*. Institute for Employment Studies for the Department for Business, Enterprise and Regulatory Reform Employment Relations Research Series No. 58.

Hyman, R. and Brough, I. 1975: *Social Values and Industrial Relations: A Study of Fairness and Inequality*. Oxford: Blackwell.

IDS 2004: *Report to the Low Pay Commission on the Impact of the National Minimum Wage in 2003 and 2004* (September).

Incomes Data Services (IDS) 2006: *An Assessment of the Causes of Pay Drift in UK Organisations*. A research report for the Office of Manpower Economics. December. http://www.ome.uk.com/downloads/An%20assessment%20of%20the%20causes%20of%20pay%20drift%20in%20UK%20organisationsDec%2006.pdf

Jackson, G. 2007: Employment adjustment and distributional conflict in Japanese firms. In Aoki, M., Jackson, G. and Miyajima, H. (eds) *Corporate Governance in Japan*. Oxford: OUP.

Kersley, B., Alpin, C., Forth, J., Bryson, A., Bewley, H., Dix, G. and Oxenbridge, S. 2006: *Inside the Workplace: Findings from the 2004 Workplace Employment Relations Survey*. London: Routledge.

Kessler, I. and Purcell, J. 1992: Performance related pay: objectives and application. *Human Resource Management Journal*, 2 (3), 16–33.

Kosseck, E. and Lambert, S. 2005: *Work and Life Integration: Organizational, Cultural, and Individual Perspectives*. London: Routledge.

Kruse, D.L., Freeman, R.B. and Blasi, J.R. (eds) 2009: *Shared Capitalism at Work: Employee Ownership, Profit and Gain Sharing, and Broad-Based Stock Options*. University of Chicago Press.

Lawler, E.E. 1971: *Pay and Organisational Effectiveness: A Psychological View*. New York: McGraw Hill.

Lazear, E. 1995: *Personnel Economics*. Cambridge, Mass.: MIT Press.

Locke, E.A. and Latham, G.P. 1990: *A Theory of Goal Setting and Task Performance*. Englewood Cliffs, NJ: Prentice-Hall.

Low Pay Commission 2003: *The National Minimum Wage: Building on Success, Fourth Report of the Low Pay Commission*. Cm 5768, London: HMSO.

Low Pay Commission 2006: *National Minimum Wage: Low Pay Commission Report 2006*, Cm 6759. Available at www.lowpay.gov.uk/lowpay/report/pdf/2006_Min_Wage.pdf.

Low Pay Commission (LPC) 2007: *National Minimum Wage: Low Pay Commission Report 2007*. Cm 7056, HMSO.

Low Pay Commission (LPC) 2008: *National Minimum Wage: Low Pay Commission Report 2008*. Cm 7333, HMSO.

Marsden, D. 2004: The role of PRP in renegotiating the 'effort bargain': the case of the British public service. *Industrial and Labor Relations Review*, 57 (3), 350–370.

Marsden, D. and French, S. 1998: What a performance: PRP in the public services. CEP Special Report, LSE (available at http://cep.lse.ac.uk/).

Marsden, D. and Richardson, R. 1994: Performing for pay? The effects of 'merit pay' on motivation in a public service. *British Journal of Industrial Relations*, 32 (2), 243–262.

Mason, G., Mayhew, K. and Osborne, M. 2008: Low-paid work in the UK: an overview. In Lloyd, C., Mason, G. and Mayhew, K. (eds) *Low-Wage Work in the UK*. New York: Russell Sage Foundation.

McBride, A. 2003: Reconciling competing pressures for working-time flexibility: an impossible task in the National Health Service (NHS)? *Work, Employment and Society*, 17 (1), 159–170, 1469–8722.

Milgrom, P. and Roberts, J. 1992: *Economics, Organization and Management*. Englewood Cliffs, NJ: Prentice-Hall.

Olsen, W. and Walby, S. 2004: Modelling gender pay gaps. EOC Working Paper Series, No. 17. Manchester: EOC.

Polanyi, K. 1957: *The Great Transformation: The Political and Economical Origins of our Time*. Boston MA: Boston Beacon Press.

Pollert, A. and Charlwood, A. 2009: The vulnerable worker in Britain and problems at work. *Work, Employment and Society*, 23(2), 343–362.

Rubery, J. 1997: Wages and the labour market. *British Journal of Industrial Relations*, 35 (3), 337–366.

Rubery, J. (ed.) 1998a: *Equal Pay in Europe? Closing the Gender Wage Gap*. London: Macmillan.

Rubery, J. 1998b: Working time in the UK. *Transfer, European Review of Labour and Research*, 4 (4), 657–677.

Rubery, J. 1998c: Part-time work: a threat to labour standards. In O'Reilly, J. and Fagan, C. (eds) *Part-time Prospects; Part-Time Employment in Europe, North America and the Pacific Rim*. London: Routledge.

Rubery, J., Ward, K., Grimshaw, D. and Beynon, H. 2005: Working time, industrial relations and the employment relationship. *Time and Society*, 14 (1), 89–111.

Shaw, S. and Clark, M. 2000: Women, pay and equal opportunities. In Thorpe, R. and Homan, G. (eds) *Strategic Reward Systems*. London: Financial Times.

Supiot, A. 2001: *Beyond Employment: Changes in Work and the Future of Labour Law in Europe*. Oxford: Oxford University Press.

Thompson, E.P. 1967: Time, work discipline and industrual capitalism. *Past and Present*, December, 56–97.

Thornley, C. and Coffey, D. 1999: The Low Pay Commission in context. *Work, Employment and Society*, 13 (3).

Toynbee, P. 2003: *Hard Work: Life in Low-Pay Britain*. London: Bloomsbury.

UK National Action Plan on Employment 2002: UK Action Plan on Employment. Report to the European Commission. http://ec.europa.eu/employment_social/employment-strategy/nap_2002/nap_uk_en.pdf

Vroom, V.H. 1964: *Work and Motivation*. New York: John Wiley & Sons.

White, M., Hill, S., McGovern, P., Mills, C. and Smeaton, D. 2003: 'High-performance' management practices, working hours and work–life balance. *British Journal of Industrial Relations*, 41 (2), 175–195.

Women and Work Commission 2006: *Shaping a Fairer Future*. London: Women and Equality Unit.

16

INDUSTRIAL RELATIONS AND ECONOMIC PERFORMANCE

PAUL EDWARDS AND SUKANYA SENGUPTA

Introduction

The debate on the effects of industrial relations on the performance of firms and whole economies has been long, heated and often inconclusive. In the UK, a key point was the late 19th century, when declining relative economic performance led to concerns about the adequacy of the country's training provision; the debate hardened in the early 20th century when various kinds of trade union 'restrictions' were identified as causes of poor performance; this view re-emerged strongly during the 1960s and 1970s (Fox 1985; Nichols 1986).

Since the 1990s, the focus has shifted from trade union 'restraints' to the positive effects on performance that may derive from a set of practices now identified as comprising a 'high performance work system' (HPWS). Debate here has addressed exclusively performance at the level of the work unit or the firm. A quite separate debate has addressed national economic performance and the effects on it of industrial relations systems such as the structure of collective bargaining (Traxler *et al.* 2001).

A single chapter cannot cover all these debates in detail. We focus on the workplace, rather than national systems, for it is here that the inputs of capital and labour are combined, and yet the relevant processes are often termed a black box (Gunderson 2002). Within this focus we begin with the HPWS approach for three reasons: it has attained a dominant position in contemporary debates on human resource management (HRM); it addresses the effects of key processes discussed in the rest of this book, such as training (see Keep *et al.*, this volume); and a critique of it will reveal the value of an alternative, 'industrial relations', approach (see Colling and Terry, this volume).

As to why the high performance model has become so dominant, we offer two suggestions. First, in academia as elsewhere, some definitions become dominant at certain times and thus define a field that becomes self-reinforcing. The 'unions and productivity' debate was powerful at one time, but it declined with the rise of HRM. The HRM paradigm developed in the USA, and it shaped British debates. Second, one reason for the change of the focus was the weakening of unions and other institutions of governance, in both the USA and the UK.

The argument of this chapter is that to ask whether HRM *directly and always* causes better performance is to invite an answer that is either banal or unconvincing. It is banal in the sense that managing employees in a consistent and fair way is likely to be 'better' than not doing so. But even this point raises questions: better in what sense and for whom; what about the costs as well as the benefits; and is managing 'fairly' the same thing across different contexts? The answer is unconvincing because, just as with the debate on union effects, piling up more and more quantitative studies has produced more data than information: fundamental issues of causality remain unresolved. That said, there has been progress in at least posing better questions and, crucially, in highlighting the 'social relations of productivity' (Edwards *et al.* 2002) as the contested arena through which 'effects' of human resources (HR) systems are mediated. Understanding HR in this way allows us to consider the complex ways in which it may contribute to performance.

The chapter begins by outlining only the main features of the HPWS approach and the main lines of criticism. This leads in the next section to an industrial relations perspective. Some key illustrations are given in the third section. The final section identifies analytical implications and also touches on national as opposed to company performance.

The HRM and Performance Debate

There has been extensive research on the relationship between HRM and performance over the past two decades. Much of this evidence points to a positive and significant association between HPWSs and performance (Huselid 1995; Guest *et al.* 2003; Patterson *et al.* 2004; Bryson *et al.* 2007). We detail below what is meant by an HPWS. As for performance, a wide variety of indicators has been used, with varying degrees of immediate connection to employment relations. Some studies use overall company measures such as profitability; others take a measure of productivity such as sales per employee; and yet others use more proximate indicators such as the rate of labour turnover.

Yet there is also widespread scepticism about many aspects of this evidence. One reason is that the studies predominantly rely on financial performance, therefore overlooking the multidimensionality of the performance construct. This practice is often misleading particularly since it is widely argued that the principal impact of HR strategies on labour productivity is different to their impact on financial performance. It is also clear that HPWS practices remain rather rare: if they really are so good why are they not used more, particularly when they have been extensively urged on firms by numerous bodies? The answer turns on several arguments: the costs as well as the benefits of an HPWS; the difficulty of establishing causation here; and the fact that the relevant practices interact with many other aspects of a firm, so that applying them in another context may not bring any benefits at all.

Conceptual issues

Recent developments suggest that there is growing consensus as to the broad areas covered by HPWS. At the core there exist a set of practices that are considered to be essential for good practice across all organizations. These include sophisticated selection, appraisal, training, teamwork, communication, job design, empowerment, participation, performance-related pay, harmonization and employment security (Wall and Wood 2005). Furthermore, terms such as high performance work systems (HPWS), high performance work practices (HPWP) and high involvement management (HIM) practices have been coined to refer to a set of practices that together would contribute to high performance in an organization.

Just what this might mean specifically is more open to dispute. A study based on WERS 1998 identified 13 measures which it saw as constituting a set of 'high commitment' practices (Bryson *et al.* 2007). At first sight, usage seems high: the mean number of practices per establishment was 6.9. But, first, some measures report presence and not the extent of coverage of employees. Second, it is not always clear how far a practice measures high performance systems rather than something else. For example, one indicator is a preference for internal over external applicants for vacancies. But this is at least as much a reflection of 'old' internal labour markets as it is of 'new' high performance systems. The inclusion of such measures may explain why public sector workplaces scored higher on the index than did private sector ones, which is not what one would expect from the high performance literature. Third, a core result of WERS is that the clearest measures of high performance systems remain very rare. Thus the 1998 study reported that only 3% of workplaces had advanced teamworking (team members work together, have responsibility for some specific activity, decide how work is to be done, and appoint their own team leaders); by 2004, this proportion had reached 4% (Kersley *et al.* 2006: 90).

Further questions concern the connections between such sets of practices. First, do these practices have independent effects, or do they combine together in some way? Some studies argue strongly that it is not individual practices that are important but their combination into bundles (Ichniowski *et al.* 1997), but others point out that the number of cases on which the claim is made is small and that there may well be diminishing returns (Godard 2004). Second, how do they combine? There is now extensive debate between 'best practice' and 'best fit' schools. The former says that the practices can be put together into a package applicable anywhere; the latter argues that the practices have to be consistent with each other ('internal fit') and with the wider operation of the organization ('external fit').

This debate has often been inconclusive. In our view, some basic points emerge. First, the 'best practice' view exaggerates. Studies finding that a common set of practices 'work' often do so within specific sectors; whether the results extend to other sectors is not demonstrated. There may nonetheless be basic components of employee management that are common at least within a sector: banks, for example, typically share some elements of pay systems, so that 'good practice' in this sector can at a basic level be identified (Boxall and Purcell 2003). Second, some degree of internal fit is essential. Group cooperation and teamwork are not consistent with pay systems stressing purely individual performance. Third, external fit is equally obvious, in broad terms. What works in retail stores may not work in management consultancies. Work in the former is much more dependent than is work in the latter on meeting specific performance targets, and performance management systems are likely to reflect this. But just how practices are put together with others, and how we know that they indeed 'fit', is far from clear. As discussed below, 'fit' is often as much to do with history and expectations as it is with some apparently technical issue of fitting HR systems to the design of tasks.

The 'best practice' and 'best fit' perspectives need not be alternatives. At one level there may be a set of basic good practices that benefit all organizations. At another level the practices may need to be tailored to the specific needs of the organization, the strategy being followed, employees' expectations and the organizational and environmental context. The relevance of context was highlighted by Harney and Dundon (2006) in their qualitative analysis of six SMEs operating in the Republic of Ireland. The findings show that a complex interplay of external structural factors (such as competitive pressures, labour markets and legislation) and internal dynamics (ownership and managerial style, managerial influence and resource constraints) shaped HRM in each of the companies. HRM was not the coherent set of practices typically identified in the literature but rather was often varied, informal and emergent depending on the context.

It may be possible to resolve this 'best practice' versus 'best fit' debate by viewing HPWS practices in terms of 'hygiene' factors and 'motivators'. There are a set of universal 'good' or 'best practices' that would benefit all organizations. While their presence may not guarantee higher performance, their absence would lead to loss of performance and costs in terms of an unhappy and dissatisfied workforce, low commitment and poor working conditions. In order to maximize returns and gain a competitive edge, a configuration of best practices tailored to the strategy and the organizational context would be relevant. These would be the 'motivators' which would correspond to the 'best fit' approach. Yet no accepted theory exists that might classify different practices into 'obligatory' and 'optional', 'hygiene' factors and 'motivators' (Boselie *et al.* 2005: 73).

Performance: concept and measurement   Identifying the appropriate performance measure is critical in assessing the true impact of HPWS practices on organizational performance. The tendency has been to focus entirely on financial measures of performance (Boselie *et al.* 2005).

Guest (1997) and several others have questioned the use of this preferred performance indicator because of the causal distance between HRM input and such outputs based on financial performance. So many other variables, both internal and external, affect organizations that this direct linkage strains credibility. Use of more 'proximal' outcome indicators, particularly those over which the workforce may enjoy some influence, is both theoretically more plausible and methodologically easier to deploy. Oddly, given how an HPWS's impact on performance is typically depicted as being refracted through changes in employee attitudes and behaviours, measures of employees' experience remain rare (Boselie *et al.* 2005: 75).

Many studies continue to rely on the subjective assessment of a single respondent (typically the manager) while measuring hard objective performance outcomes such as financial performance, labour productivity, turnover and absenteeism. There are two issues here. The first is the accuracy of self-report performance measures. Wall *et al.* (2004) compare these with objective measures and find considerable similarity, while also warning that the concordance is not exact and that the constructs may be measuring rather different things: it is thus important to be clear as to what aspects of performance are important and the best way of measuring them. Second, there is the single rater issue, and here there is general disquiet about relying on one respondent.

The multidimensionality of the performance construct raises several larger questions. Do we conceptualize organizational performance in terms of the overall well-being of the key stakeholders in the organization (employees, customers, shareholders, suppliers) or are we just interested in financial returns? The implication in the extant literature is that the interest in such returns is justified because everyone benefits from more returns. The unitarist assumptions here are evident: does everyone gain equally, and what of the different ways in which a given outcome can be achieved and the contested costs and benefits involved?

HPWSs and performance: linkages   Apart from lack of conceptual clarity with respect to the key variables, there is theoretical dispute as to the precise mechanisms through which HPWS policies and practices generate value. Becker and Gerhart (1996) pointed out that the extant literature suggests that HR practices have considerable economic potential but there is little consensus as to how to achieve this. Early in the debate Guest (1997) pointed out the need for a better theory on understanding of the linkages between HPWS and performance. Ten years on, there is still a lack of a comprehensive theory explaining the links between HPWS and performance (Fleetwood and Hesketh 2008). The widely held perception that the HPWS policies and practices have their main impact upon performance through enhanced employee attitudes and positive behavioural outcomes was a view propagated by advocates of an HPWS model, rather than something that originated from a strong theoretical understanding. While plenty of studies acknowledged the existence of the 'black box' and indulged in some speculation as to its possible contents, few studies tried to look inside (Boselie *et al.* 2005).

One of the few exceptions was the study by Ramsay *et al.* (2000). They drew on the 1998 Workplace Employee Relations Survey (WERS98) to test the view that enhanced employee experience of work and employee commitment are the primary mediating variables that explain how an HPWS feeds into improved organizational performance. The analysis provides little support for this widely held assumption.

There has been some development in this respect. The mere presence of practices does not determine that they are in fact used. What matters is the quality of implementation in terms of effectiveness and procedural justice. This realization has implications for the conceptualization and measurement of HRM. Measures of HRM should include provisions for looking at the implementation of HRM practices. An HPWS can be measured in three ways: its presence, its coverage (proportion of workforce covered) and its intensity (degree to which an individual employee is exposed to the practice or policy) (Boselie *et al.* 2005: 74). A majority relied on presence, few used coverage (Huselid 1995 and Guest *et al.* 2003) and only one looked at intensity (Truss 2001).

A fresh perspective was added to the 'best fit' argument by Kinnie *et al.* (2005). They identified the need to tailor the suitability of the practices to fit with the expectations and needs of employees. For example, managers responded favourably to career opportunities, rewards and recognition, involvement, communication and work–life balance, whereas professionals valued performance appraisal, in addition to those factors valued by management. For workers typically involved in low discretion jobs without any formal qualifications, it was rewards and recognition, communication, openness and work–life balance that were of primary importance. The findings illustrate the need to recognize the heterogeneity of employee responses towards HPWS policies and practices.

Methodological issues

Finally, decisions need to be made regarding the preferred method of investigating these arguments/theoretical frameworks. One of the key methodological limitations in the extensive HPWS/performance literature has been the inability to address the issue of causality. It is still open to debate as to whether high performing firms adopt the high performance work practices or whether the high performing firms owe their success to the adoption of these practices. Even though the issue of causality had been recognized as being important more than a decade ago, little has been done to address it. The most common research design continues to be the quantitative survey method based on cross-sectional analysis (Boselie *et al.* 2005). These studies achieve generalizability at the cost of establishing the direction of causality. A few recent studies (Guest *et al.* 2003; Truss 2001; Patterson *et al.* 2004) that have attempted to address the issue of causality by using longitudinal analysis have yielded divergent results. The results vary from showing no performance changes (Guest *et al.* 2003), to some negative outcomes (Truss 2001) to mixed results with certain practices yielding performance benefits (Patterson *et al.* 2004).

While the evidence is inconclusive, progress has been made in terms of a greater appreciation of the limitations of the longitudinal design. Longitudinal studies are limited in that they have not resolved the issue of a time lag and the issue of attribution. For example, it is unclear as to how much time should elapse in order to realistically capture the effect of an HPWS on performance. If the time lag is too long one may be measuring the effects of factors other than the HPWS, and too short a time lag may result in understating the positive effects of an HPWS on performance since the performance effects may not be evident. There is still debate as to what is the appropriate time in which to measure the performance effects of an HPWS since the benefits may not be realized for several years (Huselid and Becker 1996) or performance may dip immediately following a change in HRM (Pil and Macduffie 1996). There is no easy answer to this question since the time lag would be influenced by a number of factors such as the industry and its competitive conditions, with oligopolistic industries (such as aluminium, as discussed below) having longer time scales than competitive ones. For example, employee involvement schemes may have a more indirect effect on labour productivity in comparison to training and development which is likely to affect skill levels and have a more immediate effect on employee efficiency and productivity and ultimately financial performance. Therefore, the performance benefits for employee involvement schemes are likely to manifest themselves in a longer time in comparison to the training and development schemes. Furthermore, not all dimensions of performance may be affected at the same time by the various HR practices. For example, it is argued that HR practices have a more immediate effect on labour productivity in comparison to financial performance. Consequently, different time scales have to be considered in order to effectively capture the effect of HPWS practices on these two dimensions of performance. Therefore, time lag considerations may depend upon the performance measure under consideration. Finally, not all HPWS practices may be introduced at the same time posing further dilemmas as to what point of time performance should be measured to capture the effects of these practices. This problem is especially relevant in a study involving a group of companies implementing an HPWS at various points of time.

Overall, the review of the HPWS/performance literature reveals that the inherent weaknesses and puzzles in the literature persist even after two decades of extensive research. While there have been some attempts to address the conceptual and methodological weaknesses in the literature, progress has been restricted primarily to having a better appreciation of the limitations of the study, identifying areas of future research and asking better questions. To illustrate these points, we look in detail at one leading study which avoids some of the problems identified above but which still leaves questions unanswered.

An illustration   The study itself highlights its methodological contribution as being 'the use of independent, rather than self-report, ratings to measure practices, financial records of performance [i.e. objective measures that escape problems of single raters assessing both dependent and independent variables], and a research design controlling for prior performance' (Patterson *et al.* 2004: 660). The last characteristic is key: a cross-section design cannot eliminate reverse causality, but in this study outcome measures were related to their earlier levels, and any *additional* effects of the HR variables were then assessed. We would also underline two features particularly relevant to our discussion: the study was conducted in specific sectors such as plastics and rubber manufacture, and is thus sensitive to context; and it focused on single-site companies, so that connections between HR practices and outcomes will be more direct than in the economy-wide studies.

The central high performance indicators were job enrichment and skill enhancement which were together taken to index 'empowerment'. These predicted subsequent performance, as measured by 'labour productivity'. Importantly, effects on profit were mediated by productivity. That is, if we observed a profit effect but no productivity effect, we might argue that relevant causal mechanisms are absent, but in this case HR practice affects productivity which in turn affects profit. The study also tests the idea that packages of HR practices reinforce each other in bundles, and it rejects this view.

There are, however, several questions which start with the specific and move to the general. First, empowerment is measured by asking several managers about relevant concrete practices and then developing the researchers' own evaluations. Whether or not employees said that they were empowered is not addressed. Empowerment is also a researcher label; other studies find that managers tend to use the term rather rarely (Edwards and Collinson 2002). Second, the key dependent variable is labour productivity, defined as sales per head. This is common practice, but productivity thus defined does not measure productivity in the sense of efficiency in the use of labour inputs; for example, workers may be working harder so that efficiency in the sense of a unit of effort does not rise. It is also not clear whether other possible influences on sales per head are controlled for; amongst other things, sales may rise for reasons to do with the price of goods on the market rather than for labour-related reasons. Third, the study does not directly report employee views or responses. It mentions that, in a subset of the companies, employee surveys were carried out and that the results correlate with the measures that were used with a correlation coefficient of about 0.5; since this implies that about 75% of the variance in the chosen measures is not in fact related to employee views, the strength of this argument might be questioned.

Two wider points also arise. First, we know nothing about the process of employee management in the companies concerned, for example how empowerment schemes were implemented. Whether it was the schemes themselves or some other feature of employment relations that was crucial is impossible to say. Second, therefore, any effects of the relevant practices may well be embedded in social relations and thus not transferable. In other words, other firms even in these industries might not gain the same benefits if they simply copied the practices. This argument brings us to an alternative approach.

The Social Relations of Productivity

As noted at the start of the chapter, the HPWS debate reproduces many of the analytical issues that arose in the earlier debates on unions and productivity. The leading (American) academic study of the time concluded that unions tended to improve productivity while also raising wages, so that their net effect might be zero (or ambiguous) (Freeman and Medoff 1984). It conceded, however, that the relevant causal mechanisms were far from clear, though it did suggest that one effect might be a tendency for unions to reduce rates of absence and of labour turnover. It also remarked that union effects will vary widely according to context – an important recognition, for many studies measured simply union presence (or some other indicator) without asking whether unions in, say, coal mining had the same character and effects as those in retailing. Instead of starting where this debate left off, by examining distinct contexts and causal relationships, the HPWS approach returned to quantitative, scientistic, modelling.

A second previous debate might also give pause for thought. The idea of the psychological contract addresses individual beliefs as though these are fixed features of people's workplace behaviour and as though a workforce is simply a mass of atomized people. If we look again at earlier debates, the weaknesses of this view are, or should be, well known. The famous Luton studies developed the idea of 'orientations to work': expectations that workers form outside the workplace and take with them (Goldthorpe *et al.* 1968). One core idea was important: the concept was designed in response to then popular technological determinism, which said that workers working under a given technology will respond in identical ways, and which plainly did not fit the Luton case. Here, workers laboured under classic Fordist assembly line conditions but they did not express the expected alienation and resentment because, the Luton researchers argued, they had consciously chosen these jobs for the financial rewards that they brought. But the idea of orientations swung too far from determinism to suggest that people have consistent and purely personal sets of preferences. Later research showed that workers' attitudes were often a complex mix of ideas, which shifted over time and which reflected the social context as well as personal choice (Bulmer 1975). A re-study of Luton itself found that workers had collectivist ideas based on a sense of their shared workplace situations (Devine 1992).

The relevance of this for the HPWS debate is to underline one simple but profound point: the importance of context. 'Context' can mean at least two things. Its more basic meaning is that the specific components of a high performance system will depend on the precise situation. Thus, practices appropriate to semi-skilled manufacturing jobs would not suit professional employees. This is a standard theme in the literature: there is a broad division between those who adopt a 'best practice' view and those stressing 'fit' to particular conditions. The former focuses on universally applicable ideas and the latter on adjustment to context. There was heated debate between the two, which can be followed in many places. A reasonable conclusion is that both have strengths: universalism points to broad themes and principles, while 'fit' stresses applications.

But, and this is the second sense of context, these ideas treat an HPWS as a set of techniques that can simply be applied, rather as an engineer selects tools from a box. Workplaces are, however, spaces in which social and political relationships shape beliefs and expectations.

An overview of the theory underlying the HPWS model suggests a way forward. Many theories address institutional context or the combination of resources and practices into distinct patterns. But, therefore, 'the very uniqueness and inimitability of the HR practices presumed to generate competitive advantage . . . would very likely make the discovery of a stable empirical link between some bundle of HR practices and organizational performance most unlikely' (Fleetwood and Hesketh 2008: 134). As these authors go on, studies that identify a practice such as job rotation fail to address why workers practise rotation, how they do it, or under what conditions they do it or may cease to do it (ibid.: 138). The high performance model implicitly accepts these points in speaking of 'idiosyncratic competences' that characterize a specific firm (Becker *et al.* 2001). If these are indeed idiosyncratic, it is not clear what overall correlations can tell us, or indeed what a firm might learn from such correlations other than the benefits of good management.

An industrial relations (IR) approach tends towards an inductive rather than a deductive approach to theory, and we follow this approach here by drawing on a study from which we have taken the title of this section of the chapter (Edwards *et al.* 2002). The limitation, of course, is that it may seem hard to generalize. But the idea of idiosyncrasy abandons any attempt in this direction. We see some possibilities, though we would also stress, with Fleetwood and Hesketh (2008), that open systems such as employment relationships can never generate decisive conclusions. In other words, once we recognize that social systems are open, complex and subject to change by actors, we also have to accept that the deterministic generalizations sought by statistical studies are inherently inappropriate.

The study examined productivity trends over a 20 year period in two plants owned by the same company. It found that productivity improved throughout the period, and thus puzzled over why a component of the HPWS, teamwork, was introduced towards the end of the period. The reasons did not appear to reflect either a sense amongst managers that current workplace relationships were directly a barrier to productivity or a clear view that teamwork offered distinctive benefits. There was, rather, a much less clear view that productivity improvement needed a stimulus and that teamwork might be the answer. The rationales for an HPWS thus reflect socially based expectations and not only technical considerations.

As for the effects of teamwork, these could not be separated from the pre-existing organization of production. The plants in question were aluminium smelters owned at the time by Alcan. As in other process technologies, workers are skilled and they work together in groups rather than being organized on an assembly line; they often have considerable autonomy. Teamwork thus has an affinity with this technical division of labour. As Fleetwood and Hesketh note, it has a distinct meaning, which here was that it fitted with work organization.

Why, then, was it not introduced sooner? This is an important question for the theory of IR and performance: if a solution is feasible, what stops it from being used? The conventional answer in the debate on unions and productivity was that workers and unions resist technical innovations. The evidence for such resistance has always been weak (Daniel 1984). Important historical studies have shown that choices of technology are socially shaped. Lazonick (1986), for example, compared the UK and US cotton industries and asked why the more efficient ring spinning technology was introduced in the latter but not the former. The answer turned on several factors: UK firms had protected markets and were not under pressure to innovate; they were also small, so that they lacked not only financial resources but also the managerial skills to innovate; and there was a ready supply of labour, in contrast to the USA where labour scarcity encouraged the use of labour-saving technology. In addition, and key to the present argument, the organization of work brought benefits to management. Work groups were arranged in an accepted hierarchy which meant that they were self-disciplining and also that they recruited at the bottom through local and family links. It was thus efficient in its own terms and it was a product of a social and historical process rather than being the conscious invention of the unions or indeed anyone else.

If we return to the smelters, in pre-teamwork days there had been a drift away from cooperative workplace relations. The group solidarity promoted by the technology can lead to sectional loyalties and to the development of collectivities that distrust each other. This occurred at one of the plants (Isle Maligne in Canada) in particular, for internal reasons (the work was dirty and unpleasant, and there was an atmosphere of antagonism) and because of external factors (wider union–management relations were tense in a period of high inflation). Teamwork lacked any purchase in this context. It became meaningful after several years in which more cooperative relationships were developed, a process that reflected the age of the plant and its vulnerability to closure.

Teamwork in these workplaces eventually proved to be successful. But two implications stand out. First, its origins and nature reflected its history; it was not a technique that could simply be implemented outside this history. Second, its success also reflected these conditions. In other circumstances, teamwork has quite different effects. Comparison with a case of failure is instructive (Vallas 2003). Efforts here to increase worker autonomy were made but these foundered on an overemphasis on what the study terms the rational elements such as the need for standard procedures. These elements neglected the normative processes such as the emergence of distrust when a pay-for-skill system was not delivered. Workers were willing to participate where they could draw on 'cultural patterns that were indigenous to production crews' (Vallas 2003: 244), but they could do so only rarely. There was no one set of factors that caused this result, and it may not have been predictable. Success at Alcan was also not pre-ordained and, as we have seen, participative traditions could erode. Teamwork has its effects in a complex and to a degree unpredictable context.

Underlying these arguments is a view of workplace relations as being infused with power. Managements do not introduce new work processes because these seem to be in some intellectual sense desirable. They do so to improve output and profit. They may fail to do so because of a fear of 'losing control' if they empower workers. They will also be influenced by the political and institutional context in which they operate. The Alcan case suggests that, in the absence of pressure to change, firms, at least in the UK, tend towards the default option of 'command and control'. This point is strongly illustrated by a US study of a very advanced form of workplace participation: the Saturn subsidiary of General Motors (Rubinstein and Kochan 2001). Two points are central here. First, as at Alcan, the form of teamworking adopted reflected the powerful position of trade unions in the firm; in the absence of the pressures that the unions could make, it is unlikely that such extensive 'empowerment' would have been practised, and indeed teamwork in more weakly unionized contexts is often much more tightly constrained (Bélanger and Edwards 2007). Second, despite demonstrable successes, the Saturn model was not adopted more widely in GM, a fact that reflects the lack of institutional pressure to generalize such models and the significant monetary and political costs of investing in arrangements outside the norm.

Studies of another potential high performance practice (Total Quality Management – TQM), offer further theoretical tools (Edwards *et al.* 1998). It found that, *under certain circumstances*, TQM techniques such as performance measurement and monitoring are associated with positive results for workers such as autonomy and commitment. This result is consistent with a long line of industrial relations analyses that show that workers have interests in a productive system that meets their short and long run interests (Edwards *et al.* 2006). It goes beyond an HPWS approach by stressing that the result is dependent on certain conditions, in this case a sense of job security and a wider context in which managements introduced TQM in a way consistent with other features of the work regime such as the place of the trade union. All the organizations studied here were unionized; in some cases, TQM was introduced alongside either antipathy towards, or a disconnection from, unions, and the positive effects of TQM were much weaker.

These ideas were encapsulated in the 'disciplined worker thesis'. This states that workers value an ordered and disciplined work environment but that a set of contextual conditions are necessary for this interest to be put into practice; without relevant underpinning conditions, workers may be sceptical of empowerment schemes. It is the context and not the scheme itself that is important. The ideas have the theoretical implication that productive performance is the outcome of social relations in which worker interests in efficiency are intertwined with other interests, such as job security, and are released only under certain conditions.

Social processes and performance

To develop these points, we now give a series of illustrations of the meaning of performance in different contexts.

Case studies of employee involvement in context   Marchington *et al.* (1994) studied six contrasting cases of employee involvement, meaning systems to improve communication with employees and their engagement with the work process; such systems are one core part of HPWS models. In terms of perspective, the study underlined the importance of locating initiatives in context. It stressed the 'variable meanings' that workers may attribute to the 'same' thing.

At 'ComputerCo', for example, there was only one significant formal mechanism. Employee attitudes were, however, very positive. This reflected modest prior experience of, and expectations for, involvement schemes. Also crucial was the rapid growth of the firm and its continuing strong prospects. At a financial services firm, 'BuSoc', by contrast, there were several established initiatives. Head office policy did not, however, translate into practice on the ground; and significant business reorganization was leading to an atmosphere of distrust. It was not the involvement scheme itself which was the issue, but rather the wider context in which it was embedded.

Prior worker expectations were key. In other firms with good involvement schemes, workers expected a great deal and were frustrated when their high expectations were not met. It was the practical approach of managers that determined employee responses, in relation both to involvement and the wider running of the business.

Business uncertainty itself need not destroy employee commitment. Employment security is often seen as a key underpinning to an HPWS, but job losses themselves do not necessarily destroy commitment.

Job insecurity and its ambiguous effects   A more detailed study of one of the Alcan aluminium smelters discussed above throws light on the role of job insecurity (Wright and Edwards 1998). This plant, at Lynemouth in north-east England, had undergone major job losses entailing the closure of half the plant's capacity. This event, in the context of a strongly unionized workforce, might be expected to have undermined trust in managers. In fact, it acted as a stimulant to extensive teamworking and significant reforms to workplace practice. Reasons included a demonstrable commitment by managers to the new teamwork model, with one indicator being the willingness of senior plant managers to impose the model on sceptical middle managers. The model was, moreover, seen by workers as essential if the remaining jobs were to be retained. Several other features of the context were also identified. It was in short the specific combination of factors that was important.

Informal organization   A third theme is the role of informal organization. This is highlighted in a longitudinal study of Hewlett Packard (HP), which argues that success depends on context, including 'the way in which policies are interpreted and enacted in practice' (Truss 2001: 1122). The study argues that, though HP was successful on conventional indicators and had high performance practices in place, the linkages were complex and variable. Three headline implications may be highlighted.

First, informal practice was often more important than formal systems. For example, the formal system of career development stressed targets and appraisals, but being 'visible' and engaging in networking were seen by employees as the key factor in career success (ibid.: 1144). A correlation between the formal systems and performance would not recognize this point. Second, employee responses reflected contradiction and paradox. There was confidence in the firm's ability to perform, and substantial willingness to put in discretionary effort but there were also doubts about the appraisal system, for example, and half of respondents to a survey felt that work was not carried out efficiently. This result might be attributed to the very high expectations that HP employees had. But it shows that, even in a very successful organization with a long tradition of sophisticated HR, the elements of HRM are not necessarily tightly connected. Even here, the connections between policy and practice were shifting and variable. Third, a changing business environment was eroding some aspects of employee expectations and leading to feelings of stress and pressure.

A good illustration of the context-dependent nature of high performance systems and their links to performance comes from a study of a UK bank (Wylie 2007). Given that, like HP, the bank was performing well, what role did an HPWS play?

There was clear evidence of the presence of a large number of the relevant practices, and that these were part of the firm's strategy. This is important in that proponents of the HPWS model tend to argue that case studies that do not fit it are not 'true' tests because the relevant practices were not in fact adopted. Such an argument always looks like special pleading. In this case it is hard to make, for the practices not only existed on paper but were put into operation.

The study addressed two departments: a relatively routine back office department and a group of managers running corporate banking operations. Not surprisingly, different parts of the HPWS had different roles in the two departments. Target-setting and performance management were important in the former, while pay incentives for performance were more salient in the latter. Much more surprisingly, workers in both departments denied that the HPWS directly affected their own performance. For the managers in corporate banking, to suggest that they were driven by the carrot of a financial bonus was to impugn their professional integrity. In the back office, performance was determined by personal commitment to doing a good job and by the day-to-day practices of individual managers.

In the senses claimed by the high performance model, the relevant practices had no discernible effects: they did not directly change discretionary levels of effort or employee commitment. In a broader sense, however, they were significant in underlining that performance was an objective and defining what it meant. In the back office, for example, the measurement of work loads and the use of performance management helped to define the game that was being played. This was a matter of social relationships rather than the operation of a high performance system as such a system is identified in the HRM literature.

What makes an HPWS work? A recent study takes us further in three respects (Harley *et al.* 2007). First, like that by Wylie it is of the service sector but it embraces small organizations as well as large ones, namely, those providing aged care in Australia. Second, it returns to the disciplined worker thesis to underline the fact that an HPWS can have positive results for workers but that these turn on the wider context. Third, it uses quantitative techniques, showing that IR insights are not restricted to qualitative methods and that it is possible to deploy these insights on the same methodological terrain as that occupied by more conventional studies. It finds that an HPWS indeed promotes a number of worker interests, and it also stresses that this effect is not limited to high-skill jobs. To this extent, it is consistent with the optimistic strands of the HPWS literature. But it also stresses that the effects were mediated through workers' sense of order and predictability. And it notes that this was a study of unionized workers, so that unionization may have provided a context for positive effects to flow, though the absence of a non-union comparison here means that this point cannot be demonstrated.

Our final illustration of the importance of context is from our own study of 37 production companies in the media sector in the UK. The data include interviews with senior managers in all 37 firms and questionnaires from a total of 105 employees in 14 of these firms. These firms are of interest for two reasons. First, they are small (with a mean of nine full-time permanent employees, though freelance employees could on occasion number up to 50). Second, they can be taken to be part of the 'knowledge economy' in which performance may be driven by forces different from those discussed above. For both these reasons, the themes of contradiction and paradox noted in large organizations might be expected to be less salient. In fact, they were clearly apparent (for reasons discussed more fully in Ram and Edwards, this volume).

The findings revealed that the firms varied in terms of their performance outcomes even though they had similar HR practices (at least on paper). The firms were also similar in terms of their size and their environmental context; and they fished in the same labour market pool, and indeed employees commonly moved from one to another. The differences in the performance outcomes could be partly attributed to contextual factors like differing networking relationships and differences in business strategy. For example, the high performing firms tended to have stronger and more widely developed networking relationships with customers, suppliers and at times other media production companies. Several had also secured the ownership rights to the programmes they produced and continued to earn royalties by selling the formats of the programmes to international broadcasting corporations. It was the interaction between this context and HR practices, rather than the practices independently, that shaped performance.

Second, then, the configuration of HR practices aligned with the context played a critical role in influencing employee satisfaction in firms. For example, employee responses to training and development opportunities in two remarkably similar firms were very different owing to how the HR practices were combined. The two firms were similar in terms of their positions as market leaders, business strategy, networking relationships and size, and even shared the same pool of local talent. However, they differed with respect to the way the HR policies and practices were combined. The employees expressed greater satisfaction with training and development in the firm that integrated a formalized training and development programme with opportunities for career development and had clear channels for communication. The training needs in this firm were identified through the annual appraisal programmes. Formal training enabled the employees to acquire relevant skills which would help them fulfil their professional aspirations and move up the career ladder. In contrast, in the comparable firm which had an ad hoc and informal procedure for training and career development and had poor communication channels, less than half of the employees were satisfied with the training and development opportunities.

Third, though the policies were similar in principle, the firms differed with respect to their interpretation and implementation of the HRM practices. This could also account for the apparent differences in performance outcomes. For example, training and development opportunities in the less successful firms often meant on-the-job training or health and security training. In contrast, the more successful firms had an elaborate system of both on-the-job and off-the-job training for their employees. Furthermore, though all the firms engaged in research and development activities they differed with respect to the size of funds allocated to this activity. These funds were typically highest in the high performing firms and often there was a separate research and development fund.

Overall, these examples suggest that it is difficult to predict the impact of a set of HR practices upon different dimensions of performance without taking into account the contextual factors that mediate the HRM and performance relationship. This is not to say that the relationship does not exist or that it is unknowable or that lessons cannot be taken from one case to another. But it is deeply context-dependent, and lessons cannot be reduced to package solutions.

Discussion: The Context of Performance

As we have noted, the role of IR in performance has been debated at national as well as company level. Our purpose here is not to address this different debate, but to consider the nature of linkages between the micro and the macro.

The fundamental point here concerns institutions and the ways in which they establish a terrain on which an HPWS may have its effects. Part of the unions and productivity debate argued that UK unions as a whole had a particular character sometimes labelled 'restrictivist'; the idea here is that unions were strongly embedded in a particular trade or skill and prone to develop 'restrictive' practices such as narrow definitions of jobs, inflexibility and resistance to change. This argument identified (a) a certain form of workplace unionism which (b) affected firms and (c) was large enough to affect the economy as a whole (a view still expressed by some: Lawson 1997). But there was no evidence that the effect of (a) was so generic as to influence the whole economy. It is true that in the past the economy was characterized by sectors that are now small and that had strong workplace union organizations: coal, the docks, parts of manufacturing, and so on. But even in these sectors 'restrictivism' was far from universal; parts of the coal industry, for example, were dominated by employer paternalism. Significant parts of manufacturing had little workplace trade unionism. As for workplace unionism itself, it is true that it had restrictivist tendencies (Fox 1985), but these were balanced by a concern for productivity and, commonly, a welcome to technological innovation (Edwards and Terry 1988). Finally, unionism was itself shaped by managerial decisions, as demonstrated by studies of the cotton industry, which showed that managers made choices about technologies and the kinds of labour to be employed, choices that helped to create a specific kind of workplace unionism (Lazonick 1986). A first conclusion, therefore, is that institutions do not create a fixed pattern of constraints and opportunities within which firms make choices. Firms interact with the environment in complex ways.

As to the nature of this interaction, the HPWS model tends to assume, when in 'best practice' mode, that all firms will tend to develop schemes of empowerment. In 'best fit' terms, the argument is more subtle: firms will use such schemes to the extent that they are compatible with a firm's strategic position. But it still sees 'fit' as something that a firm can identify and secure. This assumption neglects the resources available to the firm. As the long-running debate on managerial skills has shown (see Sisson and Purcell, this volume), British firms often lacked managers with the necessary skills to identify and put into practice a strategic fit. It also neglects the product market and other conditions within which firms operate, and which their choices help to reproduce. Thus the celebrated comparative firm and sector level studies associated with the National Institute of Economic and Social Research found that British firms did indeed have relatively low-skilled workers compared to counterparts in the Netherlands and other countries (Prais 1995) but this reflected the low value-added sectors in which the firms operated. More recent research confirms that, in general, UK firms operate in sectors with a low intensity of research and development activity (DTI 2005: 13). In such a context, a high performance model would lack meaning.

Considerations such as these led to the concept of the low-skills equilibrium (see Keep *et al.*, this volume), which was seen as the result of the interaction of a set of interlocking institutions at national level (Finegold and Soskice 1988). An implication of this idea is that UK institutions create conditions where a high performance system is unlikely to flourish. The idea can, however, be as deterministic as that which says that an HPWS carries necessary competitive advantage. It is the case that elements of the system have been introduced in the UK. Indeed, it is also commonly argued that the UK institutional environment is particularly permissive precisely because it lacks strong institutions such as effectively enforced labour laws and works councils (Colling; Dickens and Hall, this volume). This apparent paradox can be resolved if we see any one institution as having mixed potentials: strong workplace unions can impose constraints on firms, but they also offer the opportunity to represent their members effectively and to create a system of workplace governance. These various institutions also do not necessarily form a coherent whole, but rather a set of differing influences, some of which will be in tension with each other.

The conclusion here is not that the institutional context is unimportant. It is, rather, that the way in which this context affects firms is variable and uncertain. It can, for example, mean that firms compete 'successfully' in certain markets and not others, rather than that they fail to compete at all. Firms are, moreover, shaped and not determined by their context.

Does this mean that nothing concrete can be said about the role of IR in performance? We have argued that the search for the concrete, in the sense of a set of practices that will improve performance, has been misconceived. Indeed, the notion of idiosyncratic competences recognizes as much. But there are certainly lessons in terms of *process*, that is, the ways in which practices are combined and used. To ask whether having an employee involvement scheme raises performance is to ask the wrong question. But one can certainly interrogate such a scheme to ask whether it is consistent with workers' social expectation, whether managers apply it consistently, how compatible it is with other goals, and so on. A particular theme to stress is the openness of a scheme: is it simply imposed, or are there means in place to debate what it does and to alter its operation? We have seen that schemes can be ignored by workers for many reasons. The point is not a scheme itself but the messages that it sends and the ways in which it is used. Thinking about process is the apparently simple lesson, which has profound consequences if it is adopted.

This conclusion has a central implication for public policy. A simple view of the high performance model says that it delivers effects in the production process, with the task of public policy being to supply skills that are then deployed in the workplace. And this supply-driven view of skills has indeed driven policy, as shown by Keep *et al.* (this volume). But there is no point supplying skills if they are not utilized in the work process, even assuming that a 'skill' has meaning outside the context in which it is deployed. A developing view of public policy says that it is the utilization of skills that is key, and that the core ideas of a high perform-ance model need to be given life within the complex of forces that determine skills utilization, rather than assuming that they are a ready-made solution (Delbridge *et al.* 2006). Thus the implicit current model says that a national training sys-tem generates skills which firms then choose to deploy through an HPWS. The alternative is a more holistic approach, of which there are examples in Australia and Finland. In a UK context it would mean that government support agencies engage directly with firms in the utilization of skills. Delbridge *et al.* (2006: 28) cite Purcell's discussion (2000: 174) of the Work Research Unit. This body, which was closed in 1993, engaged actively with firms to develop programmes of organiz-ational change; a key part of its role was to include worker representatives and to seek joint solutions to common issues. Delbridge *et al.* also argue for support to be given to voluntary bodies established by firms themselves, as opposed to blanket business support strategies.

In short, debate on the HPWS has tended to treat such a system as a set of techniques that can be deployed at will. This neglects the complex ways in which a technique in fact affects outcomes and the many constraints on its use. But the underpinning ideas have meaning and value. As Godard (2004) remarks, much of what goes under the HPWS label can be termed simply 'good management'. Pursuing the principles of skill and autonomy, within the specific contexts of a given workplace, provides a less mechanistic view of the ways in which employees contribute to workplace performance.

References

Becker, B. and Gerhart, B. 1996: The impact of human resource management on organ-izational performance: progress and prospects. *Academy of Management Journal*, 39 (4), 779–801.

Becker, B., Huselid, M. and Ulrich, D. 2001: *The HR Scorecard: Linking People, Strategy and Performance*. Cambridge, Mass.: Harvard Business School Press.

Bélanger, J. and Edwards, P. 2007: The conditions promoting compromise in the work-place. *British Journal of Industrial Relations*, 45 (4), 713–734.

Boselie, P., Dietz, G. and Boon, C. 2005: Commonalities and contradictions in HRM and performance research. *Human Resource Management Journal*, 15 (3), 67–94.

Boxall, P. and Purcell, J. 2003: *Strategy and Human Resource Management*. Basingstoke: Palgrave.

Bryson, A., Gomez, R., Kretschmer, T. and Willman, P. 2007: The diffusion of workplace voice and high-commitment human resource management practices in Britain, 1984–1998. *Industrial and Corporate Change*, 16 (3), 395–426.

Bulmer, M. (ed.) 1975: *Working-class Images of Society*. London: Routledge and Kegan Paul.

Daniel, W.W. 1984: *Workplace Industrial Relations and Technical Change*. London: Frances Pinter.

Devine, F. 1992: *Affluent Workers Revisited*. Edinburgh: Edinburgh UP.

Delbridge, R., Edwards, P., Forth, J., Miskell, P. and Payne, J. 2006: The organisation of productivity: re-thinking skills and work organisation. Advanced Institute of Management Research Report, December.

DTI (Department of Trade and Industry) 2005: R&D intensive businesses in the UK, DTI Economics Paper 11. London: DTI.

Edwards, P. and Collinson, M. 2002: Empowerment and managerial labor strategies; pragmatism regained. *Work and Occupations*, 29 (3), 272–299.

Edwards, P. and Terry, M. 1988: Conclusions: another way forward? In Terry, M. and Edwards, P. (eds) *Shopfloor Politics and Job Controls*. Oxford: Blackwell.

Edwards, P., Bélanger, J. and Wright, M. 2002: The social relations of productivity: a longitudinal and comparative study of aluminium smelters. *Relations Industrielles/Industrial Relations*, 57 (2), 309–330.

Edwards, P., Bélanger, J. and Wright, M. 2006: The bases of compromise in the workplace. *British Journal of Industrial Relations*, 44 (1), 125–146.

Edwards, P., Collinson, M. and Rees, C. 1998: The determinants of employee to Total Quality Management. *Organization Studies*, 19 (3), 449–476.

Finegold, D. and Soskice, D.1988. The failure of training in Britain. *Oxford Review of Economic Policy*, 4 (3), 21–53.

Fleetwood, S. and Hesketh, A. 2008: Theorising under-theorisation in research on the HRM-performance link. *Personnel Review*, 37 (2), 127–144.

Fox, A. 1985: *History and Heritage*. London: Allen and Unwin.

Freeman, R.B. and Medoff, J.L. 1984: *What do Unions Do?* New York: Basic.

Godard, J. 2004: A critical assessment of the high-performance paradigm. *British Journal of Industrial Relations*, 42 (2), 349–378.

Goldthorpe, J.H., Lockwood, D., Bechhofer, F. and Platt, J. 1968: *The Affluent Worker: Industrial Attitudes and Behaviour*. Cambridge: CUP.

Guest, D. 1997: Human resource management and performance: a review and research agenda. *International Journal of Human Resource Management*, 8 (3), 263–276.

Guest, D., Michie, J., Conway, N. and Sheehan, M. 2003: Human resource management and corporate performance in the UK. *British Journal of Industrial Relations*, 41 (2), 291–314.

Gunderson, M. 2002: Rethinking productivity from a workplace perspective. Canadian Policy Research Networks Discussion Paper W17.

Harley, B., Allen, B.C. and Sargent, L.D. 2007: High performance work systems and employee experience of work in the service sector: the case of aged care. *British Journal of Industrial Relations*, 45 (3), 607–633.

Harney, B. and Dundon, T. 2006: Capturing complexity: developing an integrated approach to analysing HRM in SMEs. *Human Resource Management Journal*, 16 (1), 48–73.

Huselid, M. 1995: The impact of human resource management practices on turnover, productivity and corporate financial performance. *Academy of Management Journal*, 38 (4), 635–672.

Huselid, M. and Becker, B. 1996: Methodological issues in cross-sectional and panel estimates of the human resource – firm performance link. *Industrial Relations*, 35 (3), 400–422.

Ichniowski, C., Shaw, K. and Prennushi, G. 1997: The effects of human resource management on productivity: a study of steel finishing lines. *American Economic Review*, 87 (3), 291–313.

Kersley, B., Alpin, C., Forth, J., Bryson, A., Bewley, H., Dix, G. and Oxenbridge, S. 2006: *Inside the Workplace: Findings from the 2004 Workplace Employment Relations Survey*. London: Routledge.

Kinnie, N., Hutchinson, S., Purcell, J., Rayton, B. and Swart, J. 2005: Satisfaction with HR practices and commitment to the organisation: why one size does not fit all. *Human Resource Management Journal*, 15 (4), 9–29.

Lawson, T. 1997: *Economics and Reality*. London: Routledge.

Lazonick, W. 1986: The cotton industry. In Elbaum, B. and Lazonick, W. (eds) *The Decline of the British Economy*. Oxford: Clarendon.

Marchington, M., Wilkinson, A., Ackers, P. and Goodman, J. 1994: Understanding the meaning of participation. *Human Relations*, 47 (8), 867–893.

Nichols, T. 1986: *The British Worker Question*. London: Routledge and Kegan Paul.

Patterson, M.G., West, M.A. and Wall, T.D. 2004: Integrated manufacturing, empowerment and company performance. *Journal of Organizational Behavior*, 25 (4), 641–665.

Pil, F.K. and MacDuffie, J.P. 1996: The adoption of high involvement work practices. *Industrial Relations*, 35 (3), 423–455.

Prais, S.J. 1995: *Productivity, Education and Training*. Cambridge: CUP.

Purcell, J. 2000: After collective bargaining? ACAS in the age of human resource management. In Towers, B. and Brown, W. (eds) *Employment Relations in Britain: 25 Years of the Advisory, Conciliation and Arbitration Service*. Oxford: Blackwell.

Ramsay, H., Scholarios, D. and Harley, B. 2000: Employees and high performance work systems: testing inside the black box. *British Journal of Industrial Relations*, 28 (4), 501–531.

Rubinstein, S.A. and Kochan, T.A. 2001: *Learning from Saturn*. Ithaca: ILR Press.

Traxler, F., Blaschke, S. and Kittel, B. 2001: *National Labour Relations in Internationalized Markets: a Study of Institutions, Change and Performance*. Oxford: OUP.

Truss, K. 2001: Complexities and controversies in linking HRM with organizational outcomes. *Journal of Management Studies*, 38 (8), 1121–1149.

Vallas, S. 2003: Why team work fails. *American Sociological Review*, 68 (2), 223–250.

Wall, T.D. and Wood, S.J. 2005: The romance of human resource management and business performance, and the case for big science. *Human Relations*, 58 (4), 429–462.

Wall, T.D., Michie, J., Patterson, M., Wood, S.J., Sheehan, M., Clegg, C.W. and West, M.A. 2004: On the validity of subjective measures of company performance. *Personnel Psychology*, 57 (1), 95–118.

Wright, M. and Edwards, P. 1998: Does teamworking work, and if so why? A case study in the aluminium industry. *Economic and Industrial Democracy*, 19 (1), 59–90.

Wylie, N. 2007: HRM and individual performance in a High Street bank: exploring the role of subjectivity in the HRM-performance relationship. PhD thesis, University of Warwick.

17

SKILLS POLICY AND THE DISPLACEMENT OF INDUSTRIAL RELATIONS: THE ELEPHANT IN THE CORNER?

EWART KEEP, CAROLINE LLOYD AND JONATHAN PAYNE

Introduction

> Skills is the most important lever within our control to create wealth and to reduce social deprivation. (Leitch 2006: 2)

The above statement, taken from the Treasury-sponsored Leitch Review of Skills, illustrates the central importance and weight that the UK Labour government attaches to skills as the main driver of economic success and social justice. The identification of skills as 'the most important lever' available to government is the significant phrase here. While there is no suggestion that skills are the only lever, it does elevate skills above all others. In this chapter, we argue that skills have not only become the central focus of policy intervention but that they are increasingly being conceived, at least by policy makers, as an alternative to, and replacement for, more traditional industrial relations concerns. However, if skills are to make a difference, they have to be utilized (Leitch 2006: 22). The current policy neglect of the workplace and industrial relations context in which skill is created and mobilized is therefore significant and, as we argue, impedes the development of a viable and 'joined-up' skills strategy.

It is important to note that, in the area of skills policy, devolution has already had a substantial impact. The governments of Northern Ireland, Scotland and Wales and their parliaments/assemblies have control over education and training matters, but not industrial relations and employment legislation (where jurisdiction and administrative arrangements remain UK-wide and rooted in Westminster and

Whitehall). The UK nations have evolved a varied array of institutional structures to govern and fund their education and training systems, and it is becoming increasingly apparent that they are also developing different policies and programmes. In some cases, divergent strategic paths, particularly as between England and Scotland, are introducing new fault lines and tensions within current UK policy debates about how best to make advances in this area (Payne 2008a).

The first section of the chapter charts the rise and fall of industrial relations as a policy issue from the 1960s to the present day, comparing it to the growing importance attached to skills and training. This shift in emphasis has been particularly prominent since New Labour entered office in 1997. The second section considers whether the current skills agenda has afforded new opportunities for both trade unions and employers (collectively) to influence skill and training developments. Unions have been given a new role in helping to support learning at work, while policy makers have claimed that the English vocational education and training (VET) system is increasingly 'employer-led'. Through a comparison between the early 1980s and the present day, it is argued that, notwithstanding these developments, the influence of the 'social partners' has actually declined over this period. Indeed, it is difficult to view skills policy in the UK as part of the industrial relations system, particularly when comparisons are made with arrangements elsewhere in Europe. The third section then explores some of the reasons behind the UK government's current policy focus on education and skills, together with the corresponding neglect of industrial relations issues. The chapter concludes by considering whether there is the potential for broadening current policy debates on skills, particularly given the need to address issues of skill utilization at work.

The Waxing and Waning of Industrial Relations and the Rise of Skills

From the 1960s through to the 1980s industrial relations was a central focus of policy attention in the UK. Throughout this period, the UK was frequently described as having a 'labour problem', the definition of which shifted over time. Solving that problem was seen as key to reduced industrial conflict, better economic performance and, for some at least, as a means of securing greater social equity. This section charts the shift in government policy from the 1960s through to the present day and the way in which attention has moved away from industrial relations towards skills as the main driver of both economic efficiency and social justice.

The 1960s and 1970s

In the 1960s and 1970s, deficiencies in the design and conduct of collective bargaining were regarded by government as a major factor in explaining the UK's productivity and economic growth problems. Worries centred on issues such as lack of labour flexibility and rigid demarcation lines, and the rise of informal workplace bargaining arrangements and 'leapfrog' bargaining tactics that led to wage drift and price inflation (Fox and Flanders 1969). As a result, there was substantial interest in reforming the industrial relations system, particularly to secure the orderly conduct of collective bargaining, as a means of delivering improved economic performance. Properly conducted collective bargaining was seen by government and other policy actors as essential to wage moderation, economic stability and prosperity (Ogden 1982).

National debates about industrial relations were not abstract affairs. They supported activity by government agencies (for example, the Prices and Incomes Board, ACAS, the Donovan Commission) and the work of a myriad of employer organizations and trade unions. They also gave rise to a considerable volume of legislation. Moreover, these policy debates were mirrored by extensive coverage in the media (Wilby 2007), a great deal of academic inquiry and debate, and the rise of 'schools of thought' about the best manner and direction in which policy should proceed (see Nichols 1986 for a critique of the 'accepted wisdom' on the link between industrial relations and economic performance).

Skills were not absent as a policy issue during this period, but they were largely overshadowed by industrial relations. Indeed, the notion that lack of skills and training acted as a source of national economic weakness had a long history in the UK, with the theory gaining currency at various times in the 19th century (Perry 1976; Sheldrake and Vickerstaff 1987). As the economy faltered in the early 1960s, concerns focused on the state of Britain's 'voluntarist' training system and its ability to provide training of sufficient quantity and quality. Because of the lack of any general legal obligation on employers to provide either initial or continuing training to their workforce, there was a belief that the overall volume of training was insufficient (Perry 1976). There were also concerns about the inequity of training distribution across different occupations, sectors and age groups. The Labour government's Industrial Training Act of 1964 marked a decisive break with tradition by establishing a series of Industrial Training Boards (ITBs). These were tripartite bodies, with equal employer and trade union representation, which had the power to levy firms and give grants for training.

In 1974, the Manpower Services Commission (MSC) was set up to oversee workforce planning, government training schemes and the ITBs. The MSC, like the National Economic Development Office (NEDO) which also existed at this time, was an avowedly tripartite body, with three members nominated by the Confederation of British Industry (CBI) and three by the Trades Union Congress (TUC). Insofar as skills and training were a public policy issue during this period, the national institutional mechanisms that were created to deal with them were firmly located within the machinery of corporatism and were designed through statute to deliver partnership between, and joint action by, the 'two sides of industry'. However, these institutions operated in a broader industrial relations context characterized by voluntarism, even in collective bargaining, where the 'Continental vocabulary of "social partners" was . . . almost incomprehensible in English' (Hyman 2003: 39).

Against the backdrop of the OPEC oil crisis of 1973–74, rising unemployment and stagflation, policy makers began the construction of an alternative diagnosis of the UK's economic problems. In 1976, the Labour Prime Minister, James Callaghan's

'Great Debate' speech, on the failure of the education system to meet the needs of industry, signalled a major shift of gear in terms of a determination to address perceived weaknesses in the education system (Gleeson and Keep 2004). The nature of Callaghan's framing of the skills problem – as one to do with inadequate and inappropriate supply by the education system and failure to meet the needs of employers – would strike a powerful chord with policy makers throughout the 1980s and 1990s.

The period of Conservative government (1979–97)

1979 witnessed the election of a neo-liberal Thatcher government bent on weakening trade unions and eradicating their influence within political life (Howell 2005). Trade unions, collective agreements and other traditional forms of industrial relations were now viewed by government, alongside many other aspects of the 'post-war consensus', as a major cause of Britain's economic performance woes (Taylor 1993). The aim of policy was no longer the reform of collective bargaining, but the reduction of its importance and strength, and its replacement with more individualized and managerial-led forms of pay determination (see Brown, this volume). This de-collectivization was accompanied by the rise of human resource management (HRM) and the promise of much more sophisticated approaches to managing and motivating the workforce in pursuit of organizational and national economic success (see the contributors to Storey (1989) for a flavour of these debates). In essence, industrial relations came to be seen as part of the problem, the solution to which was to bolster the 'manager's right to manage', and the introduction of an often unitarist model of HRM.

While the state of industrial relations was the government's number one priority in 1979, by the early 1990s that problem could, at least on the government's own definition, be presented as having largely been 'solved'. Trade unions were markedly weaker than at any time since the Second World War, their involvement in public policy and public life had been massively reduced, industrial action had declined sharply and unions' ability to exercise and maintain influence over decisions in the workplace was increasingly limited (see Brown; Simms and Charlwood; Terry, this volume).

In the area of training and skills, policy development quickened rapidly in the 1980s. In broad terms, the aim was to develop a 'training market' in which training decisions would be left at the discretion of employers and individuals (King 1993; Keep and Rainbird 2003). The ITBs were replaced with new, voluntary, 'employer-led' bodies as the levy system was demolished and the training system deregulated. These employer-led bodies have since undergone a series of reorganizations and name changes – Non-Statutory Training Organisations, Industry Training Organisations, National Training Organisations and, finally, Sector Skills Councils (SSCs), created in 2001. The MSC was wound up in 1988, effectively bringing to an end all formal tripartite arrangements for the governance of training in the UK. By contrast, elsewhere in Europe, social partnership-based models of training continued to flourish, with some countries, such as Spain and France, stepping up their efforts to address adult training through entitlements embedded in national and sectoral level collective agreements.

At the same time, traditional educational policy was gradually being supplanted by a broader form of skills policy that placed stress on the role of skill in securing employment in the labour market, and in delivering comparative organizational advantage in a more testing and competitive marketplace. By the early 1990s, Cutler (1992) argued that a paradigm shift was already under way, as the nature of Britain's 'labour problem' was transmuted in public debate, from an industrial relations problem to a skills problem.

Despite widespread institutional reforms to the training system, improvements in outcomes failed to materialize. Although the amount of training appeared to be increasing, there were questions over the quality of provision, particularly at lower levels, together with concerns about the sharp reduction in the number of apprenticeships (Keep and Rainbird 1995). With economic performance still a persistent problem, Finegold and Soskice argued, in a highly influential paper, that Britain was 'trapped in a low-skills equilibrium in which the majority of enterprises staffed by poorly trained managers and workers produce low-quality goods and services' (1988: 22). Their analysis indicated that rather than there being any simple causal link between weaknesses in the education and training system and poor economic performance, the UK was instead confronted with a systems problem, whereby a set of political and economic institutions acted to stifle the demand for improvements in skill. These institutions included the 'organization of industry, firms and the work process, the industrial relations system, financial markets, the state and political structure, as well as the operation of the ET [education and training] system' (ibid.: 22). Industrial relations concerns focused specifically on the absence of strong local employers' associations, the limited scope of sectoral collective bargaining, the uncoordinated nature of British trade unions and the weakness of centralizing bodies, notably the CBI and the TUC.

The UK's 'low skills model' was explicitly contrasted with the 'high skills equilibrium' or high skills, high wage approach found in the former West Germany (Finegold 1991, Streeck 1992, Culpepper 1999). Skill levels were considered to be substantially higher, as well as more evenly distributed, while German industrial performance was far superior compared with the UK (Brown *et al.* 2001). Strong employers' associations, primarily operating through local Chambers of Commerce, trade unions and works councils played a central role in training and skill formation, particularly in relation to the much-vaunted 'dual apprenticeship' system. In addition, the ability of German workers to secure relatively high wages, job security and levels of control over the work process and skill requirements was seen as part of a set of institutional constraints that forced employers to seek alternatives to low wage, low skill routes to competitive advantage (Streeck 1992). Although there has been much subsequent discussion over the extent to which the German system has collapsed since reunification in 1990, this high skills model has continued to exert a powerful influence over debates on alternatives to the UK's current approach to skills and performance (Lloyd and Payne 2003).

The New Labour government

By the time New Labour was elected in 1997 the policy discourse around education and training had, in large measure, already shifted from being concerned with national economic decline to a focus on securing relative comparative competitive advantage in an increasingly globalized economy (DTI 1995). When the Prime Minister, Tony Blair, insisted therefore that 'education is the best economic policy we have' (DfEE 1998), he was essentially continuing a line of policy argument that was already well established under his Conservative predecessors. What changed under New Labour was that these economic arguments were supplemented with another discourse, albeit a subordinate one, in which skills were presented as a central mechanism for achieving a 'fairer, more inclusive society' (DfES *et al.* 2003). New Labour was not alone in embracing the skills agenda. As Ashton and Green (1996) noted, there was already a broad consensus across the developed world, supported by policy agencies such as the OECD and World Bank, that skills were a key factor in economic competitiveness, productivity growth and rising average living standards. However, these broader international policy concerns led to very different approaches within specific national institutional contexts (Crouch *et al.* 1999; Brown *et al.* 2001).

New Labour's policy assumptions   Reflecting a similar approach to previous Conservative governments, New Labour entered office already committed to maintaining a 'flexible', deregulated labour market, albeit one supplemented with a minimum platform of employment rights, and having effectively discounted the value of an active industrial policy (Coates and Hay 2001; Lloyd and Payne 2002; Stedward 2003). The government set itself firmly against the European model of social partnership and labour market regulation, emphasizing its rigidities in the face of globalization, advocating internal reform within the EU and stressing the virtues of a resurgent Anglo-US capitalism. This position played well with UK business interests and was justified on the grounds that there was no alternative given the threat of exit from footloose global capital (see Marginson and Meardi, this volume). At the same time, it was argued that the emergence of a 'new' knowledge-based economy demanded a new role for the state in which investment in human capital took centre stage. As Tony Blair put it in his 'legacy' speech on the future of work:

> In a sense, a whole economy has passed away . . . In the new knowledge-economy, human capital, the skills that people possess, is critical . . . The rule now is not to interfere . . . in a highly fluid, rapidly changing economic market. It is to equip the employee to survive, prosper and develop in such a market, to give them the flexibility to be able to choose a wide range of jobs and to fit family and work/life together. (Blair 2007: 2–3)

The 'logic' was that if firms were to compete successfully at the higher reaches of the value chain and fend off competition from countries with lower labour costs, they needed first and foremost a highly skilled and flexible workforce. Without access to these skills, organizations would be impeded in their ability to move 'up-market' and respond effectively to the new global pressures. Increasing skill levels was seen, therefore, as both a necessary condition for taking up the new production opportunities and as a key driver in delivering competitive success and productivity growth. The *assumption* was that, faced with a more qualified and capable workforce, firms would respond by adjusting their competitive strategies and organizational approaches to make effective use of this new resource. In terms of the social inclusion agenda, offering those without qualifications the opportunity to acquire basic skills and a first Level 2 qualification[1] would allow access to the labour market and provide a platform for further progression out of low wage jobs.

The Leitch Review of Skills, commissioned by the Treasury in 2005, recommended that the government adopt a series of ambitious qualification targets designed to place the UK in the top eight of the OECD at every skill level, ranging from adult literacy and numeracy to higher education, by 2020. The targets were subsequently accepted by the government for England, with current skills policy now directed towards meeting them (DIUS 2007). The Prime Minister, Gordon Brown, has compared this stockpiling approach with the old 'arms race' between the west and the Soviet Union:

> A generation ago, a British Prime Minister had to worry about the global arms race. Today a British Prime Minister has to worry about the global skills race – because the nation that shows it can bring out the best in all its people will be the great success story of the coming decades. (Brown 2008: 1)

The assumption is that the country which amasses the biggest arsenal of skills/qualifications ultimately emerges triumphant in the global 'war' of economic competition, provided that it can maintain its position as a 'world leader' at the front of the race or 'treadmill' (Coates 2000: 254).

Problems with a skills-alone approach   There are, however, a number of well-charted problems with this policy 'logic'. Take productivity, for example. Existing research suggests that skills account for between one fifth and one eighth of the UK's relative gap with Germany and France and have little to do with poor performance vis-à-vis the USA (Leitch 2005: 4). As O'Mahony and de Boer (2002) have shown, a much bigger part of the story is the UK's weak record on capital investment and R&D (see also DTI 2005). These findings are not new and reflect long-standing concerns over the root causes of the poor performance of the UK economy (Mowery 1986; Kitson and Michie 1996). There are a number of examples of other countries which currently do better than the UK in terms of their national 'skill stocks' but which nevertheless trail behind on productivity per hour worked; Canada and New Zealand being cases in point. Scotland already has a qualifications profile, particularly in relation to graduates, that compares favourably with the rest of the UK but still lags well behind English productivity levels (Keep *et al.* 2006, Scottish Government 2007).

There is also substantial evidence to show that many UK firms continue to compete *successfully* through low skill, low value-added product market strategies

(Keep and Mayhew 1999; Brown *et al.* 2001). These firms are not necessarily acting irrationally; they are simply making the most of 'a thriving marketplace for goods and services sold on the basis of low cost and supported by low wages' (Wilson and Hogarth 2003: xvi). Given that many of these firms are 'not failing businesses' (Wilson and Hogarth 2003: 73), there must be a serious question mark over whether increasing the available supply of qualified labour will be enough to encourage them to move away from cost-based approaches towards higher value-added strategies. Neither should one expect this situation to change as a result of global competitive pressures since many of these firms operate in national or local markets (Mason 2004).

Moreover, New Labour has been reluctant to disrupt the relationship between a low-waged, flexible labour market and cost-based competitive strategies. Policies have focused on subsidizing workers on low wages, particularly those with children, through in-work benefits, rather than forcing employers to provide secure and adequate wages through a more tightly regulated labour market (Mason *et al.* 2008). The existence of a substantial number of low wage jobs, particularly in the retail, care and hospitality sectors, means that more people with qualifications are being forced to take lower skilled jobs. The 2006 Skills Survey estimated that over 7 million jobs in the UK require no qualifications in order to undertake them, while there are only around 2.5 million workers without qualifications (Felstead *et al.* 2007). Case study evidence of those working at the lower end of the labour market suggests that in many organizations there are declining opportunities for progression into better paying jobs (Lloyd *et al.* 2008).

In addition, there appears to be a general trend towards 'overqualification'. The proportion of UK employees holding qualifications higher than those required for entry to their current job is estimated to have increased from 35% in 2001 to 40% in 2006 (Felstead *et al.* 2007). The steepest rise was amongst graduates, with three in ten found to be in jobs that did not require a degree in 2006, up from one fifth in 1986 (Felstead *et al.* 2007). The possession of qualifications, including a degree, is therefore no guarantee of obtaining a job at the appropriate level. Overall, there is little evidence to suggest that a skills-alone policy, centred on driving up qualification levels, has pushed up the skill content of jobs. Economic performance also remains a major concern. The financial crisis of 2008 has highlighted the fundamental weakness and particular vulnerability of the UK economy, as growth has been heavily reliant on the financial sector, and a consumer credit and housing market boom (OECD 2008).

The role of industrial relations policy   The priority afforded to skills policy can readily be seen in the torrent of speeches, policies, white and green papers, programmes, schemes and initiatives which have emanated from central government over the last decade (Keep 2006). In comparison, there has been very little in the way of active policy engagement with industrial relations and broader employment issues. The government has introduced a minimum platform of employment rights, including a national minimum wage, but further legislation has been resisted (see Dickens and Hall; Colling, this volume). Issues such as work organization and job design, which have a vital bearing on the ability of organizations to make effective use of skills and harness them to improve performance, have been largely ignored. For instance, there are no publicly funded workplace innovation programmes of the kind found in countries such as Finland, Norway and Germany (Payne and Keep 2003; Payne 2004; Alasoini 2006).

There has been general government support for the 'high performance workplace', mainly in the form of exhortation and the publication of 'best-practice' examples, although even this now appears to have fallen off the policy agenda. The government initially encouraged a form of social partnership at work, albeit one that did not necessarily have to involve trade unions, in stark contrast to European approaches. In 1999 the Partnership at Work fund was set up to finance projects aimed at improving employment relations through partnership working (Terry, this volume). However, the initiative was closed in 2004, and, as yet, nothing else has taken its place.

Looking back over the period from the 1960s, the UK's 'labour problem' has been redefined away from one of labour *relations* to one of labour *quality* (education and skills). In a sense, it could be argued that education and training interventions can today be read as substitutes for more traditional concerns to deliver 'good' industrial relations through public policy. Issues such as the way in which people are managed and motivated at work and jobs are designed are, at best, 'bit players' within New Labour's policy agenda. Yet these factors are clearly important in affecting whether or not skills are effectively utilized within the workplace and harnessed to improved economic performance (Edwards and Sengupta, this volume). Their marginalization within the New Labour policy narrative, together with the paucity of interventions which seek to address them, leaves the skills strategy, particularly in England, lop-sided and narrowly focused.

Industrial relations may have declined as a policy issue but what about *within* the area of skills itself? The next section considers the extent to which the skills policy agenda under New Labour has presented new opportunities for both trade unions and employers to influence skill and training developments.

The Influence of Collective Organizations on Skills: Decline or Renaissance?

When New Labour was elected in 1997 it was clear that the influence of trade unions on skills had experienced a marked and substantial decline compared to the situation which existed in 1980. The contraction of manufacturing employment during the 1980s greatly accelerated the decline in traditional apprenticeships (Keep and Rainbird 2003: 408–409). The influence that craft unions had once exerted in this sphere, notably in industries such as construction, shipbuilding and engineering, was vastly diminished, with unions no longer in a position to control entry to the trade or the process of apprenticeship itself. The character of apprenticeship had also changed dramatically, with a shift to government-funded programmes, the vast bulk of which were managed, not by employers, but by private training providers (Fuller and Unwin 2004). The voluntary 'employer-led' sectoral training bodies and, in England and Wales, local Training and Enterprise Councils (TECs) were employer-dominated, with trade union involvement operating on a strictly minority 'grace and favour' basis (Clough 2007). Notwithstanding the joint TUC/TEC 'Bargaining for Skills' projects – aimed mainly at helping meet government targets on the take-up of National Vocational Qualifications (NVQs) and the Investors in People award – trade unions found themselves marginalized within the VET system.

The New Labour government made it clear that it was prepared to offer trade unions a 'new role' in training as stakeholders within the VET system and as 'trusted intermediaries' who could help employees take up learning opportunities at work (DfEE 1998; Clough 2007). To what extent, if any, has there been a renewal of social partnership within VET institutions under New Labour and what impact are trade unions currently having on skills and learning at the workplace? For social partnership to operate effectively, employers also have a role to play. In the UK, where employers associations have historically been relatively weak, has the emphasis on an 'employer-led' skills system provided the opportunity to overcome these traditional deficiencies?

No return to social partnership

Trade unions were granted formal representation on the national Learning and Skills Council (LSC) and 47 local Learning and Skills Councils, established in 2001, which assumed overall responsibility for funding all post-compulsory education and training in England outside of higher education. Employers and trade unions, along with other stakeholders, were required to apply for membership through a competitive process. However, while employers were allotted 40% of the seats on both the LSC and its local arms, trade unions were offered only a single seat. Similarly, trade unions were also given a seat on the board of the nine English Regional Development Agencies as well as on the Sector Skill Councils (SSCs).

While trade union involvement in VET institutions increased under New Labour, it would be difficult to characterize any of the aforementioned bodies as a form of social partnership. In England, the Skills Alliance, established in 2003 to oversee the development of the government's skills strategy, was initially billed as a 'new social partnership for skills' (DfES *et al.* 2003: 22). The Alliance brought together ministers, the CBI, the TUC, the Small Business Council and a range of other delivery partners. The reality, however, was that it never performed this role, meeting only twice a year and acting mainly as a 'champion' for the government's already pre-determined skills strategy (Keep 2006; Lloyd and Payne 2007).

The Leitch Review's final report recommended that the '*Ministerially-led* Skills Alliance' should be replaced with a new UK-wide Commission for Employment and Skills (UKCES) designed to '[s]trengthen the employer voice' and 'deliver greater leadership and influence' (Leitch 2006: 18, emphasis added). The TUC initially voiced disquiet over the creation of the UKCES, seeing it as a 'lost opportunity to develop a social partnership model' (TUC 2007), and pointing out that the new Commission has only 'minimum union representation' (Clough 2007: 17). The Commission became fully operational on 1 April 2008. Currently only three out of the 22 commissioners appointed are from trade unions. Indeed, despite continued pleas from the TUC, successive New Labour governments have consistently refused to contemplate any return to formal social partnership arrangements within the governance structures of the VET system.

Union learning: high hopes and hard realities

The lack of social partnership within the VET system can be contrasted with the considerable role given to unions in relation to learning at the workplace. The first major development was the establishment of the Union Learning Fund (ULF) in England in 1998, the Welsh ULF in 1999 and Scottish ULF in 2000, aimed at supporting innovative union learning activity, including partnership-based approaches with employers. Since its inception, the English ULF has involved over 50 unions in projects in 700 workplaces and supports over 100 000 learners each year, mostly undertaking ICT courses, *Skills for Life* and various further education programmes (Unionlearn 2007). Funding has grown significantly from an initial budget of £2 million in 1998 to upwards of £12 million in 2007–08. Responsibility for its management has been transferred to Unionlearn, a newly created TUC body that also provides training for union representatives and wider educational services.

The ULF has also supported the development of a new cadre of union officers – the union learning representative (ULR) – whose main role is to encourage members to take up learning or training opportunities. Under the Employment Act 2002, statutory backing was given to ULRs (where unions are recognized) in the form of paid time off to train and perform their duties. By 2007, around 18 000 ULRs had been trained in the UK. A number of evaluations provide evidence that ULRs have been relatively successful in encouraging individuals into learning (Wallis *et al.* 2005; Findlay *et al.* 2006; Shaw *et al.* 2006; Warhurst *et al.* 2006). There are many examples where individual employees have gained both in terms of their self-confidence as learners as well as in their ability to progress their careers and earnings potential (Kennedy 1995; Munro and Rainbird 2004). In many instances, the beneficiaries are drawn from marginalized groups, particularly the low qualified, who are the least likely to receive training from their employer.

Nevertheless, there are questions as to how far trade unions are able to influence the skills and learning agenda at the workplace. Funding is overwhelmingly from government and its agencies, with access to such funding increasingly tied to learners undertaking basic skills courses and achieving a first level 2 qualification. Concerns have also been raised about the ability of trade unions to pursue an independent learning agenda focused on providing employees with transferable skills and high quality learning opportunities (Lloyd and Payne 2007; Shelley 2007; McIlroy 2008).

The absence in the UK of a statutory right to bargain collectively over skills and of legally enshrined co-determination in the workplace means that unions are in a relatively weak position when it comes to challenging employer prerogative over

Table 17.1 Joint regulation of training – % of workplaces

	Nothing	Inform	Consult	Negotiate
Unionized	36%	24%	31%	9%
All	75%	10%	13%	3%

Source: Derived from Table 7.7 in Kersley *et al.* (2006: 194).

training decisions (Clough 2007). Figures from the 2004 Workplace Employment Relations Survey (see Table 17.1) show that, even where unions are recognized, negotiation over training takes place in only 9% of workplaces and consultation in just a further 31%. Training is typically an area where employees have little say, with managers in three quarters of all workplaces not even informing workers about training plans. Furthermore, the near total absence of multi-employer bargaining means that the kind of national and/or sectoral agreements over training that one finds in countries like France, Germany and Spain have virtually no equivalent in the UK (Martinez Lucio *et al.* 2007; Winterton 2007).

ULRs represent the one area where there has been a strengthening of unions' role at the workplace. There are indications that union involvement in the learning agenda can, in certain circumstances, help with the recruitment of new members and activists (Haunch and Bennett 2002; Munro and Rainbird 2004; Moore and Wood 2005; Wallis *et al.* 2005). However, that success often depends on the pre-existence of strong and supportive unions (Munro and Rainbird 2004: 163–165; Wallis *et al.* 2005: 299–300). A key problem is that by their very nature, ULRs are only found in unionized workplaces, limiting their potential reach to just 16% of private sector workplaces, and 33% of private sector employees (Kersley *et al.* 2006: 119). Moreover, in those sectors which tend to have large numbers of low paid, low qualified employees (the prime target audience for much of ULR work) union recognition is often very limited.

Finally, there is the issue of sustainability. Unionlearn has become a substantial part of the TUC infrastructure, with a staff of 145 and a budget of £26.9 million in 2007–08; the overwhelming majority of which derives from state funding. In the absence of such support – and the Conservative Party has threatened to abolish the ULF if elected – it is questionable whether union learning activities could be maintained on anything like their present scale. Indeed, research suggests that sustainability is already a major problem when funding is removed from individual projects (Findlay *et al.* 2006: 9; Finlay *et al.* 2007). Nevertheless, the importance of the skills agenda for the TUC should not be underestimated. Brendan Barber, General Secretary of the TUC, recently claimed that, 'without question, Unionlearn is the single most important development in trade unionism in a generation' (2007, foreword). It has a massive symbolic value as one of the few areas where unions can claim to have made substantial gains under New Labour. Yet this role is clearly limited, and, as the research shows, beyond some observable benefits for particular individuals, the overall impact remains questionable.

As Clough (2007: 18, 22) concedes, '[q]uantitatively, the projects have resulted in relatively modest outcomes', while '[a]t workplace level there has been little shift in the balance of power'.

The weakness of the employer voice

The weakness of trade unions within the VET systems in the UK is clearly apparent but have employers fared any better? The abolition of the MSC in 1988 not only saw trade unions removed from VET bodies but also effectively marked the end of any form of collective employer representation. Subsequent structures relied upon employers serving in a purely individual capacity rather than as representatives of industry, an approach that has continued under New Labour.

In part, this limited role is symptomatic of a much deeper structural problem linked to the weakness of employer collective bodies alluded to earlier in the chapter. Employer federations were already weak compared to the individual firm in the mid-1980s (Finegold and Soskice 1988). The subsequent collapse of multi-employer, industry-level collective bargaining left the UK without any effective bodies that could concert and mobilize employer interests around training. Certainly, there has never been anything like the German Chambers of Commerce which played a vital role in committing employers to the provision of broad transferable skills required for the functioning of the 'dual apprenticeship' system (Culpepper 1999: 45). While New Labour has repeatedly insisted that VET is moving towards an 'employer-led' system, in reality employers have been offered individual representation on what are essentially state-created and state-funded institutions which exist mainly to implement the government's own policies, targets and initiatives.

A good example of this process in action is in the operation of the LSC, where individual employers are the main stakeholder group. The role of the LSC has been to deliver policy objectives and targets that have been determined by central government, often with little or no employer input (Keep 2006). According to the LSC's former chair, Bryan Sanderson, 'It [the LSC] is not about policy making, it is about delivery of policy which national and local government has made' (House of Commons 2004: 5). For example, the Treasury's 'flagship' *Train to Gain* programme, launched across England in 2005, as a way of subsidizing employers who help members of their adult workforce to acquire basic literacy and numeracy skills and a first level 2 qualification, was designed *by* government *for* employers. The delivery and rollout of the programme was then simply handed over to the LSC. More recently, the government has followed up the Leitch recommendations by adopting the extremely ambitious target of having 400 000 people in England entering an apprenticeship programme by 2010/2011 (DCSF and DIUS 2008). This target, like the Leitch targets in general, has been arrived at without any real consultation with employers.

Similarly, the majority of the UK-wide SSCs are not 'employer-led' in any meaningful sense. Only 6.7% of income was derived from employers in 2005 (SSDA 2006a) and it is central government which determines the boundaries of the sectors they represent, along with the performance criteria against which they are judged and evaluated (Keep 2006). Although SSCs are expected to act as a key channel through which employers can make their voice heard, many have only very limited and tenuous contact with employers in their sector (SSDA 2006b; Payne 2008b). To date, there has not been a single instance where SSCs have taken the initiative and asked government to put in place new policies or programmes.

It is also important to point out that SSCs are not employer organizations and have no formalized role in either collective bargaining or indeed in any other aspect of industrial relations. They were created by government as single-purpose vehicles for delivering enhanced levels of formalized training activity and workforce qualifications. Significantly, they often have no formal relationship with employer organizations, such as the Engineering Employers Federation (EEF) or even the CBI. In some cases, relationships between SSCs and the relevant employer organizations have been strained, particularly where the latter has a prior interest in skills policy (e.g. see EEF (2006) which is less than glowing in its endorsement of the activities of its sector's SSC).

Finally, state control over the VET system is further evidenced by the way in which central institutions are created by government only to be subsequently abolished once policy makers decide they have outlived their usefulness. Most recently, the government has announced that the LSC is to be abolished in 2010 (DCSF and DIUS 2008). Funding for 16–19 year olds in England will be transferred to local authorities, aided in the process by a new 'slim' national Young People's Learning Agency. A new 'streamlined' Skills Funding Agency will also be created to oversee the development and funding of the Further Education sector. Unlike the LSC which at the time of its creation was heralded as being 'employer-led' (Hook 2000), there is no pretence that these new bodies are anything other than government agencies. Once again, it would seem that changes have been made to the institutional infrastructure of the education and training system without any real social partner consultation, confirming the position of central government as 'system architect' (Keep 2006).

The VET systems across the UK, although 'state-led', are far removed from the traditional use of the term in countries such as France. In France, VET is education-led and centred on the school, while within the workplace there are compulsory levies (instituted by the state) as well as individual rights to training. In comparison, training in the UK remains essentially 'market based' and 'voluntarist', with sectoral training levies confined to just a couple of sectors (e.g. construction and film/media) and with relatively limited licence to practice arrangements. However, in terms of policy formation and institutional design it can be considered as one of the most centrally controlled and managed systems to be found anywhere in the western world (Keep 2006). Indeed, it might be argued that the dominant role of central government within VET is a response to weak social partners, while also having the effect of reinforcing that weakness by leaving little room for them to share decision-making power.

Elsewhere in Europe, the picture remains very different. In many of the 'old' European Union (EU) countries, it is the norm for trade unions and employers to have equal representation on tripartite or bi-partite bodies set up to deal with training and skills issues. Unions have a substantial role in such bodies in Germany, the Netherlands, France, Belgium, Spain, Finland, Denmark and (non-EU) Norway, to mention only a few. At the same time, training is often subject to collective bargaining, mainly at national and sectoral levels (Crouch *et al.* 1999; Martinez Lucio *et al.* 2007; Winterton 2007). Such institutional arrangements do not automatically guarantee success. Agreements can be difficult to secure, with the state, employers and trade unions often holding opposing views on how different forms of learning should be structured and paid for (Heyes 2007). Stuart and Wallis (2007) have shown how, in certain contexts, neo-corporatist 'learning partnerships', established at national or sectoral level, can be difficult to implement on the ground, lacking the flexibility to deal with local restructuring processes and dependent upon the support and expertise of local actors. Nevertheless, such institutional arrangements provide an important framework within which employers and trade unions can shape curricula and training standards as well as 'bargain' over training, including rights to study leave and the validation of non-formal and informal learning.

There is no indication that New Labour has any wish to develop a more European style of social partnership within the governance structures of the English VET system. The new UKCES has been described by John Denham, the English Secretary of State for Innovation, Universities and Skills, as 'an unprecedented opportunity to influence the delivery of employment and skills policy, giving employers a powerful voice at the heart of government . . .' (DIUS 2008). Just how much influence or power the Commission will be able to wield in practice remains an open question. English government departments have already signalled that 'it will not have significant executive or operational functions, but will be *primarily advisory*, shaping strategy to achieve our world-class ambitions, challenging parties to raise their game on skills, and helping to shift the national culture' (DIUS 2007: 38, emphasis added). While the name of the Commission suggests that employment issues are to be a key focus, its remit appears to indicate that this relates predominantly to achieving high levels of participation in employment rather than to any broader industrial relations matters. Nevertheless, the Commission is clearly a different animal to the Skills Alliance, having its own secretariat and being comprised of an unstable coalition of ideas and interests. The commissioners include representatives from the home nations, with their own skills agenda. Whether the Commission will completely 'play ball' and limit its advice within the parameters set by the English government departments and ministers remains to be seen.

The Rise of Skills Policy and the Displacement of Industrial Relations: Reasons and Implications

So far, the chapter has argued that the influence of collective organizations on skills has been one of overall decline compared to the situation that existed in the early 1980s. Furthermore, at the macro-level of national policy, the attention once paid to industrial relations and broader employment issues has in recent years been in free fall, with a concomitant rise in the importance attached to skills as 'the key' to securing improved economic performance and, more latterly under New Labour, social justice and equity. Having charted these developments, the following section explores three key factors that contributed to this shift, along with some of the implications.

Industrial relations problems 'solved'

First, as noted above, the analysis of the 'British labour problem' as formulated by the Thatcher government could be presented as having largely been 'solved' by the late 1990s. With trade unions severely weakened and strikes at an all time low, it became harder to blame unions for the UK's persistent productivity and competitiveness problems. However, in an era of deregulation and 'letting managers manage', as Cutler (1992) argued, the list of potential actors and structural factors that were left to provide an explanation was highly problematic, since it included managers themselves and managerial decisions, along with financial institutions and other incentive structures (Finegold and Soskice 1988; Keep 2000; Lloyd and Payne 2002). The attraction of a skills supply-side strategy to Conservative governments was that it would not interfere with areas of managerial prerogative or involve any significant regulation of capital and labour markets.

By contrast, the detrimental role of the UK financial system and its relationship with the manufacturing sector had a long pedigree within academic debates over UK economic decline (Coates 1994: 151–162; Sisson and Purcell, this volume). In the 1980s and 1990s, concerns also grew about the corrosive effects of a 'hire-and-fire' labour market on firms' willingness and ability to invest in 'high road' approaches. These arguments figured prominently in Hutton's critique of Thatcherism and the elaboration of an alternative social democratic project under the banner of 'the stakeholder society' (Hutton 1995, 1997). While New Labour was prepared to debate these ideas in opposition, they were largely jettisoned once the party entered office in favour of an emphasis on flexible capital and labour markets and investment in education and skills (Lloyd and Payne 2002; Keep 2006).

New production concepts, such as 'post-Fordism' and the 'knowledge economy', popularized by policy gurus such as Leadbeater (2000) and Giddens (1998), allowed New Labour to predict the imminent arrival of a new world of work in which employees would be empowered to exercise high levels of skill, knowledge and creativity within more autonomous, team-based forms of working. The assumption was that government did not need to intervene actively to shape managerial decisions in relation to product market positioning, work design or people management. Provided organizations had the right skills, these matters would take care of themselves. This approach made it easier for policy makers to treat the firm as a 'black box' into which inputs of higher qualified labour could then be expected to feed through to improved levels of productivity and performance.

Moreover, insofar as the boost to skills supply could be delivered through the education system, the active cooperation of employers was not required. Their role became principally that of a 'consumer' of publicly funded provision or a 'passive' recipient of public subsidy or schemes designed to provide them with the skills, or to be more accurate the qualifications, which government believed they needed (Gleeson and Keep 2004). Thus, in England, the *Train to Gain* programme was introduced in 2005 as a way of offering subsidies to employers who agreed to help adult members of their workforce acquire basic skills and/or a first full level 2 qualification.

Dismantling industrial relations institutions

The second factor has been the dismantling of institutions that dealt with industrial relations and which provided industrial relations actors with an influence over the training system. When the Conservative government abolished the National Economic Development Council (NEDC), together with its sectoral working parties, in 1992, it removed the main institutional mechanisms that might have addressed the other side of the 'labour problem' coin, namely the orderly conduct of industrial relations and the productive deployment of labour within the workplace. The assumption by the Thatcher and Major Conservative governments was that enlightened management, under pressure of market forces, would, of their own volition, adopt whatever forms of employee relations and work organization were needed to maximize performance – an assumption that New Labour has, on the whole, been content to endorse. In contrast, the same approach has not been accepted in relation to employers' willingness to train, where 'market failure' is consistently used as a pretext for intervention.

At the same time, there was a sequential weakening of the very institutional mechanisms that had rooted training issues within the wider policy context of industrial relations. The abolition of the ITBs and the tripartite MSC essentially allowed the reframing of where training sat within the policy world, and ultimately enabled it to become subsumed in the machinery of central government (through the merger of the education and employment departments) and within broader debates and policies to do with education reform and the supply of skills. The removal of these tripartite governance structures for training, and the subsequent refusal by New Labour to contemplate any return to formal social partnership arrangements, has left the vast bulk of skills policy and activity *outside* the industrial relations system. The government regards the work of the union learning representatives and Unionlearn activities to be primarily part of a skills agenda rather than an industrial relations one. Attempts by the TUC to reinsert skills into more traditional industrial relations arenas, have come to nothing; witness, for example, calls for a statutory right to bargain collectively over training and an equal role with employers in VET institutions.

Elsewhere in Europe the shift in the discourse of competitiveness to embrace skills as a key element in economic success did not mean the marginalization of the social partners and industrial relations policy. If anything, the new policy priorities being placed on education and training have tended to result in the development (albeit sometimes uneven and problematic) of wider and/or deeper social dialogue on skills (Stuart and Wallis 2007). Thus, in many European countries vocational skill formation continues in large measure to be viewed as part of the (collective) industrial relations system, rather than as an element of an alternative discourse that is attached to a separate sphere of policy and activity. At present in the UK, it would seem that, outside of the union movement, there is no constituency pressing for moves that would bring policy and practice closer into line with mainstream European models.

Construction of a skills industry

A third factor is the way in which central government's policy machinery has supported and bolstered the dominance of skills. Skills have a clear champion in the shape of government departments responsible for education and skills, and after 1997 the Treasury has shown an increasing interest in this area. Since the 'machinery of government' changes in 2007, England has acquired two central government departments (and hence two Cabinet Ministers) with a direct interest in promoting the education and skills agenda – the Department for Innovation, Universities and Skills (DIUS) (subsequently subsumed into the Department for Business, Innovation and Skills (BIS)) and the Department for Children, Families and Schools.

Furthermore, the delivery of skills policy has resided in a growing array of government agencies and quangos, many with comparatively large budgets (the Learning and Skills Council has an annual budget of £11 billion) (Keep 2006). These bodies have a relatively high public profile compared to the agencies that deal with employment issues, principally ACAS and the Low Pay Commission. One of their key roles has been to heighten the public profile of skills issues and mobilize public opinion behind the government's 'skills agenda'. These quangos and agencies can be relied upon to meet, greet and publicize each new government initiative with enthusiasm (since that is what they have been ordained and funded to do). Over time, a large skills 'industry' has also arisen, comprising both individuals and institutions, with a strong material self-interest in prioritizing education and training activity. These include the Association of Learning Providers; Association of Colleges; the various teaching unions; the 157 group of FE college principals; the Campaign for Learning; and Universities UK. It is no accident that 'lifelong learning' is a sector now large enough to warrant its own Sector Skills Council – skills is an industry in its own right!

By contrast, industrial relations and workplace issues have been the concern of a subsection of what was the Department of Trade and Industry (DTI) and then the Department of Business, Enterprise and Regulatory Reform (BERR) and more recently BIS. Once New Labour had established its platform of minimum individual employment rights and the Low Pay Commission was in place, neither DTI, BERR nor BIS appeared to have placed a particularly strong emphasis upon the employee relations element of their policy portfolio. As Freeman and Kountouris argue (2006), the absence of a Ministry of Labour of the type found in most other European countries has left the UK with no powerful central policy focus for issues to do with employment, social security and industrial relations. Indeed, the Department of Work and Pensions' (DWP) employment functions are becoming more and more subsumed within wider skills policy (DIUS 2007; DCSF and DIUS 2008).

Conclusions

This chapter has argued that the UK government's policy agenda on skills as 'the key' to economic and social success can be viewed as having largely supplanted traditional concerns around collective bargaining, workplace industrial relations, industrial policy and economic development. Today, the development of a more highly skilled or qualified workforce is expected to produce better paid and more interesting work, compress wage inequalities, reduce poverty, aid social mobility and make UK enterprises more productive (Leitch 2006). Clearly, there is a danger of loading unrealistic expectations onto the education and training system. While the development of a more skilled workforce is important, ensuring that those skills are utilized and harnessed to improve performance is certainly no less vital. We have argued elsewhere that there is a strong case for rediscovering and reprioritizing the importance of a range of other factors, such as R&D and capital investment, but also industrial relations systems and policies, work organization and job design (Lloyd and Payne 2002; Keep *et al.* 2006). Rather than seeing the organization as a 'black box' into which more skills can simply be injected, policy needs to be concerned with how the different elements of production, not least labour, interact with each other, and are deployed and managed within the workplace.

Comparative research has highlighted the importance of strong collective industrial relations institutions, particularly at the industry level, to deliver improvements in skills. However, it is not just their direct role in training which is relevant but also their ability to establish higher levels of minimum wages and working conditions. These aspects, alongside labour market regulations in relation to job security and 'licence to practice' (i.e. the requirement to hold a specific qualification in order to undertake a job), constrain employers in their ability to use a cheap and disposable workforce. Cutting off 'low cost' routes to competitiveness can encourage employers to pursue more high quality, innovative product market strategies and to maximize the skills of their existing workforce. A role for trade unions at the workplace, with rights to negotiate over training and issues of work organization and job design, as is common in Germany (primarily through works councils) and the Nordic countries, provides a more positive environment for skill development and utilization.

Outside the UK, the focus of skills policy is already starting to return to the workplace and the point where skill interacts with industrial relations issues. In Ireland, for example, there has been the creation of a National Centre for Partnership and Performance, whose National Workplace Strategy aims to produce workplaces that will be 'agile; customer-centred; knowledge intensive; responsive to employee needs; networked; highly productive; involved and participatory; continually learning; and proactively diverse' (NCPP 2005: 2). In New Zealand, the government has recently announced a new Skills Strategy, based around employer and trade union partnership which will look at how skills are used, valued and retained within the workplace (Tertiary Education Commission 2008). In Australia, a skill ecosystem programme is testing a new approach to VET policy which aims to locate skills challenges in the context of wider drivers of productivity, performance and job quality including business strategy, new forms of technology, changing modes of service delivery, work organization and job design (Payne 2008c).

On an optimistic note, the time may be ripe for a renewed discussion of these topics in the UK. The Leitch Review's pronouncement that skills are *the* key lever to secure social and economic success leaves policy makers and policy itself with nowhere further to go in developing this strand of thinking (short of insisting that skills are the *only* lever). Moreover, *within* the UK, there are clear signs that, outside England at least, policy makers are becoming increasingly aware of the limitations of a narrow skill-supply strategy and are looking to evolve 'smarter' policy approaches. In Scotland, for instance, the fundamental thrust of policy has recently shifted from a 'supply alone' strategy to one where attention is also focused on the need to try to stimulate the underlying level of demand for skill within the Scottish economy, and to make greater efforts to ensure that skills, once created, are put to better use within Scottish workplaces (Scottish Government 2007). It is important to remember, however, that regulation of the labour market and employment relations, along with broader macro-economic policy decisions, remain firmly under the control of the government in Westminster. How much progress Scotland can make in advancing a new type of skills strategy, given the absence of such policy levers, remains to be seen.

Finally, the significance of the new Commission for Employment and Skills as a UK-wide body with members drawn from Northern Ireland, Scotland and Wales should not be overlooked. Some of these members may enter the Commission with a different set of assumptions and bring new concerns to the policy table. In this sense, there is the potential for the Commission to act as a transmission mechanism for new ideas and approaches, which may serve to challenge, or at least disrupt, the assumptions upon which English skills policy is based. It is possible that trade unions may also step up their efforts to advance a 'demand-side' agenda, while continuing to argue the case for 'more collective bargaining over training and a greater role for unions in policy development' (Clough 2007: 3). One thing seems certain, however. If substantive progress is to be made in tackling the UK's 'skills problem', issues such as better industrial relations policies and practice and improved work organization and job design can no longer remain the 'elephant in the corner' and will need to move from the margin to the centre of public policy debate and action.

Note

1 Level 2 is equivalent to academic qualifications of 5 GCSEs at grade A*-C that are normally taken at the end of compulsory schooling at aged 16 and vocational qualifications such as NVQ level 2. Around 30% of adults of working age do not hold this level of qualification.

References

Alasoini, T. 2006: In search of generative results: a new generation of programmes to develop work organization. *Economic and Industrial Democracy*, 27 (1), 9–37.

Ashton, D. and Green, F. 1996: *Education, Training and the Global Economy*. Cheltenham: Edward Elgar.

Barber, B. 2007: Foreword. In Shelley, S. and Calveley, M. (eds) *Learning with Trade Unions*. Aldershot: Ashgate.

Blair, T. 2007: Our nation's future – the role of work. www.number-10.gov.uk/output/Page11405.asp (accessed 15 May 2007).

Brown, G. 2008: Speech on expansion of apprenticeships, 28 January. www.number-10.gov.uk/output/Page14414.asp (accessed 6 March 2008).

Brown, P., Green, A. and Lauder, H. 2001: *High Skills: Globalization, Competitiveness and Skill Formation*. Oxford: Oxford University Press.

Clough, B. 2007: From voluntarism to post-voluntarism: the emerging role of unions in the vocational education and training system,. Research Paper 5, TUC/Unionlearn, London.

Coates, D. 1994: *The Question of UK Decline*. Hemel Hempstead: Harvester Wheatsheaf.

Coates, D. 2000: *Models of Capitalism: Growth and Stagnation in the Modern Era*. London: Polity Press.

Coates, D. and Hay, C. 2001: Home and away? The political economy of New Labour. Paper presented to the ESRC Labour Studies Seminar: The State and Labour, University of Warwick, 28–29 March.

Crouch, C., Finegold, D. and Sako, M. 1999: *Are Skills the Answer? The Political Economy of Skills Creation in Advanced Industrial Countries*. Oxford: Oxford University Press.

Culpepper, P. 1999: The future of the high-skill equilibrium in Germany. *Oxford Review of Economic Policy*, 15 (1), 43–59.

Cutler, T. 1992: Vocational training and British economic performance: a further instalment of the 'British labour problem'? *Work, Employment and Society*, 6 (2), 161–183.

DfEE (Department for Education and Employment) 1998: *The Learning Age: A Renaissance for a New Britain*. Sheffield: DfEE.

DfES (Department for Education and Skills), DTI, HM Treasury, DWP 2003: *21st Century Skills: Realising our Potential: Individuals, Employers, Nation*. Norwich: HMSO.

DCSF and DIUS (Department for Children, Schools and Families and Department for Innovation, Universities and Skills) 2008: *Raising Expectations: Enabling the System to Deliver*. Norwich: The Stationery Office.

DIUS (Department for Innovation, Universities and Skills) 2007: *World Class Skills: Implementing the Leitch Review of Skills in England*. Norwich: The Stationery Office.

DIUS 2008: New Commission puts employer voice at heart of skills policy. Press Release, 1 April. London: DIUS.

DTI (Department of Trade and Industry) 1995: *Competitiveness: Forging Ahead*. London: HMSO.

DTI 2005: R&D intensive businesses in the UK. DTI Economics Paper, No. 11, DTI.

EEF (Engineering Employers Federation) 2006: Learning to change: why the UK skills system must do better. Available at http://www.eef.org.uk

Felstead, A., Gallie, D., Green, F. and Zhou, Y. 2007: *Skills at Work 1986–2006*. Universities of Oxford and Cardiff: SKOPE.

Findlay, P., Stewart, R., Dutton, E. and Warhurst C. 2006: *Evaluation of the Scottish Union Learning Fund (SULF) (2000–2005)*. Edinburgh: Scottish Executive Social Research.

Finegold, D. 1991: Institutional incentives and skill creation: preconditions for a high skill equilibrium. In Ryan, P. (ed.) *International Comparisons of Vocational Education and Training for Intermediate Skills*. London: Falmer, pp. 93–116.

Finegold, D. and Soskice, D. 1988: The failure of training in Britain: analysis and prescription. *Oxford Review of Economic Policy*, 4 (3), 21–53.

Finlay, I., Hodgson, A. and Steer, R. 2007: Flowers in the desert: the impact of policy on basic skills provision in the workplace. *Journal of Vocational Education and Training*, 59 (2), 231–248.

Fox, A. and Flanders, A. 1969: The reform of collective bargaining: from Donovan to Durkheim. *British Journal of Industrial Relations*, 7 (2), 151–180.

Freeman, M. and Kountouris, N. 2006: The institutional face at ministerial level – not the Department of Employment. In Dickens, L. and Neal, A. (eds) *The Changing Institutional Face of British Employment Relations*. Alphen aan den Rijn: Kluwer Law International, pp. 13–24.

Fuller, A. and Unwin, L. 2004: Expansive learning environments: integrating organizational and personal development. In Rainbird, H., Fuller, A. and Munro, A. (eds) *Workplace Learning in Context*. London: Routledge, pp. 126–144.

Giddens, A. 1998: *The Third Way: The Renewal of Social Democracy*. Cambridge: Polity.

Gleeson, D. and Keep, E. 2004: Voice without accountability: the changing relationship between employers, the State and education in England. *Oxford Review of Education*, 30 (1), 37–63.

Haunch, P. and Bennett, T. 2002: Organize, educate and agitate: do learning partnerships help the employer or employee? Paper presented to IIRA CIRA conference, Toronto.

Heyes, J. 2007: Training, social dialogue and collective bargaining in Western Europe. *Economic and Industrial Democracy*, 28 (2), 239–258.

Hook, S. 2000: 'No excuses' for strong business voice. *Times Educational Supplement, FE Focus*, 17 November, 33.

House of Commons 2004: House of Commons Education and Skills Committee, uncorrected transcript of oral evidence on National Skills Strategy: 14–19 Education from Mr Bryan Sanderson and Mr Mark Haysom, Monday 17 May.

Howell, C. 2005: *Trade Unions and the State: The Construction of Industrial Relations Institutions in Britain, 1890–2000*. Princeton: Princeton University Press.

Hutton, W. 1995: *The State We're In*. London: Jonathan Cape.

Hutton, W. 1997: *The State to Come*. London: Vintage.

Hyman, R. 2003: The historical evolution of British industrial relations. In Edwards, P. (ed.) *Industrial Relations: Theory and Practice*. Oxford: Blackwell Publishing Ltd, pp. 37–57.

Keep, E. 2000: Creating a knowledge-driven economy – definitions, challenges and opportunities. *SKOPE Policy Paper* 2. Coventry: SKOPE, University of Warwick.

Keep, E. 2006: State control of the English education and training system – playing with the biggest train set in the world. *Journal of Vocational Education and Training*, 58 (1), 47–64.

Keep, E. and Mayhew, K. 1999: The assessment: education, training and economic performance. *Oxford Review of Economic Policy*, 4, 3, i–xv.

Keep, E. and Rainbird, H. 1995: Training. In Edwards, P.K. (ed.) *Industrial Relations in Britain*. Oxford: Blackwell, pp. 515–542.

Keep, E. and Rainbird, H. 2003: Training. In Edwards, P.K. (ed.) *Industrial Relations: Theory and Practice*. 2nd edition. Oxford: Blackwell, pp. 392–419.

Keep, E., Mayhew, K. and Payne, J. 2006: From skills revolution to productivity miracle – not as easy as it sounds? *Oxford Review of Economic Policy*, 22 (4), 539–559.

Kennedy, H. 1995: *Return to Learn: UNISON's Fresh Approach to Trade Union Education*. London: UNISON.

Kersley, B., Alpin, C., Forth, J., Bewley, H., Dix, G. and Oxenbridge, S. 2006: *Inside the Workplace: Findings from the 2004 Workplace Employment Relations Survey*. London: DTI.

King, D. 1993: The Conservatives and training policy 1979–1992: from a tripartite to a neo-liberal regime. *Policy Studies*, 41, 214–235.

Kitson, M. and Michie, J. 1996: Britain's industrial performance since 1960: underinvestment and relative decline. *The Economic Journal*, 106 (434), 196–212.

Leadbeater, C. 2000: *Living on Thin Air*. London: Viking.

Leitch, S. 2005: *Leitch Review of Skills: Interim Report*. London: HM Treasury.

Leitch, S. 2006: *Prosperity for All in the Global Economy – World Class Skills*. London: HM Treasury.

Lloyd, C. and Payne, J. 2002: Developing a political economy of skill. *Journal of Education and Work*, 15 (4), 365–390.

Lloyd, C. and Payne, J. 2003: What is the 'high skills society'? Some reflections on current academic and policy debates in the UK. *Policy Studies*, 24 (2), 115–133.

Lloyd, C. and Payne, J. 2007: Tackling the UK skills problem: can unions make a difference? In Shelley, S. and Calveley, M. (eds) *Learning with Trade Unions: A Contemporary Agenda in Employment Relations*. Aldershot: Ashgate Publishing Limited, pp. 57–77.

Lloyd, C., Mason, G. and Mayhew, K. 2008: *Low-Wage Work in the United Kingdom*. New York: Russell Sage Foundation.

Martinez-Lucio, M., Skule, S., Kruse, W. and Trappmann, V. 2007: Regulating skill formation in Europe: German, Norwegian and Spanish policies on transferable skills. *European Journal of Industrial Relations*, 13 (3), 323–340.

Mason, G. 2004: Enterprise product strategies and employer demand for skills in Britain: evidence form the Employers Skills Survey. *SKOPE Research Paper* No. 50. Coventry: University of Warwick, SKOPE.

Mason, G., Mayhew, K., Osborne, M. and Stevens, P. 2008: Low pay, labor market institutions, and job quality in the United Kingdom. In Lloyd, C., Mason, G. and Mayhew, K. (eds) *Low-Wage Work in the United Kingdom*. New York: Russell Sage Foundation.

McIlroy, J. 2008: Ten years of New Labour: workplace learning, social partnership and union revitalization in Britain. *British Journal of Industrial Relations*, 46 (2), 283–313.

Moore, S. and Wood, H. 2005: *The Union Learning Experience: National Survey of Union Officers and ULRs*. London: Working Lives Research Institute, London Metropolitan University.

Mowery, D. 1986: Industrial research, 1900–1950. In Elbaum, B. and Lazonick, W. (eds) *The Decline of the British Economy*. Oxford: Clarendon Press, pp. 189–222.

Munro, A. and Rainbird, H. 2004: The workplace learning agenda – new opportunities for trade unions? In Healy, G., Heery, E., Taylor, P. and Brown, W. (eds) *The Future of Worker Representation*. Basingstoke: Palgrave/Macmillan, pp. 151–166.

National Centre for Partnership and Performance 2005: Working to our advantage – a national workplace strategy, executive summary. Dublin: NCPP.

Nichols, T. 1986: *The British Worker Question*. London: Routledge.

OECD 2008: *Economic Outlook*, No. 84, November.

Ogden, S. 1982: Bargaining structure and the control of industrial relations. *British Journal of Industrial Relations*, 12 (5), 170–185.

O'Mahony, M. and de Boer, W. 2002: *Britain's Relative Productivity Performance: Updates to 1999*. London: National Institute for Economic and Social Research.

Payne, J. 2004: Re-evaluating the Finnish Workplace Development Programme: evidence from two projects in the municipal sector. *Economic and Industrial Democracy*, 25 (4), 485–524.

Payne, J. 2008a: Divergent skills policy trajectories in England and Scotland after Leitch. SKOPE Research Paper No. 82. Cardiff: SKOPE, Cardiff University.

Payne, J. 2008b: Sector skills councils and employer-engagement – delivering the 'employer-led' skills agenda in England. *Journal of Education and Work*, 21 (2), 93–113.

Payne, J. 2008c: Skills in context: what can the UK learn from Australia's skill ecosystem projects? *Policy and Politics*, 36 (3), 307–323.

Payne, J. and Keep, E. 2003: Re-visiting the Nordic approaches to work organization and job redesign: lessons for UK skills policy. *Policy Studies*, 24 (4), 205–225.

Perry, P. 1976: *The Evolution of British Manpower Policy*. London: British Association of Commercial and Industrial Training.

Scottish Government 2007: *Skills for Scotland – A Lifelong Skills Strategy*. Edinburgh: The Scottish Government.

Shaw, N., Starks, L., Hopwood, V., O'Neil, L., Wilton, M., Laxton, C. and Serr, A. 2006: *Evaluation of the Union Learning Fund (2001–2005)*. Nottingham: DfES.

Sheldrake, J. and Vickerstaff, S. 1987: *The History of Industrial Training in Britain*. Aldershot: Gower Publishing.

Shelley, S. 2007: The outcomes and usefulness of union learning. In Shelley, S. and Calveley, M. (eds) *Learning with Trade Unions*. Aldershot: Ashgate, pp. 115–130.

SSDA (Sector Skills Development Agency) 2006a: *Skills for Business Network: Phase 3 Evaluation Main Report*, Research Report 19. Wath-upon-Dearne: SSDA.

SSDA 2006b: *Skills for Business Network 2005: Survey of Employers*, Research Report 18. Wath-upon-Dearne: SSDA.

Stedward, G. 2003: Education policy as industrial policy: New Labour's marriage of the social and the economic. *Policy and Politics*, 31 (2), 139–142.

Storey, J. (ed.) 1989: *New Perspectives on Human Resource Management*. London: Routledge.

Streeck, W. 1992: *Social Institutions and Economic Performance*. London: Sage.

Stuart, M. and Wallis, E. 2007: Partnership approaches to learning: a seven country study. *European Journal of Industrial Relations*, 13 (3), 301–321.

Taylor, R. 1993: *The Trade Union Question in British Politics: Government and the Unions Since 1945*. Oxford: Blackwell Publishing Ltd.

Tertiary Education Commission 2008: Media Release: Partnership to increase workforce skills announced today. www.tec.govt.nz/ templates/NewsItem.aspx?id=2729&jssup=1 (accessed 31/03/2008).

TUC (Trades Union Congress) 2007: *Leitch Review of Skills: TUC briefing*. London: TUC.

Unionlearn 2007: *One Year On: Unionlearn Annual Report 2007*. London: Unionlearn.

Wallis, E., Stuart, M. and Greenwood, I. 2005: 'Learners of the workplace unite!': an empirical examination of the UK trade union learning representative initiative. *Work, Employment and Society*, 19 (2), 283–304.

Warhurst, C., Findlay, P. and Thompson, P. 2006: Organising to learn/learning to organise: three case studies on the effects of union-led workplace learning. SKOPE Research Paper 68. Cardiff: Cardiff University.

Winterton, J. 2007: Building social dialogue over training and learning: European and national developments. *European Journal of Industrial Relations*, 13 (3), 281–300.

Wilby, P. 2007: Why labour reporters aren't working. *The Guardian* (Media Guardian), 5 March, p. 7.

Wilson, R. and Hogarth, T. 2003: *Tackling the Low Skills Equilibrium*. London: DTI.

18

EQUALITY AND DIVERSITY: THE ULTIMATE INDUSTRIAL RELATIONS CONCERN

DEBORAH DEAN AND SONIA LIFF

Introduction

Diversity (meaning here variety) is a now a fact of life in most UK workplaces. Whereas once women were largely absent from the formal economy, the majority of UK women are now in paid work and expect to stay there even when they also have responsibilities for children or for caring for elderly or sick relatives (see Crouch, this volume). The UK has an ethnically diverse workforce which consists of people who have settled in the UK (or who have been born to families who have settled in the past) and also those who come to work for relatively short periods of time, particularly from other EU member countries. Improvements in health and more precarious pension provision mean that some employees are staying in work beyond traditional retirement age. People's working patterns and working lives are also less clear cut. Many young people enjoy interspersing periods of work with periods of travel. Fewer people than in the past work for the same organization all their lives, and people adjust their working hours to fit in other commitments and interests.

Despite this increased diversity, it remains possible to identify areas of the labour market where employees are remarkably homogeneous in terms of their gender, ethnicity and age. Segmentation of this kind is often associated with quite different outcomes for the workers involved. The well-paid boardrooms of most major companies contain only white, middle aged or elderly men (Singh and Vinnicombe 2006), whereas workplaces where fruit and vegetables are harvested or packed are likely to be staffed by younger, often migrant workers facing unsafe, low-paid and insecure conditions (Jayaweera and Anderson 2008). This chapter will explore aspects of the patterns and explanations of advantage and disadvantage in employment, which are directly linked to concepts of equality and diversity.

An industrial relations (IR) analysis is particularly appropriate to try to understand these experiences. Kaufman identifies IR's core organizing principle as the acknowledgement that *labour is human* and therefore incapable of being purely a commodity (leading to the IR focus on concepts of uncertainty, incompleteness, control and consent). This has implications for every aspect of employment relations, particularly when exploration of equality issues also highlights the human dimension of *capital*. For example, there have been studies where fake matched applications are sent to employers to see whether those purporting to come from some types of applicants tend to get a more positive response. These studies establish pervasive unfair discrimination on the basis of ethnicity, gender (in both directions in relation to sex-typed jobs) and disability (Riach and Rich 2002; Carlsson and Rooth 2008). This suggests actions are not constrained directly by legislation or equality policies (considered further below and in Colling, this volume). The organizing assumption of neo-classical economics, that labour is homogeneous and that supply and demand operate both neutrally and rationally, 'as if "all men are equal"' (Hicks 1932, cited in Kaufman 2007), is also exposed as unsustainable. IR focuses on the realities of this conceptual misattribution. In contrast to the assumptions of orthodox economics and public policy, IR scholars focus on 'context-sensitive research' (Edwards 2005) and have always recognized the 'pronounced diversity in the circumstances determining the state of firm-level employment relations' (Kaufman 2008: 326). Included in this diversity are such factors as the macro-economy (in the UK, a particular type of liberal market economy, see Colling and Terry; Crouch; Heyes and Nolan, this volume); qualities and characteristics of management and employees; and legal, political and social norms. Thus the essence of an IR analysis of work and employment relations is a multi-actor, multi-disciplinary, multi-level approach concerned, crucially, with varied and competing interests and goals (Clarke *et al.* 2008).

The first part of the chapter explores developments in IR analyses of equality and diversity issues. We then map key aspects of these issues and different ways of understanding and approaching them. The next section moves from general discussion of patterns and analyses to a closer consideration of the actions of key IR actors, enabling a more considered assessment of their aims and outcomes.

The Changing Focus of Industrial Relations

While inequality has always been a fundamental focus of IR scholarship (Webb and Webb 1897; Hyman 1974), in the past, industrial relations as a field of study was concerned primarily with white male skilled manual workers. This can be seen as a consequence of IR's policy and analytical focus on collective bargaining institutions, which have been concentrated in specific sectors; and also as a consequence of society and social science seeing (white, breadwinner) man as the norm, as synonymous with 'person' (Morgan 1981). This has been challenged increasingly by political, economic and theoretical developments. Gradual acceptance of the need to extend the scope of the subject developed following a series of studies in the 1980s documenting the experience of women and minority ethnic workers in the UK (see review in Holgate *et al.* 2006). Recent feminist critiques of IR have focused explicitly on the gendered outcomes, practices and processes within the apparently neutral concerns of *what* has been studied and *how* it has been studied (e.g. Wajcman 2000; Greene 2003; Healy *et al.* 2006). Thus it is necessary in the interests of rigorous analysis to recognize the interconnection of the cultural and the material (Holgate *et al.* 2006; Hyman 1974), reassess the categories of worker and forms and experiences of employment and regulation, to give due weight to their range and complexity. An example is Danieli's work (2006). This found that negotiations between union officials, managers and male workers in an electronics manufacturing company drew on 'natural' ideas of masculinity, in rejecting the men's redeployment to women's part-time assembly work as an alternative to redundancy. This was analysed in terms of the relevance of ideology in shaping work relations, also emphasized by Edwards (2006: 574), discussing ideology at work as 'sets of beliefs which expressed and reinforced a particular set of power relations'.

There are also significant, if less direct, moves in the mainstream of current IR thinking. Kelly (1998), writing from a different set of concerns, has criticized a traditional assumption that workers' interests are homogeneous and defined simply against those of employers; allowing space to address the more fluid notions of identity and interests raised when workers are seen as belonging to different social groups. Piore and Safford (2006), albeit writing in the distinctive US context, argue that statutory employment rights are driven by a 'shift in social and political mobilization' (2006: 304) away from occupational or workplace-specific identities and towards those rooted in social identities. Raising similar concerns in the context of the UK and France, Almond (2004) argues that there is a need to draw on different disciplines to create a wider analysis of workplace relations giving greater weight to social exclusion and cohesion, rather than simply relations between employers and employees defined by the employment contract. Ackers (2002) argues similarly for analytical emphasis on a plurality of social institutions and norms in employment relations research.

Mapping Equality Issues

The *figures* establishing pay gaps or job segregation by gender or race may not be contentious in themselves, but their *explanation* and *meaning* certainly are. For some, observed differences in outcomes are the result of some groups of employees being systematically favoured over others, giving rise to (unfair) discrimination. For others, it is more likely that different outcomes are the consequence of different *choices* made by groups in the labour market. For example, human capital theorists explain variable career outcomes with reference to patterns of investment in training and development amongst workers (see Becker 1985; Grimshaw and Rubery, this volume). Similarly, some suggest that gendered patterns of job segregation are the outcome of different levels of commitment to work, with women's divided between home, family and workplace to a greater extent than men's (Hakim 2000). Such approaches suggest workplace decisions are simply a reflection of wider social processes including socialization, education and family relationships. While these explanations have been widely critiqued as not acknowledging structural constraints such as availability of child care provision in such 'choices' (e.g. Crompton and Lyonette 2005), they do signal that categories including gender, ethnicity and age are not just salient in the workplace but are part of the way society is organized.

Unravelling this complexity requires nuanced use of employment outcome data. So, for example, in 2001 white British men had an unemployment rate of 5.7%, those from a black Caribbean background 16.8%, and those from a Bangladeshi background 20.3% (Clark and Drinkwater 2007). The type of explanation posited above might suggest that this could be the result of different levels of skills and qualification and Clark and Drinkwater tested this hypothesis, with mixed results. They found that educational achievement was indeed an important determinant of access to work. However, when they matched white and minority ethnic employees for skill levels they found that '(a)ll ethnic minorities continue to have lower earnings than comparable White groups, with large earnings differentials experienced by the Black African, Pakistani and Bangladeshi groups, while in terms of earnings within occupations, the deficits tend to be largest for professional/managerial workers for virtually all of the ethnic minorities' (2007: 54). Indicating further complexity in the same 2001 Census data (and in keeping with a focus on the cultural/material and ideology as noted above), Khattab's (2009: 319) work on educational and occupational attainment suggests that 'colour is as important as religion, but . . . that the direction and strength of their impact is likely to be determined in relation to the values, attributes and capacities attached to the various groups by the hegemonic culture'.

Similarly, women earn less on average over their lifetimes than men. If this was directly attributable to their role in childrearing we could expect the lifetime earnings of women without children to match those of men (given, for example, child care provision issues as noted above). However, data show that while childless women earn more than women with children, they still have lower lifetime average earnings than men (Sigle-Rushton and Waldfogel 2007). Again this is not accounted for by lower qualifications, with statistical data showing that the difference between men and women's average pay is *greater* for those educated to degree level than for those with lower qualifications (Women and Equality Unit 2004: 76). Purcell *et al.* (2006: 58) found that earnings of male and female graduates seven years after graduation differed markedly overall, with greatest dispersion in the private sector: 'Average earnings for high-access male graduates in the private sector seven years after graduation were £40 080 and for women were £33 210'.

A central issue here is the uneven concentration of different groups between and within occupations and sectors, known as occupational segregation. This is clear in relation to ethnicity (see TUC 2006) and particularly well established in relation to gender. Women make up 46% of the labour market in the UK but are concentrated in just over a quarter of occupations and comprise just over a third of managers (European Commission 2008: 21, 32). Divisions are most clear in relation to types of employment contract, as '59 percent of female part-time workers perform service/clerical/sales jobs (compared to 41 percent of full-time working women)' (Bardasi and Gornick 2008: 31; Thornley 2007). In a detailed exploration of earnings data over the last 30 years, Manning and Petrongolo (2008) conclude that the 22% difference in average hourly pay between full-time and part-time women workers is largely attributable to occupational segregation of these groups. Again, within this overall observation there are other complexities to consider; for example, that women of particular ethnicities are on average more or less likely to work part-time (Platt 2006). Such divisions are a worldwide phenomenon and explanations for the persistence of occupational segregation are rooted in the ideological and economic development of societies (see Estévez-Abe (2006) for a discussion of explanations and of counterintuitive institutional influences on occupational segregation).

However, notwithstanding these patterns of disadvantage, it is argued that employers can have no interest in anything other than appointing the best person for the job and aim to operate in ways to achieve this, and therefore that the workplace operates as a *meritocracy*. The objective of ensuring that decisions in the workplace are made on the basis of merit is widely endorsed and underpins the UK's legal approach to discrimination, often expressed as ensuring people are treated equally regardless of ethnicity, gender or other irrelevant characteristics (explored further below). However, research shows us that workplace processes and practices have a direct role in differential outcomes by social group. This is not necessarily the result of prejudiced individual decision making, but often that requirements which lead to discriminatory outcomes are embedded in the formal policies or informal practices of specific organizations (e.g. Acker 1990; Cockburn 1989). For this reason this is often described as *institutional discrimination* (a term made familiar from 1999 by the Macpherson Inquiry into the police investigation of the murder of black teenager Stephen Lawrence).

Thus 'merit' is a complicated concept. For example, some young people come from homes where books are owned and read and go to schools where they are taught in ways which lead them to achieve exam results permitting them to go to university. This gives them access to organizations offering graduate level opportunities to gain additional skills and experiences. On the other hand, others will drop out of education and take up jobs which offer them little opportunity to continue to develop their talents. Should we interpret the merit they display in later life as simply a reflection of their individual potential? Research indicates that parental class, amongst other 'background' factors, has a close relationship with particular career outcomes (Schroeder *et al.* 2008). Simplistic conceptions of merit do not offer much explanatory power in such comparisons.

Then we need to consider how the tasks against which people are assessed are structured. In most UK workplaces working on Sunday is not required, but working on a Saturday may be. This is a requirement that an observant Christian person can comply with, but not an observant Jewish person. So judged against this criterion the Christian will appear the better candidate for the job. But if the requirement was defined as working six days a week the result would not be such a foregone conclusion. There are many other ways in which working patterns, job requirements and the qualifications and experiences looked for have developed around the characteristics of the people who have traditionally occupied such workplaces, making the status quo look natural and therefore right, or best.

A further complicating dimension of merit is the way we assess it. For example, when a job advert specifies the need for someone with 'ambition and drive' it is likely that assessors will be affected by stereotypes relating to gender, age, ethnicity, disability and sexual orientation, which are themselves derived in part from the types of activity in which people with different characteristics are, and are not, currently engaged (Collinson *et al.* 1990). Gender stereotypes are seen as centrally connected with the existence and persistence of unequal employment outcomes (see Mills and Wilson 2001; Gorman 2005) and the elimination of these stereotypes in education, training and culture is seen by the European Commission's 'Roadmap for equality between women and men 2006–2010' (European Commission 2006: 8) as a key factor in achieving other aims, including equal economic independence for women and men. Perceptions of age are closely connected to gender and research shows that women workers suffer more as a group from negative perceptions of ageing, in particular regarding rates of employment and pay (AGE 2007; Duncan and Loretto 2004).

These complex ideas of merit are frequently implicit in ideas of equality (in their connections with 'justice'). However, equality is itself not a clear concept.

Multiple Meanings of Equality

A predominant focus on varied outcomes for members of particular social groups would imply that equality means *equal outcomes*. So while relatively few women *or* men will become managing directors, this approach would suggest that the *proportions* of women and men who do so should be similar. In fact UK women comprise barely 4% of executive directors of FTSE 100 companies: all of those women are white, and of the 14% of women non-executive directors, fewer than 5% were from minority ethnic groups (Singh and Vinnicombe 2006).

Should equality interventions therefore try to directly address such discrepancies by, say, giving preference to under-represented groups at appointment? This approach, described as positive discrimination (that is, equality as *proportionate outcomes*), is normally unlawful in the UK (although the forthcoming Single Equality Bill makes very limited provision for selection on this basis: Government Equalities Office 2008: 10). The principal exception has been in Northern Ireland, to address embedded under-representation of Catholics and Protestants in different areas of employment, involving employers in closely defined monitoring of the religious composition of their workforce and the obligation to take active remedial steps (McCrudden 2004).

Understanding equality in terms of *equal treatment* is much more widely accepted. It is commonly seen as encapsulating the merit principle and as the way to remove any discrimination that does occur at workplace level, particularly as a result of biased individual decision makers. As such it has involved attempts to ensure that managers objectively assess applicants against job-relevant criteria.

But if the competition embodies terms which are favourable to some types of people, for example by requiring working patterns some find it easier to undertake, then treating everyone the same may simply legitimate unequal outcomes. The need to consider other routes was apparent in a government review of equality approaches, which concluded that on current trends 'it will take almost 100 years for people from ethnic minorities to get the same job prospects as white people' (Government Equalities Office 2008: 7).

Equal opportunities (EO) is a term which, while widely used, does not have a clear meaning. It can mean the same as equal treatment but may also allow for wider definitions of discrimination and equality. This might involve providing some support to the individual (through, for example, providing hearing-loop technology) or changing organizational arrangements, such as allowing part-time working in senior posts (a move that might be expected to increase opportunities for promotion by those with caring responsibilities). Some measures along these lines are now required by law in the public sector through the imposition of duties to actively promote equality in relation to race/ethnicity, gender and disability.[1] These duties move away from an individualized idea of inequality (somebody suffers from someone else's action) to an effective recognition of inequality as centrally involving issues of power (conceived of as the capacity to pursue one's own interests and as embedded in existing structures and ongoing relationships (Edwards 2003: 13). That is to say that in that those who hold the balance of power (employers) are in a position to recognize and address potential barriers to potential progress.

For others, equality comes not by ensuring the same treatment or opportunities but by allowing people to demonstrate their distinctive contributions or to behave in different ways in the workplace. Such an approach, often termed *managing diversity* (MD), can provide a more radical challenge to the problem of disadvantage and discrimination by requiring organizations to adapt to individuals and groups rather than vice versa. MD perspectives attempt to positively enrol employers by privileging a 'business case' for equality beyond the social justice case. Organizations that treat everyone fairly, it is claimed, will experience a range of advantages including recruiting and retaining the best people, attracting new customers, and making it more likely that employees work productively (see CBI 2008). MD emphasizes multiple, individual difference, potentially applicable to *all* employees (e.g. Kandola and Fullerton 1998) and implicitly including the white men explicitly left out of the EO discourse (and arguably therefore sits better with the moves towards intersectionality in legal regulation we consider below). Thus corporate policy statements encouraging diversity in a workforce publicly assume a link between a multiplicity of 'difference' and adding value (Singh and Point 2006).

But the idea of a universal 'business case' has been criticized by Dickens (2000 159): 'Unfair discrimination can be rational and efficient for an individual and the organization either because of perceived cost advantages or in terms of control of the labour force.' It is also unclear whether the general corporate trend is one that, in Liff and Cameron's (1997) formulation, effectively 'dissolves' difference, focusing on the individual and their potential; or 'values' difference, where difference based on social group membership is 'acknowledged and responded to, rather than ignored', as argued to be the traditional thrust of EO approaches. However, a key point is that the *aim* of MD is not fairness and equality. This is not to say that MD does not or cannot address these issues, but that the *orientation* of policy shifts. Further, MD approaches valorize the centrality of the manager – the manager is best placed to assess the individual's needs and attributes in the context of organizational objectives that s/he is employed to deliver (see, for example, Ross and Schneider 1994). This approach sits well with dominant UK employer approaches to IR, as examined further below.

Therefore where managing diversity stresses individual differences to the exclusion of collective ones, it raises concerns about the extent to which collective experience of disadvantage is being acknowledged and the ways in which people's relative merits are being assessed. These issues, and the possibility that it might lead to the loss of gains achieved via an equal opportunities approach, have made many UK IR actors and academics wary of endorsing managing diversity whole-heartedly (Wrench 2005; Kirton and Greene 2006; Johns and Green 2009).

The Roles of IR Actors

Having considered a range of broad explanations of, and approaches to, equality and diversity issues in employment, we now explore active engagement with these issues. This section considers the approaches taken in the UK by the principal IR actors: the State, employers, employees and trade unions. These actors are essentially concerned with outcomes, both substantive (e.g. equal pay, flexible working) and procedural (e.g. equality and diversity policies).

The State

The State is involved in developing policies which impact indirectly upon employment equality. Issues such as immigration, welfare entitlement and provision of child care facilities impinge on the terms on which members of different groups work. The availability of affordable child care, for instance, will affect the 'choice' of a parent as to whether s/he works, whether s/he works part-time, and so on.

Other policy issues have more direct impact, most notably the State's major role over the last 30 years in relation to legal regulation and anti-discrimination legislation (see Dickens 2007 for a review). Basing workplace decisions on 'merit' is widely accepted as an uncontroversial aim and this underpins the UK's legal approach to discrimination: equal treatment regardless of irrelevant character-istics. The two main legal understandings (and the bases on which people can challenge employer actions/understandings of merit) are based on concepts in the Sex Discrimination Act 1975 and the Race Relations Act 1976. These are 'direct' discrimination (where, for example, a woman is treated less favourably from the way she would be if she were a man) and 'indirect' discrimination (where a requirement not strictly relevant to the job is imposed with which members of one social group would find it more difficult to comply and cannot be justified).

Indirect discrimination in particular is a potentially powerful concept through its ability to question the traditional ways in which an applicant's abilities have been assessed. However, it is open to considerable interpretation (centrally on what is a 'justifiable' condition) and Employment Tribunals (ET) and the courts have often restricted the scope of such challenges. This has effectively discouraged broader, systemic reflection that might result in the organizational rethinking argued above as necessary for meaningful change in outcomes. Such judgments have often been superseded by (EU-derived) legislation (for example, the Part-time Workers (Prevention of Less Favourable Treatment) Regulations 2000) and there have been other judgments interpreting 'justification' narrowly. However, the very inconsistency of approaches demonstrates that the actions of IR actors and institutions are never neutral, in that there are usually differing and frequently competing interests and evaluations involved in any intervention. Pay, for example, is not simply a function of the market or impartial reward for 'skills', and involves both social and economic processes: 'the reality of skill is socially constructed and contested' (Sturdy *et al.* 1992: 4; Grimshaw and Rubery, this volume). This reality has been shown to be intrinsically gendered: jobs in female-dominated sectors have been considered unskilled whether a man or a woman does them (Crompton and Sanderson 1990).

UK legislation in these areas has often been shaped at a wider European level, through the implementation of EU directives or in response to decisions of the European Court of Justice (also used by some trade unions to develop equality bargaining issues: Heery 2005; Dickens 1998). At the day-to-day level of legal regulation of equality issues in the UK, attempted resolution largely needs to be initiated by individuals, and the principal route for redress in these cases is the Tribunal system (Colling; Dickens and Hall, this volume).

If someone believes that they have been discriminated against they can make a complaint to an ET. In 2006/07, equality/discrimination cases formed 64% of the total claims accepted by ETs. However, the majority of (all) claims are withdrawn or settled through conciliation by ACAS before they are heard by an ET (ETS 2006, 2007). As Dickens and others have discussed, such conciliation is aimed at compromise between the parties, rather than judgment on the justice of the claim itself (2007: 480). This effectively lobs responsibility for thinking about equality issues back to the organizations in which the difficulties originated. Further, these statistics obscure the established findings that only up to a quarter of 'justiciable disputes' even get as far as making formal claims to ETs (for full discussion, see Colling, this volume).

Even where cases do progress to tribunal hearing, there are concerns about process which can be related back to the discussion above on our assumptions about the neutrality of 'merit' and how we come to make judgments about others. Dickens (2007) looks at Aston *et al.*'s (2006) research on the demographic characteristics of ET members, where ethnicity 'mismatch' between claimant and panel was found to have direct effects on the confidence of claimants in obtaining a fair hearing and decision (2007: 477). Dickens draws out the material significance of this lack of confidence, in Peters *et al.*'s (2006) finding that tribunals principally based decisions on their assessment of the credibility of the complainant, the respondent and their witnesses. Respondents were more likely to be white (as were tribunal members) and assessments of credibility were found to be based not only on evidential factors, but also on culturally constructed perspectives on how claimants and respondents presented and conducted themselves at the hearing (2007: 478).

There is a strained ambivalence in the State's central engagement with equality in employment. The State recognizes that experience of discrimination and disadvantage are commonly based on membership of particular social categories ('sex', 'race', and so on), but personalizes engagement with those experiences, with actions largely brought by and decided about isolated individuals. Such actions involve an individual challenging their employer (or potential employer), which can be a risky, distressing and expensive experience. A larger underlying problem is that such challenge is based on the idea of the employment contract as a bargain negotiated between equals: that each individual comes to the labour market as an individual and, according to her inclinations and qualifications, sells her capacity to labour to a particular employer. This connects to the traditional conception of merit discussed above, in that it does not acknowledge the asymmetry of power inherent in the employment contract or the complicated routes taken to arrive at the point of exchange in this contract, such as differential access to resources (e.g. education, norms in caring responsibilities).

There are signs of potential change in this approach. Pressure has been growing to allow Tribunals scope to hear 'representative actions', where the same grievance affects broader workforces, to issue action recommendations in individual cases, and to require reviews of policy and procedure, and some such measures are being debated in the Single Equality Bill (Act expected 2010). One recommendation to government was that 'socially responsible collective bodies' such as trade unions, charities and Citizens Advice Bureaux would have the right to bring representative actions (Civil Justice Council 2008: 142). One of the bodies listed also draws in the State, as government is indirectly involved in the promotion and enforcement of equality issues in its funding of the independent body, the Equality and Human Rights Commission.

In 2007 the existing single equality bodies (the Equal Opportunities Commission, Commission for Racial Equality, Disability Rights Commission) were absorbed into a single Equality and Human Rights Commission (EHRC), intended to have 'sole responsibility for promoting equality of opportunity and enforcing compliance with anti-discrimination law in Britain' (O'Cinneide 2007). The EHRC has an expanded brief to also cover other equality grounds now protected by legislation: age, religion or belief, sexual orientation or transgender status, and to encourage compliance with the Human Rights Act. There was resistance to merger from the previous equality bodies, fearing that focus and expertise on their particular areas would be lost. Another view sees creation of the EHRC (and the Single Equality Bill) as pointing toward State recognition of the simultaneous multiplicity of people's identities and, in disability and age, ongoing change in those identities.

It has been argued that the EHRC will have to compete for resources and that an opportunity has been missed to give the EHRC significantly expanded powers of investigation and enforcement (Mabbett 2008; O'Cinneide 2007; McColgan

2005). The focus therefore will be on what use the EHRC decides to make of the powers it currently has (the Single Equality Bill may expand on these). It has made a significant early move in supporting the case of a non-disabled working mother of a disabled son in an appeal to the European Court of Justice (ECJ). The ECJ agreed that she, as her son's primary carer, was covered by the Disability Discrimination Act 1995 and therefore her employer's offensive and inflexible behaviour towards her (in contrast to the employer's treatment of parents of non-disabled children) was discrimination on the grounds of disability.[2] This case also indirectly demonstrates the limitations of business case arguments and reliance on what den Dulk and de Ruijter identify as 'the variable and discretionary powers of managers' in enabling work–life balance (2008: 1223).

However, Labour governments from 1997 have largely followed previous administrations' emphasis on voluntarism in their lack of challenge to employers. The principal qualification is the public sector. The recent (2001–07) equality duties[3] require public sector employers to take positive measures to promote equality and eliminate discrimination in relation to race/ethnicity, gender and disability. Rather than just being confident that they have avoided legally defined discrimination, employers have to consider, for example, how they can improve access of women to more senior posts. There are concerns about the structure and enforcement of these duties (Fredman 2008a) but their existence is arguably *symbolically* important (Dickens 2007; see also Hepple 1992). They may signal desired outcomes and implicitly challenge the idea that social identities and advantage/disadvantage in employment are 'natural' or inevitable, or that we each create our own merit which is then appropriately rewarded. They can be seen as extending the individualized legal provision against indirect discrimination, by encouraging employers to consider what in their conventional practices might be limiting opportunity for members of some social groups.

Hopes that such an approach would be extended into the private sector were not realized in the Single Equality Bill, intended to provide an integration of the current pieces of legislation aimed at different social groups. Certainly there is potential for this new legislation to address what Hannett (2003: 65) has described as legislative and judicial failure to engage with 'equality at the intersections'. However, the preceding government paper omitted proposals to fully extend the positive equality duties imposed on the public sector to the private sector. Malik (2007: 91) summarized the government's preference for voluntarist-inclined proposals as displaying 'an underlying assumption of consensus between all parties' about challenging systemic disadvantage. Such an assumption ignores common realities of employer advantage in unfairly discriminating.

One response to problems caused by unwillingness to radically challenge the terms on which employment is offered has been legislation seeking to support employees who need to work in ways which diverge from the norm.[4] A difficulty with such an approach is that if differences are recognized through special provisions there is a risk of essentializing and perpetuating differences, rather than facilitating their breakdown. For example, planned extension of maternity leave (to 12 months) risks reinforcing the idea that women are the primary providers of child care (Brewer 2008) while leaving the traditional structures of organizations and patterns of work unchallenged. Paternity leave is now paid, increasing the likelihood of take-up, but is limited to two weeks.[5] In accordance with wider EU discourses on 'flexicurity' (e.g. European Commission 2006), the currently postponed extension of maternity leave is accompanied by a provision for parental leave that will allow fathers rights to take time away from work. However, the paid component is contingent on the mother not using all of her maternity leave; implying that equality-as-same-treatment is viewed by policy makers as a flexible concept. The fact that men frequently work in better-paid jobs also means that it is commonly harder for a family to adjust to loss of the father's wages than the mother's. Consequently, 'so far the increase [in flexible working practices] has largely been a flexing of the traditional model of working and this is not enough – more radical transformation is required' (EOC 2007: 3; see also Fleetwood 2007 for a critique of flexibility as 'employee-friendly').

Further, developments in disability anti-discrimination legislation institutionally recognize that discrimination varies in how and why it is experienced by individuals who are nominally part of the same category. In the Disability Discrimination Acts (DDA) 1995 and 2005, conceptions of disability in employment have moved from a predominantly 'medical model' (where the emphasis is on limitations imposed on the individual by their impairment) to a broader 'social model' (where the emphasis is on identifying external barriers to participation). The 1995 Act required employers to make 'reasonable adjustments' to accommodate employees with impairments and the 2005 Act, imposing the duty to promote equality for disabled people (DED), went further than either the existing race or subsequent gender duties in requiring that disabled people be *involved* in developing a disability scheme (rather than simply consulted). Both of these provisions effectively recognized the heterogeneity of disabled people's experiences (as impairments differ) and therefore that the response *could not* be 'equality as same treatment' (see Woodhams and Danieli 2000; Berthoud 2008). Centrally, the DED requires that account be taken of impairments, even where that involves treating disabled persons *more favourably than* other persons.[6] What is interesting about this provision is that it is conceptually ring-fenced: it has not been allowed to leak into consideration of the other equality categories and, so far, has not been taken up as an argument by trade unions or other interested parties. However, it should also be noted that 'age' as an employment dimension has often explicitly involved more favourable treatment (such as seniority rights, higher minimum wage rates).

Trade unions

As noted above, in the past IR actors and academics have not always been alive to the specific interests of workers who differed from what was taken as the norm; but the contexts in which they operate are now substantially changed or recognized as more complex. Trade union density has declined and both the coverage and scope of collective bargaining has narrowed (see Brown, this volume). With important elements of the employment relationship now decided by management (through unilateral policy) or the State (through statutory employment rights) the potential for action through collective bargaining is clearly constrained. The need for representation is clear, however, even in this changed landscape. Where employees advance their grievances through the tribunal systems, the complexity of discrimination cases and the fact that complainants are often from disadvantaged social groups means that support from external bodies such as trade unions can be decisive (Malik 2007; Fredman 2008b). And changes in the structure of the labour market, and thereby the pool of potential new union members, provide strong incentives to union action on equality issues.

Various dimensions of equality practice have been shown to be more likely where there is a union presence. For example, workplaces with unions are more likely to have an equality policy (Kersley *et al.* 2006: 239) and relatively compressed pay dispersal lessens the scale of race/ethnicity pay gaps (Metcalf *et al.* 2001; European Commission 2008: 88). Although Noon and Hoque (2001) found inequality of treatment between white and minority ethnic workers in unionized workplaces, Colling and Dickens (2001) found that there were, broadly, less extreme inequalities in unionized than non-unionized workplaces. While the research does not demonstrate consistent causal links, there certainly appears to be an association. Hepple *et al.*'s (2000) survey of international work on the gender pay gap found that 'Women traditionally did best in systems with not only a high level of collective bargaining but a centralised bargaining or pay awards system' (2000: 14; see also Wallerstein 1999; Heery 2006). This view is supported by Gregory's (1999) analysis of the impact of sex equality law, which also echoes criticisms of the ET process discussed above:

> Without security of employment, women are less likely to know their rights to equal treatment or be in a position to act on this knowledge. In the case of equal pay, the shift from national collective agreements to localised pay negotiation and the proliferation of individualised payment systems made it increasingly difficult for women to access the information which would provide the basis for a claim. (1999: 99; see also Pollert 2005)

As discussed above in relation to academic IR study, trade unions have traditionally treated 'economic and industrial' issues as neutral, rather than as reflecting the perspectives and interests of dominant groups (for example, issues around flexible working, or harassment: see Greene and Kirton 2009 for an overview and discussion). However, recent sectoral and labour market changes have meant that recruitment of women and minority groups is becoming an increasingly important union survival strategy (see Simms and Charlwood, this volume; Kirton 2006; Ledwith and Colgan 2002). It should be noted that this is not union movement-wide but rather where particular needs are perceived as relevant (see Heery *et al.* 2002). Special measures such as reserved seats and specialist committees are examples of a positive action approach and can be seen as linking to the legal category of indirect discrimination, in recognition that superficially neutral practices can result in effective favouring of dominant groups. Engagement with non-traditional union membership groups is also a reaction to the fact of their increasing presence (e.g. Munro 2001) and specialist committees and reserved seats on union decision-making bodies are commonplace, although these have not usually been sufficient to extend engagement with core union strategy and decision making (McBride 2001; Parker 2002). Certainly, it seems that broader internal support measures (such as availability of training and advice) are necessary in increasing the likelihood of equality bargaining (Heery 2006).

It is arguable though that trade unions also have more general 'environmental' effects, analogous to arguments in relation to law noted above, in that they raise and sustain awareness of the issues. For example, recent moves to widen protection for vulnerable workers (originally established after the deaths of 23 immigrant Chinese cockle-pickers in Morecambe Bay) are claimed to be the result of sustained union pressure (Anderson and Rogaly 2005; Brown 2007; see also BERR 2008). Vulnerable workers, defined as 'those whose participation in the labour market leaves their well-being at risk, because they have difficulty accessing work that is decently paid and/or offers conditions that meet basic social norms' (Saunders 2003: 17) are disproportionately foreign migrants of differing ethnicities and religious backgrounds (e.g. Hopkins 2009). Recent women migrants to the UK are identified as particularly at risk of poor employment practice, being 1.5 times more likely than male migrant workers to be paid less than the national minimum wage (Jayaweera and Anderson 2008), highlighting trends in conceptualizing these issues that focus on the co-construction of gender, ethnicity and class (Acker 2006; Cobble 2007; see also Soskice 2005). That is, these are not seen as separate categories that overlap, but as involved in each others' creation. Migrant women workers are disproportionately concentrated in difficult to regulate areas such as domestic service work (Jayaweera and Anderson 2008): their gender affects the terms on which they experience the work in which their ethnicity/ nationality concentrates them (and vice versa), entrenching their low socio-economic status (Peterson 2005; Soldatenko 1999).

However, increasingly visible trade union activity on equality and diversity issues (such as supporting members in anti-discrimination claims) has been part of a wider public equality and diversity discourse. Kirton and Greene (2006) note that women and minority groups are more likely to identify campaigning on specific equalities issues as an important reason for joining a union, and recent research found that 94% of workers in unionized workplaces say that 'equality' should be a union priority (TUC 2003: 19). While the connections between these findings are difficult to disentangle, we can see a potential virtuous circle (or at least chain) of regulatory pressure. This is not straightforward, either as a membership aspiration or an operational priority. The Court of Appeal judgment in *Allen v. GMB*[7] is an example of the tensions involved in making 'equality' a priority. Here, the GMB union (which had launched the first equal value pay case in 1984[8]) was found guilty of indirect sex discrimination. This was in agreeing to a low back pay settlement with Middlesbrough Borough Council in order to release more money for current pay protection and future pay. As the disadvantaged group was predominantly women, the GMB had acted in an indirectly discriminatory way in that their legitimate end goal of single status for all the council workers they represented was not achieved by proportionate means (effectively manoeuvring the women members into accepting a lower pay deal than they might otherwise have achieved). Kirton and Greene (2006) note that trade unions have been criticized for not being alert to the concerns of women and minorities; *Allen v. GMB* suggests that even where they are alert (as was specifically noted by the Court of Appeal), their primary interest is the collective's maintenance or improvement of terms and conditions. Of course how 'the collective' is identified by unions is affected by the political process of interest definition (Colling and Dickens 1998: 405; Parker 2002; Simms and Charlwood, this volume). An alternative reading is that external political decisions effectively forced the union into this position by the (in)action of local authorities and wider national governmental response: for example, trade unions had lobbied government over several years to provide additional funding to enable the Single Status agreement (Berry 2008). This reading is arguably lent some support by a government announcement, made two months after the CA decision, giving councils flexibility to raise the estimated £455 million needed to meet equal pay liabilities (Communities and Local Government 2008).

At workplace level, it is difficult to reach every union representative (where they exist, see Simms and Charlwood; Terry, this volume) and attempt to train them to identify and cope with the often complex issues involved in differential treatment in employment. Certainly, what is becoming clearer is the lack of understanding of the concepts and issues amongst union representatives at workplace level, rather than amongst union officials (Dean 2009; ACAS 2005: 1–2). But, importantly, the issues themselves are now rhetorically accepted even if translation into both bargaining agendas and outcomes does not always happen.

However, recent work on equality bargaining shows that reform of union government (in the form of specialist equality officers and committees) has fed through into general negotiator behaviour and, further, that the gender of union officials is less important in such bargaining than their expressed commitment to equal pay and their exposure to training (Heery 2006). This is important in light of earlier work by Heery (2005: 100), who reports that the pattern of findings on whether equality issues in collective bargaining are initiated by trade unions or employers suggests that 'without compulsion employers are unlikely to eliminate pay discrimination or enhance the poor conditions of part-time workers' (see Grimshaw and Rubery, this volume).

Employers, policies and practice

The initiative in addressing equality issues now rests substantially with employers, prompted and shaped to some extent by the law. There is usually an acknowledged disparity between a firm's possession of a policy addressing equality and diversity issues and outcomes reflecting the policy's aspirations. Hoque and Noon (2004) discussed 'empty shells' in the UK private sector and their exploration of WERS 98 data found that although public and private sector organizations were as likely to have equal opportunities policies, private sector organizations were significantly less likely to have practices supportive of the policy (see also Kersley *et al.* 2006: 247; Loretto and White 2006). We know that the presence of policies and practices does not necessarily imply resolution of equality issues, in the same way that unequal pay persists despite the longstanding existence of equal pay legislation (e.g. Liff and Dale 1994). It is arguable that the presence of both policies *and* practices to implement policy suggests at a minimum an organization aware of the relevance of equality and diversity issues and may indicate improved policy outcomes (Bassett-Jones *et al.* 2007). However, WERS 2004 data indicate that in three quarters of British workplaces decisions on equality matters are taken unilaterally by management without informing, consulting or negotiating with employee representatives, either union or non-union (although managerial monitoring of equality policies is more likely in unionized workplaces: Walsh 2007: 306, 308). This implies a rejection of the necessary realities of the pluralist perspective (the legitimacy of divergent interests and therefore involvement in decision making) that seems in fundamental tension with ideas of equality, although in keeping with an IR focus on the asymmetry of power in the employment relationship. However, it should also be noted that recent research suggests that there is scope for individual union representatives to play an informal role in engaging with workplace equality and diversity issues, even if management are unwilling to formally bargain with the union as a body (Greene and Kirton 2009: 209). More broadly, Walsh (2007) notes that in WERS 2004 employers and employees both reported an increase in the provision of work–life balance arrangements such as flexible working and paid leave. Elsewhere, though, it has been noted that across 21 European countries including the UK, the *effects* of working-time arrangements on employees' work–life balance are more to do with 'the practical handling of such arrangements at establishment level' (European Foundation for the Improvement of Living and Working Conditions 2006: 1, 51).

In the UK, managing diversity has been promoted by government and employer organizations as representing the 'business case' for equality: operational recognition that individuals from a range of social groups will possess talents of use to an organization widens the recruitment, promotion and innovation pools. This logically undeniable position has been thoroughly critiqued, however: principally, business benefits as drivers have been argued to be 'contingent, variable, selective and partial, and often underplay the wider context within which business case rationales are having to be pursued' (Dickens 1999: 9). For example, what if current business needs change in the light of market pressures? Bajawa and Woodall (2006) found an international airline had great difficulty maintaining diversity management objectives in the face of 'downsizing' strategies adopted in response to heightened competition, economic slowdown and terrorism fears. As downsizing alters an organization's shape and structure, comparing data (often not collected or monitored in the same way across departments) and thus providing reliable evidence on diversity initiatives, becomes problematic. Also, as Bajawa and Woodall stress, equality and diversity issues are broader than simply counting numbers of employees belonging to particular social groups in the organization overall: 'Where glass ceilings exist (especially on the boundary between middle and senior management) the cuts in absolute numbers of women and ethnic minorities may take years to redress' (2006: 58).

Such developments are in tension with increasingly formalized moves towards 'diversity' policy developments in companies based across the EU and in the USA (Grayson 2007; Singh and Point 2006). 'International framework agreements' have been concluded between a number of multinational corporations and international unions (see European Industrial Relations Review 2006; Marginson and Meardi, this volume; Riisgaard 2005), some of which specify diversity HR practices (notably the multinational Danone's agreement with the international union federation IUF on recruitment and development explicitly in pursuit of business benefits of employee diversity: Carley 2008). These agreements, which open core management practices to scrutiny by worker representatives, are in the minority. Greene and Kirton's (2009) study of contemporary diversity management practice in the UK found 'a significant shift in the way policies are formulated . . . towards recognizing the value of individual differences and the way in which these individual differences can make a difference to the organization and its business objectives' (2009: 214). However, the study also found that initiatives were almost always based around the social groups covered by legislation and equal opportunities as traditionally understood and, centrally, that there was little evidence of diversity management initiatives fundamentally challenging organizational structures and cultures.

A focus on equality outcomes also lies behind recent discussion on public sector procurement, in terms of stimulating private sector action on equality. The Women and Work Commission (2006), the Equalities Review (2007) and the Discrimination Law Review (2007) all made recommendations on use of compliance on equality issues in contracts between the public sector and private organizations. However, the document trailing the Equality Bill is vague on this issue and makes no reference to the specific proposals in these reports on using the annual £160 billion spent in procurement to strengthen equality requirements of the 30% of private sector firms contracted by the public sector (Government Equalities Office 2008: 22).

Procurement for social outcomes has been long established in the UK (since the late 19th century); however, Conservative government policy in the 1980s and 1990s restricted these possibilities and commentators have noted the constraints of both EU law and implementation problems on contract compliance equality strategies (see Fee 2002; McCrudden 2004). There are signs that an *effective* contract compliance model of sorts may be at work, in that private sector employers are aware of the public sector emphasis on equality issues and may act (sporadically and pragmatically) to meet perceived expectations to enable them to win contracts (Dean 2009: 103). However, where there is no monitoring or ongoing necessity to meet these expectations, the outcomes of such actions remain uncertain.

Nevertheless, legal compulsion in the public sector does not guarantee particular outcomes. The 'restructuring' of a large government department in 2004 had a disproportionately negative impact on its minority ethnic employees. These employees were concentrated in the lower civil service levels that were targeted for redundancy or required to move to new offices away from London (which has the largest percentage of the UK's minority ethnic population: ONS 2003) to areas of the country with predominantly white populations (Greene and Kirton

2009: 203). Arguably, a 'mainstreaming' approach to policy development, recommended in other parts of government, would have assessed this policy as indirectly discriminatory or at least disproportionately disadvantageous. Here, same treatment, unequal outcomes.

It is important not to overestimate the power of legal obligation or of organizational policies to engage with advantage and disadvantage in labour markets and in the workplace. While research indicates both may be necessary, neither is sufficient. Liff and Cameron (1997) stress the importance of gendered, racialized, organizational culture, both in managers' limited ability to compel change and the need more broadly to challenge thinking about the way the organization treats its different groups. Further, Dickens (1999) identifies three 'prongs' (business case, legal and social regulation) as necessary for equality action. The variation in presence and strength of these in the UK is suggested by the decline in union density and scope and coverage of collective bargaining, the limitations of legal regulation and also, indirectly, by research on measures of 'sophistication' in managing equality and diversity issues. Only 7% of private sector organizations were in the top 20 percentile, compared to 34% of public sector organizations and 18% of voluntary sector organizations (CIPD 2007: 5) – a very large disparity between sectors, but also not impressive overall. These findings might also be set in the context of the WERS 2004 data noted above, that decisions on equality issues are overwhelmingly taken by management alone – suggesting that most UK organizations are not, in Dickens's terms, prepared to take meaningful equality action.

Conclusions: Equality and Diversity as the Ultimate Industrial Relations Concern

The agenda of IR research concerns reflective thinking on the forces that shape the working environment (Clarke *et al.* 2008) and inequality in various forms, such as classes, wages and involvement in decision making, has always been a central part of the agenda. We increasingly recognize the salience of contemporary understanding of equality and diversity issues amongst those forces, but what 'equality' in employment would look like if achieved is not simple or commonly agreed. The same (necessarily) is true for the actions needed to arrive at this hard to define place. This is linked to our varying understandings of the primary concepts in this area. Is equality same treatment or different treatment according to needs/societal position? Equal opportunity or proportionate outcomes? Even where there is some agreement on desired ends and means, the outcomes of regulatory strategies are mediated by individuals and enterprises constituting and constrained by formal institutions (such as education, the law, collective bargaining, job design) and informal institutions (such as family, religion, gender relations, organizational custom and practice).

What we can discern are trends, some in tension with others. The State, for example, sends mixed messages. On the one hand, we have the EHRC, the Single

Equality Bill and assorted 'flexibility' provisions recognizing the multiple identities and interests of employees. At the same time, the forms of implementation and resources available have not been rethought or reprioritized in the same ways (for example, the restriction to the public sector of the duties to promote equality; limited paid paternal leave). Employers largely continue to adopt legal compliance approaches, with business case arguments deployed publicly but, in keeping with the rationale of such arguments, variably. Further, employees' protected characteristics can be experienced as conflicting, for example between religious belief and sexual orientation.[9] Thus the picture is of course not one of simple progression. However, Crouch (2007: 536, 527), heralding a 'new stage of non-determinist, actor-sensitive' institutionalist analysis, observes that 'we can never be certain that minor adjustments will not accumulate to the point where a change that retrospectively seems to have been radical takes place'. Certainly, there has been clear change in the status of these issues in public discourse and in attempts to regulate for (some idea of) justice, and in these there is potential for more. Might, for example, acknowledgement of heterogeneity in the DDA's 'more favourable' treatment aspect of reasonable adjustment act as a conceptual Trojan horse (Pandora's box)? Is it reasonable to expect a parent to demonstrate 'commitment' to jobs constructed in the disembodied shape of a worker without non-work responsibilities? This type of question draws on a social model of disadvantage, as noted above, but also engages with the 'outside' ecology of *ideas* of what is natural and appropriate; highlighting the importance for IR actors and scholars of extending boundaries in achieving and analysing outcomes.

Notes

1 Race Relations (Amendment) Act 2000; Equality Act 2006; Disability Discrimination Act 2005.
2 Coleman v. Attridge Law and another (Case C-303/06) [2008] IRLR 722.
3 See note 1 above.
4 For example the Work and Families Act 2006, which gives workers with caring responsibilities the right to request (and employers the duty to consider seriously) flexible working arrangements.
5 Employment Act 2002, s. 80A(3).
6 DDA 2005, S. 49A (1)(d).
7 *Allen & Ors v. GMB* [2008] EWCA Civ. 810 (16 July 2008).
8 *Hayward v. Cammell Laird Shipbuilders Ltd (No. 2)* [1988] 2 WLR 1134.
9 *Islington v. Ladele* [2008] UKEAT 0453/08/1912.

References

ACAS 2005: Evidence to the Women and Work Commission. Available at: http://www.acas.org.uk/CHttpHandler.ashx?id=183&p=0
Acker, J. 1990: Hierarchies, jobs, bodies: a theory of gendered organizations. *Gender and Society*, 4 (2), 139–158.
Acker, J. 2006: *Class Questions: Feminist Answers*. Lanham, MD: Rowman and Littlefield.

Ackers, P. 2002: Reframing industrial relations: the case for neo-pluralism. *Industrial Relations Journal*, 33 (1), 2–19.

AGE – the European Older People's Platform 2007: *Promoting Gender Equality for Older People in the EU*. Brussels.

Almond, P. 2004: IR as a discipline and field in France and the UK. *Relations Industrielles/Industrial Relations*, 59 (2), 321–344.

Anderson, B. and Rogaly, B. 2005: Forced labour and migration to the UK. Report to the TUC. London: TUC.

Bajawa, A. and Woodall, J. 2006: Equal opportunity and diversity management meet downsizing: a case study in the UK airline industry. *Employee Relations*, 28 (1), 46–61.

Bardasi, E. and Gornick, J.C. 2008: Working for less? Women's part-time wage penalties across countries. *Feminist Economics*, 14 (1), 37–72.

Bassett-Jones, N., Berman Brown, R. and Cornelius, N. 2007: Delivering effective diversity management through effective structures. *Systems Research and Behavioral Science*, 24, 59–67.

Becker, G.S. 1985: Human capital, effort, and the sexual division of labor. *Journal of Labor Economics*, 3 (1), S33–S58.

BERR 2008: Vulnerable Worker Enforcement Forum. Final Report and Government Conclusions. London: Department for Business, Enterprise and Regulatory Reform.

Berry, M. 2008: Pay up. *Labour & European Law Review*, Spring, 121. London: Thompsons Solicitors.

Berthoud, R. 2008: Disability employment penalties in Britain. *Work, Employment and Society*, 22(1), 129–148.

Brewer, N. 2008: Speech at launch of EHRC consultation 'Working Better', 14 July. Available at: http://www.equalityhumanrights.com/en/newsandcomment/speeches/Pages/SpeechbyNicolaBrewerlaunchof'WorkingBetter'.aspx

Brown, G. 2007: Speech to the TUC. *The Telegraph*. Available at: http://www.telegraph.co.uk/news/uknews/1562685/Gordon-Browns-speech-to-the-TUC-in-full.html Accessed 28 February 2009.

Carley, M. 2008: Danone signs international diversity agreement. *European Employment Review*, 409. Available at: http://www.xperthr.co.uk/viewarticle.aspx?id=82700&searchwords=%22danone%22 Accessed 17 March 2008.

Carlsson, M. and Rooth, D.-O. 2008: Is it your foreign name or foreign qualifications? An experimental study of ethnic discrimination in hiring. IZA Discussion Paper No. 3810. Bonn: Institute for the Study of Labor.

CBI 2008: *Talent Not Tokenism: The Business Benefits of Workforce Diversity*. London: Confederation of British Industry.

CIPD 2007: Diversity in Business: A Focus for Progress. London: Chartered Institute of Personnel and Development.

Civil Justice Council 2008: Improving access to justice through collective actions. Developing a more efficient and effective procedure for collective actions. A series of recommendations to the Lord Chancellor. Final Report. London: CJC.

Clark, K. and Drinkwater, S. 2007: *Ethnic Minorities in the Labour Market*. York: Joseph Rowntree Foundation.

Clarke, L., Donnelly, E., Hyman, R., Kelly, J., McKay, S. and Moore, S. 2008: What's the point of industrial relations? Plenary presentation to the BUIRA Conference, 26–28 June, University of West of England.

Cobble, D.S. (ed.) 2007: *The Sex of Class: Women Transforming American Labor*. Ithaca, New York: ILR Press.

Cockburn, C. 1989: Equal opportunities: the short and long agenda. *Industrial Relations Journal*, 20 (3), 213–225.

Colling, T. and Dickens, L. 1998: Selling the case for gender equality: deregulation and equality bargaining. *British Journal of Industrial Relations*, 36 (3), 389–411.

Colling, T. and Dickens, L. 2001: Gender equality and trade unions: a new basis for mobilisation? In Noon, M. and Ogbonna, E. (eds) *Equality, Diversity and Disadvantage in Employment*. Basingstoke: Palgrave.

Collinson, D., Knights, D. and Collinson, M. 1990: *Managing to Discriminate*. London: Routledge.

Communities and Local Government 2008: Healey announces support for councils to deliver equal pay. Available at: http://www.communities.gov.uk/news/corporate/977615 Accessed 6 March 2009.

Crompton, R. and Sanderson, K. 1990: *Gendered Jobs and Social Change*. London: Unwin Hyman.

Crompton, R. and Lyonette, C. 2005: The new gender essentialism: domestic and family 'choices' and their relation to attitudes. *British Journal of Sociology*, 56 (4), 601–620.

Crouch, C. 2007: How to 'do' post-determinist institutional analysis. *Socio-Economic Review*, 5, 527–537.

Danieli, A. 2006: Gender, the missing link in industrial relations. *Industrial Relations Journal*, 37 (4), 329–343.

Dean, D. 2009: Diversity in the private sector. In Greene, A.M. and Kirton, G. (eds) *Diversity Management in the UK – Organizational and Stakeholder Experiences*. Routledge Studies in Employment and Work Relations in Context. London: Routledge.

den Dulk, L. and de Ruijter, J. 2008: Managing work–life policies: disruption versus dependency arguments. Explaining managerial attitudes towards employee utilization of work–life policies. *The International Journal of Human Resource Management*, 19 (7), 1222–1236.

Dickens, L. 1998: *Equal Opportunities and Collective Bargaining in Europe: Illuminating the Process*. Dublin: European Foundation for the Improvement of Living and Working Conditions.

Dickens, L. 1999: Beyond the business case: a three-pronged approach to equality action. *Human Resource Management Journal*, 9 (1), 9–19.

Dickens, L. 2000: Still wasting resources? Equality in employment. In Bach, S. and Sisson, K. (eds) *Personnel Management*. 3rd edition. Oxford: Blackwell, pp. 137–169.

Dickens, L. 2007: The road is long: thirty years of equality legislation in Britain. *British Journal of Industrial Relations*, 45 (3), 463–494.

Duncan, C. and Loretto, W. 2004: Never the right age? Gender and age-based discrimination in employment. *Gender, Work and Organization*, 11 (1), 95–115.

Edwards, P.K. (ed.) 2003: *Industrial Relations: Theory and Practice in Britain*. Oxford: Blackwell.

Edwards, P.K. 2005: The challenging but promising future of industrial relations: developing theory and method in context-sensitive research. *Industrial Relations Journal*, 36 (4), 264–282.

Edwards, P.K. 2006: Power and ideology in the workplace: going beyond even the second version of the three-dimensional view. *Work, Employment and Society*, 20 (3), 571–581.

EOC 2007: Enter the timelords: transforming work to meet the future. Final Report. Manchester: Equal Opportunities Commission.

Equalities Review 2007: Fairness and freedom: The Final Report of the Equalities Review. Wetherby: Communities and Local Government Publications.

Estévez-Abe, M. 2006: Gendering the varieties of capitalism: a study of occupational segregation by sex in advanced industrialised societies. *World Politics*, 59, 142–175.

ETS 2006: Employment Tribunal and EAT Statistics (GB), 1 April 2006 to 31 March 2007. Available at: http://www.employmenttribunals.gov.uk/publications/documents/annual_repo rts/ETSAS06–07.pdf

European Commission Communication COM 2006 92 Final.

European Commission 2006: Flexibility and security in the EU labour markets: the effects of labour market policies and 'Flexicurity' regimes. Employment in Europe Report. Luxembourg: Office for Official Publications of the European Communities.

European Commission 2008: Report on equality between women and men 2008. Luxembourg: Office for Official Publications of the European Communities.

European Foundation for the Improvement of Living and Working Conditions 2006: Working time and work–life balance in European companies. Luxembourg: Office for Official Publications of the European Communities.

European Industrial Relations Review 2006: PSA Peugeot Citroën signs CSR/global council agreement. *European Industrial Relations Review*, Issue 388, 1/5/2006. Available at: http://www.xperthr.co.uk/article/65260/international—psa-peugeot-citroën-signs-csr-global-councilagreement.aspx?searchwords=Peugeot. Accessed 12 May 2008.

Fee, R. 2002: Contract compliance: subnational and European influences in Northern Ireland. *Journal of European Social Policy*, 12 (2), 107–121.

Fleetwood, S. 2007: Why work–life balance now? *The International Journal of Human Resource Management*, 18 (3), 387–400.

Fredman, S. 2008a: Making a difference: the promises and perils of positive duties in the equality field. In *European Anti-Discrimination Law Review*, No. 6/7.

Fredman, S. 2008b: Reforming equal pay laws. *Industrial Law Journal*, 37 (3), 193– 218.

Gorman, E.H. 2005: Gender stereotypes, same-gender preferences, and organizational variation in the hiring of women: evidence from law firms. *American Sociological Review*, 70 (4), 702–728.

Government Equalities Office 2008: *Framework for a Fairer Future – The Equality Bill*. London: Government Equalities Office.

Grayson, D. 2007: Business-Led Corporate Responsibility Coalitions: Learning from the example of Business in the Community in the UK. An Insider's Perspective. Business in the Community, Doughty Centre for Corporate Responsibility and the Kennedy School of Government, Harvard. Available at: http://www.bitc.org.uk/resources/publications/business_led.html.

Greene, A.-M. 2003: Women and industrial relations. In Ackers, P. and Wilkinson, A. (eds) *Understanding Work and Employment*. Oxford: Oxford University Press, pp. 305–315.

Greene, A.M. and Kirton, G. 2009: Trade union experiences of diversity. In Greene, A.M. and Kirton, G. (eds) *Diversity Management in the UK – Organizational and Stakeholder Experiences*. Routledge Studies in Employment and Work Relations in Context. London: Routledge.

Gregory, J. 1999: Revisiting the sex equality laws. In Walby, S. (ed.) *New Agendas for Women*. Basingstoke: Macmillan Press Ltd.

Hakim, C. 2000: *Work–Lifestyle Choice in the 21st Century: Preference Theory*. Oxford: Oxford University Press.

Hannett, S. 2003: Equality at the intersections: the legislative and judicial failure to tackle multiple discrimination. *Oxford Journal of Legal Studies*, 23 (1), 65–86.

Healy, G., Hansen, L.L. and Ledwith, S. 2006: Editorial: still uncovering gender in industrial relations. *Industrial Relations Journal*, 37 (4), 290–298.

Heery, E. 2005: Sources of change in trade unions. *Work, Employment and Society*, 19 (1), 91–106.

Heery, E. 2006: Equality bargaining: where, who, why? *Gender, Work and Organization*, 13 (2), 522–542.

Heery, E., Simms, M., Conley, H., Delbridge, R. and Stewart, P. 2002: Trade unions and the flexible workforce: a survey analysis of union policy and practice. Working Paper No. 22, ESRC Future of Work Programme.

Hepple, B. 1992: Have 25 years of the race relations act in Britain been a failure? In Hepple, B. and Szyszczak, E. (eds) *Discrimination: The Limits of Law*. London: Mansell.

Hepple, B., Coussey, M. and Choudhury, T. 2000: *Equality: A New Framework*. Oxford: Hart.

Holgate, J., Hebson, G. and McBride, A. 2006: Why gender and 'difference' matters: a critical appraisal of industrial relations research. *Industrial Relations Journal*, 37 (4), 310–328.

Hopkins, B. 2009: Inequality street? Working life in a British chocolate factory. In Bolton, S.C. and Houlihan, M. (eds) *Work Matters: Critical Reflections on Contemporary Work*. Basingstoke: Palgrave Macmillan.

Hoque, K. and Noon, M. 2004: Equal opportunities policy and practice in Britain: evaluating the 'empty shell' hypothesis. *Work, Employment & Society*, 18 (3), 481–506.

Hyman, R. 1974: Inequality, ideology and industrial relations. *British Journal of Industrial Relations*, 12 (2), 171–190.

Jayaweera, H. and Anderson, B 2008: *Migrant Workers and Vulnerable Employment: A Review of Existing Data*. Oxford: Centre on Migration, Policy and Society, University of Oxford.

Johns, N.R. and Green, A.J. 2009: Equality, equal opportunities and diversity. Obfuscation as social justice. *Equal Opportunities International*, 28 (4), 289–303.

Kandola, R. and Fullerton, J. 1998: *Managing the Mosaic: Diversity in Action*. 2nd edition. London: Chartered Institute of Personnel and Development.

Kaufman, B.E. 2007: Industrial relations: core principle and theoretical foundation. Paper to the European Regional IIRA, Manchester, 27 June.

Kaufman, B.E. 2008: Paradigms in industrial relations: original, modern and versions in-between. *British Journal of Industrial Relations*, 46 (2), 314–339.

Kelly, J. 1998: *Rethinking Industrial Relations*. London: Routledge.

Kersley, B., Alpin, C., Forth, J., Bryson, A., Bewley, H., Dix, G. and Oxenbridge, S. 2006: *Inside the Workplace: First Findings from the 2004 Workplace Employment Relations Survey*. London: Routledge.

Khattab, N. 2009: Ethno-religious background as a determinant of educational and occupational attainment in Britain. *Sociology*, 43 (2), 304–322.

Kirton, G. 2006: *The Making of Women Trade Unionists*. Aldershot: Ashgate.

Kirton, G. and Greene, A.-M. 2006: The discourse of diversity in unionised contexts: Views from trade union equality officers, *Personal Review*, 35(4), 431–448.

Ledwith, S. and Colgan, F. 2002: Tackling gender, diversity and trade union democracy. In Colgan, F. and Ledwith, S. (eds) *Gender, Diversity and Trade Unions*. Oxford: Routledge.

Liff, S. and Cameron, I. 1997: Changing equality cultures to move beyond 'women's problems'. *Gender, Work and Organization*, 4 (1), 35–46.

Liff, S. and Dale, K. 1994: Formal opportunity, informal barriers: black women managers within a local authority. *Work, Employment & Society*, 8 (2), 177–198.

Loretto, W. and White, P. 2006: Employers' attitudes, practices and policies towards older workers. *Human Resource Management Journal*, 16 (3), 313–330.

Mabbett, D. 2008: Aspirational Legalism and the Human Rights Commission in Equality Policy, *The Political Quarterley*, 79(1), 45–52.

Macpherson Report 1999: *The Stephen Lawrence Inquiry. Report of an Inquiry by Sir William Macpherson of Cluny.* London: The Stationery Office.

Malik, M. 2007: Modernising discrimination law: proposals for a Single Equality Act for Great Britain. *International Journal of Discrimination and the Law,* 9, 73–94.

Manning, A. and Petrongolo, B. 2008: The Part-Time Pay Penalty for Women in Britain. *The Economic Journal,* 118 (February), F28–F51.

McBride, A. 2001: Making it work: supporting group representation in a liberal democratic organization. *Gender, Work and Organization,* 8 (4), 411–429.

McColgan, A. 2005: *Discrimination Law.* 2nd edition. Oxford: Hart.

McCrudden, C. 2004: Using public procurement to achieve social outcomes. *National Resources Forum,* 28, 257–267.

Metcalf, D., Hansen, K. and Charlwood, A. 2001: Unions and the sword of justice: unions and pay systems, pay inequality, pay discrimination and low pay. *National Institute Economic Review,* 176, 61–75.

Mills, A.J. and Wilson, E.M. 2001: Perception and stereotyping. In Wilson, E. (ed.) *Organizational Behaviour Reassessed.* London: Sage, pp. 37–59.

Morgan, D. 1981: Men, masculinity and the process of sociological enquiry. In Roberts, H. (ed.) *Doing Feminist Research.* London: Routledge and Kegan Paul.

Munro, A. 2001: A feminist trade union agenda? The continued significance of class, gender and race. *Gender, Work and Organisation,* 8 (4), 454– 471.

Noon, M. and Hoque, K. 2001: Ethnic minorities and equal treatment: the impact of gender, equal opportunities policies and trade unions. *National Institute Economic Review,* 176, 105–116.

O'Cinneide, C. 2007: The Commission for Equality and Human Rights: a new institution for new and uncertain times. *Industrial Law Journal,* 36 (2), 141–162.

ONS 2003: Regional distribution of the minority ethnic population. Available at: http://www.statistics.gov.uk/CCI/nugget.asp?ID=263&Pos=1&ColRank=2&Rank=44. Accessed 21 June 2008.

Parker, J. 2002: Women's groups in British unions. *British Journal of Industrial Relations,* 40 (1), 23–48.

Peterson, S.V. 2005: How (the meaning of) gender matters in political economy. *New Political Economy,* 10 (4), 499–521.

Piore, M.J. and Safford, S. 2006: Changing regimes of workplace governance, shifting axes of social mobilization, and the challenge to industrial relations theory. *Industrial Relations,* 45 (3), 299–325.

Platt, L. 2006: *Pay Gaps: The Position of Ethnic Minority Women and Men.* Manchester: EOC.

Pollert, A. 2005: The unorganised worker: the decline in collectivism and new hurdles to individual employment rights. *Industrial Law Journal,* 34 (3), 217–238.

Purcell, K., Elias, P. and Wilton, N. 2006: Looking through the glass ceiling: a detailed investigation of the factors that contribute to gendered career inequalities. Warwick Institute for Employment Research. Available at: http://www2.warwick.ac.uk/fac/soc/ier/research/completed/ltgc/esfreportfinal.pdf

Riach, P.A. and Rich, J. 2002: Field experiments of discrimination in the market place. *The Economic Journal,* 112 (483), F480–F518.

Riisgaard, L. 2005: International framework agreements: a new model for securing workers rights? *Industrial Relations,* 44 (4), 707–737.

Ross, R. and Schneider, R. 1994: *From Equality to Diversity.* London: Pitman.

Saunders, R. 2003: *Defining Vulnerability in the Labour Market.* Ottawa: Canadian Policy Research Networks.

Schroeder, A., Miles, A., Savage, A., Halford, S. and Tampubolon, G. 2008: *Mobility, Careers and Inequalities: A Study of Work–Life Mobility and the Returns from Education*. London: Equality and Human Rights Commission.

Sigle-Rushton, W. and Waldfogel, J. 2007: Motherhood and women's earnings in Anglo-American, continental European and Nordic countries. *Feminist Economics*, 13 (2), 55–91.

Singh, V. and Point, S. 2006: (Re)Presentations of gender and ethnicity in diversity statements on European company websites. *Journal of Business Ethics*, 68 (4), 363–379.

Singh, V. and Vinnicombe, S. 2006: *The Female FTSE Report 2006*. Bedford: Cranfield School of Management.

Soldatenko, M.A. 1999: Made in the USA: Latinas/os? Garment work and ethnic conflict in Los Angles' sweat shops. *Cultural Studies*, 13 (2), 319–334.

Soskice, D. 2005: Varieties of capitalism and cross-national gender differences. *Social Politics*, 170–179.

Sturdy, A., Knights, D. and Willmott, H. 1992: Introduction: skill and consent in the labour process. In Sturdy, A., Knights, D. and Willmott, H. (eds) *Skill and Consent: Contemporary Studies in the Labour Process*. London: Routledge, pp. 1–24.

Thornley, C. 2007: Working part-time for the state: gender, class and the public sector pay gap. *Gender, Work and Organization*, 14 (5), 454–475.

TUC 2003: A perfect union? What workers want from unions. London: TUC.

TUC 2006: *Ten Years After: Black Workers in Employment 1997–2007*. London: TUC.

Wajcman, J. 2000: Feminism facing industrial relations in Britain. *British Journal of Industrial Relations*, 38 (2), 183–201.

Walsh, J. 2007: Equality and diversity in British Workplaces: the 2004 Workplace Employment Relations Survey, *Industrial Relations Journal*, 38(4), 303–319.

Wallerstein, M. 1999: Wage-setting institutions and pay inequality in advanced industrial societies. *American Journal of Political Science*, 43 (3), 649–680.

Webb, S. and Webb, B. 1897: *Industrial Democracy*. London: Longman and Green.

Women and Equality Unit 2004: *Interim Update of Key Indicators of Women's Position in Britain*. London: DTI.

Woodhams, C. and Danieli, A. 2000: Disability and diversity – a difference too far? *Personnel Review*, 29 (3), 402–416.

Wrench, J. 2005: Diversity management can be bad for you. *Race & Class*, 46 (3), 73–84.

INDEX

Index compiled by Terry Halliday